Teacher's Edition

# SRA OPEN COURT READING

## Level 3 • Unit 4

## Money

— PROGRAM AUTHORS —

Carl Bereiter
Ann Brown
Joe Campione
Iva Carruthers
Robbie Case
Jan Hirshberg
Marilyn Jager Adams
Anne McKeough
Michael Pressley
Marsha Roit
Marlene Scardamalia
Marcy Stein
Gerald H. Treadway, Jr.

A Division of The McGraw-Hill Companies
Columbus, Ohio

## Acknowledgments

Grateful acknowledgment is given to the following publishers and copyright owners for permissions granted to reprint selections from their publications. All possible care has been taken to trace ownership and secure permission for each selection included. In case of any errors or omissions, the Publisher will be pleased to make suitable acknowledgments in future editions.

From MONEY, MONEY, MONEY by Ruth Belov Gross. Copyright © 1971 by Ruth Belov Gross. Reprinted by permission of Scholastic, Inc.

A NEW COAT FOR ANNA by Harriet Ziefert. Text copyright © 1986 by Harriet Ziefert. Illustrations copyright © 1986 by Anita Lobel. Published by arrangement with Random House Children's Books a division of Random House, Inc., New York, New York. All rights reserved.

From ALEXANDER, WHO USED TO BE RICH LAST SUNDAY. Text copyright © 1978 by Judith Viorst. Illustrations copyright © 1978 by Ray Cruz. Reproduced by arrangement with Atheneum Books for Young Readers, Simon & Schuster Children's Publishing Division. All rights reserved.

"Smart" from WHERE THE SIDEWALK ENDS by Shel Silverstein. COPYRIGHT © 1974 BY EVIL EYE MUSIC, INC. Used by permission of HarperCollins Publishers.

"Tony and the Quarter" from ROLLING HARVEY DOWN THE HILL TEXT COPYRIGHT © 1985 BY JACK PRELUTSKY. ILLUSTRATIONS COPYRIGHT © 1985 BY YOSSI ABOLOFIA. Used by permission of HarperCollins Publishers.

"Kids Did It! in Business" from WORLD Magazine, June 1996. Judith E. Rinard/National Geographic Image collection.

From THE COBBLER'S SONG by Marcia Sewall, copyright © 1982 by Marcia Sewall. Used by permission of Dutton Children's Books, an imprint of Penguin Putnam Books for Young Readers, a division of Penguin Putnam Inc.

FOUR DOLLARS AND FIFTY CENTS by Eric A. Kimmel. Text copyright © 1989 by Eric A. Kimmel. Illustrations copyright © 1989 by Glen Rounds. All rights reserved. Reprinted by permission of Holiday House, Inc.

From THE GO-AROUND DOLLAR. Text copyright © 1992 by Barbara Johnston Adams. Illustrations copyright © 1992 by Joyce Audy Zarins. Reproduced by arrangement with Simon & Schuster Books for Young Readers, Simon & Schuster Children's Publishing Division. All rights reserved.

From UNCLE JED'S BARBER SHOP. Text copyright © 1993 by Margaree King Mitchell. Illustrations copyright © 1993 by James Ransome. Reproduced by arrangement with Simon & Schuster Books for Young Readers, Simon & Schuster Children's Publishing Division. All rights reserved.

**www.sra4kids.com**

*SRA/McGraw-Hill*

*A Division of The* **McGraw-Hill** *Companies*



Send all inquiries to:
SRA/McGraw-Hill
8787 Orion Place
Columbus, OH 43240-4027

Printed in the United States of America.

ISBN 0-07-602756-2

2 3 4 5 6 7 8 9 WEB 10 09 08 07 06 05

Making the Difference

Welcome to

# SRA Open Court Reading

# Proven Results

**Inspire a lifetime love of learning by using research-based instruction.**

***Open Court Reading*** is an instructional leader for three key reasons.

1. Research-based instruction that works
2. Teacher-tested lessons that are effective in classrooms like yours
3. Unparalleled support to help you do what you do best—Teach

# Achieve your classroom goals with ***Open Court Reading's*** proven approach.

Students attending schools using ***Open Court Reading*** score higher in basic reading skills than students attending schools that do not use ***Open Court Reading*** materials.

> "Since using ***Open Court Reading,*** our students have gone beyond even my expectations. ***Open Court Reading*** is by far the best systematic approach to instruction of reading skills that I have taught in my thirty years as an instructor or administrator."
>
> — **Gerald Judd,** 6th Grade Language Arts
> Dunbar 6th Grade Center,
> Fort Worth, TX

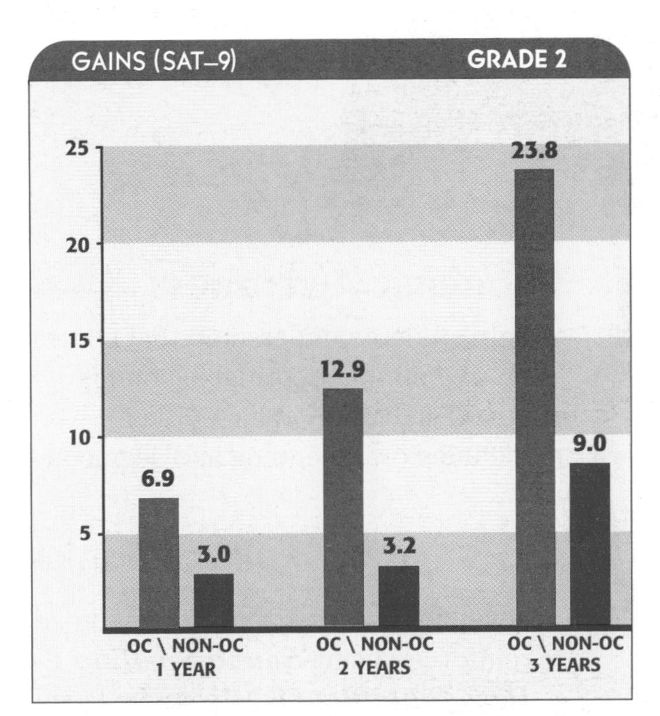


In California schools serving large concentrations of Low Socioeconomic Status students, differences over three years were most impressive.

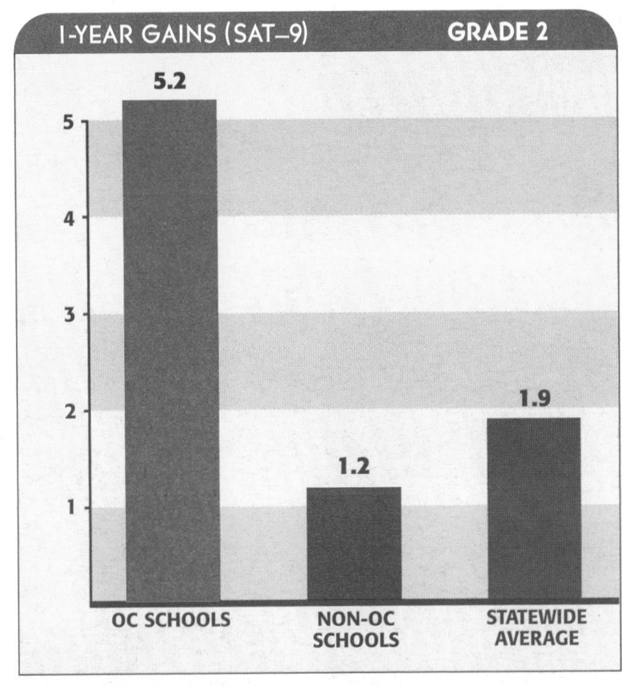


One-year gains for students in more than 700 California schools show that ***Open Court Reading*** schools outgain non-***Open Court Reading*** schools by a factor of four.

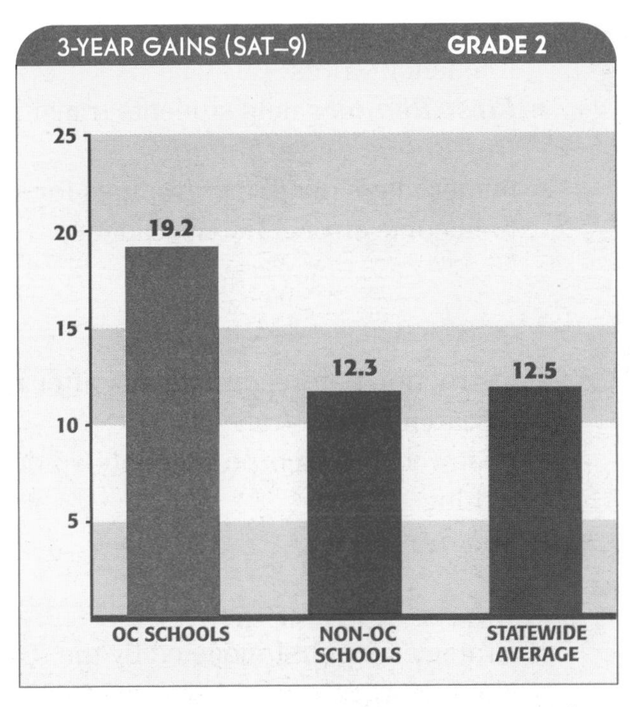


***Open Court Reading*** schools outgain demographically similar non-***Open Court Reading*** schools as well as the statewide average by 50 to 75 percent.

For a copy of the detailed ***Open Court Reading*** **Research Report** and **Results Report**, visit SRAonline.com, or contact SRA at 1-888-SRA-4543.

# Effective Instruction

**Lead the way in research-based instruction with *Open Court Reading.***

## 1 Phonemic Awareness

- help students understand that speech is made up of distinct, identifiable sounds
- quick, gamelike oral activities
- includes oral blending and segmentation

discriminating the sounds that make up words

## 2 Systematic, Explicit Phonics

- developmental sequence of sound spellings
- reinforced using ***Sound/Spelling Cards***
- ***Decodable Books*** help students apply, review, and reinforce sound/spelling correspondences

applying the links between letters and sounds to printed words

## 3 Fluency

- explicit teaching of blending and high-frequency words
- ***First Readers*** help students transition from ***Big Books*** to ***Anthologies***
- numerous reading opportunities for students to become strong, fluent readers

reading effortlessly with speed, accuracy, and expression

## 4 Vocabulary

- instruction before, during, and after reading
- research-based strategies
- reviewed and incorporated into students' writing

learning word meanings to build comprehension

## 5 Text Comprehension

- strategies are first modeled by the teacher
- graphic organizers can be used to categorize information
- skills are explicitly taught and reviewed

thinking actively before, during, and after reading

## Manage instructional time to make the most of your day.

Beginning with a strong foundation in Pre-Kindergarten, ***Open Court Reading*** effectively builds skills and strategies throughout all grade levels.

### Comprehensive Program

| Grade | | | | | | |
|---|---|---|---|---|---|---|
| Pre-K | Letter Recognition | Print/Book Awareness | Phonological and Phonemic Awareness | Phonics | Comprehension and Fluency | Writing |
| K | Letter Recognition | Print/Book Awareness | Phonological and Phonemic Awareness | Phonics | Comprehension and Fluency | Writing |
| 1 | Letter/Book/Print Awareness | Phonemic Awareness | Phonics | Comprehension and Fluency | Writing | Language Arts and Vocabulary |
| 2 | Phonics/Word Knowledge | Comprehension and Fluency | Inquiry Learning | Writing | Language Arts and Vocabulary | |
| 3 | Phonics/Word Knowledge | Comprehension and Fluency | Inquiry Learning | Writing | Language Arts and Vocabulary | |
| 4 | Word Knowledge | Comprehension and Fluency | Inquiry Learning | Writing | Language Arts and Vocabulary | |
| 5 | Word Knowledge | Comprehension and Fluency | Inquiry Learning | Writing | Language Arts and Vocabulary | |
| 6 | Word Knowledge | Comprehension and Fluency | Inquiry Learning | Writing | Language Arts and Vocabulary | |

This chart shows the time allocated for skill instruction at each grade level.

# Award-Winning Literature

## Engage students with great literature to help them become independent readers.

The literature in each theme was thoughtfully selected with the following goals in mind:

- **A variety of literature** provides a full spectrum of fiction and nonfiction.
- **Excellent literature** provides models for student writing and helps students develop their expertise as writers.
- **Award-winning authors** and different styles of writing encourage students to develop a cultural literacy.

Literature in ***Open Court Reading*** is available in a variety of formats, depending on the grade level.

- Big and Little Books
- Anthologies
- Teacher Read Alouds
- Story Time Selections (Kindergarten)
- Leveled Classroom Libraries
- First Readers

# Thought-provoking themes in ***Open Court Reading*** span grade levels.

| | Pre-K | K | 1 | 2 | 3 | 4 | 5 | 6 |
|---|---|---|---|---|---|---|---|---|
| | BIG BOOKS | BIG BOOKS | BIG BOOKS | STUDENT ANTHOLOGIES | STUDENT ANTHOLOGIES | STUDENT ANTHOLOGIES | STUDENT ANTHOLOGIES | STUDENT ANTHOLOGIES |
| Unit 1 | I'm Special | School | Let's Read! | Sharing Stories | Friendship | Risks and Consequences | Cooperation and Competition | Perseverance |
| Unit 2 | Families Everywhere | Shadows | Animals | Kindness | City Wildlife | Dollars and Sense | Astronomy | Ancient Civilizations |
| Unit 3 | All Kinds of Friends | Finding Friends | Things That Go | Look Again | Imagination | From Mystery to Medicine | Heritage | Taking a Stand |
| Unit 4 | Helping Hands | The Wind | Our Neighborhood at Work | Fossils | Money | Survival | Making a New Nation | Beyond the Notes |
| Unit 5 | Let's Go! | Stick to It | Weather | Courage | Storytelling | Communication | Going West | Ecology |
| Unit 6 | Senses | Red, White, and Blue | Journeys | Our Country and Its People | Country Life | A Changing America | Journeys and Quests | A Question of Value |
| | | | STUDENT ANTHOLOGIES | | | | | |
| Unit 7 | At the Farm | Teamwork | Keep Trying | | | | | |
| Unit 8 | Changes | By the Sea | Games | | | | | |
| Unit 9 | | | Being Afraid | | | | | |
| Unit 10 | | | Homes | | | | | |

"Reading is the basis for all learning. I applaud ***Open Court Reading*** for allowing teachers to spend so much time on reading and yet not miss out on some of the other areas of learning. So much science and social studies is built into the program that it really makes my job as a teacher easier."

– **Deanna Sinift,** Grade 1 Teacher
Woodville Elementary School,
Porterville, CA

# Comprehensive Resources

***Open Court Reading*** **materials will help your students expand their knowledge by exploring, discussing, and researching ideas.**

## Student Materials

**Big and Little Books**
- Award-winning authors and illustrators
- Variety of cultures and genres represented

**Anthologies**
- Award-winning authors and illustrators
- Wide variety of cultures and genres represented
- Concept Connections include vocabulary practice

**First and Second Readers**
- Transitions Level 1 students from ***Big Books*** to ***Anthologies***
- Reviews skills in Level 2

**Decodable Text**
- Pre-Decodable and Decodable stories in either book or takehome format
- Practice blending strategies and high-frequency words

**Story Time Selections**
- Trade books to support Kindergarten unit themes

**Leveled Classroom Libraries**
- Leveled trade books that support unit themes

**Desk Strips**
- Miniature pictures of ***Alphabet Sound Cards*** or ***Sound/Spelling Cards***

**Language Arts Big Books**
- Language arts skills for students in Kindergarten and Level 1

**Language Arts Handbooks**
- Language Arts conventions and examples for students in Levels 2–6

**Practice Books**
- Activities to practice and reinforce skills found in all parts of the lesson

**Science/Social Studies Connection Centers**
- Reinforce reading across the curriculum

### Online

**Online Phonics**
- Interactive multimedia lessons to practice phonics skills
- Includes an assessment tool to monitor student progress

**Literacy Launcher**
- ***Online Phonics*** and vocabulary instruction
- Assessment and management tools included

### CD-ROMs

**Alphabet Book Activities**
- Interactive activities to accompany ***Alphabet Big Book***

**Decodable Book Activities**
- Includes interactive activities to practice and review sound/spellings

**Spelling Software**
- Features a variety of interactive activities to review spelling patterns

**Ultimate Writing and Creativity Center**
- Activities to reinforce writing process skills

**Research Assistant**
- Provides forms to help students plan, organize, present, and assess research projects

**TechKnowledge**
- Technology skills and applications to help students research, write, calculate, and present topics more effectively
- Step-by-step instruction made easy

**Leap Into™ Phonics**
- Phonemic awareness and phonics activities

**Power Vocabulary**
- Vocabulary practice for ***Leveled Classroom Libraries*** in Levels 3–6

### Audiocassettes/CDs

**Listening Library**
- ***Big Book*** and ***Anthology*** selections available on audiocassette or compact disc

**Alphabet Sound Card Stories**
- Appropriate grade-level jingles set to music

**Sound/Spelling Card Stories**
- Appropriate grade-level jingles set to music

## Teacher materials help you make the most of your day.

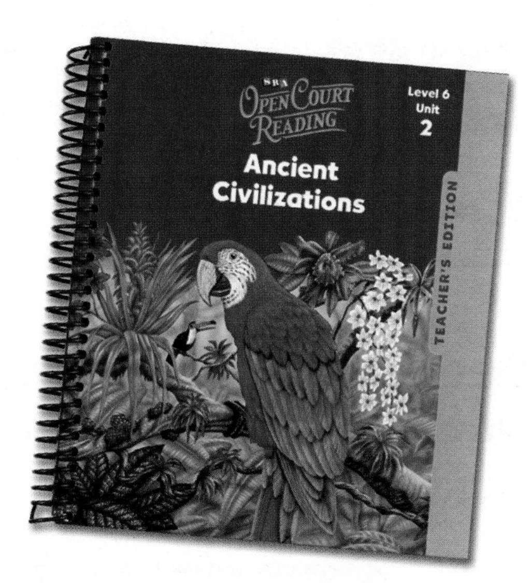


**Teacher's Editions**
- Separate books for each unit theme
- Three-part lessons, each containing phonics, reading comprehension, and language arts
- Plans to help differentiate instruction
- Tips to accommodate students learning English

**Teacher Read Alouds**
- Available in every unit for each grade level

**Phonics Packages**
- Contain manipulatives necessary for phonics instruction

**Home Connection**
- Blackline masters to inform and support ***Open Court Reading*** lessons

**Part 1 Lesson Cards**
- Easy-to-use aid to use while teaching the phonics portion of each lesson (Levels K–3)

**Teacher Management**
- Printable blackline masters of all practice, ***Reteach,*** and ***Challenge*** books

## Assessments to track and meet the needs of all students

**Program Assessment**
- Includes Pretests, Midyear Tests, and Posttests

**Unit Assessments**
- Assess skills introduced or reviewed in each lesson
- Include charts to monitor student progress

**Test Preparation and Practice**
- Prepares students for taking standardized tests

**Assessment CD-ROM**
- Printable blackline masters of all assessments
- Interactive record charts

**Online Assessment**
- Helps differentiate instruction
- Correlated to state standards
- Charts progress and monitors instruction
- Reports available at student, class, building, and district level

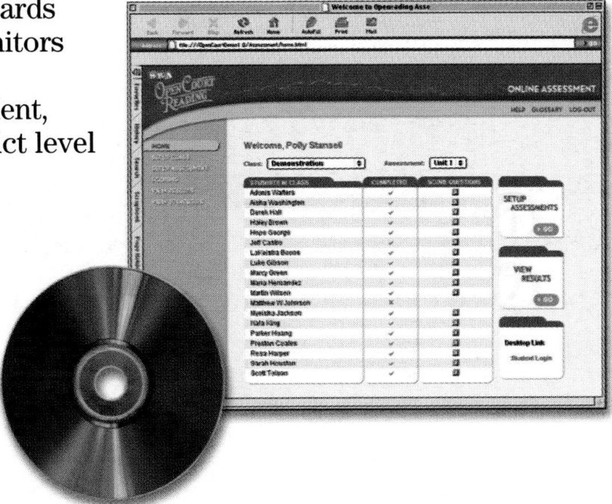


## Materials to Differentiate Instruction

**English Learner Support Guides and Activities**
- Preteach and review ***Open Court Reading*** lessons

**Intervention Guides and Workbooks**
- Support students who need remediation

**Reteach**
- Activities for students who need a skill review during the lesson

**Challenge**
- Activities for students who would benefit from a skill challenge during the lesson

**Differentiating Instruction Support Activities**
- Quick activities available at the end of the unit to address students who need an additional review before moving to the next unit
- Activities are also available for those students who would benefit from extending a skill lesson

# Differentiating Instruction

## Meet students' individual needs during Open Court Workshop.

The ***Open Court Reading Teacher's Editions*** provide easy-to-use references to ensure that you have the tools you need to help every student succeed in reading.

### English Learner Support

Lessons using English Learner routines to preteach skills and concepts critical to understanding each ***Open Court Reading*** lesson

### Reteach lessons

For those students who need extra practice on any of the lesson's skills

### Intervention lessons

More intensive support, with controlled vocabulary selections and specific skills lessons to bring students up to grade level

### Challenge activities

Continued stimulation for students working at or above grade level

### Science/Social Studies Connection Centers

Additional cross curricular support

### Differentiating Instruction Support Activities

For students who require extra practice activities to help bolster skills and extend unit instruction

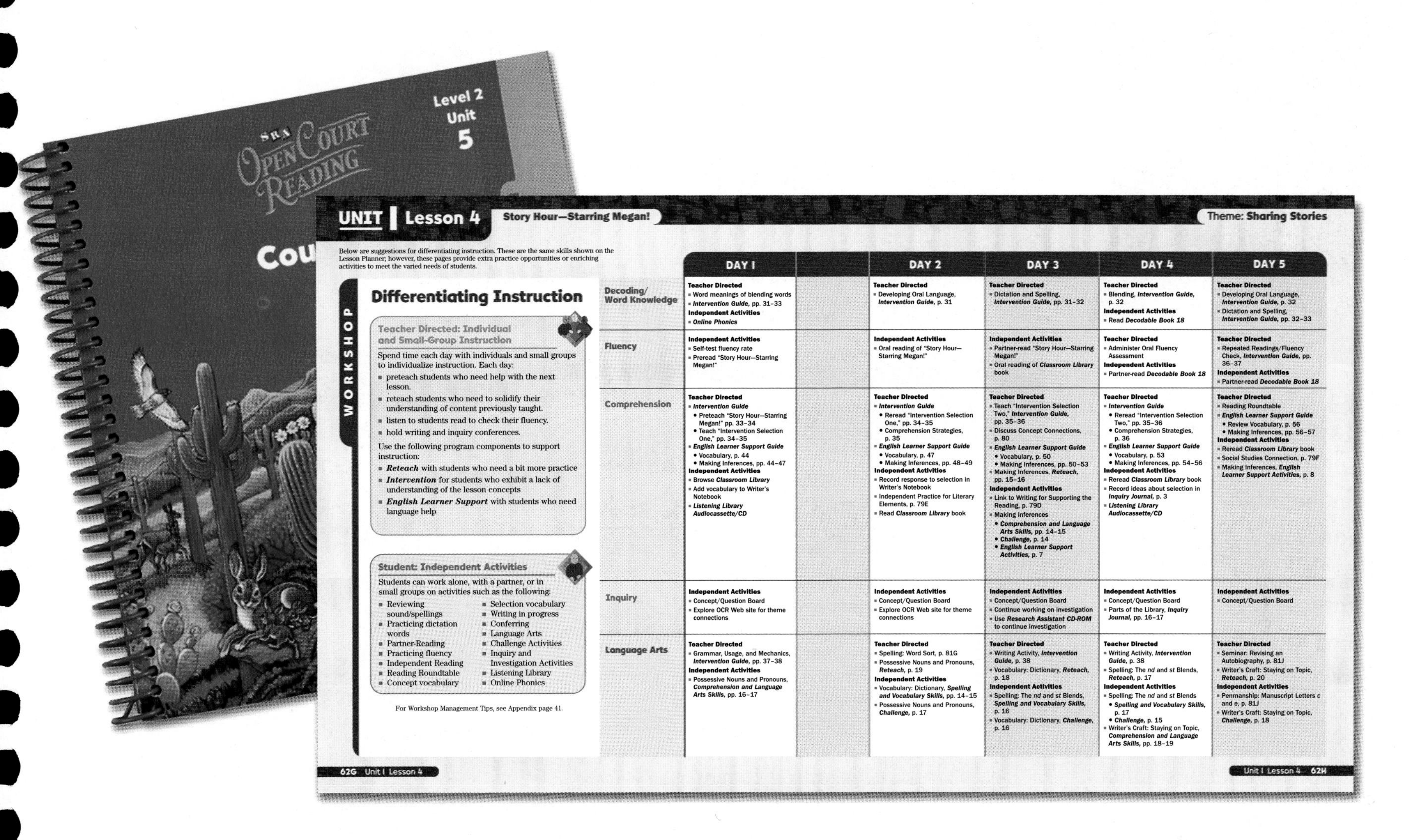


## UNIT | Lesson 4 Story Hour—Starring Megan!

Theme: Sharing Stories

Below are suggestions for differentiating instruction. These are the same skills shown on the Lesson Planner; however, these pages provide extra practice opportunities or enriching activities to meet the varied needs of students.

WORKSHOP

### Differentiating Instruction

**Teacher Directed: Individual and Small-Group Instruction**

Spend time each day with individuals and small groups to individualize instruction. Each day:

- preteach students who need help with the next lesson.
- reteach students who need to solidify their understanding of content previously taught.
- listen to students read to check their fluency.
- hold writing and inquiry conferences.

Use the following program components to support instruction:

- ***Reteach*** with students who need a bit more practice
- ***Intervention*** for students who exhibit a lack of understanding of the lesson concepts
- ***English Learner Support*** with students who need language help

**Student: Independent Activities**

Students can work alone, with a partner, or in small groups on activities such as the following:

- Reviewing sound/spellings
- Practicing dictation words
- Partner-Reading
- Practicing fluency
- Independent Reading
- Reading Roundtable
- Concept vocabulary
- Selection vocabulary
- Writing in progress
- Conferring
- Language Arts
- Challenge Activities
- Inquiry and Investigation Activities
- Listening Library
- Online Phonics

For Workshop Management Tips, see Appendix page 41.

| | DAY 1 | DAY 2 | DAY 3 | DAY 4 | DAY 5 |
|---|---|---|---|---|---|
| Decoding/ Word Knowledge | **Teacher Directed**<br>▪ Word meanings of blending words<br>▪ ***Intervention Guide,*** pp. 31–33<br>**Independent Activities**<br>▪ ***Online Phonics*** | **Teacher Directed**<br>▪ Developing Oral Language, ***Intervention Guide,*** p. 31 | **Teacher Directed**<br>▪ Dictation and Spelling, ***Intervention Guide,*** pp. 31–32 | **Teacher Directed**<br>▪ Blending, ***Intervention Guide,*** p. 32<br>**Independent Activities**<br>▪ Read ***Decodable Book 18*** | **Teacher Directed**<br>▪ Developing Oral Language, ***Intervention Guide,*** p. 32<br>▪ Dictation and Spelling, ***Intervention Guide,*** pp. 32–33 |
| Fluency | **Independent Activities**<br>▪ Self-test fluency rate<br>▪ Preread "Story Hour—Starring Megan!" | **Independent Activities**<br>▪ Oral reading of "Story Hour—Starring Megan!" | **Independent Activities**<br>▪ Partner-read "Story Hour—Starring Megan!"<br>▪ Oral reading of ***Classroom Library*** book | **Teacher Directed**<br>▪ Administer Oral Fluency Assessment<br>**Independent Activities**<br>▪ Partner-read ***Decodable Book 18*** | **Teacher Directed**<br>▪ Repeated Readings/Fluency Check, ***Intervention Guide,*** pp. 36–37<br>**Independent Activities**<br>▪ Partner-read ***Decodable Book 18*** |
| Comprehension | **Teacher Directed**<br>▪ ***Intervention Guide***<br>• Preteach "Story Hour—Starring Megan!" pp. 33–34<br>• Teach "Intervention Selection One," pp. 34–35<br>▪ ***English Learner Support Guide***<br>• Vocabulary, p. 44<br>• Making Inferences, pp. 44–47<br>**Independent Activities**<br>▪ Browse ***Classroom Library***<br>▪ Add vocabulary to Writer's Notebook<br>▪ ***Listening Library Audiocassette/CD*** | **Teacher Directed**<br>▪ ***Intervention Guide***<br>• Reread "Intervention Selection One," pp. 34–35<br>• Comprehension Strategies, p. 35<br>▪ ***English Learner Support Guide***<br>• Vocabulary, p. 47<br>• Making Inferences, pp. 48–49<br>**Independent Activities**<br>▪ Record response to selection in Writer's Notebook<br>▪ Independent Practice for Literary Elements, p. 79E<br>▪ Read ***Classroom Library*** book | **Teacher Directed**<br>▪ Teach "Intervention Selection Two," ***Intervention Guide,*** pp. 35–36<br>▪ Discuss Concept Connections, p. 80<br>▪ ***English Learner Support Guide***<br>• Vocabulary, p. 50<br>• Making Inferences, pp. 50–53<br>▪ Making Inferences, ***Reteach,*** pp. 15–16<br>**Independent Activities**<br>▪ Link to Writing for Supporting the Reading, p. 79D<br>▪ Making Inferences<br>• ***Comprehension and Language Arts Skills,*** pp. 14–15<br>• ***Challenge,*** p. 14<br>• ***English Learner Support Activities,*** p. 7 | **Teacher Directed**<br>▪ ***Intervention Guide***<br>• Reread "Intervention Selection Two," pp. 35–36<br>• Comprehension Strategies, p. 36<br>▪ ***English Learner Support Guide***<br>• Vocabulary, p. 53<br>• Making Inferences, pp. 54–56<br>**Independent Activities**<br>▪ Reread ***Classroom Library*** book<br>▪ Record ideas about selection in ***Inquiry Journal,*** p. 3<br>▪ ***Listening Library Audiocassette/CD*** | **Teacher Directed**<br>▪ Reading Roundtable<br>▪ ***English Learner Support Guide***<br>• Review Vocabulary, p. 56<br>• Making Inferences, pp. 56–57<br>**Independent Activities**<br>▪ Reread ***Classroom Library*** book<br>▪ Social Studies Connection, p. 79F<br>▪ Making Inferences, ***English Learner Support Activities,*** p. 8 |
| Inquiry | **Independent Activities**<br>▪ Concept/Question Board<br>▪ Explore OCR Web site for theme connections | **Independent Activities**<br>▪ Concept/Question Board<br>▪ Explore OCR Web site for theme connections | **Independent Activities**<br>▪ Concept/Question Board<br>▪ Continue working on investigation<br>▪ Use ***Research Assistant CD-ROM*** to continue investigation | **Independent Activities**<br>▪ Concept/Question Board<br>▪ Parts of the Library, ***Inquiry Journal,*** pp. 16–17 | **Independent Activities**<br>▪ Concept/Question Board |
| Language Arts | **Teacher Directed**<br>▪ Grammar, Usage, and Mechanics, ***Intervention Guide,*** pp. 37–38<br>**Independent Activities**<br>▪ Possessive Nouns and Pronouns, ***Comprehension and Language Arts Skills,*** pp. 16–17 | **Teacher Directed**<br>▪ Spelling: Word Sort, p. 81G<br>▪ Possessive Nouns and Pronouns, ***Reteach,*** p. 19<br>**Independent Activities**<br>▪ Vocabulary: Dictionary, ***Spelling and Vocabulary Skills,*** pp. 14–15<br>▪ Possessive Nouns and Pronouns, ***Challenge,*** p. 17 | **Teacher Directed**<br>▪ Writing Activity, ***Intervention Guide,*** p. 38<br>▪ Vocabulary: Dictionary, ***Reteach,*** p. 18<br>**Independent Activities**<br>▪ Spelling: The *nd* and *st* Blends, ***Spelling and Vocabulary Skills,*** p. 16<br>▪ Vocabulary: Dictionary, ***Challenge,*** p. 16 | **Teacher Directed**<br>▪ Writing Activity, ***Intervention Guide,*** p. 38<br>▪ Spelling: The *nd* and *st* Blends, ***Reteach,*** p. 17<br>**Independent Activities**<br>▪ Spelling: The *nd* and *st* Blends<br>• ***Spelling and Vocabulary Skills,*** p. 17<br>• ***Challenge,*** p. 15<br>▪ Writer's Craft: Staying on Topic, ***Comprehension and Language Arts Skills,*** pp. 18–19 | **Teacher Directed**<br>▪ Seminar: Revising an Autobiography, p. 81J<br>▪ Writer's Craft: Staying on Topic, ***Reteach,*** p. 20<br>**Independent Activities**<br>▪ Penmanship: Manuscript Letters *c* and *e*, p. 81J<br>▪ Writer's Craft: Staying on Topic, ***Challenge,*** p. 18 |

62G Unit 1 Lesson 4

Unit 1 Lesson 4 62H

Built into every ***Open Court Reading*** lesson, Workshop provides the time for you to meet with individuals and small groups to provide individualized, differentiated instruction based on each student's needs. Other students may be working independently on

- conducting inquiry.
- developing listening skills with audio stories.
- discussing selections in Reading Roundtable.
- reading library collections.
- completing computer activities.
- working on their writing.

# Preparing to Read

## Start by building a strong foundation for reading and fluency.

**Part 1 of every lesson contains:**

- **Sounds and Letters** (Kindergarten)
- **Phonemic Awareness** (Levels K and 1)
- **Phonics** (Levels 1–3)
- **Word Knowledge** (Levels 2–6)

Use comprehensive, explicit instruction to deliver effective learning routines.

Give added support for differentiating instruction.

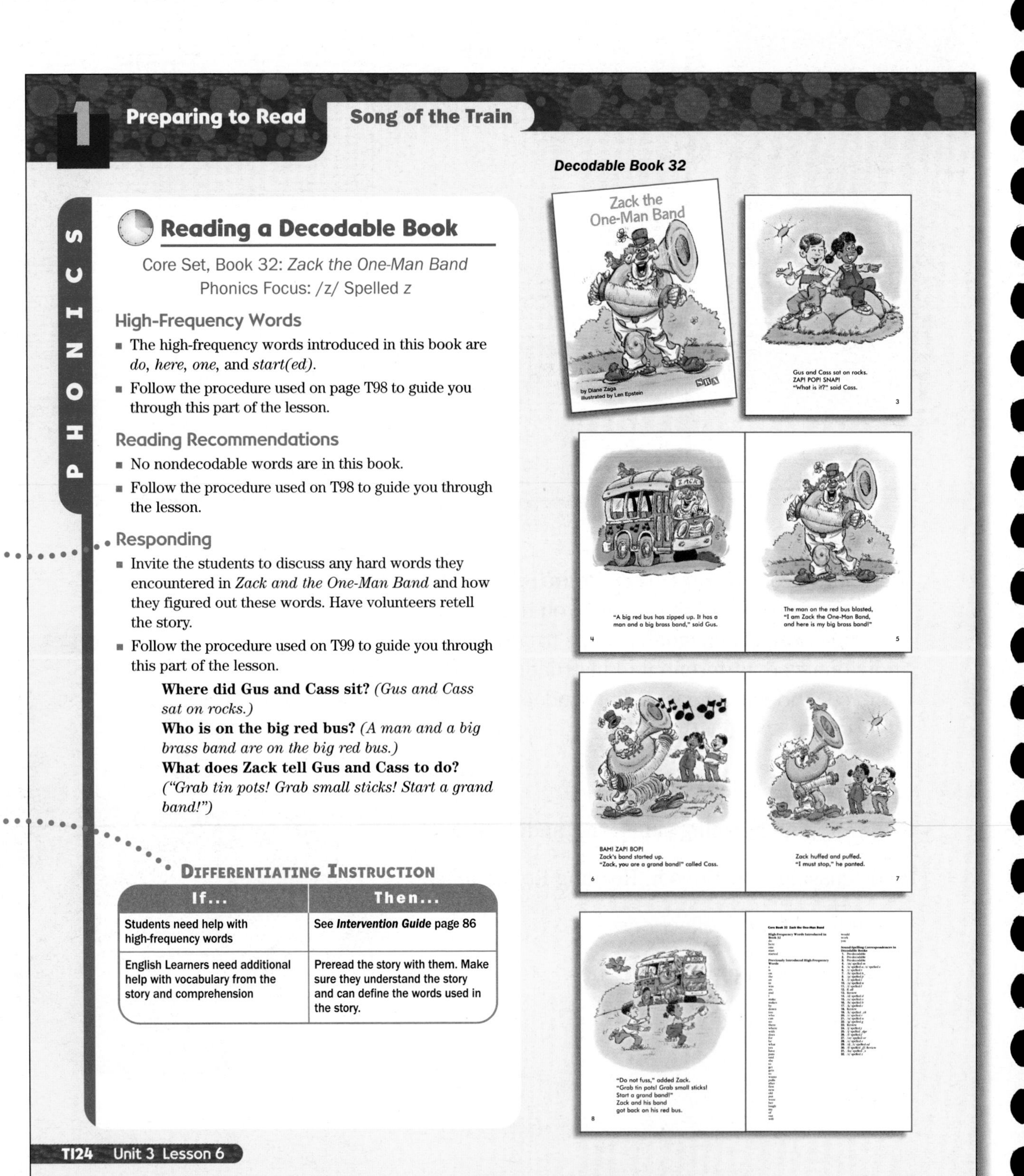

1 Preparing to Read | Song of the Train

PHONICS

### Reading a Decodable Book

Core Set, Book 32: *Zack the One-Man Band*
Phonics Focus: /z/ Spelled *z*

**High-Frequency Words**

- The high-frequency words introduced in this book are *do, here, one,* and *start(ed).*
- Follow the procedure used on page T98 to guide you through this part of the lesson.

**Reading Recommendations**

- No nondecodable words are in this book.
- Follow the procedure used on T98 to guide you through the lesson.

**Responding**

- Invite the students to discuss any hard words they encountered in *Zack and the One-Man Band* and how they figured out these words. Have volunteers retell the story.
- Follow the procedure used on T99 to guide you through this part of the lesson.

**Where did Gus and Cass sit?** *(Gus and Cass sat on rocks.)*
**Who is on the big red bus?** *(A man and a big brass band are on the big red bus.)*
**What does Zack tell Gus and Cass to do?** *("Grab tin pots! Grab small sticks! Start a grand band!")*

**Differentiating Instruction**

| If... | Then... |
|---|---|
| Students need help with high-frequency words | See *Intervention Guide* page 86 |
| English Learners need additional help with vocabulary from the story and comprehension | Preread the story with them. Make sure they understand the story and can define the words used in the story. |

**Decodable Book 32**

Zack the One-Man Band
by Diane Zaga
illustrated by Len Epstein

Gus and Cass sat on rocks.
ZAP! POP! SNAP!
"What is it?" said Cass.
3

"A big red bus has zipped up. It has a man and a big brass band," said Gus.
4

The man on the red bus blasted,
"I am Zack the One-Man Band,
and here is my big brass band!"
5

BAM! ZAP! BOP!
Zack's band started up.
"Zack, you are a grand band!" called Cass.
6

Zack huffed and puffed.
"I must stop," he panted.
7

"Do not fuss," added Zack.
"Grab tin pots! Grab small sticks!
Start a grand band!"
Zack and his band
got back on his red bus.
8

T124 Unit 3 Lesson 6

***Decodable Book 33***

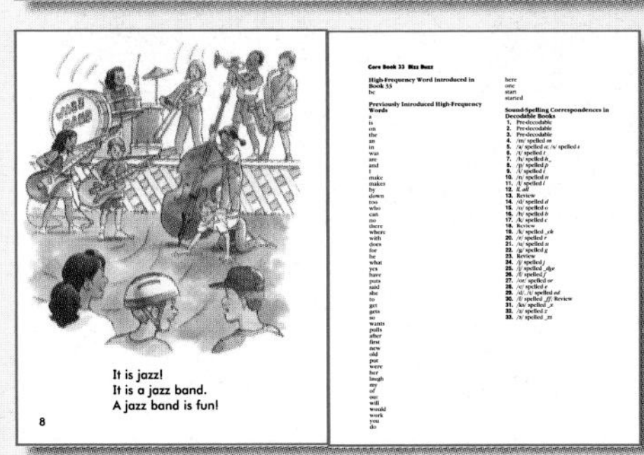


PHONICS

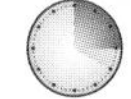

## Reading a Decodable Book

Core Set, Book 33: *Bizz Buzz*
Phonics Focus: /z/ Spelled ■*zz*

### High-Frequency Words

- The high-frequency word introduced in this book is *be*. Write *be* on the board and ask students to say it.
- Follow the procedure used on page T98 to guide you through the lesson.

### Reading Recommendations

- No nondecodable words are in this book. See page T98 for the Reading Recommendations procedures.

### Responding

- Invite the students to discuss any hard words they encountered in *Bizz Buzz* and how they figured out these words. Call on volunteers to retell the story.
- Refer back to page T99 as a guide for this portion of the lesson.

**What kind of buzz is it?** *(It is a big buzz.)*
**From where do the children think the noise comes?** *(from Dad)*
**What is the buzz?** *(It is a jazz band.)*

### Building Fluency

Encourage partners to build fluency by rereading ***Decodable Books 32*** and ***33*** of the Core Set. After the second reading, the partners should read ***Decodable Books 24***, *Liz*, and ***25***, *Fuzz on a Cuff*, of the Practice Set.

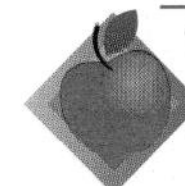

**Teacher Tip** **DECODABLE BOOKS** It is recommended that you send a story home after it has been read several times in class. Stories are available in the ***Decodable Takehome Books***.

**Informal Assessment**

**READING PROGRESS** While the students are reading to each other, invite several individuals to read with you so that you can assess their reading.

**Routine Card**
Refer to ***Routine 5*** to review the procedure for reading a ***Decodable Book***.



**Use Decodable Books in Levels K–3 to support systematic phonics instruction.**

**Focus instruction and make teaching and learning easy by using instructional routines.**

**Provide multiple opportunities to practice fluency.**

**Help guide Workshop by using Teacher Tips that suggest varied activities.**

**Monitor student progress with Informal Assessment tips to meet individual needs.**

# Reading & Responding

## Skills and strategies help students make sense of text.

**Part 2 of every lesson contains:**

- **Authentic literature**
- **Comprehension strategies and skills instruction**
- **Inquiry and Investigation**

**Teach comprehension strategies through teacher modeling.**

**Use highlighted selection words to build word knowledge or phonics sound/spellings.**

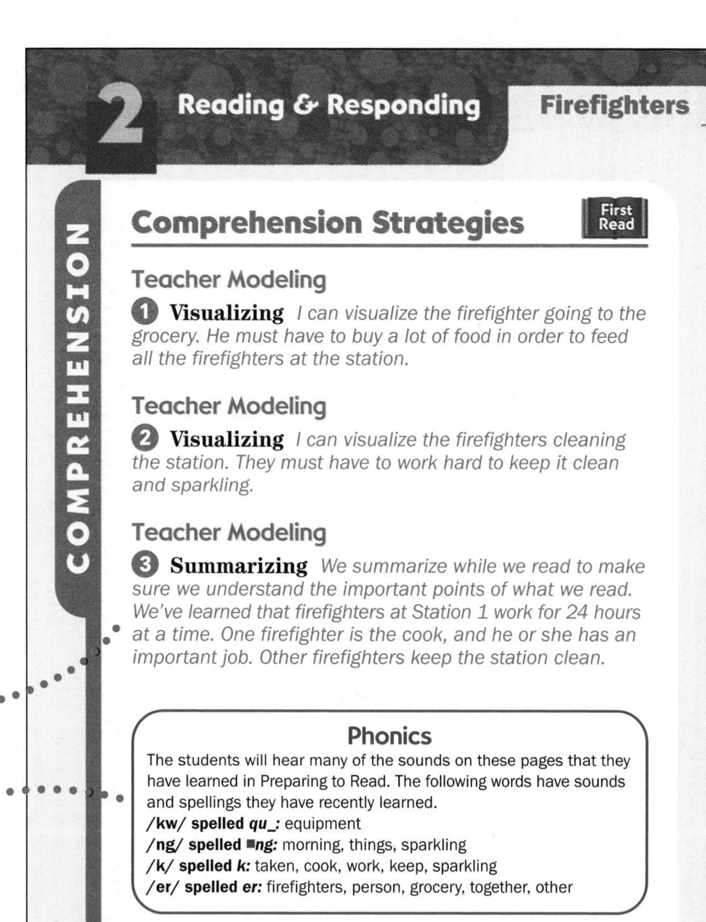

2 Reading & Responding | Firefighters

COMPREHENSION

### Comprehension Strategies

First Read

Teacher Modeling

❶ **Visualizing** *I can visualize the firefighter going to the grocery. He must have to buy a lot of food in order to feed all the firefighters at the station.*

Teacher Modeling

❷ **Visualizing** *I can visualize the firefighters cleaning the station. They must have to work hard to keep it clean and sparkling.*

Teacher Modeling

❸ **Summarizing** *We summarize while we read to make sure we understand the important points of what we read. We've learned that firefighters at Station 1 work for 24 hours at a time. One firefighter is the cook, and he or she has an important job. Other firefighters keep the station clean.*

**Phonics**

The students will hear many of the sounds on these pages that they have learned in Preparing to Read. The following words have sounds and spellings they have recently learned.

**/kw/ spelled *qu_*:** equipment
**/ng/ spelled ■*ng*:** morning, things, sparkling
**/k/ spelled *k*:** taken, cook, work, keep, sparkling
**/er/ spelled *er*:** firefighters, person, grocery, together, other

**Teacher Tip SUMMARIZING** As the students listen to the selection, have them summarize from time to time. This will help them know whether they understand the selection as well as help them remember it later.

*Focus Questions* What do firefighters do? How do firefighters help your neighborhood?

**Firefighters**

Jan Mader

*photography by Justin Shady*

*This book is dedicated to hardworking firefighters everywhere. Special thanks to Lt. John Hill.*

Inside Station 1 at 8:00 each morning roll call is taken. The firefighters live at the fire station for 24 hours at a time and there are many things to do.

24

Some firefighters think that the cook has the most important job at the station.

26

T128 Unit 4 Lesson 6

Theme: **Our Neighborhood at Work**

Review Comprehension Skills explicitly taught through all grade levels.

One of the firefighters is the cook. He collects money from each person and goes to the grocery store to buy enough food for the whole crew. 1

25

Other firefighters work together to keep the fire station sparkling clean. 2 The fire trucks are washed every morning, and the other equipment is cleaned and checked regularly, too. 3

27

## Comprehension Skills

Second Read

COMPREHENSION

### Main Idea and Details

Have the students tell what they know about Main Idea and Details. Explain that the main idea is one big idea that the author wants you to understand. Details are small pieces of information that help support the main idea.

Point out that the words *there are many things to do* are a clue to the main idea of "Firefighters." The main idea is that firefighters have many things to do at work.

### Differentiating Instruction

**Intervention Tip**

**MAIN IDEA AND DETAILS** To further help students identify the main idea, say, "Pretend you are the writer of this selection. Tell the class the big idea you would like the readers to learn."

Apply Intervention Tips given throughout each lesson in order to differentiate instruction.

Unit 4 Lesson 6 T129

# Language Arts

## Students make connections using an integrated Language Arts approach.

**Part 3 of every lesson contains:**

- Spelling
- Vocabulary
- Writing process strategies
- Writer's craft
- Grammar, usage, and mechanics
- Listening, speaking, and viewing
- Penmanship
- TechKnowledge

Present many opportunities to differentiate instruction in every part of the lesson.

Develop word-processing skills while working on the writing lesson.

Connect current research to instruction using Research in Action.

## 3 Language Arts
Firefighters

**Objectives**

**Word Analysis Vocabulary**
- **Compound Words.** Using words from "Firefighters," develop the understanding that compound words derive their meaning from the meanings of two words that are joined together to make one new word.

**Writing Process Strategies**
- **Personal Writing: Thank-you note.** Building on the theme "Our Neighborhood at Work," learn the form and purpose of a thank-you note as an expression of gratitude.

**English Language Conventions**
- **End Punctuation.** Understand correct use of end punctuation for declarative, interrogative, and exclamatory sentences.

**Materials**
- Language Arts Big Book, pp. 43, 150
- Comprehension and Language Arts Skills, pp. 52–53

**Differentiating Instruction**

***Reteach, Challenge,*** and ***Intervention*** lessons are available to support the language arts instruction in this lesson.

**Research in Action**

**Spelling**

Treat spelling as a complex process. Remember that part of the problem with the teaching and learning of spelling has been that we have treated it too simplistically: as a memorization task, as a list to be assigned, as learning that occurs incidentally, or as not important at all. Learning to spell is an important aspect of language and learning to spell is complex. (*J. Richard Gentry and Jean Wallace Gillet,* Teaching Kids to Spell)

OVERVIEW

### Language Arts Overview

#### Word Analysis

**Vocabulary** The Vocabulary activity focuses on vocabulary from "Firefighters" to discover that compound words are words that combine the meanings of two words that can stand alone, forming a new word. This activity also introduces the use of a dictionary to determine whether student-generated words are compound words or separate words.

**Vocabulary Skill Words**

| | | | | |
|---|---|---|---|---|
| firefighters* | fireman | fireplace | fireworks | firefly |
| everywhere | everyone | everything | everybody | |

*Also Selection Vocabulary*

**Additional Materials**

classroom dictionaries

#### Writing Process Strategies

The Writing Process Strategies lesson introduces the purpose of a thank-you note, a form of personal writing. A thank-you note is a form of writing that is used to express gratitude for something such as gift, a special time, special help given, or a kind deed.

To develop computer skills for writing, help students start writing a thank-you note by opening a blank word processing document and keying in text. Show students how to create new lines using the **Return** or **Enter** key. ***TechKnowledge*** Level 1 Lessons 20–21 teach these word processing skills.

**Professional Development**

***Teacher Resource Library CD-ROMs*** or ***Online Professional Development*** provides courses that help you better understand the Writing instruction in ***Open Court Reading.*** For more information about this program, visit SRAonline.com.

#### English Language Conventions

**Grammar, Usage, and Mechanics** **End Punctuation.** This lesson develops the understanding of proper use of periods, question marks, and exclamation points.

T136 Unit 4 Lesson 6

Theme: **Our Neighborhood at Work**

## Word Analysis

### Vocabulary

**Compound Words**

**Teach**

- Explain that some words are two words joined together to form a new word. For example, in today's reading selection, the word *firefighters* is a compound word formed by two separate words, *fire* and *fighters*. This new compound word takes its meaning from the words *fire* and *fighters: Firefighters are people who fight fires.*
- Write the word *fire* on the board, and ask students to suggest new compound words by joining *fire* to other words *(fireman, fireplace, fireworks, fireproof, firefly, firearm).*
- Explain that some words, such as *fire truck* and *fire station*, are not compound words, and that you will teach them later on how to use a dictionary to determine whether a word is a compound word or two separate words.

**Guided Practice**

- Explain that the word *everywhere* is also a compound word as you write it on the board. Ask students to suggest separate meanings of the words *every (all, each)*, and *where (location, place).*
- Explain that they can discover the meaning of *everywhere* in a dictionary.
- **Teacher Model:** Model using a dictionary for them by looking up the meaning of everywhere. *(in all places)*
- Encourage students to create new compound words beginning with *every (everyone, everybody, everything)* as you write their answers under the heading.
- Conclude by discussing the meanings of their new compound words.

## Writing Process Strategies

**Getting Ideas**

**Thank-You Note**

**Teach**

**Introduce Writing Form**

Read ***Language Arts Big Book*** page 43 to introduce the thank-you note writing form. Discuss the page. Point out the parts of a thank-you note, including the commas.

**Inspiration**

**Teacher Model:** Model ideas for a thank-you note related to the unit investigation and "Our Neighborhood at Work." *I want to thank someone whose job helps the community. I could thank someone who works in the school, someone who does something for all of us, or a firefighter.*

**Brainstorming**

- Using how people's jobs help others as a basis for ideas, encourage students to suggest ideas for thank-you notes they could write (thanking the school employee who came to speak to the class or a person in the community who does something for everybody (police officer, trash collector, and so on).
- Discuss ways that firefighters help the community. Have students start thinking about writing a thank-you note to a firefighter. See Inquiry, page T172.

**Guided Practice**

Have students write their ideas in their Writer's Notebook. Then have each student choose an idea to develop. Make sure the ideas are practical and sincere.

Thank-You Notes

A **thank-you note** is a short letter. It thanks someone for a gift, a nice time, or something special he or she did for you.

Take a Look

Lila wrote this thank-you note to Gracie.

Greeting — Dear Gracie,
Message — Thank you for the puzzle. It looks like fun. I can't wait to put it together.
Closing — Your friend,
Your Name — Lila

Try It! Why did Lila write the note to Gracie?

Reading Your Writing

A thank-you note must tell why you are thanking a person.

FORMS OF WRITING/Personal Writing ▲ Thank-You Notes

*Language Arts Big Book p. 43*

## English Language Conventions

**Grammar, Usage, and Mechanics**

**End Punctuation**

**Teach**

- Explain that there are three kinds of sentences.
  Some sentences tell information.
  Some sentences ask a question.
  Some sentences show strong feelings.
- Each kind of sentence has an end mark.
  A telling sentence ends with a period **(.)**.
  An asking sentence ends with a question mark **(?)**.
  A strong feeling sentence ends with an exclamation point **(!)**.
- Use ***Language Arts Big Book*** page 150 for examples of sentences with proper end marks.

**Independent Practice**

Use ***Comprehension and Language Arts Skills*** pages 52 and 53 to practice using proper end punctuation.

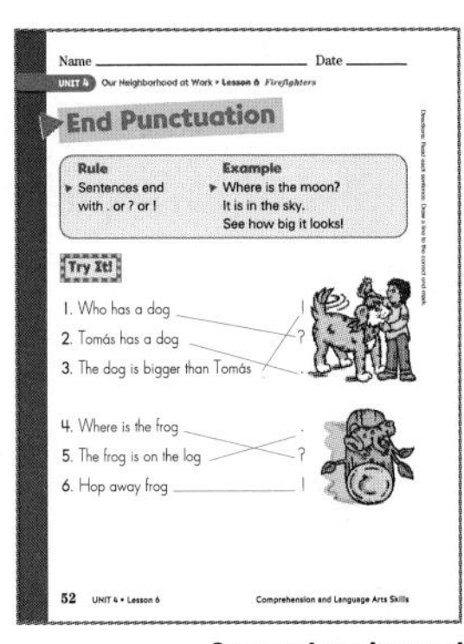

Name ______ Date ______

UNIT 4 Our Neighborhood at Work • Lesson 6 Firefighters

End Punctuation

| Rule | Example |
| --- | --- |
| ▸ Sentences end with . or ? or ! | ▸ Where is the moon? It is in the sky. See how big it looks! |

Try It!

1. Who has a dog
2. Tomás has a dog
3. The dog is bigger than Tomás
4. Where is the frog
5. The frog is on the log
6. Hop away frog

52 UNIT 4 • Lesson 6 — Comprehension and Language Arts Skills

*Comprehension and Language Arts Skills p. 52*



Offer daily practice activities for Language Arts.

Explicitly teach lessons using the Teach-and-Practice format.

Support the implementation of the writing process using Guided Practice activities.

# Professional Development

## Partner with SRA/McGraw-Hill to meet reading challenges with confidence.

At SRA/McGraw-Hill, we recognize that high-quality, long-term professional development, combined with an understanding of your needs, is critical to the successful implementation of ***Open Court Reading.*** Our commitment to systematic and sustained staff development has led to unparalleled communication between administrators, teachers, students, and SRA consultants. Our continued commitment to quality, both in product and professional development, is the hallmark of SRA, and we are fully dedicated to working with you to support your needs in the classroom.

SRA's staff development helps you teach all students to read by providing options including

- hands-on, interactive staff development.
- individual classroom demonstration and coaching by classroom-experienced consultants.
- customized workshops to meet district and staff needs.
- staff development for administrators and support staff.
- online staff development to accommodate teachers' needs and schedules.
- summer workshops and institutes.
- CD-ROMs with classroom demonstrations of best practices.

"I love ***Open Court Reading!*** It is so easy to teach (and allows me to incorporate so many creative touches), and my students just soak up the lessons."

— **Laura Ivory,** Grade K Teacher
St. James Catholic School,
Perris, CA

## Professional Development Resources

### Professional Development Guides

- Explain the research behind ***Open Court Reading***'s Comprehension, Phonics, Writing, Assessment, and Inquiry

### Online Professional Development

- Videos showing best-practice instruction at all grade levels
- Practical advice from program consultants helps support teachers and principals

### Teacher's Resource Library

- CD-ROMs showing video footage of best-practice instruction

### Lesson Model Videos

- Videos showing ***Open Court*** teachers in classroom situations

# Meet the *Open Court Reading* Authors

**Marilyn Jager Adams, Ph.D.**
Cited in the *2000 Politics of Education Yearbook* as one of the most influential people in the national reading policy arena, Dr. Adams has worked closely with a number of agencies to develop reading standards, policies, and staff development strategies.

**Carl Bereiter, Ph.D.**
An accomplished author, researcher, and professor, Dr. Bereiter has published extensively on teaching and learning. A member of the National Academy of Education, Dr. Bereiter also invented CSILE (Computer Supported Intentional Learning Environments), the first networked collaborative learning environment in schools, with Dr. Marlene Scardamalia; the current version, *Knowledge Forum®*, is in use in twelve countries.

**Joe Campione, Ph.D.**
A leading researcher on cognitive development, individual differences, assessment, and the design of innovative learning environments, Dr. Campione is currently a Professor in the School of Education at University of California, Berkeley.

**Iva Carruthers, Ph.D.**
Equipped with both hands-on and academic experience, Dr. Carruthers serves as a consultant and lecturer in both educational technology and matters of multicultural inclusion.

**Jan Hirshberg, Ed.D.**
Focusing on how children learn to read and write and the logistics of teaching reading and writing in the early grades, Dr. Hirshberg currently works as a language arts resource teacher and consultant in Alexandria, Virginia.

**Anne McKeough, Ph.D.**
A Professor in the Division of Applied Psychology and Chair of the Human Learning and Development program at the University of Calgary, Dr. McKeough has received a number of research awards and grants.

**Michael Pressley, Ph.D.**
Most recently honored by the National Reading Conference as the 2000 recipient of the Oscar Causey Award for career contributions to reading research, Dr. Pressley is Professor of Educational Psychology and Teacher Education at Michigan State University. He has authored numerous books and articles about reading instruction and comprehension.

**Marsha Roit, Ed.D.**
The Director of Professional Development for SRA/McGraw-Hill, Dr. Roit spends considerable time in classrooms developing reading curricula and working with teachers and administrators in effective instructional practices. Dr. Roit has also published in a variety of professional journals, including *Exceptional Children*, *Journal of Learning Disabilities*, and *The Elementary School Journal.*

**Marlene Scardamalia, Ph.D.**
A Professor at the Centre for Applied Cognitive Science and Department of Curriculum Teaching and Learning, Ontario Institute for Studies in Education, Dr. Scardamalia has conducted research and been published in the areas of cognitive development, psychology of writing, intentional learning, the nature of expertise, and educational uses of computers. She is also a member of the U.S. National Academy of Education.

**Marcy Stein, Ph.D.**
An Associate Professor and founding faculty member of the education program at the University of Washington, Dr. Stein currently coordinates At-Risk and Special Education graduate programs and teaches in the teacher certification program. She has served as consultant to departments of education on the translation of reading research to instructional practice.

**Gerald H. Treadway, Jr., Ph.D.**
Professor at San Diego State University, Dr. Treadway teaches classes on reading methods, balanced reading programs, bilingual methods, and reading comprehension. He is the Director of Research and Development for the California Reading & Literature Project.

UNIT 4 Table of Contents

# Money

**Lesson Skills**

| Word Knowledge | Comprehension | Language Arts |
|---|---|---|
| • Homophones<br>• Base Words and Suffixes *-ed, -ment, -tion, -sion*<br>• Word Families<br>• Double Consonants | **Strategies**<br>• Monitoring and Clarifying<br>• Predicting<br>• Summarizing<br>• Making Connections<br>**Skills**<br>• Making Inferences | • Double Consonants<br>• Writing a Friendly Letter<br>• Prepositions |



**Lesson Skills**

| Word Knowledge | Comprehension | Language Arts |
|---|---|---|
| • Synonyms<br>• Suffixes *-ly, -able*<br>• Final Double Consonants | **Strategies**<br>• Monitoring and Clarifying<br>• Summarizing<br>• Predicting<br>• Making Connections<br>**Skills**<br>• Cause and Effect | • Final Double Consonants<br>• Writing: Making a Poster<br>• Subject and Predicate |

**Lesson Skills**

| Word Knowledge | Comprehension | Language Arts |
|---|---|---|
| • Compound Words<br>• /ā/ Spelled *ai_, a_e, _ay*<br>• Base Words with Affixes<br>• Contractions | **Strategies**<br>• Monitoring and Clarifying<br>• Making Connections<br>• Summarizing<br>**Skills**<br>• Main Idea and Supporting Details | • Contractions<br>• Writing a Business Letter<br>• Parentheses and Periods |

# National Advisory Board



# Contributing Author



# Literature Consultants



# Program Reviewers

Level 3 • Unit 4

# Money

# UNIT 4 OVERVIEW

# Exploring the Theme

## Introduction

The selections in this unit are related in various ways to the idea of money as a measure of value and as a means of exchange. Students should be encouraged to use these selections as a springboard for thinking about different forms of money, how money works, and the role of money in people's lives and businesses.

All people have a natural curiosity about money. Children especially become very interested in money at this age. Some students receive allowances, and some do not. Most depend entirely on their families for any money they may receive. Students of this age are bombarded with ads enticing them to spend money—usually money they do not have. However, these enticements have little to do with value. This combination of scarcity, desirability, and need provides a good base for questions about money. Students can investigate these questions and, perhaps, gain a new understanding, appreciation, and respect for money.



***Teacher's Edition*** page numbers correspond to page numbers in the ***Student Anthology.***

## Investigation Goals

Although most students know something about money, many may not know how and why people began to use money, or how the monetary value of objects is set. One of the goals of ***Open Court Reading*** is to encourage students to question the world around them—to find out how and why the world is the way it is. A variety of text types—realistic fiction, historical fiction, expository texts, fables, humorous fiction, and poetry—help illustrate the universal curiosity about money. These stories will help students clarify their understanding of money and its role in society and their lives. These selections may even help bring about conceptual change—students may start with one idea about money but change their minds as they continue with their investigation. In addition, students will use their growing research abilities to develop their own questions and follow those questions to new learning. The investigation goals for this unit are to:

- encourage students to learn about the role money plays in their lives.
- encourage students to learn that the choices they make about money can change their lives.
- encourage students to learn the value of money.
- enable students to see that problems of significance to them can be questioned, investigated, and enlightened through their own efforts.

## Learning Goals

Within each of the general investigation goals, a number of more specific learning goals are pursued. Students will:

- **listen, write, and speak** on the topic of money.
- **participate in small and large group discussions and lead discussion** about money.
- **ask and answer questions** relevant to money.
- **relate the ideas and experiences of the texts** to their own ideas and experiences.
- **develop** a vocabulary about money.
- **make cultural connections** by reading the selections.
- **identify different types of literature**.
- **investigate, using a variety of resources,** ways to make, spend, and save money.

**Teacher Tip** Money raises a wide variety of questions. To stimulate your own thinking, you might ask students questions like the following.

- ✔ How would your life change if suddenly there was no money in the world?
- ✔ When people use credit cards to pay for something, are they paying with real money? How about when someone writes a check? Why do people so often use checks and credit cards instead of cash?
- ✔ Who decides how much money something is worth?
- ✔ Why do so many people carry debt?
- ✔ Of the things you want most, which ones can you buy with money? Which things can't you buy with money?

# Exploring the Theme

## Supporting Student Investigations

Students are encouraged throughout ***Open Court Reading*** to deepen their knowledge of each of the themes presented. In learning more about money, students will need to talk to people about money, as well as read stories and articles that revolve around the theme of money.

Encourage students to use their personal experience to interpret the literature they read about money. Because it is also important for students to extend their thinking and for their views to be challenged and developed, encourage them to use this literature to reinterpret their personal experiences.

Explain to students that they will gain a better understanding of the concept of money as they progress through the unit's selections and as they work on the unit investigation. Remind them of the investigation possibilities they were introduced to in Unit 1. These include such things as:

- A miniplay or puppet show about money.
- A role-playing game to work out a problem about money.
- A panel discussion about money-related issues.
- A debate on an issue related to money.
- An advice column dealing with money-related problems.
- A personal experience story about money.

## Unit Investigations

Unit investigations are student-driven and should emerge from students' interests, encouraged or ignited by reading and class discussions. Investigations should involve reading beyond program material and address the conceptual aims of the unit.

### Suggested Activities

Students will enjoy the independent nature of this investigation. They will use resources such as the library, the Internet, interviews, and guest speakers to gather information about money. The suggested activities below are intended to support the unit investigation.

- Plan several trips to the library. Ask the librarian to provide many resources that give information about money.
- Plan to invite a businessperson as a guest speaker. Students will benefit from a firsthand account of how a business is owned and operated.
- Encourage students to use the Internet as they research saving and investing money.

| | OVERVIEW OF SELECTION | LINK TO THE THEME | UNIT INVESTIGATIONS | SUPPORTING STUDENT INVESTIGATIONS |
|---|---|---|---|---|
| **Lesson 1** *A New Coat for Anna* | ■ Anna needs a new coat. Her mother has no money. What is she to do? Sometimes imagination and ingenuity work as well as money. | ■ There are ways of obtaining what we need without money. | ■ Discuss bartering. | ■ Students brainstorm questions about the theme. ■ Help students begin thinking about groups. ■ Discuss the difference between investigation topics and questions. |
| **Lesson 2** *Alexander, Who Used to Be Rich Last Sunday* | ■ Alexander uses ample humor to tell the story of how, in a very short time, he squandered a lot of money. | ■ It can be difficult to save money, especially when faced with so many temptations to spend it. | ■ Investigate choices related to saving and spending money. | ■ Groups form based on areas of shared interest. ■ Provide assistance in forming groups if necessary. |
| **Lesson 3** *Kids Did It! in Business* | ■ Children are ingenious, creative, and responsive in the businesses they imagine and go on to build. | ■ Some children earn money by starting their own businesses. This involves imagination and hard work. | ■ Brainstorm about turning hobbies into businesses. | ■ Demonstrate conjectures and provide necessary assistance in phrasing them. ■ Begin forming conjectures. |
| **Lesson 4** *The Cobbler's Song* | ■ The cobbler sings while he works. What makes him so happy? Why does his song so irritate his neighbor? | ■ Wealth does not necessarily bring happiness. | ■ Discuss things money cannot buy and the ways money can change people. | ■ Discuss conjectures in groups and begin plans. ■ Help groups identify investigation needs. |
| **Lesson 5** *Four Dollars and Fifty Cents* | ■ Borrowing money can lead to trouble. How far will someone go to avoid repaying a debt? | ■ Problems can beset people who live on credit. | ■ Debate on borrowing and lending money. | ■ Groups revise plans as necessary and continue investigation. ■ Help groups identify things that need revision. |
| **Lesson 6** *The Go-Around Dollar* | ■ How many times does a dollar change hands in one day? Where do dollar bills come from? This engaging nonfiction and narrative selection examines these and other questions. | ■ Paper money is carefully managed by the federal government. Money constantly changes hands. | ■ Create a story or miniplay about the journey of a dollar bill. Visit a Federal Reserve Bank if possible. | ■ Continue investigation and prepare final presentations. ■ Point out areas that might still need work. ■ Allow time for informal presentations. |
| **Lesson 7** *Uncle Jed's Barbershop* | ■ Uncle Jed had a lifelong dream of owning his own barbershop. Will a family crisis and the Great Depression make his dream impossible? | ■ Many dreams must be paid for with money. Saving the money takes patience and determination. | ■ Discuss saving money for goals. | ■ Help students with final preparations. ■ Groups give formal presentations. |

## Student Materials

### Student Anthology
**Pages 12–105**

### Inquiry Journal
**Pages 82–106**

### Writer's Workbook
**Pages 54–81**

### Comprehension and Language Arts Skills
**Pages 92–125**

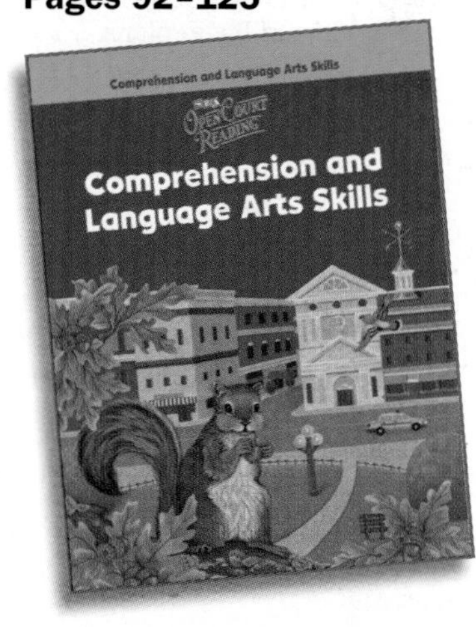


### Spelling and Vocabulary Skills
**Pages 74–101**

### Language Arts Handbook

### Additional Materials

- Listening Library Audiocassettes/CDs
- Unit 4 Assessment
- Writing Folder
- Student Research Assistant
- Science/Social Studies Connection Center

### Differentiating Instruction

- English Learner Support Activities
- Intervention Workbook
- Reteach
- Challenge
- Decodable Books
- Decodable Takehome Books
- Leveled Classroom Library

## Teacher Materials

### Teacher's Edition, Book 4
**Pages 12–105P**

### Read Aloud
*Money, Money, Money*

### Home Connection
**Pages 43–58**

### Comprehension and Language Arts Skills Teacher's Edition
**Pages 92–125**

### Spelling and Vocabulary Skills Teacher's Edition
**Pages 74–101**

### Writer's Workbook Teacher's Edition
**Pages 54–81**

### Overhead Transparencies
**Reading Numbers 23–30, 43, 46, 49, 50, 53**
**Language Arts Numbers 6, 14–15, 18, 22, 24, 27–28, 37**

### Additional Materials

- Teacher's Professional Guides
- Read Alouds
- Online Professional Development
- Teacher Resource Library
- Online Phonics
- Online Assessment

### Differentiating Instruction

- English Learner Support Guide
- Intervention Guide
- Intervention Annotated Bibliography
- Reteach Teacher's Edition
- Challenge Teacher's Edition

## Leveled Classroom Library*

### Easy

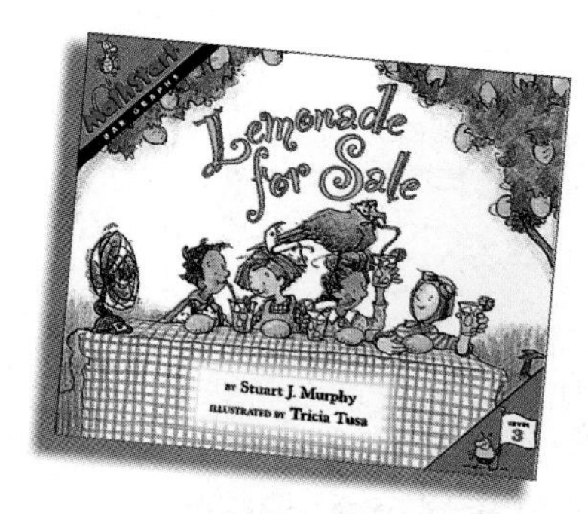

### Average

### Advanced

## Bibliography**

*The Money Tree* **by Sarah Stewart**

*One Grain of Rice* **by Demi**

*If You Made a Million* **by David M. Schwartz**

*The Gold Coin* **by Alma Flor Ada**

*A Spoon for Every Bite* **by Joe Hayes**

*Aldo Ice Cream* **by Johanna Hurwitz**

*The Treasure Bird* **by Peni R. Griffin**

*A Kid's Guide to Money: Earning It, Saving It, Spending It, Growing It, Sharing It* **by Steve Otfinoski**

Note: Teachers should preview any trade books and videos for appropriateness in their classrooms before recommending them to students.
* These books, which all support the unit theme Money, are part of a 36-book ***Leveled Classroom Library*** available for purchase from SRA/McGraw-Hill.
** Check libraries or bookstores for availability.

# TECHNOLOGY

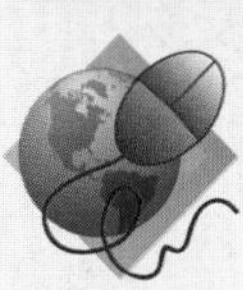

## Web Connections

### Money Web Sites

Information about Money and links to sites concerning Money can be found at **www.sra4kids.com.**

### Online Professional Development

***Online Professional Development*** delivers 20 courses with full-motion video teaching examples. Teachers can also participate in Learning Communities and Discussion Boards available through the site at **ww.SRAonline.com.**

### Online Phonics

***Online Phonics*** offers Internet-based activities that provide students with phonics practice to support ***Open Court Reading*** lessons. The management tool collects students' data and notifies the teacher of their progress. Available at **www.SRAonline.com.**

### Online Assessment

***Online Assessment*** offers automated delivery and scoring of End of Unit and Program Assessments. Data is compiled into reports that help teachers make classroom instructional decisions and guide individualized instruction. Available at **www.SRAonline.com.**

## CD-ROMs

### * Research Assistant

As students continue their investigations of money, the ***Research Assistant CD-ROM*** program will help them organize and share their findings.

### * OCR Spelling

Use this software for extra spelling practice for this unit.

### * The Ultimate Writing and Creativity Center

THE LEARNING COMPANY, 2002

Students can use this word processing software to get ideas, draft, revise, edit, and publish their Writing Process Strategies activities in this unit.

Titles preceded by an asterisk (*) are available through SRA/McGraw-Hill. Other titles can be obtained by contacting the publisher listed with the title.

### Money Town

SIMON & SCHUSTER INTERACTIVE

Students learn about earning, saving, making change, and much more as they work to reopen a park.

### * Teacher Resource Library

***Teacher Resource Library*** covers subjects such as classroom management, English Learners, assessment, and more. Included are videos of teachers and students in their classrooms and a wealth of text-based resources.

## Videocassettes

### *Learning about Money*

100% EDUCATIONAL VIDEOS, 2001

Students learn about the value of money, its different denominations, and the currencies used around the world. They also explore how coins are made. 14 min.

### * *The Talking Eggs*

A good-hearted girl is rewarded with great riches, while her sister and mother are punished for their greed. Available in English and Spanish. 21 min.

### *Uncle Jed's Barbershop*

GPN

Uncle Jed encounters several setbacks as he works to save enough money to make his dream of opening his own barbershop come true. 30 min.

## Audiocassette/CD

### * Listening Library: Money

Students will enjoy listening to the selections they have read. Encourage them to listen during Workshop.

## Computer Skills

### * TechKnowledge

***SRA TechKnowledge*** can be used to help students develop computer skills within the context of the unit theme.

# UNIT 4 OVERVIEW

UNIT SKILLS OVERVIEW

| | WORD KNOWLEDGE | COMPREHENSION | LITERARY ELEMENTS |
|---|---|---|---|
| **Lesson 1**<br>***A New Coat for Anna***<br>**Genre: Realistic Fiction** | ■ homophones; suffixes *-ed*, *-ment*, *-tion*, *-sion;* word families; double consonants | **Strategies**<br>■ Predicting<br>■ Monitoring and Clarifying<br>■ Making Connections<br>■ Summarizing<br>**Skills**<br>■ Making Inferences | ■ Plot |
| **Lesson 2**<br>***Alexander, Who Used to Be Rich Last Sunday***<br>**Genre: Realistic Fiction** | ■ synonyms; suffixes *-y*, *-able;* final double consonants | **Strategies**<br>■ Making Connections<br>■ Summarizing<br>■ Predicting<br>■ Monitoring and Clarifying<br>**Skills**<br>■ Cause and Effect | ■ Characterization |
| **Lesson 3**<br>***Kids Did It! in Business***<br>**Genre: Expository Text** | ■ compound words; base words and affixes; /ā/ sound spellings; contractions | **Strategies**<br>■ Summarizing<br>■ Monitoring and Clarifying<br>■ Making Connections<br>**Skills**<br>■ Main Idea and Supporting Details | ■ Expository Texts |
| **Lesson 4**<br>***The Cobbler's Song***<br>**Genre: Fable** | ■ review suffixes *-ed*, *-ing*, *-ful*, *-ly;* /ē/ spelled *ie* or *ei* | **Strategies**<br>■ Predicting<br>■ Summarizing<br>■ Asking Questions<br>**Skills**<br>■ Author's Purpose | ■ Recognizing and Distinguishing Fables |
| **Lesson 5**<br>***Four Dollars and Fifty Cents***<br>**Genre: Tall Tale** | ■ compound words; suffixes *-ed*, *-ing*, *-ial;* plural endings *-s*, *-es* | **Strategies**<br>■ Monitoring and Clarifying<br>■ Summarizing<br>■ Making Connections<br>■ Predicting<br>**Skills**<br>■ Author's Point of View<br>■ Drawing Conclusions | ■ Colloquial Speech |
| **Lesson 6**<br>***The Go-Around Dollar***<br>**Genre: Expository Text/Narrative** | ■ suffix *-ment;* antonyms; related words; final /nk/; /n/ spelled *gn_;* /t/ spelled *bt;* compound words | **Strategies**<br>■ Asking Questions<br>■ Making Connections<br>■ Summarizing<br>**Skills**<br>■ Sequence | ■ Dialogue |
| **Lesson 7**<br>***Uncle Jed's Barbershop***<br>**Genre: Historical Fiction** | ■ compound words; suffixes *-ment*, *-tion*, *-sion* | **Strategies**<br>■ Monitoring and Adjusting Reading Speed<br>■ Predicting<br>■ Summarizing<br>**Skills**<br>■ Cause and Effect | ■ Characterization |

| INQUIRY | WORD ANALYSIS | WRITING PROCESS STRATEGIES | ENGLISH LANGUAGE CONVENTIONS |
|---|---|---|---|
| ■ Choosing Appropriate Sources | **Spelling**<br>■ Double Consonants<br>**Vocabulary**<br>■ Base Word Families | **Persuasive Writing**<br>■ Letter<br>**Writer's Craft**<br>■ Fact and Opinion | **Grammar**<br>■ Prepositions<br>**Listening, Speaking, Viewing**<br>■ Listening: Recognizing Facts and Opinions<br>**Penmanship**<br>■ Cursive Letters *A* and *C* |
| ■ Card Catalogue | **Spelling**<br>■ Final Double Consonants<br>**Vocabulary**<br>■ The Suffix *-ly* | **Persuasive Writing**<br>■ Poster<br>**Writer's Craft**<br>■ Time and Order Words | **Grammar**<br>■ Subjects and Predicates<br>**Listening, Speaking, Viewing**<br>■ Speaking: Elements of Grammar<br>**Penmanship**<br>■ Cursive Letters *E* and *O* |
| ■ Parts of a Book | **Spelling**<br>■ Contractions<br>**Vocabulary**<br>■ Business Vocabulary | **Persuasive Writing**<br>■ Business Letter<br>**Writer's Craft**<br>■ Structure of a Business Letter | **Grammar**<br>■ Parenthesis; Periods in Abbreviations, Initials, and Titles<br>**Listening, Speaking, Viewing**<br>■ Language: Choosing Words<br>**Penmanship**<br>■ Cursive Letters *N* and *M* |
| ■ Graphs | **Spelling**<br>■ Adding *-ed* and *-ing*<br>**Vocabulary**<br>■ The Endings *-ed* and *-ing* | **Persuasive Writing**<br>■ Persuasive Paragraph<br>**Writer's Craft**<br>■ Avoiding Wordiness | **Grammar**<br>■ Possessive Pronouns<br>**Listening, Speaking, Viewing**<br>■ Viewing: Media Techniques<br>**Penmanship**<br>■ Cursive Letters *K* and *H* |
| ■ Comparing Information Across Sources | **Spelling**<br>■ Adding *-s* or *-es*<br>**Vocabulary**<br>■ Compound Words | **Persuasive Writing**<br>■ Friendly Letter<br>**Writer's Craft**<br>■ Sentence Combining | **Grammar**<br>■ Subject/Verb Agreement<br>**Listening, Speaking, Viewing**<br>■ Interacting: Conversations<br>**Penmanship**<br>■ Cursive Letters *U* and *Y* |
| ■ Diagrams | **Spelling**<br>■ Compound Words<br>**Vocabulary**<br>■ Money Words | **Persuasive Writing**<br>■ Poster<br>**Writer's Craft**<br>■ Supporting Details | **Grammar**<br>■ Adverbs<br>**Listening, Speaking, Viewing**<br>■ Presenting: Organizing a Presentation<br>**Penmanship**<br>■ Cursive Letters *Z* and *V* |
| ■ Time Lines | **Spelling**<br>■ Unit 4 Review<br>**Vocabulary**<br>■ Unit 4 Review | **Persuasive Writing**<br>■ Persuasive Paragraph<br>**Writer's Craft**<br>■ Effective Beginnings | **Grammar**<br>■ Review<br>**Listening, Speaking, Viewing**<br>■ Interacting: Engaging an Audience<br>**Penmanship**<br>■ Cursive Letters *X* and *W* |

# DIFFERENTIATING INSTRUCTION

| | Reteach | English Learner | Challenge | Intervention |
|---|---|---|---|---|
| **Lesson 1** *A New Coat for Anna* | **Language Arts**<br>■ **Spelling:** Double Consonants<br>■ **Vocabulary:** Base Word Families<br>■ **Grammar:** Prepositions<br>■ **Writer's Craft:** Fact and Opinion | **Reading and Responding**<br>■ Vocabulary<br>■ Comprehension: Making Inferences | **Language Arts**<br>■ **Spelling:** Double Consonants<br>■ **Vocabulary:** Base Word Families<br>■ **Grammar:** Prepositions<br>■ **Writer's Craft:** Fact and Opinion | **Preparing to Read**<br>■ Word Knowledge<br>**Reading and Responding**<br>■ Selection Vocabulary<br>**Language Arts**<br>■ **Vocabulary Strategies:** Grammar, Usage, and Mechanics |
| **Lesson 2** *Alexander, Who Used to Be Rich Last Sunday* | **Reading and Responding**<br>■ Cause and Effect<br>**Language Arts**<br>■ **Spelling:** Final Double Consonants<br>■ **Vocabulary:** The Suffix *-ly*<br>■ **Grammar:** Subjects and Predicates<br>■ **Writer's Craft:** Time-Order Words | **Reading and Responding**<br>■ Vocabulary<br>■ Comprehension: Cause and Effect | **Reading and Responding**<br>■ Cause and Effect<br>**Language Arts**<br>■ **Spelling:** Final Double Consonants<br>■ **Vocabulary:** The Suffix *-ly*<br>■ **Grammar:** Subjects and Predicates<br>■ **Writer's Craft:** Time-Order Words | **Preparing to Read**<br>■ Word Knowledge<br>**Reading and Responding**<br>■ Selection Vocabulary<br>**Language Arts**<br>■ **Vocabulary Strategies:** Grammar, Usage, and Mechanics |
| **Lesson 3** *Kids Did It! in Business* | **Language Arts**<br>■ **Spelling:** Contractions<br>■ **Vocabulary:** Business Vocabulary<br>■ **Grammar:** Parenthesis; Periods in Abbreviations, Initials, and Titles<br>■ **Writer's Craft:** Structure of a Business Letter | **Reading and Responding**<br>■ Vocabulary<br>■ Comprehension: Main Idea and Details | **Language Arts**<br>■ **Spelling:** Contractions<br>■ **Vocabulary:** Business Vocabulary<br>■ **Grammar:** Parenthesis; Periods in Abbreviations, Initials, and Titles<br>■ **Writer's Craft:** Structure of a Business Letter | **Preparing to Read**<br>■ Word Knowledge<br>**Reading and Responding**<br>■ Selection Vocabulary<br>**Language Arts**<br>■ **Vocabulary Strategies:** Grammar, Usage, and Mechanics |
| **Lesson 4** *The Cobbler's Song* | **Reading and Responding**<br>■ Author's Purpose<br>**Language Arts**<br>■ **Spelling:** Adding *-ed* and *-ing*<br>■ **Vocabulary:** The Endings *-ed* and *-ing*<br>■ **Grammar:** Possessive Pronouns<br>■ **Writer's Craft:** Avoiding Wordiness | **Reading and Responding**<br>■ Vocabulary<br>■ Comprehension: Summarizing | **Reading and Responding**<br>■ Author's Purpose<br>**Language Arts**<br>■ **Spelling:** Adding *-ed* and *-ing*<br>■ **Vocabulary:** The Endings *-ed* and *-ing*<br>■ **Grammar:** Possessive Pronouns<br>■ **Writer's Craft:** Avoiding Wordiness | **Preparing to Read**<br>■ Word Knowledge<br>**Reading and Responding**<br>■ Selection Vocabulary<br>**Language Arts**<br>■ **Vocabulary Strategies:** Grammar, Usage, and Mechanics |
| **Lesson 5** *Four Dollars and Fifty Cents* | **Language Arts**<br>■ **Spelling:** Plurals<br>■ **Vocabulary:** Compound Words<br>■ **Grammar:** Subject/Verb Agreement<br>■ **Writer's Craft:** Sentence Combining | **Reading and Responding**<br>■ Vocabulary<br>■ Comprehension: Drawing Conclusions; Author's Point of View | **Language Arts**<br>■ **Spelling:** Plurals<br>■ **Vocabulary:** Compound Words<br>■ **Grammar:** Subject/Verb Agreement<br>■ **Writer's Craft:** Sentence Combining | **Preparing to Read**<br>■ Word Knowledge<br>**Reading and Responding**<br>■ Selection Vocabulary<br>**Language Arts**<br>■ **Vocabulary Strategies:** Grammar, Usage, and Mechanics |
| **Lesson 6** *The Go-Around Dollar* | **Reading and Responding**<br>■ Sequence<br>**Language Arts**<br>■ **Spelling:** Compound Words<br>■ **Vocabulary:** Money Words<br>■ **Grammar:** Adverbs<br>■ **Writer's Craft:** Supporting Details | **Reading and Responding**<br>■ Vocabulary<br>■ Comprehension: Sequence | **Reading and Responding**<br>■ Sequence<br>**Language Arts**<br>■ **Spelling:** Compound Words<br>■ **Vocabulary:** Money Words<br>■ **Grammar:** Adverbs<br>■ **Writer's Craft:** Supporting Details | **Preparing to Read**<br>■ Word Knowledge<br>**Reading and Responding**<br>■ Selection Vocabulary<br>**Language Arts**<br>■ **Vocabulary Strategies:** Grammar, Usage, and Mechanics |
| **Lesson 7** *Uncle Jed's Barbershop* | **Language Arts**<br>■ **Spelling:** Unit 4 Review<br>■ **Vocabulary:** Unit 4 Review<br>■ **Grammar:** Review<br>■ **Writer's Craft:** Effective Beginnings | **Reading and Responding**<br>■ Vocabulary<br>■ Comprehension: Cause and Effect | **Language Arts**<br>■ **Spelling:** Unit 4 Review<br>■ **Vocabulary:** Unit 4 Review<br>■ **Grammar:** Review<br>■ **Writer's Craft:** Effective Beginnings | **Preparing to Read**<br>■ Word Knowledge<br>**Reading and Responding**<br>■ Selection Vocabulary<br>**Language Arts**<br>■ **Vocabulary Strategies:** Grammar, Usage, and Mechanics |

Above are suggestions for differentiating instruction to meet the individual needs of students. These are the same skills shown on the Unit Skills Overview; however, these pages provide extra practice opportunities or enriching activities to meet the varied needs of students.

| Informal Assessment | Progress Assessment | Formal Assessment |
|---|---|---|
| **Comprehension Strategies**, 14J, 14<br>**Concept Connections**, 24<br>***Grammar, Usage, and Mechanics**, 25H<br>***Listening, Speaking, Viewing**, 25I<br>***Vocabulary**, 25J<br>***Penmanship**, 25J | **Comprehension and Language Arts Skills**, 92–95<br>**Reteach**, 95–98<br>**Challenge**, 83–86<br>**Writer's Workbook**, 54–57<br>**Spelling and Vocabulary Skills**, 74–77<br>**Inquiry Journal**, 83, 87–88 | **Mid-Year Assessment**<br>**Unit 4 Assessment** **Lesson 1**<br>■ Selection Assessment, 2–5<br>■ Spelling Pretest, 30<br>■ Spelling Final Test, 31<br>*Writing Process Strategies Rubrics, 25J<br>*Research Rubrics, 14J |
| **Comprehension Strategies**, 26J, 26<br>**Concept Connections**, 34<br>***Grammar, Usage, and Mechanics**, 35H<br>***Listening, Speaking, Viewing**, 35I<br>***Vocabulary**, 35J<br>***Penmanship**, 35J | **Comprehension and Language Arts Skills**, 96–101<br>**Reteach**, 99–104<br>**Challenge**, 87–91<br>**Writer's Workbook**, 58–61<br>**Spelling and Vocabulary Skills**, 78–81<br>**Inquiry Journal**, 83, 89–92 | **Unit 4 Assessment** **Lesson 2**<br>■ Selection Assessment, 6–9<br>■ Spelling Pretest, 32<br>■ Spelling Final Test, 33<br>*Writing Process Strategies Rubrics, 35J<br>*Research Rubrics, 26J |
| **Comprehension Strategies**, 38J, 39<br>**Concept Connections**, 46<br>***Grammar, Usage, and Mechanics**, 47H<br>***Listening, Speaking, Viewing**, 47I<br>***Vocabulary**, 47J<br>***Penmanship**, 47J | **Comprehension and Language Arts Skills**, 102–105<br>**Reteach**, 105–108<br>**Challenge**, 92–95<br>**Writer's Workbook**, 62–65<br>**Spelling and Vocabulary Skills**, 82–85<br>**Inquiry Journal**, 84, 93–95 | **Unit 4 Assessment** **Lesson 3**<br>■ Selection Assessment, 10–13<br>■ Spelling Pretest, 34<br>■ Spelling Final Test, 35<br>*Writing Process Strategies Rubrics, 47J<br>*Research Rubrics, 38J |
| **Comprehension Strategies**, 48J, 49<br>**Concept Connections**, 54<br>***Grammar, Usage, and Mechanics**, 55H<br>***Listening, Speaking, Viewing**, 55I<br>***Vocabulary**, 55J<br>***Penmanship**, 55J | **Comprehension and Language Arts Skills**, 106–111<br>**Reteach**, 109–114<br>**Challenge**, 96–100<br>**Writer's Workbook**, 66–69<br>**Spelling and Vocabulary Skills**, 86–89<br>**Inquiry Journal**, 84, 96–98 | **Unit 4 Assessment** **Lesson 4**<br>■ Selection Assessment, 14–17<br>■ Spelling Pretest, 36<br>■ Spelling Final Test, 37<br>*Writing Process Strategies Rubrics, 55J<br>*Research Rubrics, 48J |
| **Comprehension Strategies**, 58J, 58<br>**Concept Connections**, 70<br>***Grammar, Usage, and Mechanics**, 71H<br>***Listening, Speaking, Viewing**, 71I<br>***Vocabulary**, 71J<br>***Penmanship**, 71J | **Comprehension and Language Arts Skills**, 112–115<br>**Reteach**, 115–118<br>**Challenge**, 101–104<br>**Writer's Workbook**, 70–73<br>**Spelling and Vocabulary Skills**, 90–93<br>**Inquiry Journal**, 85, 99–101 | **Unit 4 Assessment** **Lesson 5**<br>■ Selection Assessment, 18–21<br>■ Spelling Pretest, 38<br>■ Spelling Final Test, 39<br>*Writing Process Strategies Rubrics, 71J<br>*Research Rubrics, 58J |
| **Comprehension Strategies**, 72J, 72<br>**Concept Connections**, 92<br>***Grammar, Usage, and Mechanics**, 93H<br>***Listening, Speaking, Viewing**, 93I<br>***Vocabulary**, 93J<br>***Penmanship**, 93J | **Comprehension and Language Arts Skills**, 116–121<br>**Reteach**, 119–124<br>**Challenge**, 105–109<br>**Writer's Workbook**, 74–77<br>**Spelling and Vocabulary Skills**, 94–97<br>**Inquiry Journal**, 85, 102–103 | **Unit 4 Assessment** **Lesson 6**<br>■ Selection Assessment, 22–25<br>■ Spelling Pretest, 40<br>■ Spelling Final Test, 41<br>*Writing Process Strategies Rubrics, 93J<br>*Research Rubrics, 72J |
| **Comprehension Strategies**, 94J, 94<br>**Concept Connections**, 104<br>**Investigation Presentation**, 105C<br>***Grammar, Usage, and Mechanics**, 103H<br>***Listening, Speaking, Viewing**, 105I<br>***Vocabulary**, 105J<br>***Penmanship**, 105J | **Comprehension and Language Arts Skills**, 122–125<br>**Reteach**, 125–128<br>**Challenge**, 110–113<br>**Writer's Workbook**, 78–81<br>**Spelling and Vocabulary Skills**, 98–101<br>**Inquiry Journal**, 86, 104 | **Unit 4 Assessment** **Lesson 7**<br>■ Selection Assessment, 26–29<br>■ Spelling Pretest, 42<br>■ Spelling Final Test, 43<br>*Writing Process Strategies Rubrics, 105J<br>*Research Rubrics, 94J<br>■ End of Unit Assessment, 44–54 |

*_**Teacher's Edition**_ page reference

## Activating Prior Knowledge

Tell students that good readers relate what they know to what they are reading. Students should get into the habit of thinking about an upcoming theme and selections or activities relevant to that theme. As they are reading the upcoming selections, they should make certain to relate what they already know about money to what they are reading. Ask students questions such as the following:

- What do you know about money before we read these selections?
- How do you spend and save your money?
- Have you already read any books about money?

As students read the selections, they encounter some of these ideas, as well as new ideas. When they read something they already know, encourage them to make a note about this information. When they learn something new, have them to be sure to notice that, too. This will help students learn about money as they read the selections. Encourage students to share any stories they have already read about money. For English-language learners and others with limited language experience, exploring money on the Internet may be helpful.

When students have had some time to compose their thoughts and ideas, call on volunteers to speak. After each student expresses himself or herself, allow a few minutes for questions. As students present their ideas, add them to the Concept/Question Board.

## Read Aloud

Read aloud to students the story *Money, Money, Money* by Ruth Belov Gross. Prior to reading, provide students with the following background information.

- This is a nonfiction story that tells about where the use of money comes from and what was used before money existed.
- Money has played an important role throughout history.
- The form of money has changed significantly throughout history.

As students listen to the Read Aloud, have them think about how the information in the selection addresses their questions about money.

It is important for you as the teacher to let your students know that you use the comprehension strategies being taught in the program when you read. Thus, before you read *Money, Money, Money* make some predictions aloud as to what the selection might be about. As you read, let students know what questions occur to you, what images pop up in your mind as you read, and how points made in the reading relate to ideas you already know.

Toward the end of the reading, summarize for students. If you cannot summarize the selection well, let students see you go back and reread to fill in the gaps in your summary. One of the most powerful ways to get students to use comprehension strategies is for them to see you using them.

Students may be sensitive to some of the illustrations and captions in this trade book. Please preview the illustrations and captions in advance.

## About the Author

**Ruth Belov Gross** started out as a medical writer and later moved into the world of children's literature. She does thorough research on her topics before beginning a book. Through her books, Gross wants readers to know that adults don't have all the answers. Several of Gross's titles have been chosen as Outstanding Science Trade Books for children, Child Study Association Books of the Year, and Library of Congress Books of the Year.

READ ALOUD

***Focus Questions*** How would our lives be different if we could no longer use paper and coins for money? How do you think our current system of paper and coin money developed?

## *Money, Money, Money*

Ruth Belov Gross
*illustrated by Dave Blanchette*

A long time ago there was no money at all in the world. People didn't need money. They got everything they needed by trading things.

The people who lived in Egypt many thousands of years ago traded things. They traded some of the things they didn't need for other things they did need.

The people who lived in Greece many thousands of years ago traded things too.

All over the world, people traded with each other.

There is a special name for this kind of trading. The name is *barter*.

Most of the time, barter was a good way of getting things. There was one trouble with barter, though. What happened when you had something to trade but nobody wanted it?

If nobody wanted the things you had, you were out of luck! But—what if you had something that almost everyone wanted? Then it was easy to make a trade.

In some places, a long time ago, you could always make a trade if you had a cow. In other places, a long time ago, you could always make a trade if you had pigs or goats or sheep. In all these places, the people used their animals the way we use money. So you can say that cows and pigs and goats and sheep were an early kind of money.

Animals weren't the only things people used for money, a long time ago. In some places, people used salt for money. Everybody wanted salt for their food. In Rome, the soldiers were even paid in salt!

In some places, people used corn and grain for money.

In some places, people used little shells for money. They were called cowrie shells. You could put them on a string and wear them around your neck. They were supposed to be lucky.

In some places, people used spades and shovels and knives for money. People needed these tools for their crops and animals.

But there was one trouble with the things people used for money.

PREVIEWING THE UNIT

READ ALOUD

What if the cows or pigs or goats or sheep got sick?
What if the salt got wet—and washed away?
What if the corn or grain got spoiled?
What if the cowrie shells got smashed?
What if the tools got broken?
Then what could people use for money?

After a while, people found better things to use for money. They began to use pieces of metal—

copper and
bronze and
iron and
gold and
silver.
A piece of metal wouldn't get sick.
A piece of metal wouldn't wash away in the rain.
A piece of metal wouldn't get spoiled.
A piece of metal wouldn't get smashed.
A piece of metal wouldn't get broken.

And you could carry your metal money around with you.

You could make pots and tools and other useful things out of metal. You could make beautiful necklaces and rings and bracelets too.

When people began to use metal for money, they used all sizes and shapes of metal. They used lumps of metal, and chunks of metal, and bars of metal. How much could you buy if you had a chunk of copper? The heavier your chunk of copper was, the more you could buy with it.

But how did you know how heavy it was? You had to weigh it. When somebody gave you a piece of metal, you weighed it. When you gave somebody else a piece of metal, he weighed it. That way, nobody cheated anybody. The metal was weighed every time a person gave another person some

copper or
bronze or
iron or
gold or
silver.

Weighing the metal was a lot of trouble for everybody. Just think what it would be like if the man in the grocery store had to weigh your money every time he sold you some cookies!

At last some men had a good idea. This is what they decided to do: A man would weigh a piece of metal once. He would put a mark on it to show how much it weighed. After that, the metal would not have to be weighed again. The piece of metal was now a *coin*. Everybody could look at it and see how much it was worth.

READ ALOUD

One day, almost three thousand years ago, the king of a country called Lydia made a new law. The king said that the people of Lydia were not allowed to weigh their own metal and mark it any more. The king's men were the only ones who had the right to make metal into coins.

The king's money was the first real money people had. We say it was the first real money because it was made by the government, just like our money is today.

In Lydia it was against the law to make your own money. Any man who tried would get into trouble.

The king of Lydia made his coins out of gold and silver. The coins looked like lumpy buttons.

Soon the governments of other countries were making coins too.

Coins made in Greece a long time ago looked something like our pennies and nickels and dimes, only they were thicker and not quite round.

Some of the coins made in Rome did not look like our coins at all. This coin was bigger than a slice of bread. It weighed more than a pound. Before long, many more countries had their own metal coins.

Let's stop now to see what we know about money. This is what we know:

In the very beginning, before there was any money at all, people just traded with each other.

Later on, animals were money. Salt was money. Corn and grain and shells and tools were money too.

After a while, pieces of metal were money. And then people began to make their pieces of metal into coins.

The first real money was made by the government of a country called Lydia.

Other governments made money for their people after that. People feel safer when the government is in charge of making the money they use.

These things did not happen in a day. They took a long time to happen. And they happened at different times in different places.

People in some parts of the world were still using cows for money when people in other parts of the world were using metal coins.

About three hundred and fifty years ago, some people from England came to live in America. They came to settle in colonies.

When they lived in England, they used metal coins. But when they came to settle in America they did not bring many coins with them. And the king of England wouldn't let anyone make coins in the American colonies. So the settlers didn't have much money. But they found ways to get the things they needed.

What do you think they did?

PREVIEWING THE UNIT

READ ALOUD

They traded with each other. They used corn for money, and they used cows for money. They used beaver skins for money, and they used tobacco for money. They used fish and peas and wheat for money, and they used nails and bullets for money.

They even used these things to pay their bills and to pay their taxes. People almost always tried to pay their taxes with the skinniest cows they had.

In many of the American colonies the settlers used little beads made from shells. The shell beads were called *wampum*. Wampum was what the Indians used for money. Six white beads were worth about a penny. Black beads were worth twice as much as white beads. If you had wampum, you could buy beaver skins from the Indians. You could also buy things from other settlers.

The Indians made wampum out of clam shells and periwinkle shells. They strung the wampum beads on thin strips of deer hide. The Indians made beautiful belts and bracelets out of wampum too.

The settlers used French coins and Dutch coins and English coins and Spanish coins. They got some of the coins by selling fish and flour and lumber and furs to other countries. And they got some of the coins from pirates. The pirates came to buy food for themselves and tar and pitch and turpentine for their ships. They paid the settlers with the gold and silver coins they took from other ships at sea.

Again and again the settlers asked the king of England to let them make their own money. Every time they asked, the king said no. He said it was against the law for the settlers in the colonies to make their own money.

The settlers did not like the king's law about money. They did not like some other laws the king made for them. They decided they did not want the king of England to make any of their laws. They wanted to make their own laws.

So the colonies had a war with England. It was called the American Revolution. The colonies won the war. That was about two hundred years ago.

After the American Revolution, the colonies did not belong to England any more. They were not colonies now. They were *states*. They were the United States of America. Now they could make their own laws.

Soon the people in the United States had their own coins. The coins were made by the new government.

The United States government made the coins but for a long time it let the banks make the paper money. Now the government makes all of our money—all of our coins and all of our paper money. If anybody else tries to make coins or paper money, he gets into trouble!

The United States was not the first country to use paper money. People in China used paper money long before any settlers came to America. China was ruled by an emperor, and only the emperor's men could make paper money. If anybody else tried to make paper money, he was in trouble.

READ ALOUD

Money. Money. Money. It comes in very handy. Children use money to buy ice cream cones. They use it to buy birthday presents for their friends. Sometimes they use it to buy lunch at school.

Grownups use coins and paper money too. But they also use *checks*.

And they use *credit cards*.

Checks and credit cards are things that people can use instead of the money the government makes. A check is like a little letter to the bank. It tells the bank to give some of your money to someone. But you can only use a check if you have money in the bank!

A credit card is something people use when they want to pay later. Many people use a credit card to buy gas for their cars. Then they don't have to pay for the gas right away.

Some people think they are getting things free when they use a credit card. That isn't true at all. Even with a credit card, you have to pay for the things you buy! And sometimes you have to pay extra.

Now we know some of the things we use for money today.

We use money for money.

We use checks.

We use credit cards.

But even today some people still use barter—especially children.

## Discussing the Read Aloud

After you have finished the Read Aloud, ask students the following questions.

- What did people use before there was money? *(They bartered.)*
- What types of things did people use for money before they used metal? *(animals, beads, shells)*
- Why did people start using metal for money? *(It was easier to take care of than animals.)*
- What was the first country to make coins? *(Lydia)*
- Why did governments take over making coins? *(So people wouldn't have to weigh coins all the time and because people feel better when the government is in charge of making money.)*
- Do people still use things other than money to get what they want? *(Yes, some people use checks or credit cards. Some people still barter.)*

Remind students of some of the questions you asked them to think about before you read the story.

- What do you know about money?
- What are your saving and spending habits?

Discuss with the class how this Read Aloud is related to the theme Money. To stimulate discussion, ask students questions such as the following:

- In what ways does this Read Aloud relate to the theme?
- What did you learn about money?
- How did this story change your ideas about money?

## Concept/Question Board

The Concept/Question Board is a place for students to ask questions and find answers in order to have a better understanding of the unit theme. It is also a place to publish the results of their investigations.

This board could be a standard bulletin board or a large, three-sided board placed in the front or to the side of the classroom. The board will be a permanent place for students to ask questions, post articles or objects, add comments, and so on throughout the study of each unit theme. Students should have easy access to the Concept/ Question Board, as they will need to be able to attach items to it on their own and also read what is attached.

To get started in this unit, you could have students cut gray construction paper in the shape of a coin to represent the story, *Money, Money, Money.* Students could write their questions, comments, or theme words on these cutout shapes, which would easily identify the story in the unit.

To begin using your Concept/Question Board, ask the students to formulate statements about what they know about money or what they believe to be important about money after listening to the Read Aloud. Write these statements and attach them to the Concept side of the Board. Then, write any preliminary questions they have about money and attach those to the Question side of the Board.

Another idea to help get the students started is to put up a chart or web that they can add to throughout the unit. For example, you might put up two categories—*Things Money Can Buy* and *Things I Value That Money Cannot Buy*—and as they read the selections in the Money unit students can post examples of each concept.

As the students progress through the unit, they can refer to the Board to learn which of their classmates have interests similar to their own. This information can be used to form groups to investigate questions and ideas about money.

Throughout the unit, have the students reread and reflect on the contributions listed on the Concept/Question Board. Have them note, in their Writer's Notebooks, the contributions that mean the most to them. Suggest that they expand on the original contributions by adding their own thoughts, articles, pictures, and so on. Discuss whether the selection has provided information that might be added or that might revise existing postings.

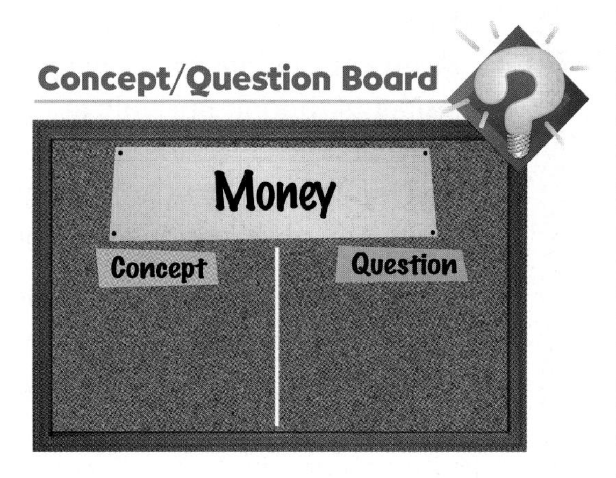

## Setting Reading Goals

Good readers regularly set goals when they are reading. Have students examine and share their thoughts on the unit opener in the ***Student Anthology,*** pages 12 and 13. Remind them that good readers are always thinking when they read. Also, remind students that good readers browse what they are going to read before reading. Guide their browsing by using the following procedure:

- Turn to the unit opener pages. First, look at the unit title. Ask what the title means and what kinds of selections may be in the unit.
- Look at the illustration on the opener pages. The illustration may answer questions about the title or prompt more questions. Post new questions on the Concept/Question Board.
- Ask students what they are thinking about as they read the unit opener.
- Invite students to browse the selections in the unit. Read the titles and quickly browse each one, looking briefly at the illustrations and the text. Encourage students to look not only at content but also at the genre: Is the selection a story? A poem? Expository text, such as an article? Encourage the students to make any observations that interest them.

When students have had sufficient time to browse the unit, encourage them to share their observations. Return to the unit opener on pages 12 and 13 and use the illustration to help initiate a discussion. Allow them to share whatever comments they have about the illustration.

Tell students that good readers make predictions about what might be in the selections they are about to read. Ask them if they are making predictions about the selections or if they are asking themselves questions about the selections they are about to read. Model asking questions that might have occurred to you as you browsed the selections.

## Inquiry Journal

- After students have discussed what they think this unit might be about, encourage them to complete page 82 in their ***Inquiry Journals.***
- Share ideas about money that they would like to investigate.

Name ______ Date ______

UNIT 4 Money

**Knowledge About Money**

- This is what I know about money before reading the unit.

Answers will vary.

- These are some things that I would like to know about money.

Answers will vary.

Reminder: When I get to the end of the unit, I should read this page again to see how much I have learned about money.

82 UNIT 4 — *Knowledge About Money* • Inquiry Journal

***Inquiry Journal p. 82***

## Professional Resources


Bereiter, C., and M. Scardamalia. *Surpassing Ourselves: An Inquiry into the Nature and Implications of Expertise*. Chicago: Open Court, 1993.

Bransford, J. D., A. L. Brown, and R. R. Cocking, eds. *How People Learn: Brain, Mind, Experience, and School*. Washington, DC: National Academy Press, 1999.

Brewer, W. F., "The Activation and Acquisition of Knowledge." S. Vosniadou & A. Ortony, eds., *Similarity and Analogical Reasoning*. (1989) New York, NY: Cambridge University Press.

Brown, A., "Metacognition, Executive Control, Self-Regulation, and Other More Mysterious Mechanisms." F. E. Weinert and R. Ho. Luwe, eds., *Metacognition, Motivation, and Understanding*. (1987) Hillsdale, NJ: L. Lawrence Erlbaum Associates.

Brown, A. and J. Campione, "Communities of Learning and Thinking, or a Context by Any Other Name," *Human Development* 21 (1990): 109-125.

Dewey, J. *How We Think*. New York: Houghton-Mifflin College, 1997.

Popper, K. *Conjectures and Refutations*. London: Routledge & Kegan Paul, 1992.

Vosniadou, S., "Children's Naïve Models and the Comprehension of Expository Text." M. Carretoero, M. Pope, R. J. Simons, and J. I. Pozo, eds., *Learning and Instruction: European Research in an International Context* 3 (1991): 325–336. Oxford: Pergamon Press.


## Home Connection

Distribute page 43 of ***Home Connection.*** Students can read books and articles about money with their families. A few stories are listed to get started. This ***Home Connection*** is also available in Spanish on page 44. Remind parents and students to review and practice the vocabulary and spelling words in preparation for the upcoming weeks.

**Money**

**A message from** ____________________

The unit our class is now reading is about money. Students will be reading stories, poems, and articles that explore the history of money, how money affects people, and the different ways people earn, save, and spend money. Students will read a story about people bartering instead of using money, another story about learning to save money, and a humorous story about the importance of paying a debt. They will also read about children who started their own businesses.

You can help your child by discussing your family values in relation to money and by encouraging your child to learn the basics of managing his or her own money. The following books explore some of the ideas your child will be learning about in this unit. You and your child will find these, and similar books, in your local library.

*Round and Round the Money Goes: What Money Is and How We Use It* by Melvin and Gilda Berger. This book discusses how the practice of using coins and paper money evolved, and explains the circle money travels.

*Sam and the Lucky Money* by Karen Chinn. As Sam searches the streets of Chinatown for ways to spend his four dollars, he meets a stranger in need.

*The Kids' Allowance Book* by Amy Nathan. A lighthearted yet informative guide on allowances from the kids' point of view.

**Next week's selection** ***A New Coat for Anna***

Your child will be studying the following vocabulary words in the upcoming week. Please review the meanings of these words with your child: **remained**—stayed the same; **bolt**—a roll of cloth or wallpaper; **weaver**—a person who uses strands of yarn to make a piece of cloth; **strung**—stretched from one place to another; **wound**—wrapped around and around.

Please review with your child the spelling words for the upcoming week: better, letter, potter, rubber, soccer, ladder, hammer, scatter, dinner, slippers, tomorrow, summer, pretty, button, happy.

***Home Connection p. 43***

## Research in Reading

### Knowledge-Building Communities

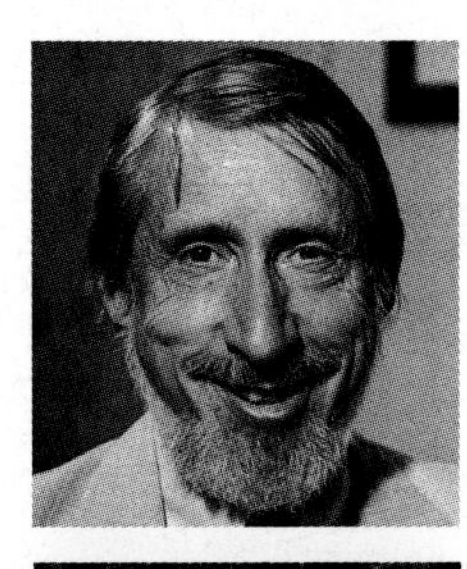

When elementary school students are given the opportunity in school to build new knowledge, they become as excited about this enterprise as scientists do. They formulate deeper and deeper questions, and propose theories that are increasingly sophisticated. They begin to see other members of the class as essential allies in this process, as members of the same research. In the process, their attitude toward their own learning becomes transformed and they begin to see reading and writing in a totally new light: not as a series of tasks that are set for them by others, but as activities that are an integral part of the knowledge-building process.

In previous decades, the question was how to optimize each child's learning potential. We now understand that this question cannot be fully answered until we address the prior question: How can we convert our schools and classrooms into knowledge-building communities? *(Carl Bereiter and Marlene Scardamalia)*

**Teacher Tip** **SETTING READING GOALS**

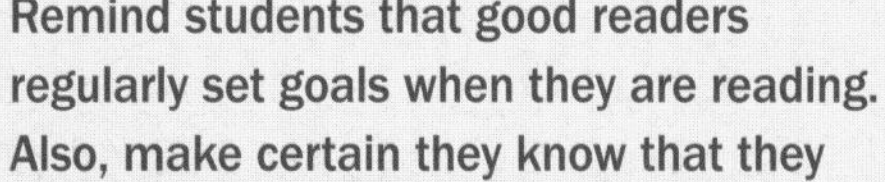

Remind students that good readers regularly set goals when they are reading. Also, make certain they know that they should get into the habit of setting reading goals for themselves, because they should know why they are reading something.

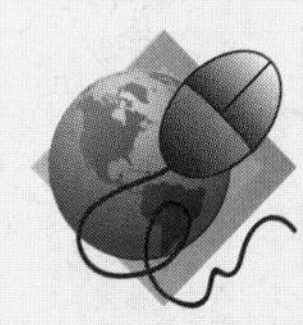

**www.toronto.edu**
**www.reading.edu**
**Web Connection**
See these Web sites for information on Research in Reading.

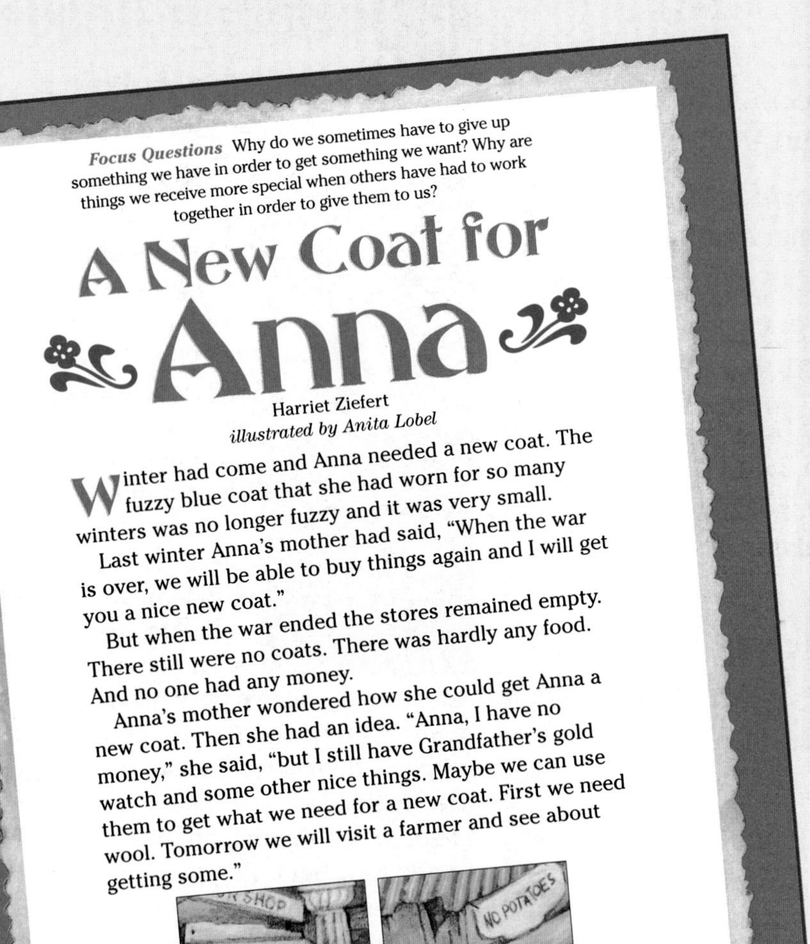

*Focus Questions* Why do we sometimes have to give up something we have in order to get something we want? Why are things we receive more special when others have had to work together in order to give them to us?

A New Coat for Anna

Harriet Ziefert
*illustrated by Anita Lobel*

Winter had come and Anna needed a new coat. The fuzzy blue coat that she had worn for so many winters was no longer fuzzy and it was very small.

Last winter Anna's mother had said, "When the war is over, we will be able to buy things again and I will get you a nice new coat."

But when the war ended the stores remained empty. There still were no coats. There was hardly any food. And no one had any money.

Anna's mother wondered how she could get Anna a new coat. Then she had an idea. "Anna, I have no money," she said, "but I still have Grandfather's gold watch and some other nice things. Maybe we can use them to get what we need for a new coat. First we need wool. Tomorrow we will visit a farmer and see about getting some."



14

SELECTION INTRODUCTION

## Selection Summary

### Genre: Realistic Fiction

"A New Coat for Anna" is based on a true story told to the author by a friend. It is a heartwarming tale of the ingenuity of a mother and her young daughter who use bartering in some very creative ways. This charming story, which is particularly evocative of the spirit of a small European village immediately following World War II, illustrates the value of resourcefulness, persistence, and cooperation.

"A New Coat for Anna" illustrates that money is not always necessary to get the things you need. When Anna's mother decides that Anna needs a new coat—whether or not she has the money for it—she finds that imagination and bartering can be just as effective as money.

Some elements of realistic fiction include:

- The characters behave as people do in real life.
- The setting of the story is a real place or could be a real place.
- The events in the story could happen in real life.

## About the Author

**Harriet Ziefert's** background in early childhood education served her well as she became a prolific author of books for primary-aged children. *A New Coat for Anna* was named an ALA Notable Children's Book. Ziefert also received the New Jersey Author's Award for *Sarah's Question* and had two picture books named Children's Choice books.

Students can read more about Harriet Ziefert on page 25 of the ***Student Anthology.***

## About the Illustrator

**Anita Lobel** is an author and illustrator known for her originality and inventiveness. Her award-winning *On Market Street* was a *New York Times* Best Illustrated Book and a Caldecott Honor Book. Anita Lobel also won awards for *The Rose in My Garden* and *Peter's Penny Dance.*

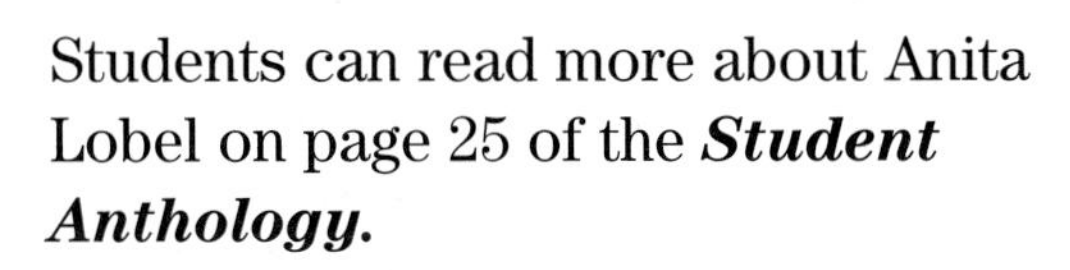

Students can read more about Anita Lobel on page 25 of the ***Student Anthology.***

## Inquiry Connections

Students are introduced to the idea of bartering—the exchange of goods or services for other goods or services. Some of the students may be very familiar with this notion. It is not unusual for children to trade their own things with friends to get what they want. They may be surprised, though, to find out that adults use barter also. Key concepts explored are:

- It sometimes takes imagination to figure out how to get the things you want.
- Sometimes other people find the things that you have are more valuable than money.
- Money is not always necessary for obtaining one's needs.

Before reading the selection:

- Point out that students may post a question, concept, word, illustration, or object on the Concept/Question Board at any time during the course of their unit investigation. Be sure that students include their name or initials on the items they post so that others will know to whom to go if they have an answer or if they wish to collaborate on a related activity.
- Students should feel free to write an answer or a note on someone else's question or to consult the Board for ideas for their own investigations throughout the unit.
- Encourage students to read about money at home and to bring in articles or pictures that are good examples to post on the Board.

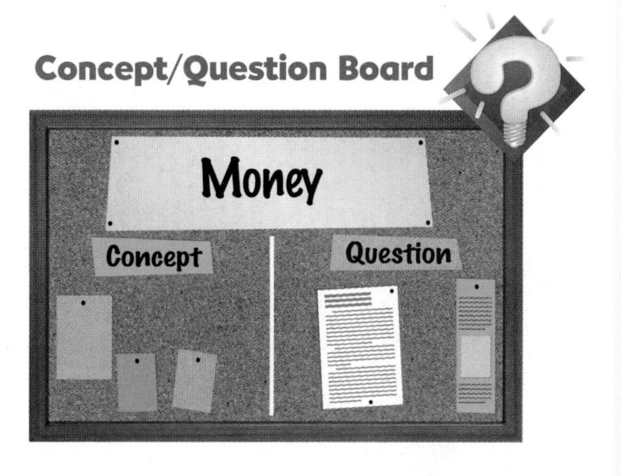

## Leveled Practice

### Reteach
**Pages 95–98**

### Challenge
**Pages 83–86**

### English Learner Support Activities

### Intervention Workbook

### Decodable Book 29

## Leveled Classroom Library*

Encourage students to read at least 30 minutes daily outside of class. Have them read books in the ***Leveled Classroom Library*** to support the unit theme and help students develop their vocabulary by reading independently.

### *The Treasure*

BY URI SHULEVITZ. FARRAR, STRAUS & GIROUX, 1978.

In this traditional English tale of a journey to find treasure, a man follows the instructions of his dream, which takes him away from his home. Upon arrival, he learns the treasure is really at his home. (Caldecott Honor Book) **(Easy)**

### *Round and Round the Money Goes*

BY MELVIN AND GILDA BERGER. HAMBLETON-HILL, 1993.

Children learn the basics about the flow of wealth, how banks work, the life span of coins and bills, and other elementary monetary issues. **(Average)**

### *Screen of Frogs*

BY SHEILA HAMANAKA. ORCHARD BOOKS, 1993.

A spoiled rich man finds respect for the world around him before it is too late. This story retells the classic Japanese folktale, "The Strange Folding Screen." **(Advanced)**

* These books, which all support the unit theme Money, are part of a 36-book ***Leveled Classroom Library*** available for purchase from SRA/McGraw-Hill. Note: Teachers should preview any trade books for appropriateness in their classrooms before recommending them to students.

## SRA TECHNOLOGY

### Web Connections

- Money Web Site
- Online Professional Development
- Online Phonics
- Online Assessment

### CD-ROMs

- Research Assistant
- The Ultimate Writing and Creativity Center
- Teacher Resource Library

### Audiocassette/CD

Listening Library: Money

### Computer Skills

TechKnowledge

Materials are available through SRA/McGraw-Hill.

Suggested Pacing: 3–5 days

LESSON PLANNER

| | DAY 1 | DAY 2 |
|---|---|---|
| **1 Preparing to Read**<br>**Materials**<br>■ Student Anthology, Book 2, pp. 14–25<br>■ Decodable Book 29<br>■ Routine Card 1, Routines 1–2<br>■ Program Assessment | ✓**Midyear Assessment**<br>■ Grade 3 Midyear Test<br>**Word Knowledge,** pp. 14K–14L<br>■ homophones<br>■ suffixes *-ed, -ment, -tion, -sion*<br>■ word families<br>■ double consonants<br>**About the Words and Sentences,** pp. 14K–14L | **Word Knowledge**<br>**Developing Oral Language,** p. 14L |
| **2 Reading & Responding**<br>**Materials**<br>■ Student Anthology, Book 2, pp. 14–25<br>■ Program Assessment<br>■ Reading Transparencies 23, 46, 49<br>■ Inquiry Journal, p. 83<br>■ Home Connection, p. 45<br>■ Unit 4 Assessment, pp. 2–5<br>■ Writer's Notebook<br>■ Routine Cards 1, 2, Routines 3–6 | **Unit Overview**<br>■ Previewing the Unit, pp. 12–13T<br>■ Read Aloud, pp. 13L–13P<br>**Build Background,** p. 14M<br>**Preview and Prepare,** pp. 14M–14N<br>**Selection Vocabulary,** p. 14N<br>**Reading Recommendations,** pp. 14O–14P | **Student Anthology,** pp. 14–23 First Read<br>✓**Comprehension Strategies**<br>■ Monitoring and Clarifying, p. 14<br>■ Summarizing, pp. 16, 22<br>■ Predicting, pp. 18, 20<br>■ Making Connections, p. 20<br>**Discussing Strategy Use,** p. 22<br>**Discussing the Selection,** p. 23A<br>■ Review Selection<br>■ Complete Discussion |
| **Inquiry**<br>**Materials**<br>■ Student Anthology, Book 2, pp. 14–25<br>■ Inquiry Journal, pp. 87–88<br>■ Research Assistant CD-ROM | **Investigation**<br>■ Investigating Concepts Beyond the Text, p. 25A | **Investigation**<br>■ Concept/Question Board, p. 25B |
| **3 Language Arts**<br>**Materials**<br>■ Spelling and Vocabulary Skills, pp. 74–77<br>■ Comprehension and Language Arts Skills, pp. 92–95<br>■ The Ultimate Writing and Creativity Center<br>■ Language Arts Handbook<br>■ Writer's Workbook, pp. 54–57<br>■ Language Arts Transparencies 6, 15, 37<br>■ Student Anthology | **Word Analysis**<br>✓■ Spelling: Double Consonants Pretest, p. 25F<br>**Writing Process Strategies**<br>■ Persuasive Writing: Friendly Letter, p. 25F<br>**English Language Conventions**<br>■ Grammar: Prepositions and Prepositional Phrases, p. 25F | **Word Analysis**<br>■ Spelling: Double Consonants, p. 25G<br>■ Vocabulary: Base Word Families, p. 25G<br>**Writing Process Strategies**<br>■ Persuasive Writing: Friendly Letter, p. 25G<br>**English Language Conventions**<br>■ Grammar: Prepositions and Prepositional Phrases, p. 25G |



P Phonics ✓Informal Assessment Available ✓Formal Assessment Available

| DAY 2 continued | DAY 3 | |
|---|---|---|
| **DAY 3** | **DAY 4** | **DAY 5** |
| **Word Knowledge**<br>**General Review** | **Word Knowledge**<br>**General Review** | **General Review** |
| **Student Anthology,** pp. 14–23 Second Read<br>**Comprehension Skills**<br>■ Making Inferences, pp. 15, 17, 19, 21, 23<br>**Checking Comprehension,** p. 23<br>**Supporting the Reading,** p. 23C<br>■ Predicting<br>**View Fine Art,** p. 23A | **Student Anthology**<br>✓■ Concept Connections, p. 24<br>■ Meet the Author and Illustrator, p. 25<br>**Review Selection Vocabulary,** p. 23B<br>**Literary Elements,** p. 23D<br>■ Plot<br>**Social Studies Connection**<br>■ Barter Systems, p. 23E | ✓**Selection Assessment**<br>■ "A New Coat for Anna," pp. 2–5<br>**Home Connection,** p. 23B<br>**Science Connection**<br>■ Symbiotic Relationships, p. 23F |
| ✓**Investigation**<br>■ Question and Problem Phase, p. 25C | **Supporting the Investigation**<br>■ Choosing Appropriate Sources, p. 25D | **Investigation**<br>■ Unit Investigation Continued<br>■ Update Concept/Question Board |
| **Word Analysis**<br>■ Spelling: Double Consonants, p. 25H<br>■ Vocabulary: Base Word Families, p. 25H<br>**Writing Process Strategies**<br>■ Persuasive Writing: Friendly Letter, p. 25H<br>■ Writer's Craft: Fact and Opinion, p. 25H<br>**English Language Conventions**<br>✓■ Grammar: Prepositions and Prepositional Phrases, p. 25H | **Word Analysis**<br>■ Spelling: Double Consonants, p. 25I<br>■ Vocabulary: Base Word Families, p. 25I<br>**Writing Process Strategies**<br>■ Persuasive Writing: Friendly Letter, p. 25I<br>**English Language Conventions**<br>✓■ Listening, Speaking, Viewing Listening: Recognizing Facts and Opinions, p. 25I | **Word Analysis**<br>✓■ Spelling: Double Consonants Final Test<br>✓■ Vocabulary: Base Word Families, p. 25J<br>**Writing Process Strategies**<br>✓■ Persuasive Writing: Friendly Letter, p. 25J<br>**English Language Conventions**<br>✓■ Penmanship: Cursive Letters *A* and *C*, p. 25J |

Below are suggestions for differentiating instruction. These are the same skills shown in the Lesson Planner; however, these pages provide extra practice opportunities or enriching activities to meet the varied needs of students.

WORKSHOP

# Differentiating Instruction

## Teacher Directed: Individual and Small-Group Instruction

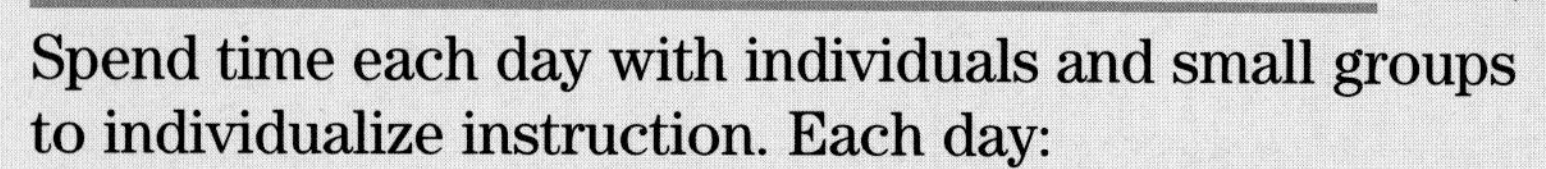

Spend time each day with individuals and small groups to individualize instruction. Each day:

- preteach students who need help with the next lesson.
- reteach students who need to solidify their understanding of content previously taught.
- listen to students read to check their fluency.
- hold writing and inquiry conferences.

Use the following program components to support instruction:

- ***Reteach*** with students who need a bit more practice
- ***Intervention*** for students who exhibit a lack of understanding of the lesson concepts
- ***English Learner Support*** with students who need language help

## Student: Independent Activities

Students can work alone, with a partner, or in small groups on such activities as:

- Review sound/spellings
- Practice dictation words
- Partner reading
- Practice fluency
- Independent reading
- Reading Roundtable
- Concept vocabulary
- Selection vocabulary
- Writing in progress
- Conference
- Language Arts
- Challenge activities
- Inquiry and Investigation activities
- Listening Library
- Online Phonics

For Workshop Management Tips, see Appendix pages 41–42.

| | DAY 1 |
|---|---|
| **Word Knowledge** | **Teacher Directed**<br>■ Reading Words: Suffixes *-ed, -ment,* and *-tion,* ***Intervention Guide,*** p. 175<br>**Independent Activities**<br>■ ***Online Phonics*** |
| **Fluency** | **Independent Activities**<br>■ Self-test fluency rate<br>■ Partner reading |
| **Comprehension** | **Teacher Directed**<br>■ Preteach "A New Coat for Anna," ***Intervention Guide,*** pp. 176–177<br>■ Preteach Intervention Selection One, ***Intervention Guide,*** pp. 177–178<br>■ ***English Learner Support Guide***<br>• Vocabulary, pp. 256–257<br>• Comprehension Skill: Making Inferences, pp. 257–258<br>**Independent Activities**<br>■ Record reaction to Read Aloud in Writer's Notebook<br>■ Browse ***Leveled Classroom Library***<br>■ Add vocabulary in Writer's Notebook |
| **Inquiry** | **Independent Activities**<br>■ Concept/Question Board<br>■ Record ideas about Money in ***Inquiry Journal,*** p. 82<br>■ Explore OCR Web site for theme connections |
| **Language Arts** | **Teacher Directed**<br>■ Grammar, Usage, and Mechanics, ***Intervention Guide,*** p. 180<br>**Independent Activities**<br>■ Prepositions and Prepositional Phrases, ***Comprehension and Language Arts Skills,*** pp. 92–93 |

| DAY 2 | DAY 3 | DAY 4 | DAY 5 |
|---|---|---|---|
| **Teacher Directed**<br>▪ Developing Oral Language, ***Intervention Guide,*** p. 175<br>**Independent Activities**<br>▪ Read ***Decodable Book 29,*** *Kitty and the Nothing Day* | **Teacher Directed**<br>▪ Dictation and Spelling: Suffixes *-ed, -ment,* and *-tion,* ***Intervention Guide,*** pp. 175–176<br>**Independent Activities**<br>▪ ***Online Phonics*** | **Teacher Directed**<br>▪ General Review<br>**Independent Activities**<br>▪ ***Online Phonics*** | **Teacher Directed**<br>▪ General Review<br>**Independent Activities**<br>▪ ***Online Phonics*** |
| **Independent Activities**<br>▪ Orally read "A New Coat for Anna"<br>▪ Partner reading of ***Decodable Book 29,*** *Kitty and the Nothing Day* | **Independent Activities**<br>▪ Partner reading of selection<br>▪ Read ***Decodable Book 29,*** *Kitty and the Nothing Day* | **Independent Activities**<br>▪ Partner reading of selection<br>▪ Reread ***Decodable Book 29,*** *Kitty and the Nothing Day* | **Teacher Directed**<br>▪ Repeated Readings/Fluency Check, ***Intervention Guide,*** p. 179<br>**Independent Activities**<br>▪ Partner reading |
| **Teacher Directed**<br>▪ Preteach "A New Coat for Anna," ***Intervention Guide,*** pp. 176–177<br>▪ Comprehension Strategies, ***Intervention Guide,*** p. 178<br>▪ Reread Intervention Selection One, ***Intervention Guide,*** pp. 177–178<br>▪ ***English Learner Support Guide***<br>• Vocabulary, pp. 259–260<br>• Comprehension Skill: Making Inferences, pp. 260–261<br>**Independent Activities**<br>▪ Choose ***Leveled Classroom Library*** book for independent reading<br>▪ Record response to selection in Writer's Notebook<br>▪ ***Listening Library Audiocassette/CD*** | **Teacher Directed**<br>▪ Reread "A New Coat for Anna," ***Intervention Guide,*** pp. 176–177<br>▪ Preteach Intervention Selection Two, ***Intervention Guide,*** pp. 178–179<br>▪ ***English Learner Support Guide***<br>• Vocabulary, pp. 261–262<br>• Comprehension Skill: Making Inferences, pp. 262–263<br>**Independent Activities**<br>▪ Read ***Leveled Classroom Library*** book<br>▪ Complete Link to Writing in Supporting the Reading, p. 23C<br>▪ ***Listening Library Audiocassette/CD***<br>▪ ***English Learner Support Activities,*** p. 31 | **Teacher Directed**<br>▪ Discuss Concept Connections, p. 24<br>▪ Reread "A New Coat for Anna," ***Intervention Guide,*** pp. 176–177<br>▪ Comprehension Strategies, ***Intervention Guide,*** p. 179<br>▪ Reread Intervention Selection Two, ***Intervention Guide,*** pp. 178–179<br>▪ ***English Learner Support Guide***<br>• Vocabulary, pp. 263–264<br>• Comprehension Skill: Making Inferences, pp. 264–265<br>**Independent Activities**<br>▪ Independent reading<br>▪ Add words to Word Bank<br>▪ Complete Independent Practice in Literary Elements, p. 23D<br>▪ Social Studies Connection, p. 23E<br>▪ ***English Learner Support Activities,*** p. 32 | **Teacher Directed**<br>▪ ***English Learner Support Guide***<br>• Review Vocabulary, p. 266<br>• Comprehension Skill: Making Inferences, pp. 266–267<br>**Independent Activities**<br>▪ Read ***Leveled Classroom Library*** book as independent reading<br>▪ Reading Roundtable<br>▪ Science Connection, p. 23F |
| **Independent Activities**<br>▪ Concept/Question Board<br>▪ Explore OCR Web site for theme connections<br>▪ Use ***Research Assistant CD-ROM*** to begin investigation | **Independent Activities**<br>▪ Investigation Ideas, ***Inquiry Journal,*** p. 87<br>▪ Concept/Question Board<br>▪ Use ***Research Assistant CD-ROM*** to begin investigation | **Independent Activities**<br>▪ Concept/Question Board<br>▪ Possible Sources, ***Inquiry Journal,*** p. 88<br>▪ Explore OCR Web site for theme connections | **Independent Activities**<br>▪ Concept/Question Board<br>▪ Continue research |
| **Teacher Directed**<br>▪ Grammar, Usage, and Mechanics, ***Intervention Guide,*** p. 180<br>▪ Prepositions, ***Reteach,*** p. 97<br>**Independent Activities**<br>▪ Seminar: Plan a Persuasive Friendly Letter, p. 25G<br>▪ Vocabulary: Base Word Families, ***Spelling and Vocabulary Skills,*** pp. 74–75<br>▪ Prepositions, ***Challenge,*** p. 85 | **Teacher Directed**<br>▪ Writing Activity, ***Intervention Guide,*** p. 181<br>▪ Vocabulary: ***Reteach,*** p. 96<br>**Independent Activities**<br>▪ Spelling: Double Consonants, ***Spelling and Vocabulary Skills,*** p. 76<br>▪ Vocabulary: ***Challenge,*** p. 84<br>▪ Writer's Craft: Fact and Opinion, ***Comprehension and Language Arts Skills,*** pp. 94–95 | **Teacher Directed**<br>▪ Writer's Craft: Fact and Opinion, ***Reteach,*** p. 98<br>▪ Writing Activity, ***Intervention Guide,*** p. 181<br>▪ Spelling: ***Reteach,*** p. 95<br>**Independent Activities**<br>▪ Spelling: Double Consonants<br>• ***Spelling and Vocabulary Skills,*** p. 77<br>• ***Challenge,*** p. 83<br>▪ Seminar: Revise a Persuasive Friendly Letter, p. 25I | **Independent Activities**<br>▪ Seminar: Edit/Proofread and Publish a Persuasive Friendly Letter, p. 25J<br>▪ Writer's Craft: Fact and Opinion, ***Challenge,*** p. 86<br>▪ Penmanship: Practice Cursive Letters *A* and *C,* p. 25J |

ASSESSMENT

# Formal Assessment Options

Use these summative assessments along with your informal observations to assess student progress.

Name ______ Date ______ Score ______

UNIT 4 Money • Lesson 1

LESSON ASSESSMENT

**A New Coat for Anna**

**Read the following questions carefully. Then completely fill in the bubble of each correct answer. You may look back at the story to find the answer to each of the questions.**

1. In addition to getting a new coat for Anna, Anna's mother
   - Ⓐ saved enough money to buy another coat
   - ● made other people in the town happy
   - Ⓒ learned how to weave cloth
2. How does Anna's mother get wool for the coat?
   - ● She gives a gold watch to a farmer.
   - Ⓑ She gives a lamp to a woman.
   - Ⓒ She gives a necklace to a weaver.

**Read the following questions carefully. Use complete sentences to answer the questions.**

3. How does Anna's mother get the wool spun into yarn?
   Anna's mother gives a lamp to a woman who spins the wool into yarn.
4. How does Anna's mother get the yarn woven into cloth?
   Anna's mother gives a necklace to a weaver who weaves the yarn into cloth.
5. How does Anna's mother get the cloth made into a coat?
   Anna's mother gives a teapot to a tailor who sews the cloth into a coat.

2 Unit 4 • Lesson 1 *A New Coat for Anna* • Unit 4 Assessment

**Unit 4 Assessment p. 2**

**A New Coat for Anna** *(continued)*

6. How does Anna's mother get the yarn to be red?
   She and Anna dye the yarn using lingonberries.
7. Why does Anna stop at every store on her way home from the tailor's shop?
   Anna is wearing her new coat and stops to look at herself in the store windows.
8. What did Anna and her mother do to celebrate Christmas?
   They had a Christmas Eve party, served cake, and invited everyone who helped with the coat.

**Read the following questions carefully. Then completely fill in the bubble of each correct answer.**

9. What did the tailor have to do before he could begin to make the coat?
   - Ⓐ pick out the buttons
   - ● take Anna's measurements
   - Ⓒ buy some red cloth
10. When did Anna finally get her new coat?
    - ● near winter
    - Ⓑ near spring
    - Ⓒ near summer

Unit 4 Assessment • *A New Coat for Anna* Unit 4 • Lesson 1 3

**Unit 4 Assessment p. 3**

**A New Coat for Anna** *(continued)*

**Read the question and statement below. Use complete sentences in your answers.**

**Linking to the Concepts** How would life change if suddenly there was no money in the world?
Answers will vary. Accept all reasonable answers.

**Personal Response** Write about a time you traded something with a friend.
Answers will vary. Accept all reasonable answers.

4 Unit 4 • Lesson 1 *A New Coat for Anna* • Unit 4 Assessment

**Unit 4 Assessment p. 4**

**A New Coat for Anna** *(continued)*

**Vocabulary**

**Read the following questions carefully. Then completely fill in the bubble of each correct answer.**

1. When the war ended, the stores remained empty. **Remained** is another word for
   - ● stayed
   - Ⓑ became
   - Ⓒ went away
2. A clothesline was strung across the kitchen. In this sentence, **strung** means about the same as
   - ● hung
   - Ⓑ stored
   - Ⓒ hidden
3. When the yarn dried, Anna and her mother wound the yarn into balls. In this sentence, **wound** means
   - Ⓐ tied
   - ● rolled
   - Ⓒ dyed
4. A **weaver** is someone who
   - Ⓐ turns cloth into clothing
   - Ⓑ turns lamb's wool into yarn
   - ● turns yarn into cloth
5. Anna and her mother take the bolt of cloth to the tailor. In this sentence, a **bolt** is like
   - ● a roll of cloth
   - Ⓑ some sewed cloth
   - Ⓒ a scrap of cloth

Unit 4 Assessment • *A New Coat for Anna* Unit 4 • Lesson 1 5

**Unit 4 Assessment p. 5**

Name ______ Date ______ Score ______

UNIT 4 Money • Lesson 1 *A New Coat for Anna*

**Spelling Pretest: Double Consonants**

**Fold this page back on the dotted line. Take the Pretest. Then correct any word you misspelled by crossing out the word and rewriting it next to the incorrect spelling.**

| | |
|---|---|
| 1. ______ | 1. better |
| 2. ______ | 2. letter |
| 3. ______ | 3. potter |
| 4. ______ | 4. rubber |
| 5. ______ | 5. soccer |
| 6. ______ | 6. ladder |
| 7. ______ | 7. hammer |
| 8. ______ | 8. scatter |
| 9. ______ | 9. dinner |
| 10. ______ | 10. slippers |
| 11. ______ | 11. tomorrow |
| 12. ______ | 12. summer |
| 13. ______ | 13. pretty |
| 14. ______ | 14. button |
| 15. ______ | 15. happy |

30 Unit 4 • Lesson 1 *Spelling Pretest: Double Consonants* • Unit 4 Assessment

**Unit 4 Assessment p. 30**

Name ______ Date ______ Score ______

UNIT 4 Money • Lesson 1 *A New Coat for Anna*

**Spelling Final Test: Double Consonants**

**Mark the letter next to the underlined word that is misspelled. Focus on the underlined word.**

1. Ⓐ Kindness makes others happy.
   ● A mailed leter needs a stamp.
   Ⓒ Some balls are made of rubber.
   Ⓓ Correct as is.
2. Ⓔ A large dinner is a feast.
   Ⓕ The day after today is tomorrow.
   ● A poter works with clay.
   Ⓗ Correct as is.
3. ● House slippars keep feet warm.
   Ⓑ Some teachers give letter grades.
   Ⓒ A button is sewn on a shirt.
   Ⓓ Correct as is.
4. Ⓔ A clay pot is made by a potter.
   Ⓕ Each fire engine has a ladder.
   Ⓖ A tire is made of rubber.
   ● Correct as is.
5. Ⓐ Some slippers are made of wool.
   Ⓑ A beach is warm in the summer.
   Ⓒ Squirrels scatter from tree to tree.
   ● Correct as is.
6. ● A smile is a hapy face.
   Ⓕ A ladder is used for climbing.
   Ⓖ Goals equal points in soccer.
   Ⓗ Correct as is.

Unit 4 Assessment • *Spelling Final Test: Double Consonants* Unit 4 • Lesson 1 31

**Unit 4 Assessment p. 31**

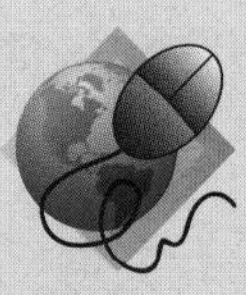

**Online Assessment** for ***Open Court Reading*** helps teachers differentiate classroom instruction based on students' scores from the weekly and end-of-unit assessments. It provides exercises best suited to meet the needs of each student. For more information, visit SRAonline.com.

## Informal Comprehension Strategies Rubrics

### Summarizing

- The student paraphrases the text, reporting main ideas and a summary of what is in the text.
- The student decides which parts of the text are important in his or her summary.
- The student draws conclusions from the text.
- The student makes global interpretations of the text, such as recognizing the genre.

### Predicting

- The student makes predictions about what the text is about.
- The student updates predictions during reading, based on information in the text.

### Monitoring and Clarifying

- The student notes characteristics of the text, such as whether it is difficult to read or whether some sections are more challenging or more important than others.
- The student shows awareness of whether he or she understands the text and takes appropriate action, such as rereading, in order to understand the text better.
- The student rereads to reconsider something presented earlier in the text.
- The student recognizes problems during reading, such as a loss of concentration, unfamiliar vocabulary, or lack of sufficient background knowledge to comprehend the text.

## Research Rubrics

During Workshop, assess students using the rubrics below. The rubrics range from 1 to 4 in most categories, with 1 being the lowest score. Record each student's score on the inside back cover of the ***Inquiry Journal***.

### Formulating Research Questions and Problems

**1** With help, identifies things he or she wonders about in relation to a topic.

**2** Expresses curiosity about topics; with help, translates this into specific questions.

**3** Poses an interesting problem or question for research; with help, refines it into a researchable question.

**4** Identifies something he or she genuinely wonders about and translates it into a researchable question.

### Objectives

- Students practice recognizing homophones.
- Students practice recognizing base words and the suffixes *-ed, -ment, -tion,* and *-sion.*
- Students practice recognizing word families.
- Students practice recognizing double consonants.

### Materials

- Student Anthology, Book 2, pp. 14–25
- Decodable Book 29
- Routine Card 1, Routines 1–2

**Teacher Tip** Starting with Unit 4, Part 1 will focus on word knowledge and word structure. If students are having problems with decoding words, stop and blend the words syllable by syllable or sound by sound. If necessary, refer to the ***Sound/Spelling Cards.***

### Differentiating Instruction

| If... | Then... |
|---|---|
| English Learners are having difficulty understanding the meaning of the blending words | Use pictures or photos, objects, board stick drawings, pantomime, or bilingual dictionaries before you do the blending exercises to help them understand each word's meaning |

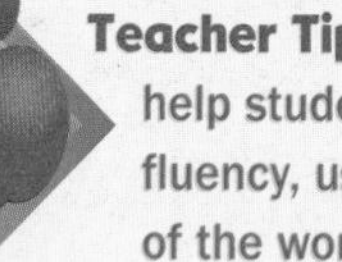

**Teacher Tip** SYLLABICATION To help students blend words and build fluency, use the syllabication below of the words in the word lines.

sheer shear dye
die hair hare
cel•e•brate cel•e•bra•tion in•vite
in•vi•ta•tion re•flect re•flec•tion
meas•ure meas•ured meas•ure•ments
di•vide di•vi•sion com•pre•hend
com•pre•hen•sion to•mor•row
sum•mer pret•ty but•ton
hap•py

WORD KNOWLEDGE

## Word Knowledge

### Reading the Words and Sentences

Use direct teaching, not varying from the routine, when instructing students in word knowledge and developing oral language activities so that students become accustomed to the routines. Use the following procedure as you have students read each line of words and the sentences in this and in subsequent lessons.

- Write each word from the word lines on the board and have students read them together. Stop and have them blend the word, sound by sound, only if they have difficulty reading it. Encourage students to pronounce the word naturally after blending. Because reading sentences helps students move from word fluency to sentence fluency, have them read each sentence in unison, then blend it word by word, using normal intonation. The words in **boldface** type appear in the selection.
- Have students complete the Developing Oral Language activities.

Line 1: sheer shear dye die hair hare
Line 2: celebrate celebration invite invitation reflect reflection
Line 3: measure measured measurements
Line 4: divide division comprehend comprehension
Line 5: tomorrow summer pretty button happy
Sentence 1: The farmer said, "What a good idea! But you will have to wait until spring when I shear my sheep's winter wool."
Sentence 2: She stopped at every store to look at her reflection in the window.
Sentence 3: "Anna, I'd be very happy to make you a new coat, but first I must take your measurements."
Sentence 4: We hope tomorrow will be a pretty summer day.

### About the Words and Sentences

- **Line 1:** Ask the students what the words in Line 1 have in common. *(They are homophones.)* Ask students to explain what a homophone is. *(Words are pronounced the same, but have different spellings and meanings.)* Have students give a definition for each word and use it in a sentence.
- **Line 2:** Line 2 contains word pairs. The first is a base word. The second word is the base word with the suffix *-tion.* Have students tell what spelling changes occurred when the suffix *-tion* was added. By this time, students should be able to determine that use of this suffix changes the word from a verb to a noun.
- **Line 3:** The words in Line 3 all have the base word *measure* and so belong in the same word family. Have students note changes in the spelling as different suffixes are added. Prompt students to identify how the meaning of the word changes. Also note the special sound/spelling of the letter *s* in the words *measure, measured,* and *measurements.* Have students say these words aloud along with you.

WORD KNOWLEDGE

- **Line 4:** Line 4 contains word pairs. The first word is a base word. The second word is the base word with the suffix *-sion.* Have students notice any spelling changes that occur when the *-sion* suffix is added. By this time, students should be able to determine that use of this suffix changes the word from a verb to a noun.
- **Line 5:** The words in the last line are found in "A New Coat for Anna" and are words with double consonants. Have students say each word, clapping the syllables. Have students identify where the words are divided into syllables.
- **Sentences 1–3:** These sentences are from the story students are about to read. Ask students to identify words that are homophones *(wait/weight, I/eye, shear/sheer).* Ask students to identify the words with a suffix *(reflection, stopped, measurements).*
- **Sentence 4:** Have students identify the words in the last sentence that contain the double consonants *rr, tt,* or *mm. (tomorrow, pretty, summer)*

## Developing Oral Language

Use direct teaching to review the words. Use one or both of the following activities to help students practice reading the words.

- Using the words from the word lines that you have written on the board, have a student choose two words and use them in a sentence; for example, "The ranger *measured* the footprints of the *hare.*" Put a check next to each word used. Then, have students take turns making sentences until all of the words have been used.
- Using the words on the board, invite a student to give a clue for one of the words; for example, "I am thinking of a word that means *to cut off*" *(shear).* Invite a volunteer to come to the board and erase the correct answer. Repeat with the remaining words.

## Building Fluency

***Decodable Books*** are used to help develop fluency for students who need extra practice. The only way to gain fluency is to read. Students will have many opportunities to read, including the ***Student Anthology,*** the ***Leveled Classroom Library,*** and their own reading. The ***Decodable Books*** can be used to practice the phonics and fluency elements being reviewed. Refer to the Appendix for the procedure on using these books. For this lesson, use ***Decodable Book 29,*** *Kitty and the Nothing Day.*

***Decodable Book 29***

### DIFFERENTIATING INSTRUCTION

| If... | Then... |
|---|---|
| Students need extra help with word families or base words with the suffixes *-tion* and *-sion* | Use ***Online Phonics*** |
| Students need extra help with base words with the suffixes *-ed, -ment,* and *-tion* | Use ***Intervention Guide*** pages 175–176 |

**Teacher Tip FLUENCY** Gaining a better understanding of the spellings of sounds and the structure of words will help students as they encounter unfamiliar words in their reading. By this time in Grade 3, students should be reading approximately 123 words per minute with fluency and expression. As students read, you may notice that some need work in building fluency. During Workshop, have these students select a section of the text (a minimum of 160 words) to read several times in order to build fluency.

**Spelling**
See pages 25E–25J for the corresponding spelling lesson for double consonants.

**Routine Card**
Refer to ***Routine 1*** for whole-word blending and ***Routine 2*** for sentence blending.

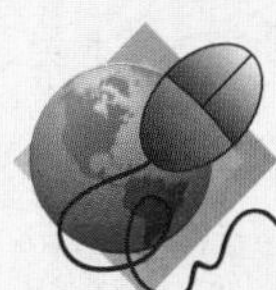
**Online Phonics**
SRA's ***Online Phonics*** program provides Web-based practice with the ***Open Court Reading*** sounds and spellings. For more information about this program, visit the SRA home page SRAonline.com

### Objectives

- Students will understand the selection vocabulary before reading, using strategies such as suffixes and structural cues.
- Students will recognize homophones and base words with the suffixes *-tion, -sion, -ed* and *-ments.*
- Students will connect prior knowledge to subjects discussed in text.
- Students will use comprehension strategies such as Monitoring and Clarifying, Summarizing, and Predicting to construct meaning from the text and monitor reading.
- Students will use the comprehension skill Making Inferences as they read the story the second time.
- Students will discuss personal reactions to the story to begin identifying their own personal reading preferences.
- Students link the selection's key concepts to their investigations.

### Materials

- Student Anthology, Book 2, pp. 14–25
- Program Assessment
- Reading Transparencies 23, 46, 49
- Inquiry Journal, p. 83
- Home Connection, p. 45
- Unit 4 Assessment, pp. 2–5
- Routine Cards 1, 2, Routines 3–6

**Routine Card**
Refer to ***Routine 4*** for the Clues, Problems, and Wonderings procedure.

| Clues | Problems | Wonderings |
|---|---|---|
| stores empty = people had to make things | shear | No one has money—how does Anna get a new coat? |

***Reading Transparency 46***

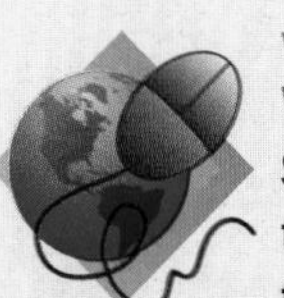

**www.sra4kids.com**
**Web Connection**
Students can use the connections to Money in the Reading link of the SRA Web page for more background information about money.

## Build Background

### Activate Prior Knowledge

Discuss the following with students to find out what they may already know about the selection and have already learned about the theme of Money.

- Preteach "A New Coat for Anna" by first determining students' prior knowledge by asking *"What is bartering?" "Have you ever traded something?" "Do you like to trade?"*
- Ask students whether they have ever traded something to a friend for another item. Explain that this type of trading is called *bartering* and that adults use it too in times when money is scarce.
- Discuss what items people can trade for other items.
- Ask students whether they are familiar with the story they are about to read, and if so, to tell a little bit about it. Remind students, however, not to give away the ending of the selection.
- Ask students if they have ever read any other stories about people who trade or barter things.

### Background Information

The following information may help students to better understand the selection they are about to read.

- Explain to students that "A New Coat for Anna" takes place in Europe following World War II, when money, food, and clothing were scarce. Many houses, factories, businesses, and transportation and communication systems were totally destroyed by aerial bombing during the war. These places and services, and the lives of the people who depended upon them, were not restored to normal until years after the war had ended.
- Tell students that "A New Coat for Anna" is based on a true story told to the author by a friend. In the dedication of the book, Harriet Ziefert writes about her friend, who as a child "waited many months for a new coat and who showed it to me some twenty-five years later," and about the friend's mother, "who at the start of it all had nothing—save persistence and determination—and who in the end fashioned a beautiful gift."

## Preview and Prepare

### Browse

- Have students read the title and the author's and illustrator's names aloud. This allows them to activate prior knowledge relevant to the story. Have students preview the selection by browsing only the first page or two of the story. Discuss with students what they think this story might reveal about money.

- Have students search for clues that tell them something about the story. Also, have students look for any problems, such as unfamiliar words, they notice while reading. Use ***Reading Transparency 46*** to record their observations as they browse. For example, students might state, "The stores were empty, so people must have made things themselves." For the *Problems* column, students might point out they are unfamiliar with the word *shear.* They might wonder how Anna gets a new coat if no one has money.
- As students prepare to read the selection, have them browse the Focus Questions on the first page of the selection. Tell them to keep these questions in mind as they read.

### Set Purposes

Encourage students to set purposes of their own for reading this selection. For example, students might think about how people can get what they need without using money. You may also have students think about how the theme of the story piques their curiosity or connects to their personal interests. As students read, have them think about what this story demonstrates about money and what characters learn about money.

## Selection Vocabulary

As students study vocabulary, they will use a variety of skills to determine the meaning of a word. These include context clues, word structure, and apposition. Students will apply these same skills while reading to clarify additional unfamiliar words. Students can write their definitions in their Writer's Notebooks.

Display ***Reading Transparency 23*** before reading the selection to introduce and discuss the following words and their meanings.

| | |
|---|---|
| **remained:** | stayed in the same place or stayed the same (page 14) |
| **strung:** | stretched from one place to another (page 19) |
| **wound:** | wrapped around and around (page 19) |
| **weaver:** | a person who makes fabric from thread or yarn (page 19) |
| **bolt:** | a roll of cloth (page 20) |

Have students read the words in the word box, stopping to blend any words that they have trouble reading. Demonstrate how to decode multisyllabic words by breaking the words into syllables and blending the syllables. Then have students try. If they still have trouble, refer them to the ***Sound/Spelling Cards.*** If the word is not decodable, give the students the pronunciation.

Have students read the sentences on ***Reading Transparency 23*** to determine the meanings of the underlined words. Each word has two sentences that students will read and from which they should be able to derive the meaning of the underlined word. Be sure students explain which skills they are using and how they figured out the meanings of the words. Have students reread the sentence, substituting the definition to see if the sentence makes sense. Have a volunteer create a new sentence using the underlined word.

**Teacher Tip** Students who set their own goals for reading read with a greater sense of engagement and notice more than students whose goals are set for them by the teacher or the reading program. The purpose of initial browsing is to help students think about what they will be reading and to build a sense of anticipation.

**Teacher Tip SELECTION VOCABULARY** To help students decode words, divide the words into syllables when you are saying them, as shown below. The information following each word tells how students can figure out the meaning of each word. When writing words on the board, do not divide them into syllables.

| | |
|---|---|
| re•mained | context clues |
| strung | context clues |
| wound | context clues |
| weav•er | context clues |
| bolt | context clues |

**Routine Card**
Refer to ***Routine 3*** for the vocabulary procedure.

OPEN COURT READING — Reading Transparency 23

remained strung wound weaver bolt

1. But when the war ended the stores remained empty.
   After the small snack the boys remained hungry.
2. Soon red yarn was hanging up to dry on a clothesline strung across the kitchen.
   Maria made a necklace of beads strung on a piece of ribbon.
3. When it dried, Anna and her mother wound the yarn into balls.
   The boys wound the rope around the tree.
4. They took the yarn to the weaver.
   At the fair this summer, we watched a weaver make rugs on a loom.
5. When Anna and her mother returned, the weaver gave them a bolt of beautiful red cloth.
   We pulled out a bolt of printed fabric to take a closer look at the pattern.

***Reading Transparency 23***

**Differentiating Instruction**

| If... | Then... |
|---|---|
| Students need extra help with selection vocabulary | Use ***Intervention Guide*** pages 176–177 |

**Teacher Tip** COMPREHENSION STRATEGIES Remind students on the second day as they read the story to summarize what they learned from the first day.

**Routine Card**
Refer to ***Routine 5*** for the procedure on reading the selection.

**DIFFERENTIATING INSTRUCTION**

| If... | Then... |
|---|---|
| Students need extra help with summarizing | Use ***Intervention Guide*** pages 177–178 |
| Students need extra help with monitoring and clarifying | Use ***Intervention Guide*** pages 178–179 |

During Workshop, and after the selection has been read at least once, have students listen to the recording of this lesson's selection on the ***Listening Library Audiocassette/CD.*** After students have listened, have them discuss their personal preferences of the selections read. Ask them what other things they have listened to and like to listen to on the radio, on audiocassettes, or on CDs.

**Teacher Tip** Have the students choose a book to read from the library relating to the theme. This book should identify their preference in either literary or nonfiction texts. Encourage students to read often from their preferred genre.

# Reading Recommendations

## Oral Reading

The simple language and narrative style of this story make it a good candidate for oral reading. Students should read aloud fluently with appropriate expression, intonation, and vocal patterns. Make sure that students attend to punctuation and read in phrases. Tell students to add a sense of feeling or anticipation as they read.

Have students make use of the comprehension strategies listed below to help them understand the selection. Have them stop reading periodically or wait until they have completed the selection to discuss the reading strategies. After the students have finished reading the selection, use the Discussing the Selection questions on page 23A to see if they understand what they have read.

## Using Comprehension Strategies 

Comprehension strategy instruction allows students to become aware of how good readers read. Good readers constantly check their understanding as they are reading and ask themselves questions. In addition, skilled readers recognize when they are having problems and stop to use various comprehension strategies to help them make sense of what they are reading.

During the first reading of "A New Coat for Anna," model and prompt the use of the following comprehension strategies. Take turns reading the story aloud with the students.

- **Summarizing** prompts readers to keep track of what they are reading and to focus their minds on important information.
- **Predicting** causes readers to analyze information given about story events and characters in the context of how it may logically connect to the story's conclusion.
- **Monitoring and Clarifying** takes different forms, including clarifying the meaning of words and clarifying difficult ideas or passages. In order to clarify meanings, students can use Context, use Structural Analysis, use Apposition, reread the text, use charts or graphic organizers, or use resources outside of the text.

As students read, they should be using a variety of strategies to help them understand the selection. Encourage students to use the strategies listed above as the class reads the story aloud. Do this by stopping at the points indicated by the numbers in the magenta circles on the reduced student page and using a particular strategy.

## Building Comprehension Skills 

Revisiting or rereading a selection allows students to apply skills that give them a more complete understanding of the text. Some follow-up comprehension skills help students organize information. Others lead to deeper understanding—to "reading between the lines," as mature readers do. In this selection, students will review the following comprehension skill:

- **Making Inferences** requires readers to activate prior knowledge and connect what they know or have experienced to what they are reading.

### Reading with a Purpose

Have students look for ways the story characters use objects instead of money throughout the selection.

### Differentiating Instruction

| If... | Then... |
| --- | --- |
| English Learners need help with the story | • Have them read it before the whole-class reading, using the ***Listening Library Audiocassette/CD***<br>• Have them associate what they see in the illustrations with the words in the story, so they learn to think English words before translating them first from their native language |

**Teacher Tip** Remember that the students' own think-alouds are always preferred to the teacher's. Continue to encourage students to model for one another when they work out problems or as they come up with ideas when they read.

### Research in Action

Students who do not seem to be using the reading strategies "on their own" should be prompted to think about, choose, and use strategies as they read. They should listen to strategy-using classmates read aloud and discuss strategies during the lesson. Students will probably notice that once they have been learned, reading strategies come naturally and enhance their understanding and enjoyment of a selection.
*(Michael Pressley)*

COMPREHENSION

Read pages 14–23.

## Comprehension Strategies

Read the story aloud, taking turns with the students. Start by modeling the use of strategies for the students.

### Teacher Modeling

**1 Monitoring and Clarifying**
*Good readers stop reading to clarify words, phrases, or concepts that they find confusing before continuing to read the story. I wonder why Anna's mother had to wait until after the war to buy Anna a new coat. First, I'll look at the illustrations, and then I'll keep on reading to help me answer my question. In the illustrations on page 14, the stores are boarded up. One has a sign on it that says "Closed," and the other store has little, if anything, to sell. The story says that when the war ended, "the stores remained empty." That tells me that the stores were empty during the war, too. Let's continue to read and remember to stop and clarify anything that we don't understand.*

### Word Knowledge

**SCAFFOLDING:** The skills students are reviewing in Word Knowledge should help them in reading the story. This lesson focuses on homophones, base words with the suffixes *-ed*, *-ment* and *-tion,* word families, and double consonants.

**homophones:** **needed** (kneaded)
**no** (know)
**new** (knew)
**see** (sea)

**Teacher Tip** Remind students to be active readers and to use the strategies that they have learned. Encourage students to make connections between the story and their own lives.

**First Reading Recommendation**

**ORAL • CHORAL**

*Focus Questions* Why do we sometimes have to give up something we have in order to get something we want? Why are things we receive more special when others have had to work together in order to give them to us?

# A New Coat for Anna

Harriet Ziefert
*illustrated by Anita Lobel*

Winter had come and Anna needed a new coat. The fuzzy blue coat that she had worn for so many winters was no longer fuzzy and it was very small.

Last winter Anna's mother had said, "When the war is over, we will be able to buy things again and I will get you a nice new coat."

But when the war ended the stores remained empty. There still were no coats. There was hardly any food. **1** And no one had any money.

Anna's mother wondered how she could get Anna a new coat. Then she had an idea. "Anna, I have no money," she said, "but I still have Grandfather's gold watch and some other nice things. Maybe we can use them to get what we need for a new coat. First we need wool. Tomorrow we will visit a farmer and see about getting some."

14

**Informal Assessment**

Observe individual students as they read and use the Teacher Observation Log found in the ***Program Assessment Teacher's Edition,*** to record anecdotal information about each student's strengths and weaknesses.

The next day Anna and her mother walked to a nearby farm.

"Anna needs a new coat," Anna's mother told the farmer. "I have no money, but I will give you this fine gold watch if you will give me enough wool from your sheep to make a coat."

The farmer said, "What a good idea! But you will have to wait until spring when I shear my sheep's winter wool. Then I can trade you their wool for your gold watch."

Anna waited for spring to come. Almost every Sunday she and her mother visited the sheep. She would always ask them, "Is your wool growing?" The sheep would always answer, "Baaa!" Then she would feed them nice fresh hay and give them hugs.

15

COMPREHENSION

## Comprehension Skills

### Making Inferences

Readers make inferences in order to figure out information and details that a writer does not actually say in a story. To make an inference, students use story clues and what they already know as a basis for determining what has happened. Help students use clues from the story to make an inference about what life was like during the war.

**Clues**

- *stores boarded up and closed; no potatoes for sale; no coats for Anna's mother to buy*

**Inferences**

- *Life was very difficult, and sometimes you might even be hungry or cold.*

### Word Knowledge

| **suffix *-ed:*** | **walked** |
|---|---|
| | **visited** |

Making Inferences

Introduced in Grade 1.
Scaffolded throughout Grades 2 and 3.

**REINTRODUCED:** Unit 3, Lesson 3
**REINFORCED:** Unit 4, Lesson 1
Unit 6, Lesson 7
**TESTED:** Unit 4 Assessment

### Differentiating Instruction

| If... | Then... |
|---|---|
| English Learners need extra help with vocabulary | Use ***English Learner Support Guide*** pages 256–257 |
| English Learners need extra help with making inferences | Use ***English Learner Support Guide*** pages 257–258 |

**Second Reading Recommendation**

ORAL • **SILENT**

COMPREHENSION

## Comprehension Strategies

Begin prompting students for responses. Praise answers that are appropriate, even if they do not match the student sample. This will encourage students to use strategies as they read.

### Prompting

**2 Summarizing** *We already have a lot of information here. Stopping to summarize what you've read helps you remember what's happened and then you understand the story better. Let's sum up what's happened so far.*

### Student Sample

**Summarizing** *Anna needed a new coat but her mother didn't have any money. Anna's mother traded a watch to a farmer for his wool. Then she gave a spinner a lamp to have the wool spun. I'll keep reading to find out more.*

### Word Knowledge

**double consonants:** **Anna**
**apples**
**getting**

**Teacher Tip** This student sample is only one example of many possible student responses. Accept other responses that are reasonable and appropriate.

**Teacher Tip** Remind students to use context clues, apposition, or word structure to figure out the meaning of difficult words as they are reading.

At Christmastime Anna brought them paper necklaces and apples and sang carols.

When spring came the farmer sheared the sheep's wool.

"Does it hurt them?" asked Anna.

"No, Anna," said the farmer. "It is just like getting a haircut."

When he had enough wool to make a coat, the farmer showed Anna how to card the wool. "It's like untangling the knots in your hair," he told Anna.

16

Then he gave Anna's mother a big bag of wool and Anna's mother gave him the gold watch.

Anna and her mother took the bag of wool to an old woman who had a spinning wheel.

"Anna needs a new coat," Anna's mother told the woman. "I have no money, but I will give you this beautiful lamp if you will spin this wool into yarn."

The woman said, "A lamp. That's just what I need. But I cannot spin quickly, for I am old and my fingers are stiff. Come back when the cherries are ripe and I will have your yarn." 2

17

# Comprehension Skills

## Making Inferences

Because there are many things a writer does not say in a story about the characters or the events, it is up to students to be good readers and to make inferences in order to grasp and understand the whole story.

Ask students to think about Anna's concern for the sheep. Encourage students to make inferences about Anna's character based on this information. What can they infer about the other characters?

- *Anna is considerate; she probably loves animals and is a very caring person.*
- *Anna's mother is working very hard to get a coat for Anna. I think her mother cares for Anna a lot and is very determined.*

COMPREHENSION

### Word Knowledge

**word families:** **spin/spinning**

**Teacher Tip** As students read aloud, listen for appropriate pacing, intonation, and expression.

**Teacher Tip COMPREHENSION** Good readers are active readers. They interact with the text as they read by emoting, reacting, responding, and problem solving in their efforts to construct and maintain meaning.

### Differentiating Instruction

| If... | Then... |
|---|---|
| English Learners need extra help with vocabulary | Use ***English Learner Support Guide*** pages 259–260 |
| English Learners need extra help with making inferences | Use ***English Learner Support Guide*** pages 260–261 |

COMPREHENSION

## Comprehension Strategies

### Teacher Modeling

③ **Predicting** *Good readers make predictions to help them understand what they've read and to help them think about what will happen next. As they read, good readers check to see if their predictions are confirmed. I wonder what will happen when Anna and her mother take the yarn to the weaver. I'll think about what I've read so far. I've read that Anna's mother gave the farmer and the spinner something they needed or wanted in return for helping with things Anna needed for a new coat. I predict that Anna's mother will find a weaver to help make the wool into cloth in exchange for something Anna's mother will barter. Let's keep reading to find clues to what might be happening next.*

### Word Knowledge

| suffix *-ed:* | answered<br>returned |
|---|---|

**Teacher Tip** During reading, encourage students to note how bartering works.

When summer came, Anna and her mother returned. Anna's mother gave the old woman the lamp and the old woman gave them the yarn—and a basket of delicious red cherries.

"Anna, what color coat would you like?" Anna's mother asked.

"A red one!" Anna answered.

"Then we will pick some lingonberries," said Anna's mother. "They make a beautiful red dye."

At the end of the summer, Anna's mother knew just the place in the woods to find the ripest lingonberries. ③

18

### Differentiating Instruction

| If... | Then... |
|---|---|
| Students are having trouble making predictions | Prompt them to first summarize what is happening in the story, to help them organize their thoughts, and then to predict |

Anna and her mother boiled water in a big pot and put the berries into it. The water turned a deep red. Anna's mother dipped the pale yarn into it.

Soon red yarn was hanging up to dry on a clothesline strung across the kitchen.

When it dried, Anna and her mother wound the yarn into balls.

They took the yarn to the weaver.

"Anna needs a new coat," Anna's mother said. "I have no money, but I will give you this garnet necklace if you will weave this yarn into cloth."

The weaver said, "What a pretty necklace. I will be happy to weave your yarn. Come back in two weeks."

19

## Comprehension Skills

### Making Inferences

Encourage students to continue to use clues from the story, from the illustrations, and from their own background knowledge to make inferences that will enhance their understanding and enjoyment of the story.

- *I know Anna saw the basket of red cherries the old woman gave her mother. Then she wanted a red coat. I can infer that perhaps the red cherries made her think of having a red coat.*
- *Anna's mother knew how to make red dye from berries. Her mother must know how to make many things. My grandfather sometimes makes new clothes and toys for me. He's really good at knowing how to put things together and make things.*

### Word Knowledge

**homophones:**
**red** (read)
**pale** (pail)
**needs** (kneads)
**new** (knew)
**no** (know)
**be** (bee)
**two** (to/too)

**Teacher Tip** Discussing problematic text will help students understand that all readers—even very good readers—sometimes have difficulty understanding what they read. Help students overcome any hesitations they have about asking for help with difficult text.

COMPREHENSION

### Differentiating Instruction

| If... | Then... |
|---|---|
| English Learners need extra help with vocabulary | Use ***English Learner Support Guide*** pages 261–262 |
| English Learners need extra help with making inferences | Use ***English Learner Support Guide*** pages 262–263 |

COMPREHENSION

## Comprehension Strategies

### Teacher Modeling

4 **Confirming Predictions** *I was right. Anna's mother did give the weaver something she needed. What will happen next? What other predictions can we make?*

### Prompting

**Making Connections** *We have read quite a few pages of the story and gathered a lot of information about how Anna and her mother are working to get Anna a new coat. Making connections between things we already know and things we are reading about helps us to understand and to remember what we have read. As you are reading, be aware of how ideas in the text remind you of things that have happened to you. When you make such connections, tell the class about them.*

### Student Sample

5 **Making Connections** *I know just how Anna feels as she is being measured by the tailor. A tailor fixed my dress when my older sister got married. I felt just like a pin cushion. He poked me with the pins and kept telling me to stand still.*

**Word Knowledge**

**suffix *-ments*: measurements**

**Teacher Tip MAKING CONNECTIONS** Tell students that good readers are active readers who make connections as they read. Encourage students to make connections between the life experiences, customs, and cultures mentioned in the text to their own experiences as they read. Ask volunteers to share them with the class.

When Anna and her mother returned, the weaver gave them a bolt of beautiful red cloth. Anna's mother gave the weaver the sparkling garnet necklace.

4 The next day Anna and her mother set off to see the tailor.

"Winter is coming and Anna needs a new coat," Anna's mother told the tailor. "I have no money, but I will give you this porcelain teapot if you will make a coat from this cloth."

The tailor said, "That's a pretty teapot. Anna, I'd be very happy to make you a new coat, but first I must take your measurements."

20

**Differentiating Instruction**

| If... | Then... |
| --- | --- |
| Students are ready for a challenge with predicting | Have them look back at events in the story and create a story map to make their predictions |
| Students are having difficulty understanding some of the story events | Invite volunteers to share their story maps with these students |

He measured her shoulders. He measured her arms. He measured from the back of her neck to the back of her knees. Then he said, "Come back next week and I will have your coat." 5

The tailor set to work making a pattern, cutting the cloth, pinning, and sewing and stitching and snipping. He worked and worked for almost a whole week. When he was finished, he found six pretty matching buttons in his button box and sewed them on the coat.

He hung the coat proudly in the window for everyone to see.

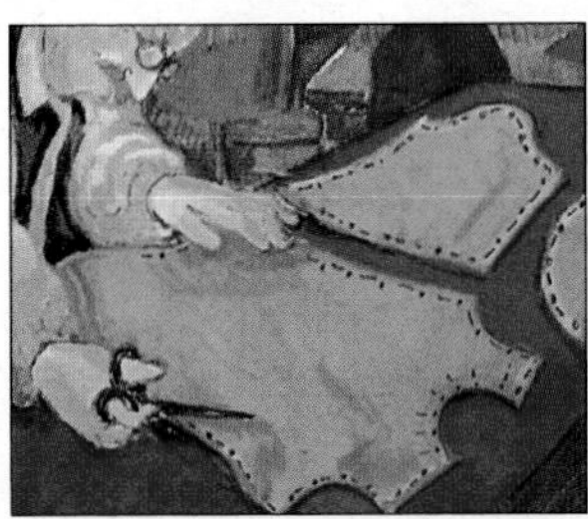

21

## Comprehension Skills

COMPREHENSION

### Making Inferences

Ask students to think about what they read in the story about Anna and all the people who helped make her new winter coat. Encourage them to make an inference about how the farmer, spinner, weaver, and tailor will feel whenever they see Anna in her new red winter coat. Then ask students to draw an inference about what the events in this story show about people working together.

- *They will probably feel proud that they helped make the coat.*
- *When people work together, they can accomplish what they set out to do.*

### Word Knowledge

**suffix *-ed*:** **measured**, **worked**, **finished**, **sewed**

**Teacher Tip** Authors purposefully cause readers to make inferences. In so doing they cause readers to project their own meaning into the text, making it mean more than is actually said in the words on the page.

**Writer's Craft: Fact and Opinion** Explain to students that a fact is something that is true, and an opinion is what someone thinks about something. Point out that in the story, it is a fact that the farmer, the spinner, the weaver, and the tailor went to Anna's house for the Christmas celebration, but it's an opinion that it was the best Christmas they had had in a long time. See Writer's Craft, page 25H.

### Differentiating Instruction

| If... | Then... |
| --- | --- |
| English Learners need extra help with vocabulary | Use ***English Learner Support Guide*** pages 263–264 |
| English Learners need extra help with making inferences | Use ***English Learner Support Guide*** pages 264–265 |

COMPREHENSION

## Comprehension Strategies

### Prompting

**6 Summarizing** *We have finished the story, and this is a good place to sum up all the steps that it took for Anna to get a new coat. Let's summarize what we learned about Anna and her new coat.*

### Student Sample

**Summarizing** *Anna needed a new coat, but her mother didn't have any money. They bartered for the things they needed. At the end, Anna had a lovely coat and many new friends.*

### Discussing Strategy Use

While they read the selection, encourage students to share any problems they encounter and to tell what strategies they use to solve them.

- What connections did they make between the reading and what they already know?
- How did they clarify confusing passages?
- Where did they pause in the reading to summarize?
- What predictions did they make?

These are questions good readers ask after they read a text. After reading, the students should always be asking, "What did I find interesting? What is important here?" Later, remind the students again that whenever they conclude a reading, they should ask themselves questions about what was in the text.

### Word Knowledge

suffix *-tion*: reflection

When Anna and her mother returned to the tailor's shop, Anna tried on her new coat. She twirled around in front of the mirror. The coat was perfect!

Anna thanked the tailor. Anna's mother thanked him, too, and gave him the pretty porcelain teapot.

Anna wore her new coat home. She stopped at every store to look at her reflection in the window.

22

### Differentiating Instruction

| If... | Then... |
|---|---|
| Students are having difficulty using any of the strategies as they read | Model and explain specific strategies with sections of the text |

**Teacher Tip BUILDING FLUENCY** As students read, you may notice that some need work in building fluency. During Workshop, have these students select a section of the text (a minimum of 160 words) to read several times in order to build fluency.

When they got home her mother said, "Christmas will soon be here, and I think this year we could have a little celebration."

Anna said, "Oh, yes, and please could we invite all the people who helped to make my coat?"

"Yes," said Anna's mother. "And I will make a Christmas cake just like I used to."

Anna gave her mother a big hug.

On Christmas Eve the farmer, the spinner, the weaver, and the tailor came to Anna's house. They all thought Anna looked beautiful in her new coat.

The Christmas cake that Anna's mother baked was delicious. Everyone agreed that this was the best Christmas they had had in a long time.

On Christmas Day Anna visited the sheep. "Thank you for the wool, sheep," she said. "Do you like my pretty new coat?"

The sheep seemed to smile as they answered, "Baaa! Baaa!"

23

## Comprehension Skills

### Making Inferences

Remind students that they must combine what they already know with information from the text to make inferences about the characters, places, things, and events in a story.

- Anna stops to look at herself in the coat at every store window. I bet having something new to wear was a very special occasion for her. She must feel very happy and proud.
- All the people who helped make the coat celebrated together. They must all be proud of their work and feel a connection to each other.

### Checking Comprehension

- What did you learn about Anna and her mother from the way that they went about getting Anna a new winter coat? *(Anna's mother was resourceful in trading what she had for something they needed.)*
- Why wasn't it necessary to pay for Anna's new coat with money? *(The people who helped make Anna's coat were willing to work in exchange for something else that they wanted or needed, such as a lamp.)*
- Who demonstrated the importance of working together in the story? *(The farmer, the spinner, the weaver, and the tailor all cooperated with Anna and her mother to make Anna's new coat. Also, Anna and her mother worked together to dye the wool for Anna's new coat.)*

COMPREHENSION

**Teacher Tip FLUENCY** By this time in third grade, good readers should be reading approximately 123 words per minute with fluency and expression. The only way to gain this fluency is through practice. Have students reread the selection to you and to each other during Workshop to help build fluency.

**Differentiating Instruction**

| If... | Then... |
|---|---|
| English Learners need extra help reviewing "A New Coat for Anna" | Use ***English Learner Support Guide*** pages 266–267 |

**Formal Assessment**

See pages 2–5 in ***Unit 4 Assessment*** to test students' comprehension of "A New Coat for Anna."

**Teacher Tip** **DISCUSSION** When you call on a student, allow him or her a few seconds to consider your question and arrive at an answer.

**Routine Card**
Refer to ***Routine* 6** for the *handing-off process.*

| Clues | Problems | Wonderings |
| --- | --- | --- |
| stores empty = people had to make things | shear | No one has money—how does Anna get a new coat? |

***Reading Transparency 46***

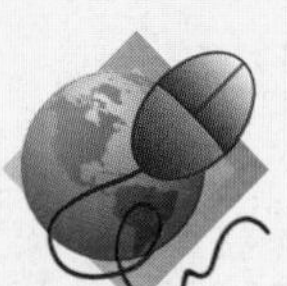

**www.sra4kids.com**
**Web Connection**
Some students may choose to conduct a computer search for additional books or information about money. Invite them to make a list of these books and sources of information to share with classmates and the school librarian. Check the Reading link of the SRA Web page for additional links to the theme-related Web site.

## Discussing the Selection

After the first read, the whole group discusses the selection and any personal thoughts, reactions, problems, or questions that it raises. To stimulate discussion, students can ask one another the kinds of questions that good readers ask themselves about a text: *How does it connect to money? What have I learned that is new? What did I find interesting about this story? What is important here? What was difficult to understand? Why would someone want to read this?* Ensure that students are using specific information from the text to support their interpretations.

**Handing-off Process** Seeing you as a contributing member of the group sets a strong example for students. To emphasize that you are part of the group, actively participate in the *handing-off process:* Raise your hand to be called on by the last speaker when you have a contribution to make. Point out unusual and interesting insights verbalized by students so that these insights are recognized and discussed. As the year progresses, students will take more and more responsibility for the discussions of the selections.

Engage students in a discussion to determine whether they have grasped the following ideas:

- why Anna's mother traded her possessions with other people
- why money was scarce
- what each of the steps was in making the coat
- what the story teaches about money or lack of money

During this time, have students return to the clues, problems, and wonderings they noted during browsing to determine whether the clues were borne out by the selection, whether and how their problems were solved, and whether their wonderings were answered or deserve further discussion and investigation. Let students decide which items deserve further discussion.

Also have students return to the Focus Questions on the first page of the selection. Select a student to read the questions aloud, and have volunteers answer the questions. If students do not know the answers to the questions, have them return to the text to find the answers.

You may wish to review the elements of realistic fiction with the students at this time. Discuss with them how they can tell that "A New Coat for Anna" is realistic fiction.

Have students break into small groups to discuss what this story tells them about money. Groups can discuss their ideas with the rest of the class.

Students may wish to record their personal responses to the selection. If students have ever traded something they own for something else, encourage them to record their experiences.

## Review Selection Vocabulary

Have students review the definitions of the selection vocabulary words that they wrote in the vocabulary section of their Writer's Notebooks. Remind them that they discussed the meanings of these words before reading the selection. Have students write sentences for each of the vocabulary words after the definitions in the same section of their Writer's Notebooks. They can use the definitions and the sentences to study for the vocabulary portion of their Lesson Assessments. Have them add to the personal dictionary section of their Writer's Notebooks any other interesting words that they clarified while reading. Encourage students to refer to the selection vocabulary words throughout the unit. The words from the selection are:

**remained** **strung** **wound** **weaver** **bolt**

Have students create a Word Bank of key words related to the unit theme Money. Encourage students to find words from other sources, in addition to their ***Anthology*** selections, to add to the Bank. Students can find words from other resources, from their investigations, and from family discussions. For this unit, have students arrange the words by the number of syllables in each word.

**Teacher Tip** It is a good idea to alert your school librarian before the start of each new unit. This will help him or her to assess the resources available and perhaps to prepare for the unit by acquiring materials specific to the topic.

## View Fine Art

Have students reflect on the photo of the wampum belt on page 57 of the ***Student Anthology*** and share their ideas with the class. Explain that wampum is formed with tubular beads made from shells, fastened together and used by the Iroquois and Algonquin of the American Northeast. Wampum was used to foretell events, declare war, and confirm treaties. At one time, wampum was used as money by the Dutch and English colonists. *Wampum* is from the Algonquin word for "strings of shell beads." The designs and colors have specific meanings: white beads refer to goodness and peace, while black beads mean war and grief.

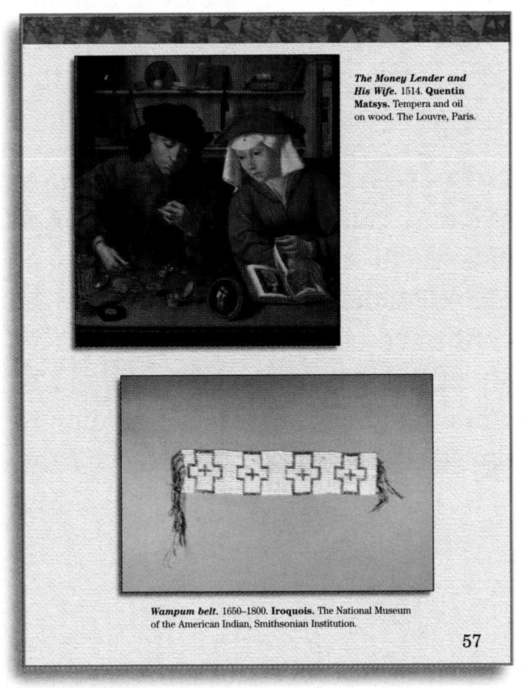

***The Money Lender and His Wife.*** 1514. **Quentin Matsys.** Tempera and oil on wood. The Louvre, Paris.

***Wampum belt.*** 1650–1800. **Iroquois.** The National Museum of the American Indian, Smithsonian Institution.

57

***Student Anthology* p. 57**

## Home Connection

Send home the letter on page 45 of ***Home Connection.*** Parents and caregivers will hear a summary of "A New Coat for Anna" from their children and also learn how to set up a barter system in their own homes. A Spanish version of this letter appears on page 46.

*A New Coat for Anna*

**A message from** ______________________

Our class has just finished reading a story called "A New Coat for Anna." This is the story of a mother who uses bartering in some very creative ways to get a new coat for her daughter. Ask your child to tell you about the story.

To help your child understand the concept of bartering, discuss an exchange of services with her or him. In this arrangement, your child agrees to complete certain jobs in your home in exchange for special privileges, such as an extra hour of free time before bed. Record the agreement on the chart below and hang it in a convenient place in your home.

**Agreement to Barter**

| Jobs | Special Privileges |
|---|---|
| | |
| | |
| | |
| | |

**Next week's selection** ***Alexander, Who Used to Be Rich Last Sunday***

Your child will be studying the following vocabulary words in the upcoming week. Please review the meanings of these words with your child: **tokens**—things that are a sign of something else, symbols; **rent**—to get the right to use in return for payment; **non-returnable**—something that cannot be taken or given back; **absolutely**—without any doubt; **positively**—for sure; certainly; confidently; **vanish**—disappear.

Please review with your child the spelling words for the upcoming week: spill, hill, gull, smell, mess, odd, add, cliff, mitt, fuzz, all, still, fall, till, guess.

***Home Connection* p. 45**

**Teacher Tip** Tell students that good readers are always making predictions as they read. Sometimes they are confirmed, and sometimes they are not. Either way, making predictions makes reading more interesting.

**Teacher Tip** **WRITING** Remind students to include the full title of the book and underline it and to include the author's name when they write about their predictions.

## Supporting the Reading

### Comprehension Strategies: Predicting

**Teach** After the first read, remind students that they need to stop periodically while reading and use clues from the story to predict what might happen next in a story. Tell students that they can use text features, such as captions, the table of contents, key words, and illustrations, as well as knowledge of formats, ideas, and plots, to help them make predictions. To use the strategy most effectively, they should return to their predictions to see whether or not further reading confirms their predictions.

**Guided Practice** Play a predicting game with students. Bring in a short, age-appropriate fiction book that you think most students have not read. Divide the class into two teams. Then read the book aloud, stopping to ask students for their prediction about what will happen next in the story. The teams of students who suggest a prediction get one point. If further reading confirms the prediction, the team receives two points. Explain to students that predictions must be based on information in the text.

**Independent Practice** Encourage students to continue making and confirming predictions as they read on their own. Students might find it helpful to keep track of their predictions in their Writer's Notebooks as they read and to note whether or not further reading confirmed the predictions they made.

**Link to Writing** Encourage students to write about their predictions. Have students choose a book from the ***Leveled Classroom Library.*** As they read, have them write their predictions and explain what information they are based on. As students read further, have them write whether their predictions were confirmed or not. They might also adjust predictions as they read, and can write about that as well. Ask students to write about at least two predictions they made while reading. Encourage students to use words that they learned while reading the selection or their ***Leveled Classroom Library*** book in their writing.

## Literary Elements

### Plot

**Instruct** Remind students that stories have plots. Ask students what they remember about plot. If necessary, review that *plot* is the sequence of events that occurs in a story. The plot usually centers around a problem and how the characters go about solving it.

**Guided Practice** Have students think about what problem needs to be solved in "A New Coat for Anna." *(Anna needs a new coat, but her mother doesn't have any money.)* Then, have students note the sequence of events that makes up the plot, beginning with the problem, followed by attempts to solve the problem, and ending with a solution to the problem. Tell students that a chart is a good way to visualize a plot's sequence of events. On the board, construct a flow chart consisting of seven empty boxes. Fill the first box in together with the phrase, "Mother says Anna needs a new coat, but she has no money." Draw a sad face above the box. Ask volunteers to supply a sequence of events to complete the chart and then fill in the boxes accordingly. Explain that these were ideas Anna's mother had to solve the problem. Draw a lightbulb over boxes 2 through 6. Draw a happy face over the box, explaining that the problem was solved—the outcome was a happy one. Possible answers include the following:

| | |
|---|---|
| First Event: | **Mother says Anna needs a new coat, but she has no money.** |
| Second: | **Mother trades watch to get wool.** |
| Third: | **Mother trades lamp to get wool spun.** |
| Fourth: | **Mother and Anna dye yarn.** |
| Fifth: | **Mother trades necklace to get yarn woven.** |
| Sixth: | **Mother trades teapot to get coat tailored.** |
| Seventh: | **Anna gets her new coat.** |

**Independent Practice** Have students look in their ***Writing Folders*** for a story they have written. Encourage them to chart the plot. What was the problem? What ideas did the characters have to solve it? What was the outcome? Do the steps in the plot make sense? Is any step missing? Invite students to make any necessary revisions to the stories. Alternatively, students can begin writing a new story by first charting out a plot. Then they can fill in details as they write the new story and use the chart as a guide. You might want to copy ***Reading Transparency 49*** to distribute to students. They can use this to help them chart a plot.

**Teacher Tip** To promote intentional learning, keep students aware of what they are learning and why, rather than letting them focus on just the activities.

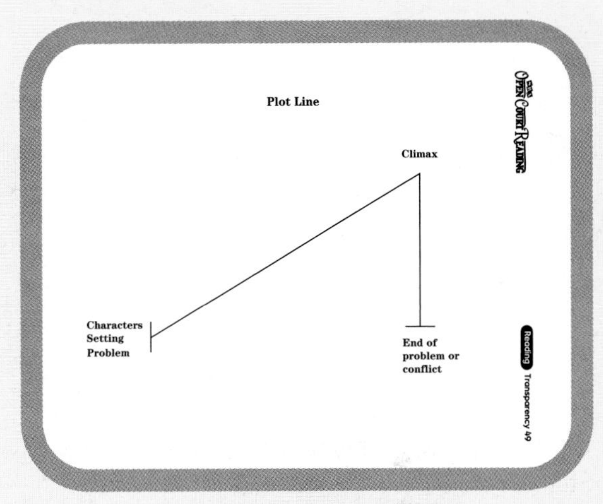


***Reading Transparency 49***

### DIFFERENTIATING INSTRUCTION

| If... | Then... |
|---|---|
| Students are having difficulty understanding plot | Have them reread "A New Coat for Anna" with you and then help them complete the plot line on ***Reading Transparency 49*** |
| English Learners need extra help with plot | Have them tell you about a story they are familiar with from their native countries. Then help them complete the plot line on ***Reading Transparency 49*** for that story. |

**Teacher Tip MATERIALS**

- poster board
- colored pencils or markers
- possibly beads (or other items that can be strung)
- string

**Teacher Tip PURPOSE** To learn about the culture of local Native Americans of the region.

**Teacher Tip** Encourage students to use their imagination for creating models. If students are making models of wampum, tell them there are many techniques for making beads to string. Students might want to make their own beads from strips of newspaper and papier mâché paste, or they can glue small stones or shells to pieces of cardboard.

## Social Studies Connection

### Barter Systems

In "A New Coat for Anna," students read about a mother that used bartering to get the materials and services she needed for a new coat for her daughter. She bartered because money was scarce. Explain to students that throughout human history, some societies have used barter or developed other forms of money that are very different from the paper money with which they are familiar.

Divide students into groups and ask them to find out more about the Native Americans of the region and to focus on how they obtained goods and services. What goods and services were considered valuable? How did people obtain them? Did the physical geography of the area influence how they adapted to the environment and what goods and services were available? Was there a system of barter? Were there objects that represented money? How did people trade with others from different cultures? Who did they trade with? Why did they trade with those people? Was there any connection between whom they traded with and the geography of the region? How did new settlers respond to the Native Americans already established in the area? Did a different system of barter develop?

Ask students to share their findings with the class, along with visuals such as drawings or models.

Suggest alternate ways for students to present their findings, such as a song, skit, artwork, written and oral report, personal account, or a media event.

After each group has finished, allow students to ask questions to the presenters about what they have seen and learned. Tell the presenters to respond to questions, clarify ideas, and paraphrase ideas as necessary for the audience. Encourage students in the audience to share any experiences they have that relate to what they have learned from the presenters.

## Science Connection

### Symbiotic Relationships

Bartering occurs not only among humans. Animals and plants share limited resources through symbiotic relationships. The remora is perhaps the best known example of a symbiotic relationship. The sucker disk on the top of its head is a modified dorsal fin that allows the fish to attach itself to another fish or turtle. The advantage of this adaptation is food for the remora and some cleanliness for the other organism. Symbiotic relationships are those in which two different types of organisms live in a close association that benefits at least one of them, like the remora. Ask the students if they can think of examples of similar relationships.

Have the students research animals or plants that live in symbiotic relationships with other organisms. The students will then draw pictures of those organisms in their habitats, to aid in the presentation of their findings. Each student should have one minute to present what he or she found.

After all students have presented, ask the students how these organisms are like Anna's mother and the townsfolk. Ask them how symbiotic relationships help animals survive.

**Teacher Tip MATERIALS**
- ✔ research materials, including encyclopedias, and the Internet
- ✔ colored pencils or crayons
- ✔ construction paper

**Teacher Tip PURPOSE** To teach how organisms survive on limited resources by working symbiotically.

## Concept Connections

### Linking the Selection

- Anna's mother traded with the farmer, the spinner, the weaver, and the tailor to have a coat made for Anna.
- Students might suggest that Anna and her mother traded their most valuable possessions to pay for the coat.

### Exploring Concept Vocabulary

The concept word for this lesson is ***barter.*** Write the word on the board. Work with students to develop a definition that clearly links to the unit theme. Have students copy the word and definition into the Vocabulary section of their Writer's Notebooks.

***Barter:*** to trade goods or services for other things without using money. For example, Anna's mother bartered her garnet necklace for a bolt of cloth.

- Bartering is a way for people to get the things they need by exchanging their possessions for them.
- Anna's mother did not have any money to pay for Anna's coat.
- Anna's mother bartered a gold watch, a lamp, a garnet necklace, and a teapot.

Remind students that their sentence endings should include a selection vocabulary word.

### Expanding the Concept

You may want to do a whole-group discussion to help students continue to develop their ability to engage in meaningful dialogue. However, students may conduct these dialogues in small groups. If students work in small groups, bring the groups together and have them share their ideas with the whole class.

Have students record their ideas and impressions about the selection on page 83 of their ***Inquiry Journals.***

# A New Coat for Anna

## Concept Connections

### Linking the Selection

Think about the following questions, and then record your responses in the Response Journal section of your Writer's Notebook.

- How was Anna's mother able to get Anna a new coat without any money?
- Why do you think Anna's new coat was valuable?

### Exploring Concept Vocabulary

The concept word for this lesson is ***barter.*** If you do not know what this word means, look it up in a dictionary. Answer these questions:

- What does the word ***barter*** have to do with money?
- Why did Anna's mother ***barter*** their possessions for a new coat?
- What did Anna's mother ***barter*** to get Anna's new coat?

Write the sentence beginning shown below. Then choose a word from the selection vocabulary, and write your own sentence ending.

Anna's mother will ***barter*** ____________________.

24

**Teacher Tip** These activities may be done during Workshop.

**Informal Assessment**

This may be a good time to observe students working in small groups and to mark your observations in the Teacher Observation Log found in the ***Program Assessment Teacher's Edition.***

## Expanding the Concept

Think about the Read Aloud "Money, Money, Money" and the story "A New Coat for Anna." What do these selections tell you about money?

Try to use the word ***barter*** in your discussion.

Add new ideas about money to the Concept/Question Board.

## Meet the Author

**Harriet Ziefert** was a schoolteacher for many years. She began looking for jobs as an editor but found that getting hired was tough. So she began writing books. She has written many books—several hundred. She likes to develop a story together with an illustrator. *"I like to work with artists and turn them into illustrators. I like finding new artists and watching them grow."*

## Meet the Illustrator

**Anita Lobel** was born in Poland and grew up during World War II. She became a very successful children's book author and illustrator. Lobel's knowledge of the theater is very important in her work as an illustrator. *"Writing and illustrating books for children is a form of drama for me. I approach the construction of a picture book as if it were a theater piece to be performed, assigning dialogue, dressing the characters, and putting them into an appropriate setting."*

25

**Teacher Tip** Encourage students to select materials for independent reading based on personal interest, knowledge of authors, and different types of texts. When students finish reading, have them conduct book talks to briefly retell their stories. Have students give their opinions about the books they read, and make recommendations to classmates and teachers.

### Differentiating Instruction

| If... | Then... |
| --- | --- |
| Students enjoyed reading "A New Coat for Anna" | Encourage them to read other stories by Harriet Ziefert, such as *A New House for Mole* |

## Meet the Author

After students read the information about Harriet Ziefert, discuss the following questions with them:

- Harriet Ziefert, like many of the authors in this textbook, was once a teacher. Why do you think so many teachers like to write? *(Possible answers: Good teachers like to tell stories to help explain what they are teaching. By being writers themselves, teachers can also help their students improve their writing by example and editing.)*
- Harriet Ziefert likes to develop her story together with the illustrator. Why? *(Possible answer: Working together, artist and writer can brainstorm about what they are trying to create.)*

## Meet the Illustrator

After students read the information about Anita Lobel, discuss the following questions with them:

- Anita Lobel grew up during World War II. How do you think this helped her develop the illustrations for "A New Coat for Anna"? *(Possible answer: Lobel probably understood about shortages. She probably remembers what some of the towns looked like and what a relief it was when the war was over.)*
- Anita Lobel says that drawing is like drama. Can you think of ways that drawing and drama are similar? *(Possible answer: Drawing and drama both tell stories. They both show emotions and feelings through the characters' faces.)*

### Objectives

- Students ask questions related to money.
- Students gain a deeper understanding of issues related to money.
- Students brainstorm questions about money and start to think about forming groups.

### Materials

- Student Anthology, Book 2, pp. 12–25
- Inquiry Journal, pp. 87–88
- Research Assistant CD-ROM

INVESTIGATION

## Investigating Concepts Beyond the Text

A major aim of ***Open Court Reading*** is knowledge building. Because inquiry is at the root of knowledge building, students are encouraged to investigate questions within each selection that relate to the unit theme.

Explain to students that for the Unit 4 investigation they will produce and present the results of an investigation of money. They will decide what questions and problems to investigate, whom they want to work with, and how to present their findings. Throughout this unit, students should work through the Research Cycle, asking questions, forming conjectures, conducting study and investigations, informally presenting findings, revising conjectures or questions, continuing with the investigation, and so on until they publish their investigation results.

The selections in this unit feature many different aspects of money. How money originated; how it is made and developed; how different people earn, save, and spend it; the value it holds for different people; and how it affects people's lives are all investigated in this unit.

To start the Research Cycle, conduct a free-floating discussion of problems and questions of interest to students. List students' questions and problems on the board. If they choose problems that are too difficult for them, help them change the objectives of their investigations rather than simply selecting an easier problem. This can be done by exploring *how* students might approach the question or problem. If the *how* cannot be determined, students will be more willing and able to refocus. Remind students that the measure of success during their investigations is not necessarily in finding answers, but in making progress.

Outline for students the schedule you have planned for the investigation of money: how long the investigation is expected to take, how much time will be available for research, and when the first presentation will be due. This schedule partly determines the scope of problems students should be encouraged to work on. Investigations should be completed at the time the unit is ending; however, some investigations may take longer. Throughout this lesson, students should pose initial questions, form groups based on areas of shared interest, and brainstorm initial plans which students can share and discuss with the class.

## Concept/Question Board

After reading each selection, students should use the Concept/Question Board to:

- Post any questions they asked about a selection before reading that haven't yet been answered.
- Refer to as they formulate statements about concepts that apply to their investigations.
- Post general statements formulated by each collaborative group.
- Continue to post news articles or other items that they find during the unit investigation.
- Read and think about posted questions, articles, or concepts that interest them and provide answers to the questions.

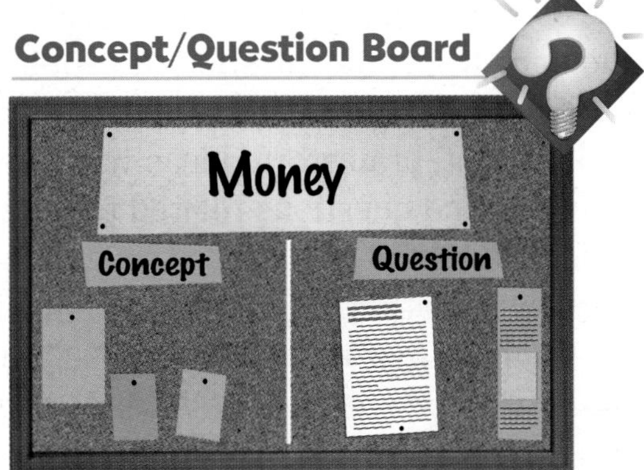


### Unit 4 Investigation Management

|  |  |
|---|---|
| Lesson 1 | Collaborative Investigation<br>**Brainstorm questions related to the theme.**<br>Supplementary Activity<br>**Investigate alternatives to money, such as bartering.** |
| Lesson 2 | Groups form based on areas of shared interest. Investigate choices related to spending and saving money. |
| Lesson 3 | Begin forming conjectures. Brainstorm about how to turn hobbies into businesses. |
| Lesson 4 | Discuss conjectures in groups and begin plans. Look for stories or illustrations about the ways that money can change people and things that money cannot buy. |
| Lesson 5 | Students revise their plans as necessary and continue investigation. Groups can debate on borrowing and lending money. |
| Lesson 6 | Continue investigation and prepare final presentations. Create a story or miniplay about how money passes from person to person, or plan a possible field trip to a Federal Reserve Bank. |
| Lesson 7 | Groups give formal presentations. Students discuss saving money for personal goals or explore the Great Depression further. |

INVESTIGATION

**Teacher Tip** Continue to encourage use of the Concept/Question Board by recognizing and thanking students for their contributions. Incorporate discussion of those items into classroom discussions whenever appropriate.

### Research Assistant

The ***Research Assistant CD-ROM*** helps students in their investigations.

**Teacher Tip** At this stage, students will be examining many possible questions. Allow enough time for them to consider different problems and questions they want to investigate. In this early stage, changing investigation problems and questions is common and even encouraged.

**Formal Assessment**

Use the Research Rubrics on page 14J to assess students' ability to research questions and problems.

### Differentiating Instruction

| If... | Then... |
|---|---|
| Students are having difficulty distinguishing between a topic and a problem | Work with them on *Inquiry Journal* page 87 during Workshop |

INVESTIGATION

## Question and Problem Phase

To start the Question and Problem Phase of the Research Cycle, conduct a free-floating discussion of problems and questions of interest to the students. Explain to the students that a good investigation problem or question will not only require them to consult multiple sources but will add to the group's knowledge of money and engage them in further discussions. Explain to students that an investigation problem is different from an investigation topic. Have them consider the difference between the topic "money" and the problem, "Why is counterfeiting a problem?" Explain that if students choose to investigate the topic "money," everything they look up under the subject heading or index entry *money* will be related in some way to their topic. Therefore, it will be quite difficult to choose what information to record. This excess of information will also create problems in organizing their research. Choosing a specific question or problem, one that particularly interests them, will help them narrow their investigation and advance their understanding. At this point, brainstorm ideas with the class to help students think about problems and questions related to money that they might like to investigate. Generate a list of these ideas on the board. Model for students how to turn their investigation ideas into good investigation problems and questions, especially if their initial responses are topics. Assign page 87 of the ***Inquiry Journal*** to be completed during Workshop.

Name ______ Date ______

Money UNIT 4

**Investigation Ideas**

Use this page to brainstorm ideas for your unit investigation.

Answers will vary.

The idea I've chosen to use for my unit investigation:

Inquiry Journal • *Investigation Ideas* UNIT 4 87

***Inquiry Journal* p. 87**

## Choosing Appropriate Sources

**Teach** Remind students that before they investigate, they need to identify exactly what they want to know and then choose the most appropriate sources for finding the answers.

**Guided Practice** Ask students to tell what sources are available to them when doing an investigation. Point out any of the following sources of information that students did not mention.

- books, magazines, encyclopedias
- charts, graphs, diagrams, maps
- Internet searches
- interviews with experts or other knowledgeable people
- videocassettes, audiocassettes, filmstrips, photographs

Remind students that they can use multiple sources in any investigation. They will most likely use both primary and secondary (or supporting) sources. Give students an example of an investigation question. Have them tell you what their primary sources would be. Then have them tell you what the possible secondary sources would be. Have them explain to you how secondary sources may not contain all of the information necessary for a particular topic, but that they provide needed additional information.

**Independent Practice** In order to facilitate student investigations, have students write all the questions they would like to have answered under the heading *What I Want to Know.* Encourage students to leave a few spaces after each entry. To the right of these questions, under the heading *Best Sources of Information*, have students list the places where they might find the answers to their questions. This method will help students narrow their searches and use the available resources more efficiently. Students can use their ***Inquiry Journals,*** page 88, to help them organize their ideas.

Remind students to consult these sources as they proceed with their unit investigations.



TECH KNOWLEDGE

Encourage students to use ***TechKnowledge*** to learn more about how to use a computer to perform various tasks.

**www.sra4kids.com**
**Web Connection**
More information about money and links to Web sites concerning money can be found at www.sra4kids.com.

Name________________ Date________

UNIT 4 Money

**Possible Sources**

Look at the list of sources below. Decide whether each will be helpful during your unit investigation. If it will be helpful, write how it will help.

Answers will vary.

| Source | Which ones? | Useful? | How? |
|---|---|---|---|
| Encyclopedias | | | |
| Books | | | |
| Magazines | | | |
| Newspapers | | | |
| Videotapes, filmstrips, etc. | | | |
| Television | | | |
| Interviews, observations | | | |
| Museums | | | |
| Internet | | | |
| Other | | | |

Use the lines below to write the names of books or other sources that will be helpful during your unit investigation.

Answers will vary.

88 UNIT 4 *Possible Sources* • Inquiry Journal

***Inquiry Journal p. 88***

### Objectives

**Word Analysis**

**Spelling**

- **Double Consonants.** Develop understanding of words containing double consonants.

**Vocabulary**

- **Base Word Families.** Using words from "A New Coat for Anna," develop an understanding of how knowing one word in a base word family can help students infer the meaning of other words in the same family.

**Writing Process Strategies**

- **Persuasive Writing: Friendly Letter.** Building on the idea of persuading others to barter for goods or services, learn the form and function of writing a persuasive friendly letter to a peer.

**English Language Conventions**

**Grammar, Usage, and Mechanics**

- **Prepositions and Prepositional Phrases.** Understand prepositions and prepositional phrases. Identify prepositions and prepositional phrases in "A New Coat for Anna."

**Listening, Speaking, Viewing**

- **Listening: Recognizing Facts and Opinions.** Develop skills to understand fact and opinion.

**Penmanship**

- **Cursive Letters *A* and *C*.** Develop handwriting skills by practicing formation of cursive *A* and *C*.

### Materials

- Spelling and Vocabulary Skills, pp. 74–77
- Language Arts Handbook
- Comprehension and Language Arts Skills, pp. 92–95
- Writer's Workbook, pp. 54–57
- Language Arts Transparencies 6, 15, 37
- Student Anthology

### Differentiating Instruction

***Reteach, Challenge,*** and ***Intervention*** lessons are available to support the language arts instruction in this lesson.

### Research in Action

Some of the usage problems that appear in writing are the result of students transporting informal speech to more formal composition... others...are rooted in a pervasive lack of reading experience among students....
(*James D. Williams*, Preparing to Teach Writing: Research, Theory, and Practice)

OVERVIEW

# Language Arts Overview

## Word Analysis

**Spelling** The Spelling activities on the following pages introduce words with double consonants. Students learn spelling strategies for recognizing how double consonants can affect the sound and meaning of a word, like the difference between *super* and *supper*.

### Selection Spelling Words

These words from "A New Coat for Anna" contain double consonants.

**tomorrow summer pretty button happy**

**Vocabulary** The Vocabulary activities extend the instruction of base word families, as introduced in Lesson 1 of Unit 3. A *base word family* is a group of words that have the same base word but with different prefixes, suffixes, or inflectional endings.

### Vocabulary Skill Words

**returned measurements reflection untangling weaver***

**Also Selection Vocabulary*

## Writing Process Strategies

The Writing Process Strategies lesson involves instruction in writing a friendly letter, with the focus on the art of persuasion.

To teach spreadsheet applications in the writing process, review how to enter data into a spreadsheet, spreadsheet features, and how to create a graph from a spreadsheet. You might want to help students create a spreadsheet listing the things they would like to trade with their brother or sister. ***TechKnowledge,*** Level 3, Lesson 67, teaches these spreadsheet application skills.

## English Language Conventions

**Grammar, Usage, and Mechanics** **Prepositions and Prepositional Phrases.** This lesson develops an understanding of prepositions and prepositional phrases through reading and writing.

**Listening, Speaking, Viewing** **Listening: Recognizing Facts and Opinions.** The Listening, Speaking, Viewing lessons are divided into six categories: Listening, Speaking, Language, Viewing, Interacting, and Presenting. In this Listening lesson, students will listen to determine fact from opinion.

**Penmanship** **Cursive Letters *A* and *C*.** This lesson develops handwriting skills by having students learn formation of *A* and *C*. Students then practice writing words from the literature selection.

# DAY 1

## Word Analysis

### Spelling

#### Assessment: Pretest

**Double Consonants**

#### Teach

Give students the Pretest on page 30 of ***Unit 4 Assessment***. Have them proofread and correct any misspelled words.

**Pretest Sentences**

1. **better** It is **better** to be kind.
2. **letter** You mail a **letter**.
3. **potter** A **potter** molds with clay.
4. **rubber** Tires contain **rubber**.
5. **soccer** In **soccer,** players kick and score goals.
6. **ladder** Painters use a **ladder**.
7. **hammer** One tool is a **hammer**.
8. **scatter** Sprinklers **scatter** water over plants.
9. **dinner** A main meal can be called **dinner**.
10. **slippers** People wear **slippers** on their feet.
11. **tomorrow** The day after today is **tomorrow**.
12. **summer** Sandals are often worn in the **summer**.
13. **pretty** A garden is **pretty**.
14. **button** A **button** helps hold fabric together.
15. **happy** A smile is the sign of a **happy** person.

Diagnose any misspellings by determining whether students misspelled the double consonant or some other part of the word. Then have students use the Pretest as a take-home list to study the spellings of words with double consonants.

## Writing Process Strategies

### Getting Ideas

**Persuasive Friendly Letter**

#### Teach

**Introduce Persuasive Writing Form**

- Read ***Language Arts Handbook,*** pages 156–157.
- Share the formal assessment rubrics with students. (See Day 5 of this lesson.)
- Discuss ***Language Arts Transparency 6,*** Models of Good Writing: Persuasive Peer Letter.

**Inspiration**

Teacher Model: "*In 'A New Coat for Anna,' Anna needed a coat, so her mother bartered what she had to get what she needed to make a coat. I'll write to a friend to see if we could trade something that she has too much of. I'll think of good reasons to persuade her to trade.*"

**Brainstorming**

Encourage students to generate ideas for what they have that they might be willing to barter with a friend.

### Guided Practice

**Getting Ideas**

Have students write ideas for a persuasive friendly letter in their Writer's Notebooks.

Persuasive Writing

Persuasive writing does two things. It can make readers think or feel a certain way. It can also make readers do something. Sometimes persuasive writing can do both of these things at the same time. Advertisements are one kind of persuasive writing. You will learn about other kinds in the following lessons.

156 / Persuasive Writing

*Language Arts Handbook p. 156*

## English Language Conventions

### Grammar, Usage, and Mechanics

**Grammar: Prepositions and Prepositional Phrases**

#### Teach

- Use ***Language Arts Handbook,*** page 254, for the definitions and examples of prepositions and prepositional phrases.
- Write *to, through, around,* and *in* on the board in one column. Write *bike, park, block, town, home, swings, tree,* and *merry-go-round* in a second column. Ask students to form prepositional phrases from the two columns.
- Write sentences on the board with prepositional phrases from these columns. Underline the prepositions and prepositional phrases.
  - Darren and Julia rode their bikes around the block. *(preposition, around; prep. phrase, around the block)*
  - They sat in the swings. *(preposition, in; prep. phrase, in the swings)*

### Independent Practice

Use ***Comprehension and Language Arts Skills,*** pages 92–93, to identify prepositions and prepositional phrases.

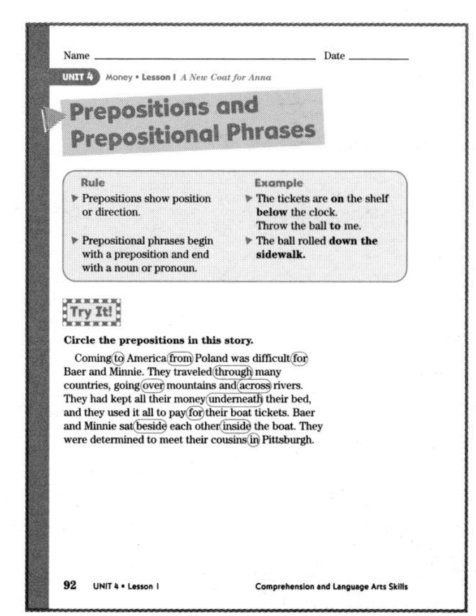

Name ______________ Date ________

UNIT 4 Money • Lesson 1 *A New Coat for Anna*

Prepositions and Prepositional Phrases

| Rule | Example |
|---|---|
| Prepositions show position or direction. | The tickets are **on** the shelf **below** the clock. Throw the ball **to** me. |
| Prepositional phrases begin with a preposition and end with a noun or pronoun. | The ball rolled **down the sidewalk.** |

Try It!

**Circle the prepositions in this story.**

Coming to America from Poland was difficult for Baer and Minnie. They traveled through many countries, going over mountains and across rivers. They had kept all their money underneath their bed, and they used it all to pay for their boat tickets. Baer and Minnie sat beside each other inside the boat. They were determined to meet their cousins in Pittsburgh.

92 UNIT 4 • Lesson 1 Comprehension and Language Arts Skills

*Comprehension and Language Arts Skills p. 92*

# DAY 2

## Word Analysis

### Spelling

**Double Consonants**

- Ask the class to say *super* and *supper*. Write the words on the board. Ask a student to circle *pp* in *supper*. Explain that double consonants come after short-vowel sounds. Point out the /ōō/ in *super* and the /u/ sound in *supper*.
- Write *better*, *soccer*, and *dinner* on the board. Have students circle the double consonants and notice the short-vowel sounds.

### Vocabulary

**Base Word Families**

#### Teach

- Write *returned* (page 18, "A New Coat for Anna") on the board, and ask a student for the base word in *returned (turn)*. Ask another student to circle the prefix in *returned (re-)*.
- Remind students that *turn*, *return*, and *returned* are part of the same base word family.

#### Guided Practice

Use ***Spelling and Vocabulary Skills,*** page 74, to reinforce the concept of base word families. Ask students to complete page 75 as independent practice.

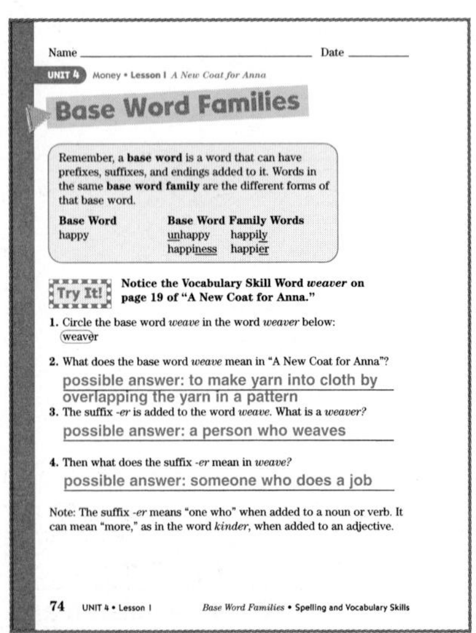

Name ______________________ Date __________

UNIT 4 Money • Lesson 1 *A New Coat for Anna*

**Base Word Families**

Remember, a **base word** is a word that can have prefixes, suffixes, and endings added to it. Words in the same **base word family** are the different forms of that base word.

| Base Word | Base Word Family Words | |
|---|---|---|
| happy | unhappy | happily |
| | happiness | happier |

**Try It!** **Notice the Vocabulary Skill Word *weaver* on page 19 of "A New Coat for Anna."**

1. Circle the base word *weave* in the word *weaver* below:
   weaver
2. What does the base word *weave* mean in "A New Coat for Anna"?
   possible answer: to make yarn into cloth by overlapping the yarn in a pattern
3. The suffix *-er* is added to the word *weave*. What is a *weaver?*
   possible answer: a person who weaves
4. Then what does the suffix *-er* mean in *weave?*
   possible answer: someone who does a job

Note: The suffix *-er* means "one who" when added to a noun or verb. It can mean "more," as in the word *kinder*, when added to an adjective.

74 UNIT 4 • Lesson 1 *Base Word Families* • Spelling and Vocabulary Skills

***Spelling and Vocabulary Skills* p. 74**

## Writing Process Strategies

### Prewriting

**Persuasive Friendly Letter**

#### Teach

- **Review** student ideas for persuasive friendly letters from Day 1.
- Read ***Writer's Workbook,*** page 54, on prewriting for a persuasive friendly letter.
- Go over ***Language Arts Transparency 15,*** Template—Friendly Letter.

#### Independent Practice

**Prewriting**

- Have students fill out their audience and purpose on page 54 of the ***Writer's Workbook.***
- Have students complete the graphic organizer on page 55 of the ***Writer's Workbook.***

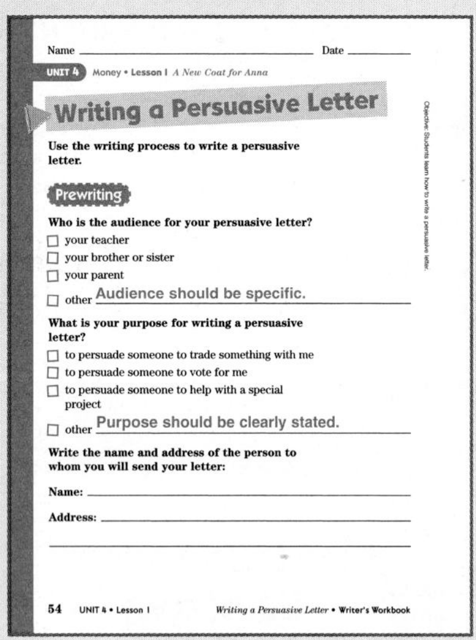

Name ______________________ Date __________

UNIT 4 Money • Lesson 1 *A New Coat for Anna*

**Writing a Persuasive Letter**

**Use the writing process to write a persuasive letter.**

**Prewriting**

**Who is the audience for your persuasive letter?**

- ☐ your teacher
- ☐ your brother or sister
- ☐ your parent
- ☐ other Audience should be specific.

**What is your purpose for writing a persuasive letter?**

- ☐ to persuade someone to trade something with me
- ☐ to persuade someone to vote for me
- ☐ to persuade someone to help with a special project
- ☐ other Purpose should be clearly stated.

**Write the name and address of the person to whom you will send your letter:**

**Name:** ______________________

**Address:** ______________________

Objective: Students learn how to write a persuasive letter.

54 UNIT 4 • Lesson 1 *Writing a Persuasive Letter* • Writer's Workbook

***Writer's Workbook* p. 54**

**Professional Development**

***Teacher Resource Library CD-ROMs*** or ***Online Professional Development*** provides courses that help you better understand the Writing instruction in ***Open Court Reading.*** For more information about this program, visit SRAonline.com.

## English Language Conventions

### Grammar, Usage, and Mechanics

**Grammar: Prepositions and Prepositional Phrases**

#### Teach

- Review prepositions and prepositional phrases using ***Comprehension and Language Arts Skills,*** pages 92–93, from Day 1.
- Write the following sentences on the board. Ask students to identify the prepositions and prepositional phrases. Ask other students if they agree or disagree.
  - The potlatch was a custom among Native Americans in the Pacific Northwest. (*prepositions*, among, in; *prep. phrases*, among Native Americans, in the Pacific Northwest)
  - At the potlatch, tribe members would give great gifts to other members. (*prepositions*, at, to; *prep. phrases*, at the potlatch, to other members)
  - People came from everywhere on foot and on horses. (*prepositions*, from, on; *prep. phrases*, from everywhere, on foot, on horses)
  - People outside the tribe would not receive gifts. (*preposition*, outside; *prep. phrase*, outside the tribe)

#### Guided Practice in Reading

Put students into small groups and have them find prepositions and prepositional phrases in "A New Coat for Anna," noting the page each comes from on a sheet of paper. Gather the sheets from the groups.

# DAY 3

## Word Analysis

### Spelling

**Double Consonants**

#### Teach

- Introduce the words found in "A New Coat for Anna" with double consonants that end in *-er*, *-on*, or *-y* and have short-vowel sounds.
- Ask students to think of parts or types of clothing that contain double consonants. *(button, zipper, slippers)*

#### Guided Practice

Have students complete page 76 from ***Spelling and Vocabulary Skills*** to learn strategies for spelling words with double consonants.

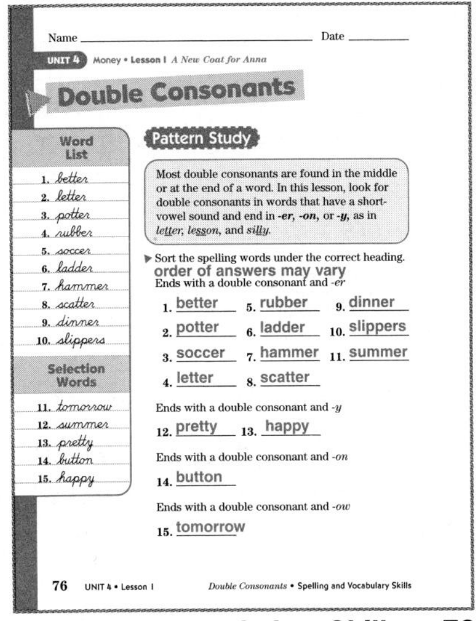
Name ______ Date ______

UNIT 4 Money • Lesson I *A New Coat for Anna*

**Double Consonants**

**Word List**
1. better
2. letter
3. potter
4. rubber
5. soccer
6. ladder
7. hammer
8. scatter
9. dinner
10. slippers

**Selection Words**
11. tomorrow
12. summer
13. pretty
14. button
15. happy

**Pattern Study**

Most double consonants are found in the middle or at the end of a word. In this lesson, look for double consonants in words that have a short-vowel sound and end in **-er**, **-on**, or **-y**, as in *letter*, *lesson*, and *silly*.

▶ Sort the spelling words under the correct heading.

order of answers may vary

Ends with a double consonant and *-er*

1. better 5. rubber 9. dinner
2. potter 6. ladder 10. slippers
3. soccer 7. hammer 11. summer
4. letter 8. scatter

Ends with a double consonant and *-y*

12. pretty 13. happy

Ends with a double consonant and *-on*

14. button

Ends with a double consonant and *-ow*

15. tomorrow

76 UNIT 4 • Lesson I *Double Consonants* • Spelling and Vocabulary Skills

***Spelling and Vocabulary Skills* p. 76**

### Vocabulary (continued)

**Base Word Families**

- Write *untangling* on the board.
- Ask a student to read the sentence in "A New Coat for Anna" (p. 16) with *untangling*, and discuss what the base word *tangle* means. *(in a knot, all tied up)*
- Ask a student to circle the prefix *un-* in *untangling.* Discuss how *un-*, meaning "not or opposite of," changes the meaning of *tangle. (to undo knots)*
- Point out how the ending *-ing* makes the word an action in the present, happening now.

## Writing Process Strategies

### Drafting

**Persuasive Friendly Letter**

#### Teach

Read ***Writer's Workbook,*** page 55, on drafting a persuasive friendly letter.

**Writer's Craft**

**Fact and Opinion**

- Explain that when you are trying to persuade someone, you may use facts or feelings to support your viewpoint. Depending on the audience, the writer will choose which will have more of an impact on the reader.
- Read ***Language Arts Handbook,*** page 159, on two ways to persuade.
- Read ***Comprehension and Language Arts Skills,*** page 94, on fact and opinion.

#### Guided Practice

**Drafting**

- Have students write their drafts on paper and put them in their ***Writing Folders.***
- If you have computers in your classroom, you may want to have students write their drafts using word processing software.

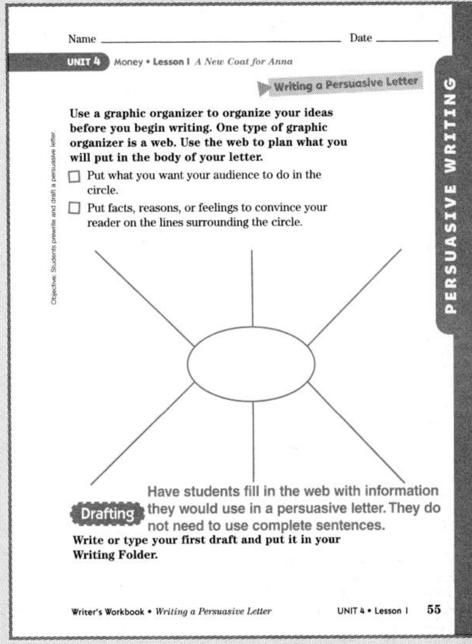
Name ______ Date ______

UNIT 4 Money • Lesson I *A New Coat for Anna*

**Writing a Persuasive Letter**

PERSUASIVE WRITING

Objective: Students prewrite and draft a persuasive letter.

**Use a graphic organizer to organize your ideas before you begin writing. One type of graphic organizer is a web. Use the web to plan what you will put in the body of your letter.**

- ☐ Put what you want your audience to do in the circle.
- ☐ Put facts, reasons, or feelings to convince your reader on the lines surrounding the circle.

Have students fill in the web with information they would use in a persuasive letter. They do not need to use complete sentences.

**Drafting**

**Write or type your first draft and put it in your Writing Folder.**

Writer's Workbook • *Writing a Persuasive Letter* UNIT 4 • Lesson I 55

***Writer's Workbook* p. 55**

## English Language Conventions

### Grammar, Usage, and Mechanics

**Grammar: Prepositions and Prepositional Phrases**

#### Teach

- Use ***Language Arts Handbook,*** page 254, to review prepositions and prepositional phrases.
- Write the following questions on the board with the suggested preposition in parentheses after them. For each, ask students to write a sentence in response.
  - In what town do you live? *(in)*
  - Where did you come from today? *(from)*
  - Where do you go to school? *(at)*
  - Where are you going after school? *(to)*

#### Guided Practice in Writing

Hand out the papers with the prepositional phrases from the Practice in Reading exercise from Day 2. Groups should not get their own papers. Ask each group to make up a story about persuading someone to barter for something the group really wants, using the prepositional phrases on their sheets, or similar ones.

**Informal Assessment**

Check students' writing to make sure they are using prepositions correctly.

# DAY 4

## Word Analysis

### Spelling

**Double Consonants**

**Teach**

Demonstrate the Consonant Substitution strategy by writing *winner* on the board. Explain how knowing the spelling of *winner* can help them know how to spell *dinner* by substituting *w* with *d*.

**Guided Practice**

Have students complete page 77 of ***Spelling and Vocabulary Skills*** to reinforce the spelling of words with double consonants.

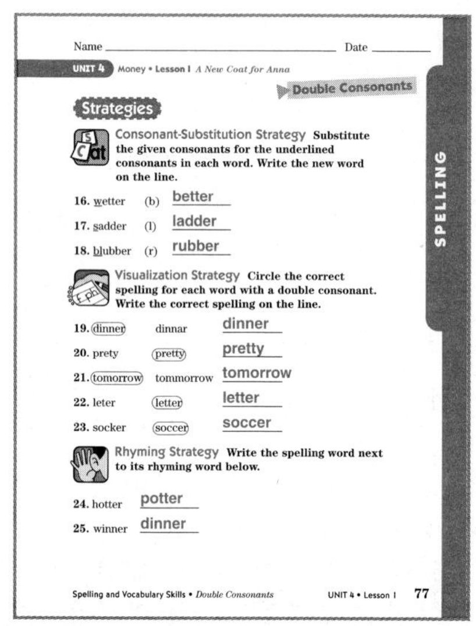

Name ______ Date ______

UNIT 4 Money • Lesson 1 *A New Coat for Anna*

Double Consonants

Strategies

**Consonant-Substitution Strategy** Substitute the given consonants for the underlined consonants in each word. Write the new word on the line.

16. wetter (b) better
17. sadder (l) ladder
18. blubber (r) rubber

**Visualization Strategy** Circle the correct spelling for each word with a double consonant. Write the correct spelling on the line.

19. dinner dinnar dinner
20. prety pretty pretty
21. tomorrow tommorrow tomorrow
22. leter letter letter
23. socker soccer soccer

**Rhyming Strategy** Write the spelling word next to its rhyming word below.

24. hotter potter
25. winner dinner

SPELLING

Spelling and Vocabulary Skills • *Double Consonants* UNIT 4 • Lesson 1 77

***Spelling and Vocabulary Skills* p. 77**

### Vocabulary (continued)

**Base Word Families**

- Write *measurements* on the board. Ask the class to find the base word in *measurements. (measure)*
- Ask a student what it means to *measure* something. *(to find the size, length, weight, or height)*
- Explain that the suffix *-ment* is added to *measure* to create *measurement.* The suffix *-ment* means "result or act of." Ask a student to define *measurement*, knowing the meaning of the base word and suffix. *(the result of measuring, the actual size)*

## Writing Process Strategies

### Revising

**Persuasive Friendly Letter**

**Teach**

- Read ***Writer's Workbook,*** page 56, on revising a persuasive friendly letter.
- Remind students that their task actually has two parts: persuasion and friendly letter. As they revise, they may want to try to separate the two and focus on one aspect at a time.

**Troubleshooting**

- Misspelling the recipient's name makes a bad impression.
- Unclear facts or feelings will confuse the reader.
- Facts or feelings that do not go with the main idea will frustrate the reader. Your reader will spend time trying to figure out why you put it in and won't be thinking about your original message.

**Guided Practice**

**Revising**

- Have students revise their writing and put it in their ***Writing Folders.***
- Have students use the checklist on ***Writer's Workbook,*** page 56, to help them revise their persuasive friendly letters.

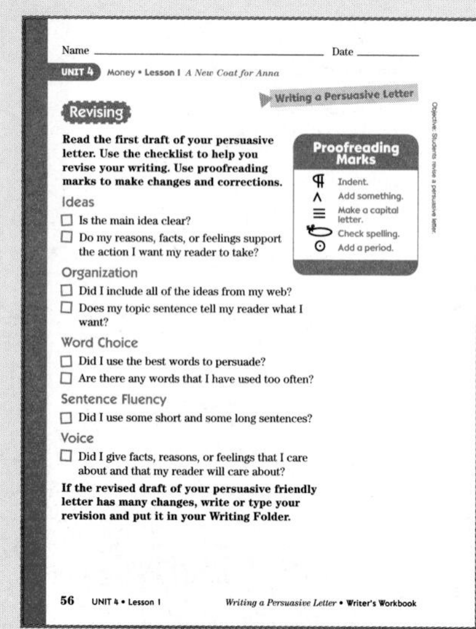

Name ______ Date ______

UNIT 4 Money • Lesson 1 *A New Coat for Anna*

Writing a Persuasive Letter

Revising

**Read the first draft of your persuasive letter. Use the checklist to help you revise your writing. Use proofreading marks to make changes and corrections.**

Ideas

- ☐ Is the main idea clear?
- ☐ Do my reasons, facts, or feelings support the action I want my reader to take?

Organization

- ☐ Did I include all of the ideas from my web?
- ☐ Does my topic sentence tell my reader what I want?

Word Choice

- ☐ Did I use the best words to persuade?
- ☐ Are there any words that I have used too often?

Sentence Fluency

- ☐ Did I use some short and some long sentences?

Voice

- ☐ Did I give facts, reasons, or feelings that I care about and that my reader will care about?

**If the revised draft of your persuasive friendly letter has many changes, write or type your revision and put it in your Writing Folder.**

**Proofreading Marks**

- ¶ Indent.
- ∧ Add something.
- ≡ Make a capital letter.
- Check spelling.
- ⊙ Add a period.

Objective: Students revise a persuasive letter.

56 UNIT 4 • Lesson 1 *Writing a Persuasive Letter* • Writer's Workbook

***Writer's Workbook* p. 56**

## English Language Conventions

### Listening, Speaking, Viewing

**Listening: Recognizing Facts and Opinions**

**Teach**

- A fact is something that actually exists or has happened. An opinion is a personal thought or feeling that may or may not be factual.
- It is important to be able to distinguish between fact and opinion. Sometimes people present ideas as facts when they are actually opinions.
- Phrases that signal a fact are: it has been proven, there is evidence, scientific proof shows. Phrases that signal opinions are: I think, I feel, it might be.

**Guided Practice**

- Make a few statements about "A New Coat for Anna," and ask students to identify them as fact or opinion. *(The story was written by Harriet Ziefert: fact. Anna's new coat is pretty: opinion. Anna and her mother make many trades to have Anna's coat made: fact.)*
- How did the students know which statements were fact or opinion? *(The story was evidence for the facts, whereas there is no actual evidence to prove the opinions.)*

Observe whether students can distinguish facts from opinions, and whether they participate in class discussions.

# DAY 5

## Word Analysis

### Spelling

#### Assessment: Final Test

**Double Consonants**

#### Teach

Repeat the Pretest or use the Final Test on page 31 of ***Unit 4 Assessment*** as summative assessment of student understanding of words with double consonants.

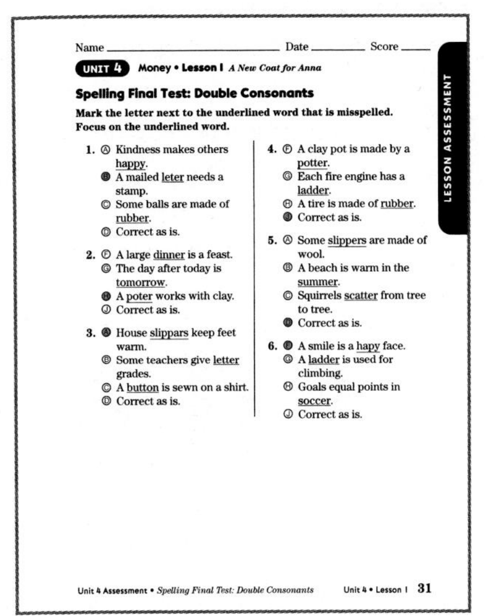

Name ______ Date ______ Score ______

UNIT 4 Money • Lesson 1 *A New Coat for Anna*

LESSON ASSESSMENT

**Spelling Final Test: Double Consonants**

**Mark the letter next to the underlined word that is misspelled. Focus on the underlined word.**

1. Ⓐ Kindness makes others happy.
   ● A mailed leter needs a stamp.
   Ⓒ Some balls are made of rubber.
   Ⓓ Correct as is.
2. Ⓕ A large dinner is a feast.
   Ⓖ The day after today is tomorrow.
   ● A poter works with clay.
   Ⓙ Correct as is.
3. ● House slippars keep feet warm.
   Ⓑ Some teachers give letter grades.
   Ⓒ A button is sewn on a shirt.
   Ⓓ Correct as is.
4. Ⓕ A clay pot is made by a potter.
   Ⓖ Each fire engine has a ladder.
   Ⓗ A tire is made of rubber.
   ● Correct as is.
5. Ⓐ Some slippers are made of wool.
   Ⓑ A beach is warm in the summer.
   Ⓒ Squirrels scatter from tree to tree.
   ● Correct as is.
6. ● A smile is a hapy face.
   Ⓖ A ladder is used for climbing.
   Ⓗ Goals equal points in soccer.
   Ⓙ Correct as is.

Unit 4 Assessment • *Spelling Final Test: Double Consonants* Unit 4 • Lesson 1 31

***Unit 4 Assessment* p. 31**

#### Guided Practice

Have students categorize any mistakes they made on the Final Test as careless errors or lesson-pattern problems.

### Vocabulary

**Informal Assessment**

Write *reflection* in "A New Coat for Anna" (p. 22). Explain that the base word of *reflection* is *reflect*. Discuss the meanings for *reflect (reflect: to give back an image, what a mirror does)*. Explain that *reflection* contains the suffix *-ion*, meaning "act of" or "result of," like the suffix *-ment*. Ask a student to define *reflection (the act of or result of reflecting)*. Check if students have added new words to their word lists in the Writer's Notebook.

## Writing Process Strategies

### Editing/Proofreading and Publishing

**Persuasive Friendly Letter**

#### Teach

- Read ***Writer's Workbook,*** page 57, on editing/proofreading and publishing.
- Discuss ***Language Arts Transparency 37,*** Presentation: Persuasive Peer Letter.

#### Guided Practice

**Editing/Proofreading and Publishing**

- Have students read their papers out loud. Ask the other students to identify the facts and opinions in the paper.
- Direct students to use the checklist on ***Writer's Workbook,*** page 57.

**Formal Assessment**

Total Point Value: 10

1. What the writer wants of the audience is clear. (2 points)
2. All facts or feelings support the main idea. (2 points)
3. The closing sentence sums up the writer's argument. (2 points)
4. The tone is friendly. (2 points)
5. The mechanics are correct. (2 points)

Name ______ Date ______

UNIT 4 Money • Lesson 1 *A New Coat for Anna*

Writing a Persuasive Letter

PERSUASIVE WRITING

Objective: Students edit/proofread and publish a persuasive letter.

**Editing/Proofreading**

**Edit your persuasive letter on paper or a computer. Then make a clean copy of your letter, and put it in your Writing Folder. Read your persuasive letter carefully. Use the checklist to help you correct any mistakes.**

Conventions

- ☐ Are your words spelled correctly?
- ☐ Do you use a capital letter correctly in your heading, greeting, closing, and signature?
- ☐ Do you use commas correctly?
- ☐ Does every sentence have a punctuation mark at the end?
- ☐ Do you indent your paragraphs?

**Publishing**

**Use this checklist to get your letter ready to mail.**

Presentation

- ☐ Make sure your writing says exactly what you want it to say.
- ☐ Make a clean copy. Make sure you have all the parts of a friendly letter in the correct place. You may want to use the computer.
- ☐ Address the envelope and send the letter.

Writer's Workbook • *Writing a Persuasive Letter* UNIT 4 • Lesson 1 57

***Writer's Workbook* p. 57**

## English Language Conventions

### Penmanship

**Cursive Letters *A* and *C***

#### Teach

- **Teacher Model:** Introduce formation of uppercase *A* and *C* as downcurve letters by demonstrating on the board.

**A** Starting point, downcurve
Undercurve to starting point
Slant down, undercurve: capital *A*

**C** Starting point, loop
Downcurve
Undercurve: capital *C*

- **Teacher Model:** Write the title "A New Coat for Anna" on the board to model proper letter formation.
- Review with students the importance of proper margins. Lines of letters should all begin at the vertical red line of a sheet of paper and end about one inch from the right edge of the paper.

#### Guided Practice

- Have students practice writing rows of *A*s and *C*s in the Writer's Notebook.
- From "A New Coat for Anna," ask students to write the words *At* and *Christmastime* in legible cursive to practice letter formation.
- Have students check their writing to see whether they stayed within the margins and if their writing is legible.

**Informal Assessment**

Check students' handwriting for proper formation of *A* and *C* and neat margins.

# Reading and Language Arts Skills Traces

## Language Arts

### WORD ANALYSIS

Skills Trace

**Spelling: Double Consonants**

Introduced in Grade 2.
Scaffolded throughout Grades 2–5.

**REINTRODUCED:** **Unit 4, Lesson 1**, p. 25E
**PRACTICED:** **Unit 4, Lesson 1**, pp. 25F–25J
*Spelling and Vocabulary Skills,* pp. 76–77
**TESTED:** **Unit 4, Lesson 1**, p. 25F (Pretest)
**Unit 4, Lesson 1**, p. 31 (Final Test)
**Unit 4 Assessment**

Skills Trace

**Vocabulary: Base Word Families**

Introduced in Grade 2.
Scaffolded throughout Grades 2–5.

**REINTRODUCED:** **Unit 4, Lesson 1**, p. 25E
**PRACTICED:** **Unit 4, Lesson 1**, pp. 25G–25J
*Spelling and Vocabulary Skills,* pp. 74–75
**TESTED:** **Unit 4 Assessment**

### WRITING PROCESS STRATEGIES

Skills Trace

**Persuasive Writing: Persuasive Letter**

Introduced in Grade 1.
Scaffolded throughout Grades 2–6.

**REINTRODUCED:** **Unit 4, Lesson 1**, p. 25F
**PRACTICED:** **Unit 4, Lesson 1**, pp. 25G–25J
*Writer's Workbook,* pp. 54–57
**TESTED:** **Unit 4, Lesson 1**, Formal Assessment, p. 25J
**Unit 4 Assessment**

Skills Trace

**Writer's Craft: Fact and Opinion**

Introduced in Grade 2.
Scaffolded throughout Grades 3, 5–6.

**REINTRODUCED:** **Unit 4, Lesson 1**, p. 25H
**PRACTICED:** **Unit 4, Lesson 1**, p. 25H
*Comprehension and Language Arts Skills,* pp. 94–95
**TESTED:** **Unit 4 Assessment**

### ENGLISH LANGUAGE CONVENTIONS

Skills Trace

**Grammar: Prepositions**

Introduced in Grade 3.
Scaffolded throughout Grades 4–6.

**INTRODUCED:** **Unit 4, Lesson 1**, p. 25F
**PRACTICED:** **Unit 4, Lesson 1**, p. 25G
**Unit 4, Lesson 1**, p. 25H
*Comprehension and Language Arts Skills,* pp. 92–93
**TESTED:** **Unit 4, Lesson 1**, Informal Assessment, p. 25H
**Unit 4 Assessment**

Skills Trace

**Listening, Speaking, Viewing**
**Listening: Recognizing Facts and Opinions**

Introduced in Grade 1.
Scaffolded throughout Grades 2–3.

**REINTRODUCED:** **Unit 4, Lesson 1**, p. 25I
**TESTED:** **Unit 4, Lesson 1**, Informal Assessment, p. 25I
**Unit 4 Assessment**

Skills Trace

**Penmanship: Cursive Letters *A* and *C***

Introduced in Grade 3.
Scaffolded throughout Grades 4–6.

**INTRODUCED:** **Unit 4, Lesson 1**
**TESTED:** **Unit 4, Lesson 1**, Informal Assessment, p. 25J

## Reading

### COMPREHENSION

**Making Inferences**

Introduced in Grade 1.
Reinforced throughout Grade 2.

**REINTRODUCED:** **Unit 3, Lesson 3**
**REINFORCED:** **Unit 4, Lesson 1**
**Unit 6, Lesson 7**
**TESTED:** **Unit 4 Assessment**

# Professional Development: Writing

## Providing Feedback: Seminar

Seminar provides yet another opportunity for students to receive feedback. Seminar is a class discussion of the work of two or three student authors, called Seminar leaders, chosen to share their work each day. As each Seminar leader reads his or her piece, the rest of the class listens, and a few students will have the chance to comment when the author is finished.

In the beginning, teachers may want to choose the Seminar leaders. They may be students who have novel topics, who have written in a particular form, who are revising, who have sloppy first drafts, and so on. After the first few weeks, post a class list, taking three students each day in the order in which their names appear on the list. Initially, it may be necessary to remind students who will be the Seminar leaders, but gradually turn the responsibility over to the class. As the year progresses, students may want to hold small-group Seminars during Workshop.

Students may use Seminar to brainstorm ideas for writing, get suggestions for revision, or focus on a particular problem. Seminar should accomplish the following:

- Provide opportunities to share and learn from each other.
- Encourage discussion and problem solving.
- Foster a sense of community.
- Allow students to share all their writing at any point in the writing process, not just work they are going to publish.
- Make students responsible for thinking and learning about writing.
- Reinforce all the language arts.
- Develop self-esteem and self-confidence.

Set up some simple rules at the beginning of the year.

1. The Seminar leader selects who will speak from among those who have raised their hands, including the teacher.
2. Seminar participants must listen carefully and provide constructive feedback. Participants should focus on what was good about a piece and ways to make it better.
3. The author has ownership and can decide which suggestions to use. The author does not have to incorporate all suggestions from participants.

Seminar usually occurs before writing so authors can apply the feedback to their work. Classmates' comments should focus on constructive changes. Be sure to model responses and questions that emphasize the *process*, not just the details in the story. As happens with writing conferences, feedback from Seminar encourages authors to grow.

Seminar for kindergarten writers initially may be sharing pictures and labels. Suggestions during Seminar may relate to comments about changing or adding to the pictures. Gradually, as children start writing words and sentences, the focus will shift to comments about the text. In the upper grades, as students start writing and sharing longer pieces of writing, they may want to share only part of a piece. When they do this, the authors should explain why they have chosen a particular section; for example, it's a part they particularly like or one with which they are having problems. Also, students should use Seminar to share their research in progress as well. During Seminar, students can get feedback on their research, refine their questions, and discuss problems finding resources.

### Professional Development

***Teacher Resource Library CD-ROMs*** or ***Online Professional Development*** provides courses that help you better understand the Writing instruction in ***Open Court Reading.*** For more information about this program, visit SRAonline.com.

Additional information about writing as well as resource references can be found in the ***Professional Development Guide: Writing.***

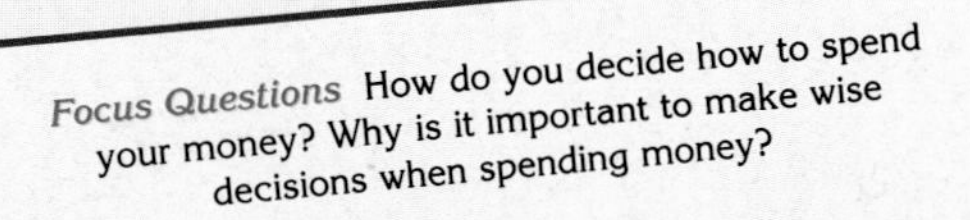

*Focus Questions* How do you decide how to spend your money? Why is it important to make wise decisions when spending money?

# Alexander, Who Used to Be Rich Last Sunday

Judith Viorst
*illustrated by Ray Cruz*

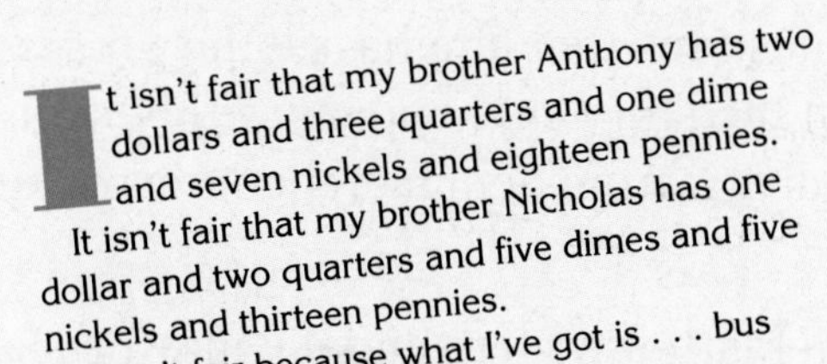

It isn't fair that my brother Anthony has two dollars and three quarters and one dime and seven nickels and eighteen pennies.

It isn't fair that my brother Nicholas has one dollar and two quarters and five dimes and five nickels and thirteen pennies.

It isn't fair because what I've got is . . . bus tokens.

And most of the time what I've mostly got is . . . bus tokens.

And even when I'm very rich, I know that pretty soon what I'll have is . . . bus tokens.

26

## Selection Summary

### Genre: Realistic Fiction

In this tale, the character Alexander uses ample humor to tell how he squandered a sum of money in a very short time. The conversational style of this selection, punctuated with the slang and the bluntness of a young boy's language, gives a delightful spin to a serious issue.

Some elements of realistic fiction include:

- The characters behave as people do in real life.
- The setting of the story is a real place or could be a real place.
- The events in the story could happen in real life.

## About the Author

**Judith Viorst** began her career as a writer by writing poetry, along with many newspaper and magazine articles. Eventually, she wrote and published children's books that were inspired by her three sons. *Alexander, Who Used to Be Rich Last Sunday* was named an IRA Children's Choice Book.

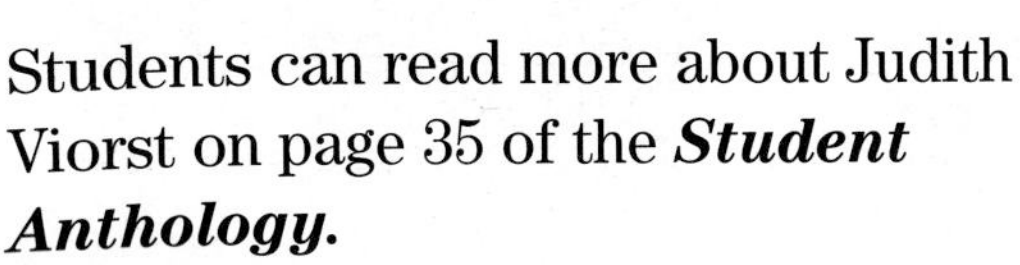

Students can read more about Judith Viorst on page 35 of the ***Student Anthology.***

## About the Illustrator

**Ray Cruz** does illustrating for advertising agencies and book publishers. He won an honorable mention in the Advertising Club of New York annual awards.

Students can read more about Ray Cruz on page 35 of the ***Student Anthology.***

## Inquiry Connections

"Alexander, Who Used to Be Rich Last Sunday" illustrates how hard it can be to save money, especially when one is faced with so many tempting ways to spend it. Key concepts explored are:

- Planning is very important in money management.
- Wise decision making, though not easy, is very important.

Before reading the selection:

- Point out that students may post a question, concept, word, illustration, or object on the Concept/Question Board at any time during the course of their unit investigation. Be sure that students include their names or initials on the items they post so that others will know to whom to go if they have an answer or if they wish to collaborate on a related activity.
- Students should feel free to write an answer or a note on someone else's question or to consult the Board for ideas for their own investigations throughout the unit.
- Encourage students to read about imagination at home and to bring in articles or pictures that are good examples to post on the Board.

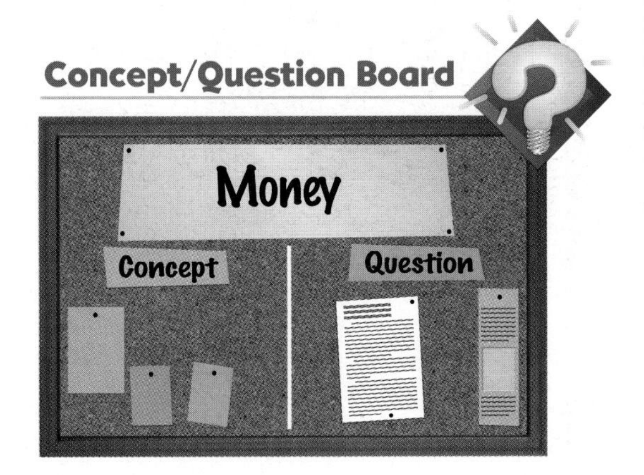

PROGRAM RESOURCES

## Leveled Practice

**Reteach**
**Pages 99–104**

**Challenge**
**Pages 87–91**

**English Learner Support Activities**

**Intervention Workbook**

**Decodable Book 30**

## Leveled Classroom Library*

Encourage students to read at least 30 minutes daily outside of class. Have them read books in the ***Leveled Classroom Library*** to support the unit theme and help students develop their vocabulary by reading independently.

### *Lemonade for Sale*

BY STUART J. MURPHY. HARPERCOLLINS JUVENILE, 1998.

The kids at the Elm Street Kids' Club use a clever combination of lemonade, bar graphs, and a juggler to make big profits that will help them repair their club. **(Easy)**

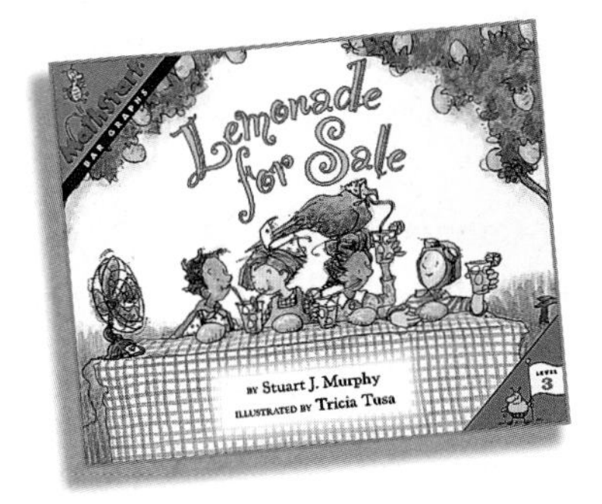


### *Saturday Sancocho*

BY LEYLA TORRES. FARRAR, STRAUS & GIROUX, 1995.

Every Saturday, Maria Lili shares a meal with her grandparents, eating Chicken Sancocho, until the weekend comes when money is tight and they are missing essential ingredients. Mama Ana barters with her eggs for the final ingredients, saving the day. **(Average)**

### *Screen of Frogs*

BY SHEILA HAMANAKA. ORCHARD BOOKS, 1993.

A spoiled rich man finds respect for the world around him before it is too late. This story retells the classic Japanese folktale, "The Strange Folding Screen." **(Advanced)**

* These books, which all support the unit theme Money, are part of a 36-book ***Leveled Classroom Library*** available for purchase from SRA/McGraw-Hill. Note: Teachers should preview any trade books for appropriateness in their classrooms before recommending them to students.

## SRA TECHNOLOGY

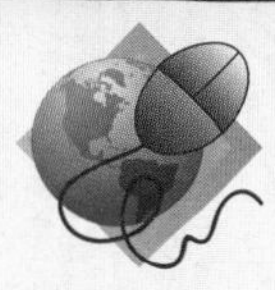

### Web Connections

- Money Web Site
- Online Professional Development
- Online Phonics
- Online Assessment

### CD-ROMs

- Research Assistant
- The Ultimate Writing and Creativity Center
- Teacher Resource Library

### Audiocassette/CD

Listening Library: Money

### Computer Skills

TechKnowledge

Materials are available through SRA/McGraw-Hill.

# UNIT 4 Lesson 2

## Alexander, Who Used to Be Rich Last Sunday

LESSON PLANNER

Suggested Pacing: 3–5 days

| | DAY 1 | DAY 2 |
|---|---|---|
| | DAY 1 | DAY 2 |
| **1 Preparing to Read**<br>**Materials**<br>■ Student Anthology, Book 2, pp. 26–37<br>■ Decodable Book 30<br>■ Routine Card 1, Routines 1–2 | **Word Knowledge, p. 26K**<br>■ synonyms<br>■ suffixes *-y, -able*<br>■ final double consonants<br>**About the Words and Sentences, p. 26K** | **Word Knowledge**<br>**Developing Oral Language, p. 26L** |
| **2 Reading & Responding**<br>**Materials**<br>■ Student Anthology, Book 2, pp. 26–37<br>■ Program Assessment<br>■ Reading Transparencies 24, 46<br>■ Inquiry Journal, p. 83<br>■ Home Connection, p. 47<br>■ Unit 4 Assessment, pp. 6–9<br>■ Writer's Notebook<br>■ Comprehension and Language Arts Skills, pp. 96–97<br>■ Routine Cards 1, 2, Routines 3–6 | **Build Background, p. 26M**<br>**Preview and Prepare, pp. 26M–26N**<br>**Selection Vocabulary, p. 26N**<br>**Reading Recommendations, pp. 26O–26P** | **Student Anthology, pp. 26–33** First Read<br>✓ **Comprehension Strategies**<br>■ Making Connections, p. 26<br>■ Predicting, pp. 28, 30<br>■ Monitoring and Clarifying, p. 30<br>■ Summarizing, p. 32<br>**Discussing Strategy Use, p. 32**<br>**Discussing the Selection, p. 33A**<br>■ Review Selection<br>■ Complete Discussion |
| **Inquiry**<br>**Materials**<br>■ Student Anthology, Book 2, pp. 26–37<br>■ Inquiry Journal, pp. 89–92<br>■ Research Assistant CD-ROM | **Investigation**<br>■ Investigating Concepts Beyond the Text, p. 35A | **Investigation**<br>■ Concept/Question Board, p. 35B |
| **3 Language Arts**<br>**Materials**<br>■ Spelling and Vocabulary Skills, pp. 78–81<br>■ Comprehension and Language Arts Skills, pp. 96–101<br>■ The Ultimate Writing and Creativity Center<br>■ Language Arts Handbook<br>■ Writer's Workbook, pp. 58–61<br>■ Language Arts Transparency 18<br>■ Student Anthology | **Word Analysis**<br>✓■ Spelling: Final Double Consonants Pretest, p. 35F<br>**Writing Process Strategies**<br>■ Persuasive Writing: Poster, p. 35F<br>**English Language Conventions**<br>■ Grammar: Subjects and Predicates, p. 35F | **Word Analysis**<br>■ Spelling: Final Double Consonants, p. 35G<br>■ Vocabulary: The Suffix *-ly*, p. 35G<br>**Writing Process Strategies**<br>■ Persuasive Writing: Poster, p. 35G<br>■ Writer's Craft: Time-Order Words, p. 35G<br>**English Language Conventions**<br>■ Grammar: Subjects and Predicates, p. 35G |

P Phonics ✓ Informal Assessment Available ✓ Formal Assessment Available

| DAY 2 continued | DAY 3 | |
|---|---|---|
| **DAY 3** | **DAY 4** | **DAY 5** |
| Word Knowledge<br>General Review | Word Knowledge<br>General Review | General Review |
| Student Anthology, pp. 26–33 Second Read<br>Comprehension Skills<br>■ Cause and Effect, pp. 27, 29, 31, 33<br>Checking Comprehension, p. 33<br>Supporting the Reading, pp. 33C–33D<br>■ Cause and Effect<br>Student Anthology<br>✓■ Concept Connections, p. 34<br>■ Meet the Author and Illustrator, p. 35 | Review Selection Vocabulary, p. 33B<br>Literary Elements, p. 33E<br>■ Characterization<br>Social Studies Connection<br>■ Costs and Benefits, p. 33F | ✓Selection Assessment<br>■ "Alexander, Who Used to Be Rich Last Sunday," pp. 6–9<br>Home Connection, p. 33B<br>Poetry<br>■ "Smart," p. 36<br>■ "Tony and the Quarter," p. 37<br>Elements of Poetry, p. 37A<br>■ Rhyme/Writing<br>Listening/Speaking/Viewing, p. 37B<br>■ Presentation/Diction |
| ✓Investigation<br>■ Problem Phase 2, p. 35C | Supporting the Investigation<br>■ Card Catalog, p. 35D | Investigation<br>■ Unit Investigation Continued<br>■ Update Concept/Question Board |
| Word Analysis<br>■ Spelling: Final Double Consonants, p. 35H<br>■ Vocabulary: The Suffix *-ly,* p. 35H<br>Writing Process Strategies<br>■ Persuasive Writing: Poster, p. 35H<br>English Language Conventions<br>✓■ Grammar: Subjects and Predicates, p. 35H | Word Analysis<br>■ Spelling: Final Double Consonants, p. 35I<br>■ Vocabulary: The Suffix *-ly,* p. 35I<br>Writing Process Strategies<br>■ Persuasive Writing: Poster, p. 35I<br>English Language Conventions<br>✓■ Listening, Speaking, Viewing Speaking: Elements of Grammar, p. 35I | Word Analysis<br>✓■ Spelling: Final Double Consonants Final Test<br>✓■ Vocabulary: The Suffix *-ly,* p. 35J<br>Writing Process Strategies<br>✓■ Persuasive Writing: Poster, p. 35J<br>English Language Conventions<br>✓■ Penmanship: Cursive Letters *E* and *O,* p. 35J |

Below are suggestions for differentiating instruction. These are the same skills shown in the Lesson Planner; however, these pages provide extra practice opportunities or enriching activities to meet the varied needs of students.

WORKSHOP

# Differentiating Instruction

## Teacher Directed: Individual and Small-Group Instruction

Spend time each day with individuals and small groups to individualize instruction. Each day:

- preteach students who need help with the next lesson.
- reteach students who need to solidify their understanding of content previously taught.
- listen to students read to check their fluency.
- hold writing and inquiry conferences.

Use the following program components to support instruction:

- ***Reteach*** with students who need a bit more practice
- ***Intervention*** for students who exhibit a lack of understanding of the lesson concepts
- ***English Learner Support*** with students who need language help

## Student: Independent Activities

Students can work alone, with a partner, or in small groups on such activities as:

- Review sound/spellings
- Practice dictation words
- Partner reading
- Practice fluency
- Independent reading
- Reading Roundtable
- Concept vocabulary
- Selection vocabulary
- Writing in progress
- Conference
- Language Arts
- Challenge activities
- Inquiry and Investigation activities
- Listening Library
- Online Phonics

For Workshop Management Tips, see Appendix pages 41–42.

| | DAY I |
|---|---|
| **Word Knowledge** | **Teacher Directed**<br>■ Reading Words: Suffixes *-ly* and *-able*, ***Intervention Guide,*** p. 183<br>**Independent Activities**<br>■ ***Online Phonics*** |
| **Fluency** | **Independent Activities**<br>■ Self-test fluency rate<br>■ Partner reading |
| **Comprehension** | **Teacher Directed**<br>■ Preteach "Alexander, Who Used to Be Rich Last Sunday," ***Intervention Guide,*** pp. 184–185<br>■ Preteach Intervention Selection One, ***Intervention Guide,*** pp. 185–186<br>■ ***English Learner Support Guide***<br>• Vocabulary, pp. 270–271<br>• Comprehension Skill: Cause and Effect, pp. 271–272<br>**Independent Activities**<br>■ Browse ***Leveled Classroom Library***<br>■ Add vocabulary in Writer's Notebook<br>■ ***English Learner Support Activities,*** p. 33 |
| **Inquiry** | **Independent Activities**<br>■ Concept/Question Board<br>■ Project Planning Calendar, ***Inquiry Journal,*** pp. 89–90<br>■ Research Cycle: Problem Phase 1, ***Inquiry Journal,*** p. 91 |
| **Language Arts** | **Teacher Directed**<br>■ Grammar, Usage, and Mechanics, ***Intervention Guide,*** p. 188<br>**Independent Activities**<br>■ Subjects and Predicates, ***Comprehension and Language Arts Skills,*** pp. 98–99 |

| DAY 2 | DAY 3 | DAY 4 | DAY 5 |
|---|---|---|---|
| **Teacher Directed**<br>■ Developing Oral Language, ***Intervention Guide,*** p. 183<br>**Independent Activities**<br>■ Read ***Decodable Book 30,*** *Traveling Star* | **Teacher Directed**<br>■ Dictation and Spelling: Suffixes *-ly* and *-able,* ***Intervention Guide,*** pp. 183–184<br>**Independent Activities**<br>■ ***Online Phonics*** | **Teacher Directed**<br>■ General Review<br>**Independent Activities**<br>■ ***Online Phonics*** | **Teacher Directed**<br>■ General Review<br>**Independent Activities**<br>■ ***Online Phonics*** |
| **Independent Activities**<br>■ Oral reading of selection for fluency<br>■ Partner reading of ***Decodable Book 30,*** *Traveling Star* | **Independent Activities**<br>■ Partner reading of selection<br>■ Read ***Decodable Book 30,*** *Traveling Star* | **Independent Activities**<br>■ Reread "Alexander, Who Used to Be Rich Last Sunday"<br>■ Partner reading of ***Decodable Book 30,*** *Traveling Star* | **Teacher Directed**<br>■ Repeated Readings/Fluency Check, ***Intervention Guide,*** p. 187 |
| **Teacher Directed**<br>■ Preteach "Alexander, Who Used to Be Rich Last Sunday," ***Intervention Guide,*** pp. 184–185<br>■ Comprehension Strategies, ***Intervention Guide,*** p. 186<br>■ Reread Intervention Selection One, ***Intervention Guide,*** pp. 185–186<br>■ ***English Learner Support Guide***<br>• Vocabulary, pp. 273–274<br>• Comprehension Skill: Cause and Effect, pp. 274–275<br>**Independent Activities**<br>■ Choose a ***Leveled Classroom Library*** book and begin independent reading<br>■ Record response to selection in Writer's Notebook<br>■ ***Listening Library Audiocassette/CD*** | **Teacher Directed**<br>■ Discuss Concept Connections, p. 34<br>■ Reread "Alexander, Who Used to Be Rich Last Sunday," ***Intervention Guide,*** pp. 184–185<br>■ Preteach Intervention Selection Two, ***Intervention Guide,*** pp. 186–187<br>■ ***English Learner Support Guide***<br>• Vocabulary, pp. 276–277<br>• Comprehension Skill: Cause and Effect, pp. 277–278<br>■ Cause and Effect, ***Reteach,*** pp. 99–100<br>**Independent Activities**<br>■ Independent reading<br>■ Complete Link to Writing in Supporting the Reading, p. 33D<br>■ Cause and Effect<br>• ***Comprehension and Language Arts Skills,*** pp. 96–97<br>• ***Challenge,*** p. 87 | **Teacher Directed**<br>■ Reread "Alexander, Who Used to Be Rich Last Sunday," ***Intervention Guide,*** pp. 184–185<br>■ Comprehension Strategies, ***Intervention Guide,*** p. 187<br>■ Reread Intervention Selection Two, ***Intervention Guide,*** pp. 186–187<br>■ ***English Learner Support Guide***<br>• Vocabulary, pp. 279–280<br>• Comprehension Skill: Cause and Effect, pp. 280–281<br>**Independent Activities**<br>■ Reread ***Leveled Classroom Library*** book<br>■ Add words to Word Bank<br>■ Complete Independent Practice in Literary Elements, p. 33E<br>■ Social Studies Connection, p. 33F<br>■ ***English Learner Support Activities,*** p. 34 | **Teacher Directed**<br>■ ***English Learner Support Guide***<br>• Review Vocabulary, p. 282<br>• Comprehension Skill: Cause and Effect, pp. 282–283<br>**Independent Activities**<br>■ Read ***Leveled Classroom Library*** book as independent reading<br>■ Reading Roundtable<br>■ Poetry Activities, pp. 36–37B |
| **Independent Activities**<br>■ Concept/Question Board<br>■ Explore OCR Web site for theme connections<br>■ Use ***Research Assistant CD-ROM*** to continue investigation | **Independent Activities**<br>■ Concept/Question Board<br>■ Research Cycle: Problem Phase 2, ***Inquiry Journal,*** p. 92<br>■ Explore OCR Web site for theme connections | **Independent Activities**<br>■ Concept/Question Board<br>■ Use ***Research Assistant CD-ROM*** to continue investigation<br>■ Complete Independent Practice in Supporting the Investigation, p. 35D | **Independent Activities**<br>■ Concept/Question Board<br>■ Continue research |
| **Teacher Directed**<br>■ Grammar, Usage, and Mechanics, ***Intervention Guide,*** p. 188<br>■ Subjects/Predicates, ***Reteach,*** p. 103<br>**Independent Activities**<br>■ Vocabulary: The Suffix *-ly,* ***Spelling and Vocabulary Skills,*** pp. 78–79<br>■ Writer's Craft: Time and Order Words, ***Comprehension and Language Arts Skills,*** pp. 100–101<br>■ Subjects/Predicates, ***Challenge,*** p. 90 | **Teacher Directed**<br>■ Writing Activity, ***Intervention Guide,*** p. 189<br>■ Vocabulary: The Suffix *-ly,* ***Reteach,*** p. 102<br>**Independent Activities**<br>■ Spelling: Final Double Consonants, ***Spelling and Vocabulary Skills,*** p. 80<br>■ Vocabulary: The Suffix *-ly,* ***Challenge,*** p. 89 | **Teacher Directed**<br>■ Writer's Craft: Time and Order Words, ***Reteach,*** p. 104<br>■ Writing Activity, ***Intervention Guide,*** p. 189<br>■ Spelling: Final Double Consonants, ***Reteach,*** p. 101<br>**Independent Activities**<br>■ Spelling: Final Double Consonants<br>• ***Spelling and Vocabulary Skills,*** p. 81<br>• ***Challenge,*** p. 88 | **Independent Activities**<br>■ Seminar: Edit/Proofread and Publish a Persuasive Poster, p. 35J<br>■ Penmanship: Practice Cursive Letters *E* and *O,* p. 35J<br>■ Writer's Craft: Time and Order Words, ***Challenge,*** p. 91 |

ASSESSMENT

# Formal Assessment Options

Use these summative assessments along with your informal observations to assess student progress.

Name ______ Date ______ Score ______

UNIT 4 Money • Lesson 2

LESSON ASSESSMENT

**Alexander, Who Used to Be Rich Last Sunday**

**Read the following questions carefully. Then completely fill in the bubble of each correct answer. You may look back at the story to find the answer to each of the questions.**

1. How much money did Alexander have when he was "rich"?
   - Ⓐ ten dollars
   - ● one dollar
   - Ⓒ fifty cents
2. Where did Alexander get the money?
   - Ⓐ from his parents
   - Ⓑ from his job
   - ● from his grandparents

**Read the following questions carefully. Use complete sentences to answer the questions.**

3. What was wrong with saving the candy bar from melting?
   It was wrong because he ate the candy bar in order to save it, and the candy bar wasn't even his.
4. What is unusual about the things Alexander buys at Cathy's garage sale?
   The things he buys are not very good things.
5. What causes Alexander to be surprised when he plays a marble trick on his mother?
   His mother guesses which hand has the marble and then surprises him by making him pay.

6 Unit 4 • Lesson 2 *Alexander, Who Used to Be Rich Last Sunday* • Unit 4 Assessment

***Unit 4 Assessment p. 6***

**Alexander: Who Used to Be Rich Last Sunday** *(continued)*

6. How do Alexander and his brothers treat each other?
   They are always teasing and saying unkind things to each other.
7. What does Alexander do with his money?
   He spends some of the money, he loses some of the money, and he makes bets with some of the money.
8. How does Alexander try to get more money?
   He tries to make a tooth fall out; he looks for coins that people forgot; he brings some bottles to the market; and he tells his grandparents to come back.

**Read the following questions carefully. Then completely fill in the bubble of each correct answer.**

9. What does Alexander's father tell him to do with the money?
   - ● save for college
   - Ⓑ save for a walkie-talkie
   - Ⓒ grow a money tree
10. What does Alexander have at the end of the story?
    - Ⓐ a walkie-talkie
    - Ⓑ a savings account
    - ● a melted candle

Unit 4 Assessment • *Alexander, Who Used to Be Rich Last Sunday* Unit 4 • Lesson 2 7

***Unit 4 Assessment p. 7***

**Alexander: Who Used to Be Rich Last Sunday** *(continued)*

**Read the questions below. Use complete sentences in your answers.**

**Linking to the Concepts** Do you think Alexander is good at keeping and using money? Why or why not?
Answers will vary. Accept all reasonable answers.

**Personal Response** Who are you more like when it comes to spending money, Alexander or his brothers? Why?
Answers will vary. Accept all reasonable answers.

8 Unit 4 • Lesson 2 *Alexander, Who Used to Be Rich Last Sunday* • Unit 4 Assessment

***Unit 4 Assessment p. 8***

**Alexander: Who Used to Be Rich Last Sunday** *(continued)*

**Vocabulary**

**Read the following questions carefully. Then completely fill in the bubble of each correct answer.**

1. At the beginning of this story, all Alexander has are bus tokens. **Tokens** are most like
   - Ⓐ seats
   - Ⓑ toys
   - ● tickets
2. Alexander absolutely thought he would save his money. **Absolutely** means
   - ● for sure
   - Ⓑ without a plan
   - Ⓒ carelessly
3. A bottle that is **non-returnable** is a bottle that you can not return or
   - ● get money for
   - Ⓑ carry yourself
   - Ⓒ find very easily
4. Nick did a magic trick that made Alexander's pennies vanish. Another word for **vanish** is
   - Ⓐ show up
   - ● disappear
   - Ⓒ increase
5. Alexander rents Eddie's snake for an hour. When you **rent** something, you
   - Ⓐ pay to have it for always
   - ● pay to keep it for a while
   - Ⓒ use it for free

Unit 4 Assessment • *Alexander, Who Used to Be Rich Last Sunday* Unit 4 • Lesson 2 9

***Unit 4 Assessment p. 9***

Name ______ Date ______ Score ______

UNIT 4 Money • Lesson 2 *Alexander, Who Used to Be Rich Last Sunday*

**Spelling Pretest: Final Double Consonants**

**Fold this page back on the dotted line. Take the Pretest. Then correct any word you misspelled by crossing out the word and rewriting it next to the incorrect spelling.**

1. ______ 1. spill
2. ______ 2. hill
3. ______ 3. gull
4. ______ 4. smell
5. ______ 5. mess
6. ______ 6. odd
7. ______ 7. add
8. ______ 8. cliff
9. ______ 9. mitt
10. ______ 10. fuzz
11. ______ 11. all
12. ______ 12. still
13. ______ 13. fall
14. ______ 14. till
15. ______ 15. guess

32 Unit 4 • Lesson 2 *Spelling Pretest: Final Double Consonants* • Unit 4 Assessment

***Unit 4 Assessment p. 32***

Name ______ Date ______ Score ______

UNIT 4 Money • Lesson 2 *Alexander, Who Used to Be Rich Last Sunday*

**Spelling Final Test: Final Double Consonants**

**Mark the letter next to the underlined word that is misspelled. Focus on the underlined word.**

1. Ⓐ The fuzz on the skin of a peach is soft.
   Ⓑ A suffix is easy to add to a word.
   ● Sliced oranges have a fresh smel.
   Ⓓ Correct as is.
2. ● Clowns fal down to be silly.
   Ⓖ New fashions look odd at first.
   Ⓗ Hawks can nest in a cliff.
   Ⓙ Correct as is.
3. ● A baseball glove is called a mit.
   Ⓑ Dust and dirt can make a mess.
   Ⓒ Leaves often change in the fall.
   Ⓓ Correct as is.
4. Ⓕ Tulips wait till spring to bloom.
   Ⓖ Mammals all have hair.
   Ⓗ Some games make players guess.
   ● Correct as is.
5. Ⓐ A catcher's mitt is padded.
   ● A gul often flies near water.
   Ⓒ Cash registers add up the price.
   Ⓓ Correct as is.
6. Ⓕ A gull is usually gray and white.
   Ⓖ Petals fall off a dead flower.
   ● My sweater was covered with fuz.
   Ⓙ Correct as is.

Unit 4 Assessment • *Spelling Final Test: Final Double Consonants* Unit 4 • Lesson 2 33

***Unit 4 Assessment p. 33***

**Online Assessment** for ***Open Court Reading*** helps teachers differentiate classroom instruction based on students' scores from the weekly and end-of-unit assessments. It provides exercises best suited to meet the needs of each student. For more information, visit SRAonline.com.

## Informal Comprehension Strategies Rubrics

### Making Connections

- The student activates prior knowledge and related knowledge.
- The student uses prior knowledge to explain something encountered in the text.
- The student connects ideas presented later in the text to ideas presented earlier in the text.
- The student notes ideas in the text that are new or conflict with what he or she thought previously.

### Predicting

- The student makes predictions about what the text is about.
- The student updates predictions during reading, based on information in the text.

### Summarizing

- The student paraphrases text, reporting main ideas and a summary of what is in the text.
- The student decides which parts of the text are important in his or her summary.
- The student draws conclusions from the text.
- The student makes global interpretations of the text, such as recognizing the genre.

### Monitoring and Clarifying

- The student notes characteristics of the text, such as whether it is difficult to read or whether some sections are more challenging or more important than others.
- The student shows awareness of whether he or she understands the text and takes appropriate action, such as rereading, in order to understand the text better.
- The student rereads to reconsider something presented earlier in the text.
- The student recognizes problems during reading, such as a loss of concentration, unfamiliar vocabulary, or lack of sufficient background knowledge to comprehend the text.

## Research Rubrics

During Workshop, assess students using the rubrics below. The rubrics range from 1 to 4 in most categories, with 1 being the lowest score. Record each student's score on the inside back cover of the ***Inquiry Journal.***

### Finding Needed Information

**1** Collects information loosely related to topic.

**2** Collects information clearly related to topic.

**3** Collects information helpful in advancing on a research problem.

**4** Collects problem-relevant information from varied sources and notices inconsistencies and missing pieces.

**5** Collects useful information, paying attention to the reliability of sources and reviewing information critically.

# 1 Preparing to Read

## Alexander, Who Used to Be Rich Last Sunday

### Objectives

- Students practice recognizing synonyms.
- Students practice recognizing base words and the suffixes *-y* and *-able*.
- Students practice recognizing final double consonants.

### Materials

- Student Anthology, Book 2, pp. 26–37
- Decodable Book 30
- Routine Card 1, Routines 1–2

### Differentiating Instruction

#### English Learner Tip

**SYNONYM GAME** Play a picture-matching game with English Learners to help them grasp the concept of synonyms. Divide the pictures into two groups of synonyms. Distribute one group and have students spread their cards out. Then you or a leader shows each master card, one at a time, calling out the word it represents. Ask the student who has a synonym that matches the card shown to show that card, and encourage the other students to call out the word.

**Teacher Tip** If necessary, remind students that a suffix is a word part that is added to the end of a word to alter its meaning. The suffix *-able* means "capable of" or "fit for."

**Teacher Tip** **SYLLABICATION** To help students blend words and build fluency, use the syllabication below of the words in the word lines.

| | | | |
|---|---|---|---|
| def•i•nite•ly | cer•tain•ly | ab•so•lute•ly | |
| pos•i•tive•ly | rat•ty | trick•y | |
| tas•ty | jump•y | re•turn•a•ble | |
| ac•cept•a•ble | de•ci•da•ble | all | |
| still | fall | till | guess |

**Teacher Tip** **BUILDING FLUENCY** As students read, you may notice that some need work in building fluency. During Workshop, have these students select a section of the text (a minimum of 160 words) to read several times in order to build fluency.

WORD KNOWLEDGE

## Word Knowledge

### Reading the Words and Sentences

Using direct teaching, have students read each line of words and the sentences in this and in subsequent lessons. The words in **boldface** type appear in the selection.

| | | | | | |
|---|---|---|---|---|---|
| Line 1: | definitely | certainly | absolutely | positively | |
| Line 2: | ratty | tricky | tasty | jumpy | |
| Line 3: | returnable | acceptable | decidable | | |
| Line 4: | all | still | fall | till | guess |
| Sentence 1: | I absolutely was saving the rest of my money. | | | | |
| Sentence 2: | I positively was saving the rest of my money. | | | | |
| Sentence 3: | My father said that there are certain words a boy can never say, no matter how ratty and mean his brothers are being. | | | | |
| Sentence 4: | Almost all pumpkins will not grow till fall. | | | | |

### About the Words and Sentences

- **Line 1:** Ask students how the words in Line 1 are related *(synonyms)*. Using the words as clues, have students explain what a synonym is *(words having the same meaning)*.
- **Line 2:** The words in Line 2 have the suffix *-y*. Have students tell about any spelling changes to the base word when we add the suffix *-y*. *(Sometimes the final consonant is doubled,* ratty; *sometimes the letter* e *is dropped,* tasty.)
- **Line 3:** The words in Line 3 have an *-able* ending. Have students note any differences in spelling when this ending is added. *(When the* -able *ending was added to the word* decide, *which has a silent* e *ending, the silent* e *was dropped before the suffix was added.)*
- **Line 4:** The words in Line 4 are found in "Alexander, Who Used to Be Rich Last Sunday" and review words with final double consonants.
- **Sentences 1–3:** These sentences are from the story students are about to read. Ask students to identify words that end in a suffix *(absolutely, positively, ratty)*.
- **Sentence 4:** Have students identify the words in the last sentence that contain a final double consonant *(all, till, fall)*.

WORD KNOWLEDGE

## Developing Oral Language

Use direct teaching to review the words. Use one or both of the following activities to help students practice reading the words.

- Read aloud sentences with words missing and ask students to suggest words from Lines 1–4 to fill in the blanks. Have students point to and read the correct word. Sentences you might read aloud include the following:

  **This math problem is ______.** *(tricky)*

  **Your answer to the problem is ______; you get the extra points.** *(acceptable)*

  **The strawberries are very ________ this year.** *(tasty)*

  **The new clothes we bought are ________, so if they do not fit we can take them back.** *(returnable)*

  **He is ________ sure of what he wants.** *(definitely/certainly/absolutely/positively)*

  **Maria had a stomach ache after eating ________ of the cookies.** *(all)*

  **The wind stopped blowing and the leaves on the trees were quiet and ________.** *(still)*

- Have a student point to one of the words in the word lines on the board. Ask him or her to identify the root word, such as *trick* in *tricky*, or *attract* in *attractive*, and then explain how the meaning of the word changed.

## Building Fluency

***Decodable Books*** are used to help develop fluency for students who need extra practice. The only way to gain fluency is to read. Students will have many opportunities to read, including the ***Student Anthology,*** the ***Leveled Classroom Library,*** and their own reading. The ***Decodable Books*** can be used to practice the phonics and fluency elements being reviewed. Refer to the Appendix for the procedure on using these books. For this lesson, use ***Decodable Book 30,*** *Traveling Star.*

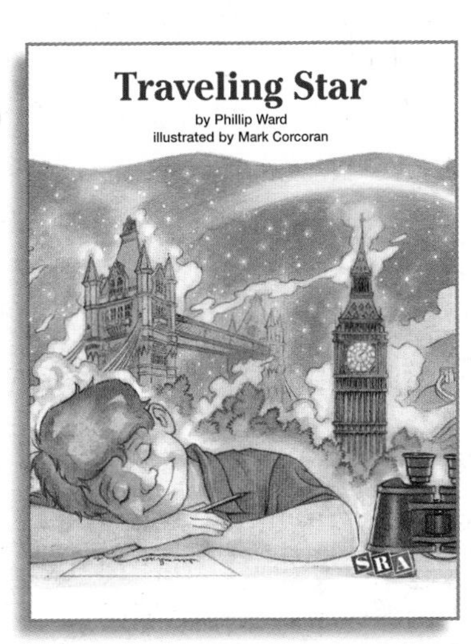


***Decodable Book 30***

**Teacher Tip** Have students name the base word of each word with an ending. Remind them that more than one consonant together in a word with an ending usually means a short vowel sound in the base word. Have students use each word they blend in a sentence. Be sure to discuss the meanings of any unfamiliar words.

### Differentiating Instruction

| If... | Then... |
|---|---|
| Students need extra help with synonyms or base words with the suffix *-ly* | Use ***Online Phonics*** |
| Students need extra help with base words and the suffixes *-ly* and *-able* | Use ***Intervention Guide*** pages 183–184 |

**Spelling**
See pages 35E–35J for the corresponding spelling lesson for final double consonants.

**Teacher Tip** **FLUENCY** Gaining a better understanding of the spellings of sounds and the structure of words will help students as they encounter unfamiliar words in their reading. By this time in Grade 3, students should be reading approximately 123 words per minute with fluency and expression.

**Routine Card**
Refer to ***Routine 1*** for whole-word blending and ***Routine 2*** for sentence blending.

### Objectives

- Students will understand the selection vocabulary before reading, using strategies such as suffixes and structural cues.
- Students will practice recognizing base words and the suffixes *-y, -ly,* and *-able.*
- Students will connect prior knowledge to subjects discussed in text.
- Students will use comprehension strategies such as Making Connections, Predicting, Monitoring and Clarifying, and Summarizing to construct meaning from the text and monitor reading.
- Students will use the comprehension skill Cause and Effect as they read the story the second time.
- Students will discuss personal reactions to the story to begin identifying their own personal reading preferences.
- Students link the selection's key concepts to their investigations.

### Materials

- Student Anthology, Book 2, pp. 26–37
- Program Assessment
- Reading Transparencies 24, 46
- Inquiry Journal, p. 83
- Home Connection, p. 47
- Comprehension and Language Arts Skills, pp. 96–97
- Unit 4 Assessment, pp. 6–9
- Routine Cards 1, 2, Routines 3–6

| Clues | Problems | Wonderings |
|---|---|---|
| used to be rich | tokens | Why is he no longer rich? |

Open Court Reading — Reading Transparency 46

*Reading Transparency 46*

### Differentiating Instruction

| If... | Then... |
|---|---|
| Students need extra help with selection vocabulary | Use ***Intervention Guide*** pages 184–185 |

## Build Background

### Activate Prior Knowledge

Discuss the following with students to find out what they may already know about the selection and may already have learned about the theme of Money.

- Preteach "Alexander, Who Used to Be Rich Last Sunday" by first determining students' prior knowledge about money by asking, "Have you ever received money as a gift? What did you do with the money? Did you save it? Did you spend it? If you spent it, what did you spend it on?"
- Ask students whether they are familiar with the story they are about to read, and if so, to tell a little bit about it. Remind students, however, that this is a fiction story and not to give away any surprises in the selection.
- Ask students if they remember any stories they have read about money.

### Background Information

The following information may help students to better understand the selection that they are about to read.

- Explain that because "Alexander, Who Used to Be Rich Last Sunday" is realistic fiction about a boy close to their age, students may be able to relate well to the character and the problems he faces.
- The conversational style of this story makes the reader feel that Alexander is talking directly to him or her. This style helps to make the story more realistic.

## Preview and Prepare

### Browse

- Have students read the title and the author's and illustrator's names aloud. This allows them to activate prior knowledge relevant to the story. Because this is a fictional piece, have students preview the selection by browsing through only the first page or two of the story. Discuss with students what they think this story might reveal about money.
- Have students search for clues that tell them something about the story. Also, have them look for any problems, such as unfamiliar words, that they notice while reading. Use ***Reading Transparency 46*** to record their observations as they browse. For example, the part of the title "Used to Be Rich" might be a clue about the story's plot. For the Problems column, students might point out they are unfamiliar with the word *tokens.* They might wonder why Alexander is no longer rich. To save time and to model note taking, write students' observations as brief notes rather than as complete sentences.
- As students prepare to read the selection, have them browse the Focus Questions on the first page of the selection. Tell them to keep these questions in mind as they read.

## Set Purposes

Encourage students to set their own purposes for reading this selection. As students read, they might think about how Alexander spent his money and how he felt about the choices he made. You may also have students think about how the theme of the story piques their curiosity or connects to their personal interests. In addition, you may wish to have students think about information in the selection that may be useful to them as they work on their own investigations.

# Selection Vocabulary

As students study vocabulary, they will use a variety of skills to determine the meaning of a word. These include context clues, word structure, and apposition. Students will apply these same skills while reading to clarify additional unfamiliar words. Students can write the definitions in their Writer's Notebooks.

Display ***Reading Transparency 24*** before reading the selection to introduce and discuss the following words and their meanings:

**tokens:** pieces of metal shaped like coins, used instead of money (page 26)
**absolutely:** without any doubt (page 29)
**positively:** for sure; certainly; confidently (page 29)
**rent:** to provide the use of something for a fee; to pay a fee in order to use something (page 29)
**vanish:** disappear (page 31)
**non-returnable:** something that cannot be taken or given back (page 33)

Have students read the words in the word box, stopping to blend any words that they have trouble reading. Demonstrate how to decode multisyllabic words by breaking the words into syllables and blending the syllables. Then let students try. If they still have trouble, refer them to the ***Sound/Spelling Cards.*** If the word is not decodable, give the students the pronunciation.

Have students read the sentences on the transparency to determine the meanings of the underlined words. Each word has two sentences that students will read and from which they should be able to derive the meaning of the underlined word. Remind them to use one or more of the skills they have learned—context clues, word structure, or apposition—to figure out the meaning before using a dictionary. Be sure students explain which skills they are using and how they figured out the meanings of the words. Have students reread the sentence, substituting the definition to see if the sentence makes sense. Have a volunteer create a new sentence using the underlined word.

**Routine Card**
Refer to ***Routine 3*** for the vocabulary procedure.

**Teacher Tip SELECTION VOCABULARY** To help students decode words, divide the words into syllables when you are saying them, as shown below. The information following each word tells how students can figure out the meaning of each word. When writing words on the board, do not divide them into syllables.

| | |
|---|---|
| to • kens | context clues |
| ab • so • lute • ly | context clues |
| pos • i • tive • ly | context clues |
| rent | context clues |
| va • nish | context clues |
| non • re • turn • a • ble | context clues |

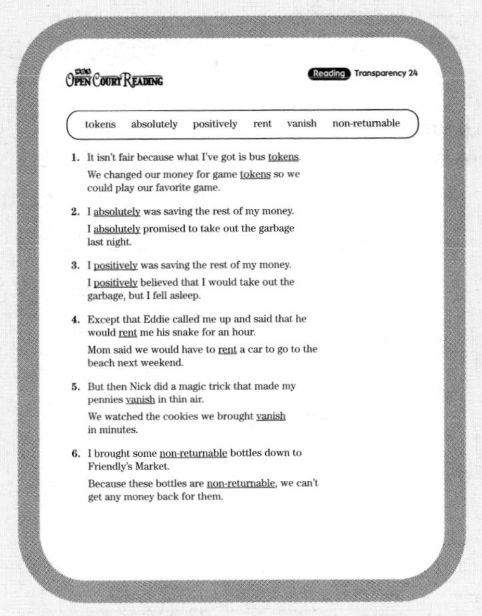

OPEN COURT READING — Reading Transparency 24

tokens absolutely positively rent vanish non-returnable

1. It isn't fair because what I've got is bus tokens.
   We changed our money for game tokens so we could play our favorite game.
2. I absolutely was saving the rest of my money.
   I absolutely promised to take out the garbage last night.
3. I positively was saving the rest of my money.
   I positively believed that I would take out the garbage, but I fell asleep.
4. Except that Eddie called me up and said that he would rent me his snake for an hour.
   Mom said we would have to rent a car to go to the beach next weekend.
5. But then Nick did a magic trick that made my pennies vanish in thin air.
   We watched the cookies we brought vanish in minutes.
6. I brought some non-returnable bottles down to Friendly's Market.
   Because these bottles are non-returnable, we can't get any money back for them.

***Reading Transparency 24***

**Teacher Tip** You may wish to point out the *-ly* endings on *positively* and *absolutely.* Prompt students to identify them as adverbs, and then use them in a sentence.

**Teacher Tip** Have students practice using each of the vocabulary words from the selection in context in a sentence. If students have trouble at first, give them an example. For instance, if the word is *tokens,* say, "The machine will accept tokens, but not coins."

**Routine Card**
Refer to ***Routine 5*** for the procedure on reading the selection.

### DIFFERENTIATING INSTRUCTION

| If... | Then... |
|---|---|
| English Learners need help with the story | Have them read it before the whole-class reading, using the ***Listening Library Audiocassette/CD.*** Encourage them to ask questions to clarify any undescribed or unspoken events that they don't understand, such as Alexander holding his breath "till 300," and the reason his father fined him. |
| Students need extra help with summarizing | Use ***Intervention Guide*** pages 185–186 |
| Students need extra help with making connections | Use ***Intervention Guide*** pages 186–187 |

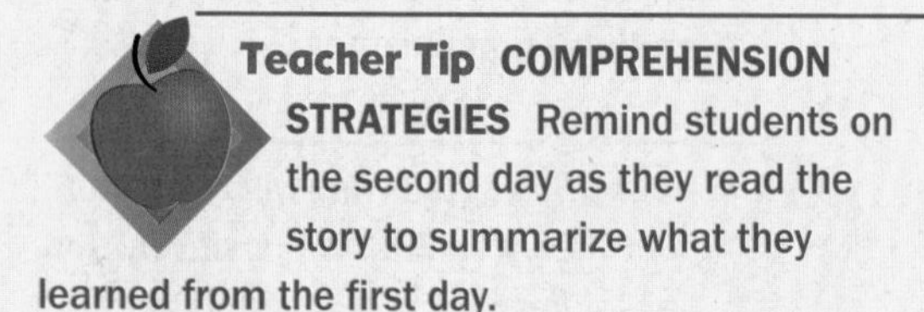

**Teacher Tip** Tell students that it is normal to encounter some difficulties in reading. Point out that even very good readers must deal with reading problems and must think carefully and question themselves to be sure they understand what they are reading.

**Teacher Tip** COMPREHENSION STRATEGIES Remind students on the second day as they read the story to summarize what they learned from the first day.

## Reading Recommendations

### Oral Reading

The simple language and conversational style of this story make it a good candidate for oral reading. Students should read aloud fluently with appropriate expression, intonation, and vocal patterns. Make sure that students attend to punctuation and read in phrases. Tell students to add a sense of feeling or anticipation as they read. Reading this story aloud will give you the opportunity to continue modeling comprehension strategies for students and give students practice using the strategies aloud.

Have students make use of the comprehension strategies listed below to help them understand the selection. Have them stop reading periodically or wait until they have completed the selection to discuss the reading strategies. After the students have finished reading the selection, use the Discussing the Selection questions on page 33A to see if they understand what they have read.

### Using Comprehension Strategies 

Comprehension strategy instruction allows students to become aware of how good readers read. Good readers constantly check their understanding as they are reading and ask themselves questions. In addition, skilled readers recognize when they are having problems and stop to use various comprehension strategies to help them make sense of what they are reading.

During the first reading of "Alexander, Who Used to Be Rich Last Sunday," you will model and prompt the use of the following comprehension strategies. Take turns reading the story aloud with the students.

- **Making Connections** requires readers to activate prior knowledge and connect what they know or have experienced to what they are reading.
- **Predicting** causes readers to analyze information given about story events and characters in the context of how it may logically connect to the story's conclusion.
- **Summarizing** prompts readers to keep track of what they are reading and to focus their minds on important information.
- **Monitoring and Clarifying** takes different forms, including clarifying the meanings of words and clarifying difficult ideas or passages. In order to clarify meanings, students can use context clues, use structural analysis, use apposition, reread the text, use charts or graphic organizers, or use resources outside of the text.

As students read, they should be using a variety of strategies to help them understand the selection. Encourage students to use the strategies listed above as the class reads the story aloud. Do this by stopping at the points indicated by the numbers in the magenta circles on the reduced student page and using a particular strategy. Students can also stop reading periodically to discuss what they have learned and what problems they may be having.

## Building Comprehension Skills 

Revisiting or rereading a selection allows students to apply skills that give them a more complete understanding of the text. Some follow-up comprehension skills help students organize information. Others lead to deeper understanding—to "reading between the lines," as mature readers do.

An extended lesson on the comprehension skill, Cause and Effect, can be found in the Supporting the Reading section on pages 33C–33D. This lesson is intended to give students extra practice with Cause and Effect. However, it may be used at this time to introduce the comprehension skill to students.

- **Cause and Effect:** Readers identify what causes events to happen or what causes characters to behave in certain ways, which helps readers put together logical explanations in the text.

### Reading with a Purpose

Have students look for ways any of the story characters learn about money throughout the selection.

**Teacher Tip** Before reading, encourage students to share how they spend their money.

During Workshop, and after the selection has been read at least once, have students listen to the recording of this lesson's selection on the ***Listening Library Audiocassette/CD.*** After students have listened, have them discuss their personal preferences of the selections read on the audiocassette. Ask them what other things they have listened to and like to listen to on the radio, on audiocassettes, or on CDs.

### Research in Action

#### Comprehension Monitoring

Good readers monitor their comprehension as they read. When they realize that they do not understand what they are reading, they apply procedures to "repair" or "fix-up" their lack of understanding. For example, they may ask themselves questions about the meaning of what they are reading, they may rephrase a passage in their own words, they may look up the meanings of difficult words, or they may outline the content of the text. *(Anne S. Palincsar and Ann L. Brown,* Cognition and Instruction)

COMPREHENSION

Read pages 26–33.

## Comprehension Strategies

First Read

Begin prompting students for responses. Praise answers that are appropriate, even if they do not match the student sample. This will encourage students to use strategies as they read.

### Prompting

**1 Making Connections** *By making connections I can better understand what I read. I know how Alexander feels. He's jealous of his brother and I can remember feeling that way when I was younger. Have you ever felt the way that Alexander does? As you are reading, be aware of how ideas in the text remind you of things that have happened to you. When you make such connections, tell the class about them. How does understanding Alexander's feelings help you to understand the story?*

### Student Sample

**Making Connections** *I know how Alexander feels. My grandmother gives me "birthday money." I always spend it on something, but later see something else I want more. Then it is too late. The money's gone.*

### Word Knowledge

**SCAFFOLDING:** The skills students are reviewing in Word Knowledge should help them in reading the story. This lesson focuses on synonyms, the suffixes *-y, -ly* and *-able,* and doubled final consonants.

**synonyms:**
**two** (a couple)
**fair** (just, right)
**rich** (wealthy)

**First Reading Recommendation**

**ORAL • CHORAL**

*Focus Questions* How do you decide how to spend your money? Why is it important to make wise decisions when spending money?

# Alexander, Who Used to Be Rich Last Sunday

Judith Viorst
*illustrated by Ray Cruz*

It isn't fair that my brother Anthony has two dollars and three quarters and one dime and seven nickels and eighteen pennies.

It isn't fair that my brother Nicholas has one dollar and two quarters and five dimes and five nickels and thirteen pennies.

It isn't fair because what I've got is . . . bus ① tokens.

And most of the time what I've mostly got is . . . bus tokens.

And even when I'm very rich, I know that pretty soon what I'll have is . . . bus tokens.

26

### Informal Assessment

Observe individual students as they read and use the Teacher Observation Log, found in the ***Program Assessment Teacher's Edition,*** to record anecdotal information about each student's strengths and weaknesses.

### Differentiating Instruction

| If... | Then... |
| --- | --- |
| Students are having difficulty comprehending the meaning of the first paragraph | Ask a volunteer to reread the paragraph as you write the individual sums of money on the board. Help the class add and compare each brother's holdings. |

I know because I used to be rich. Last Sunday.

Last Sunday Grandma Betty and Grandpa Louie came to visit from New Jersey. They brought lox because my father likes to eat lox. They brought plants because my mother likes to grow plants.

They brought a dollar for me and a dollar for Nick and a dollar for Anthony because—Mom says it isn't nice to say this—we like money.

A lot. Especially me.

My father told me to put the dollar away to pay for college.

He was kidding.

Anthony told me to use the dollar to go downtown to a store and buy a new face. Anthony stinks.

27

## Comprehension Skills

COMPREHENSION

### Cause and Effect

Point out to students that as they read, they should think about *what* happened in a story and *why* it happened. *Why* something happens is the *cause; what* happens as a result is the *effect.*

- On the board write the headings *Cause—Why It Happened* and *Effect—What Happened.* As students provide answers, help them record that information on the board under the correct heading. You can use ***Reading Transparency 48*** to record students' answers as well.
- Ask students to reread page 27 and then identify why Alexander's grandparents brought lox *(because Alexander's father liked it).*
- Then, ask students to identify why Alexander's grandparents brought plants *(because his mother liked to grow plants).*

### Word Knowledge

**synonyms:** **rich** (wealthy)
**buy** (purchase)

**Cause and Effect**

Introduced in Grade 1.
Scaffolded throughout Grades 2 and 3.

**REINTRODUCED:** Unit 1, Lesson 2
**REINFORCED:** Unit 1, Lesson 4
Unit 2, Lesson 4
Unit 2, Lesson 5
Unit 4, Lesson 2
**TESTED:** Unit 4 Assessment

**Second Reading Recommendation**

ORAL • **SILENT**

### Differentiating Instruction

| If... | Then... |
| --- | --- |
| English Learners need extra help with vocabulary | Use ***English Learner Support Guide*** pages 270–271 |
| English Learners need extra help with cause and effect | Use ***English Learner Support Guide*** pages 271–272 |

COMPREHENSION

## Comprehension Strategies

### Teacher Modeling

**2 Predicting** *I wonder what will happen to the rest of Alexander's money. He keeps saying that he was rich last Sunday. Then he talks about losing some of the dollar his grandparents gave him. And he says that saving money is hard. I think that he'll just keep losing or spending more and more of the dollar. I think some of you might be making similar predictions. What are they?*

### Word Knowledge

**doubled final consonants:** **all**

**Teacher Tip** Encourage students to identify any problems they are having with reading this selection, and then implement the strategies they can use to solve them.

**Teacher Tip** As students read aloud, listen for appropriate pacing, intonation, and expression.

**Time-Order Words**
Point out that by using time-order words like *last Sunday, after, when, then,* and *used to,* the writer helps his readers follow the story. Explain that by using time-order words in their own writing, students can also help their readers from becoming confused. See Writer's Craft, page 35G.

Nicky said to take the dollar and bury it in the garden and in a week a dollar tree would grow. Ha ha ha.

Mom said if I really want to buy a walkie-talkie, save my money.

Saving money is hard.

Because last Sunday, when I used to be rich, I went to Pearson's Drug Store and got bubble gum. And after the gum stopped tasting good, I got more gum. And after that gum stopped tasting good, I got more gum. And even though I told my friend David I'd sell him all the gum in my mouth for a nickel, he still wouldn't buy it.

Good-bye fifteen cents.

28

### Differentiating Instruction

| If... | Then... |
| --- | --- |
| Students are demonstrating an understanding of the selection and are ready for a challenge | Have them look for clues as they read that might help them make an inference to explain why Alexander's two brothers are able to save money but Alexander is not |

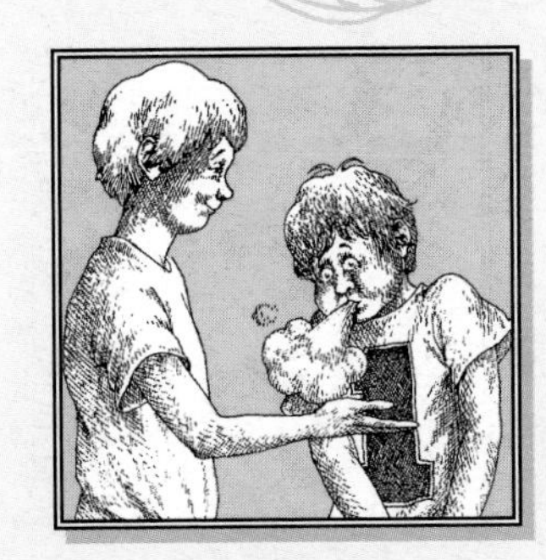

Last Sunday, when I used to be rich, I bet that I could hold my breath till 300. Anthony won. I bet that I could jump from the top of the stoop and land on my feet. Nicky won.

I bet that I could hide this purple marble in my hand, and my mom would never guess which hand I was hiding it in. I didn't know that moms made children pay.

Good-bye another fifteen cents.

I absolutely was saving the rest of my money. I positively was saving the rest of my money. Except that Eddie called me up and said that he would rent me his snake for an hour. I always wanted to rent his snake for an hour. **2**

Good-bye twelve cents.

29

# Comprehension Skills

COMPREHENSION

## Cause and Effect

Cause and effect can be applied to story events as well as to the way that story characters act.

- Ask students to reread page 28 and identify what happened when Alexander went to Pearson's Drug Store *(he spent fifteen cents)*. Ask a volunteer to identify the clue word that shows *cause* on this page *(because)*.
- Encourage volunteers to continue to record the information that they identify under the appropriate headings, either on the board or on the transparency.
- **Cause:** *Alexander went to the drugstore.*
  **Effect:** *He spent 15¢.*

### Word Knowledge

**suffix *-ly*:** **absolutely**
**positively**

**Teacher Tip** Prompt students to look at and comment on the illustrations for this selection, particularly Alexander's facial expressions.

## Differentiating Instruction

| If... | Then... |
|---|---|
| English Learners need extra help with vocabulary | Use ***English Learner Support Guide*** pages 273–274 |
| English Learners need extra help with cause and effect | Use ***English Learner Support Guide*** pages 274–275 |

COMPREHENSION

## Comprehension Strategies

### Teacher Modeling

**3 Confirming Predictions** *My prediction was confirmed. Alexander keeps losing more and more of his dollar. Keep on predicting while we are reading, and let me know what predictions you have.*

### Prompting

**4 Monitoring and Clarifying** *I wonder why Alexander said good-bye to a dime. If I think about what I've read, I can probably find the answer. Would anyone like to help me think this through? What could this mean? Who would like to help me clarify this? Let's be sure to stop and clarify everything we don't understand.*

### Student Sample

**Monitoring and Clarifying** *I know why Alexander said good-bye to a dime. He said two bad words, and his father fined him a nickel apiece. Alexander was mad at his brothers and called them bad words. Paying the 10¢ was his punishment.*

**Word Knowledge**

**suffix -y:** ratty

**Teacher Tip** Remind students that predictions should not be wild guesses. Predictions based on clues from the story are more likely to be confirmed.

**Teacher Tip** During reading, encourage students to keep track of Alexander's spending.

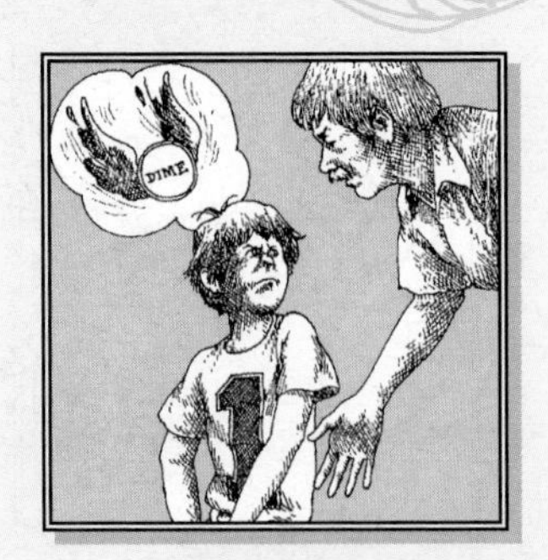


3 Anthony said when I'm ninety-nine I still won't have enough for a walkie-talkie. Nick said I'm too dumb to be let loose. My father said that there are certain words a boy can never say, no matter how ratty and mean his brothers are being. My father fined me five cents each for saying them.

Good-bye dime. 4

Last Sunday, when I used to be rich, by accident I flushed three cents down the toilet. A nickel fell through a crack when I walked on my hands. I tried to get my nickel out with a butter knife and also my mother's scissors.

Good-bye eight cents.

And the butter knife.

And the scissors.

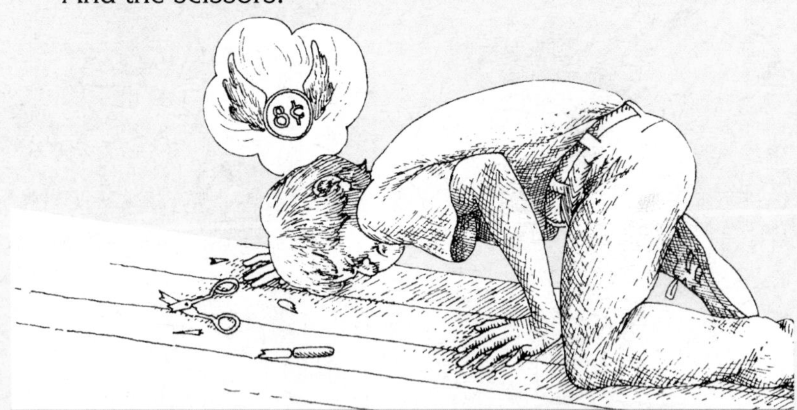


30

**Differentiating Instruction**

| If... | Then... |
|---|---|
| Students would enjoy a challenge to better understand how the characters feel and why they act as they do | Encourage small groups to dramatize scenes from the story, using dialogue from the story and original dialogue |

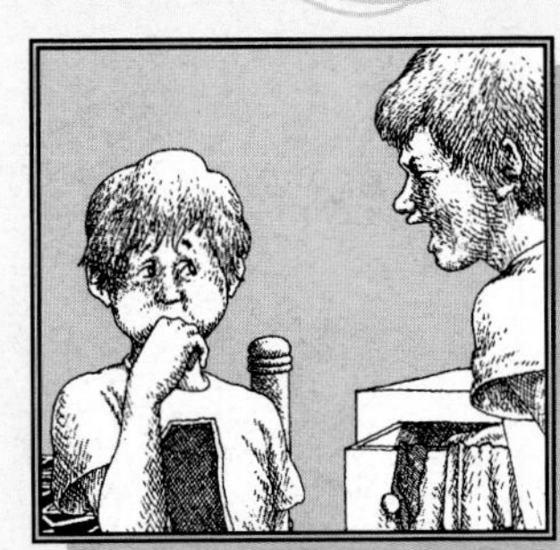

Last Sunday, when I used to be rich, I found this chocolate candy bar just sitting there. I rescued it from being melted or smushed. Except the way I rescued it from being melted or smushed was that I ate it. How was I supposed to know it was Anthony's?

Good-bye eleven cents.

I absolutely was saving the rest of my money. I positively was saving the rest of my money. But then Nick did a magic trick that made my pennies vanish in thin air. The trick to bring them back he hasn't learned yet.

Good-bye four cents.

31

## Comprehension Skills

COMPREHENSION

### Cause and Effect

Have students continue identifying causes and effects. Encourage students to use *causal indicators* as they explain causes and effects.

Causal indicators are clue words, such as *because, so,* and *in order to,* that indicate a cause-and-effect relationship.

- Alexander gave his dad a dime because he said bad words.

***Cause:*** *Alexander said bad words.*

***Effect:*** *He had to pay his dad a dime.*

- Alexander gave Anthony 11 cents in order to pay him back for the candy bar he ate.

***Cause:*** *Alexander ate his brother's candy bar.*

***Effect:*** *He had to pay his brother 11 cents.*

### Word Knowledge

**suffix -*ly*:** **absolutely**
**positively**

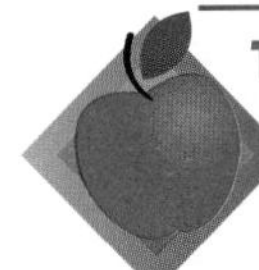

**Teacher Tip** Remind students that when authors don't use causal words like *because* or *so that,* readers must infer the cause-effect relationship.

### Differentiating Instruction

| If... | Then... |
|---|---|
| English Learners need extra help with vocabulary | Use ***English Learner Support Guide*** pages 276–277 |
| English Learners need extra help with cause and effect | Use ***English Learner Support Guide*** pages 277–278 |

COMPREHENSION

## Comprehension Strategies

### Teacher Modeling

5 **Summarizing** *This is the end of the story. It's a good place to summarize what I've read. This will show me if I understood what I read. One Sunday, Alexander's grandparents gave Alexander and his two brothers each a dollar. Alexander kept on spending the money and he ended up losing all of it. He tried to get more money, but he couldn't. Finally, he had only bus tokens left. It sounds like Alexander wishes he still had his money.*

### Discussing Strategy Use

While students read the selection, encourage them to share any problems that they encounter and to tell what strategies they use to solve them.

- What connections did they make between the reading and what they already know?
- How did they clarify confusing passages?
- Where did they pause in the reading to summarize?
- What predictions did they make?

These are questions good readers ask after they read a text. After reading, the students should always be asking, "What did I find interesting? What is important here?" Later, remind the students again that whenever they conclude a reading, they should ask themselves questions about what was in the text.

**Teacher Tip** **BUILDING FLUENCY** As students read, you may notice that some need work in building fluency. During Workshop, have these students select a section of the text (a minimum of 160 words) to read several times in order to build fluency.

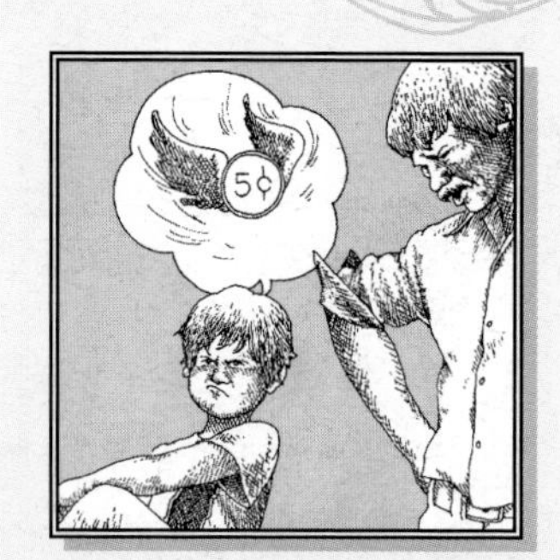


Anthony said that even when I'm 199, I still won't have enough for a walkie-talkie. Nick said they should lock me in a cage. My father said that there are certain things a boy can never kick, no matter how ratty and mean his brothers are being. My father made me pay five cents for kicking it.

Good-bye nickel.

Last Sunday, when I used to be rich, Cathy around the corner had a garage sale. I positively only went to look. I looked at a half-melted candle. I needed that candle. I looked at a bear with one eye. I needed that bear. I looked at a deck of cards that was perfect except for no seven of clubs and no two of diamonds. I didn't need that seven or that two.

Good-bye twenty cents.

32

### Differentiating Instruction

| If... | Then... |
|---|---|
| English Learners need extra help with vocabulary | Use ***English Learner Support Guide*** pages 279–280 |
| English Learners need extra help with cause and effect | Use ***English Learner Support Guide*** pages 280–281 |

I absolutely was saving the rest of my money. I positively was saving the rest of my money. I absolutely positively was saving the rest of my money. Except I needed to get some money to save.

I tried to make a tooth fall out—I could put it under my pillow and get a quarter. No loose teeth.

I looked in Pearson's telephone booths for nickels and dimes that people sometimes forget. No one forgot.

I brought some non-returnable bottles down to Friendly's Market. Friendly's Market wasn't very friendly.

I told my grandma and grandpa to come back soon.

Last Sunday, when I used to be rich, I used to have a dollar. I do not have a dollar any more. I've got this dopey deck of cards. I've got this one-eyed bear. I've got this melted candle.

5 And . . . some bus tokens.

## Comprehension Skills

COMPREHENSION

### Cause and Effect

Have students identify the primary cause and effect of this story. *(Alexander is no longer rich because he spent all his money. Alexander is unhappy due to the fact that he did not save any money.)*

### Checking Comprehension

Ask students the following questions to check their comprehension of the story.

- Do you think the author chose a good title for the story? Explain. *(Students should realize that the title repeats what Alexander says about himself and also sums up what happens to him.)*
- What makes Alexander seem like a real person to you? *(Students should note that Alexander's humor, the way he talks about himself and his family, his actions, and his relationship with his brothers are very realistic.)*
- Why is it important that this story is told by Alexander rather than by another story character or someone outside the story? *(Students should recognize that Alexander is the character who lost the dollar. By having him tell the story, readers understand more about him and about what he thinks and feels.)*
- What do you find out about Alexander by reading this story? *(He's funny; he can't save money; he fights with his brothers when they tease him.)*

### Formal Assessment

See pages 6–9 in ***Unit 4 Assessment*** to test students' comprehension of "Alexander, Who Used to Be Rich Last Sunday."

### Differentiating Instruction

| If... | Then... |
| --- | --- |
| English Learners need extra help reviewing "Alexander, Who Used to Be Rich Last Sunday" | Use ***English Learner Support Guide*** pages 282–283 |

**Teacher Tip FLUENCY** By this time in third grade, good readers should be reading approximately 123 words per minute with fluency and expression. The only way to gain this fluency is through practice. Have students reread the selection to you and to each other during Workshop to help build fluency.

**Teacher Tip** **DISCUSSION** When you call on a student, allow him or her a few seconds to consider your question and arrive at an answer.

**Routine Card**
Refer to ***Routine* 6** for the *handing-off process.*

| Clues | Problems | Wonderings |
| --- | --- | --- |
| used to be rich | tokens | Why is he no longer rich? |

Reading Transparency 46

***Reading Transparency 46***

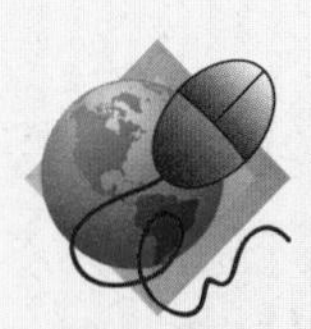
**www.sra4kids.com**
**Web Connection**
Some students may choose to conduct a computer search for additional books or information about money. Invite them to make a list of these books and sources of information to share with classmates and the school librarian. Check the Reading link of the SRA Web page for additional links to the theme-related Web site.

## Discussing the Selection

After the first read, the whole group discusses the selection and any personal thoughts, reactions, problems, or questions that it raises. To stimulate discussion, students can ask one another the kinds of questions that good readers ask themselves about a text: *How does it connect to money? What have I learned that is new? What did I find interesting about this story? What is important here? What was difficult to understand? Why would someone want to read this?* Ensure that students are using specific information from the text to support their interpretations.

**Handing-Off Process** Seeing you as a contributing member of the group sets a strong example for students. To emphasize that you are part of the group, actively participate in the *handing-off process:* Raise your hand to be called on by the last speaker when you have a contribution to make. Point out unusual and interesting insights verbalized by students so that these insights are recognized and discussed. As the year progresses, students will take more and more responsibility for the discussions of the selections.

Engage students in a discussion to determine whether they have grasped the following ideas:

- why Alexander was rich
- what happened to the money
- why he is no longer rich
- what Alexander learned about money

During this time, have students return to the clues, problems, and wonderings they noted during browsing to determine whether the clues were borne out by the selection, whether and how their problems were solved, and whether their wonderings were answered or deserve further discussion and investigation. Let the students decide which items deserve further discussion.

Also have students return to the Focus Questions on the first page of the selection. Select a student to read the questions aloud, and have volunteers answer the questions. If students do not know the answers to the questions, have them return to the text to find the answers.

You may wish to review the elements of realistic fiction with the students at this time. Discuss with them how they can tell that "Alexander, Who Used to Be Rich Last Sunday" is realistic fiction.

Have students break into small groups to discuss what this story tells them about money. Groups can discuss their ideas with the rest of the class.

Students may wish to record their personal responses to the selection. If students have ever had an experience with trying to save money or spending more than they meant to, encourage them to record their experiences.

## Review Selection Vocabulary

Have students review the definitions of the selection vocabulary words that they wrote in the vocabulary section of their Writer's Notebooks. Remind them that they discussed the meanings of these words before reading the selection. Have students write sentences for each of the vocabulary words after the definitions in the same section of their Writer's Notebooks. They can use the definitions and the sentences to study for the vocabulary portion of their Lesson Assessments. Have them add to the personal dictionary section of their Writer's Notebooks any other interesting words that they clarified while reading. Encourage students to refer to the selection vocabulary words throughout the unit. The words from the selection are:

**tokens** **absolutely** **positively** **rent** **vanish** **non-returnable**

Remind students to find words from other resources, from their investigations and from family discussions, and add them to their Unit 4 Word Banks. Remind students that they are organizing the words in Unit 4 according to syllables. Encourage students to think of other ways to group words, based on meaning, structure, or spelling.

## Home Connection

Send home the letter on page 47 of ***Home Connection.*** This letter will provide parents and caregivers the opportunity to learn about the reading selection for this lesson from their child's point of view. Information is also provided on how to set up a personal savings account at home or at a local bank. A Spanish version of this letter appears on page 48.

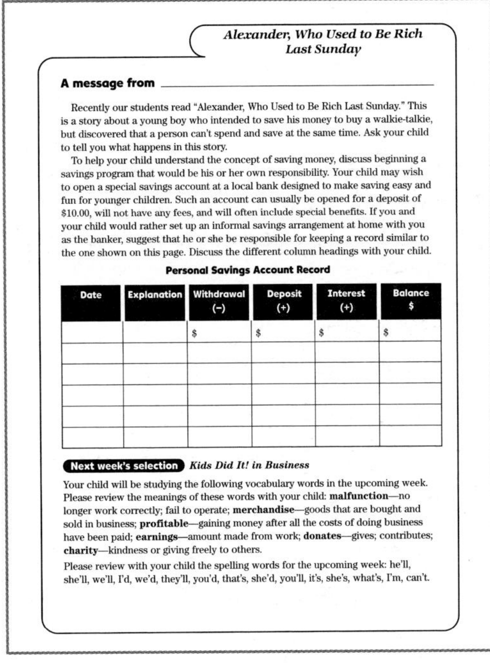

*Alexander, Who Used to Be Rich Last Sunday*

**A message from** ______________________

Recently our students read "Alexander, Who Used to Be Rich Last Sunday." This is a story about a young boy who intended to save his money to buy a walkie-talkie, but discovered that a person can't spend and save at the same time. Ask your child to tell you what happens in this story.

To help your child understand the concept of saving money, discuss beginning a savings program that would be his or her own responsibility. Your child may wish to open a special savings account at a local bank designed to make saving easy and fun for younger children. Such an account can usually be opened for a deposit of $10.00, will not have any fees, and will often include special benefits. If you and your child would rather set up an informal savings arrangement at home with you as the banker, suggest that he or she be responsible for keeping a record similar to the one shown on this page. Discuss the different column headings with your child.

**Personal Savings Account Record**

| Date | Explanation | Withdrawal (−) | Deposit (+) | Interest (+) | Balance $ |
|---|---|---|---|---|---|
| | | $ | $ | $ | $ |
| | | | | | |
| | | | | | |
| | | | | | |
| | | | | | |
| | | | | | |

**Next week's selection** ***Kids Did It! in Business***

Your child will be studying the following vocabulary words in the upcoming week. Please review the meanings of these words with your child: **malfunction**—no longer work correctly; fail to operate; **merchandise**—goods that are bought and sold in business; **profitable**—gaining money after all the costs of doing business have been paid; **earnings**—amount made from work; **donates**—gives; contributes; **charity**—kindness or giving freely to others.

Please review with your child the spelling words for the upcoming week: he'll, she'll, we'll, I'd, we'd, they'll, you'd, that's, she'd, you'll, it's, she's, what's, I'm, can't.

***Home Connection* p. 47**

### Differentiating Instruction

| If... | Then... |
|---|---|
| Students are having difficulty with vocabulary | Ask volunteers to share the sentences that they wrote in their Writer's Notebooks, using the vocabulary words |

**Teacher Tip** Have the students choose a book to read from the library relating to the theme. This book should identify their preference in either literary or nonfiction texts. Encourage students to read often from their preferred genre.

## Supporting the Reading

### Comprehension Skills: Cause and Effect

**Teach** After the second read, remind students that understanding the relationships between causes and effects in a text adds to a deeper understanding of the text, its characters, and its plot. Sometimes the effect appears before the cause. Sometimes authors indicate these relationships by using causal indicators, such as *because*, *since*, *due to the fact that*, *therefore*, *consequently*, *for*, and *as a result*, among others. Sometimes authors imply these relationships without using causal indicators, but readers can restate cause-and-effect relationships and insert causal indicators to make the relationships more clear.

**Guided Practice** Brainstorm a list of all the activities at school that are money related and ask students to add money-related activities from home as well. For example, students bring in lunch money every day and give it to the teacher. Choose several statements and establish a cause-and-effect chain with students. For example, students bring in lunch money every day *so that* they can eat a hot lunch. *Because* the lunch costs the school money, students must bring money to school to pay for it. Students give the money to teachers *so that* the lunchroom gets the money it needs to pay for the lunch, etc. Record responses on the board or on an overhead transparency.

**Independent Practice** Read through the Focus and Identify sections of ***Comprehension and Language Arts Skills,*** page 96, with students. Guide students through the Identify portion, and help them come up with examples found in the story. Then have students complete the Practice and Apply portions of ***Comprehension and Language Arts Skills,*** page 97.

**Link to Writing** Invite students to write about a money-related cause and effect with which they are familiar. The subject can be one they suggested for the practice activity, or one related to the story they just read. For example, students might write about cause-and-effect relationships related to saving money.

Tell students to use some of the causal indicators they have been taught, but to also write sentences that imply the cause-and-effect relationship without using the indicator words.

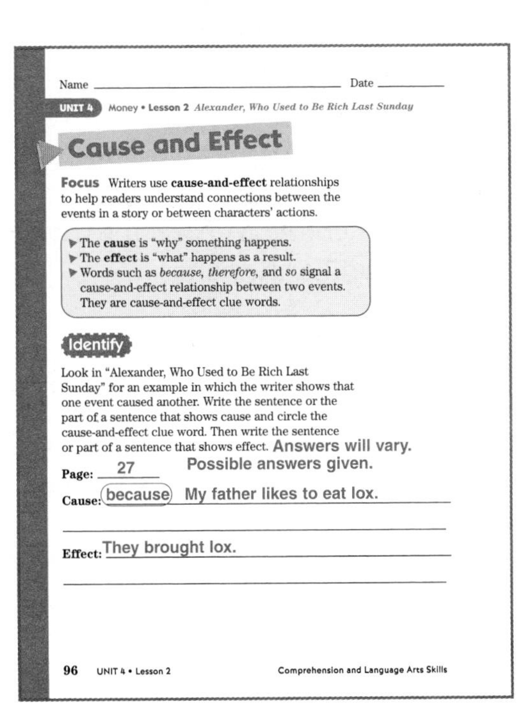

Name ____________ Date ________

UNIT 4 Money • Lesson 2 *Alexander, Who Used to Be Rich Last Sunday*

**Cause and Effect**

**Focus** Writers use **cause-and-effect** relationships to help readers understand connections between the events in a story or between characters' actions.

- The **cause** is "why" something happens.
- The **effect** is "what" happens as a result.
- Words such as *because, therefore,* and *so* signal a cause-and-effect relationship between two events. They are cause-and-effect clue words.

**Identify**

Look in "Alexander, Who Used to Be Rich Last Sunday" for an example in which the writer shows that one event caused another. Write the sentence or the part of a sentence that shows cause and circle the cause-and-effect clue word. Then write the sentence or part of a sentence that shows effect. Answers will vary. Possible answers given.

**Page:** 27

**Cause:** (because) My father likes to eat lox.

**Effect:** They brought lox.

96 UNIT 4 • Lesson 2 Comprehension and Language Arts Skills

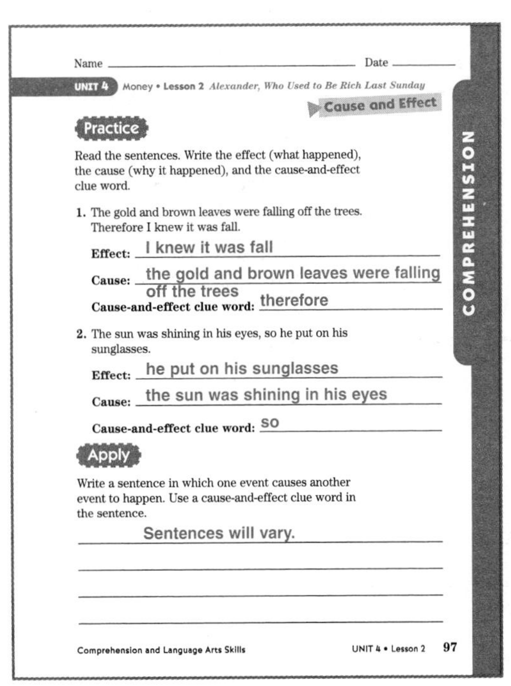

Name ____________ Date ________

UNIT 4 Money • Lesson 2 *Alexander, Who Used to Be Rich Last Sunday*

Cause and Effect

**Practice**

Read the sentences. Write the effect (what happened), the cause (why it happened), and the cause-and-effect clue word.

1. The gold and brown leaves were falling off the trees. Therefore I knew it was fall.

**Effect:** I knew it was fall

**Cause:** the gold and brown leaves were falling off the trees

**Cause-and-effect clue word:** therefore

2. The sun was shining in his eyes, so he put on his sunglasses.

**Effect:** he put on his sunglasses

**Cause:** the sun was shining in his eyes

**Cause-and-effect clue word:** so

**Apply**

Write a sentence in which one event causes another event to happen. Use a cause-and-effect clue word in the sentence.

Sentences will vary.

COMPREHENSION

Comprehension and Language Arts Skills UNIT 4 • Lesson 2 97

***Comprehension and Language Arts Skills pp. 96–97***

## Differentiating Instruction

| If... | Then... |
|---|---|
| Students need extra help with cause and effect | Use ***Reteach*** pages 99–100 |
| Students have an understanding of cause and effect and would enjoy a challenge | Use ***Challenge*** page 87 |

**Teacher Tip** Remind students to use causal indicators to explain cause-and-effect relationships. If necessary, keep a list of those on the board.

**Cause and Effect**

Introduced in Grade 1.

Scaffolded throughout Grades 2 and 3.

**REINTRODUCED:** Unit 1, Lesson 2

**REINFORCED:** Unit 1, Lesson 4
Unit 2, Lesson 4
Unit 2, Lesson 5
Unit 4, Lesson 2
Unit 4, Lesson 7
Unit 6, Lesson 6

**TESTED:** Unit 4 Assessment

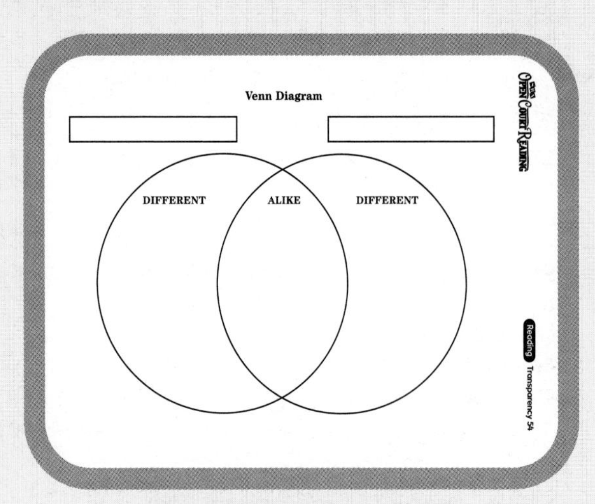


*Reading Transparency 54*

## Differentiating Instruction

| If... | Then... |
|---|---|
| Students have an understanding of characterization and would enjoy a challenge | Make copies of ***Reading Transparency 54*** and have them compare and contrast Anna's mother from "A New Coat for Anna" with Alexander |

**Teacher Tip WRITING PORTFOLIO** Over the course of the year, have students identify ten or more finished pieces of writing that reflect their abilities to write in different genres. Have students collect these pieces into a separate section of their ***Writing Folders*** to serve as a writing portfolio.

# Literary Elements

## Characterization

**Teach** Ask volunteers to tell what they know about characterization. Remind students that characterization is the way a writer shows what the characters in his or her story are like. Writers do this by telling what the characters do, say, think, and feel. Often, characters in a book can be very different from one another.

**Guided Practice** Display ***Reading Transparency 54.*** Ask students to choose two characters from "Alexander, Who Used to Be Rich Last Sunday." Have students discuss, compare, and contrast the characters. Have them use the Venn diagram to record the similarities and differences between the characters.

**Independent Practice** Have students select a piece of writing from their ***Writing Folders.*** Ask students to select one character and to list his or her thoughts, feelings, words, and actions. Invite students to think about changes or additions they could make that would make the character seem more like they want him or her to seem. For example, if students want a character to seem brave, invite them to make changes to the character's words or actions that would make him or her seem more brave. If the students create a character who is very different from the original, have them show the similarities and differences on a Venn diagram.

## Social Studies Connection

### Costs and Benefits

In "Alexander, Who Used to Be Rich Last Sunday," students read about a boy who wanted to save his money for a walkie-talkie. Instead, he spent all his money, often because the benefit of owning certain items seemed to him to be worth the cost at the time. Explain to students that in our society and throughout history, most proposed solutions to problems ultimately come down to a balance between benefits and costs.

Ask students to find a time in world history when an important decision was made. They might research, for example, times when solutions to health problems or environmental concerns had to be developed. They might investigate decisions of countries to enter or not enter a war, and explore the economic reasons for the decision. Students can ask themselves the following questions to help with the research: *What was the problem or crisis? What solution, or solutions, were proposed? What decision was made in the end? Why was that decision made? What were the advantages of the decision? What were the costs of the decision? Were advantages and costs part of the decision-making process?*

Have students present their findings to the class. Tell them to include visual aids, such as charts, graphs, maps, photographs, or diagrams, with their presentations. Also tell them to include a bibliography of the sources they used. This information might be helpful to class groups as they work on the unit investigation.

**Teacher Tip** **MATERIALS**
- ✔ poster board
- ✔ colored pencils or markers

**Teacher Tip** **PURPOSE** To learn about the balance between benefits and costs in decision making throughout history.

**Teacher Tip** Remind students that the library, as well as the Internet, provides many sources that are created especially for young students to use and that cover important periods in history. They might consider starting with such a source to look up the information for this activity.

## Concept Connections

### Linking the Selection

- He spent his money carelessly and was unhappy when he did not have any left.
- Alexander did not have self-control. He bought everything he wanted.

### Exploring Concept Vocabulary

The concept word for this lesson is ***squander.*** Write the word on the board. Work with students to develop a definition that clearly links to the unit theme. Have students copy the word and definition into the Vocabulary section of their Writer's Notebooks.

***Squander:*** to spend money in a foolish or wasteful way. For example, Alexander squandered his money when he bought a half-melted candle.

- Alexander squandered his money on things that he did not need.
- Students might suggest that Alexander will squander his money again. Alexander tells the readers that he usually has only bus tokens.

Make sure that the sentences students create show their understanding of the concept and selection vocabulary word. For example, the sentence *He positively squandered his money* does not show an understanding of the words.

### Expanding the Concept

You may want to do a whole-group discussion to help students continue to develop their ability to engage in meaningful dialogue. However, students may conduct these dialogues in small groups. If students work in small groups, bring the groups together and have them share their ideas with the whole class.

As students complete their discussions, have them record their ideas and impressions about the selection on page 83 of their ***Inquiry Journals.***

# Alexander, Who Used to Be Rich Last Sunday

## Concept Connections

### Linking the Selection

Think about the following questions, and then record your responses in the Response Journal section of your Writer's Notebook.

- How did having money cause a problem for Alexander?
- Why was it so hard for Alexander to save his money?

### Exploring Concept Vocabulary

The concept word for this lesson is ***squander.*** If you do not know what this word means, look it up in a dictionary.
Answer these questions:

- How did Alexander ***squander*** his money?
- Do you think Alexander will save or ***squander*** his money in the future? Why?

Make up an oral sentence using the word ***squander*** and one of the selection vocabulary words.

### Expanding the Concept

Think about the characters in the stories "A New Coat for Anna" and "Alexander, Who Used to Be Rich Last Sunday." How was Alexander's problem different from Anna and her mother's problem? Why is it important to be wise about the way you spend your money?

Try to use the word ***squander*** in your discussion.

Add new ideas about money to the Concept/Question Board.

34

**Informal Assessment**

This may be a good time to observe students working in small groups and to mark your observations in the Teacher Observation Log, found in the ***Program Assessment Teacher's Edition.***

**Teacher Tip CONCEPT VOCABULARY** Developing a repertoire of concept-related vocabulary will help students deepen their understanding of theme concepts, help facilitate class discussions, and help students formulate ideas, problems, and questions for inquiry.

## Meet the Author

**Judith Viorst** writes almost all of her children's stories about her sons and their adventures. *"I find my sons fierce and funny,"* she says, *"and these qualities appear in many of my characters, some of whom are named after my boys."* Judith wrote poems and stories as a child, and when she was older, she kept writing. She has also written books with her husband and has had her own column in a magazine.

## Meet the Illustrator

**Ray Cruz** was born and raised in New York City. He went to an art and design school during his high school years and then went on to study art in college. Being an illustrator has allowed him to work in many different types of jobs. He has worked for advertising agencies, cosmetic companies, textile companies, and of course, publishing companies. Besides illustration, his interests are art history, archaeology, and conservation.

35

## Meet the Author

After students read the information about Judith Viorst, discuss the following questions with them:

- Judith Viorst says almost all of her stories are based on her sons. After reading this story how do you think her sons get along? *(Possible answer: They probably fight like normal brothers and sisters. They like to tease one another, but they really do care for one another deep down.)*
- The theme of this unit is Money. Why do you think Judith Viorst's story was included? *(Possible answer: It's not always easy to hold on to your money. Sometimes money gets wasted on useless things instead of being saved.)*

## Meet the Illustrator

After students read the information about Ray Cruz, discuss the following questions with them:

- Why do you think being an illustrator allowed Ray Cruz to work the many jobs he described? *(Possible answer: Many projects need good illustrators to make them successful. Any type of advertising for any company has to be sketched out. Also, the designs for products need to be created.)*
- Ray Cruz is interested in art history and archaeology. Why would these areas help his illustrating? *(Possible answer: By studying other artists and old artifacts, he can learn different techniques to improve his own artwork.)*

## Objectives

- Students ask questions related to money.
- Students gain a deeper understanding of issues related to money.
- Students form groups and decide on initial investigation questions.

## Materials

- Student Anthology, Book 2, pp. 26–37
- Inquiry Journal, pp. 89–92
- Research Assistant CD-ROM

INVESTIGATION

# Investigating Concepts Beyond the Text

At this point in the Research Cycle, students are still in the first problem phase and will move into the second problem phase by the end of the lesson. This means that students need to form their groups based on areas of interest. As the lesson progresses, students should form groups based on areas of shared interest, settle on a question to investigate, and brainstorm initial plans, which students can share and discuss with the class.

During this time, you might find it helpful for students to plan the schedule for their investigations on money that you previously outlined. Help students complete ***Inquiry Journal,*** pages 89–90, to plan the schedule.

Have students begin planning their investigations. Then have them complete ***Inquiry Journal,*** page 91, to help them start thinking about their investigation problems and questions.

In "Alexander, Who Used to Be Rich Last Sunday," students read about a boy who regretted his decisions about spending. Invite students to investigate this idea further. They can generate a list of ways that Alexander spent his money and another list of reasons he could have given himself for not spending it. Students can further investigate the idea of spending and saving by picking a sum of money and an activity such as a trip to an amusement park, a visit to a state or county fair, or a shopping spree. Encourage students to investigate the costs of items, such as tickets, rides, food, and gifts. Then, have students break down the amounts they might spend on each facet of the activity, perhaps using columns labeled *Good Decision* and *Poor Decision.* Provide time for students to share their information and ideas.

Name ______ Date ______
Money UNIT 4

**Research Cycle: Problem Phase I**

A good problem to research:
Answers will vary.

Why this is an interesting research problem:
Answers will vary.

Some other questions about this problem:
Answers will vary.

Inquiry Journal • *Research Cycle: Problem Phase I* UNIT 4 91

***Inquiry Journal p. 91***

Name ______ Date ______
Money UNIT 4

**Project Planning Calendar**

Use the calendar to help schedule your Money unit investigation. Fill in the dates. Make sure that you mark any days you know you will not work on the investigation. Choose the date on which you will start.

| Sunday | Monday | Tuesday | Wednesday |
|---|---|---|---|
| | | | |
| | | | |
| | | | |
| | | | |
| | | | |
| | | | |

Inquiry Journal • *Project Planning Calendar* UNIT 4 89

**Project Planning Calendar** *(continued)*

Then choose the date on which you hope to finish. You may also find it helpful to mark the dates by which you hope to complete different parts of the investigation. Record what you accomplish each day.

| Thursday | Friday | Saturday |
|---|---|---|
| | | |
| | | |
| | | |
| | | |
| | | |
| | | |

90 UNIT 4 *Project Planning Calendar* • Inquiry Journal

***Inquiry Journal pp. 89–90***

## Concept/Question Board

After reading each selection, students should use the Concept/Question Board to:

- Post any questions they asked about a selection before reading that have not been answered yet.
- Refer to as they formulate statements about concepts that apply to their investigations.
- Post general statements formulated by each collaborative group.
- Continue to post news articles or other items that they find during the unit investigation.
- Read and think about posted questions, articles, or concepts that interest them and provide answers to the questions.

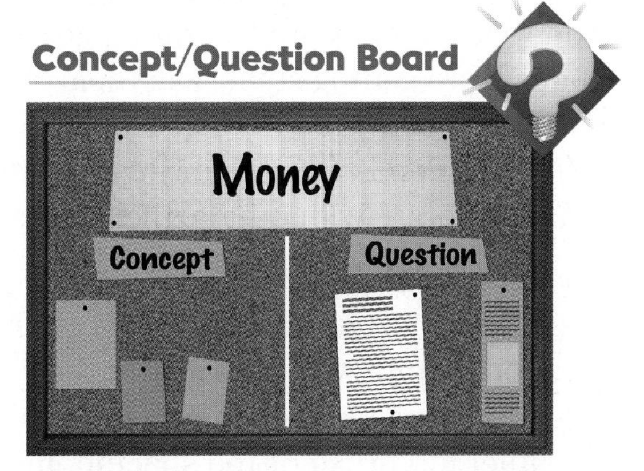


## Unit 4 Investigation Management

| | |
|---|---|
| Lesson 1 | Brainstorm questions related to the theme. Investigate alternatives to money, such as bartering. |
| Lesson 2 | **Collaborative Investigation**<br>**Groups form based on areas of shared interest.**<br>**Supplementary Activity**<br>**Investigate choices related to spending and saving money.** |
| Lesson 3 | Begin forming conjectures. Brainstorm about how to turn hobbies into businesses. |
| Lesson 4 | Discuss conjectures in groups and begin plans. Look for stories or illustrations about the ways that money can change people and things that money cannot buy. |
| Lesson 5 | Students revise their plans as necessary and continue investigation. Groups can debate on borrowing and lending money. |
| Lesson 6 | Continue investigation and prepare final presentations. Create a story or miniplay about how money passes from person to person, or plan a possible field trip to a Federal Reserve Bank. |
| Lesson 7 | Groups give formal presentations. Students discuss saving money for personal goals or explore the Great Depression further. |

INVESTIGATION

**Teacher Tip** Continue to encourage use of the Concept/Question Board by recognizing and thanking students for their contributions. Incorporate discussion of those items into classroom discussions whenever appropriate.

### Research Assistant

The ***Research Assistant CD-ROM*** assists students in their investigations.

### Differentiating Instruction

| If... | Then... |
|---|---|
| Students are having difficulty with their Inquiry activities | Help them formulate questions for the Concept/Question Board |

Open Court Reading Reading Transparency 55

_______________ Web

Reading Transparency 55

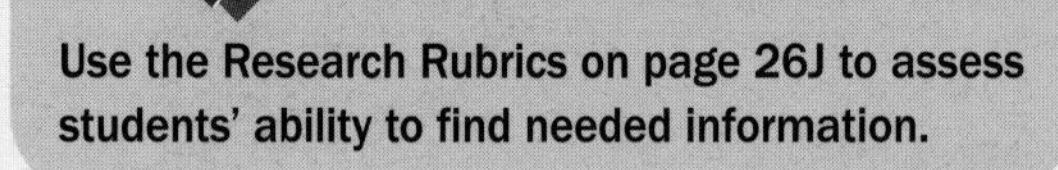

**Formal Assessment**

Use the Research Rubrics on page 26J to assess students' ability to find needed information.

Name_______________ Date_______

UNIT 4 Money

**Research Cycle: Problem Phase 2**

My research group's problem:

Answers will vary.

What our research will contribute to the unit investigation and to the rest of the class:

Answers will vary.

Some other questions about this problem:

Answers will vary.

92 UNIT 4 *Research Cycle: Problem Phase 2* • Inquiry Journal

***Inquiry Journal p. 92***

INVESTIGATION

## Problem Phase 2

To continue guiding students through the Problem Phase of the Research Cycle, have students talk about things they wonder about that are related to the unit theme. For example, students might wonder where money in a money machine comes from or how prices are determined. Help students formulate their wondering into investigation questions. If necessary, continue to model the difference between an investigation topic and question by providing students with examples. Further ideas can also be generated as you and the students create a web of their questions or problems related to money. You may want to use ***Reading Transparency 55*** to continue generating ideas.

Point out that a good investigation problem or question not only requires the students to consult a variety of sources, but is engaging and adds to the group's knowledge. Furthermore, good problems generate more questions. If students are getting stuck, ask them "What aspect of the topic really interests you?" and "Can you turn that idea into a question?" Keep in mind that this initial question is a guide for investigation, and as students collect information and collaborate with others, their ideas will change.

Revision is also a part of the research cycle. As students settle on initial investigation problems and questions, have students present their proposed questions, along with reasons for their choices, to the class for discussion of how promising proposed problems are. Students should avoid problems that are either too broad or too specific. Instead, they should focus on ones that help the group understand the investigation concepts.

Help the students settle into groups. To facilitate forming groups, you can record students' questions on the board or on self-sticking notes. During class discussion, draw arrows to link related problems. Final groups should be created in the way you find best for your class—by self-selection, by assignment on the basis of common interests, or by some combination of methods. Students can use Workshop to work on their investigations. Assign page 92 of the ***Inquiry Journal*** to be completed during Workshop.

## Card Catalog

**Teach** Invite students to review aloud what they already know about card catalogs. Answers will vary but should include the following facts.

- A card catalog has alphabetically arranged cards containing information about all the books in the library.
- Usually there are three cards for each book: an author card, a title card, and a subject card.

**Guided Practice** Give each student three index cards. Have students write a card for Author, a card for Title, and a card for Subject. Read aloud the following situations, and ask students to hold up the type of card that they would look for in the card catalog.

- You enjoy books by Judith Viorst and want to see if she has written any more books. *(author)*
- You want to see if there are any more books in the library about money. *(subject)*
- You want to find out who wrote the book *Freckle Juice. (title)*
- You want to see if there are any books about Bill Peet. *(subject)*
- You want to see if Shel Silverstein has written any other books of poetry in addition to *Where the Sidewalk Ends. (author)*
- Someone recommended a book called *Stone Fox*. You want to see if it is in your library. *(title)*

**Independent Practice** Ask students to take their investigation questions with them to the library and begin a card catalog search for titles they might use. Ask them to find at least three different sources.

SUPPORTING THE INVESTIGATION

### Differentiating Instruction

| If... | Then... |
|---|---|
| Students are showing an understanding of the card catalog and would enjoy a challenge | Have them use the card catalog to make a list of books written by the authors of the selections in the Money unit |

**Teacher Tip** Many libraries use computerized catalog systems. Review the system used in your school library with students. Consider making a field trip to the local public library to learn about their catalog system.

Encourage students to use ***TechKnowledge*** to learn more about how to use a computer to perform various tasks.

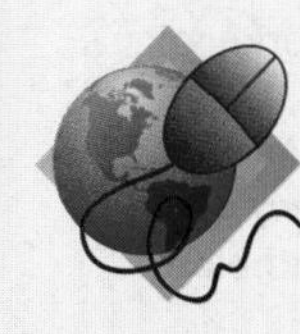

**www.sra4kids.com**
**Web Connection**
More information about money and links to Web sites concerning money can be found at www.sra4kids.com.

### Objectives

**Word Analysis**

**Spelling**
- **Final Double Consonants.** Develop understanding of how to spell words with final double consonants.

**Vocabulary**
- **Suffixes.** Using words from "Alexander, Who Used to Be Rich Last Sunday," learn how the suffix *-ly* can change the spellings and meanings of base words.

**Writing Process Strategies**
- **Persuasive Writing—Poster.** Building on the idea of saving money for a purpose, learn to use persuasive writing to create a poster.

**English Language Conventions**

**Grammar, Usage, and Mechanics**
- **Subjects and Predicates.** Understand and use simple and compound subjects and predicates. Find simple and compound subjects in "Alexander, Who Used to Be Rich Last Sunday."

**Listening, Speaking, Viewing**
- **Speaking: Elements of Grammar.** Develop speaking skills by using elements of grammar.

**Penmanship**
- **Cursive Letters *E* and *O*.** Develop handwriting skills by practicing formation of cursive *E* and *O*.

### Materials

- Spelling and Vocabulary Skills, pp. 78–81
- Language Arts Handbook
- Comprehension and Language Arts Skills, pp. 96–101
- Writer's Workbook, pp. 58–61
- Language Arts Transparency 18
- Student Anthology

### Differentiating Instruction

***Reteach, Challenge,*** and ***Intervention*** lessons are available to support the language arts instruction in this lesson.

### Research in Action

The writing of a word inherently forces attention to its full sequence of letters. For a student, the thought that somebody else might evaluate one's products may encourage such attention all the more.
(*Marilyn Adams,* Beginning to Read: Thinking and Learning About Print)

OVERVIEW

# Language Arts Overview

## Word Analysis

**Spelling** The Spelling activities on the following pages introduce words with the final double consonants *ll, ss, dd, ff, tt,* and *zz.*

### Selection Spelling Words

These words from "Alexander, Who Used to Be Rich Last Sunday" contain final double consonants.

**all still fall till guess**

**Vocabulary** The Vocabulary activities extend the instruction of the Vocabulary Skill Words from "Alexander, Who Used to Be Rich Last Sunday" to recognize how the suffix *-ly* can add new meanings and create spelling changes to base words. A *suffix,* as first taught in Lesson 2 of Unit 3, is added to the end of a base word and adds new meaning to the word. Knowing the meanings of suffixes can help students infer the meanings of words with suffixes.

### Vocabulary Skill Words

**absolutely* positively* mostly friendly really**
**Also Selection Vocabulary*

## Writing Process Strategies

The Writing Process Strategies lesson involves instruction in using persuasive writing to create a poster, providing reasons, facts, or feelings to support one's viewpoint.

To teach spreadsheet applications in the writing process, show students how to edit data in a spreadsheet. You might want to help students create a spreadsheet to organize their ideas for a poster and show them how to change incorrect information. ***TechKnowledge,*** Level 3, Lesson 68, teaches these spreadsheet application skills.

## English Language Conventions

**Grammar, Usage, and Mechanics** **Subjects and Predicates.** This lesson develops an understanding of subjects and predicates in sentences.

**Listening, Speaking, Viewing** **Speaking: Elements of Grammar.** In this Speaking lesson, students will discuss the importance of using elements of grammar in their speech.

**Penmanship** **Cursive Letters *E* and *O*.** This lesson develops handwriting skills by having students learn formation of *E* and *O*. Students then write words from the literature selection.

# DAY 1

## Word Analysis

### Spelling

**Assessment: Pretest**

**Final Double Consonants**

**Teach**

Give students the Pretest on page 32 of ***Unit 4 Assessment.*** Have them proofread and correct any misspelled words.

**Pretest Sentences**

1. **spill** Red juice on white carpet is a **spill** that will stain.
2. **hill** A **hill** is smaller than a mountain.
3. **gull** A sea bird with gray and white feathers is a **gull**.
4. **smell** Some people like the **smell** of a burning fire.
5. **mess** A wet dog can make a **mess** of a clean house.
6. **odd** The number three is an **odd** number.
7. **add** Flowers **add** color to a room.
8. **cliff** A **cliff** is the edge of a rock.
9. **mitt** The catcher's **mitt** in baseball is heavily padded.
10. **fuzz** The **fuzz** on the skin of a peach is soft.
11. **all** Americans **all** have the freedom of speech.
12. **still** A tiger is **still** as it sleeps.
13. **fall** Leaves begin to turn colors during the **fall** season.
14. **till** Baseball fans cannot wait **till** the World Series.
15. **guess** On some tests, it is better to **guess** an answer than to leave a blank.

Diagnose any misspellings by determining whether students misspelled final double consonants or some other part of the word. Then use the Pretest as a take-home list to study the spellings of words with final double consonants.

## Writing Process Strategies

### Getting Ideas

**Persuasive Poster**

**Teach**

**Introduce Persuasive Writing Form**

Read ***Language Arts Handbook,*** pages 156–157, on persuasive writing. If you have completed Lesson 1 of this unit, this will be a review.

**Inspiration**

Teacher Model: *"I saw a sign in a store window the other day that said there was a circus coming to town. I know there are lots of things to buy at a circus. I'm going to make a poster to remind children to save their money to spend at the circus."*

**Brainstorming**

Using the idea of saving money as a springboard for ideas, encourage students to generate ideas for what they would encourage others to save money for. Make a list of these ideas on the board.

**Guided Practice**

**Getting Ideas**

Have students write ideas for a persuasive poster in their Writer's Notebooks.

Persuasive Writing

Persuasive writing does two things. It can make readers think or feel a certain way. It can also make readers do something. Sometimes persuasive writing can do both of these things at the same time. Advertisements are one kind of persuasive writing. You will learn about other kinds in the following lessons.

156 Persuasive Writing

*Language Arts Handbook p. 156*

## English Language Conventions

### Grammar, Usage, and Mechanics

**Grammar: Subjects and Predicates**

**Teach**

- **Review** the four kinds of sentences using ***Language Arts Handbook,*** page 181.
- Remind students that sentences contain a complete thought. Tell them that sentences form a complete thought by having subjects and predicates.
- Use ***Language Arts Handbook,*** page 256, for the definition and examples of subjects and predicates.
- Write the following sentences on the board and ask students to identify subjects and predicates.
  - Mrs. Davis lived in Mississippi. (*subject*, Mrs. Davis; *predicate*, lived)
  - Tammy worked as a maid and raised her children. (*subject*, Tammy; *predicates*, worked *and* raised)
  - Mrs. Davis and Tammy attended the same school. (*subject*, Mrs. Davis and Tammy; *predicate*, attended)

**Independent Practice**

Use ***Comprehension and Language Arts Skills,*** pages 98–99, to identify subjects and predicates.

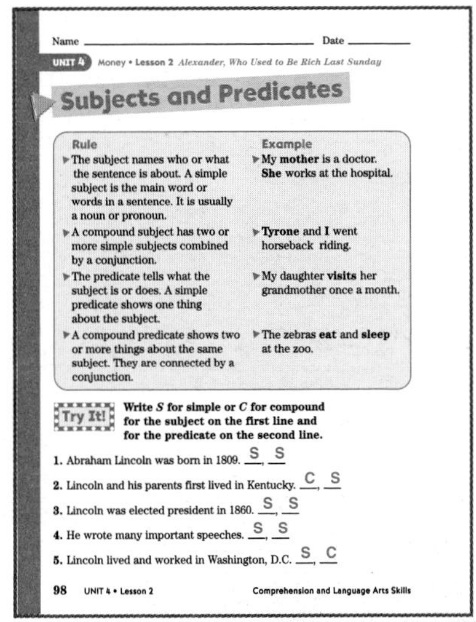

Name ______________________ Date __________

UNIT 4 Money • Lesson 2 *Alexander, Who Used to Be Rich Last Sunday*

Subjects and Predicates

| Rule | Example |
| --- | --- |
| The subject names who or what the sentence is about. A simple subject is the main word or words in a sentence. It is usually a noun or pronoun. | My **mother** is a doctor. **She** works at the hospital. |
| A compound subject has two or more simple subjects combined by a conjunction. | **Tyrone** and **I** went horseback riding. |
| The predicate tells what the subject is or does. A simple predicate shows one thing about the subject. | My daughter **visits** her grandmother once a month. |
| A compound predicate shows two or more things about the same subject. They are connected by a conjunction. | The zebras **eat** and **sleep** at the zoo. |

**Try It!** **Write *S* for simple or *C* for compound for the subject on the first line and for the predicate on the second line.**

1. Abraham Lincoln was born in 1809. S, S
2. Lincoln and his parents first lived in Kentucky. C, S
3. Lincoln was elected president in 1860. S, S
4. He wrote many important speeches. S, S
5. Lincoln lived and worked in Washington, D.C. S, C

98 UNIT 4 • Lesson 2 Comprehension and Language Arts Skills

***Comprehension and Language Arts Skills p. 98***

# DAY 2

## Word Analysis

### Spelling

**Final Double Consonants**

**Word Sorting**

- Write *fill* on the board. Point out that the word has a double consonant in the final position, the *ll*, and that the letter *i* makes the short i sound.
- **Board Word Sort.** Write on the board: *ladder, smell, add, little, mitt,* and *happy.* Have students look at each word and recognize the position of the double consonant.

### Vocabulary

**The Suffix -*ly***

#### Teach

- Write *absolutely* ("Alexander, Who Used to be Rich Last Sunday," p. 29) on the board and circle the *-ly.*
- Explain that the suffix *-ly* means "in a certain way," so *absolutely* means "in an absolute way."

#### Guided Practice

Use ***Spelling and Vocabulary Skills,*** page 78, to teach students how to add the suffix *-ly* to a word to change the meaning of a base word. Ask students to complete page 79 as independent practice.

Name ____________ Date ______

UNIT 4 Money • Lesson 2 *Alexander, Who Used to be Rich Last Sunday*

**The Suffix -*ly***

Remember, the suffix **-*ly*** can be added to the end of an adjective and change the meaning of the word.

| Base Word | + | Suffix (Meaning) | = | New Word | New Meaning |
|---|---|---|---|---|---|
| safe | + | -ly ("in a ___ way") | = | safely | "in a safe way" |

Adding some suffixes, such as **-*ly***, to words changes the spelling of base words that end in the letter *y*. If a base word ends in *y*, change the *y* to *i* before adding **-*ly***.

happy + -ly = happily (the *y* changed to an *i*)

**Try It!** **Notice the word *positively* on page 29 of "Alexander, Who Used to be Rich Last Sunday."**

1. Circle the base word *positive* in the word below: positively
2. Knowing the meaning of the suffix *-ly*, what does the word *positively* mean? possible answer: in a positive way
3. Did the spelling of the word *positive* change or stay the same when the suffix *-ly* was added? stayed the same
4. Add *-ly* to the words below. Change the *y* to *i* if necessary.

| | New Word | New Meaning |
|---|---|---|
| near | nearly | in a near way |
| lucky | luckily | in a lucky way |

78 UNIT 4 • Lesson 2 *The Suffix -ly* • Spelling and Vocabulary Skills

***Spelling and Vocabulary Skills* p. 78**

## Writing Process Strategies

### Prewriting

**Persuasive Poster**

#### Teach

- **Review** the use of reasons/facts or feelings to support the main idea in persuasive writing.
- Read ***Writer's Workbook,*** page 58, on prewriting for a persuasive poster.

**Writer's Craft**

**Time-Order Words**

- Introduce the idea of time-order words by saying, *"First, I got a job delivering newspapers. Next, I opened a savings account at the bank. Then, I worked and saved. Finally, I had enough to go to the circus."*
- Read ***Language Arts Handbook,*** pages 198–199, on time-order words.
- Read ***Comprehension and Language Arts Skills,*** pages 100–101, on time-order words.

#### Independent Practice

**Prewriting**

- Have students write their audience and purpose on the appropriate lines in the ***Writer's Workbook,*** page 58.
- Have students fill in the graphic organizer on page 59 of the ***Writer's Workbook.***

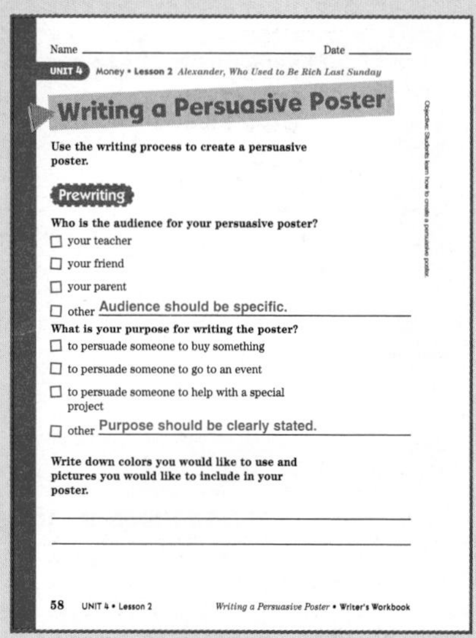

Name ____________ Date ______

UNIT 4 Money • Lesson 2 *Alexander, Who Used to Be Rich Last Sunday*

**Writing a Persuasive Poster**

**Use the writing process to create a persuasive poster.**

**Prewriting**

**Who is the audience for your persuasive poster?**

- ☐ your teacher
- ☐ your friend
- ☐ your parent
- ☐ other Audience should be specific.

**What is your purpose for writing the poster?**

- ☐ to persuade someone to buy something
- ☐ to persuade someone to go to an event
- ☐ to persuade someone to help with a special project
- ☐ other Purpose should be clearly stated.

**Write down colors you would like to use and pictures you would like to include in your poster.**

______________________

______________________

Objective: Students learn how to create a persuasive poster.

58 UNIT 4 • Lesson 2 *Writing a Persuasive Poster* • Writer's Workbook

***Writer's Workbook* p. 58**

## English Language Conventions

### Grammar, Usage, and Mechanics

**Grammar: Subjects and Predicates**

#### Teach

- **Review** subjects and predicates using ***Language Arts Handbook,*** page 256.
- Write two columns on the board, one titled *Subjects* and the other titled *Predicates.*
- Ask students to look around the room and name people and objects. Write these in the *Subjects* column.
- Then ask students to think of verbs. Write these in the *Predicates* column.
- Ask students to combine words from the two columns to make the silliest sentences they can think of. Have them use *and, or,* and *but* to form compound subjects and predicates.
- Write their sentences on the board and mark the subjects with an *S* and the predicates with a *P.*

#### Guided Practice in Reading

Have students find subjects and predicates in sentences in "Alexander, Who Used to Be Rich Last Sunday." Ask them to note the page number. Have some students share their answers with the class.

# DAY 3

## Word Analysis

### Spelling

**Final Double Consonants**

#### Teach

- Introduce the words with final double consonants found in "Alexander, Who Used to Be Rich Last Sunday."
- Ask students to think of words that contain final double consonants around the school. *(bell, hall)*

#### Guided Practice

Have students complete page 80 from ***Spelling and Vocabulary Skills*** to learn strategies for spelling words with final double consonants.

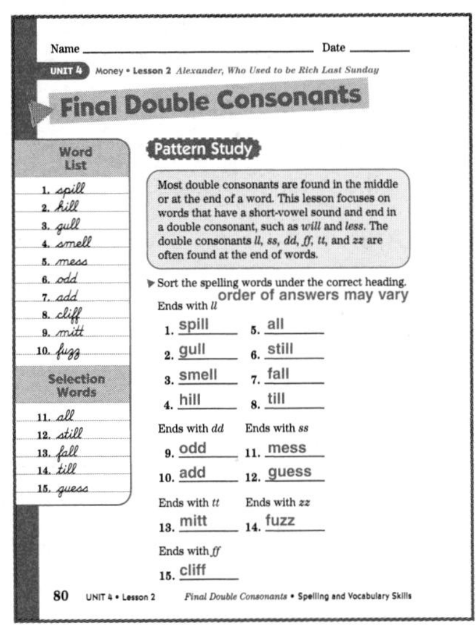

Name ______ Date ______

UNIT 4 Money • Lesson 2 *Alexander, Who Used to be Rich Last Sunday*

**Final Double Consonants**

**Word List**

1. spill
2. hill
3. gull
4. smell
5. mess
6. odd
7. add
8. cliff
9. mitt
10. fuzz

**Selection Words**

11. all
12. still
13. fall
14. till
15. guess

**Pattern Study**

Most double consonants are found in the middle or at the end of a word. This lesson focuses on words that have a short-vowel sound and end in a double consonant, such as *will* and *less*. The double consonants *ll*, *ss*, *dd*, *ff*, *tt*, and *zz* are often found at the end of words.

▸ Sort the spelling words under the correct heading.

order of answers may vary

Ends with *ll*

1. spill 5. all
2. gull 6. still
3. smell 7. fall
4. hill 8. till

Ends with *dd*

9. odd
10. add

Ends with *ss*

11. mess
12. guess

Ends with *tt*

13. mitt

Ends with *zz*

14. fuzz

Ends with *ff*

15. cliff

80 UNIT 4 • Lesson 2 *Final Double Consonants* • Spelling and Vocabulary Skills

***Spelling and Vocabulary Skills* p. 80**

### Vocabulary (continued)

**The Suffix *-ly***

- Write *mostly* on the board.
- Ask a student to read the sentence in "Alexander, Who Used to Be Rich Last Sunday" (p. 26) with *mostly.* Ask a student to write the base word for *mostly* that is also found in the sentence. *(most)*
- Ask the students what *mostly* means. *(in most ways)*
- Explain to students that they are proving their knowledge of suffixes and therefore a new knowledge of certain words.

## Writing Process Strategies

### Drafting

**Persuasive Poster**

#### Teach

- Read ***Writer's Workbook,*** page 59, on drafting a persuasive poster.
- Remind students to look over their prewriting plans to review the reasons they came up with to persuade their readers.
- Model for students how you would begin to arrange your poster persuading children to save money. Explain ideas you have for art and text placement, as well as for the content of your text. For example, you could tell them you will put a picture of a circus in the middle with sentences at the top that read: The circus is coming! Will you be able to afford it?

#### Guided Practice

**Drafting**

- Have students write or type their drafts and put them in their ***Writing Folders,*** including any artwork they want to use.
- Encourage students to write each idea for persuading as a sentence that can be included on their posters.

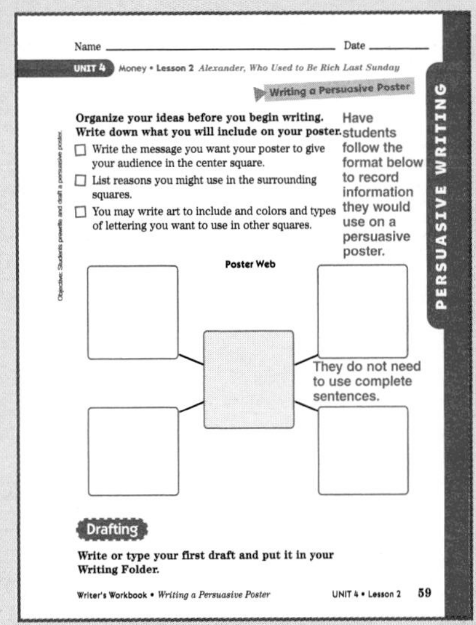

Name ______ Date ______

UNIT 4 Money • Lesson 2 *Alexander, Who Used to Be Rich Last Sunday*

Writing a Persuasive Poster

PERSUASIVE WRITING

Objective: Students prewrite and draft a persuasive poster.

**Organize your ideas before you begin writing. Write down what you will include on your poster.**

Have students follow the format below to record information they would use on a persuasive poster.

- ☐ Write the message you want your poster to give your audience in the center square.
- ☐ List reasons you might use in the surrounding squares.
- ☐ You may write art to include and colors and types of lettering you want to use in other squares.

**Poster Web**

They do not need to use complete sentences.

**Drafting**

**Write or type your first draft and put it in your Writing Folder.**

Writer's Workbook • *Writing a Persuasive Poster* UNIT 4 • Lesson 2 59

***Writer's Workbook* p. 59**

## English Language Conventions

### Grammar, Usage, and Mechanics

**Grammar: Subjects and Predicates**

#### Teach

- Review subjects and predicates using ***Comprehension and Language Arts Skills,*** pages 98–99.
- Write the following definitions on the board and lead a discussion about them.
  - *Sentence: a group of words that contains a complete thought*
  - *Subject: names who or what a sentence is about*
  - *Predicate: tells what the subject is or does*
- Encourage students to ask questions about anything they don't understand.

#### Guided Practice in Writing

Have students think of something expensive they want. Ask them to write a paragraph about how they might earn the money to buy it. Have some students read their paragraphs slowly, as you write each sentence on the board. Ask students to identify the subjects and predicates.

**Informal Assessment**

Check students' writing to make sure all of their sentences include a subject and a predicate.

# DAY 4

## Word Analysis

### Spelling

**Final Double Consonants**

#### Teach

- Explain that these exercises in ***Spelling and Vocabulary Skills*** are designed to help them learn to become better spellers of words with final double consonants.
- Demonstrate the Rhyming Strategy by writing *will* and *spill* on the board. Explain how knowing the spelling pattern of *will* can help them know how to spell other rhyming words, such as *spill*, *hill*, and *still*.

#### Guided Practice

Have students complete page 81 of ***Spelling and Vocabulary Skills*** to reinforce the spelling patterns for words with final double consonants.

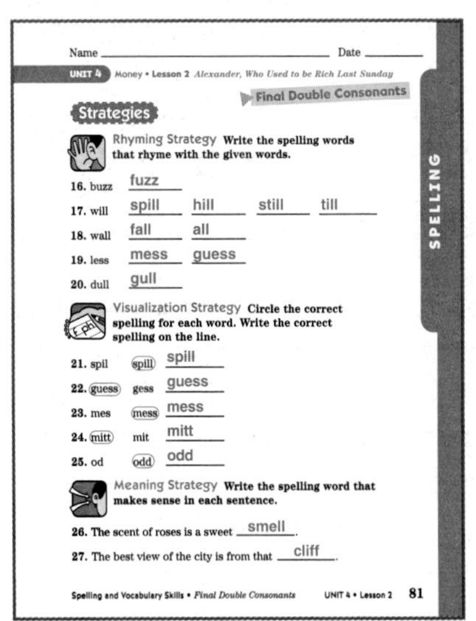

Name ______ Date ______

UNIT 4 Money • Lesson 2 *Alexander, Who Used to be Rich Last Sunday*

Final Double Consonants

SPELLING

Strategies

Rhyming Strategy **Write the spelling words that rhyme with the given words.**

16. buzz fuzz
17. will spill hill still till
18. wall fall all
19. less mess guess
20. dull gull

Visualization Strategy **Circle the correct spelling for each word. Write the correct spelling on the line.**

21. spil (spill) spill
22. (guess) gess guess
23. mes (mess) mess
24. (mitt) mit mitt
25. od (odd) odd

Meaning Strategy **Write the spelling word that makes sense in each sentence.**

26. The scent of roses is a sweet smell.
27. The best view of the city is from that cliff.

Spelling and Vocabulary Skills • *Final Double Consonants* UNIT 4 • Lesson 2 81

***Spelling and Vocabulary Skills* p. 81**

### Vocabulary (continued)

**The Suffix *-ly***

- Write *really* on the board. Ask one student to circle the suffix *-ly* in *really*.
- Ask the students what the word *really* means. *(in a real way)*
- Ask a student to write a sentence on the board that uses and defines *really*. *(The students really wanted to do well on the test.)*

## Writing Process Strategies

### Revising

**Persuasive Poster**

#### Teach

- Read ***Writer's Workbook,*** page 60, on revising a persuasive poster.
- Discuss ***Language Arts Transparency 18,*** Revising: Deleting Copy. Discuss with students that too much copy on a poster may make it difficult to read.
- Remind students to view their posters with their audience and purpose in mind.

**Troubleshooting**

- Too many words on the poster will make it look cluttered and difficult to read.
- Too few words on the poster may make it difficult for readers to understand the point.

#### Guided Practice

**Revising**

- Have students revise their persuasive posters and put them in their ***Writing Folders.***
- Have students use the checklist on ***Writer's Workbook,*** page 60, to revise their posters.

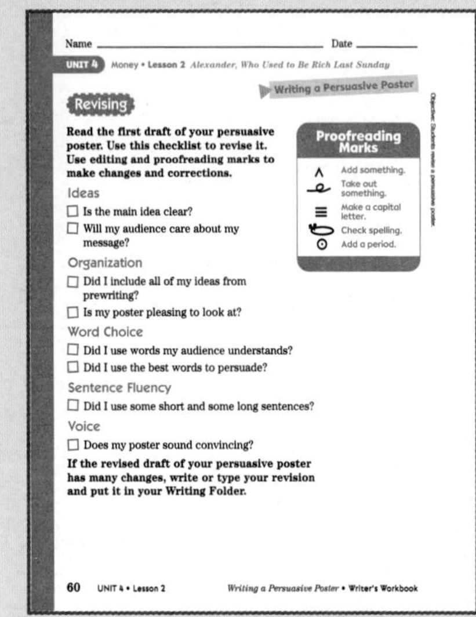

Name ______ Date ______

UNIT 4 Money • Lesson 2 *Alexander, Who Used to Be Rich Last Sunday*

Writing a Persuasive Poster

Revising

**Read the first draft of your persuasive poster. Use this checklist to revise it. Use editing and proofreading marks to make changes and corrections.**

Ideas

- ☐ Is the main idea clear?
- ☐ Will my audience care about my message?

Organization

- ☐ Did I include all of my ideas from prewriting?
- ☐ Is my poster pleasing to look at?

Word Choice

- ☐ Did I use words my audience understands?
- ☐ Did I use the best words to persuade?

Sentence Fluency

- ☐ Did I use some short and some long sentences?

Voice

- ☐ Does my poster sound convincing?

**If the revised draft of your persuasive poster has many changes, write or type your revision and put it in your Writing Folder.**

Proofreading Marks

- ∧ Add something.
- Take out something.
- ≡ Make a capital letter.
- Check spelling.
- ⊙ Add a period.

Objective: Students revise a persuasive poster.

60 UNIT 4 • Lesson 2 *Writing a Persuasive Poster* • Writer's Workbook

***Writer's Workbook* p. 60**

## English Language Conventions

### Listening, Speaking, Viewing

**Speaking: Elements of Grammar**

#### Teach

Explain the importance of using proper grammar and clear, specific words when we speak. What we say is often taken more seriously when we use clear words and proper English grammar.

#### Guided Practice

- In small groups, have students discuss the plot of the poem "Smart" and their personal reactions. *(Do they like the poem; did they find it amusing; is the boy really "smart"?)* Remind students to use proper grammar to discuss the poem. Instruct them to use the appropriate verb for the subject, to use singular and plural nouns correctly, and to use a variety of verb tenses in order to add dimension to their discussions.
- As a class, observe and discuss the grammar of the poem. Have students use clear and specific vocabulary to communicate their ideas. When does the speaker of the poem use improper grammar? *("he don't know")* Why is this incorrect? *(According to the subject, he, the correct verb would be "does" instead of "do.")*

**Informal Assessment**

Observe whether students understand how using correct elements of grammar can aid their speech.

# DAY 5

## Word Analysis

### Spelling

#### Assessment: Final Test

**Final Double Consonants**

**Teach**

Repeat the Pretest or use the Final Test on page 33 of ***Unit 4 Assessment*** as summative assessment of student understanding of spelling words with final double consonants.

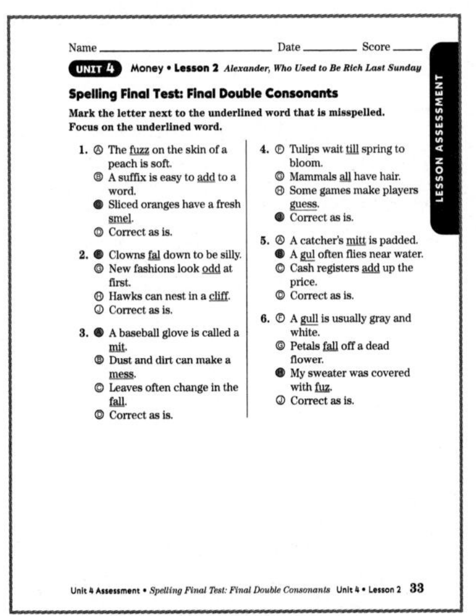

Name ________ Date ______ Score ____

UNIT 4 Money • **Lesson 2** *Alexander, Who Used to Be Rich Last Sunday*

LESSON ASSESSMENT

**Spelling Final Test: Final Double Consonants**

**Mark the letter next to the underlined word that is misspelled. Focus on the underlined word.**

1. Ⓐ The fuzz on the skin of a peach is soft.
   Ⓑ A suffix is easy to add to a word.
   ● Sliced oranges have a fresh smel.
   Ⓓ Correct as is.
2. ● Clowns fal down to be silly.
   Ⓖ New fashions look odd at first.
   Ⓗ Hawks can nest in a cliff.
   Ⓙ Correct as is.
3. ● A baseball glove is called a mit.
   Ⓑ Dust and dirt can make a mess.
   Ⓒ Leaves often change in the fall.
   Ⓓ Correct as is.
4. Ⓕ Tulips wait till spring to bloom.
   Ⓖ Mammals all have hair.
   Ⓗ Some games make players guess.
   ● Correct as is.
5. Ⓐ A catcher's mitt is padded.
   ● A gul often flies near water.
   Ⓒ Cash registers add up the price.
   Ⓓ Correct as is.
6. Ⓕ A gull is usually gray and white.
   Ⓖ Petals fall off a dead flower.
   ● My sweater was covered with fuz.
   Ⓙ Correct as is.

Unit 4 Assessment • *Spelling Final Test: Final Double Consonants* Unit 4 • Lesson 2 33

***Unit 4 Assessment p. 33***

**Guided Practice**

Have students categorize any mistakes they made on the Final Test as careless errors or lesson-pattern problems.

### Vocabulary

**Informal Assessment**

**Periodically check students' writing assignments to see that students are properly changing the *y* to *i* when adding the suffix *-ly* to words that end in *y*. Have students add any new words to the running Vocabulary Word List in the Writer's Notebook.**

## Writing Process Strategies

### Editing/Proofreading and Publishing

**Persuasive Poster**

**Teach**

Read ***Writer's Workbook,*** page 61, on editing/proofreading and publishing.

**Guided Practice**

**Editing/Proofreading and Publishing**

- Have students edit/proofread their posters.
- Direct students to use the checklist on ***Writer's Workbook,*** page 61, to help them edit their posters.
- Refer to the Grammar, Usage, and Mechanics Subjects and Predicates lesson on page 35F.
- Have students hang their posters in the classroom.

**Formal Assessment**

**Total Point Value: 10**

1. **Color and design have been used effectively. (2 points)**
2. **The main idea is clearly stated. (2 points)**
3. **Reasons supporting the main idea are clear and precise. (2 points)**
4. **Every sentence has a subject and predicate. (2 points)**
5. **The mechanics are correct. (2 points)**

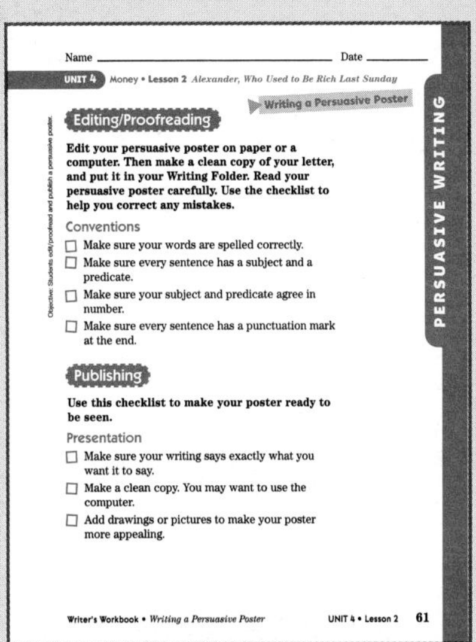

Name ________ Date ______

UNIT 4 Money • **Lesson 2** *Alexander, Who Used to Be Rich Last Sunday*

Writing a Persuasive Poster

PERSUASIVE WRITING

Objective: Students edit/proofread and publish a persuasive poster.

**Editing/Proofreading**

**Edit your persuasive poster on paper or a computer. Then make a clean copy of your letter, and put it in your Writing Folder. Read your persuasive poster carefully. Use the checklist to help you correct any mistakes.**

Conventions

- ☐ Make sure your words are spelled correctly.
- ☐ Make sure every sentence has a subject and a predicate.
- ☐ Make sure your subject and predicate agree in number.
- ☐ Make sure every sentence has a punctuation mark at the end.

**Publishing**

**Use this checklist to make your poster ready to be seen.**

Presentation

- ☐ Make sure your writing says exactly what you want it to say.
- ☐ Make a clean copy. You may want to use the computer.
- ☐ Add drawings or pictures to make your poster more appealing.

Writer's Workbook • *Writing a Persuasive Poster* UNIT 4 • Lesson 2 61

***Writer's Workbook p. 61***

## English Language Conventions

### Penmanship

**Cursive Letters *E* and *O***

**Teach**

- **Teacher Model:** Introduce formation of uppercase *E* and *O* as downcurve letters by demonstrating on the board.

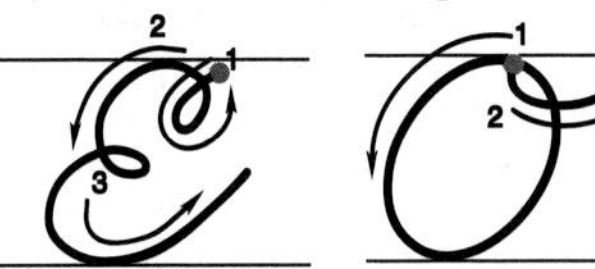

**E** Starting point, loop around left
Downcurve
Loop back, downcurve
Undercurve: capital *E*

**O** Starting point, downcurve left
Undercurve
Loop and curve right: capital *O*

- **Teacher Model:** Write the following sentence to model proper letter formation: "Edgar lives in Oakland."
- Use the example sentence to show students how they should leave enough space between the letters so that they do not touch, except for where they join.

**Guided Practice**

- Have students practice writing rows of *E*s and *O*s in the Writer's Notebook.
- From "Alexander, Who Used to be Rich Last Sunday," have students write the words *Except*, *some*, and *money* to practice letter formation.

**Informal Assessment**

**Check students' handwriting for proper spacing between letters in a word and proper formation of *E* and *O*.**

# Reading and Language Arts Skills Traces

## Language Arts

### WORD ANALYSIS

**Skills Trace**

**Spelling: Final Double Consonants**

Introduced in Grade 3.
Scaffolded throughout Grades 3–5.

**INTRODUCED:** **Unit 4, Lesson 2**, p. 35E
**PRACTICED:** **Unit 4, Lesson 2**, pp. 35F–35J
*Spelling and Vocabulary Skills,* pp. 80–81
**TESTED:** **Unit 4, Lesson 2**, p. 35F (Pretest)
**Unit 4, Lesson 2**, p. 33 (Final Test)
**Unit 4 Assessment**

**Skills Trace**

**Vocabulary: The Suffix *-ly***

Introduced in Grade 2.
Scaffolded throughout Grades 2–5.

**REINTRODUCED:** **Unit 4, Lesson 2**, p. 35E
**PRACTICED:** **Unit 4, Lesson 2**, pp. 35G–35J
*Spelling and Vocabulary Skills,* pp. 78–79
**TESTED:** **Unit 4 Assessment**

### WRITING PROCESS STRATEGIES

**Skills Trace**

**Persuasive Writing: Persuasive Poster**

Introduced in Grade K.
Scaffolded throughout Grades 1–3, 5.

**REINTRODUCED:** **Unit 4, Lesson 2**, p. 35F
**PRACTICED:** **Unit 4, Lesson 2**, pp. 35G–35J
*Writer's Workbook,* pp. 58–61
**TESTED:** **Unit 4, Lesson 2,**
Formal Assessment, p. 35J
**Unit 4 Assessment**

**Skills Trace**

**Writer's Craft: Time-Order Words**

Introduced in Grade K.
Scaffolded throughout Grades 1–6.

**REINTRODUCED:** **Unit 4, Lesson 2**, p. 35G
**PRACTICED:** **Unit 4, Lesson 2**, p. 35G
*Comprehension and Language Arts Skills,* pp. 100–101
**TESTED:** **Unit 4 Assessment**

### ENGLISH LANGUAGE CONVENTIONS

**Skills Trace**

**Grammar: Subject and Predicates**

Introduced in Grade 1.
Scaffolded throughout Grades 2–6.

**REINTRODUCED:** **Unit 4, Lesson 2**, p. 35F
**PRACTICED:** **Unit 4, Lesson 2**, p. 35G
**Unit 4, Lesson 2**, p. 35H
*Comprehension and Language Arts Skills,* pp. 98–99
**TESTED:** **Unit 4, Lesson 2,**
Informal Assessment, p. 35H
**Unit 4 Assessment**

**Skills Trace**

**Listening, Speaking, Viewing Speaking: Elements of Grammar**

Introduced in Grade 3.
Scaffolded throughout Grades 4–6.

**INTRODUCED:** **Unit 4, Lesson 2**, p. 35I
**TESTED:** **Unit 4, Lesson 2,**
Informal Assessment, p. 35I

**Skills Trace**

**Penmanship: Cursive Letters *E* and *O***

Introduced in Grade 3.
Scaffolded throughout Grades 4–6.

**INTRODUCED:** **Unit 4, Lesson 2**, p. 35J
**TESTED:** **Unit 4, Lesson 2,**
Informal Assessment, p. 35J

## Reading

### COMPREHENSION

**Skills Trace**

**Cause and Effect**

Introduced in Grade 1.
Scaffolded throughout Grades 2 and 3.

**REINTRODUCED:** **Unit 1, Lesson 2**
**REINFORCED:** **Unit 1, Lesson 4**
**Unit 2, Lesson 4**
**Unit 2, Lesson 5**
**Unit 4, Lesson 2**
**Unit 4, Lesson 7**
**Unit 6, Lesson 6**
**TESTED:** **Unit 4 Assessment**

# Professional Development: Assessment

## The Changing Face of Reading Assessment

Reading assessment has moved away from being based predominantly on multiple-choice items and toward requiring students to be more active, or *constructive*, in responding. Formal, standardized assessment, while retaining an important role in education, is being supplemented by teacher observations, samples of students' work, and other activities that can be used to infer achievement and reading progress. The new, or *alternative*, forms of assessment are called by several names, including *authentic* assessment and *performance-based* assessment. Whatever the name, the idea behind alternative assessment is that testing should be an integral part of instruction, not the end purpose of learning (Reichel, 1994).

One reason for the shift in reading assessment is that traditional, standardized tests provide relatively little instructional guidance (García & Pearson, 1994; Shepard, 1989; Stallman & Pearson, 1990). Although alternative assessments have shortcomings that prevent their widespread use for accountability purposes, they provide a great deal of meaningful instructional guidance (Pearson et al., 1998). A second reason for the shift is a new concept of reading. The traditional perspective of reading was more or less that students either did or did not read and comprehend what they read. Recent views of reading interpret reading as a more dynamic act that includes a variety of skills and active processing by the reader—processing that reflects the reader's background, prior knowledge, preferences, and so forth (Anderson & Pearson, 1984; Rumelhart, 1985).

One of the greatest advantages of alternative assessments is that students actually may learn in the process of engaging in assessment. From taking a traditional multiple-choice comprehension test, students may learn little more than surface knowledge of a passage (Winograd, Paris, & Bridge, 1991). An alternative assessment that involves having a student write or tell about a passage that she or he has read, engage in a reading-related investigations, or make a presentation about the reading often creates highly motivating learning opportunities and gives the teacher great insights into a student's ability.

Another advantage of alternative assessment is that students have more time to respond than they do when they take a standardized test. The lack of a time anchor diminishes the psychometric or scientific measurement properties of alternative assessment, though it gives students an opportunity to demonstrate what they really can do under conditions that reflect real reading.

Assessment, whether traditional or alternative, is only a sample of behavior from which conclusions can be drawn and generalizations made. In the case of a traditional test, the behavior sample is a single event that occurs in a relatively short duration of time. In alternative assessment, the sample is drawn over a longer time period and involves complex thinking, problem solving, and continuous feedback (Wiggins, 1993). Students:

- construct responses instead of choosing one correct answer.
- solve a problem or apply principles instead of responding to text by choosing an answer, usually from four options, that is "more correct" than the others.
- apply several skills at once, rather than depending on an isolated skill.

Although alternative assessments have enjoyed increasing popularity, their widespread use has been limited by a number of factors. They are difficult to score and are highly susceptible to subjective interpretation. The time and effort involved mean they cost more to develop and to score. They lack the rigor of traditional assessments. Finally, for certain students, alternative assessments may be just as unfair as traditional assessments. For example, students who are good at presenting their ideas may be overrated when compared to students who comprehend what they read just as well but cannot present their ideas as clearly as other students (Mehrens, 1992; Pearson et al., 1998).

Additional information about assessment as well as resource references can be found in the ***Professional Development Guide: Assessment.***

## Activating Prior Knowledge

- Ask students if they have ever counted change back. Have they wondered how fewer coins can be worth more than more coins?
- Ask students if they have ever lost money. How did they lose it? How did that make them feel?

## Reading the Poem

- Read the poems aloud twice in a voice that reflects the humor of each poem. Encourage students to close their eyes as you read and listen very carefully.
- Help students understand the meaning of *swapped. (traded)*
- Prompt students to share the emotions that they feel while listening to this poem.
- In the time you designate for Workshop, you may encourage students to listen to the poems recorded on the ***Listening Library Audiocassette/CD.***

**Teacher Tip** Students may be familiar with books written by Shel Silverstein. The illustrations and short poems in Silverstein's books could be used to prompt a lively discussion about Author's Purpose. *(to entertain)*

**Focus Questions** What is it like to trade something you have for something you want? How do you know that what you get from a trade is more valuable to you than what you give?

# Smart

Shel Silverstein

My dad gave me one dollar bill
'Cause I'm his smartest son,
And I swapped it for two shiny quarters
'Cause two is more than one!

And then I took the quarters
And traded them to Lou
For three dimes—I guess he don't know
That three is more than two!

Just then, along came old blind Bates
And just 'cause he can't see
He gave me four nickels for my three dimes,
And four is more than three!

And I took the nickels to Hiram Coombs
Down at the seed-feed store,
And the fool gave me five pennies for them,
And five is more than four!

And then I went and showed my dad,
And he got red in the cheeks
And closed his eyes and shook his head—
Too proud of me to speak!

36

### Differentiating Instruction

| If... | Then... |
|---|---|
| Students are having difficulty understanding the meaning of the poem | Make available the different denominations mentioned in the poem and help students compare the sums |

*Focus Questions* When you have extra money to spend, what do you do with it? What do you think is more valuable, money or friendship?

# Tony and the Quarter

Jack Prelutsky • *illustrated by Victoria Chess*

Tony's my neighbor
and Tony's my friend.
Today Tony's ma
gave him money to spend.

He slapped my behind
and he said with a laugh,
"Whatever I get,
you can have almost half.

I got a whole quarter,
I'll split it with you.
Let's go get some candy
and bubble gum too."

So happily downhill
the two of us tore,
to see what a quarter
would buy at the store.

But things didn't work
just the way that we planned,
Tony tripped—and the quarter
flew out of his hand.

It rolled down the sidewalk
and oh, what a pain!
We couldn't catch up
and it went down the drain.

Such a dumb thing to do,
oh, it made me so sore.
Still, I guess I like Tony
as much as before.

37

## Writer's Notebook

Have the students print the following question in their Writer's Notebooks.

- What lesson do the poems teach about money?

Then have students write their answers in the response section of their Writer's Notebooks.

## Meet the Poets

Shel Silverstein was a cartoonist, recording artist, writer, playwright, actor, composer of movie soundtracks, and a songwriter. He wrote and illustrated fiction for both children and adults.

Silverstein began writing and illustrating as a child growing up in Chicago. Today his children's book and poetry collections include *A Light in the Attic*, *Where the Sidewalk Ends*, and *The Giving Tree.*

Jack Prelutsky has many different interests, including baseball, cooking, photography, and collecting frog figurines. Prelutsky's childhood experiences in New York City often turn up again in his stories for children. Books by Prelutsky include *The New Kid on the Block*, *Ride a Purple Pelican*, and *Tyrannosaurus Was a Beast.* Several of Prelutsky's works, including *The Snopp on the Sidewalk and Other Poems*, were honored as ALA Notable Books. He has said that the book he treasures the most is *The New Kid on the Block*, although his favorite book is usually the one he's working on at the time.

**Teacher Tip** You may want to tie the friendship aspect of this poem to knowledge that students gleaned from the Friendship unit.

## Differentiating Instruction

| If... | Then... |
| --- | --- |
| Students need extra practice identifying the words that rhyme | Have them listen to the poems on the ***Listening Library Audiocassette/CD*** |

## ELEMENTS OF POETRY

As students study poetry, they will learn that there are many elements that make up a poem. Have students look at "Smart" and "Tony and the Quarter" and discuss the following elements with them.

### Rhyme

Explain that in these two poems words at the end of certain lines rhyme. Reread "Smart." Then ask students to identify the words that rhyme at the end of certain lines. Ask students to identify which lines rhyme. Explain that many poets write verses with rhyming lines occurring in a regular pattern. If poets vary the pattern, they usually do so for some significant reason that affects the meaning of the poem. For example, a poem about something scary might have an irregular rhyming pattern during a verse to communicate a feeling of anxiousness. These poems, however, both feature a regular rhyming pattern. This is part of the light, upbeat, and humorous tones of the poems. Reread "Tony and the Quarter" and again, ask students to identify which words rhyme and which lines rhyme.

### Writing

Have students respond to poetry by writing poems of their own. Have students think about a time when they lost money or spent more than they meant to spend. Tell them they can use the poems they just read as a model. Have them experiment with rhyming lines two and four, and encourage them to write at least one full verse of four lines.

## Presentation

### Diction

Poetry is a special kind of writing that is most often meant to be read aloud. Poems, more than any other type of writing, often emphasize rhythm and rhyme. When reading a poem aloud, readers should properly emphasize the rhythm and rhyme of the poem without overexaggerating to the point that the reading seems forced. One way to emphasize rhyme is simply to pronounce words clearly when reading.

Often when reading in public, speakers feel shy and mumble the words through half-closed mouths. Remind students to speak clearly and move their mouths enough to fully pronounce each syllable they read. They should pay special attention to the ends of words and the ends of lines, which many speakers drop to the point that they are practically inaudible to the audience.

Have students practice reading the poems in pairs or in small groups, paying particular attention to completely pronouncing the ends of words and lines. Then, when students feel comfortable with the exercise, invite them to read for the whole class one of the poems they studied as a group or one of their own creation.



**Teacher Tip** PRESENTATION If students are reading "Smart" or "Tony and the Quarter" to the class, have them read it as the character would read it. For example, when reading "Tony and the Quarter," students should be reading the poem as if they were Tony's neighbor. Tell them to adopt the attitude and frame of mind of the character. Tell them to read the poem as if they really were that character, using the character's tone of voice, pacing, volume, accents, and so on.

### Differentiating Instruction

| If... | Then... |
|---|---|
| Students need practice building fluency | Have them read the poems aloud into a tape recorder and then listen to how they read |

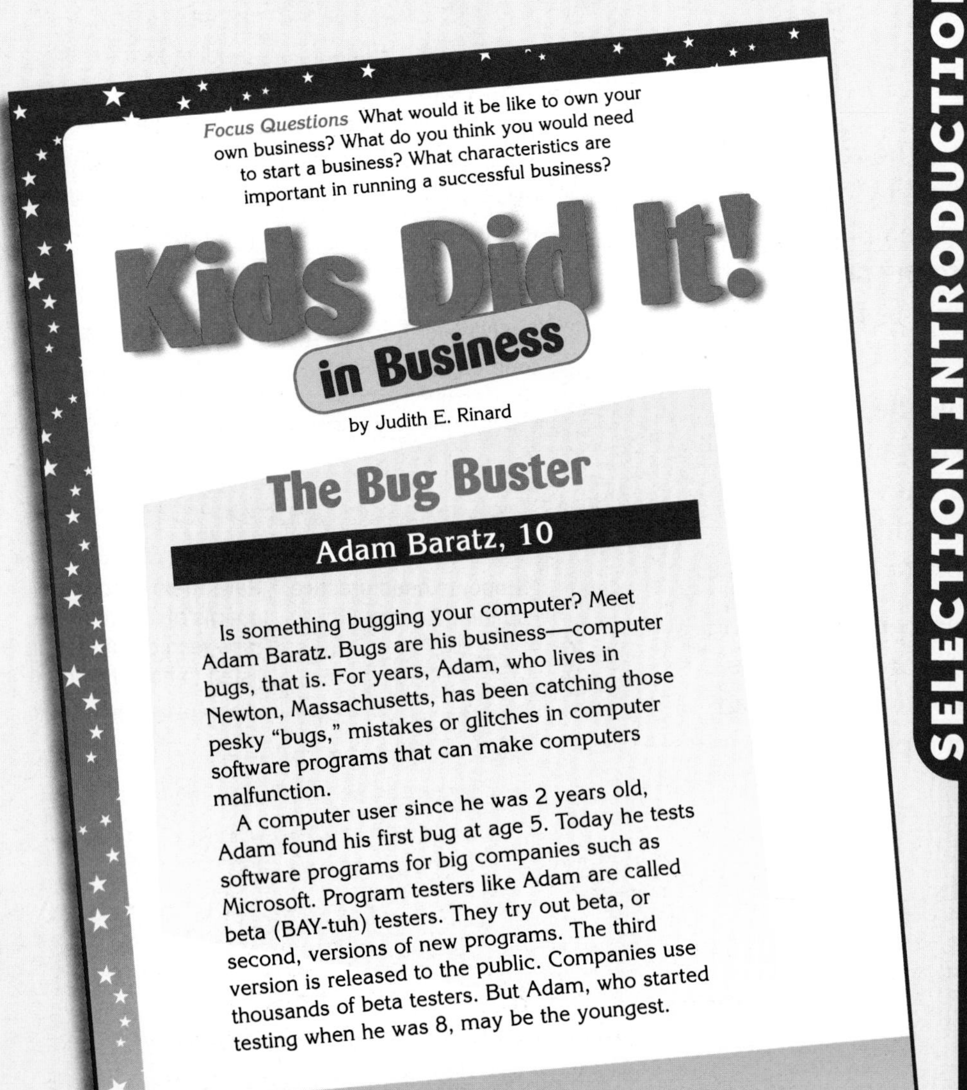

*Focus Questions* What would it be like to own your own business? What do you think you would need to start a business? What characteristics are important in running a successful business?

# Kids Did It! in Business

by Judith E. Rinard

## The Bug Buster

### Adam Baratz, 10

Is something bugging your computer? Meet Adam Baratz. Bugs are his business—computer bugs, that is. For years, Adam, who lives in Newton, Massachusetts, has been catching those pesky "bugs," mistakes or glitches in computer software programs that can make computers malfunction.

A computer user since he was 2 years old, Adam found his first bug at age 5. Today he tests software programs for big companies such as Microsoft. Program testers like Adam are called beta (BAY-tuh) testers. They try out beta, or second, versions of new programs. The third version is released to the public. Companies use thousands of beta testers. But Adam, who started testing when he was 8, may be the youngest.

38

SELECTION INTRODUCTION

## Selection Summary

### Genre: Expository Text

"Kids Did It! in Business" features four successful businesspeople. What makes these four people unique in the business world is their age—they're all kids! Their businesses include finding bugs in computer programs, inventing a gadget that has become the family business, catering parties, and designing and selling greeting cards. The article profiles each child, with quotes and photographs.

Major elements of expository text include:

- Expository text gives information. It tells people something.
- It contains facts about real events or people.
- It presents information in a straightforward way.
- It may be organized by topics.
- It may contain diagrams, photographs, and other illustrations.
- It contains information that can be checked by looking at other sources.

## About the Author

**JUDITH RINARD** was born in Mason City, Iowa. She attended Drake University and the University of Toronto, where she was awarded a Bachelor of Arts in Religion.

A resident of Silver Spring, Maryland, Rinard enjoys traveling, painting, and camping. She has many titles to her credit and enjoys writing on the subjects of Spanish-speaking Latin Americans and Native Americans. Rinard believes children share her enthusiasm for learning about people and cultures different from their own.

Students can read more about Judith Rinard on page 47 of the ***Student Anthology.***

## Inquiry Connections

Children are ingenious, creative, and responsive in the businesses they imagine and go on to build. "Kids Did It! in Business" is an article about young people who develop their own ways of making money. Whether it is a computer business or making and selling fashion accessories, greeting cards, or a cooking device, these children have learned some of the basics of successful business. Key concepts explored are:

- Understanding that starting a business is one way to make money.
- Understanding that kids can start businesses.
- Learning about what is involved in starting and running a business.

Before reading the selection:

- Point out that students may post a question, concept, word, illustration, or object on the Concept/Question Board at any time during the course of their unit investigations. Be sure that students include their name or initials on the items they post so that others will know to whom to go if they have an answer or if they wish to collaborate on a related activity.
- Students should feel free to write an answer or a note on someone else's question or to consult the Board for ideas for their own investigations throughout the unit.
- Encourage students to read about money at home and to bring in articles or pictures that are good examples to post on the Board.

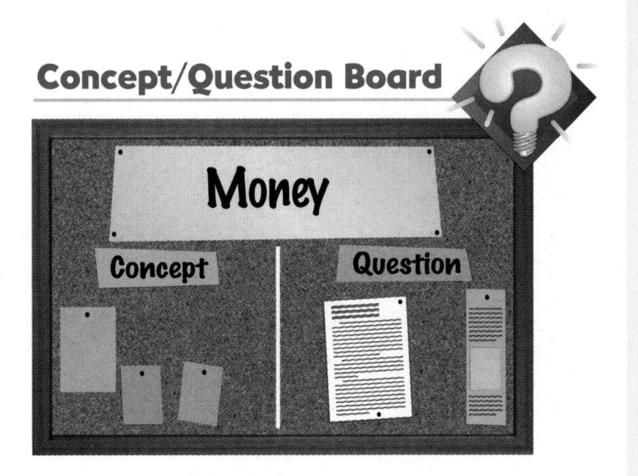

## Leveled Practice

**Reteach**
**Pages 105–108**

**Challenge**
**Pages 92–95**

**English Learner Support Activities**

**Intervention Workbook**

**Decodable Book 31**

## Leveled Classroom Library*

Encourage students to read at least 30 minutes daily outside of class. Have them read books in the ***Leveled Classroom Library*** to support the unit theme and help students develop their vocabulary by reading independently.

### *Lemonade for Sale*

BY STUART J. MURPHY. HARPERCOLLINS JUVENILE, 1998.

The kids at the Elm Street Kids' Club use a clever combination of lemonade, bar graphs, and a juggler to make big profits that will help them repair their club. **(Easy)**

### *Saturday Sancocho*

BY LEYLA TORRES. FARRAR, STRAUS & GIROUX, 1995.

Every Saturday, Maria Lili shares a meal with her grandparents, eating Chicken Sancocho, until the weekend comes when money is tight and they are missing essential ingredients. Mama Ana barters with her eggs for the final ingredients, saving the day. **(Average)**

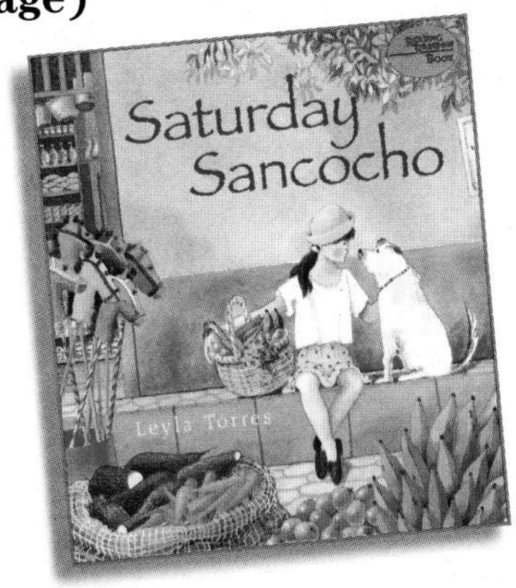


### *Our Money*

BY KAREN BORNEMANN SPIES. THE MILLBROOK PRESS, 1994.

Chronicling the changes American money has undergone, this book explains money ranging from wampum to today's currency. Also discussed are counterfeiting and minting procedures. **(Advanced)**

* These books, which all support the unit theme Money, are part of a 36-book ***Leveled Classroom Library*** available for purchase from SRA/McGraw-Hill. Note: Teachers should preview any trade books for appropriateness in their classrooms before recommending them to students.

## SRA TECHNOLOGY

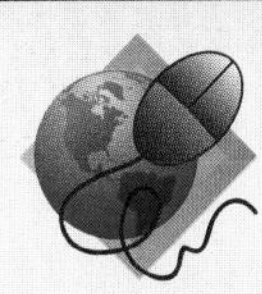

### Web Connections

- Money Web Site
- Online Professional Development
- Online Phonics
- Online Assessment

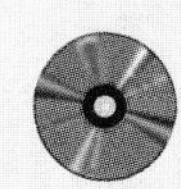

### CD-ROMs

- Research Assistant
- The Ultimate Writing and Creativity Center
- Teacher Resource Library

### Audiocassette/CD

Listening Library: Money

### Computer Skills

TechKnowledge

Materials are available through SRA/McGraw-Hill.

# UNIT 4 Lesson 3 Kids Did It! in Business

LESSON PLANNER

Suggested Pacing: 3–5 days

| | DAY 1 | DAY 2 |
|---|---|---|
| | DAY 1 | DAY 2 |
| **1 Preparing to Read**<br>**Materials**<br>■ Student Anthology, Book 2, pp. 38–47<br>■ Decodable Book 31<br>■ Routine Card 1, Routines 1–2 | **Word Knowledge,** pp. 38K–38L<br>■ compound words<br>■ base words and affixes<br>■ contractions<br>■ /ā/ sound spellings<br>**About the Words and Sentences,** p. 38K | **Word Knowledge**<br>**Developing Oral Language,** p. 38L |
| **2 Reading & Responding**<br>**Materials**<br>■ Student Anthology, Book 2, pp. 38–47<br>■ Program Assessment<br>■ Reading Transparencies 25, 46, 50<br>■ Inquiry Journal, p. 84<br>■ Science/Social Studies Connection Center Card 34<br>■ Home Connection, p. 49<br>■ Unit 4 Assessment, pp. 10–13<br>■ Writer's Notebook<br>■ Routine Cards 1, 2, Routines 3–6 | **Build Background,** p. 38M<br>**Preview and Prepare,** pp. 38M–38N<br>**Selection Vocabulary,** p. 38N<br>**Reading Recommendations,** pp. 38O–38P | **Student Anthology,** pp. 38–45 First Read<br>✓ **Comprehension Strategies**<br>■ Summarizing, p. 38<br>■ Making Connections, p. 40<br>■ Monitoring and Clarifying, pp. 42, 44<br>**Discussing Strategy Use,** p. 44<br>**Discussing the Selection,** p. 45A<br>■ Review Selection<br>■ Complete Discussion |
| **Inquiry**<br>**Materials**<br>■ Student Anthology, Book 2, pp. 38–47<br>■ Inquiry Journal, pp. 93–95<br>■ Research Assistant CD-ROM | **Investigation**<br>■ Investigating Concepts Beyond the Text, p. 47A | **Investigation**<br>■ Concept/Question Board, p. 47B |
| **3 Language Arts**<br>**Materials**<br>■ Spelling and Vocabulary Skills, pp. 82–85<br>■ Comprehension and Language Arts Skills, pp. 102–105<br>■ The Ultimate Writing and Creativity Center<br>■ Language Arts Handbook<br>■ Writer's Workbook, pp. 62–65<br>■ Language Arts Transparency 14<br>■ Student Anthology<br>■ Routine Card 2, Routine 7 | **Word Analysis**<br>✓■ Spelling: Contractions Pretest, p. 47F<br>**Writing Process Strategies**<br>■ Persuasive Writing: Business Letter, p. 47F<br>**English Language Conventions**<br>■ Mechanics: Periods in Abbreviations, Initials, and Titles; Parentheses, p. 47F | **Word Analysis**<br>■ Spelling: Contractions, p. 47G<br>■ Vocabulary: Business Vocabulary, p. 47G<br>**Writing Process Strategies**<br>■ Persuasive Writing: Business Letter, p. 47G<br>■ Writer's Craft: Structure of a Business Letter, p. 47G<br>**English Language Conventions**<br>■ Mechanics: Periods in Abbreviations, Initials, and Titles; Parentheses, p. 47G |



Ⓟ Phonics ✓ Informal Assessment Available ✓ Formal Assessment Available

| DAY 2 continued | DAY 3 | |
|---|---|---|
| **DAY 3** | **DAY 4** | **DAY 5** |
| **Word Knowledge**<br>**General Review** | **Word Knowledge**<br>**General Review** | **General Review** |
| **Student Anthology,** pp. 38–45 Second Read<br>**Comprehension Skills**<br>■ Main Idea and Details, pp. 39, 41, 43, 45<br>**Checking Comprehension,** p. 45<br>**Supporting the Reading,** p. 45C<br>■ Making Connections<br>**Student Anthology**<br>✓■ Concept Connections, p. 46<br>■ Meet the Author, p. 47 | **Review Selection Vocabulary,** p. 45B<br>**Literary Elements,** p. 45D<br>■ Expository Texts<br>**Social Studies Connection**<br>■ Money in History, p. 45E | ✓**Selection Assessment**<br>■ "Kids Did It! in Business," pp. 10–13<br>**Home Connection,** p. 45B<br>**Science Connection**<br>■ Inventions and Inventors, p. 45F |
| ✓**Investigation**<br>■ Conjecture Phase, p. 47C | **Supporting the Investigation**<br>■ Parts of a Book, p. 47D | **Investigation**<br>■ Unit Investigation Continued<br>■ Update Concept/Question Board |
| **Word Analysis**<br>■ Spelling: Contractions, p. 47H<br>■ Vocabulary: Business Vocabulary, p. 47H<br>**Writing Process Strategies**<br>■ Persuasive Writing: Business Letter, p. 47H<br>**English Language Conventions**<br>✓■ Mechanics: Periods in Abbreviations, Initials, and Titles; Parentheses, p. 47H | **Word Analysis**<br>■ Spelling: Contractions, p. 47I<br>■ Vocabulary: Business Vocabulary, p. 47I<br>**Writing Process Strategies**<br>■ Persuasive Writing: Business Letter, p. 47I<br>**English Language Conventions**<br>✓■ Listening, Speaking, Viewing Language: Choosing Words, p. 47I | **Word Analysis**<br>✓■ Spelling: Contractions Final Test<br>✓■ Vocabulary: Business Vocabulary, p. 47J<br>**Writing Process Strategies**<br>✓■ Persuasive Writing: Business Letter, p. 47J<br>**English Language Conventions**<br>✓■ Penmanship: Cursive Letters *N* and *M,* p. 47J |

Below are suggestions for differentiating instruction. These are the same skills shown in the Lesson Planner; however, these pages provide extra practice opportunities or enriching activities to meet the varied needs of students.

WORKSHOP

# Differentiating Instruction

## Teacher Directed: Individual and Small-Group Instruction

Spend time each day with individuals and small groups to individualize instruction. Each day:

- preteach students who need help with the next lesson.
- reteach students who need to solidify their understanding of content previously taught.
- listen to students read to check their fluency.
- hold writing and inquiry conferences.

Use the following program components to support instruction:

- ***Reteach*** with students who need a bit more practice
- ***Intervention*** for students who exhibit a lack of understanding of the lesson concepts
- ***English Learner Support*** with students who need language help

## Student: Independent Activities

Students can work alone, with a partner, or in small groups on such activities as:

- Review sound/spellings
- Practice dictation words
- Partner reading
- Practice fluency
- Independent reading
- Reading Roundtable
- Concept vocabulary
- Selection vocabulary
- Writing in progress
- Conference
- Language Arts
- Challenge activities
- Inquiry and Investigation activities
- Listening Library
- Online Phonics

| | DAY 1 |
|---|---|
| **Word Knowledge** | **Teacher Directed**<br>▪ Reading Words: Suffixes *-ful* and *-er*, ***Intervention Guide,*** p. 191<br>**Independent Activities**<br>▪ ***Online Phonics*** |
| **Fluency** | **Independent Activities**<br>▪ Self-test fluency rate<br>▪ Partner reading |
| **Comprehension** | **Teacher Directed**<br>▪ Preteach "Kids Did It! in Business," ***Intervention Guide,*** pp. 192–193<br>▪ Preteach Intervention Selection One, ***Intervention Guide,*** pp. 193–194<br>▪ ***English Learner Support Guide***<br>• Vocabulary, pp. 286–287<br>• Comprehension Skill: Main Idea/Details, pp. 287–288<br>**Independent Activities**<br>▪ Browse ***Leveled Classroom Library***<br>▪ Add vocabulary in Writer's Notebook |
| **Inquiry** | **Independent Activities**<br>▪ Concept/Question Board<br>▪ Explore OCR Web site for theme connections<br>▪ Ways to Earn Money Chart, ***Inquiry Journal,*** pp. 93–94 |
| **Language Arts** | **Teacher Directed**<br>▪ Grammar, Usage, and Mechanics, ***Intervention Guide,*** p. 196<br>**Independent Activities**<br>▪ Parentheses and Periods, ***Comprehension and Language Arts Skills,*** pp. 102–103 |

| DAY 2 | DAY 3 | DAY 4 | DAY 5 |
|---|---|---|---|
| **Teacher Directed**<br>▪ Developing Oral Language, ***Intervention Guide,*** p. 191<br>**Independent Activities**<br>▪ ***Online Phonics***<br>▪ Read ***Decodable Book 31,*** *Whales* | **Teacher Directed**<br>▪ Dictation and Spelling: Suffixes *-ful* and *-er,* ***Intervention Guide,*** pp. 191–192<br>**Independent Activities**<br>▪ ***Online Phonics*** | **Teacher Directed**<br>▪ General Review<br>**Independent Activities**<br>▪ ***Online Phonics*** | **Teacher Directed**<br>▪ General Review<br>**Independent Activities**<br>▪ ***Online Phonics*** |
| **Independent Activities**<br>▪ Oral reading of selection for fluency<br>▪ Partner reading of ***Decodable Book 31,*** *Whales* | **Independent Activities**<br>▪ Partner reading of selection<br>▪ Read ***Decodable Book 31,*** *Whales* | **Independent Activities**<br>▪ Reread "Kids Did It! in Business"<br>▪ Partner reading of ***Decodable Book 31,*** *Whales* | **Teacher Directed**<br>▪ Repeated Readings/Fluency Check, ***Intervention Guide,*** p. 195<br>**Independent Activities**<br>▪ Reread ***Decodable Book 31,*** *Whales* |
| **Teacher Directed**<br>▪ Preteach "Kids Did It! in Business," ***Intervention Guide,*** pp. 192–193<br>▪ Comprehension Strategies, ***Intervention Guide,*** p. 194<br>▪ Reread Intervention Selection One, ***Intervention Guide,*** pp. 193–194<br>▪ ***English Learner Support Guide***<br>• Vocabulary, pp. 288–290<br>• Comprehension Skill: Main Idea/Details, pp. 290–291<br>**Independent Activities**<br>▪ Choose a ***Leveled Classroom Library*** book for independent reading<br>▪ Record response to selection in Writer's Notebook<br>▪ ***Listening Library Audiocassette/CD*** | **Teacher Directed**<br>▪ Discuss Concept Connections, p. 46<br>▪ Reread "Kids Did It! in Business," ***Intervention Guide,*** pp. 192–193<br>▪ Preteach Intervention Selection Two, ***Intervention Guide,*** pp. 194–195<br>▪ ***English Learner Support Guide***<br>• Vocabulary, pp. 291–292<br>• Comprehension Skill: Main Idea/Details, pp. 292–293<br>**Independent Activities**<br>▪ Read ***Leveled Classroom Library*** book<br>▪ Complete Link to Writing in Supporting the Reading, p. 45C<br>▪ ***English Learner Support Activities,*** p. 35 | **Teacher Directed**<br>▪ Reread "Kids Did It! in Business," ***Intervention Guide,*** pp. 192–193<br>▪ Comprehension Strategies, ***Intervention Guide,*** p. 195<br>▪ Reread Intervention Selection Two, ***Intervention Guide,*** pp. 194–195<br>▪ ***English Learner Support Guide***<br>• Vocabulary, pp. 293–295<br>• Comprehension Skill: Main Idea/Details, pp. 295–296<br>**Independent Activities**<br>▪ Independent reading<br>▪ Add words to Word Bank<br>▪ Complete Independent Practice in Literary Elements, p. 45D<br>▪ Social Studies Connection, p. 45E<br>▪ ***English Learner Support Activities,*** p. 36 | **Teacher Directed**<br>▪ Informal Assessment for Intervention<br>▪ ***English Learner Support Guide***<br>• Review Vocabulary, p. 296<br>• Comprehension Skill: Main Idea/Details, pp. 296–297<br>**Independent Activities**<br>▪ Read ***Leveled Classroom Library*** book as independent reading<br>▪ Reading Roundtable<br>▪ Science Connection, p. 45F<br>▪ ***English Learner Support Activities,*** p. 37 |
| **Independent Activities**<br>▪ Concept/Question Board<br>▪ Explore OCR Web site for theme connections<br>▪ Use ***Research Assistant CD-ROM*** to continue investigation | **Independent Activities**<br>▪ Concept/Question Board<br>▪ Discuss and share conjectures<br>▪ Research Cycle: Conjecture Phase, ***Inquiry Journal,*** p. 95 | **Independent Activities**<br>▪ Concept/Question Board<br>▪ Complete Independent Practice in Supporting the Investigation, p. 47D | **Independent Activities**<br>▪ Concept/Question Board<br>▪ Use ***Research Assistant CD-ROM*** to continue investigation |
| **Teacher Directed**<br>▪ Grammar, Usage, and Mechanics, ***Intervention Guide,*** p. 196<br>▪ Parentheses and Periods, ***Reteach,*** p. 107<br>**Independent Activities**<br>▪ Vocabulary: Business and Technology Words, ***Spelling and Vocabulary Skills,*** pp. 82–83<br>▪ Parentheses and Periods, ***Challenge,*** p. 94<br>▪ Writer's Craft: Structure of a Business Letter, ***Comprehension and Language Arts Skills,*** pp. 104–105 | **Teacher Directed**<br>▪ Writing Activity, ***Intervention Guide,*** p. 197<br>▪ Vocabulary: Business Vocabulary, ***Reteach,*** p. 106<br>**Independent Activities**<br>▪ Spelling: Contractions, ***Spelling and Vocabulary Skills,*** p. 84<br>▪ Vocabulary: Business Vocabulary, ***Challenge,*** p. 93<br>▪ Seminar: Draft a Persuasive Business Letter, p. 47H | **Teacher Directed**<br>▪ Writer's Craft: Structure of a Business Letter, ***Reteach,*** p. 108<br>▪ Writing Activity, ***Intervention Guide,*** p. 197<br>▪ Spelling: Contractions, ***Reteach,*** p. 105<br>**Independent Activities**<br>▪ Spelling: Contractions<br>• ***Spelling and Vocabulary Skills,*** p. 85<br>• ***Challenge,*** p. 92<br>▪ Seminar: Revise a Persuasive Business Letter, p. 47I | **Independent Activities**<br>▪ Seminar: Edit/Proofread and Publish a Persuasive Business Letter, p. 47J<br>▪ Penmanship: Practice Cursive Letters *N* and *M,* p. 47J<br>▪ Writer's Craft: Structure of a Business Letter, ***Challenge,*** p. 95 |

ASSESSMENT

# Formal Assessment Options

Use these summative assessments along with your informal observations to assess student progress.

Name ______ Date ______ Score ______

UNIT 4 Money • Lesson 3

LESSON ASSESSMENT

**Kids Did It! in Business**

**Read the following questions carefully. Then completely fill in the bubble of each correct answer. You may look back at the story to find the answer to each of the questions.**

1. What does Adam Baratz, the Bug Buster, do for big companies?
   - Ⓐ designs software programs
   - ● tests software programs
   - Ⓒ sells software programs
2. What is a "bug" in a computer program?
   - ● a mistake
   - Ⓑ a fancy picture
   - Ⓒ a command

**Read the following questions carefully. Use complete sentences to answer the questions.**

3. How did Ebony Hood learn about business?
   Ebony learned about business in a special course at her high school.
4. What does Ebony Hood think is important in order to succeed in business?
   Ebony thinks honesty, a good personality, and hard work are important.
5. How did Marc Wright get started in business?
   Marc drew a picture, and his mother suggested he put the picture on a greeting card.

10 Unit 4 • Lesson 3 *Kids Did It! in Business* • Unit 4 Assessment

**Unit 4 Assessment p. 10**

**Kids Did It! in Business** *(continued)*

LESSON ASSESSMENT

6. How does Marc's business help others?
   Ten percent of the money Marc makes goes to a children's charity.
7. Describe Abbey Fleck's invention.
   Abbey Fleck's invention cooks bacon in a microwave.
8. What is a health benefit of Abbey's invention?
   Bacon cooked with Abby's invention is less greasy than bacon cooked the regular way.

**Read the following questions carefully. Then completely fill in the bubble of each correct answer.**

9. What do all of these "business kids" have in common?
   - ● They turned ideas into businesses.
   - Ⓑ They live outside the United States.
   - Ⓒ They get help from their parents.
10. This story is mostly about
    - Ⓐ why young people should pay attention in school
    - Ⓑ how different young people are interested in different things
    - ● some young people who have been successful in business

Unit 4 Assessment • *Kids Did It! in Business* Unit 4 • Lesson 3 11

**Unit 4 Assessment p. 11**

**Kids Did It! in Business** *(continued)*

LESSON ASSESSMENT

**Read the questions below. Use complete sentences in your answers.**

**Linking to the Concepts** What are some of the advantages of a young person being in business?

Answers will vary. Accept all reasonable answers.

**Personal Response** Suppose you wanted to start a business. What are some of the problems you would have to solve?

Answers will vary. Accept all reasonable answers.

12 Unit 4 • Lesson 3 *Kids Did It! in Business* • Unit 4 Assessment

**Unit 4 Assessment p. 12**

**Kids Did It! in Business** *(continued)*

LESSON ASSESSMENT

**Vocabulary**

**Read the following questions carefully. Then completely fill in the bubble of each correct answer.**

1. Adam finds software bugs that can make computers malfunction. When something **malfunctions**, it
   - Ⓐ can not be returned
   - Ⓑ works perfectly
   - ● does not work correctly
2. Selling pins and scarves is fun and profitable for Ebony Hood. Something is **profitable** if you
   - ● make money from it
   - Ⓑ enjoy doing it
   - Ⓒ do it all by yourself
3. Marc Wright donates some of his profits. Another way to say **donates** is
   - ● gives away
   - Ⓑ spends on himself
   - Ⓒ buys nice things
4. Marc donates 10 percent of his profits to a children's charity. A **charity** is a group that
   - Ⓐ is owned and run by children
   - ● helps people who are in need
   - Ⓒ sells cards to cheer people up
5. Ebony learned how to set up a business, order merchandise, and keep records. **Merchandise** is the word for
   - Ⓐ how you let people know about your business
   - Ⓑ people who help make your business successful
   - ● things that are bought and sold in a business

Unit 4 Assessment • *Kids Did It! in Business* Unit 4 • Lesson 3 13

**Unit 4 Assessment p. 13**

Name ______ Date ______ Score ______

UNIT 4 Money • Lesson 3 *Kids Did It! in Business*

LESSON ASSESSMENT

**Spelling Pretest: Contractions**

**Fold this page back on the dotted line. Take the Pretest. Then correct any word you misspelled by crossing out the word and rewriting it next to the incorrect spelling.**

| | |
|---|---|
| 1. ______ | 1. he'll |
| 2. ______ | 2. she'll |
| 3. ______ | 3. we'll |
| 4. ______ | 4. I'd |
| 5. ______ | 5. we'd |
| 6. ______ | 6. they'll |
| 7. ______ | 7. you'd |
| 8. ______ | 8. that's |
| 9. ______ | 9. she'd |
| 10. ______ | 10. you'll |
| 11. ______ | 11. it's |
| 12. ______ | 12. she's |
| 13. ______ | 13. what's |
| 14. ______ | 14. I'm |
| 15. ______ | 15. can't |

34 Unit 4 • Lesson 3 *Spelling Pretest: Contractions* • Unit 4 Assessment

**Unit 4 Assessment p. 34**

Name ______ Date ______ Score ______

UNIT 4 Money • Lesson 3 *Kids Did It! in Business*

LESSON ASSESSMENT

**Spelling Final Test: Contractions**

**Mark the letter next to the underlined word that is misspelled. Focus on the underlined word.**

1. Ⓐ Salt is a spice that's in soups.
   Ⓑ I think I'd like some candy.
   Ⓒ Simon thinks he'll go for a walk.
   ● Correct as is.
2. ● To fly, youl'l need a ticket.
   Ⓖ Ostriches can't fly in the air.
   Ⓗ A runner races so she'll win.
   Ⓙ Correct as is.
3. ● At the south pole, its' very cold.
   Ⓑ Teams hope they'll win games.
   Ⓒ Golf is a game that's fun to play.
   Ⓓ Correct as is.
4. Ⓕ Shantel knows she's smart.
   ● Fish caint live out of water.
   Ⓗ Each year, you'll get older.
   Ⓙ Correct as is.
5. Ⓐ At midnight, it's 12:00 a.m.
   Ⓑ I think that I'm going to smile.
   ● A raisin is a grape thati's dried.
   Ⓓ Correct as is.
6. Ⓕ I'd like to go to the beach.
   Ⓖ Teachers hope you'll learn.
   Ⓗ People can't fly like birds.
   ● Correct as is.

Unit 4 Assessment • *Spelling Final Test: Contractions* Unit 4 • Lesson 3 35

**Unit 4 Assessment p. 35**

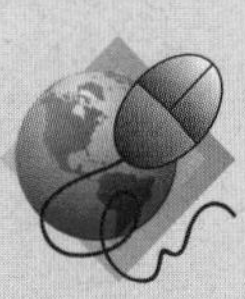

**Online Assessment** for ***Open Court Reading*** helps teachers differentiate classroom instruction based on students' scores from the weekly and end-of-unit assessments. It provides exercises best suited to meet the needs of each student. For more information, visit SRAonline.com.

## Informal Comprehension Strategies Rubrics

### Summarizing

- The student paraphrases the text, reporting main ideas and a summary of what is in the text.
- The student decides which parts of the text are important in his or her summary.
- The student draws conclusions from the text.
- The student makes global interpretations of the text, such as recognizing the genre.

### Making Connections

- The student activates prior knowledge and related knowledge.
- The student uses prior knowledge to explain something encountered in the text.
- The student connects ideas presented later in the text to ideas presented earlier in the text.
- The student notes ideas in the text that are new or conflict with what he or she thought previously.

### Monitoring and Clarifying

- The student notes characteristics of the text, such as whether it is difficult to read or whether some sections are more challenging or more important than others.
- The student shows awareness of whether he or she understands the text and takes appropriate action, such as rereading, in order to understand the text better.
- The student rereads to reconsider something presented earlier in the text.
- The student recognizes problems during reading, such as a loss of concentration, unfamiliar vocabulary, or lack of sufficient background knowledge to comprehend the text.

## Research Rubrics

During Workshop, assess students using the rubrics below. The rubrics range from 1 to 4 in most categories, with 1 being the lowest score. Record each student's score on the inside back cover of the ***Inquiry Journal.***

### Making Conjectures

**1** Offers conjectures that are mainly expressions of fact or opinion. ("I think the Anasazi lived a long time ago." "I think tigers should be protected.")

**2** Offers conjectures that partially address the research question. ("I think germs make you sick because they get your body upset." "I think germs make you sick because they multiply really fast.")

**3** Offers conjectures that address the research question with guesses. ("I think the Anasazi were wiped out by a meteor.")

**4** Offers reasonable conjectures that address the question and that can be improved through further research.

# 1 Preparing to Read



### Objectives

- Students practice recognizing compound words, /ā/ spelled *ai_, a_e,* and *_ay,* and base words with the suffixes *-ful, -er,* and *-ation.*
- Students practice recognizing contractions.

### Materials

- Student Anthology, Book 2, pp. 38–47
- Decodable Book 31
- Routine Card 1, Routines 1–2

### Differentiating Instruction

| If... | Then... |
|---|---|
| English Learners need extra help with compound words | Have English-speaking volunteers write compound words on the board and read them. Then have English Learners identify the two smaller words in the compound words and draw a chalk line between them. |
| Students need extra help with compound words | Write the two words that make up the compound words on individual cards and have students match the words to make compound words |

**Teacher Tip SYLLABICATION** To help students blend words and build fluency, use the syllabication below of the words in the word lines.

| | | |
|---|---|---|
| news • pa • per | soft • ware | world • wide |
| mic • ro • wave | suc • ceed | suc • cess |
| suc • cess • ful | com • pute | com • pu • ter |
| com • pu • ta • tion | ed • u • cate | ed • u • ca • tion |
| ed • u • ca • tion • al | make | play |
| paid | cake | drain |
| mail | it's | she's |
| what's | I'm | can't |

**Routine Card**
Refer to ***Routine 1*** for whole-word blending and ***Routine 2*** for sentence blending.

WORD KNOWLEDGE

## Word Knowledge

### Reading the Words and Sentences

- Use direct teaching to teach the following lesson.
- Using the established procedure, have students read each line of words and sentences in this and in subsequent lessons. The words in **boldface** type appear in the selection.

| | | | | | | |
|---|---|---|---|---|---|---|
| Line 1: | newspaper | software | worldwide | microwave | | |
| Line 2: | succeed | success | successful | compute | computer | |
| Line 3: | computation | educate | education | educational | | |
| Line 4: | make | play | paid | cake | drain | mail |
| Line 5: | it's | she's | what's | I'm | can't | |

Sentence 1: Adam, who lives in Newton, Massachusetts, has been catching those pesky "bugs," mistakes or glitches in computer software programs that can make computers malfunction.
Sentence 2: But Adam, who started testing when he was 8, may be the youngest.
Sentence 3: The best part of the business? "Being able to do things like take my mom on a vacation to Walt Disney World," says Marc.
Sentence 4: It's true that ostriches can't fly high in the air.

### About the Words and Sentences

- **Line 1:** The words in Line 1 are compound words. Have students explain what a compound word is. Ask if the two words that make up the compound word help us understand the meaning.
- **Lines 2–3:** The words in Lines 2–3 are base words and base words with affixes. Explain to students that sometimes affixes added to words change the whole meaning of the word. Prompt students to tell how each of the words in Lines 2–3 changes in meaning as it changes spelling.
- **Line 4:** The words in Line 4 have the /ā/ sound. After the words have been read, have students identify the vowel sound and tell how the /ā/ sound is spelled in each word.
- **Line 5:** The words in the last line are found in "Kids Did It! in Business" and review contractions. Have students tell what two words make up each contraction. Then have them tell you what the contraction means.
- **Sentences 1–3:** These sentences are from the story students are about to read. Ask students to identify the compound word *(software).* Ask students to identify the words with the /ā/ sound *(make, may, take, vacation).* Ask students to identify the words with suffixes *(computer, vacation).*
- **Sentence 4:** Have students identify the contractions in Sentence 4 *(It's, can't).*

## Developing Oral Language

- Have individual students point to a word in Lines 1–5, say it, and use it in a sentence. Then have them underline the word. Have students extend the sentences at the beginning and at the end by asking questions such as *Who? What? When? Where? Why?* and *How?*
- Ask students to find words in Lines 1–5 for each of the following clues. As each word is identified and read, have students circle it.

**The news is printed in it every day** *(newspaper).*
**To do something well** *(succeed).*
**The opening in a sink** *(drain).*
**A favorite dessert** *(cake).*
**What the postman delivers to your house** *(mail).*

## Building Fluency

***Decodable Books*** are used to help develop fluency for students who need extra practice. The only way to gain fluency is to read. Students will have many opportunities to read, including the ***Student Anthology,*** the ***Leveled Classroom Library,*** and their own reading. The ***Decodable Books*** can be used to practice the phonics and fluency elements being reviewed. Refer to the Appendix for the procedure on using these books. For this lesson, use ***Decodable Book 31,*** *Whales.*

***Decodable Book 31***

**Teacher Tip** With multiple spellings for a sound, it is especially important that students ask "Which spelling?" when they are unsure about which spelling to use in a given word.

### DIFFERENTIATING INSTRUCTION

| If... | Then... |
|---|---|
| Students need extra help with base words with the suffixes *-er* and *-ation* | Use ***Online Phonics*** |
| Students need extra help with base words with the suffixes *-ful* and *-er* | Use ***Intervention Guide*** pages 191–192 |

**Teacher Tip** FLUENCY Gaining a better understanding of the spellings of sounds and structure of words will help students as they encounter unfamiliar words in their reading. By this time in Grade 3 students should be reading approximately 123 words per minute with fluency and expression. As students read, you may notice that some need work in building fluency. During Workshop, have these students select a section of the text (a minimum of 160 words) to read several times in order to build fluency.

**Teacher Tip** Encourage students to just read the words. Stop and blend only those words that give them problems.

**Spelling**
See pages 47E–47J for the corresponding spelling lesson for contractions.

## Objectives

- Students will understand the selection vocabulary before reading, using strategies such as suffixes and structural cues.
- Students will recognize compound words; /ā/ spelled *ai_, a_e,* and *_ay;* suffixes *-ful, -er, -tation;* and contractions.
- Students will connect prior knowledge to subjects discussed in text.
- Students will use comprehension strategies such as Summarizing, Making Connections, and Monitoring and Clarifying to construct meaning from the text and monitor reading.
- Students will use the comprehension skill Main Idea and Supporting Details as they read the story the second time.
- Students will discuss personal reactions to the story to begin identifying their own personal reading preferences.
- Students link the selection's key concepts to their investigations.

## Materials

- Student Anthology, Book 2, pp. 38–47
- Program Assessment
- Reading Transparencies 25, 46, 50
- Science/Social Studies Connection Center Card 34
- Inquiry Journal, p. 84
- Home Connection, p. 49
- Unit 4 Assessment, pp. 10–13
- Routine Cards 1, 2, Routines 3–6

**Routine Card**
Refer to ***Routine 4*** for the Clues, Problems, and Wonderings procedure.

| Clues | Problems | Wonderings |
|---|---|---|
| facts about the children = informa-tional article about them | catering | How can kids run a business? |

***Reading Transparency 46***

**www.sra4kids.com**
**Web Connection**
Students can use the connections to Money in the Reading link of the SRA Web page for more background information about money.

# Build Background

## Activate Prior Knowledge

Discuss the following with students to find out what they may already know about the selection and have already learned about the unit theme, Money.

- Preteach "Kids Did It! in Business" by asking students whether they are familiar with the story they are about to read, and if so, to tell a little bit about it.
- Ask students if they have ever worked for money and invite them to share their experiences.
- Ask students if they remember any other stories that tell about children earning money.
- Ask students if they have ever come up with a business idea and, if so, to share their ideas.

## Background Information

The following information may help students to better understand the selection they are about to read.

- Tell students that "Kids Did It! in Business" is expository text like they might find in a magazine. Expository texts give factual information that interests readers.
- A profile is a short, written sketch of a person. In this selection, four children and the businesses that they created are profiled.

# Preview and Prepare

## Browse

- Have students read the title and the author's name aloud. This allows students to activate prior knowledge relevant to the story. Have students preview the selection by browsing through the first page or two of the selection. Because this is expository text, you may encourage students to browse quickly through the entire text with no danger of disclosing a surprise ending, as with fiction. Ask students to pay attention to photographs and headings. Have students discuss what they think this story might reveal about money.
- Have students search for clues that tell them something about the selection. Also have students look for any problems, such as unfamiliar words or long sentences, that they notice while reading. Use ***Reading Transparency 46*** to record their observations as they browse. For example, the presentation of facts is a *clue* that this selection is an informational article. For the Problems column, students might point out that they are unfamiliar with the word *catering.* They might *wonder* how kids can run a business. To save time and to model note taking, write students' observations as brief notes rather than as complete sentences.

- As students prepare to read the selection, have them browse the Focus Questions on the first page of the selection. Tell them to keep these questions in mind as they read.

### Set Purposes

Encourage students to set their own purposes for reading this selection. For example, you might have students think about children earning money. In addition, you may wish to have students think about information in the selection that may be useful to them as they work on their investigations. Encourage students to develop additional purposes for reading.

## Selection Vocabulary

As students study vocabulary, they will use a variety of skills to determine the meaning of a word. These include context clues, word structure, and apposition. Students will apply these same skills while reading to clarify additional unfamiliar words. Students can write their definitions in their Writer's Notebooks.

Display ***Reading Transparency 25*** before reading the selection to introduce and discuss the following words and their meanings:

**malfunction:** no longer work correctly; fail to operate (page 38)
**profitable:** gaining money after all the costs of doing business have been paid (page 40)
**merchandise:** goods that are bought and sold in business (page 40)
**earnings:** money that is paid for doing a job (page 41)
**donates:** gives money or objects as a gift (page 42)
**charity:** a group that provides help to those in need (page 42)

Have students read the words in the word box, stopping to blend any words that they have trouble reading. Demonstrate how to decode multisyllabic words by breaking the words into syllables and blending the syllables. Then let students try. If they still have trouble, refer them to the ***Sound/Spelling Cards.*** If the word is not decodable, give the students the pronunciation.

Have students read the sentences on the transparency to determine the meaning of the underlined words. Each word has two sentences that students will read and from which they should be able to derive the meaning of the underlined word. Remind them to use one or more of the skills they have learned—context clues, word structure, or apposition—to figure out the meaning before using a dictionary. Be sure students explain which skills they are using and how they figured out the meanings of the words. Have students reread the sentence, substituting the definition to see if the sentence makes sense. Have a volunteer create a new sentence using the underlined word.

**Teacher Tip** During browsing, students should notice section headings.

**Routine Card**
Refer to ***Routine 5*** for the vocabulary procedure.

**Teacher Tip** SELECTION VOCABULARY To help students decode words, divide the words into syllables when you are saying them, as shown below. The information following each word tells how students can figure out the meaning of each word. When writing words on the board, do not divide them into syllables.

| | |
|---|---|
| mal • func • tion | context clues |
| prof • it • a • ble | context clues |
| mer • chan • dise | context clues |
| earn • ings | context clues |
| do • nates | context clues |
| char • i • ty | context clues |

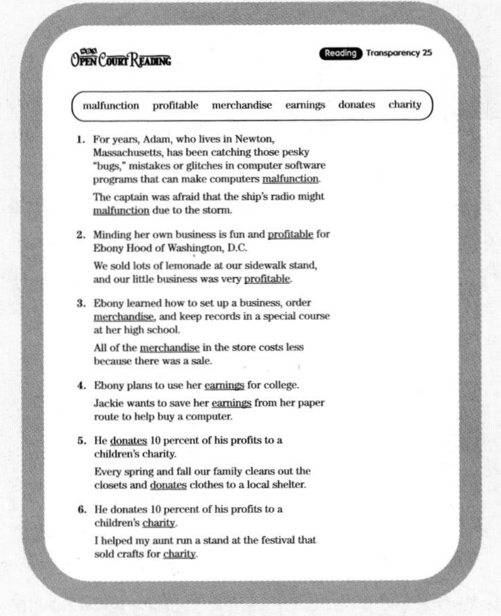

OPEN COURT READING — Reading Transparency 25

malfunction profitable merchandise earnings donates charity

1. For years, Adam, who lives in Newton, Massachusetts, has been catching those pesky "bugs," mistakes or glitches in computer software programs that can make computers malfunction.
   The captain was afraid that the ship's radio might malfunction due to the storm.
2. Minding her own business is fun and profitable for Ebony Hood of Washington, D.C.
   We sold lots of lemonade at our sidewalk stand, and our little business was very profitable.
3. Ebony learned how to set up a business, order merchandise, and keep records in a special course at her high school.
   All of the merchandise in the store costs less because there was a sale.
4. Ebony plans to use her earnings for college.
   Jackie wants to save her earnings from her paper route to help buy a computer.
5. He donates 10 percent of his profits to a children's charity.
   Every spring and fall our family cleans out the closets and donates clothes to a local shelter.
6. He donates 10 percent of his profits to a children's charity.
   I helped my aunt run a stand at the festival that sold crafts for charity.

***Reading Transparency 25***

### Differentiating Instruction

| If... | Then... |
|---|---|
| Students need extra help with selection vocabulary | Use ***Intervention Guide*** pages 192–193 |

**Teacher Tip** COMPREHENSION STRATEGIES Remind students on the second day as they read the story to summarize what they learned from the first day.

**Teacher Tip** SET PURPOSES Remind students that good readers have a purpose when they read. Let them know that they should make sure they know the purpose for reading whenever they read.

**Routine Card**
Refer to ***Routine 5*** for the procedure on reading the selection.

**DIFFERENTIATING INSTRUCTION**

| If... | Then... |
|---|---|
| Students need extra help with summarizing | Use ***Intervention Guide*** pages 193–195 |

During Workshop, and after the selection has been read at least once, have students listen to the recording of this lesson's selection on the ***Listening Library Audiocassette/CD.*** After students have listened, have them discuss their personal preferences of the selections read. Ask them what other things they have listened to and like to listen to on the radio, on audiocassettes, or on CDs.

**Teacher Tip** For extra practice in oral fluency, have individual students read aloud to you a selection they have previously read, either from a ***Decodable Book*** or a passage from the ***Student Anthology.*** Time each student for one minute. If the student reads more than 123 words correctly, have the student retell the selection he or she has just read. Use one prompt if the student seems to be stuck, and allow a maximum of one minute for the student to retell the story. If the student does not read more than 123 words correctly, have the student try reading from an earlier ***Decodable Book*** to help you determine where the problem lies.

# Reading Recommendations

## Oral Reading

This story lends itself to being read aloud because it contains many facts and points of discussion. Students should read aloud fluently with appropriate expression, intonation, and vocal patterns. Make sure that students attend to punctuation and read in phrases. Tell students to add a sense of feeling or anticipation as they read. You may want to stop after each profile and discuss what exciting things the child in that section of the article is doing.

Have students make use of the comprehension strategies listed below to help them understand the selection. Have them stop reading periodically or wait until they have completed the selection to discuss the reading strategies. After the students have finished reading the selection, use the Discussing the Selection questions on page 45A to see if they understand what they have read.

## Using Comprehension Strategies 

Comprehension strategy instruction allows students to become aware of how good readers read. Good readers constantly check their understanding as they are reading and ask themselves questions. In addition, skilled readers recognize when they are having problems and stop to use various comprehension strategies to help them make sense of what they are reading.

During the first reading of "Kids Did It! in Business," you will model and prompt the use of the following comprehension strategies:

- **Summarizing** prompts readers to keep track of what they are reading and to focus their minds on important information.
- **Making Connections** requires readers to activate prior knowledge and connect what they know or have experienced to what they are reading.
- **Monitoring and Clarifying** takes different forms, including clarifying the meaning of words and clarifying difficult ideas or passages. In order to clarify meanings, students can use context clues, use structural analysis, use apposition, use charts or graphic organizers, use resources outside of the text, or reread the text.

As students read, they should be using a variety of strategies to help them understand the selection. Encourage students to use the strategies listed above as the class reads the story aloud. Do this by stopping at the points indicated by the numbers in the magenta circles on the reduced student page and using a particular strategy. Students can also stop reading periodically to discuss what they have learned and what problems they may be having.

An extended lesson on the comprehension strategy, Making Connections, can be found on page 45C.

## Building Comprehension Skills 

Revisiting or rereading a selection allows students to apply skills that give them a more complete understanding of the text. Some follow-up comprehension skills help students organize information. Others lead to deeper understanding—to "reading between the lines," as mature readers do. In this selection, students will review the following comprehension skill:

- **Main Idea and Details:** Readers identify relevant information in a text, including main ideas and the relationships among ideas.

### Reading with a Purpose

Have students look for ways any of the kids in the article learn about money.

**Teacher Tip** Tell students that good readers keep thinking about the questions that come up about the topic, and they keep coming back to those questions. As they read, tell them to keep the questions on the Concept/Question Board in mind. Have them making notes to themselves in the Response Journal section of their Writer's Notebooks about which questions seem most important. Tell them that good readers always think about what is important in selections, and they try to remember this important information.

### Differentiating Instruction

| If... | Then... |
|---|---|
| English Learners need extra support reading "Kids Did It! in Business" | Have them listen to the selection on the ***Listening Library Audiocassette/CD*** and then read it aloud |

### Research in Action

Students who set their own goals for reading read with a greater sense of engagement and notice more than students whose goals are set for them by you or the reading program. The purpose of the initial browsing is to help students think about what they will be reading and to build a sense of anticipation for the reading they will do. As students progress, they will be noticing titles, headings, and the first sentences of paragraphs.
*(Carl Bereiter)*

COMPREHENSION

Read pages 38–45.

## Comprehension Strategies

Read the story aloud, taking turns with the students. Start by modeling the use of strategies for the students.

### Teacher Modeling

1 **Summarizing** *Summarizing as you read will help you to better understand the main idea of a selection. Since this is the end of a section, I'll sum up the information. I learned that ten-year-old Adam Baratz tests software programs for big computer companies. He uses the second version of a program and tries to find any mistakes in it. Instead of earning money, Adam gets lots of free software. Let's continue reading, and as we do, remember to summarize what we are reading. Make sure you understand what you have just read. Let me know if you would like to share your summary with the group.*

### Word Knowledge

**SCAFFOLDING:** The skills students are reviewing in Word Knowledge should help them in reading the story. This lesson focuses on compound words, the /ā/ sound spelled *ai, a_e* and *_ay,* and any base words with the suffixes *-ful, -er,* and *-tation.*

**suffix *-er*:** **computer**

**Teacher Tip** During Workshop have students find multisyllabic words in their anthology selection and list them under columns for two- or three-syllable words. Have them underline the vowel spellings.

**First Reading Recommendation**

**ORAL • CHORAL**

*Focus Questions* What would it be like to own your own business? What do you think you would need to start a business? What characteristics are important in running a successful business?

# Kids Did It! in Business

by Judith E. Rinard

## The Bug Buster

### Adam Baratz, 10

Is something bugging your computer? Meet Adam Baratz. Bugs are his business—computer bugs, that is. For years, Adam, who lives in Newton, Massachusetts, has been catching those pesky "bugs," mistakes or glitches in computer software programs that can make computers malfunction.

A computer user since he was 2 years old, Adam found his first bug at age 5. Today he tests software programs for big companies such as Microsoft. Program testers like Adam are called beta (BAY-tuh) testers. They try out beta, or second, versions of new programs. The third version is released to the public. Companies use thousands of beta testers. But Adam, who started testing when he was 8, may be the youngest.

38

### Differentiating Instruction

| If... | Then... |
| --- | --- |
| Students need help summarizing | Have them reread the section carefully and put the main idea into their own words |

### Informal Assessment

Observe individual students as they read and use the Teacher Observation Log, found in the ***Program Assessment Teacher's Edition,*** to record anecdotal information about each student's strengths and weaknesses.

How does Adam test for bugs? "I play around with the program to see what it can do," he says. "I feel like a detective. You have to work hard to track down bugs or they can really mess up your computer." Adam gets paid for his skills with free copies of the programs. "The best part is that I get to look at the programs before anyone else," he says. Adam has also written newspaper columns reviewing educational software for kids. Adam enjoys his job. "It's fun," he says. "I just really like computers!" (1)

39

## Comprehension Skills

COMPREHENSION

### Main Idea and Supporting Details

Remind students that a main idea is what a selection is mostly about. Usually, the author provides a topic sentence that sums up this main idea. Sometimes, however, the main idea is implied; this is often the case with fiction. Supporting details are the smaller pieces of information that support or tell more about the main idea.

Ask students to find the sentence that sums up the main idea of pages 38–39.

- *Adam Baratz has made a business by finding bugs in computer programs.*

Then help students find three important facts that give information or support this main idea.

- *He tests programs for big companies.*
- *He explains that his work is like being a detective.*
- *He gets paid with free software.*

**Word Knowledge**

/ā/: **paid**

**Skills Trace**

Main Idea and Details

Introduced in Grade 1.

Scaffolded throughout Grades 2 and 3.

**REINTRODUCED:** Unit 1, Lesson 5

**REINFORCED:** Unit 4, Lesson 3; Unit 5, Lesson 6; Unit 6, Lesson 6

**TESTED:** Unit 4 Assessment

**Second Reading Recommendation**

ORAL • **SILENT**

## Differentiating Instruction

| If... | Then... |
|---|---|
| English Learners need extra help with vocabulary | Use ***English Learner Support Guide*** pages 286–287 |
| English Learners need extra help with main idea and supporting details | Use ***English Learner Support Guide*** pages 287–288 |

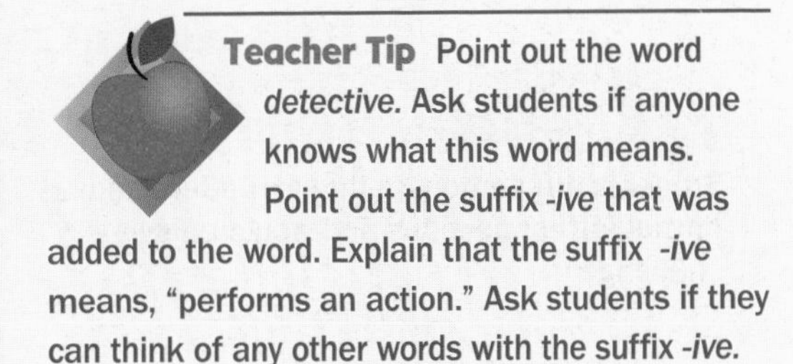

**Teacher Tip** Point out the word *detective.* Ask students if anyone knows what this word means. Point out the suffix *-ive* that was added to the word. Explain that the suffix *-ive* means, "performs an action." Ask students if they can think of any other words with the suffix *-ive.*

COMPREHENSION

## Comprehension Strategies

### Teacher Modeling

**2 Making Connections** *Good readers make connections between what they read and what they know in order to better understand how the people in a selection think or feel. I can understand how Ebony Hood feels. Earning your own money by starting your own business makes you feel good about yourself. I once had a dog-walking business. It was fun and made me feel very good. As we are reading, be aware of how ideas in the text remind you of things that have really happened to you. Be sure to tell the class. Has anyone ever earned their own money? If so, how did you feel?*

**Word Knowledge**

/ā/: **catering**

**Teacher Tip** As students read aloud, listen for appropriate pacing, intonation, and expression.

# Fashioning a Success

## Ebony Hood, 18

Minding her own business is fun and profitable for Ebony Hood of Washington, D.C. She's started her own business selling fashion pins and scarves like the ones she's modeling here. Ebony learned how to set up a business, order merchandise, and keep records in a special course at her high school.

Ebony sells her brightly colored fashions at school and in friends' homes. During her first four months in business, she earned nearly $1,000.

"I love being in charge, being my own boss, and dealing with people," says Ebony. Now she's added a new business: baking fancy cakes and catering parties. What's her most challenging catering task? "Not breaking the cakes!"

40

### Differentiating Instruction

| If... | Then... |
|---|---|
| Students are demonstrating an understanding of making connections and would enjoy a challenge | Ask them to provide several connections between what they are reading and what they already know. Write their connections on the board and ask volunteers to explain how what they know helps them to understand the selection. |

Ebony plans to use her earnings for college. To succeed in business, she advises, requires "honesty, a good personality, and hard work." ❷

## Comprehension Skills

COMPREHENSION

### Main Idea and Supporting Details

Ask students to identify the sentence that sums up the main idea of the selection about Ebony Hood.

- *Ebony has her own business selling fashion pins and scarves.*

Then ask them to identify at least three supporting details that are facts in the selection.

- *She learned how to run the business in a special course at school.*
- *She sells these items in friends' homes and at school.*
- *She has made $1,000 so far.*

**Teacher Tip** Ask students one or more of the following questions to make sure they understand what they are reading: Is anyone confused? Do you need clarification? Can you summarize what you have read so far? Does what you are reading make sense to you?

**Teacher Tip** Remind students to use context clues, apposition, or word structure to figure out the meaning of difficult words as they are reading.

### Differentiating Instruction

| If... | Then... |
|---|---|
| English Learners need extra help with vocabulary | Use ***English Learner Support Guide*** pages 288–290 |
| English Learners need extra help with main idea and supporting details | Use ***English Learner Support Guide*** pages 290–291 |

COMPREHENSION

## Comprehension Strategies

First Read

Begin prompting students for responses. Praise answers that are appropriate, even if they do not match the student sample. This will encourage students to use strategies as they read.

### Prompting

**3 Monitoring and Clarifying**

*There is a lot of information in this section, including some new terms. I think I need to stop and clarify some things. What do you need to stop and clarify in this section?*

### Student Sample

**Monitoring and Clarifying** *I don't get it. What does "mail orders worldwide" mean? I'll try reading this last part again and then think about what I know. Okay, rereading helped me to order my thoughts. I already know that you can order things by mail. I think "worldwide" has to do with being all over the world. So I guess Marc was selling cards to people from all over the world, in lots of different countries, who ordered by mail.*

### Word Knowledge

/ā/: **day**
**make**
**made**
**pays**

**Teacher Tip** Some students may have difficulty understanding the concept of children establishing businesses. Be prepared to supply additional background information and clarification as needed, but also encourage students to use expository texts and research technology to find answers to their questions.

# Greetings!

## Marc Wright, 10

When Marc Wright lays his cards on the table, he has quite a few. Marc owns his own greeting card company, called Kiddie Cards. He started the company four years ago when he was just 6. "I wanted to make extra money," says Marc of Windsor, Ontario, in Canada. "One day I drew a picture. My mom suggested I put it on a greeting card." Marc did, and his company was launched.

At first Marc made and sold his own cards, going door to door. The cards really caught on, and people wanted more. "So I hired friends to help," he says. About 20 young artists ages 5 to 13 now work for Marc. He pays them 25 cents a card and sells the cards for about $1. He donates 10 percent of his profits to a children's charity.

42

### Differentiating Instruction

**English Learner Tip**

The short sections of "Kids Did It! in Business" provide brief, compartmentalized text for you to use as a teaching tool when working individually with English Learners. Encourage these students to ask questions, clarify problems, and make connections to better understand the selection.

Marc's business has earned up to $3,000 a year and now includes mail orders worldwide. The best part of the business? "Being able to do things like take my mom on a vacation to Walt Disney World," says Marc. **3**

43

## Comprehension Skills

### Main Idea and Supporting Details

Have students continue to search for the main idea, along with details that add information or clarify the main idea.

Ask students to identify a sentence that sums up the main idea of this selection.

- *Marc owns his own greeting card company, called Kiddie Cards.*

Then ask students to find as many important facts as they can in the selection that support the main idea.

- *He started the company four years ago.*
- *He sold his cards door to door.*
- *Twenty artists work for him.*

**Word Knowledge**

**compound words:** worldwide

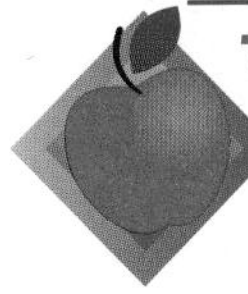

**Teacher Tip** Good readers constantly evaluate their understanding of what they read. Stop often to make sure students are doing this.

**Teacher Tip COMPREHENSION** Good readers are active readers. They interact with the text as they read by emoting, reacting, responding, and problem solving in their efforts to construct and maintain meaning.

COMPREHENSION

**Differentiating Instruction**

| If... | Then... |
| --- | --- |
| English Learners need extra help with vocabulary | Use ***English Learner Support Guide*** pages 291–292 |
| English Learners need extra help with main idea and supporting details | Use ***English Learner Support Guide*** pages 292–293 |

COMPREHENSION

## Comprehension Strategies

### Prompting

**4 Monitoring and Clarifying**
*I need to stop and clarify something. I wonder why the bacon turns out to be crispier and healthier? I'll go back over what I just read to understand. It says the fat drips off the bacon as it cooks. If the bacon has less fat, I guess it is crispier and healthier for people to eat. Does anybody else wish to clarify something from the selection?*

### Student Sample

**Monitoring and Clarifying** *What exactly is a "gadget"? I'll read this again to try to figure this out. As I reread about Abbey's invention, I realized a "gadget" is a kind of special tool that might seem strange but that really works and is useful.*

### Discussing Strategy Use

While students read the selection, encourage them to share any problems that they encounter and to tell what strategies they use to solve them.

- What connections did they make between the reading and what they already know?
- How did they clarify confusing passages?
- Where did they pause in the reading to summarize?

These are questions good readers ask after they read a text. After reading, the students should always be asking, "What did I find interesting? What is important here?" Later, remind the students again that whenever they conclude a reading, they should ask themselves questions about what was in the text.

**Word Knowledge**
**compound words:** **microwave**

# A Sizzling Idea

## Abbey Fleck, 12

Abbey Fleck of St. Paul, Minnesota, really knows how to bring home the bacon. In fact, when she was 8, she invented a gadget that does just that! (4) Called "Makin' Bacon," her invention is a plastic dish with T-shaped bars. You hang bacon over the bars to cook in the microwave oven. The fat drips off the bacon as it cooks, producing a crisper, healthier bacon with less mess. Abbey's invention is now her family's business. How did Abbey think of it? "I was watching my dad cook bacon one morning," says Abbey. "When he ran out of paper towels to drain the grease, I said, 'Why not just hang it up while it's cooking?'" Abbey and her dad designed and perfected "Makin' Bacon." Now it's widely sold. "I'm proud I thought of it," says Abbey. "And it's neat to know my idea is now supporting my family!"

44

**Science/Social Studies Connection Center**
Refer to the ***Science/Social Studies Connection Center*** Card 34 for a science activity that students can investigate.

45

## Comprehension Skills

### Main Idea and Supporting Details

Remind students that although main ideas are often implied, articles such as this one state it directly. Authors include details that support the main idea. What is the main idea of this article? What are the major supporting details?

- *Main idea: Kids can earn money by starting their own businesses.*
- *Major supporting details: Adam, Ebony, Marc, and Abbey have all started their own businesses.*

### Checking Comprehension

- Why is this selection called "Kids Did It! in Business"? *(It is about kids who are in business for themselves.)*
- What does this selection tell us about money? *(Kids can earn money by working.)*
- In what ways are the kids who are discussed in this selection alike? *(Students should note the kids' resourcefulness, hard work, dedication to their businesses, and pride in their achievements.)*

**Teacher Tip FLUENCY** By this time in third grade, good readers should be reading approximately 123 words per minute with fluency and expression. The only way to gain this fluency is through practice. Have students reread the selection to you and to each other during Workshop to help build fluency. As students read, you may notice that some need work in building fluency. During Workshop, have these students select a section of the text (a minimum of 160 words) to read several times in order to build fluency.

**Formal Assessment**

See pages 10–13 in ***Unit 4 Assessment*** to test students' comprehension of "Kids Did It! in Business."

### Differentiating Instruction

| If... | Then... |
|---|---|
| English Learners need extra help with vocabulary | Use ***English Learner Support Guide*** pages 293–295 |
| English Learners need extra help with main idea and supporting details | Use ***English Learner Support Guide*** pages 295–296 |
| English Learners need extra help reviewing the article | Use ***English Learner Support Guide*** pages 296–297 |

COMPREHENSION

**Teacher Tip** DISCUSSION When you call on a student, allow him or her a few seconds to consider your question and arrive at an answer.

**Routine Card**
Refer to ***Routine* 6** for the *handing-off process.*

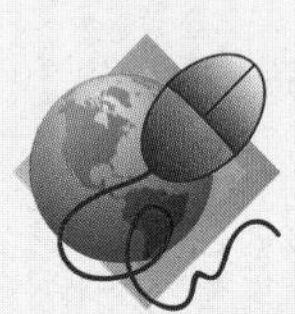

**www.sra4kids.com**
**Web Connection**
Some students may choose to conduct a computer search for additional books or information about money. Invite them to make a list of these books and sources of information to share with classmates and the school librarian. Check the Reading link of the SRA Web page for additional links to the theme-related Web site.

| Clues | Problems | Wonderings |
|---|---|---|
| facts about the children = informa-tional article about them | catering | How can kids run a business? |

***Reading Transparency* 46**

## Discussing the Selection

After the first read, the whole group discusses the selection and any personal thoughts, reactions, problems, or questions that it raises. To stimulate discussion, students can ask one another the kinds of questions that good readers ask themselves about a text: *How does it connect to money? What have I learned that is new? What did I find interesting about this story? What is important here? What was difficult to understand? What information surprised me? Why would someone want to read this?* Ensure that students are using specific information from the text to support their interpretations.

**Handing-off Process** Seeing you as a contributing member of the group sets a strong example for students. To emphasize that you are part of the group, actively participate in the *handing-off process:* Raise your hand to be called on by the last speaker when you have a contribution to make. Point out unusual and interesting insights verbalized by students so that these insights are recognized and discussed. As the year progresses, students will take more and more responsibility for the discussions of the selections.

Engage students in a discussion to determine whether they have grasped the following ideas:

- what the meaning of the article title is
- what the children did in business
- how all the children ran their businesses
- what all the children have in common

During this time, have students return to the clues, problems, and wonderings they noted during browsing to determine whether the clues were borne out by the selection, whether and how their problems were solved, and whether their wonderings were answered or deserve further discussion and investigation. Let students decide which items deserve further discussion.

Also have students return to the Focus Questions on the first page of the selection. Select a student to read the questions aloud, and have volunteers answer the questions. If students do not know the answers to the questions, have them return to the text to find the answers.

You may wish to review the elements of expository text with the students at this time. Discuss with them how they can tell that "Kids Did It! in Business" is expository text.

Have students break into small groups to discuss what this story tells them about money. Groups can discuss their ideas with the rest of the class.

Students may wish to record their personal responses to the selection. If students have ever had an experience with being in business, having a business idea, or creating something original, encourage them to record these events.

## Review Selection Vocabulary

Have students review the definitions of the selection vocabulary words that they wrote in the vocabulary section of their Writer's Notebooks. Remind them that they discussed the meanings of these words before reading the selection. Have students write sentences for each of the vocabulary words after the definitions in the same section of their Writer's Notebooks. They can use the definitions and the sentences to study for the vocabulary portion of their Lesson Assessments. Have them add to the personal dictionary section of their Writer's Notebooks any other interesting words that they clarified while reading. Encourage students to refer to the selection vocabulary words throughout the unit. The words from the selection are:

**malfunction** **profitable** **merchandise** **earnings** **donates** **charity**

Remind students to add the selection vocabulary to their Word Banks and to find words from other resources, from their investigations, and from family discussions and add them to the Word Bank as well.

## Home Connection

Distribute ***Home Connection,*** page 49. Parents and caregivers may enjoy working with their children to create a business plan for starting their own business. Encourage students to share their business plans with the class. A Spanish version of this letter appears on page 50.

*Kids Did It! in Business*

**A message from** ______________________

As part of our unit on money, our class has read "Kids Did It! in Business," an article about four young people, each with her or his own business. Ranging in age from ten to eighteen, these young entrepreneurs are an inspiration to readers.

You and your child might enjoy brainstorming ideas for a business he or she could start to earn extra money. To stimulate ideas, ask your child to tell you more about the businesses that the young people in the article started. Then encourage him or her to use the space below to create a preliminary "business plan" by writing a paragraph to answer each of the following questions.

**My Business Plan**

I. What is the name of my business?

______________________

II. What type of business and what services will I offer?

______________________

III. Who will my customers be and why will they hire me?

______________________

IV. How much will I charge for my services?

______________________

**Next week's selection** *The Cobbler's Song*

Your child will be studying the following vocabulary words in the upcoming week. Please review the meanings of these words with your child: **cobbler**—a person who makes or repairs shoes; **safekeeping**—guarding in safety; **workbench**—strong table used for working; **treasure**—something valuable; **mended**—fixed, repaired; **recognizing**—suddenly aware that someone or something is familiar.

Please review with your child the spelling words for the upcoming week: making, biting, diving, hiking, skated, prized, shaking, skating, hiding, shining, thinking, entered, opened, passing, safekeeping.

***Home Connection p. 49***

**Teacher Tip** Encourage students to write a sentence using these vocabulary words. In order to provide additional help in remembering words, students may write a synonym or an antonym for the word if it is appropriate. Some students may even draw something that helps them to remember the meaning of the word.

### Differentiating Instruction

| If... | Then... |
| --- | --- |
| Students enjoyed reading the article "Kids Did It! in Business" | Challenge them to read articles from other student-oriented magazines and to identify similarities and differences between the various magazines |

Reading Transparency 50

**Teacher Tip** WRITING Remind students to practice proofreading skills after they write a first draft. Students can proofread their own papers, or they can exchange papers with a classmate for proofreading.

### Differentiating Instruction

| If... | Then... |
|---|---|
| Students need extra help making connections | • Reread the article with them and provide additional modeling of the strategy<br>• Help them write an informative piece about their personal connections to the article during Workshop |

**Teacher Tip** Have the class develop a revision checklist, using what they know about the elements of informative writing and the revision process. Encourage students to use this checklist to revise their writing.

## Supporting the Reading

### Comprehension Strategies: Making Connections

**Teach** During the first read, remind students that making connections involves paying attention to what they are reading and noticing how their own experiences and knowledge relate to the text. Thinking about how a text reminds us of our own experiences helps us as readers to more fully understand what we read.

**Guided Practice** Read through the article again with students. This time, ask students to pay special attention to any fact or detail that reminds them of something with which they are already familiar. For example, as students read the first page of the article, they might make a connection with experiences they have had with computers, or more specifically, with software or perhaps bugs that cause crashes. Invite students to share their connections with the class. Record their responses on the board or on the two-column chart on ***Reading Transparency 50.*** You can use the following as an example to get started.

| Passage from Article | Student Connection |
|---|---|
| Adam Baratz looks for software bugs that make computers malfunction. | I know why this is important because sometimes when I use the library computer for my schoolwork, it crashes. |

**Independent Practice** Have students focus on the strategy Making Connections as they read selections in the ***Student Anthology,*** the ***Leveled Classroom Library,*** and Bibliography.

**Link to Writing** Invite students to write about their personal connections to the article they have just read. What are their connections? Do they relate to the children featured in the article? Do students have a connection to the products discussed in the article? Do students have their own experiences with being in business, working for money, or creating or inventing something original? Ask students to explain what their connection is to the article, in a small informative piece of their own. Explain to students that with informative writing, they need to pay special attention to the details that answer the questions *Who? What? When? Where? Why?* and *How?* Encourage students to use words that they learned while reading the article in their writing.

## Literary Elements

### Expository Texts

**Teach** Ask students to tell you what they know about expository texts. If necessary, remind them that expository texts inform readers about a subject by supplying facts and informative details. Expository texts are sometimes called informational texts or articles, and they are a type of nonfiction literature. If necessary, review with students the meaning of the terms *fiction* and *nonfiction.*

**Guided Practice** Draw four web charts on the board. You may also choose to make copies of ***Reading Transparency 55*** to distribute to each of the groups. Have students identify the names of the four children in the article "Kids Did It! in Business." Write one of the names *(Adam, Ebony, Marc,* and *Abbey)* in the center of each circle. Divide the class into four groups and assign one of these names to each group. Have each group complete their web with factual information about the person in their web. Allow time for each group to report their findings to the class by explaining their web charts.

**Independent Practice** Ask students to look up some expository texts in the school library or on the Internet. They can look for a text related to their investigation question if they like. Ask students to identify at least two expository texts. If the texts seem promising, students might want to check them out or print them out, as necessary.

**Teacher Tip INVESTIGATE** Before students begin their search for expository texts, go over with them ways to identify reliable sources on the Internet. Reliable sources will be published by a well-known, reputable organization, such as an educational organization, university, or governmental organization. Many of these sites end with the suffixes *.com, .gov,* or *.edu.*

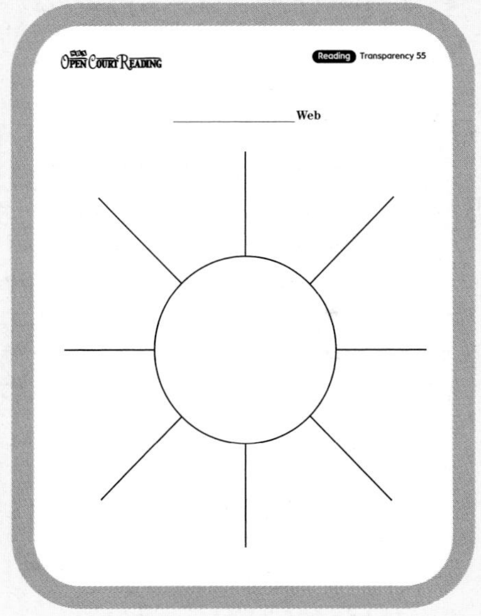


***Reading Transparency 55***

### Differentiating Instruction

| If... | Then... |
|---|---|
| Students are having difficulty with the Independent Practice portion of this activity and need help identifying expository texts | • Review the elements of expository text with them<br>• Have them find examples of expository texts in their ***Anthologies.*** Have them explain how these selections were different from the fictional stories that they read.<br>• Help them locate expository texts in the library or on the Internet |

**Teacher Tip MATERIALS**
- ✔ poster board
- ✔ colored pencils or markers
- ✔ cardboard
- ✔ gold- or silver-colored foil

**Teacher Tip PURPOSE** To learn about the role money has played in the development of an ancient civilization.

**Teacher Tip** Remind students that the library as well as the Internet provides many sources that cover important periods in history and that are created especially for young students to use. They might consider starting with such a source to look up the information in this activity.

## Social Studies Connection

### Money in History

In "Kids Did It! in Business," students read about kids who have started their own businesses to make money. In our society, selling goods or services for money is how money is generated and circulated for people to make a living and obtain the things they need. Throughout history, different societies developed different means of establishing currency and creating and distributing money. Different societies also placed different emphasis on private property and entrepreneurship.

Ask students to focus on one particular ancient society and conduct research to discover how money developed in that culture and how money influenced the development of that culture. Have them trace it to the present day, taking special note of what has changed and what has remained the same. To help students get started on the research, remind them of the Read Aloud selection *Money, Money, Money.*

On the board, list the names of the societies discussed in that selection. Ask students to work in pairs or small groups and to prepare a presentation of their findings, accompanied by visuals. Students might wish to create diagrams showing money-related developments, a time line, graphs, charts, photographs, diagrams of different types of money used, or models of currency used.

## Science Connection

### Inventions and Inventors

Invite students to give examples of products they use, such as the ink pen, the microwave, the calculator, and the shovel. Have them think about what problem each of the inventions has solved. Remind students of the "Makin' Bacon," invented by Abbey Fleck, described in the article "Kids Did It! in Business." Organize the students into groups of five or six, and have them come up with their own inventions. The students will present their concepts to the classroom. Ask the students to consider the following questions:

- How will their invention make life easier or better?
- Are there any negative consequences if their invention is made?
- What will their invention be made of?
- Who will use their invention?

Remind students that while inventions are intended to be helpful, they can also have negative consequences, for example, cloning.

Once they have completed their presentations, ask the audience if they think the invention is feasible. Make them support their answers. If the invention is feasible, encourage students to create their inventions.

**Teacher Tip** MATERIALS

- ✔ pencils
- ✔ paper
- ✔ research materials

**Teacher Tip** PURPOSE To allow students to use their creativity to come up with new inventions. To show the importance of inventions and the propriety necessary when inventing.

**Teacher Tip** Encourage students to use strategies when responding to speakers. Tell them that by asking questions, making contributions, and paraphrasing, they are clarifying a speaker's words for the entire class.

## Concept Connections

### Linking the Selection

- They had good ideas for a product or service, and they all worked to turn their ideas into successful businesses.
- One possible answer: Ebony is saving for college.

### Exploring Concept Vocabulary

The concept word for this lesson is ***worth.*** Write the word on the board. Work with students to develop a definition that clearly links to the unit theme. Have students copy the word and definition into the Vocabulary section of their Writer's Notebooks.

***Worth:*** the importance, value, or usefulness of something; the monetary value of something. For example, in "A New Coat for Anna," Anna's mother thought a new coat was worth more than the possessions she bartered.

- A service or product is worth what people will pay for it. Adam's services were worth free products. The other children's products were worth varying amounts of money.
- People show a product's worth by buying it and taking care of it.

Make sure that each student's sentence contains the concept word ***worth*** and one of the selection vocabulary words.

### Expanding the Concept

You may want to do a whole-group discussion to help students continue to develop their ability to engage in meaningful dialogue. However, students may conduct these dialogues in small groups. If students work in small groups, bring the groups together and have them share their ideas with the whole class.

As students complete their discussions, have them record their ideas and impressions about the selection on page 84 of their ***Inquiry Journals.***

# Kids Did It! in Business

## Concept Connections

### Linking the Selection

Think about the following questions, and then record your responses in the Response Journal section of your Writer's Notebook.

- What do all the children in this article have in common?
- What kinds of things do the children do with the money they earn?

### Exploring Concept Vocabulary

The concept word for this lesson is ***worth.*** If you do not know what this word means, look it up in a dictionary. Answer these questions:

- What determines a service's or product's ***worth?*** In the article, what were the children's services' or products' ***worth?***
- How do people show a product's ***worth?***

Make up an oral sentence using the word ***worth*** and one of the selection vocabulary words.

### Expanding the Concept

Think about the article "Kids Did It! in Business." What did you learn about money from this article?

Try to use the word ***worth*** in your discussion.

Add new ideas about money to the Concept/Question Board.

46

**Teacher Tip** These activities may be done during Workshop.

**Informal Assessment**

This may be a good time to observe students working in small groups and to mark your observations in the Teacher Observation Log in the ***Program Assessment Teacher's Edition.***

## Meet the Author

**Judith E. Rinard** writes for the National Geographic Society. Besides writing, she loves drawing, painting, traveling, and camping. Most of her writing is about nature and foreign cultures.

## Meet the Author

After students read the information about Judith E. Rinard, discuss the following questions with them:

- Judith E. Rinard writes for the National Geographic Society. How do you think this type of writing would be different from writing stories? *(Possible answers: Articles have to be shorter and based on fact. A writer might need to do more research on a factual piece of writing to be sure it is accurate.)*
- Judith E. Rinard likes to travel and camp, and most of her writing is about nature and foreign cultures. How do these two ideas fit together? *(Possible answers: By traveling and camping, she can observe nature and foreign cultures herself. She knows more about what they are like because she has lived in them.)*

## Objectives

- Students ask questions related to money.
- Students gain a deeper understanding of issues related to money.
- Student groups form conjectures.

## Materials

- Student Anthology, Book 2, pp. 38–47
- Inquiry Journal, pp. 93–95
- Research Assistant CD-ROM

**Teacher Tip** Remind students that they can use any of the activities performed during the unit to help them come up with their investigation questions, problems, and conjectures. The various activities, readings, and writing projects should generate ideas. Also remind them that the investigation they choose should be one that really interests them. They should be excited about seeking the answers to their questions.

## Differentiating Instruction

| If... | Then... |
| --- | --- |
| Students are having difficulty with the Inquiry activities | • Help them brainstorm ideas for turning one of their hobbies into a business<br>• Help them fill in the Ways to Earn Money Chart on pages 93–94 in their ***Inquiry Journals*** |

INVESTIGATION

# Investigating Concepts Beyond the Text

At this point in the research cycle, students will continue identifying problems and questions and will begin forming conjectures based on their questions and initial investigations. Continue monitoring and directing the process when necessary, but do not lose sight of the fact that these investigations are student-directed. These groups will move at different rates and go in different directions throughout the unit, as they follow their own questions and develop their own presentations.

In "Kids Did It! in Business," students read about children who run their own businesses. Ask students to list on the board any hobbies that interest them. In small groups, students can choose a particular hobby and brainstorm ideas for turning it into a business. Ask students to think about and share the questions they would have to ask themselves before starting a business. Ask small groups to plan a business around one of the hobbies listed on the board. Encourage each group to investigate the particular type of business they have chosen. Invite students to share their research findings and to describe their businesses. To begin this activity, have students work in their groups to complete ***Inquiry Journal,*** pages 93–94.

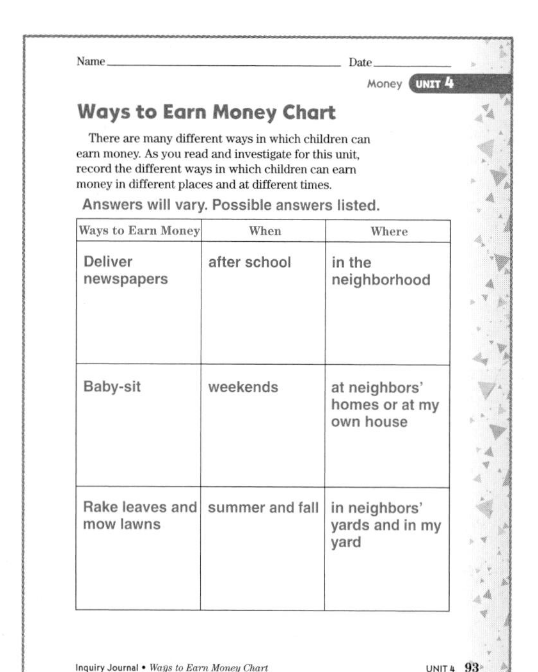

Name_______________ Date_______________

Money UNIT 4

**Ways to Earn Money Chart**

There are many different ways in which children can earn money. As you read and investigate for this unit, record the different ways in which children can earn money in different places and at different times.

Answers will vary. Possible answers listed.

| Ways to Earn Money | When | Where |
| --- | --- | --- |
| Deliver newspapers | after school | in the neighborhood |
| Baby-sit | weekends | at neighbors' homes or at my own house |
| Rake leaves and mow lawns | summer and fall | in neighbors' yards and in my yard |

Inquiry Journal • *Ways to Earn Money Chart* UNIT 4 93

**Ways to Earn Money Chart** *(continued)*

| Ways to Earn Money | When | Where |
| --- | --- | --- |
| Shovel snow | winter | my driveway and neighbors' driveways |
| Walk dogs | after school and weekends | in my neighborhood |
| Perform | weekends and after school | parties |
| Make jewelry and sell it | weekends and after school | to stores and friends |

94 UNIT 4 *Ways to Earn Money Chart* • Inquiry Journal

***Inquiry Journal pp. 93–94***

## Concept/Question Board

After reading each selection, students should use the Concept/Question Board to:

- Post any questions they asked about a selection before reading that have not been answered yet.
- Refer to as they formulate statements about concepts that apply to their investigations.
- Post general statements formulated by each collaborative group.
- Continue to post news articles or other items that they find during the unit investigation.
- Read and think about posted questions, articles, or concepts that interest them and provide answers to the questions.

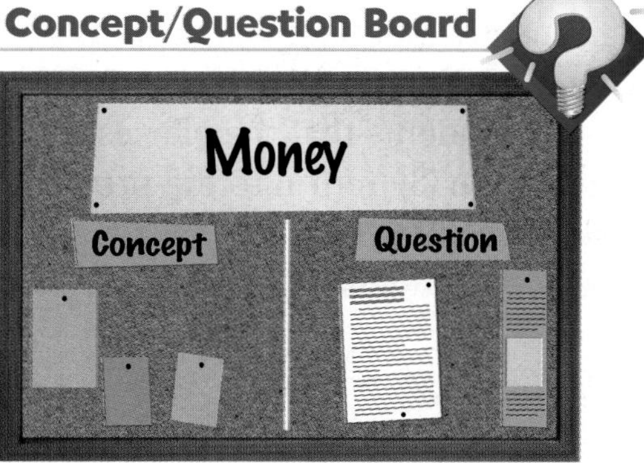


## Unit 4 Investigation Management

| | |
|---|---|
| Lesson 1 | Brainstorm questions related to the theme. Investigate alternatives to money, such as bartering. |
| Lesson 2 | Groups form based on areas of shared interest. Investigate choices related to spending and saving money. |
| Lesson 3 | Collaborative Investigation<br>**Begin forming conjectures.**<br>Supplementary Activity<br>**Brainstorm about how to turn hobbies into businesses.** |
| Lesson 4 | Discuss conjectures in groups and begin plans. Look for stories or illustrations about the ways that money can change people and things that money cannot buy. |
| Lesson 5 | Students revise their plans as necessary and continue investigation. Groups can debate on borrowing and lending money. |
| Lesson 6 | Continue investigation and prepare final presentations. Create a story or miniplay about how money passes from person to person, or plan a field trip to a Federal Reserve Bank. |
| Lesson 7 | Groups give formal presentations. Students discuss saving money for personal goals or explore the Great Depression further. |

INVESTIGATION

**Teacher Tip** Continue to encourage use of the Concept/Question Board by recognizing and thanking students for their contributions. Incorporate discussion of those items into classroom discussions whenever appropriate.

### Research Assistant

The ***Research Assistant CD-ROM*** helps students in their investigations.

**Teacher Tip** Ensure that students understand that conjectures can and should change over the course of their investigations.

**Formal Assessment**

Use the Research Rubrics on page 38J to assess students' ability to make conjectures.

INVESTIGATION

## Conjecture Phase

Explain to students that a conjecture is a kind of hypothesis that lacks evidence, an explanation that one suggests before having a great deal of proof or support. Conjectures may be proved right, or proved wrong, or modified in some way by the evidence. Have students join their groups to work on the Conjecture Phase on page 95 in their ***Inquiry Journals.*** Prior to this, it will be helpful to have group discussion and to model conjectures. For this, you might choose a problem that has already been suggested for investigation but has not been chosen by any group. Using this problem, the whole class can engage in conjecturing without anything being taken away from a group investigation.

As students share their conjectures, record them on the board. Explain that consensus is not necessary at this point. As students begin investigations, they will revisit their conjectures and revise them based on new information. Remind students that the phases of the Research Cycle are recursive; students will continually return to the previous phases of the cycle and assess how the problem and the conjectures have changed and what new information is necessary. Students can use Workshop time to work on their investigations.

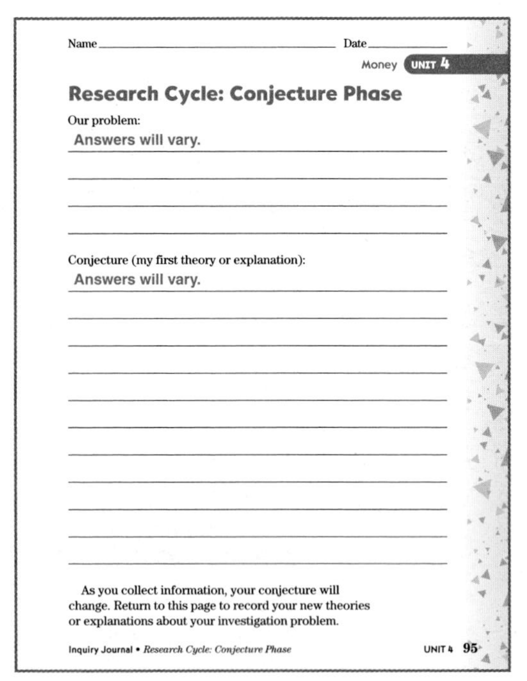

Name ________ Date ________

Money UNIT 4

**Research Cycle: Conjecture Phase**

Our problem:

Answers will vary.

Conjecture (my first theory or explanation):

Answers will vary.

As you collect information, your conjecture will change. Return to this page to record your new theories or explanations about your investigation problem.

Inquiry Journal • *Research Cycle: Conjecture Phase* UNIT 4 95

***Inquiry Journal p. 95***

**Teach** Review with students the parts of a book and what purpose each serves. Students should mention that the *title page* is at the beginning of a book and gives the title, author's name, and the publisher's full name; the *copyright page* follows the title page and gives the publisher's name, as well as the place and year of publication; the *table of contents* appears in the front of the book and lists units, chapters, or stories, along with the page on which each begins; the *glossary* appears at the back of the book and lists definitions alphabetically and sometimes pronunciations of new or special words used in the book; the *index* is found at the back of the book and alphabetically lists names, places, and topics included in the book, with page numbers showing where the information can be found; and the *bibliography* appears at the back of the book and lists alphabetically, by title or author, books or articles the author used or other writings that might interest the reader. Remind students that not all kinds of books contain all of these book parts.

**Guided Practice** List the book parts on the board as students mention them. If students fail to mention a specific part, direct them to that part in the anthology, using page numbers and asking students what they find on those pages.

**Independent Practice** Ask students questions that require them to use the different parts of the anthology or any nonfiction book to find the answers. Students may work in pairs. You may list questions on the board and require written answers, or you may proceed orally. If written answers are required, students may check each other's work. You can address the following with students:

- What title is shown on the title page?
- Write three words and their definitions from the glossary.
- Write one name, one place, and one topic found in the index, along with their page numbers.
- Write the page numbers for the first and last chapters.
- Write the title of one other book used by the author as a reference when he or she was writing this book.
- When was this book copyrighted?



choose a book to read from the library relating to the theme. This book should identify their preference in either literary or nonfiction texts. Encourage students to read often from their preferred genre. Make sure students utilize the appropriate areas of the library to select reading materials. If necessary, review these areas with students before they visit the library.

Encourage students to use ***TechKnowledge*** to learn more about using a computer to assist in their investigations.

## Differentiating Instruction

| If... | Then... |
| --- | --- |
| Students need extra help identifying the parts of a book | • Point to the different parts as students name them, using the list on the board<br>• Help them point to the different parts as you name them<br>• Review the parts of a book during Workshop |

Spelling

- **Contractions.** Develop understanding of how to spell contractions.

Vocabulary

- **Business and Technology Vocabulary.** Using words from "Kids Did It! in Business," learn the meanings of words that relate to business and technology.

**Writing Process Strategies**

- **Persuasive Writing: Business Letter.** Building on the idea of young people starting businesses, students will learn the form and function of writing a persuasive business letter.

**English Language Conventions**

Grammar, Usage, and Mechanics

- **Mechanics: Periods in Abbreviations, Titles, and People's Initials; and Parentheses.** Learning to identify and use periods in abbreviations, titles, and people's initials, and to identify abbreviations and parentheses in "Kids Did It! in Business." Locate periods in titles and initials in classroom library selections.

Listening, Speaking, Viewing

- **Language: Choosing Words.** Use appropriate words to express an intended message.

Penmanship

- **Cursive Letters *N* and *M*.** Develop handwriting skills by practicing formation of cursive *N* and *M*.

### Materials

- Spelling and Vocabulary Skills, pp. 82–85
- Language Arts Handbook
- Comprehension and Language Arts Skills, pp. 102–105
- Writer's Workbook, pp. 62–65
- Language Arts Transparency 14
- Student Anthology
- Routine Card 2, Routine 7

## Differentiating Instruction

***Reteach, Challenge,*** and ***Intervention*** lessons are available to support the language arts instruction in this lesson.

## Research in Action

The first property of effective vocabulary instruction is integration—tying in new words with familiar concepts and experiences. *(William E. Nagy,* Teaching Vocabulary to Improve Reading Comprehension)

OVERVIEW

## Word Analysis

**Spelling** The Spelling activities introduce how to spell contractions. A contraction is a shortened form of two or more words. When the words come together, some letters are taken out, and an apostrophe (') marks the place.

### Selection Spelling Words

These words from "Kids Did It! in Business" are contractions. Notice the apostrophe in each word.

**can't I'm what's she's it's**

**Vocabulary** The Vocabulary activities introduce how business trends and new technology add new words to our vocabulary.

### Vocabulary Skill Words

**software profitable* merchandise* donates* invention**

**Also Selection Vocabulary*

**Additional Materials:** dictionary

## Writing Process Strategies

The Writing Process Strategies lesson involves instruction in writing a business letter with the focus on the art of persuasion, using reasons, facts, or feelings to support one's viewpoint.

To teach spreadsheet applications in the writing process, help students become familiar with the idea that spreadsheets can calculate. You might want to help students create a spreadsheet to organize ideas for a business they would like to start; show them how to automatically add numbers to a spreadsheet to create a total. ***TechKnowledge,*** Level 3, Lesson 69, teaches these spreadsheet application skills.

## English Language Conventions

**Grammar, Usage, and Mechanics** **Mechanics: Periods with Abbreviations, Titles, and People's Initials; and Parentheses.** This lesson develops an understanding of using periods with abbreviations, titles, and people's initials, and using parentheses.

**Listening, Speaking, Viewing** **Language: Choosing Words.** In this Language lesson, students will choose appropriate words for an advertisement.

**Penmanship** **Cursive Letters *N* and *M*.** This lesson develops handwriting skills by having students learn formation of *N* and *M*. Students then write words from the literature selection.

# DAY 1

## Word Analysis

### Spelling

**Assessment: Pretest**

**Contractions**

**Teach**

Give students the Pretest on page 34 of ***Unit 4 Assessment.*** Have them proofread and correct any misspelled words.

**Pretest Sentences**

1. **he'll** If a male gorilla feels threatened, **he'll** attack.
2. **she'll** She knows **she'll** go.
3. **we'll** Scientists dream that **we'll** find a cure for all diseases.
4. **I'd** I studied so **I'd** succeed.
5. **we'd** If **we'd** eat healthful foods, then **we'd** feel better.
6. **they'll** Geese know **they'll** fly south when it gets cold.
7. **you'd** If **you'd** study for tests, you'd get good grades.
8. **that's** Bread is made from dough **that's** left out to rise.
9. **she'd** Rosa Parks knew **she'd** made a difference.
10. **you'll** If you visit a foreign country, **you'll** need a passport.
11. **it's** At midnight, **it's** 12:00 a.m.
12. **she's** My sister is proud because **she's** the fastest runner in her class.
13. **what's** A chef is proud to tell **what's** in his or her meals.
14. **I'm** **I'm** made of cells.
15. **can't** Little chicks **can't** fly when they first hatch.

Diagnose any misspellings by determining whether students misspelled the formation of the contraction or some other part of the word. Use the Pretest as a take-home list to study the spellings of contractions.

## Writing Process Strategies

### Getting Ideas

**Persuasive Business Letter**

**Teach**

**Introduce Persuasive Writing**

- Read ***Language Arts Handbook,*** pages 156–157.
- Read ***Language Arts Handbook,*** pages 72–77.
- Discuss ***Language Arts Transparency 14,*** Template—Business Letter.
- Share the formal assessment rubrics with students. (See Day 5 of this lesson.)

**Inspiration**

Teacher Model: *"I have an idea for a business. I want to write a letter to my principal to ask him to help."*

**Brainstorming**

Encourage students to suggest businesses they could start. Make a list of these ideas on the board.

**Guided Practice**

**Getting Ideas**

Have students write ideas for a persuasive business letter in their Writer's Notebooks.

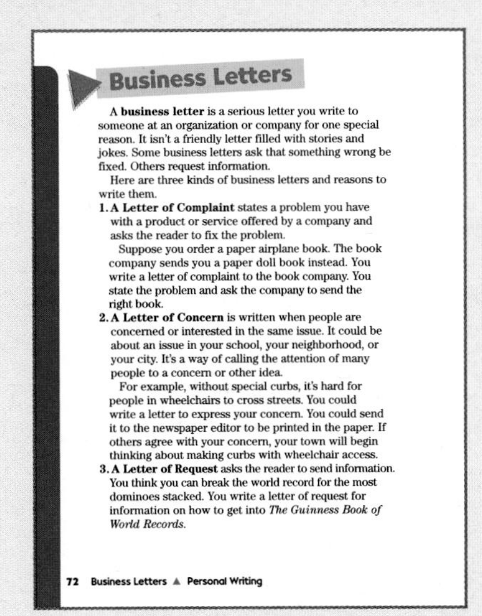

**Business Letters**

A **business letter** is a serious letter you write to someone at an organization or company for one special reason. It isn't a friendly letter filled with stories and jokes. Some business letters ask that something wrong be fixed. Others request information.

Here are three kinds of business letters and reasons to write them.

1. **A Letter of Complaint** states a problem you have with a product or service offered by a company and asks the reader to fix the problem.
   Suppose you order a paper airplane book. The book company sends you a paper doll book instead. You write a letter of complaint to the book company. You state the problem and ask the company to send the right book.
2. **A Letter of Concern** is written when people are concerned or interested in the same issue. It could be about an issue in your school, your neighborhood, or your city. It's a way of calling the attention of many people to a concern or other idea.
   For example, without special curbs, it's hard for people in wheelchairs to cross streets. You could write a letter to express your concern. You could send it to the newspaper editor to be printed in the paper. If others agree with your concern, your town will begin thinking about making curbs with wheelchair access.
3. **A Letter of Request** asks the reader to send information. You think you can break the world record for the most dominoes stacked. You write a letter of request for information on how to get into *The Guinness Book of World Records.*

72 Business Letters ▲ Personal Writing

***Language Arts Handbook* p. 72**

## English Language Conventions

### Grammar, Usage, and Mechanics

**Mechanics: Periods with Abbreviations and People's Initials, and Parentheses**

**Teach**

- Read ***Language Arts Handbook,*** pages 270 and 274, for rules and examples concerning periods with abbreviations, titles, and people's initials, and using parentheses.
- Write the following items on the board and explain the rule for each.
  - Ms. Tammy Wilkin *(period in title)*
  - W.C. Fields *(periods in initials)*
  - Washington, D.C. *(periods in abbreviations)*
  - I ate (almost) all of it in one bite. *(parentheses)*

  (Point out that initials are capitalized and have a period after each one.)

**Guided Practice**

Use ***Comprehension and Language Arts Skills,*** pages 102–103, to identify the use of periods with abbreviations, titles, and initials, and the use of parentheses.

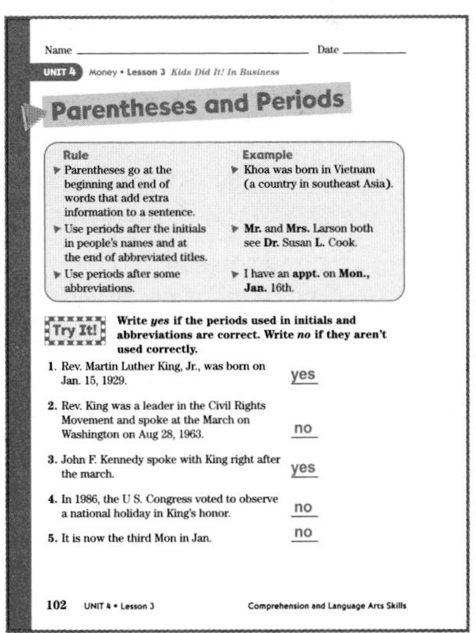

Name ____________ Date ______

UNIT 4 Money • Lesson 3 *Kids Did It! In Business*

**Parentheses and Periods**

| Rule | Example |
|---|---|
| Parentheses go at the beginning and end of words that add extra information to a sentence. | Khoa was born in Vietnam (a country in southeast Asia). |
| Use periods after the initials in people's names and at the end of abbreviated titles. | **Mr.** and **Mrs.** Larson both see **Dr.** Susan **L.** Cook. |
| Use periods after some abbreviations. | I have an **appt.** on **Mon.**, **Jan.** 16th. |

**Try It!** **Write *yes* if the periods used in initials and abbreviations are correct. Write *no* if they aren't used correctly.**

1. Rev. Martin Luther King, Jr., was born on Jan. 15, 1929. yes
2. Rev. King was a leader in the Civil Rights Movement and spoke at the March on Washington on Aug 28, 1963. no
3. John F. Kennedy spoke with King right after the march. yes
4. In 1986, the U S. Congress voted to observe a national holiday in King's honor. no
5. It is now the third Mon in Jan. no

102 UNIT 4 • Lesson 3 Comprehension and Language Arts Skills

***Comprehension and Language Arts Skills* p. 102**

## DAY 2

## Word Analysis

### Spelling

**Contractions**

**Board Work.** Write *can't* on the board. Explain that contractions are shortened words with letters taken out. An apostrophe (') marks the space. Write *can + not* under *can't.* Ask a student to circle the letters taken out to spell *can't (n* in *can* and *o* in *not).*

### Vocabulary

**Business and Technology Vocabulary**

#### Teach

- Write *software* ("Kids Did It! in Business," p. 38) on the board and ask what the word relates to *(computers, programs, games).* Ask students to find context clues for the meaning of the word.
- Explain that without computers, *software* would not be part of our vocabulary. Business and technology both add new words to our language.
- Ask a student to find *software* in the dictionary. *(a computer program)*

#### Guided Practice

Use ***Spelling and Vocabulary Skills,*** page 82, to teach students to use strategies to learn the meaning of a word. Ask students to complete page 83 as independent practice.

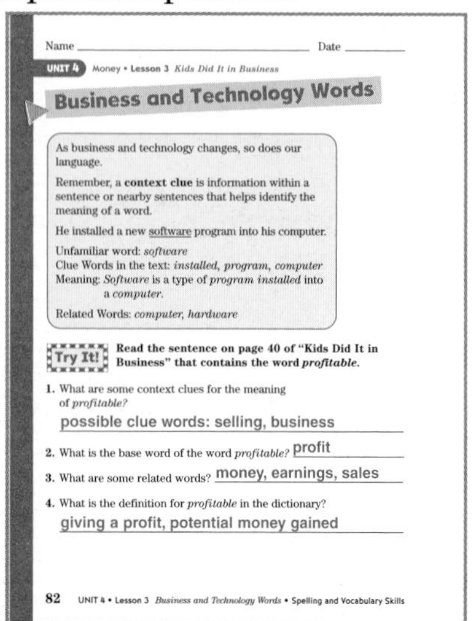
Name ______ Date ______

UNIT 4 Money • Lesson 3 *Kids Did It in Business*

**Business and Technology Words**

As business and technology changes, so does our language.

Remember, a **context clue** is information within a sentence or nearby sentences that helps identify the meaning of a word.

He installed a new software program into his computer.

Unfamiliar word: *software*
Clue Words in the text: *installed, program, computer*
Meaning: *Software* is a type of *program installed* into a *computer.*

Related Words: *computer, hardware*

**Try It!** **Read the sentence on page 40 of "Kids Did It in Business" that contains the word *profitable.***

1. What are some context clues for the meaning of *profitable?* possible clue words: selling, business
2. What is the base word of the word *profitable?* profit
3. What are some related words? money, earnings, sales
4. What is the definition for *profitable* in the dictionary? giving a profit, potential money gained

82 UNIT 4 • Lesson 3 *Business and Technology Words* • Spelling and Vocabulary Skills

***Spelling and Vocabulary Skills* p. 82**

## Writing Process Strategies

### Prewriting

**Persuasive Business Letter**

#### Teach

- **Review** student ideas for persuasive business letters from Day 1.
- Read ***Writer's Workbook,*** page 62, on prewriting for a persuasive business letter.

**Writer's Craft**

**Structure of a Business Letter**

- Discuss that a business letter has the same parts as a friendly letter but is more formal.
- Read ***Language Arts Handbook,*** page 74, on the parts of a business letter.
- Read ***Comprehension and Language Arts Skills,*** pages 104–105, on the structure of a business letter.

#### Independent Practice

**Prewriting**

- Have students fill out their audience and purpose on ***Writer's Workbook,*** page 62.
- Have students complete the graphic organizer on ***Writer's Workbook,*** page 63.

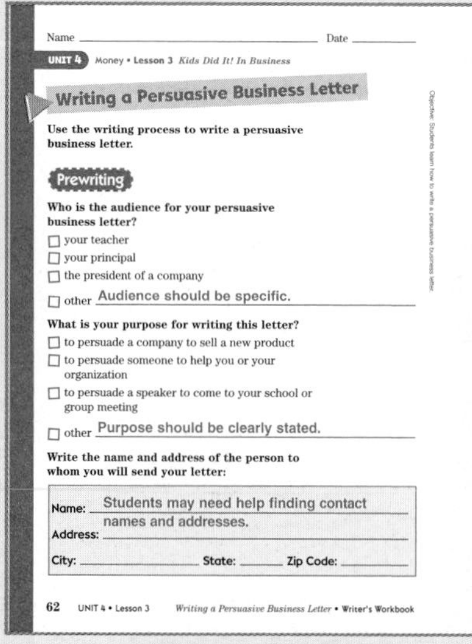
Name ______ Date ______

UNIT 4 Money • Lesson 3 *Kids Did It! In Business*

**Writing a Persuasive Business Letter**

**Use the writing process to write a persuasive business letter.**

**Prewriting**

**Who is the audience for your persuasive business letter?**

- ☐ your teacher
- ☐ your principal
- ☐ the president of a company
- ☐ other Audience should be specific.

**What is your purpose for writing this letter?**

- ☐ to persuade a company to sell a new product
- ☐ to persuade someone to help you or your organization
- ☐ to persuade a speaker to come to your school or group meeting
- ☐ other Purpose should be clearly stated.

**Write the name and address of the person to whom you will send your letter:**

Name: Students may need help finding contact names and addresses.
Address: ______
City: ______ State: ______ Zip Code: ______

Objective: Students learn how to write a persuasive business letter.

62 UNIT 4 • Lesson 3 *Writing a Persuasive Business Letter* • Writer's Workbook

***Writer's Workbook* p. 62**

## English Language Conventions

### Grammar, Usage, and Mechanics

**Mechanics: Periods with Abbreviations and People's Initials; Parentheses**

#### Teach

- **Review** the use of periods with abbreviations, titles, and people's initials, and the use of parentheses using ***Language Arts Handbook,*** pages 270 and 274.
- Write the following examples on the board and ask students to tell you which rule is being followed.
  - Dr. Clark took his temperature. *(period in title)*
  - J.R.R. Tolkien was an author. *(periods in initials)*
  - Feb. *(periods in abbreviations)*
- Explain that parentheses set off additional, but nonessential, information in a sentence. Explain that parentheses go around both sides of the words expressing this information. Then write these sentences on the board. Ask students where the parentheses should go.
  - A newspaper published in Manhattan costs 50 cents. *(published in Manhattan)*
  - Printers they make a good living come to work in the early evening. *(they make a good living)*
  - They work until late how tiring at night. *(how tiring)*
  - Printers work and it's noisy work those hours so readers can have the latest news in the morning. *(and it's noisy work)*

#### Guided Practice in Reading

Have students find parentheses, and periods in abbreviations, in "Kids Did It! in Business." Have students look for periods in initials and titles in the classroom library literature.

# DAY 3

## Word Analysis

### Spelling

**Contractions**

#### Teach

- Introduce words that are contractions found in "Kids Did It! in Business."
- Ask students to think of three contractions that can be made from *I*. (possible answers: *I'm, I'd, I'll)*

#### Guided Practice

Have students complete page 84 from ***Spelling and Vocabulary Skills*** to learn strategies for spelling contractions.

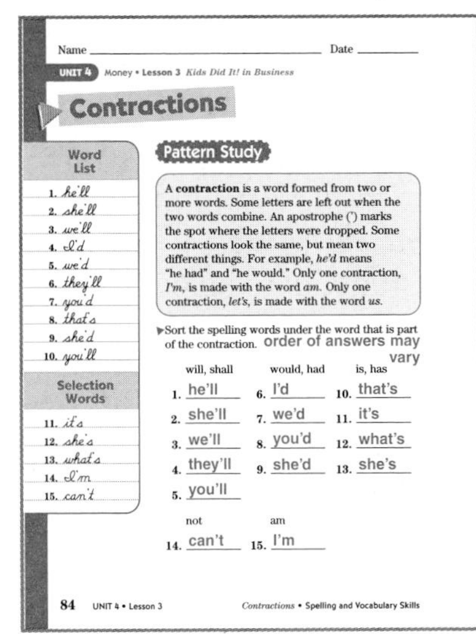

Name ______________________ Date ________

UNIT 4 Money • Lesson 3 *Kids Did It! in Business*

**Contractions**

Word List: 1. he'll 2. she'll 3. we'll 4. I'd 5. we'd 6. they'll 7. you'd 8. that's 9. she'd 10. you'll

Selection Words: 11. it's 12. she's 13. what's 14. I'm 15. can't

**Pattern Study**

A **contraction** is a word formed from two or more words. Some letters are left out when the two words combine. An apostrophe (') marks the spot where the letters were dropped. Some contractions look the same, but mean two different things. For example, *he'd* means "he had" and "he would." Only one contraction, *I'm*, is made with the word *am*. Only one contraction, *let's*, is made with the word *us*.

Sort the spelling words under the word that is part of the contraction. order of answers may vary

| will, shall | would, had | is, has |
|---|---|---|
| 1. he'll | 6. I'd | 10. that's |
| 2. she'll | 7. we'd | 11. it's |
| 3. we'll | 8. you'd | 12. what's |
| 4. they'll | 9. she'd | 13. she's |
| 5. you'll | | |

| not | am |
|---|---|
| 14. can't | 15. I'm |

84 UNIT 4 • Lesson 3 *Contractions* • Spelling and Vocabulary Skills

***Spelling and Vocabulary Skills* p. 84**

### Vocabulary (continued)

**Business and Technology Vocabulary**

- Write *donates* on the board.
- Ask a student to read the sentence in "Kids Did It! in Business" (page 42) with *donates*. Ask the class what *donates* means in the story *(gives away as a gift)*.
- Ask the class if the words *charity* and *profits* gave them clues to the meaning.
- Ask a student to explain how *donates* and *donor* relate to one another *(a donor donates something, the suffix* or *means "one who")*.

## Writing Process Strategies

### Drafting

**Persuasive Business Letter**

#### Teach

- Read ***Writer's Workbook,*** page 63, on drafting a persuasive business letter.
- Have students reread the information they recorded in their ***Writer's Workbooks*** during prewriting. As they read, they may begin formulating a topic sentence in their minds. All of the prewriting information should be included in their drafts.

#### Guided Practice

**Drafting**

Have students write or type the drafts of them persuasive business letters and put them in their ***Writing Folders.***

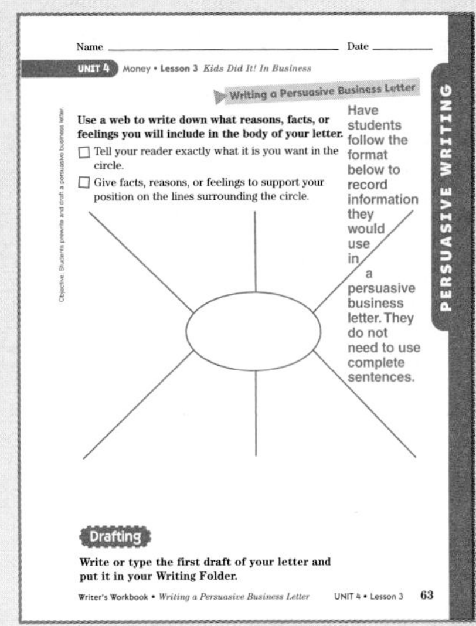

Name ______________________ Date ________

UNIT 4 Money • Lesson 3 *Kids Did It! In Business*

Writing a Persuasive Business Letter

PERSUASIVE WRITING

Objective: Students prewrite and draft a persuasive business letter.

**Use a web to write down what reasons, facts, or feelings you will include in the body of your letter.**

☐ Tell your reader exactly what it is you want in the circle.

☐ Give facts, reasons, or feelings to support your position on the lines surrounding the circle.

Have students follow the format below to record information they would use in a persuasive business letter. They do not need to use complete sentences.

**Drafting**

**Write or type the first draft of your letter and put it in your Writing Folder.**

Writer's Workbook • *Writing a Persuasive Business Letter* UNIT 4 • Lesson 3 63

***Writer's Workbook* p. 63**

**Professional Development**

***Teacher Resource Library CD-ROMs*** or ***Online Professional Development*** provides courses that help you better understand the Writing instruction in ***Open Court Reading.*** For more information about this program, visit SRAonline.com.

## English Language Conventions

### Grammar, Usage, and Mechanics

**Mechanics: Periods with Abbreviations and People's Initials; Parentheses**

#### Teach

- Review the use of periods with abbreviations and people's initials and the use of parentheses using ***Comprehension and Language Arts Skills,*** pages 102–103.
- Ask students to think up fun occupations for each other. For example, dancer, toy maker, emperor, etc. Ask students to imagine abbreviations for these occupations, then write down three, adding them to their own names or the names of friends or relatives. Ask students to write the names in sentences using initials for the first name, with the full name in parentheses. *[dancer could be Dc. so if the name was Sally Brown, it would be Dc. S. Brown (Dancer Sally Brown)]*

#### Guided Practice in Writing

Ask students to imagine that a doctor or general has come to their school and given a speech about their occupation. Students should write thank-you notes which include titles, dates, addresses, and names, using initials for the first and middle names. Challenge them to include nonessential information once, using parentheses.

**Informal Assessment**

Check students' writing to make sure they are using periods and parentheses correctly.

# DAY 4

## Word Analysis

### Spelling

**Contractions**

#### Teach

Explain to students that these exercises in ***Spelling and Vocabulary Skills*** are designed to help them learn to become better spellers of contractions.

#### Guided Practice

Have students complete page 85 of the ***Spelling and Vocabulary Skills*** to reinforce the spelling patterns for contractions.

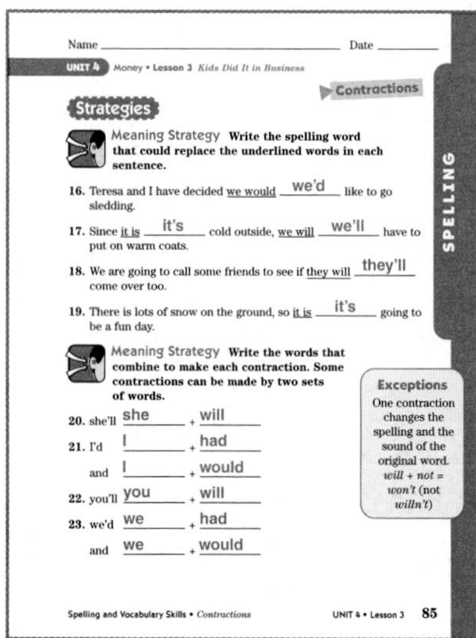

Name ______ Date ______

UNIT 4 Money • Lesson 3 *Kids Did It in Business*

Contractions

**Strategies**

Meaning Strategy **Write the spelling word that could replace the underlined words in each sentence.**

16. Teresa and I have decided we would we'd like to go sledding.
17. Since it is it's cold outside, we will we'll have to put on warm coats.
18. We are going to call some friends to see if they will they'll come over too.
19. There is lots of snow on the ground, so it is it's going to be a fun day.

Meaning Strategy **Write the words that combine to make each contraction. Some contractions can be made by two sets of words.**

20. she'll she + will
21. I'd I + had
    and I + would
22. you'll you + will
23. we'd we + had
    and we + would

**Exceptions**
One contraction changes the spelling and the sound of the original word. *will* + *not* = *won't* (not *willn't*)

SPELLING

Spelling and Vocabulary Skills • *Contractions* UNIT 4 • Lesson 3 85

***Spelling and Vocabulary Skills* p. 85**

### Vocabulary (continued)

**Business and Technology Vocabulary**

- Write *invention* on the board. Write *An inventor invented the invention.* Explain that Abbey Fleck, from "Kids Did It! in Business," is an *inventor.*
- Write *Abbey Fleck invented the invention.* Ask a student what could replace *invention* in the sentence *("Makin' Bacon").* Replace *invention* with *"Makin' Bacon."* Ask another student what could replace *invented* in the sentence *(thought of, created).*
- Write *Abbey Fleck (thought of* or *created) the "Makin' Bacon."*

## Writing Process Strategies

### Revising

**Persuasive Business Letter**

#### Teach

Read ***Writer's Workbook,*** page 64, on revising a persuasive business letter.

**Troubleshooting**

- Misspelling the recipient's name or address makes a bad impression.
- An incorrect format will affect the appearance of your letter.
- Even though you may be expressing feelings, you should be in control of those feelings. You should never use exclamation marks in a business letter.
- Forgetting to thank the reader is impolite.

#### Guided Practice

**Revising**

- Have students revise their drafts and put them in their ***Writing Folders***.
- Have students use the checklist in the ***Writer's Workbook,*** page 64, to revise their persuasive business letters.

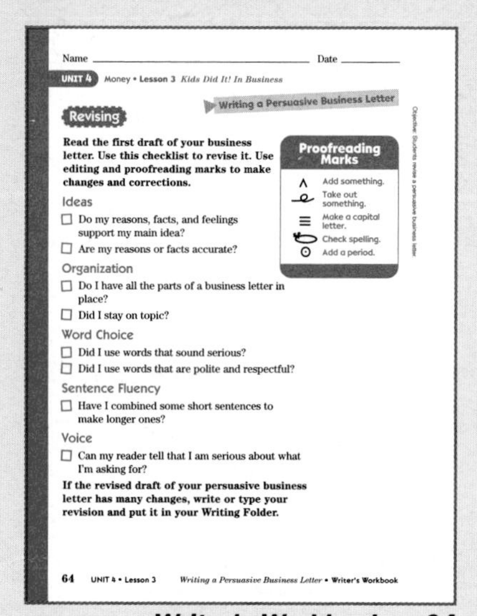

Name ______ Date ______

UNIT 4 Money • Lesson 3 *Kids Did It! In Business*

Writing a Persuasive Business Letter

**Revising**

**Read the first draft of your business letter. Use this checklist to revise it. Use editing and proofreading marks to make changes and corrections.**

Ideas
- ☐ Do my reasons, facts, and feelings support my main idea?
- ☐ Are my reasons or facts accurate?

Organization
- ☐ Do I have all the parts of a business letter in place?
- ☐ Did I stay on topic?

Word Choice
- ☐ Did I use words that sound serious?
- ☐ Did I use words that are polite and respectful?

Sentence Fluency
- ☐ Have I combined some short sentences to make longer ones?

Voice
- ☐ Can my reader tell that I am serious about what I'm asking for?

**If the revised draft of your persuasive business letter has many changes, write or type your revision and put it in your Writing Folder.**

**Proofreading Marks**
- ^ Add something.
- Take out something.
- ≡ Make a capital letter.
- Check spelling.
- ⊙ Add a period.

Objective: Students revise a persuasive business letter.

64 UNIT 4 • Lesson 3 *Writing a Persuasive Business Letter* • Writer's Workbook

***Writer's Workbook* p. 64**

**Routine Card**

Refer to ***Routine 7*** for the Writing Conferences.

## English Language Conventions

### Listening, Speaking, Viewing

**Language: Choosing Words**

#### Teach

- It takes a lot of time and dedication to think of a business, supply the product, and sell that product successfully.
- Explain that the characters in "Kids Did It! in Business" probably advertise their products or services in order to sell them. Using certain words can shape different reactions and perceptions.

#### Guided Practice

- In groups, have students work together to write an advertisement slogan for one of the three services from the story. Instruct the groups to think of the message that they want to express. *(Quality; Fun; Fashionable; Important; Helpful)*
- Remind students to select clear, specific words to communicate ideas and tone. The words they use should reflect what they want to sell. *(If Ebony Hood wanted to advertise her scarves as "fun," she might use words such as vibrant and exciting.)*
- Invite students to share their advertisement slogans with the class.

**Informal Assessment**

Observe whether students can choose appropriate words for an intended message.

# DAY 5

## Word Analysis

### Spelling

#### Assessment: Final Test

**Contractions**

#### Teach

Repeat the Pretest or use the Final Test on page 35 of ***Unit 4 Assessment*** as summative assessment of student understanding of spelling patterns for contractions.

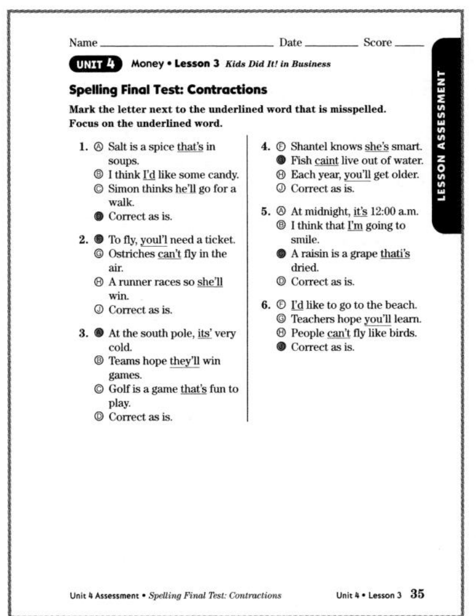

Name ______________ Date ________ Score ______

UNIT 4 Money • Lesson 3 *Kids Did It! in Business*

**Spelling Final Test: Contractions**

**Mark the letter next to the underlined word that is misspelled. Focus on the underlined word.**

1. Ⓐ Salt is a spice that's in soups.
   Ⓑ I think I'd like some candy.
   Ⓒ Simon thinks he'll go for a walk.
   ● Correct as is.
2. ● To fly, youl'l need a ticket.
   Ⓖ Ostriches can't fly in the air.
   Ⓗ A runner races so she'll win.
   Ⓙ Correct as is.
3. ● At the south pole, its' very cold.
   Ⓑ Teams hope they'll win games.
   Ⓒ Golf is a game that's fun to play.
   Ⓓ Correct as is.
4. Ⓕ Shantel knows she's smart.
   ● Fish caint live out of water.
   Ⓗ Each year, you'll get older.
   Ⓙ Correct as is.
5. Ⓐ At midnight, it's 12:00 a.m.
   Ⓑ I think that I'm going to smile.
   ● A raisin is a grape thati's dried.
   Ⓓ Correct as is.
6. Ⓕ I'd like to go to the beach.
   Ⓖ Teachers hope you'll learn.
   Ⓗ People can't fly like birds.
   ● Correct as is.

LESSON ASSESSMENT

Unit 4 Assessment • *Spelling Final Test: Contractions* Unit 4 • Lesson 3 35

***Unit 4 Assessment* p. 35**

#### Guided Practice

Have students categorize any mistakes they made on the Final Test as careless errors or lesson-pattern problems.

### Vocabulary

**Informal Assessment**

Periodically check students' writing assignments to see if students are using words related to either business or technology. Offer praise or encouragement as needed. Have students add any new words to the running Vocabulary Word List in the Writer's Notebook.

## Writing Process Strategies

### Editing/Proofreading and Publishing

**Persuasive Business Letter**

#### Teach

Read ***Writer's Workbook,*** page 65, on editing/proofreading and publishing a persuasive business letter.

#### Guided Practice

**Editing/Proofreading and Publishing**

- Have students edit/proofread their letters.
- Have students use the checklist on ***Writer's Workbook,*** page 65.
- Refer to the Grammar, Usage, and Mechanics lesson on page 47F.
- Have students make a neat final copy of their letters in their best cursive handwriting.

**Formal Assessment**

Total Point Value: 10

1. The topic sentence clearly states the purpose. (2 points)
2. The strongest reason or feeling is given last. (2 points)
3. The tone is formal but polite. (2 points)
4. All the parts of a business letter are in place. (2 points)
5. Capitalization and punctuation are correct. (2 points)

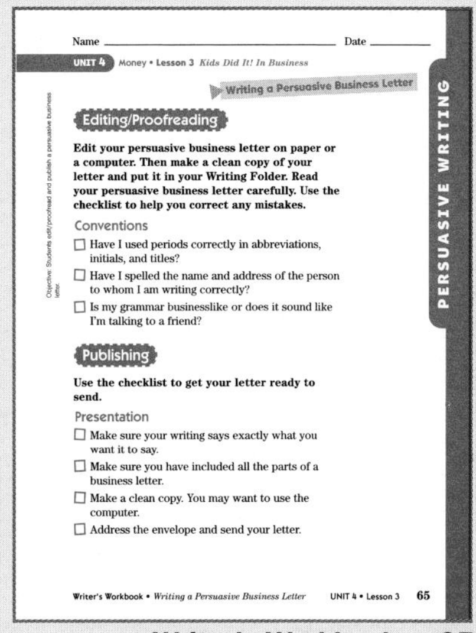

Name ______________ Date ________

UNIT 4 Money • Lesson 3 *Kids Did It! In Business*

Writing a Persuasive Business Letter

Objective: Students edit/proofread and publish a persuasive business letter.

**Editing/Proofreading**

**Edit your persuasive business letter on paper or a computer. Then make a clean copy of your letter and put it in your Writing Folder. Read your persuasive business letter carefully. Use the checklist to help you correct any mistakes.**

Conventions

- ☐ Have I used periods correctly in abbreviations, initials, and titles?
- ☐ Have I spelled the name and address of the person to whom I am writing correctly?
- ☐ Is my grammar businesslike or does it sound like I'm talking to a friend?

**Publishing**

**Use the checklist to get your letter ready to send.**

Presentation

- ☐ Make sure your writing says exactly what you want it to say.
- ☐ Make sure you have included all the parts of a business letter.
- ☐ Make a clean copy. You may want to use the computer.
- ☐ Address the envelope and send your letter.

PERSUASIVE WRITING

Writer's Workbook • *Writing a Persuasive Business Letter* UNIT 4 • Lesson 3 65

***Writer's Workbook* p. 65**

## English Language Conventions

### Penmanship

**Cursive Letters *N* and *M***

#### Teach

- **Teacher Model:** Introduce formation of uppercase *N* and *M* as curve-forward letters by demonstrating on the board.

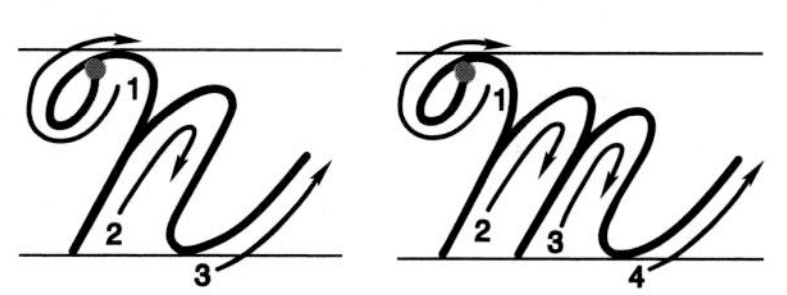


**N** Starting point, loop
Curve forward
Slant down, retrace back up
Overcurve down
Undercurve: capital *N*

**M** Starting point, loop
Curve forward, slant down
Retrace up slant, overcurve
Slant down, retrace up slant
Overcurve, undercurve: capital *M*

- **Teacher Model:** Write the following sentence to model proper letter formation: "Many people live in New York."
- Tell students they should leave a space the size of a small *o* between their words.

#### Guided Practice

- Have students practice writing rows of *N*s and *M*s in their Writer's Notebooks.
- From "Kids Did It! In Business" have students write the words *Newton* and *Massachusetts* to practice letter formation.

**Informal Assessment**

Check students' handwriting for proper formation of *N* and *M* and space between words in a sentence.

# Reading and Language Arts Skills Traces

## Language Arts

### WORD ANALYSIS

Skills Trace

**Spelling: Contractions**

Introduced in Grade 2.
Scaffolded throughout Grades 2–5.

**REINTRODUCED:** **Unit 4, Lesson 3**, p. 47E
**PRACTICED:** **Unit 4, Lesson 3**, pp. 47F–47J
*Spelling and Vocabulary Skills*, pp. 82–83
**TESTED:** **Unit 4, Lesson 3**, p. 47F (Pretest)
**Unit 4, Lesson 3**, p. 35 (Final Test)
**Unit 4 Assessment**

Skills Trace

**Vocabulary: Business Vocabulary**

Introduced in Grade 3.
Scaffolded throughout Grades 3–5.

**INTRODUCED:** **Unit 4, Lesson 3**, p. 47E
**PRACTICED:** **Unit 4, Lesson 3**, pp. 47G–47J
*Spelling and Vocabulary Skills*, pp. 82–83
**TESTED:** **Unit 4 Assessment**

### WRITING PROCESS STRATEGIES

Skills Trace

**Persuasive Writing: Persuasive Business Letter**

Introduced in Grade 2.
Scaffolded throughout Grades 3–6.

**REINTRODUCED:** **Unit 4, Lesson 3**, p. 47F
**PRACTICED:** **Unit 4, Lesson 3**, pp. 47G–47J
*Writer's Workbook*, pp. 62–65
**TESTED:** **Unit 4, Lesson 3**,
Formal Assessment, p. 47J
**Unit 4 Assessment**

Skills Trace

**Writer's Craft: Structure of a Business Letter**

Introduced in Grade 2.
Scaffolded throughout Grades 3–6.

**REINTRODUCED:** **Unit 4, Lesson 3**, p. 47G
**PRACTICED:** **Unit 4, Lesson 3**, p. 47G
*Comprehension and Language Arts Skills*, pp. 104–105
**TESTED:** **Unit 4 Assessment**

### ENGLISH LANGUAGE CONVENTIONS

Skills Trace

**Grammar: Parentheses and Periods in Abbreviations, Initials, and Titles**

Introduced in Grade 3.
Scaffolded throughout Grades 4–6.

**INTRODUCED:** **Unit 4, Lesson 3**, p. 47F
**PRACTICED:** **Unit 4, Lesson 3**, p. 47G
**Unit 4, Lesson 3**, p. 47H
*Comprehension and Language Arts Skills*, pp. 102–103
**TESTED:** **Unit 4, Lesson 3**,
Informal Assessment, p. 47H
**Unit 4 Assessment**

Skills Trace

**Listening, Speaking, Viewing Language: Choosing Words**

Introduced in Grade K.
Scaffolded throughout Grades 1–6.

**REINTRODUCED:** **Unit 4, Lesson 3**, p. 47I
**TESTED:** **Unit 4, Lesson 3**,
Informal Assessment, p. 47I

Skills Trace

**Penmanship: Cursive Letters *N* and *M***

Introduced in Grade 3.
Scaffolded throughout Grades 4–6.

**INTRODUCED:** **Unit 4, Lesson 3**, p. 47J
**TESTED:** **Unit 4, Lesson 3**,
Informal Assessment, p. 47J

## Reading

### COMPREHENSION

**Main Idea and Supporting Details**

Introduced in Grade 1.
Scaffolded throughout Grades 2 and 3.

**REINTRODUCED:** **Unit 1, Lesson 5**
**REINFORCED:** **Unit 4, Lesson 3**
**Unit 5, Lesson 6**
**Unit 6, Lesson 6**
**TESTED:** **Unit 4 Assessment**

# Professional Development: Phonics

## Word Recognition/Decoding

Once the alphabetic principle is established and children are able quickly and automatically to translate the spelling patterns of written words into their phonological counterparts, they can begin to focus more attention on getting meaning from what they are reading. Indeed, without an efficient strategy for reading words, children tend to devote too much mental energy to figuring out words, leaving them with too little energy for comprehension (Stanovich, 1991).

*Word recognition* refers to the ability to associate a printed word with its meaning. As children begin to read real stories and informational texts, they need to develop effective word recognition strategies that will permit them to identify words effortlessly and to figure out the increasing number of unfamiliar words they will encounter.

### What Does Research Tell Us about Word Recognition/Decoding?

The goal of reading is not to sound out words—it is to comprehend. The reason for helping children learn to sound out and read words is to give them a strategy for understanding text on their own (Adams, 1990). Without such a strategy, children tend to rely too much on context to get meaning from words. Using context is an unreliable way to identify and read words (Schatz & Baldwin, 1986). The problem is that the words likely to contribute most to the meaning of a text are words that occur less frequently in written language, and are, thus, words that are less familiar to children (Finn, 1977–1978). Therefore, children rely on a text's context to determine the meaning of its unfamiliar words, but the meaning of the context depends in large part on the meanings of its unfamiliar words (Adams, 1990).

This is not to say that children should *never* use context; rather, teaching children to rely only on context may interfere with learning to recognize and process words. When children encounter a word they do not recognize, they should learn to think about the word's spelling and consider its meaning. After this, the information available from the context will be more helpful to them (Adams, 1990).

To develop fast and accurate—fluent—word recognition, children require a great deal of practice in applying what they are learning about the sounds and spellings of English. Research suggests that children can benefit from five kinds of practice opportunities to build word-recognition fluency:

- reading words in isolation.
- reading words in decodable text.
- repeated reading of words in real text.
- writing words from dictation and invented spelling.
- working with word families, or phonograms.

**Professional Development**

***Teacher Resource Library CD-ROMs*** or ***Online Professional Development*** provides courses that help you better understand the Phonics and Fluency instruction in ***Open Court Reading.*** For more information about this program, visit SRAonline.com.

Additional information about phonics as well as resource references can be found in the ***Professional Development Guide: Phonics.***

*Focus Questions* How can people have happy and meaningful lives without a great deal of money? Why would money have a greater value if it is well earned?

# The Cobbler's Song

a fable by Jean de La Fontaine
*adapted and illustrated by Marcia Sewall*

Once upon a time a poor cobbler lived in the basement of a large house in Paris. He had to work from early morning until late at night to make enough money to keep himself and his wife and children. But he was happy in his dark little rooms, and he sang all day as he mended old shoes.

On the floor above him lived a very rich man. His rooms were large and sunny. He wore fine clothes and had plenty of good things to eat. Still, he was never happy.

All night long he lay awake thinking about his money—how to make more, or fearing lest it be stolen. Often the sun was shining in at his windows before he fell asleep.

Now, as soon as it grew light enough to see, the cobbler always got up and went about his work. And as he hammered, he sang. His songs floated up to the rooms of the rich man and woke him.

48

SELECTION INTRODUCTION

## Selection Summary

### Genre: Fable

Many people think that if they had lots of money, they would be happy. "The Cobbler's Song" is a story about a man who is happy even though he has very little money. This poor cobbler, or shoemaker, is so happy that he always sings. The cobbler's upstairs neighbor has lots of money but is always unhappy. One day, the rich man gives the poor cobbler a bag full of money. Suddenly, the cobbler is rich! How will the newfound wealth affect him?

Major elements of a fable may include:

- A fable is a very short story.
- It usually has only two or three characters.
- Often the characters are animals or things that talk and act.

## About the Author

**JEAN DE LA FONTAINE** was born in Champagne, France, in 1621. For 19 years La Fontaine held the public office of Inspector of Forests and Waterways, a post he inherited from his father. La Fontaine was respected as a poet, philosopher, and writer. He published his first volume of fables at the age of 47. Over the course of 25 years, La Fontaine published more than 250 fables comprising a total of 12 books. His fables were adored by French youth of the time and are still widely read today.

Students can read more about Jean de La Fontaine on page 55 of the ***Student Anthology.***

## About the Illustrator

**MARCIA SEWALL** was born in Providence, Rhode Island. Before becoming a full-time illustrator, she was a high school art teacher and she also worked as a staff artist at Boston's Children's Museum.

Sewall credits her mother's numerous artistic abilities and her father's love for telling stories and reciting long humorous poems for inspiring her to turn to art. Four of her books have been named Best Illustrated Books of the Year by *The New York Times*, and two others have been selected as Notable Books by the American Library Association.

Students can read more about Marcia Sewall on page 55 of the ***Student Anthology.***

## Inquiry Connections

Students have been discussing what money is and ways to make money. In "The Cobbler's Song," students will consider the true value of money. The cobbler is happy with his work—and his life. When he is given a large amount of money, he finds his life changing. But is it for the better?

- Joy in work does not necessarily depend on the money one makes.
- Having money can bring its own set of concerns and worries.

Before reading the selection:

- Point out that students may post a question, concept, word, illustration, or object on the Concept/Question Board at any time during the course of their unit investigation. Be sure that students include their name or initials on the items they post so that others will know to whom to go if they have an answer or if they wish to collaborate on a related activity.
- Students should feel free to write an answer or a note on someone else's question or to consult the Board for ideas for their own investigations throughout the unit.
- Encourage students to read about money at home and to bring in articles or pictures that are good examples to post on the Board.

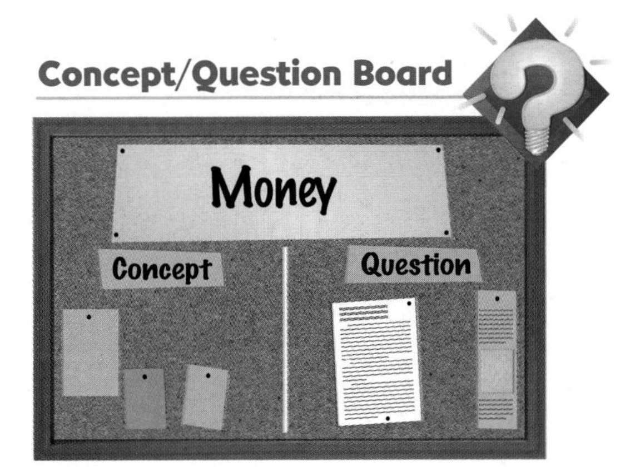

## Leveled Practice

**Reteach**
Pages 109–114

**Challenge**
Pages 96–100

**English Learner Support Activities**

**Intervention Workbook**

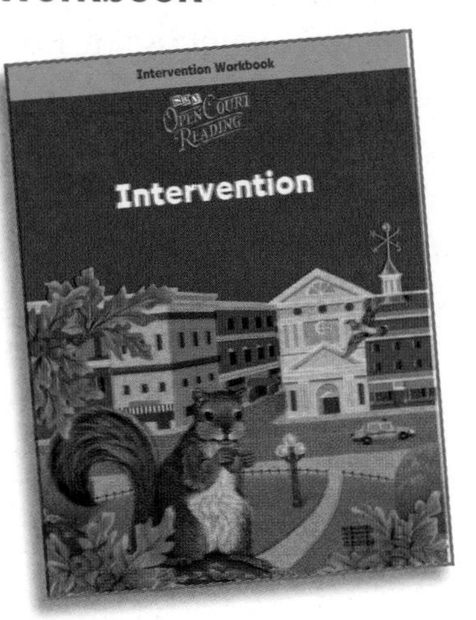


**Decodable Book 32**

## Leveled Classroom Library*

Encourage students to read at least 30 minutes daily outside of class. Have them read books in the ***Leveled Classroom Library*** to support the unit theme and help students develop their vocabulary by reading independently.

### *Lemonade for Sale*

BY STUART J. MURPHY. HARPERCOLLINS JUVENILE, 1998.

The kids at the Elm Street Kids' Club use a clever combination of lemonade, bar graphs, and a juggler to make big profits that will help them repair their club. **(Easy)**

### *Round and Round the Money Goes*

BY MELVIN AND GILDA BERGER. HAMBLETON-HILL, 1993.

Children learn the basics about the flow of wealth, how banks work, the life span of coins and bills, and other elementary monetary issues. **(Average)**

### *Screen of Frogs*

BY SHEILA HAMANAKA. ORCHARD BOOKS, 1993.

A spoiled rich man finds respect for the world around him before it is too late. This story retells the classic Japanese folktale, "The Strange Folding Screen." **(Advanced)**

*These books, which all support the unit theme Money, are part of a 36-book ***Leveled Classroom Library*** available for purchase from SRA/McGraw-Hill. Note: Teachers should preview any trade books for appropriateness in their classrooms before recommending them to students.

## SRA TECHNOLOGY

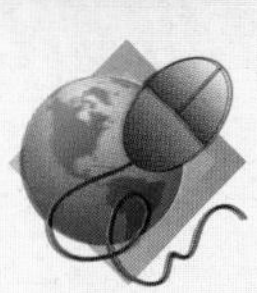

### Web Connections

- Money Web Site
- Online Professional Development
- Online Phonics
- Online Assessment

### CD-ROMs

- Research Assistant
- The Ultimate Writing and Creativity Center
- Teacher Resource Library

### Audiocassette/CD

Listening Library: Money

### Computer Skills

TechKnowledge

Materials are available through SRA/McGraw-Hill.

# UNIT 4 Lesson 4 The Cobbler's Song

LESSON PLANNER

Suggested Pacing: 3–5 days

| | DAY 1 | DAY 2 |
|---|---|---|
| **1 Preparing to Read**<br><br>**Materials**<br>■ Student Anthology, Book 2, pp. 48–57<br>■ Sound/Spelling Card 37<br>■ Routine Card 1, Routines 1–2<br>■ Decodable Book 32 | **Word Knowledge,** p. 48K<br>■ Suffix *-ed, -ing, -ful, -ly*<br>■ /ē/ spelled *_ie_* and *ei*<br>**About the Words and Sentences,** p. 48K | **Developing Oral Language,** p. 48L |
| **2 Reading & Responding**<br><br>**Materials**<br>■ Student Anthology, Book 2, pp. 48–57<br>■ Program Assessment<br>■ Reading Transparencies 26, 46, 53<br>■ Inquiry Journal, p. 84<br>■ Home Connection, p. 51<br>■ Unit 4 Assessment, pp. 14–17<br>■ Writer's Notebook<br>■ Comprehension and Language Arts Skills, pp. 106–107<br>■ Routine Cards 1, 2, Routines 3–6 | **Build Background,** p. 48M<br>**Preview and Prepare,** p. 48M<br>**Selection Vocabulary,** p. 48N<br>**Reading Recommendations,** p. 480<br>**Student Anthology,** pp. 48–53 First Read<br>✓**Comprehension Strategies**<br>■ Predicting, pp. 48, 50<br>■ Asking Questions, p. 50<br>■ Summarizing, p. 52<br>**Discussing Strategy Use,** p. 52<br>**Discussing the Selection,** p. 53A | **Student Anthology,** pp. 48–53 Second Read<br>**Comprehension Skills**<br>■ Author's Purpose, pp. 49, 51, 53<br>**Checking Comprehension,** p. 53<br>**Supporting the Reading,** pp. 53C–53D<br>■ Author's Purpose |
| **Inquiry**<br><br>**Materials**<br>■ Student Anthology, Book 2, pp. 48–57<br>■ Inquiry Journal, pp. 96–98<br>■ Research Assistant CD-ROM | **Investigation**<br>■ Investigating Concepts Beyond the Text, p. 55A | **Investigation**<br>■ Concept/Question Board, p. 55B |
| **3 Language Arts**<br><br>**Materials**<br>■ Spelling and Vocabulary Skills, pp. 86–89<br>■ Comprehension and Language Arts Skills, pp. 106–111<br>■ The Ultimate Writing and Creativity Center<br>■ Language Arts Handbook<br>■ Writer's Workbook, pp. 66–69<br>■ Language Arts Transparency 27<br>■ Student Anthology | **Word Analysis**<br>✓■ Spelling: Adding *-ed* and *-ing* Pretest, p. 55F<br>**Writing Process Strategies**<br>■ Persuasive Writing: Persuasive Paragraph, p. 55F<br>**English Language Conventions**<br>■ Grammar: Possessive Pronouns, p. 55F | **Word Analysis**<br>■ Spelling: Adding *-ed* and *-ing*, p. 55G<br>■ Vocabulary: Inflectional Endings *-ed* and *-ing*, p. 55G<br>**Writing Process Strategies**<br>■ Persuasive Writing: Persuasive Paragraph, p. 55G<br>**English Language Conventions**<br>■ Grammar: Possessive Pronouns, p. 55G |

Ⓟ Phonics ✓ Informal Assessment Available ✓ Formal Assessment Available

| DAY 2 continued | DAY 3 | |
|---|---|---|
| **DAY 3** | **DAY 4** | **DAY 5** |
| **General Review** | **General Review** | **Review Word Knowledge** |
| **Student Anthology**<br>✓ ■ Concept Connections, p. 54<br>■ Meet the Author/Illustrator, p. 55<br>**Review Selection Vocabulary,** p. 53B<br>**View Fine Art,** p. 53B | **Literary Elements,** p. 53E<br>■ Recognize and Distinguish Fables<br>**Social Studies Connection**<br>■ History of Costs, Goods, and Services, p. 53F | ✓ **Comprehension Test**<br>■ "The Cobbler's Song," pp. 14–17<br>**Home Connection,** p. 53B |
| ✓ **Investigation**<br>■ Needs and Plans Phase 1, p. 55C | **Supporting the Investigation**<br>■ Graphs, p. 55D | **Investigation**<br>■ Unit Investigation Continued<br>■ Update Concept/Question Board |
| **Word Analysis**<br>■ Spelling: Adding *-ed* and *-ing,* p. 55H<br>■ Vocabulary: Inflectional Endings *-ed* and *-ing,* p. 55H<br>**Writing Process Strategies**<br>■ Persuasive Writing: Persuasive Paragraph, p. 55H<br>■ Writer's Craft: Avoiding Wordiness, p. 55H<br>**English Language Conventions**<br>✓ ■ Grammar: Possessive Pronouns, p. 55H | **Word Analysis**<br>■ Spelling: Adding *-ed* and *-ing,* p. 55I<br>■ Vocabulary: Inflectional Endings *-ed* and *-ing,* p. 55I<br>**Writing Process Strategies**<br>■ Persuasive Writing: Persuasive Paragraph, p. 55I<br>**English Language Conventions**<br>✓ ■ Listening, Speaking, Viewing Viewing: Media Techniques, p. 55I | **Word Analysis**<br>✓ ■ Spelling: Adding *-ed* and *-ing* Final Test<br>✓ ■ Vocabulary: Inflectional Endings *-ed* and *-ing,* p. 55J<br>**Writing Process Strategies**<br>✓ ■ Persuasive Writing: Persuasive Paragraph, p. 55J<br>**English Language Conventions**<br>✓ ■ Penmanship: Cursive Letters *K* and *H,* p. 55J |

Below are suggestions for differentiating instruction. These are the same skills shown in the Lesson Planner; however, these pages provide extra practice opportunities or enriching activities to meet the varied needs of students.

WORKSHOP

# Differentiating Instruction

## Teacher Directed: Individual and Small-Group Instruction

Spend time each day with individuals and small groups to individualize instruction. Each day:

- preteach students who need help with the next lesson.
- reteach students who need to solidify their understanding of content previously taught.
- listen to students read to check their fluency.
- hold writing and inquiry conferences.

Use the following program components to support instruction:

- ***Reteach*** with students who need a bit more practice
- ***Intervention*** for students who exhibit a lack of understanding of the lesson concepts
- ***English Learner Support*** with students who need language help

## Student: Independent Activities

Students can work alone, with a partner, or in small groups on such activities as:

- Review sound/spellings
- Practice dictation words
- Partner reading
- Practice fluency
- Independent reading
- Reading Roundtable
- Concept vocabulary
- Selection vocabulary
- Writing in progress
- Conference
- Language Arts
- Challenge activities
- Inquiry and Investigation activities
- Listening Library
- Online Phonics

For Workshop Management Tips, see Appendix pages 41–42.

| | DAY I |
|---|---|
| **Word Knowledge** | **Teacher Directed**<br>▪ Reading Words: Suffixes *-ful* and *-ly*, ***Intervention Guide,*** p. 199<br>**Independent Activities**<br>▪ ***Online Phonics*** |
| **Fluency** | **Independent Activities**<br>▪ Self-test fluency rate<br>▪ Oral reading of selection for fluency |
| **Comprehension** | **Teacher Directed**<br>▪ Preteach "The Cobbler's Song," ***Intervention Guide,*** pp. 200–201<br>▪ Preteach Intervention Selection One, ***Intervention Guide,*** pp. 201–202<br>▪ ***English Learner Support Guide***<br>• Vocabulary, pp. 300–301<br>• Comprehension Strategy: Summarizing, pp. 300–302<br>**Independent Activities**<br>▪ Browse and choose ***Leveled Classroom Library*** book for independent reading<br>▪ Add vocabulary in Writer's Notebook<br>▪ Record response to selection in Writer's Notebook<br>▪ ***Listening Library Audiocassette/CD*** |
| **Inquiry** | **Independent Activities**<br>▪ Concept/Question Board<br>▪ Explore OCR Web site for theme connections<br>▪ Things Worth More Than Money, ***Inquiry Journal,*** pp. 96–97 |
| **Language Arts** | **Teacher Directed**<br>▪ Grammar, Usage, and Mechanics, ***Intervention Guide,*** p. 204<br>**Independent Activities**<br>▪ Pronouns, ***Comprehension and Language Arts Skills,*** pp. 108–109 |

| DAY 2 | DAY 3 | DAY 4 | DAY 5 |
|---|---|---|---|
| **Teacher Directed**<br>▪ Developing Oral Language, ***Intervention Guide,*** p. 199<br>**Independent Activities**<br>▪ Read ***Decodable Book 32,*** *The Stone Wall* | **Teacher Directed**<br>▪ Dictation and Spelling: Suffixes *-ful* and *-ly*, ***Intervention Guide,*** pp. 199–200<br>**Independent Activities**<br>▪ ***Online Phonics*** | **Teacher Directed**<br>▪ General Review<br>**Independent Activities**<br>▪ ***Online Phonics*** | **Teacher Directed**<br>▪ General Review<br>**Independent Activities**<br>▪ ***Online Phonics*** |
| **Independent Activities**<br>▪ Reread "The Cobbler's Song" for fluency<br>▪ Partner reading of ***Decodable Book 32,*** *The Stone Wall* | **Independent Activities**<br>▪ Partner reading of selection<br>▪ Oral reading of ***Decodable Book 32,*** *The Stone Wall* | **Independent Activities**<br>▪ Reread "The Cobbler's Song"<br>▪ Partner reading of ***Decodable Book 32,*** *The Stone Wall* | **Teacher Directed**<br>▪ Repeated Readings/Fluency Check, ***Intervention Guide,*** p. 203 |
| **Teacher Directed**<br>▪ Preteach "The Cobbler's Song," ***Intervention Guide,*** pp. 200–201<br>▪ Comprehension Strategies, ***Intervention Guide,*** p. 202<br>▪ Reread Intervention Selection One, ***Intervention Guide,*** pp. 201–202<br>▪ ***English Learner Support Guide***<br>• Vocabulary, pp. 302–303<br>• Comprehension Strategy: Summarizing, pp. 303–304<br>▪ Author's Purpose, ***Reteach,*** pp. 109–110<br>**Independent Activities**<br>▪ Independent reading<br>▪ Complete Link to Writing in Supporting the Reading, p. 53D<br>▪ Author's Purpose<br>• ***Comprehension and Language Arts Skills,*** pp. 106–107<br>• ***Challenge,*** p. 96<br>▪ ***English Learner Support Activities,*** p. 38 | **Teacher Directed**<br>▪ Discuss Concept Connections, p. 54<br>▪ Reread "The Cobbler's Song," ***Intervention Guide,*** pp. 200–201<br>▪ Preteach Intervention Selection Two, ***Intervention Guide,*** pp. 202–203<br>▪ ***English Learner Support Guide***<br>• Vocabulary, pp. 304–305<br>• Comprehension Strategy: Summarizing, pp. 305–306<br>**Independent Activities**<br>▪ Read ***Leveled Classroom Library*** book<br>▪ Add words to Word Bank<br>▪ ***Listening Library Audiocassette/CD*** | **Teacher Directed**<br>▪ Reread "The Cobbler's Song," ***Intervention Guide,*** pp. 200–201<br>▪ Comprehension Strategies, ***Intervention Guide,*** p. 203<br>▪ Reread Intervention Selection Two, ***Intervention Guide,*** pp. 202–203<br>▪ ***English Learner Support Guide***<br>• Review Vocabulary, pp. 306–307<br>• Comprehension Strategy: Summarizing, pp. 306–308<br>**Independent Activities**<br>▪ Read ***Leveled Classroom Library*** book<br>▪ Complete Independent Practice in Literary Elements, p. 53E<br>▪ Social Studies Connection, p. 53F | **Teacher Directed**<br>▪ ***English Learner Support Guide***<br>• Review Vocabulary, p. 308<br>• Comprehension Strategy: Summarizing, pp. 308–309<br>**Independent Activities**<br>▪ Read ***Leveled Classroom Library*** book as independent reading<br>▪ Reading Roundtable<br>▪ ***English Learner Support Activities,*** p. 39 |
| **Independent Activities**<br>▪ Concept/Question Board<br>▪ Use ***Research Assistant CD-ROM*** to continue investigation | **Independent Activities**<br>▪ Concept/Question Board<br>▪ Research Cycle: Needs and Plans Phase 1, ***Inquiry Journal,*** p. 98<br>▪ Explore OCR Web site for theme connections | **Independent Activities**<br>▪ Concept/Question Board<br>▪ Complete Independent Practice in Supporting the Investigation, p. 55D | **Independent Activities**<br>▪ Concept/Question Board<br>▪ Use ***Research Assistant CD-ROM*** to continue investigation |
| **Teacher Directed**<br>▪ Grammar, Usage, and Mechanics, ***Intervention Guide,*** p. 204<br>▪ Pronouns, ***Reteach,*** p. 113<br>**Independent Activities**<br>▪ Vocabulary: The Endings *-ed* and *-ing*, ***Spelling and Vocabulary Skills,*** pp. 86–87<br>▪ Pronouns, ***Challenge,*** p. 99 | **Teacher Directed**<br>▪ Writing Activity, ***Intervention Guide,*** p. 205<br>▪ Vocabulary: ***Reteach,*** p. 112<br>**Independent Activities**<br>▪ Spelling: Adding *-ed* and *-ing*, ***Spelling and Vocabulary Skills,*** p. 88<br>▪ Vocabulary: ***Challenge,*** p. 98<br>▪ Writer's Craft: Avoiding Wordiness, ***Comprehension and Language Arts Skills,*** pp. 110–111 | **Teacher Directed**<br>▪ Writer's Craft: Avoiding Wordiness, ***Reteach,*** p. 114<br>▪ Writing Activity, ***Intervention Guide,*** p. 205<br>▪ Spelling: Adding *-ed* and *-ing*, ***Reteach,*** p. 111<br>**Independent Activities**<br>▪ Spelling: Adding *-ed* and *-ing*<br>• ***Spelling and Vocabulary Skills,*** p. 89<br>• ***Challenge,*** p. 97 | **Independent Activities**<br>▪ Seminar: Edit/Proofread and Publish a Persuasive Paragraph, p. 55J<br>▪ Penmanship: Practice Cursive Letters *K* and *H*, p. 55J<br>▪ Writer's Craft: Avoiding Wordiness, ***Challenge,*** p. 100 |

ASSESSMENT

# Formal Assessment Options

Use these summative assessments along with your informal observations to assess student progress.

Name ____________ Date ________ Score ______

UNIT 4 Money • Lesson 4

**The Cobbler's Song**

LESSON ASSESSMENT

**Read the following questions carefully. Then completely fill in the bubble of each correct answer. You may look back at the story to find the answer to each of the questions.**

1. What was the cobbler's shop like?
   - ● small and dark
   - Ⓑ large and sunny
   - Ⓒ bright and cute
2. At the beginning of the story, the rich man was
   - Ⓐ always happy
   - Ⓑ sometimes happy
   - ● never happy

**Read the following questions carefully. Use complete sentences to answer the questions.**

3. What does the rich man think men worry about the most?
   He thinks men worry about having too little or too much money.
4. What makes it difficult for the rich man to sleep during the day?
   It is difficult for him to sleep because the cobbler is always singing.
5. Why does the rich man give the cobbler a hundred pieces of gold?
   He wants to give the cobbler something to worry about so he will stop singing.

14 Unit 4 • Lesson 4 *The Cobbler's Song* • Unit 4 Assessment

*Unit 4 Assessment p. 14*

**The Cobbler's Song** *(continued)*

6. How does the cobbler's life change after he gets the money?
   He worries all the time that someone will steal the money.
7. After a month, what does the cobbler tell his wife?
   The cobbler tells his wife how he got the money and that he can't stand the worrying anymore.
8. What does the wife tell the cobbler to do?
   She tells the cobbler to give the money back to the rich man.

**Read the following questions carefully. Then completely fill in the bubble of each correct answer.**

9. Which of these best describes the cobbler at the beginning of the story?
   - ● always happy
   - Ⓑ sometimes happy
   - Ⓒ never happy
10. The author wrote this story to
    - Ⓐ show how to save money
    - ● teach a lesson
    - Ⓒ explain how to make friends

LESSON ASSESSMENT

Unit 4 Assessment • *The Cobbler's Song* Unit 4 • Lesson 4 15

*Unit 4 Assessment p. 15*

**The Cobbler's Song** *(continued)*

**Read the questions below. Use complete sentences in your answers.**

**Linking to the Concepts** Does having money always make people happy? Why?
Answers will vary. Accept all reasonable answers.

**Personal Response** Suppose someone gave you a lot of money. How would it change your life?
Answers will vary. Accept all reasonable answers.

LESSON ASSESSMENT

16 Unit 4 • Lesson 4 *The Cobbler's Song* • Unit 4 Assessment

*Unit 4 Assessment p. 16*

**The Cobbler's Song** *(continued)*

**Vocabulary**

**Read the following questions carefully. Then completely fill in the bubble of each correct answer.**

1. A **cobbler** is someone who
   - ● fixes old shoes
   - Ⓑ sews fine clothing
   - Ⓒ builds nice houses
2. The cobbler sang all day as he mended shoes. Another word for **mended** is
   - Ⓐ designed
   - Ⓑ organized
   - ● repaired
3. "What can I do for you?" asked the cobbler, recognizing his neighbor. To **recognize** someone means you
   - Ⓐ want to make friends with that person
   - Ⓑ talk to that person
   - ● know who that person is
4. The cobbler hides the coins for safekeeping. When you put something away for **safekeeping**, it means you want to
   - Ⓐ spend it all
   - ● protect it
   - Ⓒ show it off
5. First, the cobbler hid the coins under the covers at the foot of his bed, which he could see from his workbench. A **workbench** is
   - Ⓐ a stool that does not work
   - Ⓑ a large comfortable sofa
   - ● a table used for working

LESSON ASSESSMENT

Unit 4 Assessment • *The Cobbler's Song* Unit 4 • Lesson 4 17

*Unit 4 Assessment p. 17*

Name ____________ Date ________ Score ______

UNIT 4 Money • Lesson 4 *The Cobbler's Song*

**Spelling Pretest: Adding –ed and –ing**

LESSON ASSESSMENT

**Fold this page back on the dotted line. Take the Pretest. Then correct any word you misspelled by crossing out the word and rewriting it next to the incorrect spelling.**

| | |
|---|---|
| 1. ________ | 1. making |
| 2. ________ | 2. biting |
| 3. ________ | 3. diving |
| 4. ________ | 4. hiking |
| 5. ________ | 5. skated |
| 6. ________ | 6. prized |
| 7. ________ | 7. shaking |
| 8. ________ | 8. skating |
| 9. ________ | 9. hiding |
| 10. ________ | 10. shining |
| 11. ________ | 11. thinking |
| 12. ________ | 12. entered |
| 13. ________ | 13. opened |
| 14. ________ | 14. passing |
| 15. ________ | 15. safekeeping |

36 Unit 4 • Lesson 4 *Spelling Pretest: Adding –ed and –ing* • Unit 4 Assessment

*Unit 4 Assessment p. 36*

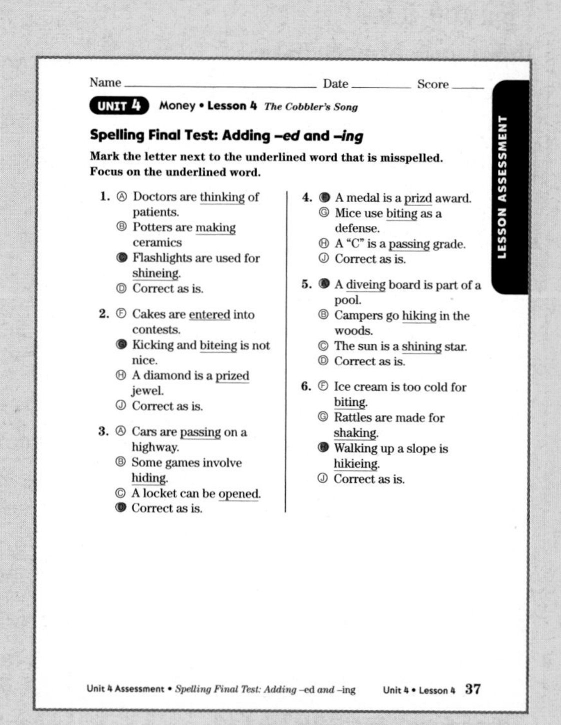

Name ____________ Date ________ Score ______

UNIT 4 Money • Lesson 4 *The Cobbler's Song*

**Spelling Final Test: Adding –ed and –ing**

**Mark the letter next to the underlined word that is misspelled. Focus on the underlined word.**

1. Ⓐ Doctors are thinking of patients.
   Ⓑ Potters are making ceramics
   ● Flashlights are used for shineing.
   Ⓓ Correct as is.
2. Ⓔ Cakes are entered into contests.
   ● Kicking and biteing is not nice.
   Ⓖ A diamond is a prized jewel.
   Ⓙ Correct as is.
3. Ⓐ Cars are passing on a highway.
   Ⓑ Some games involve hiding.
   Ⓒ A locket can be opened.
   ● Correct as is.
4. ● A medal is a prizd award.
   Ⓖ Mice use biting as a defense.
   Ⓗ A "C" is a passing grade.
   Ⓙ Correct as is.
5. ● A diveing board is part of a pool.
   Ⓑ Campers go hiking in the woods.
   Ⓒ The sun is a shining star.
   Ⓓ Correct as is.
6. Ⓕ Ice cream is too cold for biting.
   Ⓖ Rattles are made for shaking.
   ● Walking up a slope is hikeing.
   Ⓙ Correct as is.

LESSON ASSESSMENT

Unit 4 Assessment • *Spelling Final Test: Adding –ed and –ing* Unit 4 • Lesson 4 37

*Unit 4 Assessment p. 37*

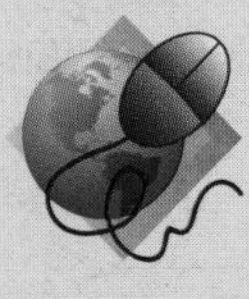

**Online Assessment** for ***Open Court Reading*** helps teachers differentiate classroom instruction based on students' scores from the weekly and end-of-unit assessments. It provides exercises best suited to meet the needs of each student. For more information, visit SRAonline.com.

# Informal Comprehension Strategies Rubrics

## Predicting

- The student makes predictions about what the text is about.
- The student updates predictions during reading, based on information in the text.

## Asking Questions

- The student asks questions about ideas or facts presented in the text and attempts to answer these questions by reading the text.

## Summarizing

- The student paraphrases the text, reporting main ideas and a summary of what is in the text.
- The student decides which parts of the text are important in his or her summary.
- The student draws conclusions from the text.
- The student makes global interpretations of the text, such as recognizing the genre.

# Research Rubrics

During Workshop, assess students using the rubrics below. The rubrics range from 1 to 4 in most categories, with 1 being the lowest score. Record each student's score on the inside back cover of the ***Inquiry Journal***.

## Recognizing Information Needs

**1** Identifies topics about which more needs to be learned. ("I need to learn more about the brain.")

**2** Identifies information needs that are relevant though not essential to the research question. ("To understand how Leeuwenhoek invented the microscope, I need to know what size germs are.")

**3** Identifies questions that are deeper than the one originally asked. (Original question: "How does the heart work?" Deeper question: "Why does blood need to circulate?")

### Objectives

- Students practice recognizing base words and the suffixes *-ful, -ly, -ing,* and *-ed.*
- Students practice recognizing the /ē/ sound spelled *_ie_* and *ei.*

### Materials

- Student Anthology, Book 2, pp. 48–57
- Sound/Spelling Card 37
- Routine Card 1, Routines 1–2
- Decodable Book 32

### Differentiating Instruction

| If... | Then... |
|---|---|
| Students need extra help with the suffix *-ly* | Use ***Online Phonics*** |
| Students need extra help with base words with the suffixes *-ful* and *-ly* | Use ***Intervention Guide*** pages 199–200 |

**Teacher Tip** SYLLABICATION To help students blend words and build fluency, use the syllabication below of the words in the word lines.

| | | | |
|---|---|---|---|
| dread•ful | thank•ful | force•ful | fright•ful |
| drows•i•ly | un•hap•pi•ly | sleep•i•ly | has•ti•ly |
| re•lieved | thief | re•ceived | de•ceit |
| think•ing | en•tered | o•pened | pass•ing |
| safe•keep•ing | | | |

**Routine Card**
Refer to ***Routine 1*** for whole-word blending and ***Routine 2*** for sentence blending.

WORD KNOWLEDGE

## Word Knowledge

### Reading the Words and Sentences

- Use direct teaching to teach the following lesson.
- Display ***Sound/Spelling Card 37.***
- Use the established procedure as you have students read each line of words and sentences in this and in subsequent lessons. The words in **boldface** type appear in the selection.

| | | | | | |
|---|---|---|---|---|---|
| Line 1: | **dreadful** | thankful | forceful | frightful | |
| Line 2: | **drowsily** | unhappily | sleepily | hastily | |
| Line 3: | **relieved** | thief | received | deceit | |
| Line 4: | **thinking** | **entered** | **opened** | **passing** | **safekeeping** |
| Sentence 1: | "This is just dreadful!" said the rich man. | | | | |
| Sentence 2: | He quickly hid the gold. | | | | |
| Sentence 3: | "One hundred pieces of gold! How rich I am!" | | | | |
| Sentence 4: | A lock box is opened for the safekeeping of something valuable. | | | | |

### About the Words and Sentences

- **Line 1:** These words are descriptive words that end in the suffix *-ful.* Have students explain what this suffix means *(full of).* As each word is read have the students give a definition of the word.
- **Line 2:** These are words with the suffix *-ly.* Explain that this ending shows that something is being done in a certain way. Point out to students that the ending *y* changes to an *i* before adding *-ly.*
- **Line 3:** These words have the /ē/ sound spelled *_ie_* and *ei.* Point out the difference in spellings when the letters follow a *c.*
- **Line 4:** These words are found in "The Cobbler's Song" and review words with the suffixes *-ed* and *-ing.*
- **Sentences 1–3:** These sentences are from the story the students are about to read. Ask students to identify words with the suffixes *-ful* or *-ly (dreadful, quickly).* Ask students to identify the word with the /ē/ sound spelled *_ie_* or *ei (pieces).*
- **Sentence 4:** Have students identify that the words in the last sentence contain the suffixes *-ed* and *-ing (opened, safekeeping).*

WORD KNOWLEDGE

## Developing Oral Language

- Have students recall that the suffix *-ful* means "full of." Say to the class, *I'm thinking of a word that means full of… joy, sorrow, deceit, mercy, art, plenty, gratitude, revenge.* Ask for volunteers to supply the correct word. Write the word on the board, and review its formation and usage.
- Use each word in Line 2 in a sentence. Ask volunteers to use other words to describe the behavior, attitude, or appearance of a person modified by the adverb *(for example, to describe a person who is speaking drowsily).*

## Building Fluency

***Decodable Books*** are used to help develop fluency for students who need extra practice. The only way to gain fluency is to read. Students will have many opportunities to read, including the ***Student Anthology,*** the ***Leveled Classroom Library,*** and their own reading. The ***Decodable Books*** can be used to practice the phonics and fluency elements being reviewed. Refer to the Appendix for the procedure on using these books. For this lesson, use ***Decodable Book 32,*** *The Stone Wall.*

***Decodable Book 32***

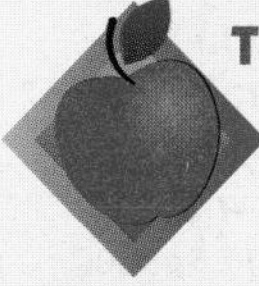

**Teacher Tip** Remember to point out and remind students that sentences begin with a capital letter and end with a period, question mark, or exclamation mark.

**Teacher Tip** **FLUENCY** Gaining a better understanding of the spellings of sounds and structure of words will help students as they encounter unfamiliar words in their reading. By this time in Grade 3 students should be reading approximately 123 words per minute with fluency and expression. As students read, you may notice that some need work in building fluency. During Workshop, have these students select a section of the text (a minimum of 160 words) to read several times in order to build fluency.

**Spelling**
See pages 55E–55J for the corresponding spelling lesson for adding *-ed* and *-ing*.

### Differentiating Instruction

| If... | Then... |
| --- | --- |
| Students need help building fluency | Have them take turns reading ***Decodable Book 32,*** *The Stone Wall,* out loud to a partner |

### Objectives

- Students will understand the selection vocabulary before reading, using strategies such as suffixes and structural cues.
- Students will recognize base words with the suffixes *-ful* and *-ly,* and the /ē/ sound spelled *_ie_* and *ei.*
- Students will connect prior knowledge to subjects discussed in the text.
- Students will use comprehension strategies such as Predicting, Asking Questions, and Summarizing to construct meaning from the text and monitor reading.
- Students will use the comprehension skill Author's Purpose as they read the story the second time.
- Students will discuss personal reactions to the story to begin identifying their own personal reading preferences.
- Students link the selection's key concepts to their investigations.

### Materials

- Student Anthology, Book 2, pp. 48–57
- Program Assessment
- Reading Transparencies 26, 46, 53
- Inquiry Journal, p. 84
- Home Connection, p. 51
- Comprehension and Language Arts Skills, pp. 106–107
- Unit 4 Assessment, pp. 14–17
- Routine Cards 1, 2, Routines 3–6

**Teacher Tip** Before reading, discuss with students the idea of wealth.

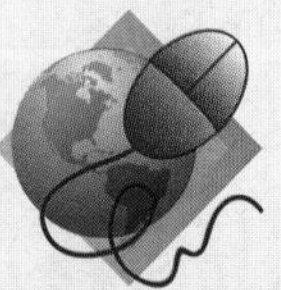

**www.sra4kids.com**
**Web Connection**
Students can use the connections to Money in the Reading link of the SRA Web page for more background information about money.

| Clues | Problems | Wonderings |
| --- | --- | --- |
| pictures mean? | cobbler | Is this a story about money and a song? |

*Reading Transparency 46*

## Build Background

### Activate Prior Knowledge

Preteach this selection by discussing the following with students to find out what they may already know about the selection and what they have already learned about the unit theme of Money.

- Ask students whether they are familiar with the story they are about to read, and if so, to tell a little bit about it. Remind students, because this is a fictional piece, not to give away the ending of the story.
- Ask students if they think money has anything to do with happiness. Ask them to explain their answers.
- Ask students if they have ever read any stories about money and happiness.

### Background Information

The following information may help students to better understand the selection they are about to read.

- "The Cobbler's Song" is a fable. A fable is a fictional story that teaches a lesson. In "The Cobbler's Song" all of the characters are people, but many fables have animals that talk, think, and act like humans. Ask students to name other fables.
- "The Cobbler's Song" takes place in Paris. Explain that Paris is a city in France, a European country. This story was originally written by a French writer named Jean de la Fontaine (1621–1695). La Fontaine was a poet who became famous for writing fables. "The Cobbler's Song" was adapted, or changed, for a certain audience, by Marcia Sewall. Marcia Sewall adapted this fable so it would read like a story instead of a poem, and so that modern readers could more easily understand the story.

## Preview and Prepare

### Browse

- Have students read the title and the author's and adapter/illustrator's names aloud. Have students preview the selection by browsing only the first page or two of the story. Discuss with students what they think this story might reveal about money.
- Have students search for clues that tell them something about the selection, such as pictures and words or descriptive phrases. Also, have students look for any problems, such as unfamiliar words or long sentences, that they notice while reading. Use ***Reading Transparency 46*** to record their observations as they browse. For example, the pictures in the story might be a clue that the cobbler is happy. For the Problems column, students might point out that they are unfamiliar with the word *cobbler.* They might wonder why a story about money has the word *song* in the title. To save time and to model note taking, write students' observations as brief notes rather than as complete sentences.

- As students prepare to read the selection, have them browse the Focus Questions on the first page of the selection. Tell them to keep these questions in mind as they read.

### Set Purposes

Encourage students to set their own purposes for reading. As they read, suggest that students think about the idea that having money makes people happy. You may also have students think about how the theme of the story piques their curiosity or connects to their personal interests. In addition, you may wish to have students think about information in the selection that may be useful to them as they work on their investigations and activities.

## Selection Vocabulary

As students study vocabulary, they will use a variety of skills to determine the meaning of a word. These include context clues, word structure, and apposition. Students will apply these same skills while reading to clarify additional unfamiliar words.

Display ***Reading Transparency 26*** before reading the selection to introduce and discuss the following words and their meanings.

| | |
|---|---|
| **cobbler:** | a person who makes or repairs shoes (page 48) |
| **mended:** | repaired (page 48) |
| **recognizing:** | identifying people we know or previously saw (page 49) |
| **safekeeping:** | so as to be protected or safe (page 51) |
| **workbench:** | a strong table used for working (page 51) |
| **treasure:** | items of great value (page 52) |

Have students read the words in the Word Box, stopping to blend any words that they have trouble reading. Demonstrate how to decode multisyllabic words by breaking the words into syllables and blending the syllables. Then have the students try. If they still have trouble, refer them to the ***Sound/Spelling Cards.*** If the word is not decodable, give the students the pronunciation.

Have students read the sentences on the transparency to determine the meaning of the underlined words. Each word has two sentences that students will read and from which they should be able to derive the meaning of the underlined word. Remind them to use one or more of the skills they have learned—context clues, word structure, or apposition—to figure out the meaning before using a dictionary. Be sure students explain which skills they are using and how they figured out the meanings of the words. Have students reread the sentence, substituting the definition to see if the sentence makes sense. Have a volunteer create a new sentence using the underlined word.

**Teacher Tip SELECTION VOCABULARY** To help students decode words, divide them into syllables when you are saying them, as shown below. The information following each word tells how students can figure out the meaning of each word. When writing words on the board, do not divide them into syllables.

| | |
|---|---|
| **cob • bler** | context clues |
| **mend • ed** | context clues |
| **re • cog • niz • ing** | context clues |
| **safe • keep • ing** | context clues |
| **work • bench** | context clues |
| **treas • ure** | context clues |

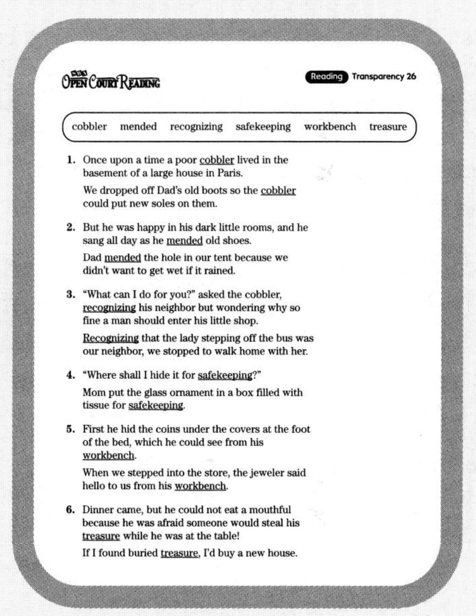

OPEN COURT READING — Reading Transparency 26

cobbler mended recognizing safekeeping workbench treasure

1. Once upon a time a poor cobbler lived in the basement of a large house in Paris.
   We dropped off Dad's old boots so the cobbler could put new soles on them.
2. But he was happy in his dark little rooms, and he sang all day as he mended old shoes.
   Dad mended the hole in our tent because we didn't want to get wet if it rained.
3. "What can I do for you?" asked the cobbler, recognizing his neighbor but wondering why so fine a man should enter his little shop.
   Recognizing that the lady stepping off the bus was our neighbor, we stopped to walk home with her.
4. "Where shall I hide it for safekeeping?"
   Mom put the glass ornament in a box filled with tissue for safekeeping.
5. First he hid the coins under the covers at the foot of the bed, which he could see from his workbench.
   When we stepped into the store, the jeweler said hello to us from his workbench.
6. Dinner came, but he could not eat a mouthful because he was afraid someone would steal his treasure while he was at the table!
   If I found buried treasure, I'd buy a new house.

***Reading Transparency 26***

**Teacher Tip** Encourage students to comment on one another's ideas.

**Routine Card**
Refer to ***Routine 3*** for the vocabulary procedure.

### DIFFERENTIATING INSTRUCTION

| If... | Then... |
|---|---|
| Students need extra help with selection vocabulary | Use ***Intervention Guide*** pages 200–201 |

**Teacher Tip** COMPREHENSION STRATEGIES Remind students on the second day as they read the story to summarize what they learned from the first day.

**Routine Card**
Refer to ***Routine 5*** for the procedure on reading the selection.

During Workshop, and after the selection has been read at least once, have students listen to the recording of this lesson's selection on the ***Listening Library Audiocassette/CD.*** After students have listened, have them discuss their personal preferences of the selections read. Ask them what other things they have listened to and like to listen to on the radio, on audiocassettes, or on CDs.

### DIFFERENTIATING INSTRUCTION

| If... | Then... |
|---|---|
| Students need extra help with summarizing | Use ***Intervention Guide*** pages 201–202 |
| Students need extra help with asking questions | Use ***Intervention Guide*** pages 202–203 |

# Reading Recommendations

## Oral Reading

The narrative style of this story makes it enjoyable for oral reading. Students should read aloud fluently with appropriate expression and intonation. Make sure that students attend to punctuation and read in phrases. Tell students to add a sense of feeling or anticipation as they read.

Have students make use of the comprehension strategies listed below to help them understand the selection. Have them stop reading periodically or wait until they have completed the selection to discuss the reading strategies. After the students have finished reading the selection, use the Discussing the Selection questions on page 53A to see if they understand what they have read.

## Using Comprehension Strategies

Comprehension strategy instruction allows students to become aware of how good readers read. Good readers constantly check their understanding as they are reading and ask themselves questions. In addition, skilled readers recognize when they are having problems and stop to use various comprehension strategies to help them make sense of what they are reading.

During the first reading of "The Cobbler's Song," you will model and prompt the use of the following reading strategies:

- **Predicting** causes readers to analyze information given about story events and characters in the context of how it may logically connect to the story's conclusion.
- **Asking Questions** helps readers focus attention on what they are reading and engages them in deeper understanding of themes, concepts, and ideas.
- **Summarizing** prompts readers to keep track of what they are reading and to focus their minds on important information.

As students read, they should be using a variety of strategies to help them understand the selection. Encourage students to use the strategies listed above as the class reads the story aloud. Do this by stopping at the points indicated by the numbers in the magenta circles on the reduced student page and modeling for the students the use of a particular strategy. Students can also stop reading periodically to discuss what they have learned and what problems they may be having.

## Building Comprehension Skills 

Revisiting or rereading a selection allows readers to apply skills that give them a more complete understanding of the text. Some follow-up comprehension skills help students organize information. Others lead to deeper understanding—to "reading between the lines," as mature readers do.

An extended lesson on Comprehension Skill: Author's Purpose can be found in the Supporting the Reading section on pages 53C–53D. This lesson is intended to give students extra practice with Author's Purpose. However, it may be used at this time to introduce the comprehension skill to students.

- **Author's Purpose:** Readers determine the purpose the author had for writing the text. Readers can then sort out what is important in a text from what is less important. Knowing the author's purpose also gives readers an idea of what they can expect to find in the text.

### Reading with a Purpose

Have students look for ways any of the story characters learn about money throughout the selection.

**Teacher Tip** As often as possible, ask questions that are not specific to the selection. Students should be able to apply most of your questions to many different selections.

### Research in Action

Instruction designed to build and support students' metacognitive skills leads to improved reading comprehension. Such instruction is most effective when teachers help students develop the strategies necessary for deep comprehension by modeling and explaining the behaviors and strategies used by expert readers as they tackle a text; guiding students in using strategies appropriately; asking students to apply the strategies on their own; and gradually shifting responsibility to the students for their own learning.

Strategic reading seems to promote the development of comprehension ability most when teachers encourage students to make associations between what they read and their own experiences, to interpret, and to create summaries of what they find important in a text.
*(Michael Pressley)*

COMPREHENSION

Read pages 48–53.

## Comprehension Strategies

Read the story aloud, taking turns with the students. Start by modeling the use of strategies for the students.

### Teacher Modeling

**1 Predicting** *Predicting what might happen next helps me organize my thoughts about the selection I'm reading. I'm going to try to figure out what's in the purse that the rich man gave to the cobbler. The rich man wanted to give the cobbler something to worry about. The rich man knew that people worry when they have too much money. I think he's giving the cobbler money so he'll worry. Now I'll keep on reading to see if I'm right.*

### Word Knowledge

**SCAFFOLDING** The skills students are reviewing in Word Knowledge should help them in reading the story. This lesson focuses on the /ē/ sound spelled *ie* and *ei* and base words with the suffixes *-ful, -ing, -ed,* and *-ly.*

**suffix *-ing:***
**thinking** **fearing** **shining**

**Teacher Tip** Good readers constantly evaluate their understanding of what they read. Stop often to make sure students are doing this.

**First Reading Recommendation**

**ORAL • CHORAL**

*Focus Questions* How can people have happy and meaningful lives without a great deal of money? Why would money have a greater value if it is well earned?

# The Cobbler's Song

a fable by Jean de La Fontaine
*adapted and illustrated by Marcia Sewall*

Once upon a time a poor cobbler lived in the basement of a large house in Paris. He had to work from early morning until late at night to make enough money to keep himself and his wife and children. But he was happy in his dark little rooms, and he sang all day as he mended old shoes.

On the floor above him lived a very rich man. His rooms were large and sunny. He wore fine clothes and had plenty of good things to eat. Still, he was never happy.

All night long he lay awake thinking about his money—how to make more, or fearing lest it be stolen. Often the sun was shining in at his windows before he fell asleep.

Now, as soon as it grew light enough to see, the cobbler always got up and went about his work. And as he hammered, he sang. His songs floated up to the rooms of the rich man and woke him.

48

### Differentiating Instruction

| If... | Then... |
|---|---|
| English Learners need extra help with vocabulary | Use ***English Learner Support Guide*** pages 300–301 |
| English Learners need extra help with summarizing | Use ***English Learner Support Guide*** pages 300–302 |

COMPREHENSION

## Comprehension Strategies

### Teacher Modeling

**2 Confirming Predictions** *My prediction was confirmed. There was money in the purse.*

Begin prompting students for responses. Praise answers that are appropriate, even if they do not match the student sample. This will encourage students to use strategies as they read.

### Prompting

**3 Asking Questions** *Why did the cobbler hide the gold pieces when he saw a man passing by the window? Why did he then go into the bedroom to count them? What will the cobbler do with so much gold? When I reread carefully I learned that the cobbler was a poor man. Now the rich man has given him money. I think the cobbler is afraid that someone will steal the money from him. Who else has any questions we can consider as we read?*

### Student Sample

**Answering Questions** *I think the cobbler went to his bedroom to hide his money because he was afraid somebody would steal it.*

**Word Knowledge**

the /ē/ sound: **pieces** **happiest**

**Teacher Tip** Be sure students answer questions with appropriate elaboration.

The cobbler opened it and saw that it was full of shining gold pieces.

2 "I cannot take all this money!" cried he. "I have not earned it. Take it back."

"No," answered the rich man, "you have earned it by your songs. I give it to you because you are the happiest man I know."

Without waiting for any thanks, the rich man left the shop.

The cobbler turned the gold pieces out on his table and began to count them. He had counted to fifty-two, when he looked up and saw a man passing by the window. He quickly hid the gold. Then he went into 3 the bedroom to count it where no one could see him.

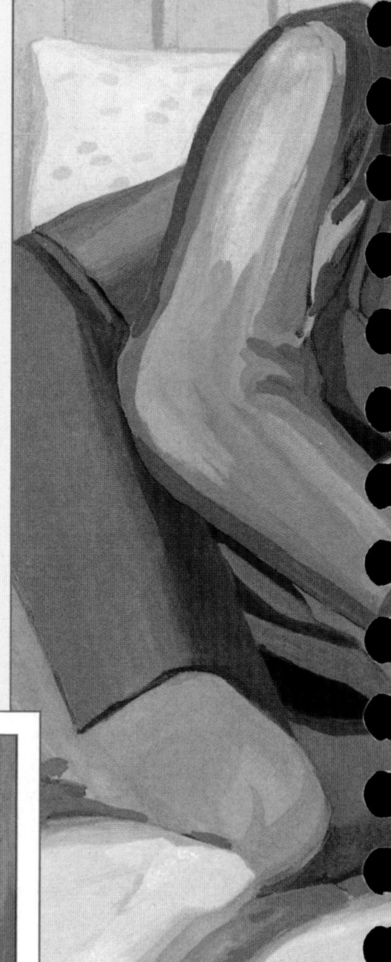

50

**Differentiating Instruction**

| If... | Then... |
|---|---|
| English Learners need extra help with vocabulary | Use ***English Learner Support Guide*** pages 302–303 |
| English Learners need extra help with summarizing | Use ***English Learner Support Guide*** pages 303–304 |

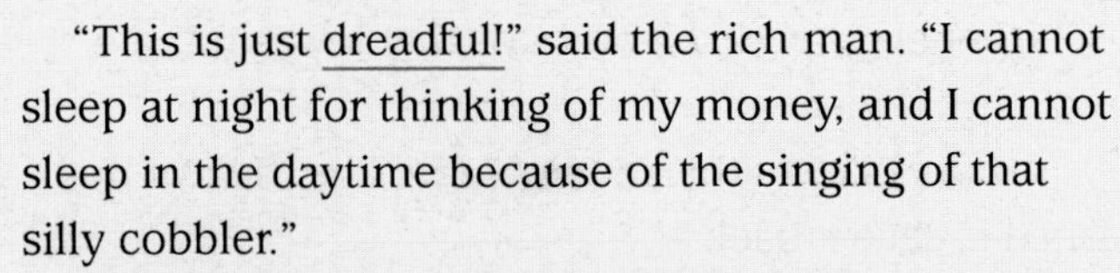

"This is just dreadful!" said the rich man. "I cannot sleep at night for thinking of my money, and I cannot sleep in the daytime because of the singing of that silly cobbler."

So the rich man sat down and thought the matter over.

"Hmm," he said to himself, "if the cobbler had something to worry about, he would not sing so much. I must think of a plan to stop him. Let me see, what worries men most?

"Why money, to be sure! Some men worry because they have so little. The cobbler has little enough, it's true, but that does not worry him. In fact, he is the happiest man I know.

"Other men worry because they have too much money, which is my trouble. I wonder if it would worry the cobbler if he had too much. That's the idea! Now I know what I shall do!"

A few minutes later, the rich man entered the cobbler's poor home.

"What can I do for you?" asked the cobbler, recognizing his neighbor but wondering why so fine a man should enter his little shop.

"Here, I have brought you a present," said the rich man, and he gave the poor man a purse. **1**

## Comprehension Skills

### Author's Purpose

Students should be able to define the Author's Purpose as the main reason for writing a story or selection and for presenting it in a certain way. The author's purpose can be to *entertain*—to tell students a story they will enjoy and perhaps laugh at; to *inform*—to tell students about something; to *explain;* or to *persuade*—to get readers to think about something the way that the author does. There can be more than one purpose for writing a story or selection.

Ask students to identify the author's purpose for writing this story *(to entertain or to persuade)*. What clues let you know? *(Starts with "Once upon a time"; has a moral.)*

### Word Knowledge

**suffix *-ful*:** **dreadful**

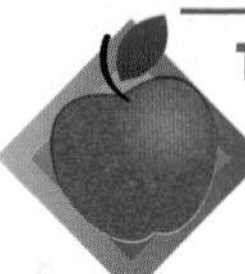

**Teacher Tip** By this time in the school year, students should be using all of the reading strategies with confidence.

### Skills Trace

**Author's Purpose**

Introduced in Grade 2.

Scaffolded throughout Grade 3.

**REINTRODUCED:** Unit 2, Lesson 6

**REINFORCED:** Unit 3, Lesson 1
Unit 4, Lesson 4
Unit 5, Lesson 2
Unit 5, Lesson 3
Unit 6, Lesson 4

**TESTED:** Unit 4 Assessment

**Second Reading Recommendation**

ORAL • **SILENT**

COMPREHENSION

### Informal Assessment

Observe individual students as they read and use the Teacher Observation Log, found in the ***Program Assessment Teacher's Edition,*** to record anecdotal information about each student's strengths and weaknesses.

He piled the coins up on the bed. How golden they were! How bright! He had never seen so much money before. He looked and looked at the money until everything in the room seemed golden and bright. Then he counted it slowly.

"One hundred pieces of gold! How rich I am! Where shall I hide it for safekeeping?"

First he hid the coins under the covers at the foot of the bed, which he could see from his workbench.

"The money makes quite a lump under the covers," he said. "Perhaps someone else will see it and steal it. I think I should hide it under the pillow."

51

## Differentiating Instruction

| If... | Then... |
| --- | --- |
| Students have an understanding of "The Cobbler's Song" | Have small groups of students take turns acting out the parts of the story characters. Encourage them to add dialogue to enrich the scenes. Have the class evaluate peer performances based on a set of criteria or a rubric developed by the class prior to the performances. |

COMPREHENSION

## Comprehension Skills

### Author's Purpose

Inform students that the author can accomplish his or her purpose through descriptions of story events, the use of illustrations, the dialogue, and the details. Students know that the author's purpose in writing this story is to entertain and to persuade. Encourage students to identify specific events, descriptions, illustrations, and dialogue in this story that help the writer accomplish this purpose.

- *Author uses dialogue.* That's part of a fiction story, which is mainly to entertain.
- *Author uses conflict in the plot.* That's also part of a fiction story.
- *Author ends with a moral.* This is common in a persuasive piece.

### Word Knowledge

**suffix *-ly*:** **slowly**

**Teacher Tip** As students read aloud, listen for appropriate pacing, intonation, and expression.

**Teacher Tip** Tell students that good readers keep thinking about the questions that come up about the topic, and they keep coming back to those questions. As they read, tell them to keep the questions on the Concept/Question Board in mind. Have them make notes to themselves in the Response Journal section of their Writer's Notebooks about which questions seem most important. Tell them that good readers always think about what is important in selections, and they try to remember this important information.

COMPREHENSION

## Comprehension Strategies

### Teacher Modeling

**4 Summarizing** *This is a good time to sum up what I've read. A rich man was bothered by a cobbler's song. So the rich man gave the cobbler a purse with gold coins so that he would worry about his money and stop singing. The cobbler worried about the gold for a month. He finally returned the coins to the rich man. Who would like to continue this summary in their own words?*

### Discussing Strategy Use

After students have read the selection, encourage them to share any problems they encountered and to tell what strategies they used to solve them.

- What questions did they ask as they read?
- Where did they pause in the reading to summarize?
- On what basis did they make and confirm predictions?

These are questions good readers ask after they read a text. After reading, the students should always be asking, "What did I find interesting? What is important here?" Later, remind the students again that whenever they conclude a reading, they should ask themselves questions about what was in the text.

### Word Knowledge

**suffix *-ly*:** **drowsily**

**Teacher Tip** During reading, have students explain why the cobbler sings.

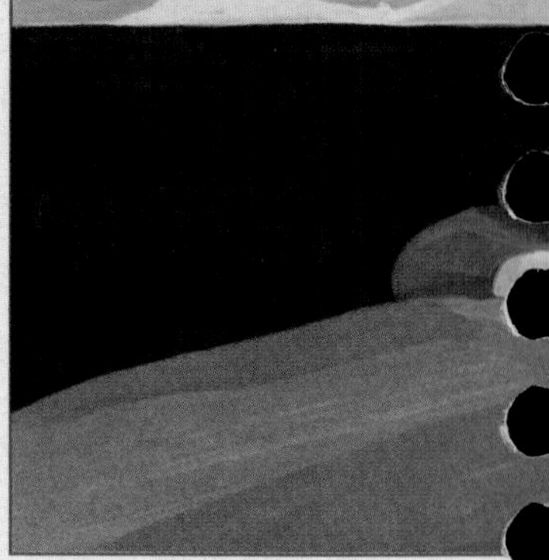

While he was putting it under the pillow, his wife came into the room.

"What is the matter with the bed?" she asked.

The cobbler glared at her, and drove her from the room with angry words—the first cross words he had ever spoken to her.

Dinner came, but he could not eat a mouthful because he was afraid someone would steal his treasure while he was at the table! As he worked, not a note did he sing. By suppertime he felt worse. Not a kind word did he speak to his wife.

Day after day and night after night, the cobbler grew more and more unhappy, worrying about his money. He dared not go to sleep, lest he should wake to find that his gold had disappeared. He tossed and turned on his pillow.

But upstairs, the rich man was happy. "That was a fine idea," he said to himself drowsily. "Now I can sleep all day without being awakened by the cobbler's song."

52

### Differentiating Instruction

| If... | Then... |
|---|---|
| English Learners need extra help with vocabulary | Use ***English Learner Support Guide*** pages 304–305 |
| English Learners need extra help with summarizing | Use ***English Learner Support Guide*** pages 305–306 |

For a month, the cobbler worried over the hundred gold pieces. He grew thin and pale, and his wife and children were most unhappy. At last he could bear the worry no longer, so he called his wife and told her the whole story.

"Dear husband," she said, "take back the gold. All the gold in the world is not worth as much to me as your happiness and one of your glad songs."

How relieved the cobbler felt to hear her say this. He picked up the purse and ran upstairs to the rich man's home. Throwing the gold on the table, he smiled and said: "Here is your purse of gold. Take it back! I can live without your money, but I cannot live without my song." 4

53

## Comprehension Skills

COMPREHENSION

### Author's Purpose

Remind students that authors can have more than one main purpose. What might other main purposes be for this piece? Ask students to give support from the text for their answers.

- *One reason might be to teach. La Fontaine wants to teach that money can cause unhappiness.*
- *Marcia Sewall's purpose was to share the stories of La Fontaine with a modern audience. That's why she translated and illustrated the story.*

### Checking Comprehension

- What does the cobbler learn about the value of money and about the value of his own happiness? *(He realizes that happiness and peace of mind are more important than money.)*
- What do we learn about the cobbler's wife in this story? *(She loves her husband very much and believes his happiness is more important than money.)*
- What do you think the cobbler means when he tells the rich man, "I can live without your money, but I cannot live without my song"? *(The cobbler cannot live without his happiness and peace of mind.)*

**Teacher Tip** **FLUENCY** By this time in third grade, good readers should be reading approximately 123 words per minute with fluency and expression. The only way to gain this fluency is through practice. Have students reread the selection to you and each other during Workshop to help build fluency. As students read, you may notice that some need work in building fluency. During Workshop, have these students select a section of the text (a minimum of 160 words) to read several times in order to build fluency.

### Differentiating Instruction

| If... | Then... |
| --- | --- |
| English Learners need extra help reviewing "The Cobbler's Song" | Use ***English Learner Support Guide*** pages 306–309 |

### Formal Assessment

See pages 14–17 in ***Unit 4 Assessment*** to test students' comprehension of "The Cobbler's Song."

**Teacher Tip** DISCUSSION When you call on a student, allow him or her a few seconds to consider your question and arrive at an answer.

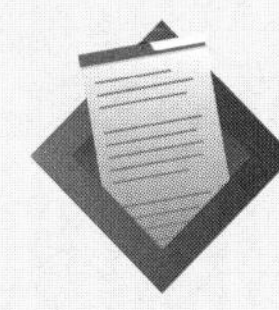

**Routine Card**
Refer to ***Routine 6*** for the *handing-off process.*

| Clues | Problems | Wonderings |
|---|---|---|
| pictures mean? | cobbler | Is this a story about money and a song? |

***Reading Transparency 46***

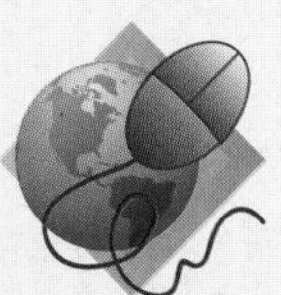

**www.sra4kids.com**
**Web Connection**
Some students may choose to conduct a computer search for additional books or information about money. Invite them to make a list of these books and sources of information to share with classmates and the school librarian. Check the Reading link of the SRA Web page for additional links to the theme-related Web site.

## Discussing the Selection

After the first read, the whole group discusses the selection and any personal thoughts, reactions, problems, or questions that it raises. To stimulate discussion, students can ask one another the kinds of questions good readers ask themselves about a text: *How does it connect to the theme of Money? What have I learned that is new? What did I find interesting? What is important here? What was difficult to understand? Why would someone want to read this?*

**Handing-off Process** Seeing you as a contributing member of the group sets a strong example for students. To emphasize that you are part of the group, actively participate in the *handing-off process:* Raise your hand to be called on by the last speaker when you have a contribution to make. Point out unusual and interesting insights verbalized by students so that these insights are recognized and discussed. As the year progresses, students will take more and more responsibility for the discussions of the selections.

Engage students in a discussion to determine whether they have grasped the following ideas:

- why the rich man wanted to give the cobbler money
- how the cobbler changed after receiving the money
- why the selection was named "The Cobbler's Song"

During this time, have students return to the clues, problems, and wonderings they noted during browsing to determine whether the clues were borne out by the selection, whether and how their problems were solved, and whether their wonderings were answered or deserve further discussion and investigation. Let students decide which items deserve further discussion.

Also have students return to the Focus Questions on the first page of the selection. Select a student to read the questions aloud, and have volunteers answer the questions. If students do not know the answers to the questions, have them return to the text to find the answers.

You may wish to review the elements of a fable with the students at this time. Discuss with them how they can tell "The Cobbler's Song" is a fable.

Have students break into small groups to discuss what this story tells about money. Groups can then share their ideas with the rest of the class.

If they have ever received money as a surprise, ask them to think about how their behavior changed. Encourage them to record their thoughts.

## Review Selection Vocabulary

Have students review the definitions of the selection vocabulary words that they wrote in the vocabulary section of their Writer's Notebooks. Remind them that they discussed the meanings of these words before reading the selection. Have students write sentences for each of the vocabulary words after the definitions in the same section of their Writer's Notebooks. They can use the definitions and the sentences to study for the vocabulary portion of their Lesson Assessments. Have them add to the personal dictionary section of their Writer's Notebooks any other interesting words that they clarified while reading. Encourage students to refer to the selection vocabulary words throughout the unit. The words from the selection are:

**cobbler** **mended** **recognizing** **safekeeping** **workbench** **treasure**

If you created a Word Bank of key words related to the theme of Money, remind students to find words from other resources, from their investigations, and from family discussions and add them to the Word Bank. Organize your Word Bank by the number of syllables in a word.

**Teacher Tip** After reading, discuss with students what the cobbler might have done differently.

## View Fine Art

Have students reflect on the painting ***The Money Lender and His Wife*** on page 57 of the ***Student Anthology*** and share their thoughts and reactions with the class. Explain that the painting by Quentin Matsys portrays a man counting his money as his wife looks on and thumbs through a book. During this time, books were so costly that only the wealthy were able to afford them. Notice the miniature painting in the foreground and how the couple is surrounded by material objects.

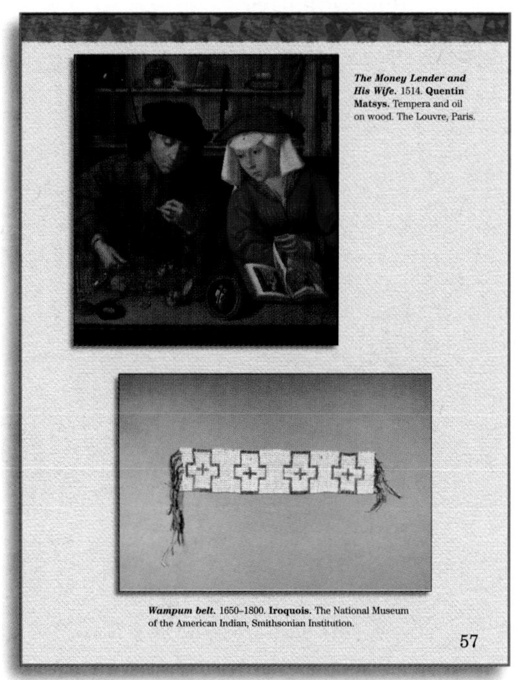

***The Money Lender and His Wife.*** 1514. **Quentin Matsys.** Tempera and oil on wood. The Louvre, Paris.

***Wampum belt.*** 1650–1800. **Iroquois.** The National Museum of the American Indian, Smithsonian Institution.

57

***Student Anthology* p. 57**

## Home Connection

Distribute ***Home Connection,*** page 51. Parents and caregivers will have the opportunity to hear about "The Cobbler's Song" from their children. After discussing the relationship between money and happiness at home, students can share their thoughts with the class. A Spanish version of this letter appears on page 52.

*The Cobbler's Song*

**A message from** ______________________

We've just read "The Cobbler's Song," a fable about a hardworking, but happy, cobbler and his rich, but unhappy, neighbor. In this story, the cobbler discovers that he would rather be poor and happy than rich and worried about his money. Ask your child to tell you the story.

Discuss with your child the issue of money and happiness that the story raises. What does your child think? Is it better to be poor and happy? Or, is it better to be rich, but worried about someone stealing your money? Ask your child to write his or her thoughts on this page and bring it to school to share and discuss with classmates.

**Rich and Unhappy or Poor and Happy?**

**Next week's selection** ***Four Dollars and Fifty Cents***

Your child will be studying the following vocabulary words in the upcoming week. Please review the meanings of these words with your child: **blacksmith**—person who makes and repairs iron objects; **determined**—firm and unwilling to change; **decent**—fairly good, proper; **collecting**—getting payment for a debt; **volunteered**—offered to help or do something by choice and without pay.

Please review with your child the spelling words for the upcoming week: berries, bunnies, guppies, hobbies, pennies, puppies, ponies, babies, donkeys, families, dollars, horses, sleeves, cowboys, britches.

***Home Connection* p. 51**

**Reading Transparency 53**

### Research in Action
#### Author's Purpose

Although texts can have multiple purposes, typically we think that the purpose of narrative text is to entertain while the purpose of expository text is to inform. However, research has shown that narratives also inform. Stories tell us about the social world—how people act and what they think and feel. They link story characters' actions and intentions to consequences so as to provide models of human behavior. In so doing they help us to interpret our own and others' actions and intentions and thus, to order the events of our lives into meaningful experiences.
*(Anne McKeough)*

## Supporting the Reading

### Comprehension Skills: Author's Purpose

**Teach** After the second read, ask students what they know about author's purpose. If necessary, explain that every text is written for a purpose. Good readers use their knowledge of the author's purpose to help sort out what is important in a text from what is less important. Understanding an author's purpose also helps readers know what they can expect to find in a text.

**Guided Practice** Use the three-column chart on ***Reading Transparency 53*** to record students' responses. Ask them to think about the stories they have read so far in this unit. Write the titles in the first column of the chart. Then ask students to tell you what the author's main purpose was for each selection. Place that information in the second column. Then ask students to give examples from the text that support their answer. Record examples in the third column. You can use the following example to get started.

| Selection Title | Author's Purpose | Examples from Text |
|---|---|---|
| A New Coat for Anna | To entertain and to inform | Author writes an interesting story based on the true experience of a friend. |

**Independent Practice** Read through the Focus and Identify sections of ***Comprehension and Language Arts Skills,*** page 106, with students. Guide students through the Identify portion, and help them come up with examples found in the story. Then have students complete the Practice and Apply portions of ***Comprehension and Language Arts Skills,*** page 107.

**Link to Writing** Separate students into groups. Then pass out two slips of paper to each student. Ask students to write a subject, such as *baseball, snow,* or *school lunch,* on one slip of paper. Mix them in a hat or a box and have each student select a slip. Next have students write a purpose, such as *inform, persuade,* or *entertain,* on the other slip of paper. Again, mix and distribute the slips. Each student will then have a subject and a purpose. Ask students to write one paragraph about the subject they chose with the purpose they chose. If students have trouble making the two fit, provide assistance or allow them to change one or the other.

Name ______ Date ______

UNIT 4 Money • Lesson 4 *The Cobbler's Song*

**Author's Purpose**

**Focus** An **author's purpose** is the author's reason for writing or presenting a selection in a certain way.

- The four main reasons for writing are *to inform, to entertain, to persuade,* and *to explain.*
- A writer can have more than one purpose for writing a story.

**Identify**

The author's purpose in "The Cobbler's Song" is to entertain the reader. Look through the story to find three examples that show it was written mainly to entertain.

Answers will vary. Possible answers given.

1. Page: 48 Example The story starts with "Once upon a time."
2. Page: ______ Example ______
3. Page: ______ Example ______

106 UNIT 4 • Lesson 4 Comprehension and Language Arts Skills

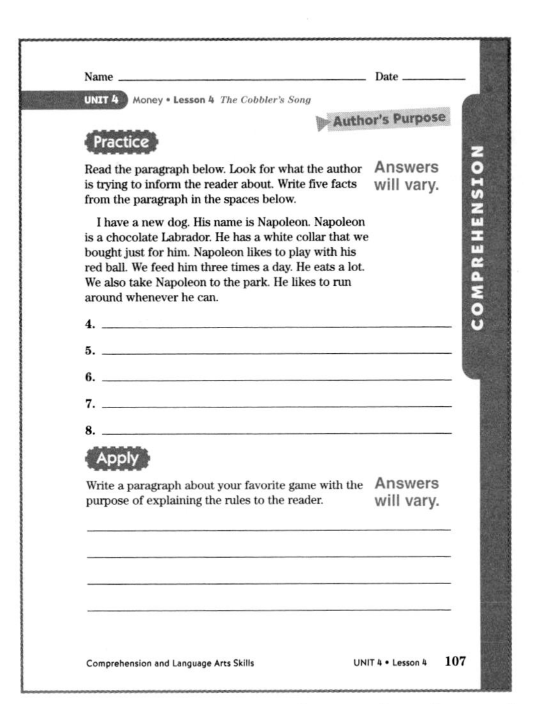

Name ______ Date ______

UNIT 4 Money • Lesson 4 *The Cobbler's Song*

Author's Purpose

**Practice**

Read the paragraph below. Look for what the author is trying to inform the reader about. Write five facts from the paragraph in the spaces below.

Answers will vary.

I have a new dog. His name is Napoleon. Napoleon is a chocolate Labrador. He has a white collar that we bought just for him. Napoleon likes to play with his red ball. We feed him three times a day. He eats a lot. We also take Napoleon to the park. He likes to run around whenever he can.

4. ______
5. ______
6. ______
7. ______
8. ______

**Apply**

Write a paragraph about your favorite game with the purpose of explaining the rules to the reader.

Answers will vary.

COMPREHENSION

Comprehension and Language Arts Skills UNIT 4 • Lesson 4 107

***Comprehension and Language Arts Skills pp. 106–107***

## Differentiating Instruction

| If... | Then... |
| --- | --- |
| Students need extra help with author's purpose | Use ***Reteach*** pages 109–110 |
| Students have an understanding of author's purpose and would enjoy a challenge | Use ***Challenge*** page 96 |

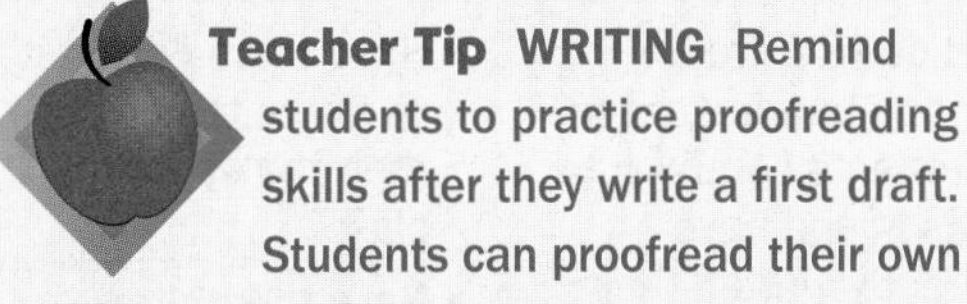

**Teacher Tip** WRITING Remind students to practice proofreading skills after they write a first draft. Students can proofread their own papers, or they can exchange papers with a classmate for proofreading.

**Author's Purpose**

Introduced in Grade 2.

Scaffolded throughout Grade 3.

**REINTRODUCED:** Unit 2, Lesson 6

**REINFORCED:** Unit 3, Lesson 1
Unit 4, Lesson 4
Unit 5, Lesson 2
Unit 5, Lesson 3
Unit 6, Lesson 4

**TESTED:** Unit 4 Assessment

**Teacher Tip** Some investigation groups might wish to write or dramatize a fable about their research topic, if applicable.

### Differentiating Instruction

| If... | Then... |
| --- | --- |
| Students are having difficulty recognizing fables | Read a fable with them and help them identify the elements found in that fable |
| Students have an understanding of the elements common to fables and have already written their own fables | • Have them work with partners to perform their fables for the class<br>• Have them draw illustrations to go along with their fables |

## Literary Elements

### Recognize and Distinguish Fables

**Teach** Have students tell what they know about fables. If necessary, point out that a fable is much like a folktale. It is a very short story that teaches a moral or lesson. List the following elements common to fables on the board and review them with students:

- Fables are short.
- There are only a few characters in the story.
- Animals and objects talk and act like humans.
- Fables teach a lesson called a moral.

**Guided Practice** Provide students with several fables from which to choose. Have them read at least one fable and identify the elements listed above. Invite students to summarize their fables for the class and tell which elements were present.

**Independent Practice** Ask students to write a fable about the subject of money. List the characteristics of fables on the board. Ask students to share their fables with the class.

## Social Studies Connection

### History of Costs, Goods, and Services

In "The Cobbler's Song," students read about a fictional family who lived in medieval times. The cobbler worked hard to make a living for his family by practicing a trade, one that he likely learned as an apprentice when he was a boy. As an adult, he was likely part of a guild, or organization of others in the same trade. During those times, many people earned their living by practicing a particular trade or craft.

Ask students to investigate the tradition of tradesmen and apprentices in medieval times. Ask them to investigate the following questions in their research: *How did the system of tradesmen, craftsmen, and apprentices affect the costs of goods and services? How did the system affect the amount of goods and services produced? How were the different tradesmen and craftsmen dependent on each other?* Ask students to prepare a presentation to share their findings with the class. Students might wish to draw a diagram of the flow of goods, services, and money between tradesmen and craftsmen, perhaps by focusing on one item, such as wool, cotton, paper, or leather, and its final product, such as clothing, linens, books, or shoes.

**Teacher Tip** **MATERIALS**
- ✔ poster board
- ✔ colored pencils or markers

**Teacher Tip** **PURPOSE** To learn about how economic specialization, especially in medieval times, affects costs and amounts of goods and services.

**Teacher Tip** Remind students that the library as well as the Internet provides many sources that cover important periods in history and that are created especially for young students to use. They might consider starting with such a source to look up the information for this activity.

## Concept Connections

### Linking the Selection

- The rich man and the cobbler were unhappy when they had a lot of money.
- The cobbler realized that he was happier without the gold.

### Exploring Concept Vocabulary

The concept word for this lesson is ***value.*** Write the word on the board. Work with students to develop a definition that links to the unit theme. Have students copy the word and definition into the Vocabulary section of their Writer's Notebooks.

***Value:*** to consider something as important or useful. For example, the cobbler's wife valued her husband's songs.

- People show that they value something by working hard to get or keep it. For example, using the money you saved to buy a new basketball shows that you value the basketball.
- Students might suggest that both men valued their happiness. For the rich man, happiness was being able to sleep during the day so he could protect his money at night. For the cobbler, happiness was the freedom from worrying about money.

Each student's sentence should demonstrate an understanding of the concept and selection vocabulary word.

### Expanding the Concept

You may want to do a whole-group discussion to help students continue to develop their ability to engage in meaningful dialogue. However, students may conduct these dialogues in small groups. If students work in small groups, bring the groups together and have them share their ideas with the whole class.

Have students record their ideas and impressions about the selection on page 84 of their ***Inquiry Journals.***

# The Cobbler's Song

## Concept Connections

### Linking the Selection

Think about the following questions, and then record your responses in the Response Journal section of your Writer's Notebook.

- How did money affect the rich man and the cobbler?
- Why did the cobbler give the gold back to the rich man?

### Exploring Concept Vocabulary

The concept word for this lesson is ***value.*** If you do not know what this word means, look it up in a dictionary. Answer these questions:

- How do people show that they ***value*** something?
- What did the rich man ***value*** most? What did the cobbler ***value*** most?

In the Vocabulary section of your Writer's Notebook, write a sentence that includes the word ***value*** as well as one of the selection vocabulary words.

### Expanding the Concept

Think about the stories "Alexander, Who Used to Be Rich Last Sunday" and "The Cobbler's Song." How did money cause problems in these stories? How were the characters alike and different?

Try to use the word ***value*** in your discussion.

Add new ideas about money to the Concept/Question Board.

54

**Informal Assessment**

This may be a good time to observe students working in small groups and to mark your observations in the Teacher Observation Log found in the ***Program Assessment Teacher's Edition.***

**Teacher Tip** **CONCEPT VOCABULARY** Developing a repertoire of concept-related vocabulary will help students deepen their understanding of theme concepts, help facilitate class discussions, and help students formulate ideas, problems, and questions for inquiry.

## Meet the Author

**Jean de La Fontaine** was born in France in 1621. He is best known for his collection of nearly 250 fables. In six volumes of writing, he took existing fables, built on them, and turned them into poetry. His writings about everyday life and the choices people face have remained popular for more than 350 years.

## Meet the Illustrator

**Marcia Sewall** adapted and illustrated this fable written by Jean de La Fontaine. Her home and family have been very influential in her life and career. *"The interests of my family have come together in my own desire to illustrate books. My father was full of good tales, particularly of Maine, and would love to entertain us with long humorous poems memorized, and anecdotes* [stories] *of people. My mother has always been artistic in so many different ways."*

55

## Meet the Author

After students have read about Jean de La Fontaine have them answer the following questions:

- Jean de La Fontaine's stories are still popular after over 350 years. Why do you think this is true and what does this say about him as a writer? *(Possible answer: His stories are popular because they are about everyday life and the choices people face. He must be a good writer if people can still enjoy his tales after all of this time.)*
- Jean de La Fontaine is best known for his collection of fables, which he built on and turned into poetry. Why do you think this story lends itself well to adaptation? *(Possible answer: This story has a simple plot that can be modified with lots of details and descriptive phrases.)*

## Meet the Illustrator

After students read about Marcia Sewall have them answer the following questions:

- Look back at the illustrations in "The Cobbler's Song." Why do you think Marcia Sewall decided to use colors the way she did in her illustrations? *(Possible answer: She wanted the colors to express the changing moods and feelings of the story.)*
- Family has always been important to Marcia Sewall. How does this reflect in her drawings? *(Possible answer: She clearly shows the relationship between the husband and wife in good and bad times, much like any family might have.)*

### Objectives

- Students ask questions related to money.
- Students gain a deeper understanding of issues related to money.
- Students discuss conjectures and begin making plans.

### Materials

- Student Anthology, Book 2, pp. 48–57
- Inquiry Journal, pp. 96–98
- Research Assistant CD-ROM

**Teacher Tip** The supplementary activities are suggestions for further investigation. They do not have to be completed within the days devoted to this lesson.

INVESTIGATION

## Investigating Concepts Beyond the Text

Students should already have produced conjectures regarding their chosen investigations and discussed them in their investigation groups. A whole-class discussion of these may now be conducted, in which problems and conjectures are briefly presented and all students have a chance to contribute suggestions, criticisms, and questions. These ideas should help the investigation groups as they enter the next phase, Needs and Plans.

In "The Cobbler's Song," students read about a man who went through a change after he received money. Students might wish to further investigate the theme of the story through discussion. They might recall true stories in which money changed a person's life. They may share details of the stories with others in small groups, either orally or in writing. Have students complete ***Inquiry Journal,*** pages 96–97, during Workshop and then have them share their responses during the discussion. Additionally, students might draw pictures of things that cannot be bought or sold that make them happy.

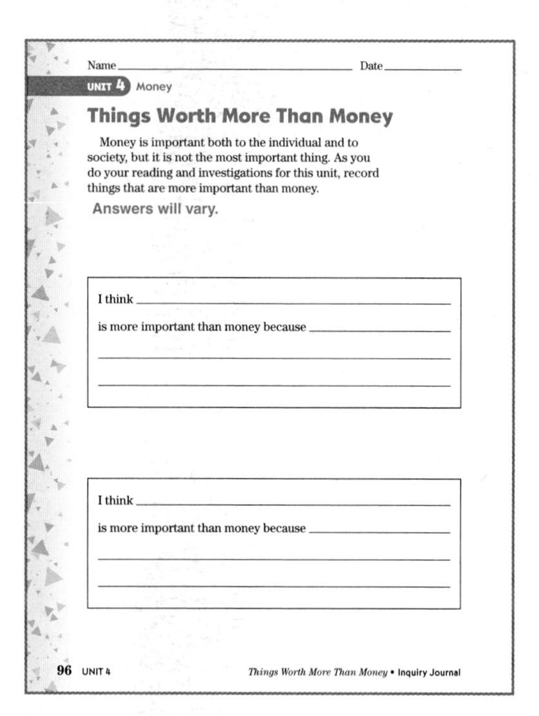
Name ______________________ Date __________

UNIT 4 Money

**Things Worth More Than Money**

Money is important both to the individual and to society, but it is not the most important thing. As you do your reading and investigations for this unit, record things that are more important than money.

Answers will vary.

I think ______________________
is more important than money because ______________________

I think ______________________
is more important than money because ______________________

96 UNIT 4 *Things Worth More Than Money* • Inquiry Journal

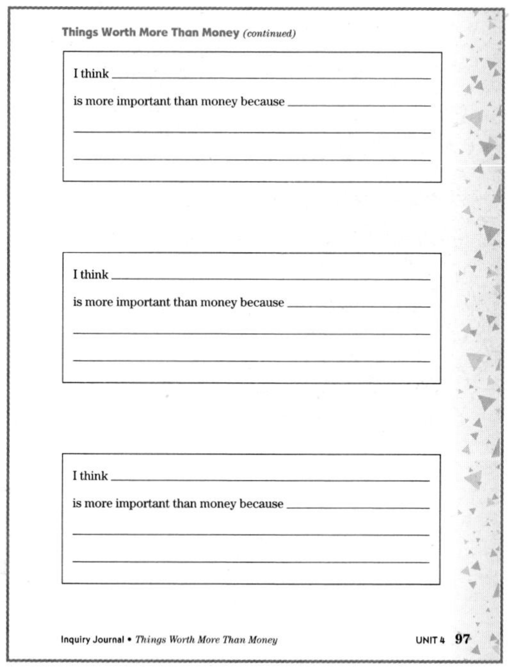
**Things Worth More Than Money** *(continued)*

I think ______________________
is more important than money because ______________________

I think ______________________
is more important than money because ______________________

I think ______________________
is more important than money because ______________________

Inquiry Journal • *Things Worth More Than Money* UNIT 4 97

***Inquiry Journal pp. 96–97***

## Concept/Question Board

Tell students this is a good time to post on the Concept/Question Board any new questions they have about money that "The Cobbler's Song" might have raised. Remind them of your earlier discussion about the Concept/Question Board and ask them to tell what they remember about that discussion.

After reading each selection, students should use the Concept/Question Board to:

- Post any questions they asked about a selection before reading that have not yet been answered.
- Refer to as they formulate statements about concepts that apply to their investigations.
- Post general statements formulated by each collaborative group.
- Continue to post news articles or other items that they find during the unit investigation.
- Read and think about posted questions, articles, or concepts that interest them and provide answers to the questions.
- Students might wish to bring in articles about things that money cannot buy or about how money can change people's lives.

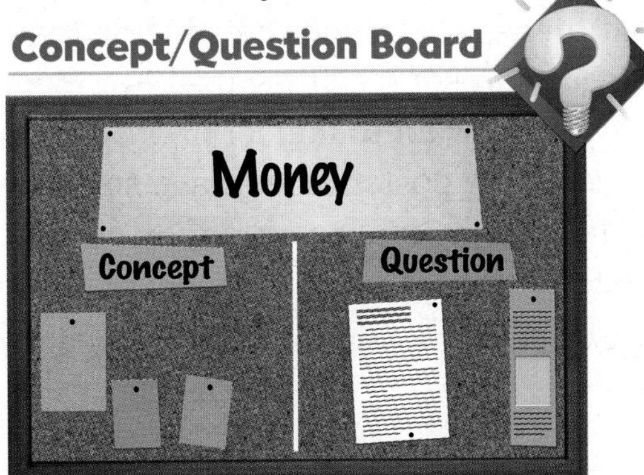


## Unit 4 Investigation Management

|  |  |
|---|---|
| Lesson 1 | Brainstorm questions related to the theme. Investigate alternatives to money, such as barter. |
| Lesson 2 | Groups form based on areas of shared interest. Investigate choices related to spending and saving money. |
| Lesson 3 | Begin forming conjectures. Brainstorm about how to turn hobbies into businesses. |
| Lesson 4 | **Collaborative Investigation**<br>**Discuss conjectures in groups and begin plans.**<br>**Supplementary Activity**<br>**Look for stories or illustrations about the ways that money can change people and things that money cannot buy.** |
| Lesson 5 | Students revise their plans as necessary and continue investigations. Groups can debate on borrowing and lending money. |
| Lesson 6 | Continue investigating and prepare final presentations. Create a story or miniplay about how money passes from person to person, or plan a field trip to a Federal Reserve Bank. |
| Lesson 7 | Groups give formal presentations. Students discuss saving money for personal goals or explore the Great Depression further. |

INVESTIGATION

**Teacher Tip** Continue to encourage use of the Concept/Question Board by recognizing and thanking students for their contributions. Incorporate discussion of those items into classroom discussions whenever appropriate.

### Research Assistant

The ***Research Assistant CD-ROM*** helps students with their investigations.

**Teacher Tip** Remind students of the recursive nature of the investigation process. Students will be continually finding and discussing new information and revising questions and conjectures. Their readings, activities, and research will assist them as they continue through the investigation cycle.

**Formal Assessment**

Use the Research Rubrics on page 48J to assess students' ability to recognize information needs.

**DIFFERENTIATING INSTRUCTION**

| If... | Then... |
|---|---|
| Students are having difficulty identifying the information they will need to find out in order to investigate their problems | Help them complete ***Inquiry Journal*** page 98 during Workshop |
| Students are having difficulty identifying resources that will help them investigate their problems | • Discuss with them the various resources that might be beneficial to their investigations during Workshop<br>• Review the resources on ***Inquiry Journal*** page 98 |

INVESTIGATION

## Needs and Plans Phase I

Remind students that *needs* refers to things they need to find out or understand. To help groups get started in identifying knowledge needs related to their problems, you might pose the following questions: *What facts will we need to help us decide whether this conjecture is right? Where can we find these facts? What do we need to understand to make our conjecture better? What would an expert on this problem know that we do not know?*

Have students examine the resources listed on ***Inquiry Journal,*** page 98. If they are unfamiliar with any of these resources, briefly explain the purpose of each and where it can be found. The students may be unaware of alternate sources of information for this unit theme, such as interviews, films, and primary source materials. Highlight these sources of information and have the students discuss how each might be useful to their investigation. Tell students that the way in which they decide to present their investigations might also affect the resources they use. For example, if they decide to make a poster, they might want to collect photographs and illustrations from magazines to place on the poster. Encourage students to begin thinking of interesting ways to present the information they collect. These might include reports, posters, dioramas, video presentations, plays, or a combination of methods. During Workshop, ask students to fill in page 98 of the ***Inquiry Journal.***

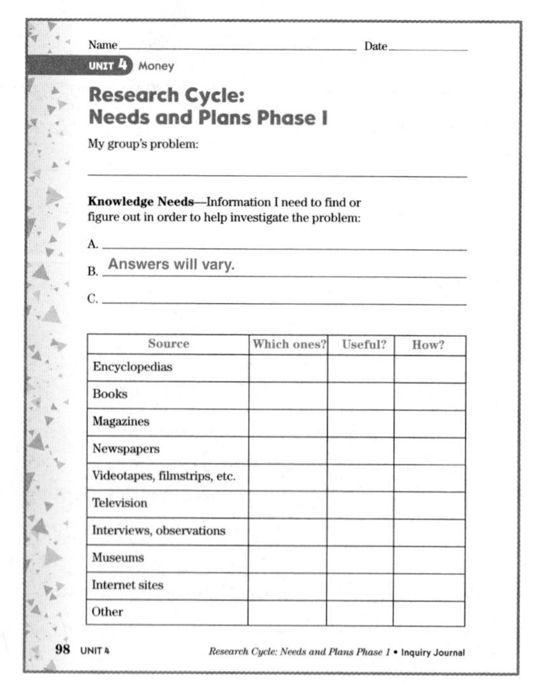

Name ______ Date ______

UNIT 4 Money

**Research Cycle: Needs and Plans Phase I**

My group's problem:

**Knowledge Needs**—Information I need to find or figure out in order to help investigate the problem:

A. ______

B. Answers will vary.

C. ______

| Source | Which ones? | Useful? | How? |
|---|---|---|---|
| Encyclopedias | | | |
| Books | | | |
| Magazines | | | |
| Newspapers | | | |
| Videotapes, filmstrips, etc. | | | |
| Television | | | |
| Interviews, observations | | | |
| Museums | | | |
| Internet sites | | | |
| Other | | | |

98 UNIT 4 *Research Cycle: Needs and Plans Phase I* • Inquiry Journal

***Inquiry Journal p. 98***

## Graphs

**Teach** Ask students to tell what a graph is and to give examples of graphs they have seen or used. If necessary, tell students that graphs can show a lot of information in a small amount of space.

**Guided Practice** Present the following guidelines for making a graph.

- Collect the data related to the topic of interest, and needed to show change over time.
- Select a name for the graph that describes the information it will contain.
- On a paper or poster board, write the time intervals used for the study across the bottom.
- Write the numbers that represent the units counted over time along the left side of the paper or poster board.
- Place dots at the location where imaginary lines would cross if one line was drawn upward from a date to meet another line that was drawn across from the number of items counted on that date. Repeat this step for all of the dates on the graph. **Do not draw the lines;** just place dots.

Explain that readers will follow the up and down movements depicted by the line to see how things changed over time.

**Independent Practice** For homework, have students make a graph of how they spend their free time. Tell them they should organize their graphs so that all information is easily understood. Have them share their graphs with classmates.

SUPPORTING THE INVESTIGATION

Encourage students to use ***TechKnowledge*** to learn more about how to use a computer to complete various tasks.

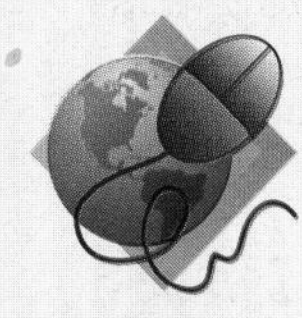

**www.sra4kids.com**
**Web Connection**
Students can use the connections to Money in the Reading link of the SRA Web page for more background information about money.

### Differentiating Instruction

| If... | Then... |
|---|---|
| Students are having difficulty understanding the concept of a graph | Provide them with an example of a graph and review the guidelines, using the example |

### Objectives

**Word Analysis**

**Spelling**

- **Adding *-ed* and *-ing*.** Develop understanding of how to add *-ed* and *-ing* to words.

**Vocabulary**

- **Inflectional Endings *-ed* and *-ing*.** Using words from "The Cobbler's Song," learn how the endings *-ed* and *-ing* affect the meaning of a word.

**Writing Process Strategies**

- **Persuasive Writing—Persuasive Paragraph.** Building on the theme of Money, learn the form of writing a persuasive paragraph.

**English Language Conventions**

**Grammar, Usage, and Mechanics**

- **Pronouns: Possessive and Personal; Singular and Plural.** Understand the concepts of singular and plural possessive pronouns. Identify personal and possessive singular and plural pronouns in "A Cobbler's Song."

**Listening, Speaking, Viewing**

- **Viewing: Media Techniques.** Observe and discuss persuasive techniques and purposes in the media.

**Penmanship**

- **Cursive Letters *K* and *H*.** Develop handwriting skills by practicing formation of cursive *K* and *H*.

### Materials

- Spelling and Vocabulary Skills, pp. 86–89
- Language Arts Handbook
- Comprehension and Language Arts Skills, pp. 106–111
- Writer's Workbook, pp. 66–69
- Language Arts Transparency 27
- Student Anthology

### Differentiating Instruction

***Reteach, Challenge,*** and ***Intervention*** lessons are available to support the language arts instruction in this lesson.

### Research in Action

Gaining insight into the cognitive processes of writing is seen as especially important as a basis for changing from knowledge telling to knowledge transforming. *(Carl Bereiter* and *Marlene Scardamalia,* The Psychology of Written Composition)

OVERVIEW

# Language Arts Overview

## Word Analysis

**Spelling** The Spelling activities on the following pages introduce how to add *-ed* and *-ing* to base words. For words with a *short vowel-consonant* pattern, double the final consonant before adding *-ed* or *-ing.* For words with a silent *e* drop the *e* before adding the *-ed* or *-ing.* For words ending in *consonant-y,* change the *y* to *i* before adding *-ed.*

### Selection Spelling Words

These words from "The Cobbler's Song" have the ending *-ed* or *-ing.*

**thinking   entered   opened   passing   safekeeping**

**Vocabulary** The Vocabulary activities extend the instruction of the Vocabulary Skill Words from "The Cobbler's Song" to recognize how the endings *-ed* and *-ing* affect the meaning of a word. The ending *-ed* means that an action has happened in the past. The ending *-ing* means that an action is happening now, in the present.

### Vocabulary Skill Words

**glared   safekeeping*   relieved   recognizing*   mended***

**Also Selection Vocabulary*

## Writing Process Strategies

The Writing Process Strategies lesson involves instruction in writing a persuasive paragraph. Three parts of a persuasive paragraph are emphasized: a topic sentence that grabs a reader; reasons, facts, or feelings used to support the topic sentence; and a strong closing sentence.

To teach spreadsheet applications in the writing process, show students how to modify a spreadsheet by deleting a row of information. ***TechKnowledge,*** Level 3, Lesson 70, teaches these spreadsheet application skills.

## English Language Conventions

**Grammar, Usage, and Mechanics** **Pronouns: Possessive and Personal; Singular and Plural.** This lesson develops an understanding of singular and plural possessive pronouns.

**Listening, Speaking, Viewing** **Viewing: Media Techniques.** In this Viewing lesson, students will observe and discuss persuasive techniques and purposes in the media.

**Penmanship** **Cursive Letters *K* and *H*.** This lesson develops handwriting skills by having students learn formation of *K* and *H*. Students then write words from the literature selection that contain those letters.

# DAY 1

## Word Analysis

### Spelling

#### Assessment: Pretest

**Adding *-ed* and *-ing***

#### Teach

Give students the Pretest on page 36 of ***Unit 4 Assessment.*** Have them proofread and correct any misspelled words.

**Pretest Sentences**

1. **making** A pastry chef is skilled in **making** pastries.
2. **biting** Sprays can prevent mosquitoes from **biting.**
3. **diving** A **diving** board is above a swimming pool.
4. **hiking** Mountains have trails for **hiking.**
5. **skated** Peggy Fleming **skated** in the 1968 Olympics.
6. **prized** The farmer was famous for his **prized** cow.
7. **shaking** Foreign leaders agree by **shaking** hands.
8. **skating** An ice skate is a boot worn for ice **skating.**
9. **hiding** Rabbits like **hiding** in their burrows.
10. **shining** The sun is always **shining**.
11. **thinking** Inventors like **thinking** of new ideas.
12. **entered** The contestant **entered** a contest.
13. **opened** A door can be **opened.**
14. **passing** A **passing** grade is good.
15. **safekeeping** Money is kept in a bank for **safekeeping.**

Diagnose any misspellings by determining whether students misspelled the way the ending was to be added or some other part of the word. Then use the Pretest as a take-home list to study the ways *-ed* and *-ing* are added.

## Writing Process Strategies

### Getting Ideas

**Persuasive Paragraph**

#### Teach

**Introduce Persuasive Paragraph Writing Form**

Read ***Language Arts Handbook,*** page 187, to introduce persuasive paragraphs.

**Inspiration**

Teacher Model: *"I think everyone deserves to know that it is better to be happy than to be rich. I am going to write a persuasive paragraph to convince people that this is true."*

**Brainstorming**

Encourage students to generate ideas for what they think or feel about money. Make a list of their responses on the board.

### Guided Practice

**Getting Ideas**

Have students write ideas for a persuasive paragraph in their Writer's Notebooks.

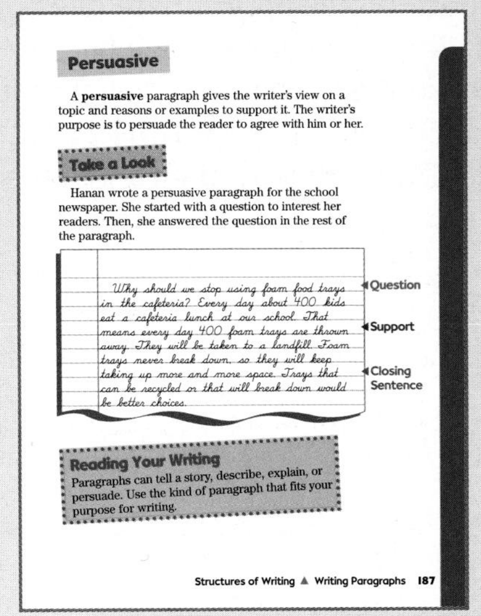

**Persuasive**

A **persuasive** paragraph gives the writer's view on a topic and reasons or examples to support it. The writer's purpose is to persuade the reader to agree with him or her.

**Take a Look**

Hanan wrote a persuasive paragraph for the school newspaper. She started with a question to interest her readers. Then, she answered the question in the rest of the paragraph.

*Why should we stop using foam food trays in the cafeteria? Every day about 400 kids eat a cafeteria lunch at our school. That means every day 400 foam trays are thrown away. They will be taken to a landfill. Foam trays never break down, so they will keep taking up more and more space. Trays that can be recycled or that will break down would be better choices.*

Question

Support

Closing Sentence

**Reading Your Writing**

Paragraphs can tell a story, describe, explain, or persuade. Use the kind of paragraph that fits your purpose for writing.

Structures of Writing ▲ Writing Paragraphs 187

***Language Arts Handbook p. 187***

## English Language Conventions

### Grammar, Usage, and Mechanics

**Grammar: Pronouns: Possessive, Singular and Plural**

#### Teach

- Use ***Language Arts Handbook,*** pages 248–249, for the definition and examples of pronouns.
- Point to yourself, individual students, and groups of students. Refer to them with the appropriate pronouns—*I, she,* and so on. Make up a sentence with the pronoun for each individual or group.
- Review possession and the use of the apostrophe in possession, and that possessive pronouns do not use the apostrophe. Write the following examples on the board.
  - Rod's racquet/His racquet *(singular)*
  - Sheila's computer/Her computer *(singular)*
  - My parents' hometown/Their hometown *(plural)*

### Independent Practice

Use ***Comprehension and Language Arts Skills,*** pages 108–109, to identify singular and plural possessive pronouns.

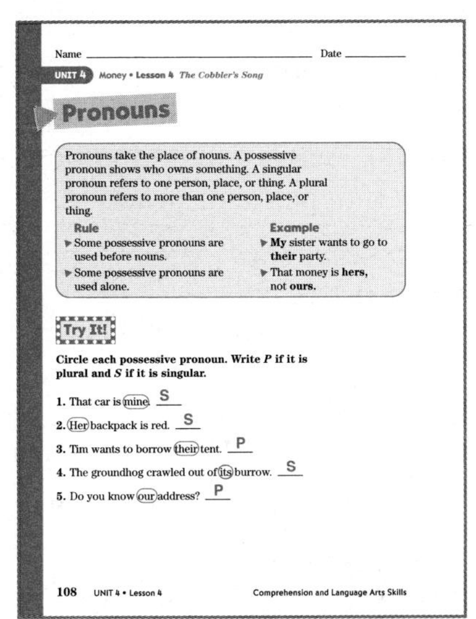

Name ____________ Date ______

UNIT 4 Money • Lesson 4 *The Cobbler's Song*

**Pronouns**

Pronouns take the place of nouns. A possessive pronoun shows who owns something. A singular pronoun refers to one person, place, or thing. A plural pronoun refers to more than one person, place, or thing.

| Rule | Example |
|---|---|
| Some possessive pronouns are used before nouns. | **My** sister wants to go to **their** party. |
| Some possessive pronouns are used alone. | That money is **hers,** not **ours.** |

**Try It!**

**Circle each possessive pronoun. Write *P* if it is plural and *S* if it is singular.**

1. That car is mine. S
2. Her backpack is red. S
3. Tim wants to borrow their tent. P
4. The groundhog crawled out of its burrow. S
5. Do you know our address? P

108 UNIT 4 • Lesson 4 Comprehension and Language Arts Skills

***Comprehension and Language Arts Skills p. 108***

# DAY 2

## Word Analysis

### Spelling

**Adding *-ed* and *-ing***

#### Board Work

Write *skate*, *skated*, and *skating* on the board. Underline *-ed* and *-ing*. Explain that adding *-ed* or *-ing* changes the spelling of many words. The silent *e* is dropped in *skated* and *skating*. Ask one student to add *-ed* and *-ing* to the word *hike*. *(hiked* and *hiking)*

### Vocabulary

**Inflectional Endings *-ed* and *-ing***

#### Teach

- Write *mended* ("The Cobbler's Song," page 48) on the board.
- Say: "The cobbler *mended* the shoes yesterday." Ask when he fixed the shoes *(yesterday)*. Explain that *yesterday* is in the past. Ask what *mended* means *(to have already repaired)*. Explain that *-ed* makes the action happen in the past.
- Say: "The cobbler is *mending* the shoes now." Explain that *-ing* makes the verb in the present.

#### Guided Practice

Use ***Spelling and Vocabulary Skills***, page 86, to teach about the endings *-ed* and *-ing*. Ask students to complete page 87 as independent practice.

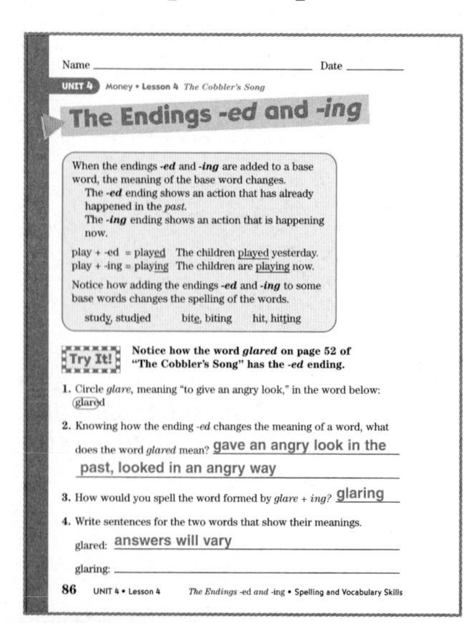

Name ______________________ Date __________

UNIT 4 Money • Lesson 4 *The Cobbler's Song*

**The Endings *-ed* and *-ing***

When the endings ***-ed*** and ***-ing*** are added to a base word, the meaning of the base word changes.
The ***-ed*** ending shows an action that has already happened in the *past.*
The ***-ing*** ending shows an action that is happening now.

play + -ed = played The children played yesterday.
play + -ing = playing The children are playing now.

Notice how adding the endings ***-ed*** and ***-ing*** to some base words changes the spelling of the words.

study, studied  bite, biting  hit, hitting

**Try It!** **Notice how the word *glared* on page 52 of "The Cobbler's Song" has the *-ed* ending.**

1. Circle *glare*, meaning "to give an angry look," in the word below: glared
2. Knowing how the ending *-ed* changes the meaning of a word, what does the word *glared* mean? gave an angry look in the past, looked in an angry way
3. How would you spell the word formed by *glare* + *ing*? glaring
4. Write sentences for the two words that show their meanings.
   glared: answers will vary
   glaring: ______________

86 UNIT 4 • Lesson 4 *The Endings* -ed *and* -ing • Spelling and Vocabulary Skills

***Spelling and Vocabulary Skills* p. 86**

## Writing Process Strategies

### Prewriting

**Persuasive Paragraph**

#### Teach

- **Review** the ideas for a persuasive paragraph that students generated on Day 1.
- Read ***Writer's Workbook,*** page 66, on prewriting for a persuasive paragraph.
- Model for students the process you go through to generate ideas for your topic by filling in a web for your own writing. In the center of the web, you may wish to write, "Better to be happy than rich." Write supporting reasons next to each spoke. Examples may include: "It feels good not to worry." "Enjoy life." "Friends like you for you." "Nothing to lose."

#### Independent Practice

**Prewriting**

- Have students write their audience and purpose on the appropriate lines on ***Writer's Workbook,*** page 66.
- Have students complete the graphic organizer on ***Writer's Workbook,*** page 67, to organize their thoughts.

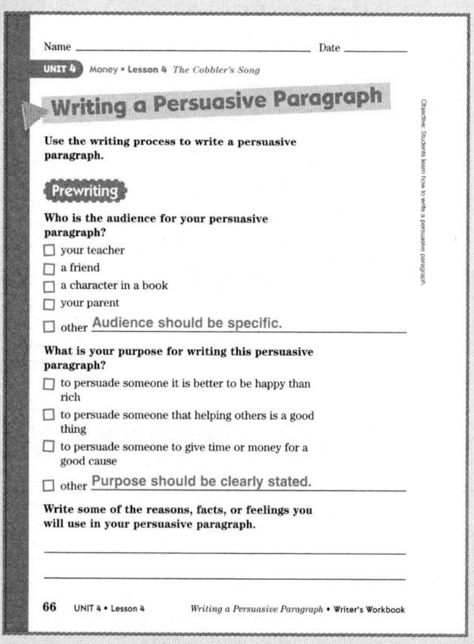

Name ______________________ Date __________

UNIT 4 Money • Lesson 4 *The Cobbler's Song*

**Writing a Persuasive Paragraph**

**Use the writing process to write a persuasive paragraph.**

Prewriting

**Who is the audience for your persuasive paragraph?**

- ☐ your teacher
- ☐ a friend
- ☐ a character in a book
- ☐ your parent
- ☐ other Audience should be specific.

**What is your purpose for writing this persuasive paragraph?**

- ☐ to persuade someone it is better to be happy than rich
- ☐ to persuade someone that helping others is a good thing
- ☐ to persuade someone to give time or money for a good cause
- ☐ other Purpose should be clearly stated.

**Write some of the reasons, facts, or feelings you will use in your persuasive paragraph.**

______________

______________

Objective: Students learn how to write a persuasive paragraph.

66 UNIT 4 • Lesson 4 *Writing a Persuasive Paragraph* • Writer's Workbook

***Writer's Workbook* p. 66**

## English Language Conventions

### Grammar, Usage, and Mechanics

**Grammar: Pronouns: Possessive, Singular and Plural**

#### Teach

- Review ***Language Arts Handbook,*** pages 248–249, on pronouns.
- Remind students that the possessive pronouns *my, your, its, her, his* (singular) and *our, their* (plural) are used before nouns.
- Review with students that a personal pronoun refers to people or things. Write the following sentences on the board and ask students to change the noun to a personal pronoun.
  - Cindy likes it. *(She likes it.)*
  - Stacy and Vince live next door. *(They live next door.)*
  - Michael and Jason like to talk to Alissa. *(They like to talk to her.)*

#### Guided Practice in Reading

Have students find singular and plural possessive pronouns in "The Cobbler's Song." Write them on the board.

# DAY 3

## Word Analysis

### Spelling

**Adding *-ed* and *-ing***

**Teach**

- Introduce the words with *-ed* or *-ing* found in "The Cobbler's Song."
- Ask students to think of words that end in *e* that would lose the *e* when adding *-ed* or *-ing*. *(love, live, give)*

**Guided Practice**

Have students complete page 88 from ***Spelling and Vocabulary Skills*** to learn strategies for adding *-ed* or *-ing* to words.

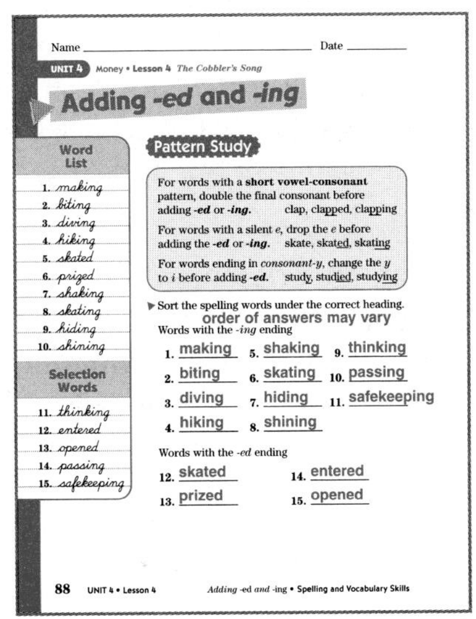
Name ______________________ Date ________

UNIT 4 Money • Lesson 4 *The Cobbler's Song*

**Adding -ed and -ing**

**Word List**
1. making
2. biting
3. diving
4. hiking
5. skated
6. prized
7. shaking
8. skating
9. hiding
10. shining

**Selection Words**
11. thinking
12. entered
13. opened
14. passing
15. safekeeping

**Pattern Study**

For words with a **short vowel-consonant** pattern, double the final consonant before adding ***-ed*** or ***-ing***. clap, clapped, clapping

For words with a silent *e*, drop the *e* before adding the ***-ed*** or ***-ing***. skate, skated, skating

For words ending in *consonant-y*, change the *y* to *i* before adding ***-ed***. study, studied, studying

▶ Sort the spelling words under the correct heading.
order of answers may vary

Words with the *-ing* ending

1. making 5. shaking 9. thinking
2. biting 6. skating 10. passing
3. diving 7. hiding 11. safekeeping
4. hiking 8. shining

Words with the *-ed* ending

12. skated 14. entered
13. prized 15. opened

88 UNIT 4 • Lesson 4 *Adding* -ed *and* -ing • Spelling and Vocabulary Skills

***Spelling and Vocabulary Skills* p. 88**

### Vocabulary (continued)

**Inflectional Endings *-ed* and *-ing***

- Write *relieved* on the board.
- Ask a student to read the sentence in "The Cobbler's Song" (p. 53) with *relieved*. Ask how *-ed* affects the meaning of the base word *relieve*. *(-ed makes the word in the past)*
- Explain that *relieve* means "to free from discomfort or pain."
- Ask for a possible meaning for *relieved*. *(to have been happy, freed, no longer in pain)*

## Writing Process Strategies

### Drafting

**Persuasive Paragraph**

**Teach**

Read ***Writer's Workbook***, page 67, on drafting a persuasive letter.

Writer's Craft 
**Avoiding Wordiness**

- Remind students that their readers will have trouble following along if they find too many words that say the same thing.
- Tell students they need to choose words carefully. Ask them which is better to say: "the man who has a lot of money" or "the rich man."
- Caution students to watch for wordiness in their own writing.
- Read ***Language Arts Handbook***, page 13, on word choice.
- Read ***Comprehension and Language Arts Skills***, pages 110–111, on avoiding wordiness.

**Guided Practice**

**Drafting**

- Have students draft their persuasive paragraphs and put them in their ***Writing Folders***.
- If you have computers in the classroom, you may want to give students the option of using word processing software to do their drafts.

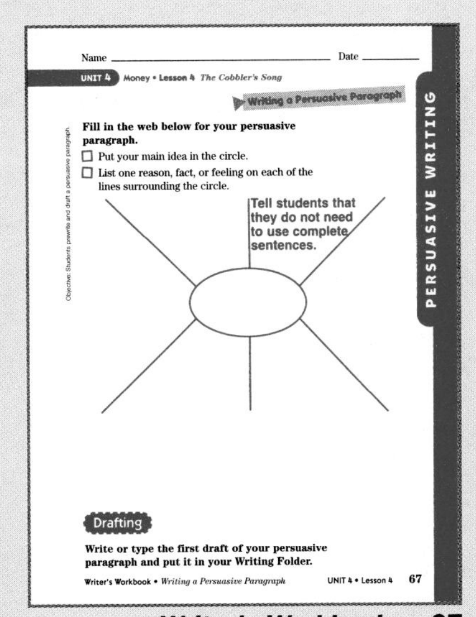
Name ______________________ Date ________

UNIT 4 Money • Lesson 4 *The Cobbler's Song*

**Writing a Persuasive Paragraph**

PERSUASIVE WRITING

Objective: Students prewrite and draft a persuasive paragraph.

**Fill in the web below for your persuasive paragraph.**

- [ ] Put your main idea in the circle.
- [ ] List one reason, fact, or feeling on each of the lines surrounding the circle.

Tell students that they do not need to use complete sentences.

**Drafting**

**Write or type the first draft of your persuasive paragraph and put it in your Writing Folder.**

Writer's Workbook • *Writing a Persuasive Paragraph* UNIT 4 • Lesson 4 67

***Writer's Workbook* p. 67**

## English Language Conventions

### Grammar, Usage, and Mechanics

**Grammar: Pronouns: Possessive, Singular and Plural**

**Teach**

- Review possessive pronouns using ***Comprehension and Language, Arts Skills***, pages 108–109.
- Write the following phrases on the board. Ask students to substitute possessive pronouns, then cross out the possessive noun and write the possessive pronoun above it.
  - Betty's pet snake *(Her pet snake)*
  - Leo's pet anteater *(His pet anteater)*
  - My friends' strange pets *(Their strange pets)*
  - Leo's and my strange petting zoo *(Our strange petting zoo)*

**Guided Practice in Writing**

Have students write a paragraph to the rich man in "The Cobbler's Song," giving him reasons why it is better to be happy than rich. Discuss possible reasons with students first.

**Informal Assessment**

Check students' writing for the correct use of possessive pronouns.

# DAY 4

## Word Analysis

### Spelling

**Adding -ed and -ing**

**Teach**

Explain that exercises in ***Spelling and Vocabulary Skills*** are designed to help them learn to correctly add *-ed* and *-ing* to words.

**Guided Practice**

Have students complete page 89 of ***Spelling and Vocabulary Skills*** to reinforce how to add *-ed* and *-ing* to words.

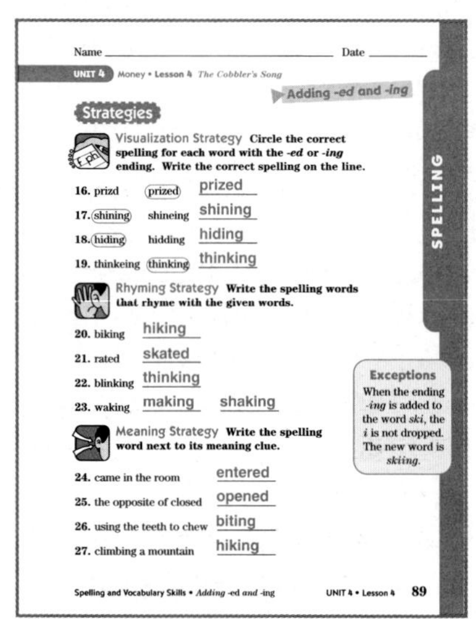
Name ______________________ Date ________

UNIT 4 Money • Lesson 4 *The Cobbler's Song*

Adding -ed and -ing

Strategies

Visualization Strategy **Circle the correct spelling for each word with the *-ed* or *-ing* ending. Write the correct spelling on the line.**

16. prizd (prized) prized
17. (shining) shineing shining
18. (hiding) hidding hiding
19. thinkeing (thinking) thinking

Rhyming Strategy **Write the spelling words that rhyme with the given words.**

20. biking hiking
21. rated skated
22. blinking thinking
23. waking making shaking

Meaning Strategy **Write the spelling word next to its meaning clue.**

24. came in the room entered
25. the opposite of closed opened
26. using the teeth to chew biting
27. climbing a mountain hiking

Exceptions
When the ending *-ing* is added to the word *ski*, the *i* is not dropped. The new word is *skiing*.

SPELLING

Spelling and Vocabulary Skills • *Adding* -ed *and* -ing UNIT 4 • Lesson 4 89

***Spelling and Vocabulary Skills* p. 89**

### Vocabulary (continued)

**Inflectional Endings -ed and -ing**

- Write *safekeeping* on the board.
- Ask how *-ing* affects the meaning of a base word. *(-ing makes the word in the present)*
- Ask a student to read the sentence in "The Cobbler's Song" (p. 51) with *safekeeping*. Explain that *-ing* in *safekeeping* makes the action continue into the present.
- Ask students for meanings of *safekeeping* by reading for context clues *(saving, to keep safe)*. Have a student tell what he or she might hide for *safekeeping (allowance, jewelry)*.

## Writing Process Strategies

### Revising

**Persuasive Paragraph**

**Teach**

Read ***Writer's Workbook,*** page 68, on revising a persuasive paragraph.

**Troubleshooting**

- Topic sentence does not catch the reader's interest. If your reader is not interested right away, chances are he or she will not go on.
- Supporting reasons are not strong enough. If your reasons are not good ones or do not fit your main idea, your reader may end up doing exactly the opposite of what you suggest.
- The closing sentence does not say what the writer wants the reader to do or think. This is the writer's last chance to clearly state what action they want the reader to take.

**Guided Practice**

**Revising**

- Have students revise their paragraphs in their Writer's Notebooks.
- Have students use the checklist on ***Writer's Workbook,*** page 68, to revise their persuasive paragraphs.

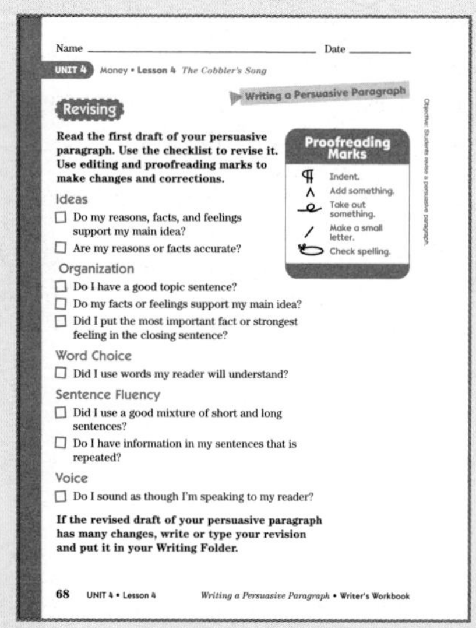
Name ______________________ Date ________

UNIT 4 Money • Lesson 4 *The Cobbler's Song*

Writing a Persuasive Paragraph

Revising

**Read the first draft of your persuasive paragraph. Use the checklist to revise it. Use editing and proofreading marks to make changes and corrections.**

Ideas
- ☐ Do my reasons, facts, and feelings support my main idea?
- ☐ Are my reasons or facts accurate?

Organization
- ☐ Do I have a good topic sentence?
- ☐ Do my facts or feelings support my main idea?
- ☐ Did I put the most important fact or strongest feeling in the closing sentence?

Word Choice
- ☐ Did I use words my reader will understand?

Sentence Fluency
- ☐ Did I use a good mixture of short and long sentences?
- ☐ Do I have information in my sentences that is repeated?

Voice
- ☐ Do I sound as though I'm speaking to my reader?

Proofreading Marks
¶ Indent.
^ Add something.
Take out something.
/ Make a small letter.
Check spelling.

Objective: Students revise a persuasive paragraph.

**If the revised draft of your persuasive paragraph has many changes, write or type your revision and put it in your Writing Folder.**

68 UNIT 4 • Lesson 4 *Writing a Persuasive Paragraph* • Writer's Workbook

***Writer's Workbook* p. 68**

## English Language Conventions

### Listening, Speaking, Viewing

**Viewing: Media Techniques**

**Teach**

- Explain how media advertisements use facts and opinions or different points of view to persuade people.
- Explain how the media uses fact and opinion in advertisements. Some ads send various factual messages to gain the trust of the audience. When an opinion is expressed *("this product is the best" or "the product you are using is no good")* the audience often believes it to be true because they trust the message being expressed.
- Explain that the point of view of an advertisement is the position or belief that the ad is expressing. *(In my point of view, baseball is the best sport.)*

**Guided Practice**

- Provide an advertisement or commercial and show it to the class.
- Ask questions to further students' understanding of the purposes, techniques, and effects of media messages, including main concepts and supporting details. *(What is it saying about its product in order to sell it? Does it use fact and opinion? How? What is the main idea of the advertisement? What is it trying to sell and to whom?)*
- Individually or with a partner, have students respond to the example of media viewed in class. Encourage students to respond in a variety of ways, such as through art, writing, or a play. You might also have students find and respond to their own examples of media.

**Informal Assessment**

Observe whether students understand different persuasive techniques of the media.

# DAY 5

## Word Analysis

### Spelling

#### Assessment: Final Test

**Adding *-ed* and *-ing***

#### Teach

Repeat the Pretest or use the Final Test on page 37 of ***Unit 4 Assessment*** as summative assessment of student understanding of spelling patterns for inflectional endings.

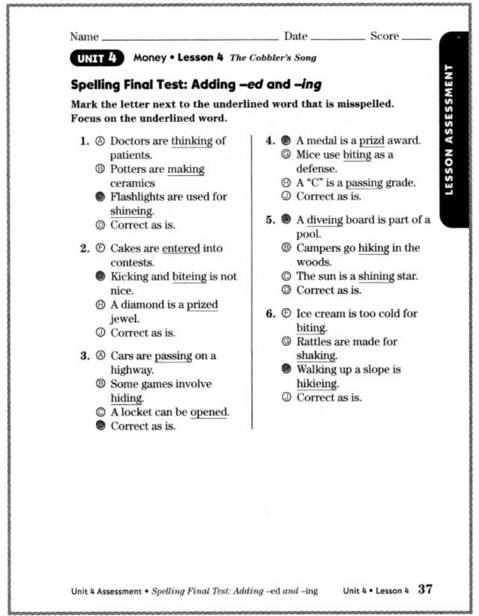

Name ______ Date ______ Score ______

UNIT 4 Money • Lesson 4 *The Cobbler's Song*

**Spelling Final Test: Adding *–ed* and *–ing***

**Mark the letter next to the underlined word that is misspelled. Focus on the underlined word.**

1. Ⓐ Doctors are thinking of patients.
   Ⓑ Potters are making ceramics
   ● Flashlights are used for shineing.
   Ⓓ Correct as is.
2. Ⓕ Cakes are entered into contests.
   ● Kicking and biteing is not nice.
   Ⓗ A diamond is a prized jewel.
   Ⓙ Correct as is.
3. Ⓐ Cars are passing on a highway.
   Ⓑ Some games involve hiding.
   Ⓒ A locket can be opened.
   ● Correct as is.
4. ● A medal is a prizd award.
   Ⓖ Mice use biting as a defense.
   Ⓗ A "C" is a passing grade.
   Ⓙ Correct as is.
5. ● A diveing board is part of a pool.
   Ⓑ Campers go hiking in the woods.
   Ⓒ The sun is a shining star.
   Ⓓ Correct as is.
6. Ⓕ Ice cream is too cold for biting.
   Ⓖ Rattles are made for shaking.
   ● Walking up a slope is hikieing.
   Ⓙ Correct as is.

LESSON ASSESSMENT

Unit 4 Assessment • *Spelling Final Test: Adding –ed and –ing* Unit 4 • Lesson 4 37

***Unit 4 Assessment p. 37***

#### Guided Practice

Have students categorize any mistakes they made on the Final Test as careless errors or lesson-pattern problems.

### Vocabulary

#### Informal Assessment

Periodically check students' writing assignments to see if they understand verb tenses and spell words with *-ed* and *-ing* correctly. Offer praise or encouragement as needed. Have students add any new words to the running Vocabulary Word List in the Writer's Notebook.

## Writing Process Strategies

### Editing/Proofreading and Publishing

**Persuasive Paragraph**

#### Teach

- Read ***Writer's Workbook,*** page 69, on editing/proofreading and publishing.
- Discuss ***Language Arts Transparency 27,*** Editing: Grammar.

#### Guided Practice

**Editing/Proofreading and Publishing**

- Have students edit/proofread their persuasive paragraphs.
- Direct students to use the checklist on ***Writer's Workbook,*** page 69, to help them edit their paragraphs.
- Have students make a clean copy of their paragraphs in their best cursive handwriting.

#### Formal Assessment

Total Point Value: 10

1. Topic sentence grabs the reader's attention. (2 points)
2. Topic sentence clearly states the writer's main idea and viewpoint. (2 points)
3. All of the reasons support the topic sentence. (2 points)
4. The strongest reason is given last. (2 points)
5. The paragraph is indented. (2 points)

Name ______ Date ______

UNIT 4 Money • Lesson 4 *The Cobbler's Song*

Writing a Persuasive Paragraph

Editing/Proofreading

**Edit your persuasive paragraph on paper or a computer. Then make a clean copy of your paragraph and put it in your Writing Folder. Read your persuasive paragraph carefully. Use the checklist to help you correct any mistakes.**

Objective: Students edit/proofread and publish a persuasive paragraph.

Conventions

- ☐ Have I added *-s* or *-es* correctly?
- ☐ Did I spell possessive nouns correctly?
- ☐ Is it clear which nouns my pronouns replace?
- ☐ Did I use end punctuation correctly?
- ☐ Did I capitalize all proper nouns and the first word of every sentence?

Publishing

**Use this checklist to get your persuasive paragraph ready for your reader.**

Presentation

- ☐ Make sure your writing says exactly what you want it to say.
- ☐ Make a clean copy. You may want to use the computer.
- ☐ Practice reading your persuasive paragraph out loud if you plan to give an oral presentation.

PERSUASIVE WRITING

Writer's Workbook • *Writing a Persuasive Paragraph* UNIT 4 • Lesson 4 69

***Writer's Workbook p. 69***

## English Language Conventions

### Penmanship

**Manuscript Letters *K* and *H***

#### Teach

- **Teacher Model:** Introduce formation of uppercase *K* and *H* as curve forward letters by demonstrating on the board.

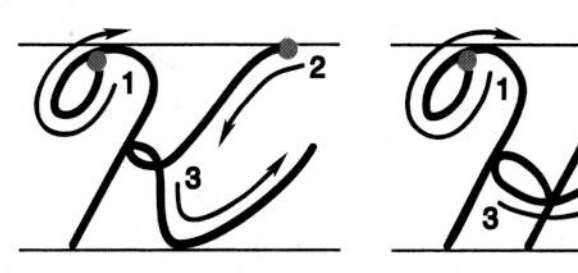

**K**
Starting point, loop
Curve forward, slant down to end point
Starting point
Double curve back to slant
Curve forward
Undercurve: capital *K*

**H**
Starting point, loop
Curve forward, slant down to end point
Starting point
Curve back and slant down
Retrace up slant, loop left
Curve right: capital *H*

- **Teacher Model:** Write the words *Hawaii* and *Kenya* to model proper letter formation.
- Tell the students that they should leave enough space between the letters in a word so that they do not touch, except for where they join.

#### Guided Practice

- Have students practice writing rows of *K*s and *H*s in the Writer's Notebook.
- From "The Cobbler's Song," have students write the words *Here, take,* and *back* to practice letter formation.
- Have students check for proper spacing between letters in words.

#### Informal Assessment

Check students' handwriting for proper formation of *K* and *H* and space between letters.

# Reading and Language Arts Skills Traces

## Language Arts

### WORD ANALYSIS

**Skills Trace**

**Spelling: Adding *-ed* and *-ing***

Introduced in Grade 2.
Scaffolded throughout Grades 2–5.

**REINTRODUCED:** Unit 4, Lesson 4, p. 55E
**PRACTICED:** Unit 4, Lesson 4, pp. 55F–55J
*Spelling and Vocabulary Skills,* pp. 88–89
**TESTED:** Unit 4, Lesson 4, p. 55F (Pretest)
Unit 4, Lesson 4, p. 37 (Final Test)
Unit 4 Assessment

**Skills Trace**

**Vocabulary: Inflectional Endings *-ed* and *-ing***

Introduced in Grade 2.
Scaffolded throughout Grades 2–5.

**REINTRODUCED:** Unit 4, Lesson 4, p. 55E
**PRACTICED:** Unit 4, Lesson 4, pp. 55G–55J
*Spelling and Vocabulary Skills,* pp. 86–87
**TESTED:** Unit 4 Assessment

## Reading

### COMPREHENSION

**Author's Purpose**

Introduced in Grade 2.
Scaffolded throughout Grade 3.

**REINTRODUCED:** Unit 2, Lesson 6
**REINFORCED:** Unit 3, Lesson 1
Unit 4, Lesson 4
Unit 5, Lesson 2
Unit 5, Lesson 3
Unit 6, Lesson 4
**TESTED:** Unit 4 Assessment

### WRITING PROCESS STRATEGIES

**Skills Trace**

**Persuasive Writing: Persuasive Paragraph**

Introduced in Grade 1.
Scaffolded throughout Grades 2–5.

**REINTRODUCED:** Unit 4, Lesson 4, p. 55F
**PRACTICED:** Unit 4, Lesson 4, pp. 55G–55J
*Writer's Workbook,* pp. 66–69
**TESTED:** Unit 4, Lesson 4, Formal Assessment, p. 55J
Unit 4 Assessment

**Skills Trace**

**Writer's Craft: Avoiding Wordiness**

Introduced in Grade 3.
Scaffolded throughout Grades 4 and 6.

**INTRODUCED:** Unit 4, Lesson 4, p. 55H
**PRACTICED:** Unit 4, Lesson 4, p. 55H
*Comprehension and Language Arts Skills,* pp. 110–111
**TESTED:** Unit 4 Assessment

### ENGLISH LANGUAGE CONVENTIONS

**Skills Trace**

**Grammar: Possessive Pronouns**

Introduced in Grade 1.
Scaffolded throughout Grades 2–6.

**REINTRODUCED:** Unit 4, Lesson 4, p. 55F
**PRACTICED:** Unit 4, Lesson 4, p. 55G
Unit 4, Lesson 4, p. 55H
*Comprehension and Language Arts Skills,* pp. 108–109
**TESTED:** Unit 4, Lesson 4, Informal Assessment, p. 55H
Unit 4 Assessment

**Skills Trace**

**Listening, Speaking, Viewing Viewing: Media Techniques**

Introduced in Grade 3.
Scaffolded throughout Grades 4–6.

**INTRODUCED:** Unit 4, Lesson 4, p. 55I
**TESTED:** Unit 4, Lesson 4
Informal Assessment, p. 55I

**Skills Trace**

**Penmanship: Cursive Letters *K* and *H***

Introduced in Grade 3.
Scaffolded throughout Grades 4–6.

**INTRODUCED:** Unit 4, Lesson 4, p. 55J
**TESTED:** Unit 4, Lesson 4
Informal Assessment, p. 55J

# Professional Development: Comprehension

## Modeling and Thinking Aloud: Predicting

One of the most effective ways to help students use and understand the strategies good readers use is to make strategic thinking public. Modeling these behaviors and encouraging students to think aloud as they attempt to understand text can demonstrate for everyone in a class how these behaviors are put into practice. Suggestions for think-alouds are provided throughout the ***Teacher's Edition.***

### Modeling Predicting

Predicting can be appropriate at the beginning of a selection—on the basis of the titles and the illustrations—or at any point while reading a selection. At first, your modeling will take the form of speculation about what might happen next, but tell students from the start what clues in the text or illustrations helped you predict, in order to make it clear that predicting is not just guessing. When a student makes a prediction—especially a far-fetched one—ask what in the selection or in his or her own experience the prediction is based on. If the student can back up the prediction, let the prediction stand; otherwise, suggest that the student make another prediction on the basis of what he or she already knows.

Often it is appropriate to sum up before making a prediction. This will help students consider what has come before as they make their predictions about what will happen next. When reading aloud, stop whenever a student's prediction has been confirmed or contradicted. Have students tell whether the prediction was correct. If students seem comfortable with the idea of making predictions but rarely do so on their own, encourage them to discuss how to find clues in the text that will help them.

**Professional Development**

***Teacher Resource Library CD-ROMs*** or ***Online Professional Development*** provides courses that help you better understand the Comprehension/Knowledge Building instruction in ***Open Court Reading.*** For more information about this program, visit SRAonline.com.

Additional information about comprehension as well as resource references can be found in the ***Professional Development Guide: Comprehension.***

## Viewing the Theme Through Fine Art

Students can use the artworks on these pages to investigate the unit theme of Money in images rather than in words. Encourage students to talk about their impressions of the artworks and about how each piece of art might relate to the unit theme, Money.

Below is some background information about each of the artworks. Share with students whatever you feel is appropriate.

### *80 Two-Dollar Bills*

**ANDY WARHOL** (1928–1987) began his career as a commercial artist. In the 1960s, he was part of a group of artists who produced works based on popular culture.

***80 Two-Dollar Bills*** was Warhol's first silkscreen print, the technique that later made him famous. He liked this process of creating art because he was able to reproduce the same image several times. Warhol believed that by repeating an image in a work of art he was better able to reflect society's love of quantity and conformity.

### *Daric Coin*

This Daric coin was created by a skilled laborer. This coin was found in Persia, now known as Iran. It was made by placing a sheet of metal between two plates with incised images. A mallet was used to hammer the plates together so that the design would be embossed onto the metal.

The Daric coin is named after Darius I, the emperor of Persia from 522 B.C.E.–486 B.C.E. The artist stylized the features of the ruler. The artist also included a lance and a bow shape, both symbols of power, and gave the coin the name "archer."

This Daric coin is one of the most valuable ancient coins.

# Fine Art

## Money

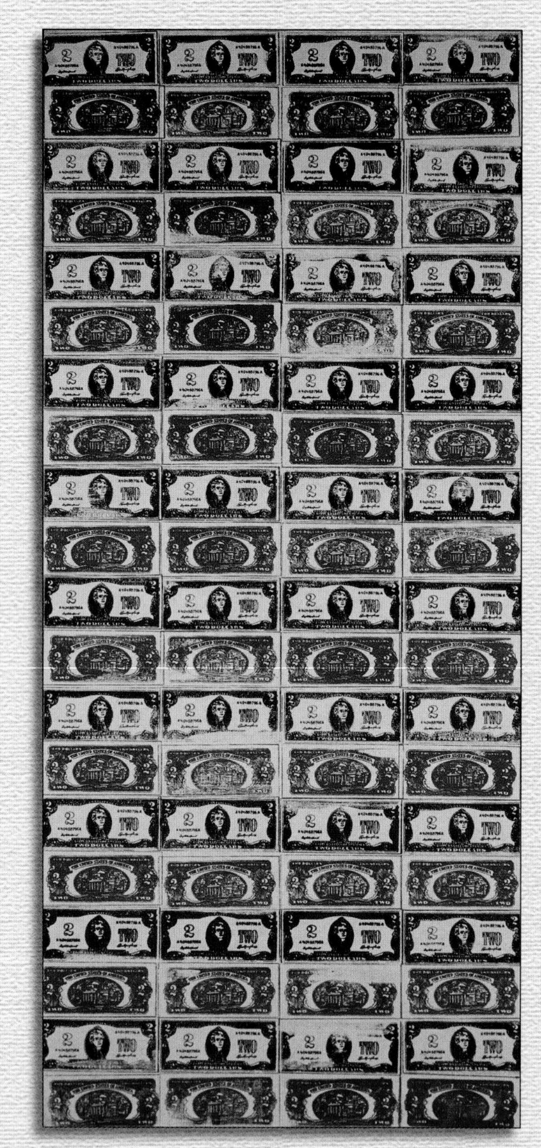

***80 Two-Dollar Bills*** (front and rear). 1962. **Andy Warhol.** Silkscreen on canvas. Museum Ludwig, Cologne, Germany. 

***Daric coin, first minted under Darius I of Persia.*** 4th century B.C. Gold. Diameter: $\frac{9}{16}$". Ashmolean Museum, Oxford, England.

56

**Teacher Tip** Some may be unfamiliar with the abbreviation B.C.E. Explain that B.C.E. means "Before Common Era" and that it denotes the time previously known as B.C. Tell them to note that C.E., "Common Era," has replaced A.D. in usage. This labeling is used to be inclusive to all cultural and religious backgrounds.

***The Money Lender and His Wife.*** 1514. **Quentin Matsys.** Tempera and oil on wood. The Louvre, Paris.

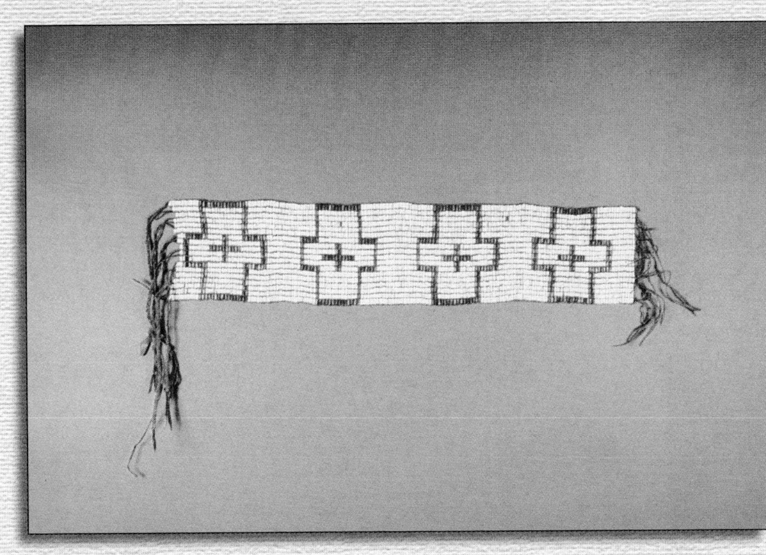

***Wampum belt.*** 1650–1800. **Iroquois.** The National Museum of the American Indian, Smithsonian Institution.



## *The Money Lender and His Wife*

**QUENTIN MATSYS** (c.1465–1530) was born in the Netherlands and lived in Antwerp, Belgium, where many of the wealthy merchants purchased works of art. During this time, people began buying landscapes, still lifes, and scenes from daily life, instead of the traditional religious subject matter which had been so popular.

***The Money Lender and His Wife*** portrays a man counting his money as his wife looks on and thumbs through a book. During this time, books were so costly that only the wealthy were able to afford them. Notice the miniature painting in the foreground and how the couple are surrounded with material objects.

## *Wampum Belt*

Wampum is formed with tubular beads made from shells, fastened together and used by the Iroquois and Algonquin of the American Northeast. Wampum was used to foretell events, declare war, and confirm treaties. At one time, wampum was used as money by the Dutch and English colonists.

*Wampum* is from the Algonquin word for "strings of shell beads." The designs and colors have specific meanings: white beads refer to goodness and peace, while black beads mean war and grief.

**Teacher Tip** Students may benefit by referring to the selection "Money, Money, Money" to review the descriptions and discussion of ancient metal coins and wampum.

*Focus Questions* What does it mean to be in debt? Why is it so important to pay back debts?

Eric A. Kimmel
*illustrated by Glen Rounds*

It's a terrible thing to call a cowboy a deadbeat, but in Shorty Long's case it was true. He owed everybody money, from Big Oscar the blacksmith to Widow Macrae, who ran the Silver Dollar Cafe and baked the best biscuits west of the Rockies.

"Shorty ain't a bad sort. He just hates to pay for anything he thinks he can get free," Big Oscar told the widow one afternoon over coffee at the Silver Dollar.

The widow brought Oscar another plate of biscuits. "How am I gonna keep this place going if folks won't pay their bills? Shorty's the worst. He owes me four dollars and fifty cents."

Big Oscar shook his head. "You got as much chance of collecting that money as seeing Custer ride back from the Little Bighorn."

Widow Macrae picked up her rolling pin. "That's what you think. I'm driving out to the Circle K this afternoon. If Shorty won't pay what he owes, I'll lay him out flatter 'n the bottom of a skillet."

58

SELECTION INTRODUCTION

## Selection Summary

### Genre: Tall Tale

"Four Dollars and Fifty Cents" is a humorous story set in the Old West. Shorty Long is a cowboy who owes everybody money. One day Widow Macrae, who runs the Silver Dollar Café, decides she's tired of Shorty not paying his bills. Shorty owes her four dollars and fifty cents, and she wants him to pay up. When Widow Macrae goes to the ranch where Shorty works, Shorty pretends he's dead so he won't have to pay her. Well, if Shorty is dead, he has to be buried. Widow Macrae takes Shorty's body to Boot Hill, where dead cowboys are buried. That's when the outlaw, Big Nose George Parrott, and some of his gang come riding along and Shorty's troubles multiply.

Some elements of a tall tale include:

- A tall tale uses humorous exaggeration to tell of the adventures of a fictional character, such as Paul Bunyan.
- Tall tales build upon improbable incidents and unusual problems that are solved in creative ways.

## About the Author

**Eric A. Kimmel** "never wanted to be anything else" but a writer. He was inspired by his grandmother, a natural storyteller who filled his childhood with countless stories peopled by real and fictional characters from European history and folktales. His numerous awards include a Sydney Taylor Book Award, an Evelyn Sibley Lampman Award, and an Aesop Prize.

Students can read more about Eric A. Kimmel on page 71 of the ***Student Anthology.***

## About the Illustrator

Before becoming a full-time author and illustrator, **Glen Rounds** worked as a mule-skinner, cowboy, sign painter, railroad hand, and carnival medicine man. He has written and illustrated nearly 50 books, and has artwork in more than 60 publications. His many awards include six Lewis Carroll Shelf Awards and two *Parents' Choice* awards.

Students can read more about Glen Rounds on page 71 of the ***Student Anthology.***

## Inquiry Connections

"Four Dollars and Fifty Cents" takes a humorous view of a serious subject—borrowing and lending money and the possible consequences. When Shorty decides to go to great lengths to avoid paying a debt, he faces dire consequences.

- Living on credit can have serious consequences.
- Collecting on debts can be very difficult.

Before reading the selection:

- Point out that students may post a question, concept, word, illustrations, or object on the Concept/Question Board at any time during the course of their unit investigations. Be sure that students include their name or initials on the items they post so that others will know to whom to go if they have an answer or if they wish to collaborate on a related activity.
- Students should feel free to write an answer or a note on someone else's question or to consult the Board for ideas for their own investigations throughout the unit.
- Encourage students to read about money at home and to bring in articles or pictures that are good examples to post on the Board.

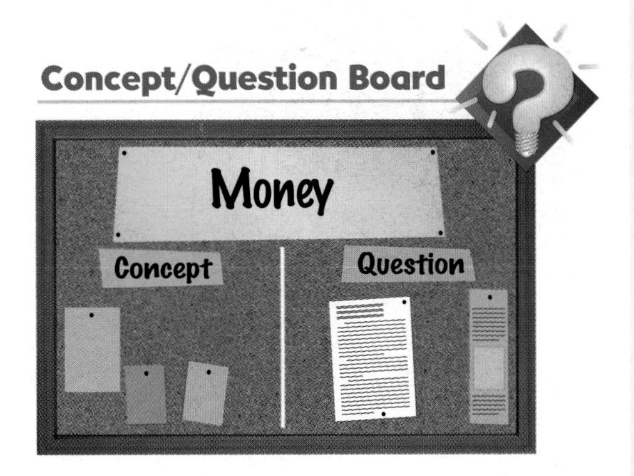

## Leveled Practice

### Reteach
**Pages 115–118**

### Challenge
**Pages 101–104**

### English Learner Support Activities

### Intervention Workbook

### Decodable Book 33

## Leveled Classroom Library*

Encourage students to read at least 30 minutes daily outside of class. Have them read books in the ***Leveled Classroom Library*** to support the unit theme and help students develop their vocabulary by reading independently.

### *Lemonade for Sale*

BY STUART J. MURPHY. HARPERCOLLINS JUVENILE, 1998.

The kids at the Elm Street Kids' Club use a clever combination of lemonade, bar graphs, and a juggler to make big profits that will help them repair their club. **(Easy)**

### *Saturday Sancocho*

BY LEYLA TORRES. FARRAR, STRAUS & GIROUX, 1995.

Every Saturday, Maria Lili spends a meal with her grandparents, eating Chicken Sancocho, until the weekend comes when money is tight and they are missing essential ingredients. Mama Ana barters with her eggs for the final ingredients, saving the day. **(Average)**

### *Our Money*

BY KAREN BORNEMANN SPIES. THE MILLBROOK PRESS, 1994.

Chronicling the changes American money has undergone, this book explains money ranging from wampum to today's currency. Also discussed are counterfeiting and minting procedures. **(Advanced)**

* These books, which all support the unit theme Money, are part of a 36-book ***Leveled Classroom Library*** available for purchase from SRA/McGraw-Hill. Note: Teachers should preview any trade books for appropriateness in their classrooms before recommending them to students.

## SRA TECHNOLOGY

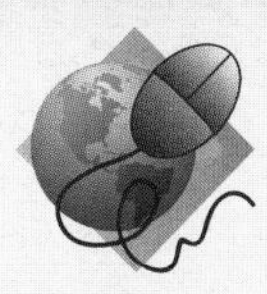

### Web Connections

- Money Web Site
- Online Professional Development
- Online Phonics
- Online Assessment

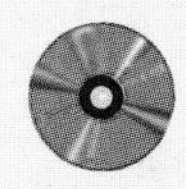

### CD-ROMs

- Research Assistant
- The Ultimate Writing and Creativity Center
- Teacher Resource Library

### Audiocassette/CD

Listening Library: Money

### Computer Skills

TechKnowledge

Materials are available through SRA/McGraw-Hill.

# UNIT 4 Lesson 5 Four Dollars and Fifty Cents

LESSON PLANNER

Suggested Pacing: 3–5 days

| | DAY 1 | DAY 2 |
|---|---|---|
| | DAY 1 | DAY 2 |
| **1 Preparing to Read**<br>**Materials**<br>■ Student Anthology, Book 2, pp. 58–71<br>■ Sound/Spelling Cards<br>■ Routine Card 1, Routines 1–2<br>■ Decodable Book 33 | **Word Knowledge,** p. 58K<br>■ compound words<br>■ base word and suffixes<br>■ plurals *-es* and *-s*<br>**About the Words and Sentences,** p. 58K | **Developing Oral Language,** p. 58L |
| **2 Reading & Responding**<br>**Materials**<br>■ Student Anthology, Book 2, pp. 58–71<br>■ Program Assessment<br>■ Reading Transparencies 27, 46, 50<br>■ Inquiry Journal, p. 85<br>■ Home Connection, p. 53<br>■ Unit 4 Assessment, pp. 18–21<br>■ Writer's Notebook<br>■ Routine Cards 1, 2, Routines 3–6 | **Build Background,** p. 58M<br>**Preview and Prepare,** pp. 58M–58N<br>**Selection Vocabulary,** p. 58N<br>**Reading Recommendations,** pp. 58O–58P<br>**Student Anthology,** pp. 58–63 First Read<br>✓**Comprehension Strategies**<br>■ Monitoring and Clarifying, pp. 58, 60<br>■ Making Connections, p. 60<br>■ Predicting, p. 62 | **Student Anthology,** pp. 64–69 First Read<br>**Comprehension Strategies**<br>■ Monitoring and Clarifying, pp. 64, 66<br>■ Predicting, pp. 64, 68<br>■ Summarizing, p. 68<br>**Discussing Strategy Use,** p. 68<br>**Discussing the Selection,** p. 69A<br>■ Review Selection<br>■ Complete Discussion<br>**Supporting the Reading,** p. 69C<br>■ Monitoring and Clarifying |
| **Inquiry**<br>**Materials**<br>■ Student Anthology, Book 2, pp. 58–71<br>■ Inquiry Journal, pp. 99–101<br>■ Research Assistant CD-ROM | **Investigation**<br>■ Investigating Concepts Beyond the Text, p. 71A | **Investigation**<br>■ Concept/Question Board, p. 71B |
| **3 Language Arts**<br>**Materials**<br>■ Spelling and Vocabulary Skills, pp. 90–93<br>■ Comprehension and Language Arts Skills, pp. 112–115<br>■ Student Anthology<br>■ The Ultimate Writing and Creativity Center<br>■ Language Arts Handbook<br>■ Writer's Workbook, pp. 70–73<br>■ Language Arts Transparency 22 | **Word Analysis**<br>✓■ Spelling: Adding *-s* or *-es* Pretest, p. 71F<br>**Writing Process Strategies**<br>■ Persuasive Writing: Friendly Letter, p. 71F<br>**English Language Conventions**<br>■ Grammar: Subject/Verb Agreement, p. 71F | **Word Analysis**<br>■ Spelling: Adding *-s* or *-es*, p. 71G<br>■ Vocabulary: Compound Words, p. 71G<br>**Writing Process Strategies**<br>■ Persuasive Writing: Friendly Letter, p. 71G<br>■ Writer's Craft: Sentence Combining, p. 71G<br>**English Language Conventions**<br>■ Grammar: Subject/Verb Agreement, p. 71G |



Ⓟ Phonics ✓Informal Assessment Available ✓Formal Assessment Available

| DAY 2 continued | DAY 3 | |
|---|---|---|
| **DAY 3** | **DAY 4** | **DAY 5** |
| **General Review** | **General Review** | **Review Word Knowledge** |
| **Student Anthology, pp. 58–63** Second Read<br>**Comprehension Skills**<br>■ Drawing Conclusions, pp. 59, 61, 63<br>✓**Concept Connections,** p. 70<br>**Meet the Author/Illustrator,** p. 71<br>**Math Connection**<br>■ The Interest Game I, p. 69E | **Student Anthology, pp. 64–69** Second Read<br>**Comprehension Skills**<br>■ Author's Point of View, pp. 65, 67, 69<br>**Checking Comprehension,** p. 69<br>**Review Selection Vocabulary,** p. 69B<br>**View Fine Art,** p. 69B<br>**Literary Elements,** p. 69D<br>■ Colloquial Speech | ✓**Selection Assessment**<br>■ "Four Dollars and Fifty Cents," pp. 18–21<br>**Home Connection,** p. 69B<br>**Social Studies Connection**<br>■ Civic Laws, p. 69F |
| ✓**Investigation**<br>■ Needs and Plans Phase 2/Reevaluating Problems and Conjectures, p. 71C | **Supporting the Investigation**<br>■ Compare Information Across Sources, p. 71D | **Investigation**<br>■ Unit Investigation Continued<br>■ Update Concept/Question Board |
| **Word Analysis**<br>■ Spelling: Adding -s or -es, p. 71H<br>■ Vocabulary: Compound Words, p. 71H<br>**Writing Process Strategies**<br>■ Persuasive Writing: Friendly Letter, p. 71H<br>**English Language Conventions**<br>✓■ Grammar: Subject/Verb Agreement, p. 71H | **Word Analysis**<br>■ Spelling: Adding -s or -es, p. 71I<br>■ Vocabulary: Compound Words, p. 71I<br>**Writing Process Strategies**<br>■ Persuasive Writing: Friendly Letter, p. 71I<br>✓**English Language Conventions**<br>■ Listening, Speaking, Viewing Interacting: Conversations, p. 71I | **Word Analysis**<br>✓■ Spelling: Adding -s or -es Final Test<br>✓■ Vocabulary: Compound Words, p. 71J<br>**Writing Process Strategies**<br>✓■ Persuasive Writing: Friendly Letter, p. 71J<br>**English Language Conventions**<br>✓■ Penmanship: Cursive Letters *U* and *Y*, p. 71J |

Below are suggestions for differentiating instruction. These are the same skills shown in the Lesson Planner; however, these pages provide extra practice opportunities or enriching activities to meet the varied needs of students.

WORKSHOP

# Differentiating Instruction

## Teacher Directed: Individual and Small-Group Instruction

Spend time each day with individuals and small groups to individualize instruction. Each day:

- preteach students who need help with the next lesson.
- reteach students who need to solidify their understanding of content previously taught.
- listen to students read to check their fluency.
- hold writing and inquiry conferences.

Use the following program components to support instruction:

- ***Reteach*** with students who need a bit more practice
- ***Intervention*** for students who exhibit a lack of understanding of the lesson concepts
- ***English Learner Support*** with students who need language help

## Student: Independent Activities

Students can work alone, with a partner, or in small groups on such activities as:

- Review sound/spellings
- Practice dictation words
- Partner reading
- Practice fluency
- Independent reading
- Reading Roundtable
- Concept vocabulary
- Selection vocabulary
- Writing in progress
- Conference
- Language Arts
- Challenge activities
- Inquiry and Investigation activities
- Listening Library
- Online Phonics

For Workshop Management Tips, see Appendix pages 41–42.

| | DAY 1 |
|---|---|
| **Word Knowledge** | **Teacher Directed**<br>■ Reading Words: Suffixes *-ed* and *-ing*, ***Intervention Guide***, p. 207<br>**Independent Activities**<br>■ ***Online Phonics*** |
| **Fluency** | **Independent Activities**<br>■ Self-test fluency rate<br>■ Oral reading of selection for fluency |
| **Comprehension** | **Teacher Directed**<br>■ Preteach "Four Dollars and Fifty Cents," ***Intervention Guide***, pp. 208–209<br>■ Preteach Intervention Selection One, ***Intervention Guide***, pp. 209–210<br>■ ***English Learner Support Guide***<br>• Vocabulary, pp. 312–313<br>• Comprehension Skill: Drawing Conclusions, pp. 313–314<br>**Independent Activities**<br>■ Browse ***Leveled Classroom Library***<br>■ Add vocabulary in Writer's Notebook |
| **Inquiry** | **Independent Activities**<br>■ Concept/Question Board<br>■ Explore OCR Web site for theme connections<br>■ Investigating Concepts Beyond the Text, p. 71A |
| **Language Arts** | **Teacher Directed**<br>■ Grammar, Usage, and Mechanics, ***Intervention Guide***, p. 212<br>**Independent Activities**<br>■ Subject/Verb Agreement, ***Comprehension and Language Arts Skills***, pp. 112–113 |

| DAY 2 | DAY 3 | DAY 4 | DAY 5 |
|---|---|---|---|
| **Teacher Directed**<br>▪ Developing Oral Language, ***Intervention Guide,*** p. 207<br>**Independent Activities**<br>▪ Read ***Decodable Book 33,*** *Say It in Code* | **Teacher Directed**<br>▪ Dictation and Spelling: Suffixes *-ed* and *-ing,* ***Intervention Guide,*** pp. 207–208<br>**Independent Activities**<br>▪ ***Online Phonics*** | **Teacher Directed**<br>▪ General Review<br>**Independent Activities**<br>▪ ***Online Phonics*** | **Teacher Directed**<br>▪ General Review<br>**Independent Activities**<br>▪ ***Online Phonics*** |
| **Independent Activities**<br>▪ Oral reading of "Four Dollars and Fifty Cents"<br>▪ Partner reading of ***Decodable Book 33,*** *Say It in Code* | **Independent Activities**<br>▪ Partner reading of selection<br>▪ Read ***Decodable Book 33,*** *Say It in Code* | **Independent Activities**<br>▪ Reread "Four Dollars and Fifty Cents" for fluency<br>▪ Partner reading of ***Decodable Book 33,*** *Say It in Code* | **Teacher Directed**<br>▪ Repeated Readings/Fluency Check, ***Intervention Guide,*** p. 212<br>**Independent Activities**<br>▪ Reread ***Decodable Book 33*** |
| **Teacher Directed**<br>▪ Preteach "Four Dollars and Fifty Cents," ***Intervention Guide,*** pp. 208–209<br>▪ Comprehension Strategies, ***Intervention Guide,*** p. 210<br>▪ Reread Intervention Selection One, ***Intervention Guide,*** pp. 209–210<br>▪ ***English Learner Support Guide***<br>• Vocabulary, pp. 314–316<br>• Comprehension Skill: Drawing Conclusions, pp. 316–317<br>**Independent Activities**<br>▪ Independent reading<br>▪ Record response to selection in Writer's Notebook<br>▪ Complete Link to Writing in Supporting the Reading, p. 69C | **Teacher Directed**<br>▪ Discuss Concept Connections, p. 70<br>▪ Reread "Four Dollars and Fifty Cents," ***Intervention Guide,*** pp. 208–209<br>▪ Preteach Intervention Selection Two, ***Intervention Guide,*** pp. 210–211<br>▪ ***English Learner Support Guide***<br>• Vocabulary, pp. 317–319<br>• Comprehension Skill: Author's Point of View, pp. 319–320<br>▪ Math Connection, p. 69E<br>**Independent Activities**<br>▪ Read ***Leveled Classroom Library*** book<br>▪ ***Listening Library Audiocassette/CD*** | **Teacher Directed**<br>▪ Reread "Four Dollars and Fifty Cents," ***Intervention Guide,*** pp. 208–209<br>▪ Comprehension Strategies, ***Intervention Guide,*** p. 211<br>▪ Reread Intervention Selection Two, ***Intervention Guide,*** pp. 210–211<br>▪ ***English Learner Support Guide***<br>• Review Vocabulary, pp. 320–321<br>• Comprehension Skill: Author's Point of View, pp. 320–321<br>**Independent Activities**<br>▪ Add words to Word Bank<br>▪ Complete Independent Practice in Literary Elements, p. 69D<br>▪ ***English Learner Support Activities,*** p. 40 | **Teacher Directed**<br>▪ ***English Learner Support Guide***<br>• Review Vocabulary, p. 322<br>• Comprehension Skills: Drawing Conclusions; Author's Point of View, pp. 322–323<br>**Independent Activities**<br>▪ Read ***Leveled Classroom Library*** book as independent reading<br>▪ Reading Roundtable<br>▪ Social Studies Connection, p. 69F<br>▪ ***English Learner Support Activities,*** p. 41 |
| **Independent Activities**<br>▪ Concept/Question Board<br>▪ Use ***Research Assistant CD-ROM*** to continue investigation | **Independent Activities**<br>▪ Concept/Question Board<br>▪ Research Cycle: Needs and Plans Phase 2, ***Inquiry Journal,*** p. 99<br>▪ Explore OCR Web site for theme connections | **Independent Activities**<br>▪ Concept/Question Board<br>▪ Complete Independent Practice in Supporting the Investigation, p. 71D<br>▪ Comparing Information Across Sources, ***Inquiry Journal,*** pp. 100–101 | **Independent Activities**<br>▪ Concept/Question Board<br>▪ Continue research |
| **Teacher Directed**<br>▪ Grammar, Usage, and Mechanics, ***Intervention Guide,*** p. 212<br>▪ Subject/Verb Agreement, ***Reteach,*** p. 117<br>**Independent Activities**<br>▪ Vocabulary: Compound Words, ***Spelling and Vocabulary Skills,*** pp. 90–91<br>▪ Writer's Craft: Sentence Combining, ***Comprehension and Language Arts Skills,*** pp. 114–115<br>▪ Subject/Verb Agreement, ***Challenge,*** p. 103 | **Teacher Directed**<br>▪ Writing Activity, ***Intervention Guide,*** p. 213<br>▪ Vocabulary: Compound Words, ***Reteach,*** p. 116<br>**Independent Activities**<br>▪ Spelling: Adding *-s* or *-es,* ***Spelling and Vocabulary Skills,*** p. 92<br>▪ Vocabulary: Compound Words, ***Challenge,*** p. 102 | **Teacher Directed**<br>▪ Writer's Craft: Sentence Combining, ***Reteach,*** p. 118<br>▪ Writing Activity, ***Intervention Guide,*** p. 213<br>▪ Spelling: Plurals, ***Reteach,*** p. 115<br>**Independent Activities**<br>▪ Spelling: Adding *-s* or *-es*<br>• ***Spelling and Vocabulary Skills,*** p. 93<br>• ***Challenge,*** p. 101<br>▪ Seminar: Revise a Persuasive Friendly Letter, p. 71I | **Independent Activities**<br>▪ Seminar: Edit/Proofread and Publish a Persuasive Friendly Letter, p. 71J<br>▪ Penmanship: Practice Cursive Letters *U* and *Y,* p. 71J<br>▪ Writer's Craft: Sentence Combining, ***Challenge,*** p. 104 |

ASSESSMENT

# Formal Assessment Options

Use these summative assessments along with your informal observations to assess student progress.

Name ______________________ Date __________ Score ______

LESSON ASSESSMENT

UNIT 4 Money • Lesson 5

**Four Dollars and Fifty Cents**

**Read the following questions carefully. Then completely fill in the bubble of each correct answer. You may look back at the story to find the answer to each of the questions.**

1. From what you read in this story, you can conclude that Shorty
   - Ⓐ is a nice person who can be trusted
   - Ⓑ pays other people as soon as he can
   - ● is not very concerned about other people
2. How do the Circle K boys help Shorty?
   - Ⓐ They give him some money.
   - Ⓑ They help him run away.
   - ● They pretend he is dead.

**Read the following questions carefully. Use complete sentences to answer the questions.**

3. Why does Widow Macrae take the coffin from the Circle K boys?
   She wants to see if Shorty is really dead.
4. What does Widow Macrae tell Shorty up at Boot Hill?
   She tells Shorty that she doesn't know if he is really dead, but she's going to watch him all night. If he doesn't move by morning, she will bury him.
5. What do the outlaws do when they find Shorty's coffin at Boot Hill?
   They are surprised and decide to close the lid.

18 Unit 4 • Lesson 5 *Four Dollars and Fifty Cents* • Unit 4 Assessment

**Unit 4 Assessment p. 18**

**Four Dollars and Fifty Cents** *(continued)*

LESSON ASSESSMENT

6. Why does Shorty start yelling?
   Big Nose George is going to cut off Shorty's nose.
7. Why do the outlaws leave the money behind?
   They are frightened and run away because they think Shorty is a ghost.
8. How does the story end?
   Shorty and the Widow Macrae share a $500 reward, but Shorty still doesn't pay his debt.

**Read the following questions carefully. Then completely fill in the bubble of each correct answer.**

9. This story is being told by
   - Ⓐ Widow Macrae
   - Ⓑ Shorty
   - ● someone not in the story
10. Why couldn't the outlaws get the coffin to shut all the way?
    - ● Shorty's nose was too big.
    - Ⓑ The strongbox was inside.
    - Ⓒ Shorty's feet stuck out.

Unit 4 Assessment • *Four Dollars and Fifty Cents* Unit 4 • Lesson 5 19

**Unit 4 Assessment p. 19**

**Four Dollars and Fifty Cents** *(continued)*

LESSON ASSESSMENT

**Read the questions below. Use complete sentences in your answers.**

**Linking to the Concepts** Do you think Shorty has learned a lesson about paying on time? Why or why not?

Answers will vary. Accept all reasonable answers.

**Personal Response** Why is it important to pay your bills as soon as you have the money?

Answers will vary. Accept all reasonable answers.

20 Unit 4 • Lesson 5 *Four Dollars and Fifty Cents* • Unit 4 Assessment

**Unit 4 Assessment p. 20**

**Four Dollars and Fifty Cents** *(continued)*

LESSON ASSESSMENT

**Vocabulary**

**Read the following questions carefully. Then completely fill in the bubble of each correct answer.**

1. Shorty owed everybody money, from Big Oscar the blacksmith to Widow Macrae. A **blacksmith** is a person who
   - Ⓐ cleans out dirty chimneys
   - Ⓑ takes care of horses
   - ● makes things out of iron
2. Big Oscar does not think Widow Macrae has much chance of collecting the money from Shorty. **Collecting** means
   - ● getting the money he owes
   - Ⓑ making him work for money
   - Ⓒ taking him to the cemetery
3. Widow Macrae wants Shorty to have a decent burial. **Decent** means
   - Ⓐ free
   - Ⓑ rude
   - ● nice
4. Duck Pooley volunteered to nail down the lid of the coffin. To **volunteer** to do something means to
   - Ⓐ want someone else to do it
   - ● say you will do it
   - Ⓒ refuse to do it
5. Shorty was determined not to pay that four dollars and fifty cents, so he lay still. To be **determined** about something means you
   - ● don't want to change your mind
   - Ⓑ ask a lot of questions about it
   - Ⓒ have learned a lesson

Unit 4 Assessment • *Four Dollars and Fifty Cents* Unit 4 • Lesson 5 21

**Unit 4 Assessment p. 21**

Name ______________________ Date __________ Score ______

LESSON ASSESSMENT

UNIT 4 Money • Lesson 5 *Four Dollars and Fifty Cents*

**Spelling Pretest: Plurals**

**Fold this page back on the dotted line. Take the Pretest. Then correct any word you misspelled by crossing out the word and rewriting it next to the incorrect spelling.**

| | | | |
|---|---|---|---|
| 1. | ______ | 1. | berries |
| 2. | ______ | 2. | bunnies |
| 3. | ______ | 3. | guppies |
| 4. | ______ | 4. | hobbies |
| 5. | ______ | 5. | pennies |
| 6. | ______ | 6. | puppies |
| 7. | ______ | 7. | ponies |
| 8. | ______ | 8. | babies |
| 9. | ______ | 9. | donkeys |
| 10. | ______ | 10. | families |
| 11. | ______ | 11. | dollars |
| 12. | ______ | 12. | horses |
| 13. | ______ | 13. | sleeves |
| 14. | ______ | 14. | cowboys |
| 15. | ______ | 15. | britches |

38 Unit 4 • Lesson 5 *Spelling Pretest: Plurals* • Unit 4 Assessment

**Unit 4 Assessment p. 38**

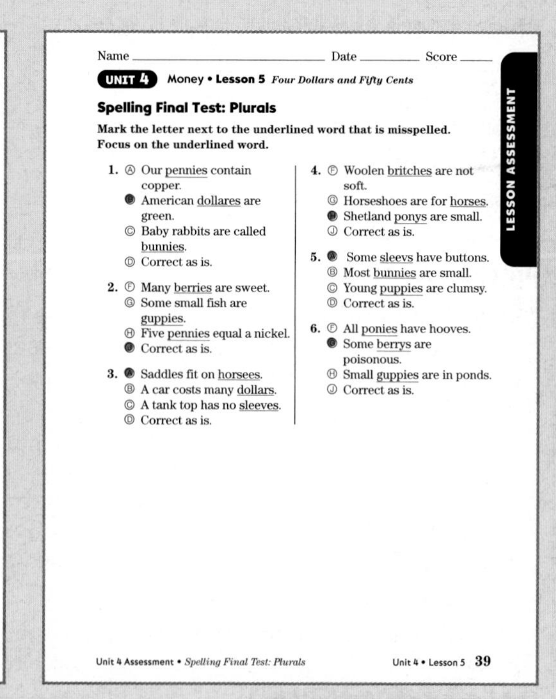

Name ______________________ Date __________ Score ______

UNIT 4 Money • Lesson 5 *Four Dollars and Fifty Cents*

LESSON ASSESSMENT

**Spelling Final Test: Plurals**

**Mark the letter next to the underlined word that is misspelled. Focus on the underlined word.**

1. Ⓐ Our pennies contain copper.
   ● American dollares are green.
   Ⓒ Baby rabbits are called bunnies.
   Ⓓ Correct as is.
2. Ⓔ Many berries are sweet.
   Ⓕ Some small fish are guppies.
   Ⓖ Five pennies equal a nickel.
   ● Correct as is.
3. ● Saddles fit on horsees.
   Ⓑ A car costs many dollars.
   Ⓒ A tank top has no sleeves.
   Ⓓ Correct as is.
4. Ⓔ Woolen britches are not soft.
   Ⓕ Horseshoes are for horses.
   ● Shetland ponys are small.
   Ⓙ Correct as is.
5. ● Some sleevs have buttons.
   Ⓑ Most bunnies are small.
   Ⓒ Young puppies are clumsy.
   Ⓓ Correct as is.
6. Ⓔ All ponies have hooves.
   ● Some berrys are poisonous.
   Ⓗ Small guppies are in ponds.
   Ⓙ Correct as is.

Unit 4 Assessment • *Spelling Final Test: Plurals* Unit 4 • Lesson 5 39

**Unit 4 Assessment p. 39**

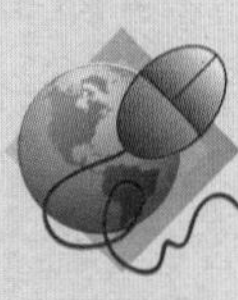

**Online Assessment** for ***Open Court Reading*** helps teachers differentiate classroom instruction based on students' scores from the weekly and end-of-unit assessments. It provides exercises best suited to meet the needs of each student. For more information, visit SRAonline.com.

# Informal Comprehension Strategies Rubrics

### Monitoring and Clarifying

- The student notes characteristics of the text, such as whether it is difficult to read or whether some sections are more challenging or more important than others.
- The student rereads to reconsider something presented earlier in the text.
- The student recognizes problems during reading, such as a loss of concentration, unfamiliar vocabulary, or lack of sufficient background knowledge to comprehend the text.

### Making Connections

- The student activates prior knowledge and related knowledge.
- The student uses prior knowledge to explain something encountered in text.
- The student connects ideas presented later in the text to ideas presented earlier in the text.
- The student notes ideas in the text that are new or conflict with what he or she thought previously.

### Predicting

- The student makes predictions about what the text is about.
- The student updates predictions during reading, based on information in the text.

### Summarizing

- The student paraphrases the text, reporting main ideas and a summary of what is in the text.
- The student decides which parts of the text are important in his or her summary.
- The student draws conclusions from the text.
- The student makes global interpretations of the text, such as recognizing the genre.

# Research Rubrics

During Workshop, assess students using the rubrics below. The rubrics range from 1 to 4 in most categories, with 1 being the lowest score. Record each student's score on the inside back cover of the ***Inquiry Journal.***

### Finding Needed Information

**1** Collects information loosely related to the topic.

**2** Collects information clearly related to the topic.

**3** Collects information helpful in advancing a research problem.

**4** Collects problem-relevant information from varied sources and notices inconsistencies and missing pieces.

**5** Collects useful information, paying attention to the reliability of sources and reviewing information critically.

### Objectives

- Students practice recognizing compound words.
- Students practice recognizing base words and the suffixes *-ed*, *-ing*, and *-ial*.
- Students practice making a word plural by adding *-s* or *-es*.

### Materials

- Student Anthology, Book 2, pp. 58–71
- Phonics CD-ROM
- Sound/Spelling Cards
- Routine Card 1, Routines 1–2
- Decodable Book 33

**Teacher Tip** Have students name the base word in each word with an ending. Remind them that more than one consonant together in a word with an ending usually means a short vowel sound in the base word. Have them use each word they blend in a sentence. Be sure to discuss the meanings of any unfamiliar words.

### Differentiating Instruction

| If... | Then... |
|---|---|
| Students need extra practice making words plural by adding *-s* or *-es* | Use *Online Phonics* |
| Students need extra help with base words and the suffixes *-ed* and *-ing* | Use *Intervention Guide* pages 207–208 |

**Teacher Tip** SYLLABICATION To help students blend words and build fluency, use the syllabication below of the words in the word lines.

| | | |
|---|---|---|
| black•smith | grave•yard | fire•works |
| tomb•stone | buck•board | clenched |
| lugged | growled | owed |
| leaned | bur•y | bur•y•ing |
| bur•ied | bur•i•al | dol•lars |
| hors•es | sleeves | cow•boys |
| britch•es | | |

WORD KNOWLEDGE

## Word Knowledge

### Reading the Words and Sentences

- Use direct teaching to teach the following lesson.
- Use the established procedure as you have students read each line of words and the sentences in this and in subsequent lessons. The words in **boldface** type appear in the selection.

| | | | | | |
|---|---|---|---|---|---|
| Line 1: | blacksmith | graveyard | fireworks | tombstone | buckboard |
| Line 2: | clenched | lugged | growled | owed | leaned |
| Line 3: | bury | burying | buried | burial | |
| Line 4: | dollars | horses | sleeves | cowboys | britches |

Sentence 1: "I'm driving out to the Circle K this afternoon."

Sentence 2: As soon as Oscar left, Widow Macrae hitched her two horses, Clementine and Evangeline, to the buckboard and drove out to the Circle K ranch.

Sentence 3: One lit a lantern while the other two lugged an iron strongbox over to the open grave.

Sentence 4: Cowboys used to wear leather britches when riding on their horses.

### About the Words and Sentences

- **Line 1:** The words in Line 1 are compound words. Have students explain what compound words are and then tell what words make up each compound word. Ask if the two words help us understand the meaning.
- **Line 2:** Line 2 has words with the suffix *-ed*. The suffix *-ed* indicates an action has taken place in the past. Have students note spelling changes that occur when the base word was changed to *-ed*.
- **Line 3:** Line 3 has the base word *bury*. Have students note spelling changes when a suffix is added to the base word.
- **Line 4:** The words in the last line are found in "Four Dollars and Fifty Cents" and review how to make words plural by adding *-s* or *-es*. Ask students to give the singular form for each word and note any spelling changes when the suffix is added.
- **Sentences 1–3:** These sentences are from the story students are about to read. Ask students to identify the compound words *(afternoon, buckboard, strongbox)*. Ask students to identify the words with suffixes *-ed* and *-ing* *(driving, hitched, lugged)*.
- **Sentence 4:** Have students identify the plural words in the last sentence *(cowboys, britches, horses)*.

## Developing Oral Language

- Using the sentences on the board as examples, ask a student to begin a sentence using one of the words from Lines 1–4. Write that word on the board. Have other students add words from Lines 1–4, one at a time, to form a sentence that includes as many of these words as possible. Students may use some new words to help with sentence meaning and context, but encourage them to try using the board words first.
- List the following words on the board: *cow, hand, girl, stage, coach, fire, works.* Explain that these words can be used to form compound words. Ask volunteers to combine these words to form compound words and explain what the new words mean. Compare these compound words to the compound words in Line 1. Students should use these new compound words in a sentence.

## Building Fluency

***Decodable Books*** are used to help develop fluency for students who need extra practice. The only way to gain fluency is to read. Students will have many opportunities to read, including the ***Student Anthology,*** the ***Leveled Classroom Library,*** and their own reading. The ***Decodable Books*** can be used to practice the phonics and fluency elements being reviewed. Refer to the Appendix for the procedure on using these books. For this lesson, use ***Decodable Book 33,*** *Say It in Code.*

***Decodable Book 33***

**Teacher Tip FLUENCY** Gaining a better understanding of the spellings of sounds and structure of words will help students as they encounter unfamiliar words in their reading. By this time in Grade 3 students should be reading approximately 123 words per minute with fluency and expression. As students read, you may notice that some need work in building fluency. During Workshop, have these students select a section of the text (a minimum of 160 words) to read several times in order to build fluency.

**Spelling**
See pages 71E–71J for the corresponding spelling lesson for adding *-s* or *-es*.

**Routine Card**
Refer to ***Routine 1*** for whole-word blending and ***Routine 2*** for sentence blending.

## Objectives

- Students will understand the selection vocabulary before reading, using strategies such as suffixes and structural cues.
- Students will recognize compound words and base words with the suffixes *-ed, -ing* and *-ial.*
- Students will connect prior knowledge to subjects discussed in text.
- Students will use Comprehension Strategies such as Monitoring and Clarifying, Making Connections, Predicting and Summarizing to construct meaning from the text, and monitor reading.
- Students will use the comprehension skills Drawing Conclusions and Author's Point of View as they read the story the second time.
- Students will discuss personal reactions to the story to begin identifying their own personal reading preferences.
- Students link the selection's key concepts to their investigations.

## Materials

- Student Anthology, Book 2, pp. 58–71
- Teacher Observation Log
- Reading Transparencies 27, 46, 50
- Inquiry Journal, p. 85
- Home Connection, p. 53
- Unit 4 Assessment, pp. 18–21
- Program Assessment
- Routine Cards 1, 2, Routines 3–6

**Teacher Tip** Before reading, introduce the idea of borrowing and credit.

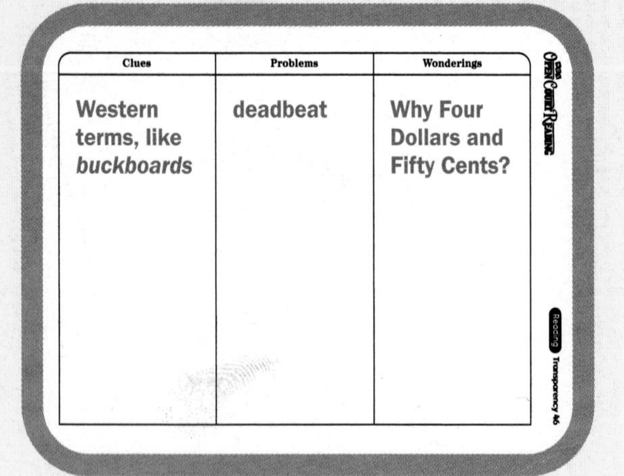

| Clues | Problems | Wonderings |
|---|---|---|
| Western terms, like *buckboards* | deadbeat | Why Four Dollars and Fifty Cents? |



***Reading Transparency 46***

**www.sra4kids.com**
**Web Connection**
Students can use the connections to Money in the Reading link of the SRA Web page for more background information about money.

## Build Background

### Activate Prior Knowledge

Preteach this selection by discussing the following with students to find out what they may already know about the selection and what they already have learned about the unit theme of Money:

- Ask students to think of a time they borrowed money from someone. How did they feel about it? Did they pay back the money? Ask students whether they have ever loaned money to someone. What was that like? Did the person pay them back?
- The theme of managing money was wisely expressed in "Alexander, Who Used to Be Rich Last Sunday." Students should recall that Alexander has a problem with money. Alexander gets what he wants, but does not choose wisely and later regrets his choices. In "Four Dollars and Fifty Cents," Shorty Long gets what he wants but refuses to pay for it. Ask students to discuss how the two are similar.

### Background Information

The following information may help students to better understand the selection they are about to read.

- We can buy things without paying for them immediately. We do this by agreeing to pay at a later time. This is called *buying on credit.* Today, people often use credit cards to buy things they want.
- This story takes place in the Old West. When we refer to the Old West, we often mean the part of the United States west of the Mississippi River, during the years 1840–1890. This story refers to some things that were used in the Old West. A *skillet* is a frying pan. A *buckboard* is an open carriage pulled by horses. To *rein in* means "to stop your horse." *Mosey* means "to walk slowly." *Greenbacks* was a word for paper money.

## Preview and Prepare

### Browse

- Have students read the title and the author's and illustrator's names aloud. Because this is a fictional piece, have the students preview the selection by browsing through only the first page or two of the story so as not to disclose any surprise ending. Discuss with them what they think this story might reveal about money.
- Have students search for clues that tell them something about the story. The students should look briefly at the pictures and the name of the story, and then search for any problems or unfamiliar words or for Old West references that they notice while reading. Use ***Reading Transparency 46*** to record their observations as they browse. For example, students might notice the dialectical flavor of the selection as a clue to what characters will be like. For the Problems column, students might point out they are unfamiliar with the word *deadbeat.*

They might wonder why the story is called "Four Dollars and Fifty Cents." To save time and to model note taking, write students' observations as notes rather than as sentences.

- As students prepare to read the selection, have them browse the Focus Questions on the first page of the selection. Tell them to keep these questions in mind as they read.

### Set Purposes

Encourage students to set their own purpose for reading this selection. As they read, have students think about managing and spending money. You may also have students think about how the theme of the story piques their curiosity or connects to their personal interests. In addition, you may wish to have students think about information in the selection that may be useful to them as they work on their investigations.

## Selection Vocabulary

As students study vocabulary, they will use a variety of skills to determine the meaning of a word. These include context clues, word structure, and apposition. Students will apply these same skills while reading to clarify additional unfamiliar words (*examples: bronco, sagebrush).* Students can write their definitions in their Writer's Notebooks.

Display ***Reading Transparency 27*** before reading the selection to introduce and discuss the following words and their meanings.

**blacksmith:** a person who makes objects from iron, which is heated and then hammered to the desired shape (page 58)
**collecting:** getting payment for a debt (page 58)
**decent:** proper; respectable; acceptable to the community (page 60)
**volunteered:** offered to do (page 61)
**determined:** firm and unwilling to change; stubbornly continuing as planned (page 62)

Have students read the words, stopping to blend any words that they have trouble reading. Help students decode multisyllabic words by breaking the words into syllables and blending the syllables. If students still have trouble, refer them to the ***Sound/Spelling Cards.*** If the word is not decodable, give the students the pronunciation.

Have students read the sentences on the transparency to determine the meaning of the underlined words. Each word has two sentences that students will read and from which they should be able to derive the meaning of the underlined word. Remind them to use one or more of the skills they have learned—context clues, word structure, or apposition—to figure out the meaning before using a dictionary. Be sure students explain which skills they are using and how they figured out the meanings of the words. Have students reread the sentence, substituting the definition to see if the sentence makes sense. Have a volunteer create a new sentence using the underlined word.

**Teacher Tip** The point of setting reading goals is to prepare the reader for an attentive and appreciative reading of the material. Encourage students to set multiple reading goals. Have students record their reading goals in their Writer's Notebooks.

**Teacher Tip** SELECTION VOCABULARY To help students decode words, divide them into syllables when you are saying them, as shown below. The information following each word tells how students can figure out the meaning of each word. When writing words on the board, do not divide them into syllables.

| | |
|---|---|
| **black • smith** | context clues |
| **col • lect • ing** | context clues |
| **de • cent** | context clues |
| **vol • un • teered** | context clues |
| **de • ter • mined** | context clues |

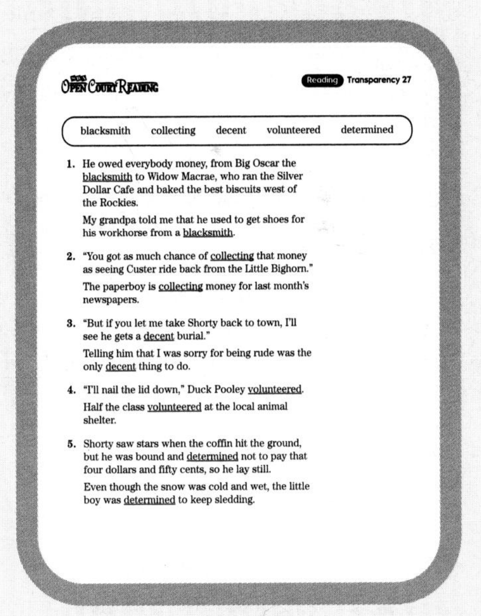
OPEN COURT READING — Reading Transparency 27

blacksmith   collecting   decent   volunteered   determined

1. He owed everybody money, from Big Oscar the blacksmith to Widow Macrae, who ran the Silver Dollar Cafe and baked the best biscuits west of the Rockies.
   My grandpa told me that he used to get shoes for his workhorse from a blacksmith.
2. "You got as much chance of collecting that money as seeing Custer ride back from the Little Bighorn."
   The paperboy is collecting money for last month's newspapers.
3. "But if you let me take Shorty back to town, I'll see he gets a decent burial."
   Telling him that I was sorry for being rude was the only decent thing to do.
4. "I'll nail the lid down," Duck Pooley volunteered.
   Half the class volunteered at the local animal shelter.
5. Shorty saw stars when the coffin hit the ground, but he was bound and determined not to pay that four dollars and fifty cents, so he lay still.
   Even though the snow was cold and wet, the little boy was determined to keep sledding.

***Reading Transparency 27***

### Differentiating Instruction

| If... | Then... |
|---|---|
| Students need extra help with selection vocabulary | Use ***Intervention Guide*** pages 208–209 |

## Differentiating Instruction

| If... | Then... |
|---|---|
| English Learners need support reading "Four Dollars and Fifty Cents" | • Have them read the story with you during Workshop<br>• Have them listen to the story on the ***Listening Library Audiocassette/CD*** a day or two before the whole-class oral reading |
| Students need extra help with summarizing | Use ***Intervention Guide*** pages 209–210 |
| Students need extra help with clarifying | Use ***Intervention Guide*** pages 210–211 |

**Routine Card**
Refer to ***Routine 5*** for the procedure on reading the selection.

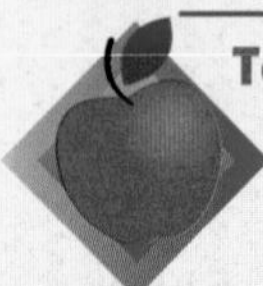

**Teacher Tip** Remember to "think aloud" often as you read, making connections, wondering, and so on.

During Workshop, and after the selection has been read at least once, have students listen to the recording of this lesson's selection on the ***Listening Library Audiocassette/CD.*** After students have listened, have them discuss their personal preferences of the selections read. Ask them what other things they have listened to and like to listen to on the radio, on audiocassettes, or on CDs.

**Teacher Tip** COMPREHENSION STRATEGIES Remind students on the second day as they read the story to summarize what they learned from the first day.

## Reading Recommendations

### Oral Reading

This story lends itself to oral reading because of its playful language, colorful dialogue, and use of Old West expressions. Students should read aloud fluently with appropriate expression and intonation. Make sure that students attend to punctuation and read in phrases. Tell students to add a sense of feeling or anticipation as they read. Have students make use of the comprehension strategies listed below to help them understand the selection. Have them stop reading periodically or wait until they have completed the selection to discuss the reading strategies. After the students have finished reading the selection, use the Discussing the Selection questions on page 69A to see if they understand what they have read.

### Using Comprehension Strategies 

Comprehension strategy instruction allows students to become aware of how good readers read. Good readers constantly check their understanding as they are reading and ask themselves questions. In addition, skilled readers recognize when they are having problems and stop to use various comprehension strategies to help them make sense of what they are reading. An extended lesson on Comprehension Strategy: Monitoring and Clarifying can be found in the Supporting the Reading section on page 69C. This lesson is intended to give students extra practice with Monitoring and Clarifying. However, it may be used at this time to introduce the comprehension strategy to students.

During the first reading of "Four Dollars and Fifty Cents," you will model the use of the following reading strategies:

- **Monitoring and Clarifying** takes different forms, including clarifying the meaning of words and clarifying difficult ideas or passages. In order to clarify meanings, students can use context clues, use structural analysis, use apposition, use charts or graphic organizers, use resources outside of the text, or reread the text.
- **Making Connections** requires readers to activate prior knowledge and connect what they know or have experienced to what they are reading.
- **Predicting** causes readers to analyze information given about story events and characters in the context of how it may logically connect to the story's conclusion.
- **Summarizing** prompts readers to keep track of what they are reading and to focus their minds on important information.

As students read, they should be using a variety of strategies to help them understand the selection. Encourage students to use the strategies listed above as the class reads the story aloud. Do this by stopping at the points indicated by the numbers in the magenta circles on the reduced student page and modeling for the students the use of a particular strategy. Students can also stop reading periodically to discuss what they have learned and what problems they may be having.

## Building Comprehension Skills 

Revisiting or rereading a selection allows readers to apply skills that give them a more complete understanding of the text. Some follow-up comprehension skills help students organize information. Others lead to deeper understanding—to "reading between the lines," as mature readers do. In this selection, students will review the following comprehension skills. Since there are two skills in this lesson, review one skill in its entirety and then review the second skill.

- **Drawing Conclusions:** Readers draw conclusions using what they already know, together with what they know about characters and events, to understand the total picture in a story.
- **Author's Point of View:** Readers determine the perspective from which an author presents the actions and events in the story, generally either first-person or third-person.

### Reading with a Purpose

Have students look for ways any of the story characters learn about money throughout the selection.

### Research in Action

Discussing strategy use and evaluating class discussions as a group will help students understand that they must remain aware of the ways that help them make sense of what they read. Encourage each student to actively participate in these discussions.
*(Michael Pressley)*

**Teacher Tip** After students have read through this story once, they may enjoy reading it a second time in play form. Assign students characters and have them read through the dialogue as if acting out a play. If time permits, create and use props to increase the excitement of the story.

**Teacher Tip** For extra practice in oral fluency, have individual students read aloud to you a selection they have previously read, either from a ***Decodable Book*** or a passage from the ***Student Anthology.*** Time each student for one minute. If the student reads more than 123 words correctly, have the student retell the selection he or she has just read. Use one prompt if the student seems to be stuck, and allow a maximum of one minute for the student to retell the story. If the student does not read more than 123 words correctly, have the student try reading from an earlier ***Decodable Book*** to help you determine where the problem lies.

COMPREHENSION

This selection is broken into two parts.
On the first day, read pages 58–63.
On the second day, read pages 64–69.

## Comprehension Strategies

Read the story aloud, taking turns with the students. Start by modeling the use of strategies for the students.

### Teacher Modeling

**1 Monitoring and Clarifying**

*I'm not sure what "deadbeat" means so I'll continue to read and look for clues. Now, I see that Shorty "owed everybody money" and "he just hates to pay for anything he thinks he can get for free." Maybe a "deadbeat" is someone who doesn't pay his bills. Let's continue to clarify as we read.*

### Teacher Modeling

**2 Monitoring and Clarifying**

*I'm not sure what Big Oscar means when he says, "You got as much chance of collecting that money as seeing Custer ride back from the Little Bighorn." By thinking about what I already know about American history, I remember that Custer was an American general who was killed during the Battle of the Little Bighorn in 1876. If Custer was killed in battle, then he couldn't be seen riding back from battle! Big Oscar says that you are as likely to see Custer as you are to see that money again. Big Oscar must believe that there is no way to collect the money from Shorty.*

### Word Knowledge

**SCAFFOLDING** The skills students are reviewing in Word Knowledge should help them in reading the story. This lesson focuses on compound words, base words with suffixes and plurals.

**compound words:** **deadbeat**, **blacksmith**, **afternoon**

**First Reading Recommendation**

**ORAL • CHORAL**

*Focus Questions* What does it mean to be in debt? Why is it so important to pay back debts?

Eric A. Kimmel
*illustrated by Glen Rounds*

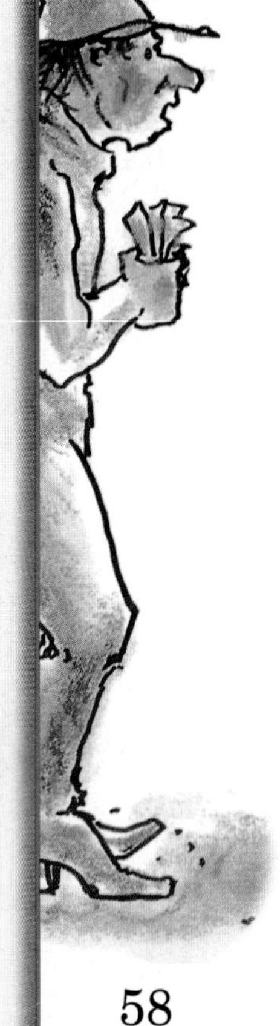

It's a terrible thing to call a cowboy a deadbeat, (1) but in Shorty Long's case it was true. He owed everybody money, from Big Oscar the blacksmith to Widow Macrae, who ran the Silver Dollar Cafe and baked the best biscuits west of the Rockies.

"Shorty ain't a bad sort. He just hates to pay for anything he thinks he can get free," Big Oscar told the widow one afternoon over coffee at the Silver Dollar.

The widow brought Oscar another plate of biscuits. "How am I gonna keep this place going if folks won't pay their bills? Shorty's the worst. He owes me four dollars and fifty cents."

(2) Big Oscar shook his head. "You got as much chance of collecting that money as seeing Custer ride back from the Little Bighorn."

Widow Macrae picked up her rolling pin. "That's what you think. I'm driving out to the Circle K this afternoon. If Shorty won't pay what he owes, I'll lay him out flatter 'n the bottom of a skillet."

58

### Informal Assessment

Observe individual students as they read and use the Teacher Observation Log found in the ***Program Assessment Teacher's Edition*** to record anecdotal information about each student's strengths and weaknesses.

**Teacher Tip** Point out to students that clarifying is a process that has several steps. It is important to pause and carefully clarify, using all of the clues available. Students should reread the phrase or word that is being clarified after each new idea is developed, in order to see if additional new thoughts occur.

As soon as Oscar left, Widow Macrae hitched her two horses, Clementine and Evangeline, to the buckboard and drove out to the Circle K ranch. Duck Pooley saw her coming. He rode back to the corral to warn Shorty.

"Widow Macrae's coming! She's got a rolling pin in her hand and an awful mean look in her eye. You better come up with that money, Shorty."

"Boys, you gotta help me!" Shorty yelped.

"Why don't you just pay what you owe?"

"It ain't that simple. If I paid the widow back, everybody I owe money to'd expect the same. I'd end up broker 'n a mess of eggs."

The Circle K boys decided to help Shorty out just for the fun of seeing what would happen. They knocked together a few boards to make a coffin. When Widow Macrae drove up, she found Shorty lying in it. He looked real peaceful. The Circle K boys stood around blubbering, wiping their noses on their sleeves.

Widow Macrae got down from the buckboard. "What happened to Shorty?" she asked.

59

## Comprehension Skills

COMPREHENSION

### Drawing Conclusions

A *conclusion* is a reader's general idea about a story character or event that's based on small pieces of information. A conclusion should be supported in the text by statements, or by clues from which the reader can infer things that the author does not say directly.

Have students look for clues that the author provides about Shorty's character. *(Shorty doesn't pay his bills; he is not trustworthy.)*

What is one conclusion that students can draw about the way Shorty treats other people? *(He thinks about himself first.)*

**Word Knowledge**

**compound words:** **buckboard**

Drawing Conclusions

Introduced in Grade 1.

Scaffolded throughout Grades 2 and 3.

**REINTRODUCED:** Unit 2, Lesson 2

**REINFORCED:** Unit 4, Lesson 5

Unit 6, Lesson 3

**TESTED:** Unit 4 Assessment

**Teacher Tip** Remind students to use context clues, apposition, or word structure to figure out the meaning of difficult words as they are reading.

**Differentiating Instruction**

| If... | Then... |
|---|---|
| English Learners need extra help with vocabulary | Use ***English Learner Support Guide*** pages 312–313 |
| English Learners need extra help with drawing conclusions | Use ***English Learner Support Guide*** pages 313–314 |

**Second Reading Recommendation**

ORAL • **SILENT**

COMPREHENSION

## Comprehension Strategies

### Teacher Modeling

**3 Monitoring and Clarifying** *I wonder what the Circle K boys mean when they tell the Widow Macrae that Shorty's "gone to the last roundup"? I'll keep on reading. I know that the Circle K boys tell the Widow Macrae that Shorty fell on his head. "Gone to the last roundup" is another way of saying he's dead.*

Begin prompting students for responses. Praise answers that are appropriate, even if they do not match the student sample. This will encourage students to use strategies as they read.

### Prompting

**4 Making Connections** *When readers can make a connection to their own experiences, they can understand the story better. Who can make connections with what they've read to their own experiences?*

### Student Sample

**Making Connections** *It says in the story that Shorty saw stars when the coffin hit the ground. He must have hit his head inside the coffin when it landed on the ground. That reminds me of a cartoon I saw when the character fell down and a circle of stars moved around his head.*

**Word Knowledge**

**suffixes -ing and -ial:** burying, burial

**Teacher Tip** Invite students to support and model the strategy for asking questions.

"He's gone to the last roundup," the Circle K boys told her. "A bronco threw him. He landed on his head." 3

The widow leaned over for a closer look. Shorty looked deader 'n a Christmas tree in August. But she still wasn't sold, although she kept her suspicions to herself.

"Poor Shorty. It hurts my heart to see him like this. Where do you boys figure on burying him?"

"Why, here on the ranch. Somewheres."

Widow Macrae frowned. "That's not right. Shorty deserves better than sagebrush and coyotes. I know you don't have time to spare, what with the spring roundup coming on. But if you let me take Shorty back to town, I'll see he gets a decent burial."

60

### Differentiating Instruction

| If... | Then... |
|---|---|
| Students are having difficulty comprehending "Four Dollars and Fifty Cents" | Have them reread the first three pages of the story, in small sections of text, and then help them identify each main event in the order in which it took place |

The Circle K boys could hardly refuse.

"Then it's settled. Some of you boys load Shorty onto the buckboard. Try not to bounce him around too much."

"I'll nail the lid down," Duck Pooley volunteered.

"Not just yet," said Widow Macrae. "I want to see him one last time before I put him in the ground. Shorty Long was my friend."

That sure was news to Shorty. He didn't say a word, but he was thinking hard, mostly about what he'd like to do to Duck Pooley.

With the coffin loaded, Widow Macrae headed back towards town. She turned off onto the Boot Hill road. Boot Hill is where they bury cowboys like Shorty, who die with their boots on. It's a mighty rough road for a feller's last journey.

Widow Macrae reined in at the top of the hill next to a freshly dug grave. She got down from the buckboard, unhitched the horses, and turned them loose to graze. Then she took hold of the coffin and dragged it out of the wagon. Shorty saw stars when the coffin hit the ground, but he

4

61

## Comprehension Skills

### Drawing Conclusions

Encourage students to continue drawing conclusions about the story based on clues and inferences about things that the author does not say directly. Explain that a *conclusion* is a statement about a character or event that is made by building on small pieces of information that the author supplies.

- Ask students to tell what they learn about the Widow Macrae on pages 60–61. *(The widow takes a second look at Shorty's "dead body"; she was suspicious but did not tell anybody about her suspicions, and so on.)*
- Ask students to make a conclusion based on the information. *(The Widow Macrae is clever and won't be outsmarted.)*

### Word Knowledge

**suffix *-ed*:** **settled**, **volunteered**, **headed**, **unhitched**, **dragged**

**Teacher Tip** During reading, have students note Shorty's excuses and how he avoids paying his debts.

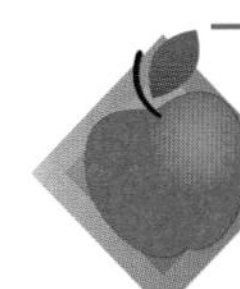

**Teacher Tip** As students read aloud, listen for appropriate pacing, intonation, and expression.

### Differentiating Instruction

| If... | Then... |
|---|---|
| English Learners need extra help with vocabulary | Use ***English Learner Support Guide*** pages 314–316 |
| English Learners need extra help with drawing conclusions | Use ***English Learner Support Guide*** pages 316–317 |

COMPREHENSION

COMPREHENSION

## Comprehension Strategies

### Teacher Modeling

**5 Predicting** *I wonder what's going to happen to Shorty. Will the riders get him? Will he admit that he isn't dead? I know that the widow is suspicious. I predict that the widow will find out for sure that Shorty is alive. What do you think? We can continue to read to see if this prediction is confirmed. We can always revise the prediction as we read further. Who would like to make another prediction about the story?*

### Word Knowledge

| | |
|---|---|
| **suffix *-ed*:** | **determined** |
| | **moved** |

**Teacher Tip** By this time in the school year, students, on their own, should be able to suggest strategies to use while reading.

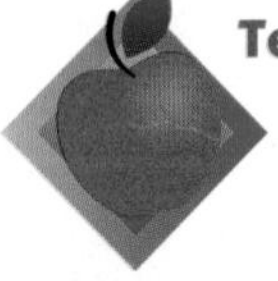

**Teacher Tip COMPREHENSION** Good readers are active readers. They interact with the text as they read by emoting, reacting, responding, and problem solving in their efforts to construct and maintain meaning.

was bound and determined not to pay that four dollars and fifty cents, so he lay still. 5

The widow studied him hard. "Can you hear me, Shorty? If you can, listen good. I don't know if you're dead or not, but I'm gonna keep my eyes on you all night. If you ain't moved by morning, into the ground you go!"

62

### Differentiating Instruction

| If... | Then... |
|---|---|
| English Learners are having difficulty understanding the "Old West" setting and plot | Use ***English Learner Support Guide*** page 312 to provide them with additional background information |

Poor Shorty! It was pay up or be buried alive—and he couldn't make up his mind which was worse! The sun went down. With Widow Macrae's eyes fixed on him tight, Shorty lay still in his coffin, not moving a muscle, not hardly breathing, waiting for something to happen.

On about midnight something did. Riders! He heard them coming up the Boot Hill road. Widow Macrae ducked behind a tombstone. As for Shorty, he was sure it was a posse of dead cowboys riding back from the grave for one last roundup. He lay in his coffin, stiff as rawhide, hoping that with all the graves up there they wouldn't notice one extra corpse.

63

## Comprehension Skills

COMPREHENSION

### Drawing Conclusions

Remind students to draw conclusions as they gather more information from a story. What conclusions can they draw about the characters in this story?

- *Widow Macrae is not easily fooled. She must know Shorty pretty well.*
- *Shorty is not very smart. The easy thing to do would be to pay the money back. He hasn't thought what he would do if his trick worked either. He would probably have to leave town.*

### Word Knowledge

**compound words:** **midnight** **tombstone** **rawhide**

**Teacher Tip** Ask students one or more of the following questions to make sure they understand what they are reading: Is anyone confused? Do you need clarification? Can you summarize what you have read so far? Does what you are reading make sense to you?

COMPREHENSION

## Comprehension Strategies

### Teacher Modeling

**6 Monitoring and Clarifying** *I'm not sure what "nearly gave up the ghost" means. Maybe I can figure it out by continuing to read the story. It says that Shorty "thought the bullet was meant for him." He must have been really scared. I think "nearly gave up the ghost" means he almost died of fright.*

### Prompting

**7 Predicting** *Predictions are based on what you know and what's happening in the story. Who has predictions about the characters in this selection?*

### Student Sample

**Predicting** *By predicting, I can figure out what will happen next. I wonder what the Oregon Kid and Smiley will do now? Will they find Shorty? Will they find the widow? I think somehow Shorty gets the money away from the outlaws. I'll keep reading to see if my prediction is confirmed, like the teacher said to do.*

#### Word Knowledge

**compound words:** strongbox, graveyard

Three riders reined in at the top of Boot Hill. They got off their horses. One lit a lantern while the other two lugged an iron strongbox over to the open grave. Anyone would recognize them at once. It was Big Nose George Parrott and two of his gang, Smiley Dunlap and the Oregon Kid. The outlaws started bragging about a train they robbed that afternoon. They came to the graveyard to divide the loot. No one would think of looking for outlaws on Boot Hill. Not live ones, anyway.

Shorty was in a heap of trouble. If those outlaws caught him spying on them, he wouldn't

64

### Differentiating Instruction

| If... | Then... |
|---|---|
| Students are demonstrating an understanding of author's point of view | Challenge them to speculate on when an author might wish to use a first-person narrator *(when the feelings and experiences of the main character are to be expressed)* or a third-person narrator *(when the thoughts and feelings of more than just the main character are to be expressed)* |

have to worry about being a fake corpse.
Big Nose George drew his six-gun.

"Stand back, boys! I'll settle this business!"

He fired a shot into the strongbox padlock. (6) Shorty nearly gave up the ghost. He thought that bullet was meant for him.

"Yahoo! We struck it rich!"

The Oregon Kid kicked open the lid. He and Smiley reached inside and began throwing fistfuls of hundred dollar bills into the air. That made Big Nose George real mad.

"Quit that clowning! This ain't the circus! You boys pick up them greenbacks and put 'em back where you found 'em!" (7)

"Aw, George!"

65

## Differentiating Instruction

| If... | Then... |
| --- | --- |
| English Learners need extra help with vocabulary | Use ***English Learner Support Guide*** pages 317–319 |
| English Learners need extra help with author's point of view | Use ***English Learner Support Guide*** pages 319–320 |

COMPREHENSION

## Comprehension Skills

### Author's Point of View

Students should be able to explain that the author's point of view refers to the kind of narrator or speaker that the writer uses to tell the story. In the first-person narrative, the writer tells the story as if the storyteller were a character in the story. Ask students to name clue words that are used with a first-person narrative *(I, me, we, us).* Students should be able to explain that in a third-person narrative, the writer tells the story as if the narrator or storyteller were someone outside of the story.

Have students name clue words for a third-person narrative *(he, him, her, she, they, them, it).*

Ask students to think about the story so far and to identify the author's point of view. *(It's told in the third-person narrative by an outside narrator.)*

### Word Knowledge

**suffix *-ing*:** **throwing**
**clowning**

Author's Point of View

Introduced in Grade 2.
Scaffolded throughout Grade 3.

**REINTRODUCED:** Unit 3, Lesson 6
**REINFORCED:** Unit 4, Lesson 5
Unit 5, Lesson 7
**TESTED:** Unit 4 Assessment

**Teacher Tip** Remind students that the writer chooses the point of view appropriate to each particular piece of writing.

COMPREHENSION

## Comprehension Strategies

### Teacher Modeling

**8 Monitoring and Clarifying** *I'm not sure what "divvy it up" means. But I'll keep reading so that I can find clues to help me figure it out. Now, I know that Big George says they're going to "divvy it up businesslike. No grabbing!" I think he means they are going to divide the money in a businesslike way, without grabbing it. "Divvy" is probably slang for "divide." What else have we clarified at this point?*

### Word Knowledge

**suffix *-ing*:** **grabbing**
**picking**
**burying**
**leaving**

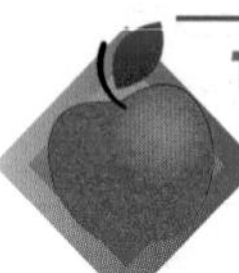

**Teacher Tip** Encourage students to model the use of different reading strategies.

**Teacher Tip** Tell students that good readers keep thinking about the questions that come up about the topic, and they keep coming back to those questions. As they read, tell them to keep the questions on the Concept/Question Board in mind. Have them make notes to themselves in the Response Journal section of their Writer's Notebooks about which questions seem most important. Tell them that good readers always think about what is important in selections, and they try to remember this important information.

"Aw, George nothing! We're gonna divvy it up business-like. No grabbing!" 8

The Kid and Smiley started picking up the money. One of the bills landed in Shorty's coffin.

"Holy Hannah! What's this? There's a dead 'un here!"

"Don't drop your britches, boys. Dead 'uns don't bite." Big Nose George moseyed over for a closer look. "Why, it's some poor cowpoke whose burying had to wait till morning. They should've covered him up, though. It ain't decent leaving a feller out in the open where the buzzards can get at him. But that ain't none of our concern. Bring over them bills and let's get started."

66

## Differentiating Instruction

### Intervention Tip

**CLARIFYING** Invite students to listen to volunteers read small sections of the story aloud. Have students make up questions that can be answered by clues stated directly in each section. Encourage students to model the clarifying process as they answer these questions.

"Can't we close that coffin first?" the Kid asked. "Dead 'uns give me the willies."

"Sure, go ahead," said Big Nose George.

The Kid slammed the coffin lid right down on Shorty's nose! Tears came to Shorty's eyes. He clenched his teeth to keep from yelling.

"What's the matter?" Smiley asked.

"This lid don't fit."

"Let me try." Smiley sat down hard on the coffin. He packed a lot of weight. The lid mashed Shorty's nose into his face. Shorty saw stars, but not the ones in the sky.

"What's keeping you two?" Big Nose George growled.

"This lid won't lay flat."

"Let me see." Big Nose George had a look. "Are you both crack-brained? Use your eyes. This feller's nose sticks up a mile. It's way too long for the coffin."

"What'll we do?"

"Easy! He don't need a sniffer where he's going. I'll cut it off with my bowie knife!"

67

## Comprehension Skills

COMPREHENSION

### Author's Point of View

Prompt students to tell you what they know about Author's Point of View. Students should tell that every story is told from a specific point of view. It can be told directly by the author in a third-person narrative, or it can be told by a story character in a first-person narrative. In the first-person narrative, readers learn a lot about the character telling the story, but in a third-person narrative readers can learn a lot about what different story characters do and feel.

Ask students to identify clue words on pages 66–67 that indicate this story is told in the third person *(they, he)*.

- What other clues are in the story? *(The narrator is observing the action and is not a part of it.)*

**Word Knowledge**

| **suffix *-ed:*** | **clenched** |
| --- | --- |
| | **packed** |

COMPREHENSION

## Comprehension Strategies

### Teacher Modeling

**9 Confirming Predictions** *Our predictions were confirmed. The widow does find out that Shorty is not dead, and Shorty does save the money from the outlaws.*

### Teacher Modeling

**10 Summarizing** *I think this is a good place to sum up what happened. Shorty is a cowboy who didn't want to pay the Widow Macrae the four dollars and fifty cents that he owed her. Instead, Shorty made believe that he was dead. Who would like to continue the summary in their own words?*

### Discussing Strategy Use

After students have read the selection, encourage them to share any problems that they encountered and to tell what strategies they used to solve them.

- What connections did they make between the reading and what they already know?
- How did they clarify confusing passages?
- Where did they pause in the reading to summarize?
- How did they make, confirm, and revise predictions as they read?

These are questions good readers ask after they read a text. After reading, the students should always be asking, "What did I find interesting? What is important here?" Later, remind the students again that whenever they conclude a reading, they should ask themselves questions about what was in the text.

### Word Knowledge

**compound words:** graveyard, fireworks

That was enough for Shorty. He sat up in his coffin and hollered, "Hold on, boys! I ain't that dead!"

Big Nose George nearly dropped his teeth.

Smiley let out a yell as the whole gang ran for their horses.

Those outlaws shot out of that graveyard faster than fireworks!

Widow Macrae laughed fit to bust. When she was all laughed out, she came from behind the tombstone and gave Shorty the scolding of his life.

"I hope you learned your lesson. You nearly got your nose cut off for four dollars and fifty cents!"

Shorty was too embarrassed to say anything. He and Widow Macrae gathered up the money the outlaws left behind. In the morning they took it to the railroad agent in town. He gave (9)

68

### Differentiating Instruction

| If... | Then... |
|---|---|
| Students are having difficulty understanding the concepts being discussed | Expand, restate, and reinforce important points often, and work with individual students as necessary |

them a five-hundred-dollar reward to divide between them.

Shorty rubbed his nose. "I reckon we're even now."

"Not quite," said Widow Macrae. "You still owe me four dollars and fifty cents."

Shorty stared glumly at his pile of fifty-dollar bills. "I don't have no change. How about if I come by tomorrow and settle up?"

"I'll expect you," Widow Macrae said.

But so far as anyone knows, he hasn't paid her yet. (10)

69

## Comprehension Skills

Second Read

### Author's Point of View

Remind students that story clues tell readers what the author's point of view is. Ask students to identify story clues that tell them that this story is told from a third-person point of view.

- *The narrator is describing the action as it happens to other people.*
- *The narrator talks about other characters, but never himself.*

### Checking Comprehension

- Why is this story called "Four Dollars and Fifty Cents"? *(The title sums up the most important story event; Shorty owes four dollars and fifty cents to Widow Macrae.)*
- What are some ways that the writer makes this story funny? *(Students may refer to story dialogue, characters' actions, and the silly situation.)*
- What does this story reveal about money? *(It illustrates what happens when people refuse to pay their debts and also emphasizes the problems that can result.)*

**Teacher Tip FLUENCY** By this time in third grade, good readers should be reading approximately 123 words per minute with fluency and expression. The only way to gain this fluency is through practice. Have students reread the selection to you and to each other during Workshop to help build fluency. As students read, you may notice that some need work in building fluency. During Workshop, have these students select a section of the text (a minimum of 160 words) to read several times in order to build fluency.

COMPREHENSION

### Differentiating Instruction

| If... | Then... |
|---|---|
| English Learners need extra help reviewing "Four Dollars and Fifty Cents" | Use ***English Learner Support Guide*** pages 320–323 |

**Formal Assessment**

See pages 18–21 in ***Unit 4 Assessment*** to test students' comprehension of "Four Dollars and Fifty Cents."

**Teacher Tip DISCUSSION** When you call on a student, allow him or her a few seconds to consider your question and arrive at an answer.

**Routine Card**
Refer to ***Routine 6*** for the *handing-off process.*

| Clues | Problems | Wonderings |
|---|---|---|
| Western terms, like *buckboards* | deadbeat | Why Four Dollars and Fifty Cents? |

***Reading Transparency 46***

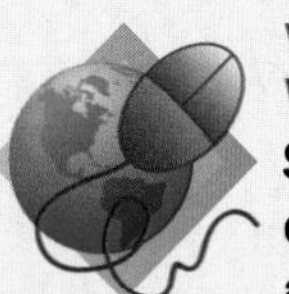

**www.sra4kids.com**
**Web Connection**
Some students may choose to conduct a computer search for additional books or information about money. Invite them to make a list of these books and sources of information to share with classmates and the school librarian. Check the Reading link of the SRA Web page for additional links to the theme-related Web site.

## Discussing the Selection

After the first read, the whole group discusses the selection and any personal thoughts, reactions, problems, or questions that it raises. To stimulate discussion, students can ask one another the kinds of questions good readers ask themselves about a text: *How does it connect to money? What have I learned that is new? What did I find interesting about this story? What is important here? What was difficult to understand? Why would someone want to read this?* Ensure that students are using specific information from the text to support their interpretations.

**Handing-Off Process** Seeing you as a contributing member of the group sets a strong example for students. To emphasize that you are part of the group, actively participate in the *handing-off process:* Raise your hand to be called on by the last speaker when you have a contribution to make. Point out unusual and interesting insights verbalized by students so that these insights are recognized and discussed. As the year progresses, students will take more and more responsibility for the discussions of the selections.

Engage students in a discussion to determine whether they have grasped the following ideas:

- why Shorty behaved as he did
- what the story teaches about lending and borrowing
- why the selection was named "Four Dollars and Fifty Cents"

During this time, have students return to the clues, problems, and wonderings they noted during browsing to determine whether the clues were borne out by the selection, whether and how their problems were solved, and whether their wonderings were answered or deserve further discussion and investigation. Let students decide which items deserve further discussion.

Also have students return to the Focus Questions on the first page of the selection. Select a student to read the questions aloud, and have volunteers answer the questions. If students do not know the answers to the questions, have them return to the text to find the answers.

You may wish to review the elements of a tall tale with the students at this time. Discuss with them how they can tell that "Four Dollars and Fifty Cents" is a tall tale.

Have students break into small groups to discuss what this story tells them about money. Groups can then discuss their ideas with the rest of the class.

If students have ever received, lent or borrowed money, or read a story about lending and borrowing, encourage them to record their experiences.

## Review Selection Vocabulary

Have students review the definitions of the selection vocabulary words that they wrote in the vocabulary section of their Writer's Notebooks. Remind them that they discussed the meanings of these words before reading the selection. Have students write sentences for each of the vocabulary words after the definitions in the same section of their Writer's Notebooks. They can use the definitions and the sentences to study for the vocabulary portion of their Lesson Assessments. Have them add to the personal dictionary section of their Writer's Notebooks any other interesting words that they clarified while reading. Encourage students to refer to the selection vocabulary words throughout the unit. The words from the selection are:

**blacksmith** **collecting** **decent** **volunteered** **determined**

If you created a Word Bank of key words related to the theme of Money, remind students to find words from other resources, from their investigations, and from family discussions and add them to the Word Bank, organizing the words by the number of syllables.

**Teacher Tip** Encourage students to write a sentence using these vocabulary words. In order to provide additional help in remembering words, students can write a synonym or an antonym for the word if it is appropriate. Some students may even draw something that helps them to remember the meaning of the word.

## View Fine Art

Have students reflect on the print ***80 Two-Dollar Bills*** on page 56 of the ***Student Anthology*** and share their thoughts and reactions with the class. Explain that the print by Andy Warhol was his first silkscreen print, the technique that later made him famous. He liked this process of creating art because he was able to reproduce the same image several times. Warhol believed that by repeating an image in a work of art he was better able to reflect society's love of quantity and conformity.

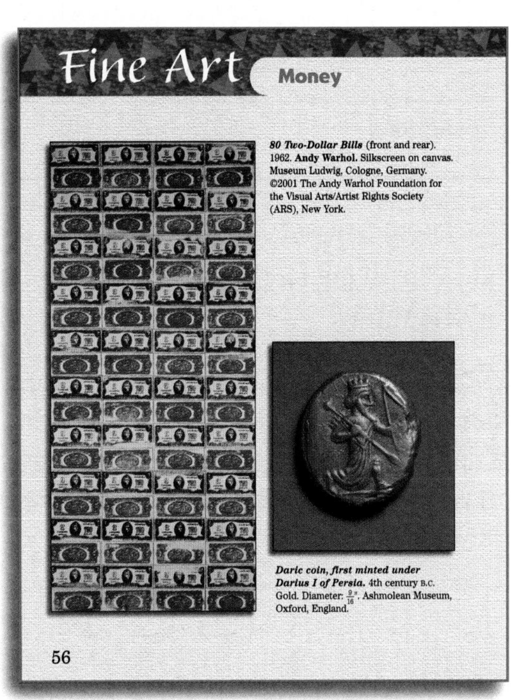
Fine Art Money

***80 Two-Dollar Bills*** (front and rear). 1962. **Andy Warhol.** Silkscreen on canvas. Museum Ludwig, Cologne, Germany. ©2001 The Andy Warhol Foundation for the Visual Arts/Artist Rights Society (ARS), New York.

***Daric coin, first minted under Darius I of Persia.*** 4th century B.C. Gold. Diameter: $\frac{9}{16}$". Ashmolean Museum, Oxford, England.

56

***Student Anthology* p. 56**

## Home Connection

Distribute ***Home Connection,*** page 53. Parents and caregivers will be provided with a recipe for traditional biscuits similar to those discussed in the story "Four Dollars and Fifty Cents." A Spanish version of this letter appears on page 54.

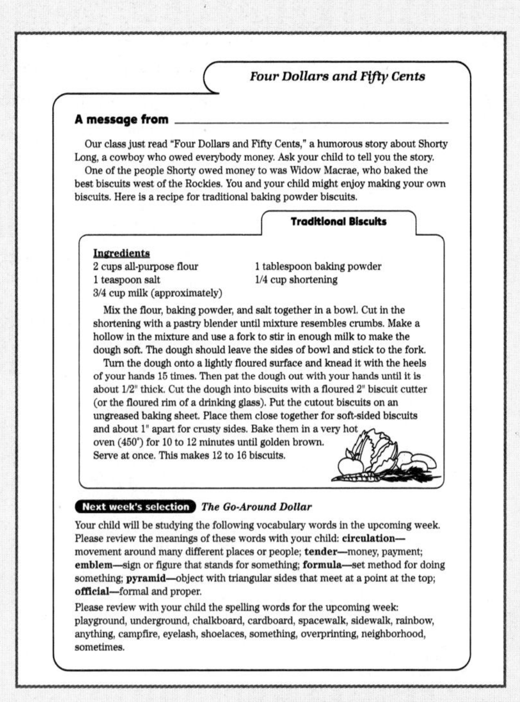
*Four Dollars and Fifty Cents*

**A message from** ______________________

Our class just read "Four Dollars and Fifty Cents," a humorous story about Shorty Long, a cowboy who owed everybody money. Ask your child to tell you the story.

One of the people Shorty owed money to was Widow Macrae, who baked the best biscuits west of the Rockies. You and your child might enjoy making your own biscuits. Here is a recipe for traditional baking powder biscuits.

**Traditional Biscuits**

Ingredients
2 cups all-purpose flour
1 teaspoon salt
3/4 cup milk (approximately)
1 tablespoon baking powder
1/4 cup shortening

Mix the flour, baking powder, and salt together in a bowl. Cut in the shortening with a pastry blender until mixture resembles crumbs. Make a hollow in the mixture and use a fork to stir in enough milk to make the dough soft. The dough should leave the sides of bowl and stick to the fork.

Turn the dough onto a lightly floured surface and knead it with the heels of your hands 15 times. Then pat the dough out with your hands until it is about 1/2" thick. Cut the dough into biscuits with a floured 2" biscuit cutter (or the floured rim of a drinking glass). Put the cutout biscuits on an ungreased baking sheet. Place them close together for soft-sided biscuits and about 1" apart for crusty sides. Bake them in a very hot oven (450°) for 10 to 12 minutes until golden brown. Serve at once. This makes 12 to 16 biscuits.

**Next week's selection** *The Go-Around Dollar*

Your child will be studying the following vocabulary words in the upcoming week. Please review the meanings of these words with your child: **circulation**—movement around many different places or people; **tender**—money, payment; **emblem**—sign or figure that stands for something; **formula**—set method for doing something; **pyramid**—object with triangular sides that meet at a point at the top; **official**—formal and proper.

Please review with your child the spelling words for the upcoming week: playground, underground, chalkboard, cardboard, spacewalk, sidewalk, rainbow, anything, campfire, eyelash, shoelaces, something, overprinting, neighborhood, sometimes.

***Home Connection* p. 53**

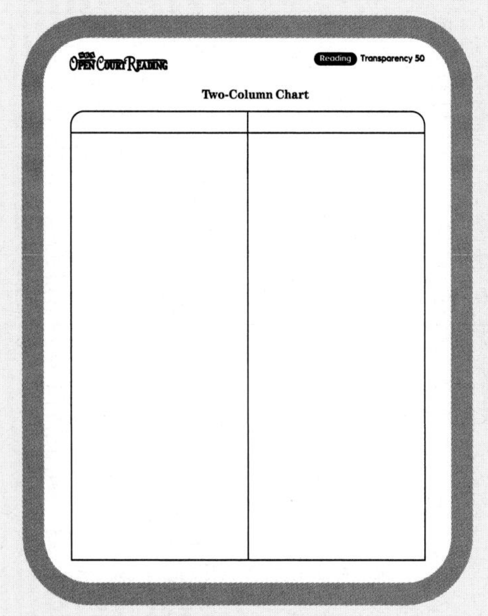

***Reading Transparency 50***

**Teacher Tip** **WRITING** Remind students to respond to the writing of others by providing specific feedback on clarity, coherency, and logical order. Remind students to also practice proofreading skills after they write a first draft. Students can proofread their own papers, or they can exchange papers with a classmate for proofreading.

### Differentiating Instruction

| If... | Then... |
|---|---|
| Students are having difficulty with the strategy Monitoring and Clarifying | • Point out a specific passage in the story and have them read it with you, focusing on the strategy<br>• Reread "Four Dollars and Fifty Cents" with them and provide additional modeling of the strategy |

## Supporting the Reading

### Comprehension Strategies: Monitoring and Clarifying

**Teach** After the first read, ask students what they know about Monitoring and Clarifying. If necessary, explain that this strategy takes several forms, including monitoring comprehension and clarifying the meaning of words and difficult ideas or passages. To clarify the meaning of words, students can use context clues, structural analysis, apposition, or outside resources. To clarify difficult ideas or passages, students must first recognize that some part of the text does not make sense by monitoring their own comprehension. If they detect problems, they can reread the difficult parts to see if they missed something the first time, use graphic organizers, use other comprehension strategies, or ask someone for help.

**Guided Practice** Use the two-column chart on ***Reading Transparency 50*** to record students' responses. In the first column, ask students for suggestions of things they wrote in the Problems section of the Clues, Problems, and Wonderings sheet. Then ask students to explain how they clarified the information for themselves. You can use the following as an example to get started.

| Problems | Method of Clarifying |
|---|---|
| deadbeat | Context clues |

**Independent Practice** Have students focus on the strategy Monitoring and Clarifying as they read selections in the anthology, classroom library, and bibliography.

**Link to Writing** Ask students to think of a new word that they learned from reading the selection. Then ask them to use the word in an interesting sentence. Encourage them to add more sentences so they have a paragraph. Some students may wish to continue until they have an entire story. Invite students to share what they write with the class.

## Literary Elements

### Colloquial Speech

**Teach** Ask students to tell you what colloquial speech is. If necessary, tell them that colloquial speech is the way people in a particular place speak. Most people do not use standard English all the time. Every region has its own colloquial speech. Time periods have colloquial speech as well. Some writers use colloquial speech in stories to help readers have a clearer picture of the setting and characters.

**Guided Practice** Tell students that the colloquial speech used in "Four Dollars and Fifty Cents" is from the Old West. The pronunciation and expressions were characteristic of that place and time. As a group, go back through the selection and identify words, expressions, and spellings that reflect the colloquial speech used in the story. Record answers on the board or on an overhead transparency.

**Independent Practice** Ask students to pay attention to their own conversations. Do they use special expressions that are not part of the standard language? Ask them to pay attention to pronunciation. Do they leave off word endings when they speak? If a writer were writing a story about them, what sorts of expressions and spellings would he or she use? Ask students, as they read on their own, to look for examples of writers using colloquial speech in fiction.

**Teacher Tip** You might point out authors, such as Mark Twain or Lucille Clifton, known for using colloquial speech in their writing.

**Differentiating Instruction**

| If... | Then... |
|---|---|
| Students have an understanding of colloquial speech and would enjoy a challenge | • Have them write a story using the expressions and spellings unique to their own conversation style<br>• Have them find examples of colloquial speech in their own reading to share with the class |

**Teacher Tip** MATERIALS
- ✔ chalk
- ✔ board

**Teacher Tip** PURPOSE To help students understand how loans work and accrue interest.

**Teacher Tip** To keep the math interesting, use the characters and situations in the story as part of the story problem. For example: Shorty owed $4.50. If Widow Macrae charged five cents a day for every day he kept the loan, how much interest would have accumulated after one week? *(5 x 7 = 35)*

## Math Connection

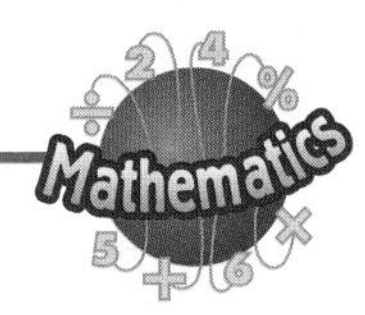


### The Interest Game I

Explain that Shorty, in essence, took a loan from the Widow Macrae for four dollars and fifty cents. Though this story did not employ interest, modern loans involve interest. Ask students if they know what that means. If they do not know, ask them how someone like Widow Macrae might make money by the loan she gave Shorty.

Figure some simple interest problems on the board together. Focus primarily on multiplication tables, multiplying a flat-rate interest for x amount of days. To complicate the problems, you might ask students how much *total* would be owed. It might be helpful to write out the formulas for the students. *(days* x *interest amount, days* x *interest amount + loan amount = total)*

Have students break into two groups and, two at a time, have them come to the board. Ask them to figure out simple interest problems using addition, multiplication, and subtraction. Keep track of the team scores by counting a point for every right answer. Make sure every student gets an opportunity to participate. If the students at the board are stumped, allow the members of their teams to help them.

End the game with a discussion of the importance of paying back loans. Ask the students if they have any insights they would like to share about interest and loans. Ask them if they think it would be a good idea to take out a loan they cannot repay.

Shape this exercise to fit the needs of your classroom. The guidelines of this math connection are merely suggestions of starting points.

## Social Studies Connection

### Civic Laws

In "Four Dollars and Fifty Cents," students read about a cowboy who did not want to pay back the money he had borrowed. Ask students what they think about Shorty's actions. Was it wrong for him not to pay back his debts? Why or why not? Discuss the idea of respecting the rights of others. Were Widow Macrae's rights respected? Ask students to explore laws in their city or state that deal with the issue of borrowing and lending money, and laws dealing with respecting the rights of others. How are individuals protected? What are individuals' responsibilities? Are these laws important? Why or why not? Students can work in groups to explore these questions. Ask groups to make a presentation of their findings, accompanied by visuals explaining the laws they learned about.

**Teacher Tip** MATERIALS
- ✔ poster board
- ✔ colored pencils or markers

**Teacher Tip** PURPOSE To learn about civic laws and responsibilities.

**Teacher Tip** Remind students that the library as well as the Internet provide many sources that cover civic issues that are created especially for young students to use. They might consider starting with such a source to look up the information for this activity.

## Concept Connections

### Linking the Selection

- Widow Macrae wanted to find Shorty to make him pay back the money that he owed her.
- The outlaws showed that money was important to them by robbing a train. The outlaws wanted money so badly that they were willing to do something wrong to get it.

### Exploring Concept Vocabulary

The concept word for this lesson is ***debt.*** Write the word on the board. Work with students to develop a definition that links to the unit theme. Have students copy the word and definition into the Vocabulary section of their Writer's Notebooks.

***Debt:*** the condition of owing money; something that is owed to someone. For example, Shorty's debt to Widow Macrae was $4.50.

- Shorty tried to trick Widow Macrae, but embarrassed himself instead.
- Shorty could have avoided being in debt by paying for the goods and services that he used.

The sentences that students write should show an understanding of the concept word and the selection vocabulary word.

### Expanding the Concept

You may want to do a whole-group discussion to help students continue to develop their ability to engage in meaningful dialogue. However, students may conduct these dialogues in small groups. If the students work in small groups, bring the groups together and have them share their ideas with the whole class.

As students complete their discussions, have them record their ideas and impressions about the selection on page 85 of their ***Inquiry Journals.***

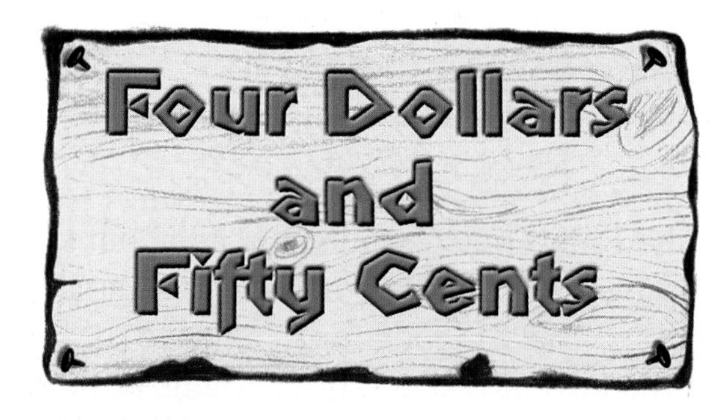


## Concept Connections

### Linking the Selection

Think about the following questions, and then record your responses in the Response Journal section of your Writer's Notebook.

- Why did Widow Macrae set out to find Shorty in the beginning of the story?
- Was money important to the outlaws? How do you know?

### Exploring Concept Vocabulary

The concept word for this lesson is ***debt.*** If you do not know what this word means, look it up in a dictionary. Answer these questions:

- What kinds of problems did Shorty's ***debt*** cause him in the story?
- How could Shorty have avoided being in ***debt?***

In the Vocabulary section of your Writer's Notebook, write a sentence using the word ***debt*** and one of the selection vocabulary words.

### Expanding the Concept

Think about Anna's mother in "A New Coat for Anna." How were her ideas about money different from Shorty's ideas about money?

Try to include the word ***debt*** in your discussion.

Add new ideas about money to the Concept/Question Board.

70

**Informal Assessment**

This may be a good time to observe students working in small groups and to mark your observations in the Teacher Observation Log found in the ***Program Assessment Teacher's Edition.***

## Meet the Author

**Eric A. Kimmel** loved stories as a child. As he was growing up, his grandmother (who spoke five languages besides English) would tell him wild stories that would go on for days. Her storytelling inspired him to become a great storyteller himself. He also loved books. He remembers how he felt when he first realized that real people wrote the books. *"I felt electrified. I wanted that. I wanted to have my name on the cover of a book. It was the most wonderful thing I could imagine. I still get a shiver of excitement whenever I take a new book out of the envelope and hold it for the first time. Wow, I did that! I wrote a book! It never fails to amaze me."*

## Meet the Illustrator

**Glen Rounds** held many jobs before becoming an author and illustrator. He was a cowboy, sign painter, railroad section hand, baker, carnival medicine man, textile designer, and staff sergeant in the army, among other things. Eventually he went to New York to get into the book business. He wrote more than 50 books and illustrated over 60 other publications by other authors. Although he is classified as a children's author, he insists that his works are meant for all age groups.

71

## Meet the Author

After students read the information about Eric A. Kimmel, discuss the following questions with them:

- Eric Kimmel's grandmother told stories that went on for days. How do you think this helped Kimmel as a writer? *(Possible answer: He felt challenged. He wanted to be a storyteller like she was and entertain other people.)*
- Eric Kimmel was excited when he thought about authors being the real people behind the book. He wanted this for himself. Why is it important to remember that authors are real people? *(Possible answer: It's easy to forget that authors are real people when you get wrapped up with their characters.)*

## Meet the Illustrator

After students read the information about Glen Rounds, discuss the following questions with them:

- What jobs in Glen Rounds's past helped him illustrate this story and why? *(Possible answer: Being a cowboy helped him because he was familiar with details such as clothing, scenery, horses, etc.)*
- Although Glen Rounds is classified as a children's author, he insists that his works are meant for all age groups. Why do you think he says this? *(Possible answer: Even though a story may be written at a level for children, it might be entertaining and educational for any age. People should never limit themselves on the types of stories they enjoy.)*

**Teacher Tip WRITER'S NOTEBOOK** Have students keep a reading log, interest list, and a set of reading goals as a part of their Writer's Notebooks.

### Differentiating Instruction

| If... | Then... |
| --- | --- |
| Students enjoyed reading "Four Dollars and Fifty Cents" | Challenge them to find other stories, folk tales, and tall tales by Eric Kimmel to read and share with the class |

### Objectives

- Students ask questions related to money.
- Students gain a deeper understanding of issues related to money.
- Students continue identifying needs and making plans.

### Materials

- Student Anthology, Book 2, pp. 58–71
- Inquiry Journal, pp. 99–101
- Research Assistant CD-ROM

### Differentiating Instruction

| If... | Then... |
|---|---|
| Students have an understanding of the story and would enjoy a challenge | Have them write a new ending to the story, beginning when Shorty and Widow Macrae receive the cash reward |

INVESTIGATION

## Investigating Concepts Beyond the Text

At this point in the investigation, students should continue identifying needs and discussing plans. Your role is to see how students are progressing and provide necessary discussion or guidance as students move into Needs and Plans, Phase 2.

In "Four Dollars and Fifty Cents," students read about a cowboy who did not want to pay his debts. Ask students to host a panel discussion or a debate on the subject of lending and borrowing money. They can discuss questions such as the following: *Should friends lend money to friends? Why or why not? Should people pay their debts? Why or why not? If they should, what should happen to them when they don't?* Then ask students to think about the end of the story when both Shorty and Widow Macrae received the cash reward. Students might wish to discuss the following questions: *Should Shorty still pay the money he owes? Why or why not? What should happen to him if he doesn't?*

INVESTIGATION

## Concept/Question Board

Tell students this is a good time to post on the Concept/Question Board any new questions they have about money that "Four Dollars and Fifty Cents" might have raised. Remind them of your earlier discussion about the Concept/Question Board and ask them to tell what they remember about that discussion.

After reading each selection, students should use the Concept/Question Board to:

- Post any questions they asked about a selection before reading that have not yet been answered.
- Refer to as they formulate statements about concepts that apply to their investigations.
- Post general statements formulated by each collaborative group.
- Continue to post news articles or other items that they find during the unit investigation.
- Read and think about posted questions, articles, or concepts that interest them and provide answers to the questions.
- Students might wish to bring in articles about borrowing and lending money.

Concept/Question Board

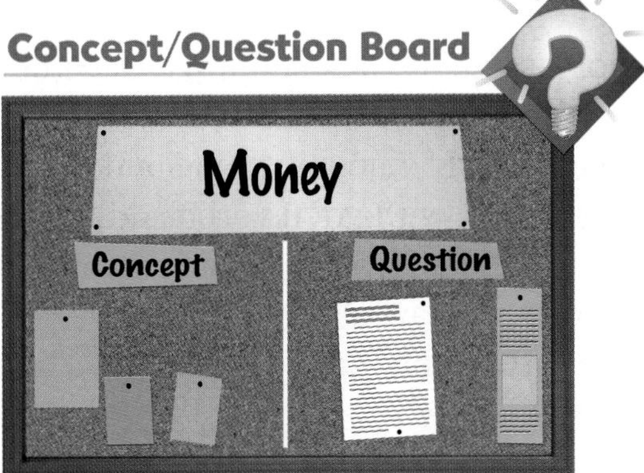


## Unit 4 Investigation Management

| | |
|---|---|
| Lesson 1 | Brainstorm questions related to the theme. Investigate alternatives to money, such as barter. |
| Lesson 2 | Groups form based on areas of shared interest. Investigate choices related to spending and saving money. |
| Lesson 3 | Begin forming conjectures. Brainstorm about how to turn hobbies into businesses. |
| Lesson 4 | Discuss conjectures in groups and begin plans. Look for stories or illustrations about the ways that money can change people and things that money cannot buy. |
| Lesson 5 | **Collaborative Investigation** **Students revise their plans as necessary and continue investigations.** **Supplementary Activity** **Groups can debate on borrowing and lending money.** |
| Lesson 6 | Continue investigations and prepare final presentations. Create a story or miniplay about how money passes from person to person, or plan a field trip to a Federal Reserve Bank. |
| Lesson 7 | Groups give formal presentations. Students discuss saving money for personal goals or investigate the Great Depression further. |

**Teacher Tip** Continue to encourage use of the Concept/Question Board by recognizing and thanking students for their contributions. Incorporate discussion of those items into classroom discussions whenever appropriate.

### Research Assistant

The ***Research Assistant CD-ROM*** can assist students in their investigations.

**Teacher Tip** At this point in the year, students should move through the investigation process more readily. Encourage them to take risks, such as changing their conjectures, as they discover new ideas about money.

**Formal Assessment**

Use the Research Rubrics on page 58J to assess students' ability to find needed information.

**DIFFERENTIATING INSTRUCTION**

| If... | Then... |
|---|---|
| Students are having difficulty assigning individual jobs | Help groups assign tasks related to each member's strengths and preferences during Workshop |

**Teacher Tip** As students are choosing sources for their investigations, remind them to keep in mind their personal interests, knowledge of authors, and the need to choose information from a variety of texts and types of media.

INVESTIGATION

## Needs and Plans Phase 2/Reevaluating Problems and Questions

Before the investigation groups meet to settle on definite investigation plans, conduct a whole-class discussion to help identify groups that need help. Some students might be having trouble identifying knowledge needs related to their conjectures. Additionally, remind investigation groups that they can still change their investigation problems. Some groups may have discovered by this time that their problem is not very promising. A group may choose to keep the same general problem but reformulate it more precisely. Some students might want to change groups because they have become more interested in the problem of another group.

Assign page 99 of the ***Inquiry Journal*** to be completed after each planning group has agreed on a final statement of its problem, its knowledge needs, and its individual job assignments. As you observe the groups making their job assignments, encourage the students to take on tasks that are related to their strengths and likings. For example, a student who loves to draw might particularly enjoy planning and making the visual portion of the investigations. A student with good verbal skills might benefit from conducting interviews, while a less verbal student might primarily contribute information located in books, magazines, and other references. Whatever the job assignment, it is important that each student have a significant role in the group.

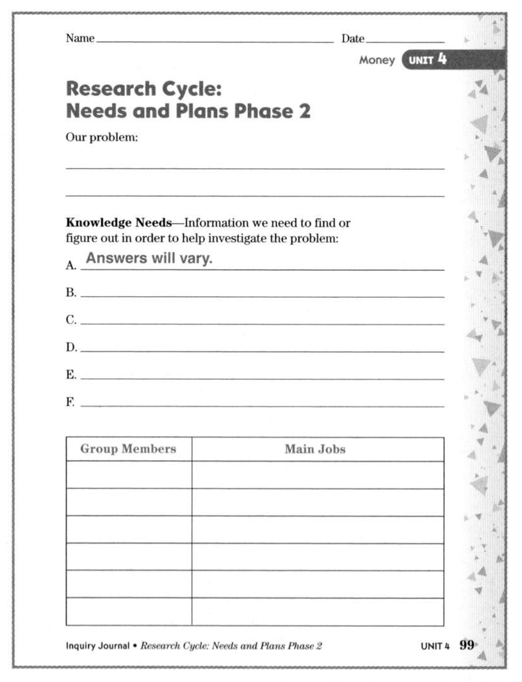
Name ______ Date ______

Money UNIT 4

**Research Cycle: Needs and Plans Phase 2**

Our problem:

**Knowledge Needs**—Information we need to find or figure out in order to help investigate the problem:

A. Answers will vary.

B.

C.

D.

E.

F.

| Group Members | Main Jobs |
|---|---|
| | |
| | |
| | |
| | |
| | |
| | |

Inquiry Journal • *Research Cycle: Needs and Plans Phase 2* UNIT 4 99

***Inquiry Journal* p. 99**

SUPPORTING THE INVESTIGATION

## Compare Information Across Sources

**Teach** Provide students with different sources, such as encyclopedias, biographies, magazines, and technology resources. Ask students why they might need more than one source of information when investigating. Point out, if necessary, that good writers use the most reliable sources available, and that cross-checking between sources is sometimes necessary. Tell students that they can make sure their sources are reliable by considering the following points:

- Is the source written by an expert? Book jackets and notes at the beginning or the end of articles sometimes give information about the authors.
- Is the source up to date? Would another source be more up to date?
- Is the information detailed enough?
- Is the information relevant to their topic?

**Guided Practice** Ask each student to choose a famous person that he or she admires. Have students use multiple sources to answer the following questions:

- What is (or was) this person really like? What character traits does (or did) this person have?
- What evidence supports this?
- In what source or sources did you find this evidence?

**Independent Practice** Invite students to write a paragraph about the person they chose, focusing on character traits that they discovered in their investigations. For additional practice, have students complete ***Inquiry Journal,*** pages 100–101.

Name ______ Date ______

UNIT 4 Money

### Comparing Information Across Sources

Good writers use the most reliable sources available. To make sure that information is correct, cross-checking between sources is sometimes necessary.

To make sure that your sources are reliable, consider the following points:

- Is the source written by an expert? Book jackets and notes at the beginning or end of articles sometimes give information about the authors.
- Is the source up-to-date? Would another source be more up-to-date?
- Is the information detailed enough?
- Is the information relevant to the topic?

Sources you might have used:

| | | |
|---|---|---|
| Encyclopedias | Books | Magazines |
| Newspapers | Videos | Interviews |
| Personal Experiences | Museums | Internet |

100 UNIT 4 *Comparing Information Across Sources* • Inquiry Journal

**Comparing Information Across Sources** *(continued)*

Think about your unit investigation. On the lines below, list the sources that you are using. Then, write what other sources you can use to check the information that you received from the original sources.

Source used: Answers will vary.
Sources to check against: ______

Source used: ______
Sources to check against: ______

Source used: ______
Sources to check against: ______

Source used: ______
Sources to check against: ______

Source used: ______
Sources to check against: ______

Inquiry Journal • *Comparing Information Across Sources* UNIT 4 101

***Inquiry Journal pp. 100–101***

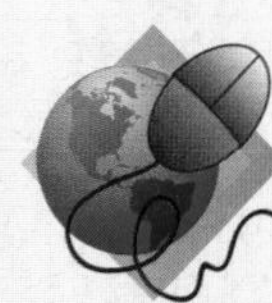

**Teacher Tip** Remind students about the difference between primary and secondary sources.

**www.sra4kids.com**
**Web Connection**
Students may wish to use the Money connections found on the Reading Web site.

Encourage students to use ***TechKnowledge*** to learn more about how to use a computer to complete various investigation tasks.

### Differentiating Instruction

| If... | Then... |
|---|---|
| Students are having difficulty with the Inquiry activities | • Help them brainstorm a list of famous people they admire and find interesting<br>• Help them find reliable sources consistent with their reading levels |

**Teacher Tip** As students are choosing sources for their investigations, encourage them to sort the information they are gathering based on its relevance and appropriateness to their investigation purposes and reading tasks. Remind students also to use text features of nonfiction, such as headings, subheading, bold print, and italics, to locate information.

## Objectives

**Word Analysis**

**Spelling**

- **Adding -s or -es.** Develop understanding of how to add -s or -es to make words plural.

**Vocabulary**

- **Compound Words.** Using words from "Four Dollars and Fifty Cents," learn the meanings of compound words in the context of the Old West.

**Writing Process Strategies**

- **Persuasive Writing: Friendly Letter.** Building on the theme of Money, learn the form and function of writing a persuasive friendly letter.

**English Language Conventions**

**Grammar, Usage, and Mechanics**

- **Subject/Verb Agreement: Singular and Plural; Regular and Irregular.** Understand and identify subject/verb agreement of regular, irregular, singular, and plural verbs. Identify subject/verb agreement in "Four Dollars and Fifty Cents."

**Listening, Speaking, Viewing**

- **Interacting: Conversations.** Develop conversation skills through participating in group discussions.

**Penmanship**

- **Cursive Letters *U* and *Y*.** Develop handwriting skills by practicing formation of cursive *U* and *Y*.

## Materials

- Spelling and Vocabulary Skills, pp. 90–93
- Language Arts Handbook
- Comprehension and Language Arts Skills, pp. 112–115
- Writer's Workbook, pp. 70–73
- Language Arts Transparency 22
- Student Anthology

## Differentiating Instruction

***Reteach, Challenge,*** and ***Intervention*** lessons are available to support the language arts instruction in this lesson.

## Research in Action

The goal of teaching handwriting is to help children write *legibly* and *comfortably.* Effective writing must be readable in order to convey a message, but it must be done without frustrating or fatiguing the writer.
*(Charles Temple and Jean Wallace Gillet,* Language Arts: Learning Processes and Teaching Practices)

OVERVIEW

# Language Arts Overview

## Word Analysis

**Spelling** The Spelling activities on the following pages introduce how to make base words plural, meaning more than one, by adding the ending *-s* or *-es.* The ending *-s* is added to most words to make them plural. The ending *-es* is added to words that end in *ch, sh, s, ss, x, z,* or *zz.*

### Selection Spelling Words

These words from "Four Dollars and Fifty Cents" are plural with the ending *-s* or *-es.*

**dollars horses sleeves cowboys britches**

**Vocabulary** The Vocabulary activities introduce how a compound word is formed from two words. A compound word can have the same meaning as the two words in it, as in *bedroom,* or it can have a new meaning, as in *jellyfish.*

### Vocabulary Skill Words

**blackshmith* buckboard rawhide sagebrush padlock**

**Also Selection Vocabulary*

**Additional Materials:** dictionary

## Writing Process Strategies

The Writing Process Strategies lesson involves instruction in writing a persuasive friendly letter to an adult audience. The format and tone of a friendly letter will be addressed, as well as instruction in using facts, reasons, and feelings to persuade.

To teach spreadsheet applications in the writing process, show students how to modify a spreadsheet by deleting a column of data. ***TechKnowledge,*** Level 3, Lesson 71, teaches these spreadsheet application skills.

## English Language Conventions

**Grammar, Usage, and Mechanics** **Subject/Verb Agreement: Singular and Plural; Regular and Irregular.** This lesson develops an understanding of subject/verb agreement with regular, irregular, singular and plural verbs.

**Listening, Speaking, Viewing** **Interacting: Conversations.** In this Interacting lesson, students will develop conversation skills through participating in group discussions.

**Penmanship** **Cursive Letters *U* and *Y*.** This lesson develops handwriting skills by having students learn formation of *U* and *Y.* Students then write words from the literature selection.

# DAY 1

## Word Analysis

### Spelling

#### Assessment: Pretest

**Adding -s and -es**

#### Teach

Give students the Pretest on page 38 of ***Unit 4 Assessment.*** Have them proofread and correct any misspelled words.

**Pretest Sentences**

1. **berries** Some **berries** found on bushes are poisonous.
2. **bunnies** Small **bunnies** are cute.
3. **guppies** Small fish are **guppies**.
4. **hobbies** Quilting, painting, and fishing are **hobbies**.
5. **pennies** People throw **pennies** into fountains.
6. **puppies** Young dogs are called **puppies**.
7. **ponies** Shetland **ponies** are strong.
8. **babies** Young **babies** drink milk.
9. **donkeys** Most **donkeys** are tame.
10. **families** Some **families** join together for reunions.
11. **dollars** A five-dollar bill is equal to five **dollars**.
12. **horses** Stallions are **horses**.
13. **sleeves** Arms fit into **sleeves**.
14. **cowboys** In the Old West, **cowboys** rode on horses.
15. **britches** Most **britches** are long.

Diagnose any misspellings by determining whether students misspelled the way the ending was added or some other part of the word. Then, have the students use the Pretest as a take-home list to study the ways *-s* and *-es* are added to words to make them plural.

## Writing Process Strategies

### Getting Ideas

**Persuasive Friendly Letter**

#### Teach

**Review Friendly Letters**

- Read ***Language Arts Handbook,*** pages 68–71, to review the form and function of a friendly letter.
- Read ***Language Arts Handbook,*** pages 156–157, to review persuasive writing.
- Discuss ***Language Arts Transparency 22,*** Revising: Ideas.
- Share the formal assessment rubrics with students. (See Day 5 of this lesson.)

**Inspiration**

Teacher Model: *"I think my brother should pay back the money he owes me, and I am going to write him a letter telling him so."*

**Brainstorming**

Encourage students to name situations in which money has been a problem. Make a list of these ideas on the board.

#### Guided Practice

**Getting Ideas**

Have students write ideas for a persuasive friendly letter in their Writer's Notebooks.

**Friendly Letters**

A **friendly letter** is a letter you write to a relative or a friend. It's also a letter you write to someone you would like to get to know. Friendly letters can be written to a pen pal. They can also be written to a favorite author, actor, actress, or athlete.

Friendly letters help you share news, stories, and thoughts. They help you start or continue friendships with people who live far away.

**The Parts of a Friendly Letter**

Heading

The *heading* is your address and the date. The heading goes in the upper right corner of the friendly letter.

Greeting

The *greeting* tells who will receive the letter. Many greetings begin with *Dear,* but you can also use words like *Hi.* Put a comma after the person's name.

Body

The *body* is the main part of the letter. This is where you write the news, stories, and thoughts you want to tell.

Closing

The *closing* lets the person know you are ending the letter. Words like *Love, Your friend,* and *Sincerely* are often used as closings. Be sure to put a comma after the closing.

Signature

The *signature* is your name.

68 Friendly Letters ▲ Personal Writing

***Language Arts Handbook* p. 68**

## English Language Conventions

### Grammar, Usage, and Mechanics

**Usage: Subject/Verb Agreement: Singular and Plural; Regular and Irregular**

#### Teach

- **Review** the concepts of sentences, subjects, and verbs. Ask students what they know and fill in any gaps. Reference ***Language Arts Handbook,*** pages 176 and 250–251.
- Use ***Language Arts Handbook,*** page 264, for definitions and examples of subject/verb agreement with regular verbs.
- Write the sentences below on the board. Ask students to identify which sentences have subject/verb agreement.
  - *He take a nap at noon.* (No agreement)
  - *Lydia has a camper.* (Subject, "Lydia," agrees with verb, "has")
  - *They was flying over New York.* (No agreement)
- Read ***Language Arts Handbook,*** page 265, on subject/verb agreement of irregular verbs.

#### Independent Practice

Use ***Comprehension and Language Arts Skills,*** pages 112–113, to identify subject/verb agreement.

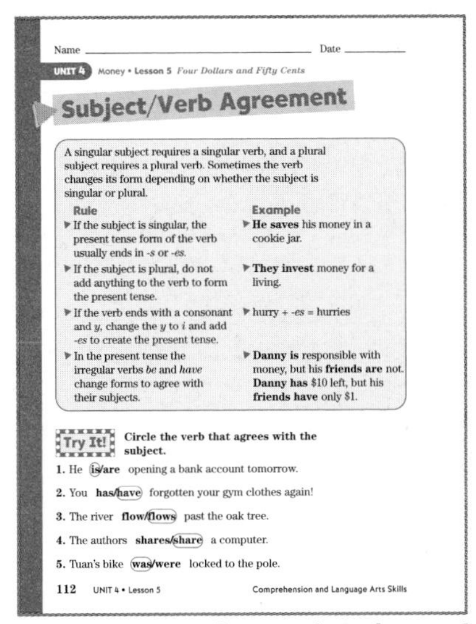

Name ______________ Date ________

UNIT 4 Money • Lesson 5 *Four Dollars and Fifty Cents*

**Subject/Verb Agreement**

A singular subject requires a singular verb, and a plural subject requires a plural verb. Sometimes the verb changes its form depending on whether the subject is singular or plural.

| Rule | Example |
|---|---|
| If the subject is singular, the present tense form of the verb usually ends in *-s* or *-es*. | **He saves** his money in a cookie jar. |
| If the subject is plural, do not add anything to the verb to form the present tense. | **They invest** money for a living. |
| If the verb ends with a consonant and *y*, change the *y* to *i* and add *-es* to create the present tense. | hurry + *-es* = hurries |
| In the present tense the irregular verbs *be* and *have* change forms to agree with their subjects. | **Danny is** responsible with money, but his **friends are** not. **Danny has** $10 left, but his **friends have** only $1. |

**Try It!** **Circle the verb that agrees with the subject.**

1. He **is/are** opening a bank account tomorrow.
2. You **has/have** forgotten your gym clothes again!
3. The river **flow/flows** past the oak tree.
4. The authors **shares/share** a computer.
5. Tuan's bike **was/were** locked to the pole.

112 UNIT 4 • Lesson 5 Comprehension and Language Arts Skills

***Comprehension and Language Arts Skills* p. 112**

# DAY 2

## Word Analysis

### Spelling

**Adding -s or -es**

#### Board Work

- Write *baby* on the board. Explain that *plural* means "more than one." When a word ends in *consonant-y,* change *y* to *i,* and add *-es* to make a plural word. Write *babies.* If a word ends in *vowel-y,* just add *-s.* Write the plural of *donkey* on the board. *(donkeys)*

### Vocabulary

**Compound Words**

#### Teach

- Write *sagebrush* (p. 60) on the board. Explain that *sagebrush* is made from *sage* and *brush.* A compound word is formed from two words.
- Ask a student to find *sage* and *brush* in a dictionary *(a wise person* or *an herb; a bush* or *a tool for hair).* Explain that *sagebrush* has a new meaning *(a plant with silver leaves and yellow flowers).*

#### Guided Practice

Use ***Spelling and Vocabulary Skills,*** page 90, to teach the meanings of compound words. Ask students to complete page 91 as independent practice.

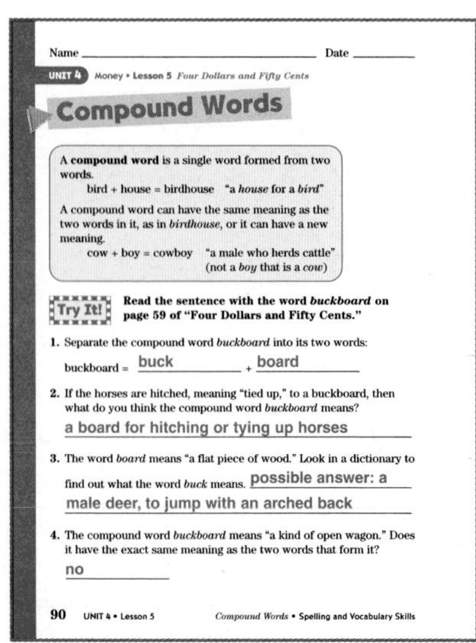

Name ____________ Date ______

UNIT 4 Money • Lesson 5 *Four Dollars and Fifty Cents*

**Compound Words**

A **compound word** is a single word formed from two words.
bird + house = birdhouse "a *house* for a *bird*"

A compound word can have the same meaning as the two words in it, as in *birdhouse,* or it can have a new meaning.
cow + boy = cowboy "a male who herds cattle" (not a *boy* that is a *cow*)

Try It! **Read the sentence with the word *buckboard* on page 59 of "Four Dollars and Fifty Cents."**

1. Separate the compound word *buckboard* into its two words:
buckboard = buck + board
2. If the horses are hitched, meaning "tied up," to a buckboard, then what do you think the compound word *buckboard* means?
a board for hitching or tying up horses
3. The word *board* means "a flat piece of wood." Look in a dictionary to find out what the word *buck* means. possible answer: a male deer, to jump with an arched back
4. The compound word *buckboard* means "a kind of open wagon." Does it have the exact same meaning as the two words that form it?
no

90 UNIT 4 • Lesson 5 *Compound Words* • Spelling and Vocabulary Skills

***Spelling and Vocabulary Skills p. 90***

## Writing Process Strategies

#### Prewriting

**Persuasive Friendly Letter**

#### Teach

- Read ***Writer's Workbook,*** page 70, on prewriting for a persuasive friendly letter.
- **Review** the ideas students generated for persuasive friendly letters on Day 1.

Writer's Craft

**Sentence Combining**

- Write two short sentences with related ideas on the chalkboard, such as "Mary is tall. She plays basketball."
- Model for students how the sentences can sound more fluent by combining them. *"Mary is tall, and she plays basketball."*
- Read ***Language Arts Handbook,*** pages 178–179, on combining sentences.
- Read ***Comprehension and Language Arts Skills,*** pages 114–115, on sentence combining.

#### Independent Practice

**Prewriting**

- Have students write their audience and purpose on the appropriate lines of ***Writer's Workbook,*** page 70.
- Have students complete the graphic organizer on ***Writer's Workbook,*** page 71.

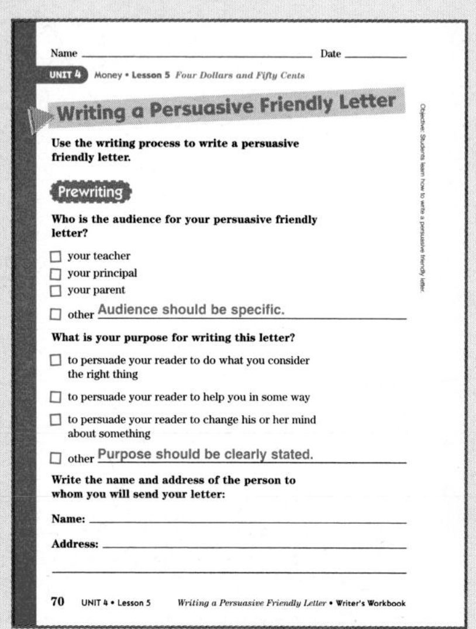

Name ____________ Date ______

UNIT 4 Money • Lesson 5 *Four Dollars and Fifty Cents*

**Writing a Persuasive Friendly Letter**

**Use the writing process to write a persuasive friendly letter.**

Prewriting

**Who is the audience for your persuasive friendly letter?**

- ☐ your teacher
- ☐ your principal
- ☐ your parent
- ☐ other Audience should be specific.

**What is your purpose for writing this letter?**

- ☐ to persuade your reader to do what you consider the right thing
- ☐ to persuade your reader to help you in some way
- ☐ to persuade your reader to change his or her mind about something
- ☐ other Purpose should be clearly stated.

**Write the name and address of the person to whom you will send your letter:**

**Name:** ____________

**Address:** ____________

Objective: Students learn how to write a persuasive friendly letter.

70 UNIT 4 • Lesson 5 *Writing a Persuasive Friendly Letter* • Writer's Workbook

***Writer's Workbook p. 70***

## English Language Conventions

#### Grammar, Usage, and Mechanics

**Usage: Subject/Verb Agreement: Singular and Plural; Regular and Irregular**

#### Teach

- Review subject/verb agreement using ***Language Arts Handbook,*** page 264.
- Write the following sentences on the board. Have students come up and correct them.
  - Many inventions helps people. *(Many inventions help people.)*
  - The inventor work all day. *(The inventor worked all day.)*
  - Joseph makes invention in his garage. *(Joseph makes inventions in his garage.)*
  - Thomas Edison's inventions is numerous. *(Thomas Edison's inventions are numerous.)*
- Use ***Language Arts Handbook,*** page 265, for subject/verb agreement of irregular verbs. Ask students to make up sentences that have subject/verb agreement using the verbs *be* and *have.* Ask them to come up with some that are past tense and some that are present tense. Write these sentences on the board as examples.
  - I had my tonsils removed. *(past tense of* have; *subject* I *agrees with verb* had*)*
  - The houses are falling over. *(present tense of* be; *subject* houses *agrees with verb* are*)*

#### Guided Practice in Reading

Put students into small groups. Have them identify subject/verb agreements in "Four Dollars and Fifty Cents."

# DAY 3

## Word Analysis

### Spelling

**Adding -s or -es**

#### Teach

Introduce the spelling words *horses* and *britches.* Ask students if they know the idioms "You bet your *britches*" or "Hold your *horses.*" Discuss how idioms do not have literal meanings. Ask students for other idioms that use plural words. *(raining cats and dogs)*

#### Guided Practice

Have students complete page 92 from ***Spelling and Vocabulary Skills*** to learn strategies for spelling plural words.

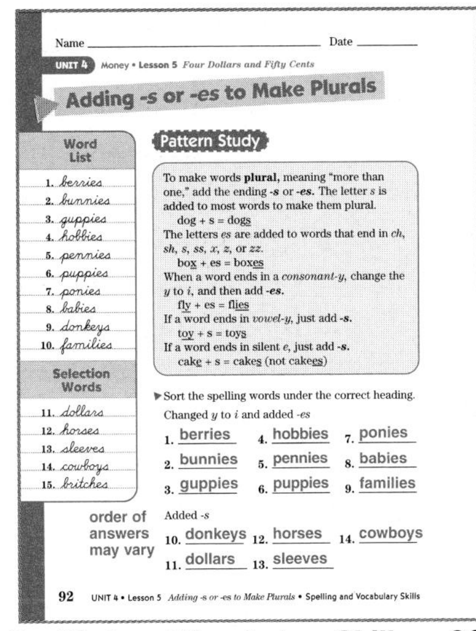

Name ______________ Date ________

UNIT 4 Money • Lesson 5 *Four Dollars and Fifty Cents*

**Adding -s or -es to Make Plurals**

**Word List**

1. berries
2. bunnies
3. guppies
4. hobbies
5. pennies
6. puppies
7. ponies
8. babies
9. donkeys
10. families

**Selection Words**

11. dollars
12. horses
13. sleeves
14. cowboys
15. britches

**Pattern Study**

To make words **plural,** meaning "more than one," add the ending **-s** or **-es.** The letter *s* is added to most words to make them plural.
dog + s = dogs
The letters *es* are added to words that end in *ch, sh, s, ss, x, z,* or *zz.*
box + es = boxes
When a word ends in a *consonant-y,* change the *y* to *i,* and then add **-es.**
fly + es = flies
If a word ends in *vowel-y,* just add **-s.**
toy + s = toys
If a word ends in silent *e,* just add **-s.**
cake + s = cakes (not cakees)

▶ Sort the spelling words under the correct heading.

Changed *y* to *i* and added *-es*

1. berries 4. hobbies 7. ponies
2. bunnies 5. pennies 8. babies
3. guppies 6. puppies 9. families

Added *-s*

10. donkeys 12. horses 14. cowboys
11. dollars 13. sleeves

order of answers may vary

92 UNIT 4 • Lesson 5 *Adding -s or -es to Make Plurals* • Spelling and Vocabulary Skills

***Spelling and Vocabulary Skills* p. 92**

### Vocabulary (continued)

**Compound Words**

Write *blacksmith* on the board. Ask a student to write the words that form *blacksmith (black, smith).* Explain that *black* relates to hot black coals that heat and shape iron. Explain that *smith* means "one who works with metal." Ask a student to explain what the *blacksmith* does for a living *(he heats and shapes iron).* Have students write notes on compound words for future reference.

## Writing Process Strategies

### Drafting

**Persuasive Friendly Letter**

#### Teach

- Review with students how to combine sentences.
- Read ***Writer's Workbook,*** page 71, on drafting a persuasive friendly letter. Encourage students to review the information they recorded in their graphic organizers on Day 2.
- Review with students ways to get the most out of the drafting process, such as skipping lines, circling words they may change, and leaving a blank when they cannot think of a word. Ask students to share any other hints they have that help them.

#### Guided Practice

**Drafting**

- Have students draft their letters and put them in their ***Writing Folders,*** keeping in mind that they will go back later to revise, edit, and recopy them.
- If you have computers in the classroom, you may want to give students the option of using word processing software to write their drafts.

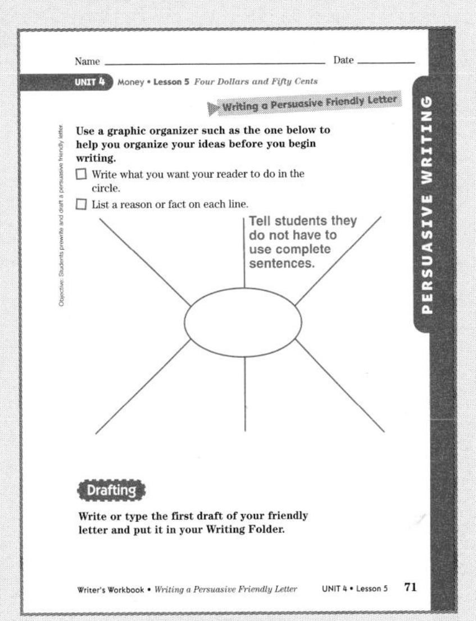

Name ______________ Date ________

UNIT 4 Money • Lesson 5 *Four Dollars and Fifty Cents*

**Writing a Persuasive Friendly Letter**

PERSUASIVE WRITING

Objective: Students prewrite and draft a persuasive friendly letter.

**Use a graphic organizer such as the one below to help you organize your ideas before you begin writing.**

☐ Write what you want your reader to do in the circle.

☐ List a reason or fact on each line.

Tell students they do not have to use complete sentences.

**Drafting**

**Write or type the first draft of your friendly letter and put it in your Writing Folder.**

Writer's Workbook • *Writing a Persuasive Friendly Letter* UNIT 4 • Lesson 5 71

***Writer's Workbook* p. 71**

## English Language Conventions

### Grammar, Usage, and Mechanics

**Usage: Subject/Verb Agreement: Singular and Plural; Regular and Irregular**

#### Teach

- Review subject/verb agreement using ***Comprehension and Language Arts Skills,*** pages 112–113.
- Write the following words on the board and ask students to write short sentences using them.
  - *buy, buys*
  - *is, are*
  - *has, have*
  - *wish, wishes*
  - *was, were*
- Have some students read their sentences out loud.

#### Guided Practice in Writing

Have students write a friendly letter to Shorty from "Four Dollars and Fifty Cents," persuading him to pay Widow Macrae back. Instruct them to include good reasons why he should pay her back.

**Informal Assessment**

Check students' writing for correct subject/verb agreement.

# DAY 4

## Word Analysis

### Spelling

**Adding -s or -es**

#### Teach

Explain that these exercises in ***Spelling and Vocabulary Skills*** are designed to help them learn to become better spellers of plural words.

#### Guided Practice

Have students complete page 93 of ***Spelling and Vocabulary Skills*** to reinforce how to spell plural words.

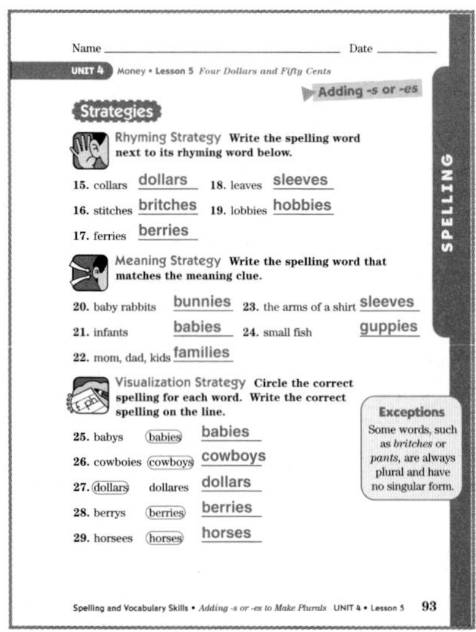

Name ____________ Date ______

UNIT 4 Money • Lesson 5 *Four Dollars and Fifty Cents*

Adding -s or -es

SPELLING

**Strategies**

Rhyming Strategy **Write the spelling word next to its rhyming word below.**

15. collars dollars
16. stitches britches
17. ferries berries
18. leaves sleeves
19. lobbies hobbies

Meaning Strategy **Write the spelling word that matches the meaning clue.**

20. baby rabbits bunnies
21. infants babies
22. mom, dad, kids families
23. the arms of a shirt sleeves
24. small fish guppies

Visualization Strategy **Circle the correct spelling for each word. Write the correct spelling on the line.**

25. babys (babies) babies
26. cowboies (cowboys) cowboys
27. (dollars) dollares dollars
28. berrys (berries) berries
29. horsees (horses) horses

**Exceptions**
Some words, such as *britches* or *pants*, are always plural and have no singular form.

Spelling and Vocabulary Skills • *Adding -s or -es to Make Plurals* UNIT 4 • Lesson 5 93

***Spelling and Vocabulary Skills* p. 93**

### Vocabulary (continued)

**Compound Words**

- Write *padlock* ("Four Dollars and Fifty Cents," p. 65) on the board.
- Ask what a *lock* is *(a fastener with a key or combination)*. Ask a student to find *pad* in a dictionary *(material for protection or comfort)*. Have a student find *padlock* in a dictionary *(a lock with a U-shaped bar that is hinged at one end)*. Discuss how the words that make *padlock* help explain its meaning *(a padlock is a lock to protect something)*.

## Writing Process Strategies

### Revising

**Persuasive Friendly Letter**

#### Teach

Read ***Writer's Workbook,*** page 72, on revising a persuasive friendly letter.

**Troubleshooting**

- Your letter sounds too familiar or demanding. You must always remember that you do not want to insult your reader. Your tone should be informal, but polite.
- The main idea is unclear or missing. Your topic sentence should clearly state the main idea of your letter. It should leave no doubt in your reader's mind what you are trying to say.
- Unimportant or unrelated information has been added. Your reader will probably get confused.
- Words are misspelled. You should always try your best to spell words correctly, then recheck your spelling later.

#### Guided Practice

**Revising**

- Have students revise their letters and put them in their ***Writing Folders.***
- Have students use the checklist on ***Writer's Workbook,*** page 72, to revise their persuasive friendly letters.

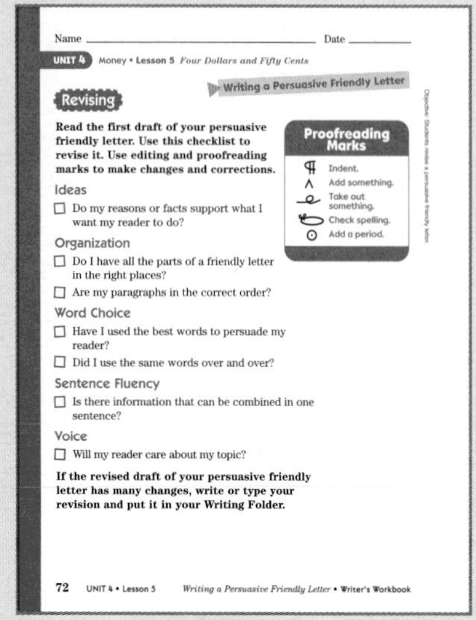

Name ____________ Date ______

UNIT 4 Money • Lesson 5 *Four Dollars and Fifty Cents*

Writing a Persuasive Friendly Letter

**Revising**

**Read the first draft of your persuasive friendly letter. Use this checklist to revise it. Use editing and proofreading marks to make changes and corrections.**

Ideas
- ☐ Do my reasons or facts support what I want my reader to do?

Organization
- ☐ Do I have all the parts of a friendly letter in the right places?
- ☐ Are my paragraphs in the correct order?

Word Choice
- ☐ Have I used the best words to persuade my reader?
- ☐ Did I use the same words over and over?

Sentence Fluency
- ☐ Is there information that can be combined in one sentence?

Voice
- ☐ Will my reader care about my topic?

**If the revised draft of your persuasive friendly letter has many changes, write or type your revision and put it in your Writing Folder.**

**Proofreading Marks**
¶ Indent.
∧ Add something.
Take out something.
Check spelling.
⊙ Add a period.

Objective: Students revise a persuasive friendly letter.

72 UNIT 4 • Lesson 5 *Writing a Persuasive Friendly Letter* • Writer's Workbook

***Writer's Workbook* p. 72**

## English Language Conventions

### Listening, Speaking, Viewing

**Interacting: Conversations**

#### Teach

- Explain what kinds of problems Shorty created by not paying back his debts. He inconvenienced a lot of people who depended on his money, he made people mad at him, and he had to waste a lot of time and energy to avoid the people he owed.

#### Guided Practice

- In small groups, have students share a time when they let someone borrow something. What happened? Did they get it back? Remind students to take turns speaking and listening, and to be considerate of one another.
- Remind the groups to make an effort to include each of its members in the conversation. Students should participate in the discussion by developing and presenting their ideas and asking and responding to questions. Tell students to also provide supportive verbal and nonverbal cues to participants during the conversation. Explain that these cues, such as asking questions and eye contact, will encourage the exchange of ideas and opinions.

**Informal Assessment**

Observe whether students engage in conversation and use strategies to ask and respond to questions.

# DAY 5

## Word Analysis

### Spelling

#### Assessment: Final Test

**Adding -s and -es**

#### Teach

Repeat the Pretest or use the Final Test on page 39 of ***Unit 4 Assessment*** as summative assessment of student understanding of spelling patterns for plurals.

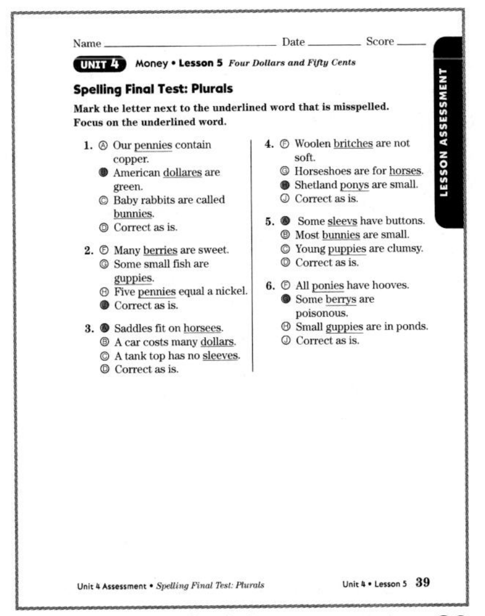

Name ______________ Date ________ Score ______

UNIT 4 Money • Lesson 5 *Four Dollars and Fifty Cents*

**Spelling Final Test: Plurals**

**Mark the letter next to the underlined word that is misspelled. Focus on the underlined word.**

1. Ⓐ Our pennies contain copper.
   ● American dollares are green.
   Ⓒ Baby rabbits are called bunnies.
   Ⓓ Correct as is.
2. Ⓕ Many berries are sweet.
   Ⓖ Some small fish are guppies.
   Ⓗ Five pennies equal a nickel.
   ● Correct as is.
3. ● Saddles fit on horsees.
   Ⓑ A car costs many dollars.
   Ⓒ A tank top has no sleeves.
   Ⓓ Correct as is.
4. Ⓕ Woolen britches are not soft.
   Ⓖ Horseshoes are for horses.
   ● Shetland ponys are small.
   Ⓙ Correct as is.
5. ● Some sleevs have buttons.
   Ⓑ Most bunnies are small.
   Ⓒ Young puppies are clumsy.
   Ⓓ Correct as is.
6. Ⓕ All ponies have hooves.
   ● Some berrys are poisonous.
   Ⓗ Small guppies are in ponds.
   Ⓙ Correct as is.

LESSON ASSESSMENT

Unit 4 Assessment • *Spelling Final Test: Plurals* Unit 4 • Lesson 5 39

***Unit 4 Assessment* p. 39**

#### Guided Practice

Have students categorize any mistakes they made on the Final Test as careless errors or lesson-pattern problems.

### Vocabulary

#### Informal Assessment

Ask how the meanings of *safe* and *keeping,* that form *safekeeping* learned in Lesson 4, help explain the meaning of the compound word. *(safekeeping is keeping something safe)* Have students add any new words to the running Vocabulary Word List in the Writer's Notebook.

## Writing Process Strategies

### Editing/Proofreading and Publishing

**Persuasive Friendly Letter**

#### Teach

Read ***Writer's Workbook,*** page 73, on editing/proofreading and publishing a persuasive friendly letter.

#### Guided Practice

**Editing/Proofreading and Publishing**

- Have students edit/proofread their writing.
- Direct students to use the checklist on ***Writer's Workbook,*** page 73, to help them edit/proofread.
- Refer to the ***Grammar, Usage, and Mechanics*** agreement lesson on page 71F.
- Have students produce a clean copy of their persuasive friendly letter using their best cursive handwriting.

#### Formal Assessment

Total Point Value: 10

1. The writer's main idea is in the topic sentence. (2 points)
2. All facts or feelings support the main idea. (2 points)
3. All parts of a friendly letter are included. (2 points)
4. Sentences read fluently. (2 points)
5. Mechanics are correct. (2 points)

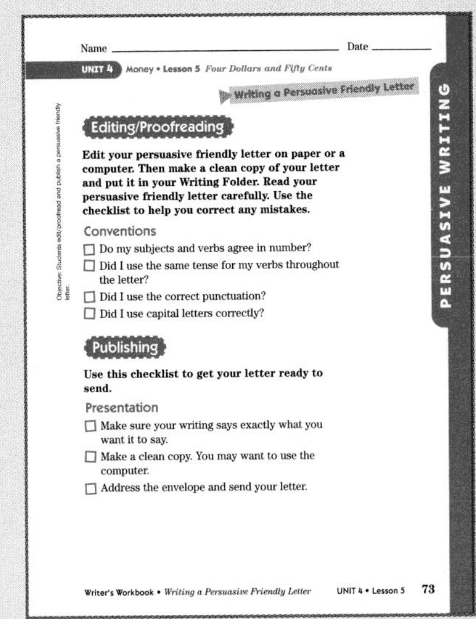

Name ______________ Date ________

UNIT 4 Money • Lesson 5 *Four Dollars and Fifty Cents*

Writing a Persuasive Friendly Letter

Objective: Students edit/proofread and publish a persuasive friendly letter.

**Editing/Proofreading**

**Edit your persuasive friendly letter on paper or a computer. Then make a clean copy of your letter and put it in your Writing Folder. Read your persuasive friendly letter carefully. Use the checklist to help you correct any mistakes.**

Conventions

- ☐ Do my subjects and verbs agree in number?
- ☐ Did I use the same tense for my verbs throughout the letter?
- ☐ Did I use the correct punctuation?
- ☐ Did I use capital letters correctly?

**Publishing**

**Use this checklist to get your letter ready to send.**

Presentation

- ☐ Make sure your writing says exactly what you want it to say.
- ☐ Make a clean copy. You may want to use the computer.
- ☐ Address the envelope and send your letter.

PERSUASIVE WRITING

Writer's Workbook • *Writing a Persuasive Friendly Letter* UNIT 4 • Lesson 5 73

***Writer's Workbook* p. 73**

## English Language Conventions

### Penmanship

**Cursive Letters *U* and *Y***

#### Teach

- **Teacher Model:** Introduce formation of uppercase *U* and *Y* as curve forward letters by demonstrating on the board.

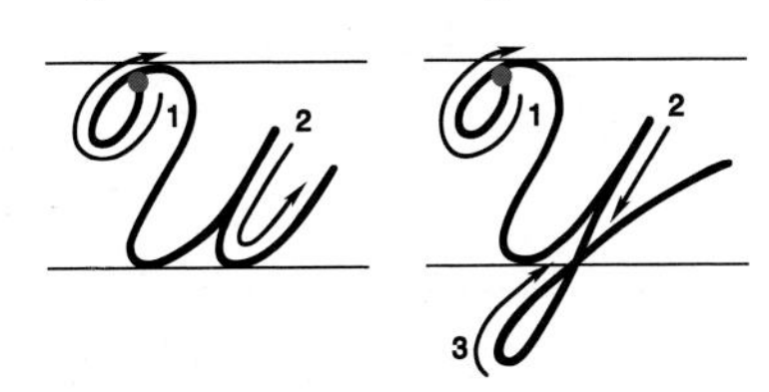

**U** Starting point, loop
Curve forward, slant into undercurve
Slant down, undercurve: capital *U*

**Y** Starting point, loop
Curve forward, slant down
Undercurve, slant down
Loop back, overcurve: capital *Y*

- **Teacher Model:** Write the following sentence to model proper letter formation: "Yuri visited the United States."
- Draw circles between the words to demonstrate proper spacing.

#### Guided Practice

- Have students practice writing rows of *U*s and *Y*s in their Writer's Notebooks.
- From "Four Dollars and Fifty Cents," have students write the following sentence to practice letter formation: "Yahoo! We struck it rich!"
- Have students draw circles between their words to check for proper spacing.

#### Informal Assessment

Check students' handwriting for proper formation of *U* and *Y* and space between words.

# Reading and Language Arts Skills Traces

## Language Arts

### WORD ANALYSIS

Skills Trace

**Spelling: Adding -s or -es**

Introduced in Grade 1.
Scaffolded throughout Grades 2–5.

**REINTRODUCED:** Unit 4, Lesson 5, p. 71E
**PRACTICED:** Unit 4, Lesson 5, pp. 71F–71J
*Spelling and Vocabulary Skills,* pp. 92–93
**TESTED:** Unit 4, Lesson 5, p. 71F (Pretest)
Unit 4, Lesson 5, p. 39 (Final Test)
Unit 4 Assessment

Skills Trace

**Vocabulary: Compound Words**

Introduced in Grade 1.
Scaffolded throughout Grades 2–5.

**REINTRODUCED:** Unit 4, Lesson 5, p. 71E
**PRACTICED:** Unit 4, Lesson 5, pp. 71G–71J
*Spelling and Vocabulary Skills,* pp. 90–91
**TESTED:** Unit 4 Assessment

### WRITING PROCESS STRATEGIES

Skills Trace

**Persuasive Writing: Persuasive Friendly Letter**

Introduced in Grade 1.
Scaffolded throughout Grades 2–6.

**REINTRODUCED:** Unit 4, Lesson 5, p. 71F
**PRACTICED:** Unit 4, Lesson 5, pp. 71G–71J
*Writer's Workbook,* pp. 70–73
**TESTED:** Unit 4, Lesson 5, Formal Assessment, p. 71J
Unit 4 Assessment

Skills Trace

**Writer's Craft: Sentence Combining**

Introduced in Grade 1.
Scaffolded throughout Grades 2–6.

**REINTRODUCED:** Unit 4, Lesson 5, p. 71G
**PRACTICED:** Unit 4, Lesson 5, p. 71G
*Comprehension and Language Arts Skills,* pp. 114–115
**TESTED:** Unit 4 Assessment

### ENGLISH LANGUAGE CONVENTIONS

Skills Trace

**Grammar: Subject/Verb Agreement**

Introduced in Grade 1.
Scaffolded throughout Grades 2–6.

**REINTRODUCED:** Unit 4, Lesson 5, p. 71F
**PRACTICED:** Unit 4, Lesson 5, p. 71G
Unit 4, Lesson 5, p. 71H
*Comprehension and Language Arts Skills,* pp. 112–113
**TESTED:** Unit 4, Lesson 5, Informal Assessment, p. 71H
Unit 4 Assessment

Skills Trace

**Listening, Speaking, Viewing Interacting: Conversations**

Introduced in Grade 2.
Scaffolded throughout Grades 3–6.

**REINTRODUCED:** Unit 4, Lesson 5, p. 71I
**TESTED:** Unit 4, Lesson 5, Informal Assessment, p. 71I

Skills Trace

**Penmanship: Cursive Letters *U* and *Y***

Introduced in Grade 3.
Scaffolded throughout Grades 4–6.

**INTRODUCED:** Unit 4, Lesson 5, p. 71J
**TESTED:** Unit 4, Lesson 5, Informal Assessment, p. 71J

## Reading

### COMPREHENSION

**Author's Point of View**

Introduced in Grade 2.
Scaffolded throughout Grade 3.

**REINTRODUCED:** Unit 3, Lesson 6
**REINFORCED:** Unit 4, Lesson 5
Unit 5, Lesson 7
**TESTED:** Unit 4 Assessment

# Professional Development: Inquiry

## How Does the Inquiry/Investigation Procedure Differ from Conventional Research Instruction?

In conventional elementary school classrooms, *research* generally means having students collect information and prepare a paper. They conduct their research by following a procedure that usually involves a series of steps such as the following: (1) select a topic, (2) narrow the topic, (3) collect materials, (4) take notes, (5) organize notes, (6) make an outline, (7) write the paper, and (8) present the paper.

Topic selection usually means choosing from a list of topics suggested or directed by the teacher. The remainder of the steps usually requires students to locate encyclopedia entries or articles easily found in a library or on the Internet—then write down information from them (Schack, 1993).

Although this procedure may result in the preparation of an adequate paper, it does not constitute *research* in any meaningful or useful sense. Indeed, it gives students a distorted and depressing idea of what real research is all about.

Ample evidence exists that elementary school students *can* do descriptive, historical, and experimental research that seeks answers to real questions or solutions to real problems (Schack, 1993). To do this kind of work, however, students need a better research procedure than the one provided by the traditional approach.

The inquiry/investigation procedure is based on the assumption that students *can* do research that will result in the construction of deeper knowledge. The procedure presents research as a never-ending, recursive cycle. Like real-world researchers, students produce their own questions, develop ideas or conjectures about why something is the way it is, then pursue the answers. The answers, as for real researchers, may never come. What will come are more questions. Developing the questions, pursuing the answers, developing conjectures, revising ideas, and setting off on new avenues of research and exploration are the stuff of which strong, deep knowledge and expertise are made. The web of knowledge expands in ways that no teacher or student can predict easily.

Translated into instruction, the inquiry/investigation procedure provides enough structure that students do not get lost or bogged down as they explore concepts, while it preserves the open-ended character of real research, which can lead to unexpected findings and to questions that students did not consider originally. To do this, the procedure follows these important principles (Bereiter & Scardamalia, 1993):

- Research focuses on problems, not topics.
- Conjectures guide the research rather than the reverse.
- New information is gathered to test and revise conjectures.
- Discussion, constant feedback, and constructive criticism are important in all phases of the research, especially in the revising of problems and conjectures.
- The cycle of true research is essentially endless, although findings are presented from time to time; new findings give rise to new problems and conjectures, and thus to new cycles of research.

Additional information about inquiry and investigation as well as resource references can be found in the ***Professional Development Guide: Inquiry and Investigation.***

*Focus Questions* How do you think paper money is made? Who do you think makes paper money? What do you think the symbols on the one-dollar bill represent?

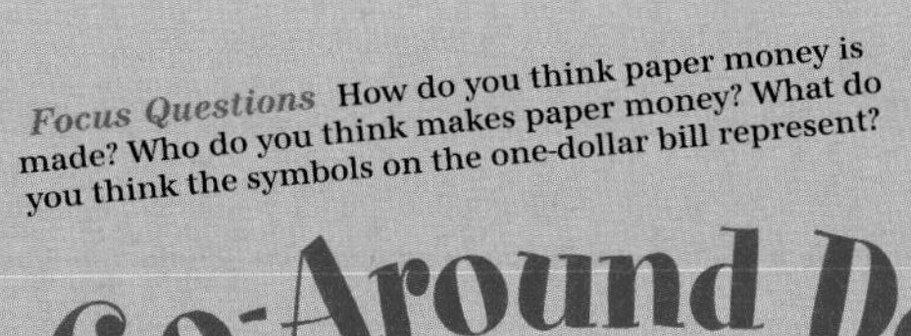


Barbara Johnston Adams
*illustrated by Joyce Audy Zarins*

Every dollar travels from person to person in a different way. But each dollar starts out in the same place—the Bureau of Engraving and Printing in Washington, D.C. Since 1862, this is where our nation's paper money has been produced. The Bureau is part of the United States Treasury Department. At the Bureau, huge printing presses run around the clock, turning out dollar bills. In twenty-four hours, ten million one-dollar bills can be printed.

Dollars are printed in big sheets of thirty-two bills. First the basic design is printed. Then the sheets are cut in half and go back to the presses for an overprinting. This second printing adds information such as the serial numbers and the Treasury seal.

72

SELECTION INTRODUCTION

## Selection Summary

### Genre: Combined Expository Text and Realistic Fiction

"The Go-Around Dollar" is an entertaining look at the journey of a dollar bill as it passes from person to person. Throughout the story are informational references to the real journey of a dollar bill, from its creation at the Bureau of Engraving and Printing, to Federal Reserve Banks, and out to the public.

This selection is unique in that it is a combination of two genres: realistic fiction and expository text. Review elements of each genre with the students to aid in their comprehension of the two different parts of the selection.

Some elements of realistic fiction include:

- The characters behave as people do in real life.
- The setting of the story is a real place or could be a real place.
- The events in the story could happen in real life.

Some of the elements of expository text include:

- The text gives information. It tells people something.
- It contains facts about real events or people.
- It presents information in a straightforward way.
- It gives events in the order in which they happen.
- It might contain diagrams, photographs, and other illustrations.
- It contains information that can be checked by looking at other sources.

## About the Author

**BARBARA JOHNSTON** is a writer of nonfiction children's books. Two of her most notable books are *Winners: Women and the Nobel Prize* and *The Picture Life of Bill Cosby.* Another book about New York City gives children in Grades 2 through 5 a tour of the complex city.

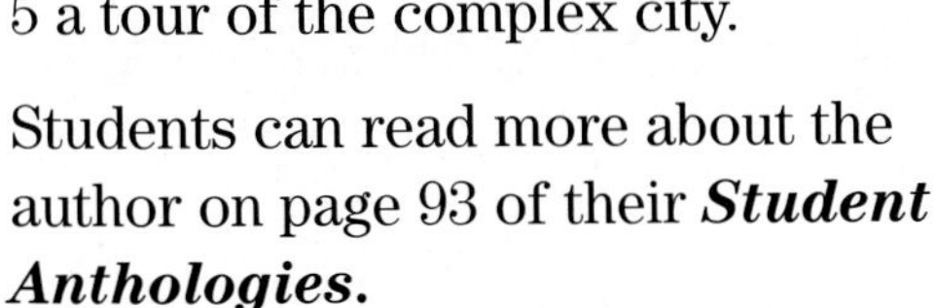

Students can read more about the author on page 93 of their ***Student Anthologies.***

## About the Illustrator

**JOYCE AUDY ZARINS** has written as well as illustrated children's books. On a regular basis, she illustrates for children's magazines.

Students can read more about the illustrator on page 93 of the ***Student Anthology.***

## Inquiry Connections

This book informs students of the production of American money and, at the same time, stirs their thoughts about how money circulates in our society. This book provides a rare opportunity to see a bit of fiction accompanied by the factual information that provides the background for the story.

- The government is in charge of printing and regulating paper currency.
- Strict regulations govern the printing and replacement of paper currency.
- Paper currency travels an unpredictable journey through our society.

Before reading the selection:

- Point out that students may post a question, concept, word, illustration, or object on the Concept/Question Board at any time during the course of their unit investigation. Be sure that students include their name or initials on the items they post so that others will know to whom to go if they have an answer or if they wish to collaborate on a related activity.
- Students should feel free to write an answer or a note on someone else's question or to consult the Board for ideas for their own investigations throughout the unit.
- Encourage students to read about money at home and to bring in articles or pictures that are good examples to post on the Board.

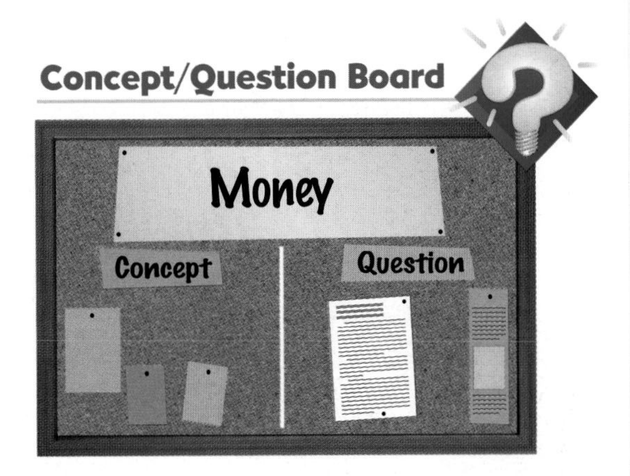

## Leveled Practice

### Reteach
**Pages 119–124**

### Challenge
**Pages 105–109**

### English Learner Support Activities

### Intervention Workbook

### Decodable Book 34

## Leveled Classroom Library*

Encourage students to read at least 30 minutes daily outside of class. Have them read books in the ***Leveled Classroom Library*** to support the unit theme and help students develop their vocabulary by reading independently.

### *The Treasure*

BY URI SHULEVITZ. FARRAR, STRAUS & GIROUX, 1978.

In this traditional English tale of a journey to find treasure, a man follows the instructions of his dream, which takes him away from his home. Upon arrival, he learns the treasure is really at his home. (Caldecott Honor Book) **(Easy)**

### *Saturday Sancocho*

BY LEYLA TORRES. FARRAR, STRAUS & GIROUX, 1995.

Every Saturday, Maria Lili shares a meal with her grandparents, eating Chicken Sancocho, until the weekend comes when money is tight and they are missing essential ingredients. Mama Ana barters with her eggs for the final ingredients, saving the day. **(Average)**

### *Screen of Frogs*

BY SHEILA HAMANAKA. ORCHARD BOOKS, 1993.

A spoiled rich man finds respect for the world around him before it is too late. This story retells the classic Japanese folktale, "The Strange Folding Screen." **(Advanced)**

* These books, which all support the unit theme Money, are part of a 36-book ***Leveled Classroom Library*** available for purchase from SRA/McGraw-Hill. Note: Teachers should preview any trade books for appropriateness in their classrooms before recommending them to students.

## SRA TECHNOLOGY

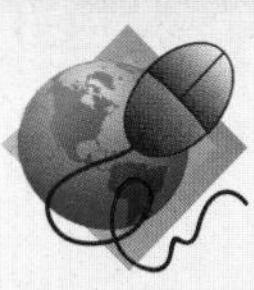

### Web Connections

- Money Web Site
- Online Professional Development
- Online Phonics
- Online Assessment

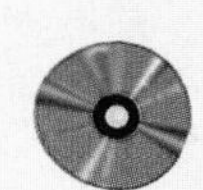

### CD-ROMs

- Research Assistant
- The Ultimate Writing and Creativity Center
- Teacher Resource Library

### Audiocassette/CD

- Listening Library: Money

### Computer Skills

TechKnowledge

Materials are available through SRA/McGraw-Hill.

LESSON PLANNER

Suggested Pacing: 3–5 days

| | DAY 1 | DAY 2 |
|---|---|---|
| **1 Preparing to Read**<br>**Materials**<br>■ Student Anthology, Book 2, pp. 72–93<br>■ Sound/Spelling Cards<br>■ Routine Card 1, Routines 1–2<br>■ Decodable Book 34 | **Word Knowledge,** p. 72K<br>■ suffix *-ment*<br>■ antonyms<br>■ related words<br>■ final /nk/<br>■ /n/ spelled *gn_*<br>■ /t/ spelled *bt*<br>■ compound words<br>**About the Words and Sentences,** pp. 72K–72L | **Developing Oral Language,** p. 72L |
| **2 Reading & Responding**<br>**Materials**<br>■ Student Anthology, Book 2, pp. 72–93<br>■ Program Assessment<br>■ Reading Transparencies 28, 46<br>■ Inquiry Journal, p. 85<br>■ Home Connection, p. 55<br>■ Unit 4 Assessment, pp. 22–25<br>■ Writer's Notebook<br>■ Comprehension and Language Arts Skills, pp. 116–117<br>■ Routine Cards 1, 2, Routines 3–6<br>■ Science/Social Studies Connection Center Card 32 | **Build Background,** p. 72M<br>**Preview and Prepare,** pp. 72M–72N<br>**Selection Vocabulary,** p. 72N<br>**Reading Recommendations,** pp. 72O–72P<br>**Student Anthology,** pp. 72–81 First Read<br>✓**Comprehension Strategies**<br>■ Asking Questions, pp. 72, 74<br>■ Making Connections, pp. 76, 78<br>■ Summarizing, p. 80 | **Student Anthology,** pp. 82–91 First Read<br>**Comprehension Strategies**<br>■ Asking Questions, pp. 82, 86<br>■ Making Connections, p. 84, 88<br>■ Summarizing, p. 90<br>**Discussing Strategy Use,** p. 90<br>**Discussing the Selection,** p. 91A<br>■ Review Selection<br>■ Complete Discussion |
| **Inquiry**<br>**Materials**<br>■ Student Anthology, Book 2, pp. 72–93<br>■ Inquiry Journal, pp. 102–103<br>■ Research Assistant CD-ROM<br>■ Reading Transparency 29 | **Investigation**<br>■ Investigating Concepts Beyond the Text, p. 93A | **Investigation**<br>■ Concept/Question Board, p. 93B |
| **3 Language Arts**<br>**Materials**<br>■ Spelling and Vocabulary Skills, pp. 94–97<br>■ Comprehension and Language Arts Skills, pp. 116–121<br>■ The Ultimate Writing and Creativity Center<br>■ Language Arts Handbook<br>■ Writer's Workbook, pp. 74–77<br>■ Language Arts Transparency 24<br>■ Student Anthology | **Word Analysis**<br>✓■ Spelling: Compound Words Pretest, p. 93F<br>**Writing Process Strategies**<br>■ Persuasive Writing: Poster, p. 93F<br>**English Language Conventions**<br>■ Grammar: Comparative and Superlative Adverbs, p. 93F | **Word Analysis**<br>■ Spelling: Compound Words, p. 93G<br>■ Vocabulary: Money Words, p. 93G<br>**Writing Process Strategies**<br>■ Persuasive Writing: Poster, p. 93G<br>**English Language Conventions**<br>■ Grammar: Comparative and Superlative Adverbs, p. 93G |



Ⓟ Phonics ✓Informal Assessment Available ✓Formal Assessment Available

| DAY 2 continued | DAY 3 | |
|---|---|---|
| **DAY 3** | **DAY 4** | **DAY 5** |
| **General Review** | **General Review** | **Review Word Knowledge** |
| **Student Anthology,** pp. 72–81 Second Read<br>**Comprehension Skills**<br>■ Sequence, pp. 73, 75, 77, 79, 81<br>✓**Concept Connections,** p. 92<br>**Meet the Author/Illustrator,** p. 93 | **Student Anthology,** pp. 82–91 Second Read<br>**Comprehension Skills**<br>■ Sequence, pp. 83, 85, 87, 89, 91<br>**Supporting the Reading,** pp. 91C–91D<br>■ Sequence<br>**Checking Comprehension,** p. 91<br>**Review Selection Vocabulary,** p. 91B<br>**Literary Elements,** p. 91E<br>■ Dialogue | ✓**Comprehension Test**<br>■ "The Go-Around Dollar," pp. 22–25<br>**Home Connection,** p. 91B<br>**View Fine Art,** p. 91B<br>**Social Studies Connection**<br>■ Government and Money, p. 91F |
| ✓**Investigation**<br>■ Revising Conjectures, p. 93C | **Supporting the Investigation**<br>■ Diagrams, p. 93D | **Investigation**<br>■ Unit Investigation Continued<br>■ Update Concept/Question Board |
| **Word Analysis**<br>■ Spelling: Compound Words, p. 93H<br>■ Vocabulary: Money Words, p. 93H<br>**Writing Process Strategies**<br>■ Persuasive Writing: Poster, p. 93H<br>■ Writer's Craft: Supporting Details, p. 93H<br>**English Language Conventions**<br>✓■ Grammar: Comparative and Superlative Adverbs, p. 93H | **Word Analysis**<br>■ Spelling: Compound Words, p. 93I<br>■ Vocabulary: Money Words, p. 93I<br>**Writing Process Strategies**<br>■ Persuasive Writing: Poster, p. 93I<br>**English Language Conventions**<br>✓■ Listening, Speaking, Viewing Presenting: Organizing a Presentation, p. 93I | **Word Analysis**<br>✓■ Spelling: Compound Words Final Test<br>✓■ Vocabulary: Money Words, p. 93J<br>**Writing Process Strategies**<br>✓■ Persuasive Writing: Poster, p. 93J<br>**English Language Conventions**<br>✓■ Penmanship: Cursive Letters *Z* and *V*, p. 93J |

Below are suggestions for differentiating instruction. These are the same skills shown in the Lesson Planner; however, these pages provide extra practice opportunities or enriching activities to meet the varied needs of students.

WORKSHOP

# Differentiating Instruction

## Teacher Directed: Individual and Small-Group Instruction

Spend time each day with individuals and small groups to individualize instruction. Each day:

- preteach students who need help with the next lesson.
- reteach students who need to solidify their understanding of content previously taught.
- listen to students read to check their fluency.
- hold writing and inquiry conferences.

Use the following program components to support instruction:

- ***Reteach*** with students who need a bit more practice
- ***Intervention*** for students who exhibit a lack of understanding of the lesson concepts
- ***English Learner Support*** with students who need language help

## Student: Independent Activities

Students can work alone, with a partner, or in small groups on such activities as:

- Review sound/spellings
- Practice dictation words
- Partner reading
- Practice fluency
- Independent reading
- Reading Roundtable
- Concept vocabulary
- Selection vocabulary
- Writing in progress
- Conference
- Language Arts
- Challenge activities
- Inquiry and Investigation activities
- Listening Library
- Online Phonics

For Workshop Management Tips, see Appendix pages 41–42.

| | DAY I |
|---|---|
| **Word Knowledge** | **Teacher Directed**<br>▪ Reading Words: Suffix *-ment*, ***Intervention Guide,*** p. 215<br>**Independent Activities**<br>▪ ***Online Phonics*** |
| **Fluency** | **Independent Activities**<br>▪ Self-test fluency rate<br>▪ Oral reading of selection for fluency |
| **Comprehension** | **Teacher Directed**<br>▪ Preteach "The Go-Around Dollar," ***Intervention Guide,*** pp. 216–217<br>▪ Preteach Intervention Selection One, ***Intervention Guide,*** pp. 217–218<br>▪ ***English Learner Support Guide***<br>• Vocabulary, pp. 326–327<br>• Comprehension Skill: Sequence, pp. 326–328<br>**Independent Activities**<br>▪ Browse ***Leveled Classroom Library***<br>▪ Add vocabulary in Writer's Notebook |
| **Inquiry** | **Independent Activities**<br>▪ Concept/Question Board<br>▪ Explore OCR Web site for theme connections |
| **Language Arts** | **Teacher Directed**<br>▪ Grammar, Usage, and Mechanics, ***Intervention Guide,*** p. 220<br>**Independent Activities**<br>▪ Comparative and Superlative Adverbs, ***Comprehension and Language Arts Skills,*** pp. 118–119 |

| DAY 2 | DAY 3 | DAY 4 | DAY 5 |
|---|---|---|---|
| **Teacher Directed**<br>▪ Developing Oral Language, ***Intervention Guide,*** p. 215<br>**Independent Activities**<br>▪ Read ***Decodable Book 34,*** *Peace and Quiet* | **Teacher Directed**<br>▪ Dictation and Spelling: Suffix *-ment,* ***Intervention Guide,*** pp. 215–216<br>**Independent Activities**<br>▪ ***Online Phonics*** | **Teacher Directed**<br>▪ General Review<br>**Independent Activities**<br>▪ ***Online Phonics*** | **Teacher Directed**<br>▪ General Review<br>**Independent Activities**<br>▪ ***Online Phonics*** |
| **Independent Activities**<br>▪ Oral reading of selection<br>▪ Partner reading of ***Decodable Book 34,*** *Peace and Quiet* | **Independent Activities**<br>▪ Partner reading of selection<br>▪ Reread ***Decodable Book 34,*** *Peace and Quiet* | **Independent Activities**<br>▪ Reread "The Go-Around Dollar"<br>▪ Partner reading of ***Decodable Book 34,*** *Peace and Quiet* | **Teacher Directed**<br>▪ Repeated Readings/Fluency Check, ***Intervention Guide,*** p. 219 |
| **Teacher Directed**<br>▪ Preteach "The Go-Around Dollar," ***Intervention Guide,*** pp. 216–217<br>▪ Comprehension Strategies, ***Intervention Guide,*** p. 218<br>▪ Reread Intervention Selection One, ***Intervention Guide,*** pp. 217–218<br>▪ ***English Learner Support Guide***<br>• Vocabulary, pp. 328–329<br>• Comprehension Skill: Sequence, pp. 329–330<br>**Independent Activities**<br>▪ Choose a ***Leveled Classroom Library*** book for independent reading<br>▪ Record response to selection in Writer's Notebook<br>▪ ***Listening Library Audiocassette/CD***<br>▪ ***English Learner Support Activities,*** p. 42 | **Teacher Directed**<br>▪ Discuss Concept Connections, p. 92<br>▪ Reread "The Go-Around Dollar," ***Intervention Guide,*** pp. 216–217<br>▪ Preteach Intervention Selection Two, ***Intervention Guide,*** pp. 218–219<br>▪ ***English Learner Support Guide***<br>• Vocabulary, pp. 330–331<br>• Comprehension Skill: Sequence, pp. 331–332<br>**Independent Activities**<br>▪ Read ***Leveled Classroom Library*** book<br>▪ ***Listening Library Audiocassette/CD*** | **Teacher Directed**<br>▪ Reread "The Go-Around Dollar," ***Intervention Guide,*** pp. 216–217<br>▪ Comprehension Strategies, ***Intervention Guide,*** p. 219<br>▪ Reread Intervention Selection Two, ***Intervention Guide,*** pp. 218–219<br>▪ ***English Learner Support Guide***<br>• Vocabulary, pp. 333–334<br>• Comprehension Skill: Sequence, pp. 334–335<br>▪ Sequence, ***Reteach,*** pp. 119–120<br>**Independent Activities**<br>▪ Add words to Word Bank<br>▪ Complete Link to Writing in Supporting the Reading, p. 91D<br>▪ Sequence<br>• ***Comprehension and Language Arts Skills,*** pp. 116–117<br>• ***Challenge,*** p. 105<br>▪ Complete Independent Practice in Literary Elements, p. 91E | **Teacher Directed**<br>▪ ***English Learner Support Guide***<br>• Review Vocabulary, pp. 335–336<br>• Comprehension Skill: Sequence, pp. 335–337<br>**Independent Activities**<br>▪ Read ***Leveled Classroom Library*** book as independent reading<br>▪ Reading Roundtable<br>▪ Social Studies Connection, p. 91F<br>▪ ***English Learner Support Activities,*** p. 43 |
| **Independent Activities**<br>▪ Concept/Question Board<br>▪ Use ***Research Assistant CD-ROM*** to continue investigation<br>▪ Varieties of Money Chart, ***Inquiry Journal,*** p. 102 | **Independent Activities**<br>▪ Concept/Question Board<br>▪ Recording Concept Information, ***Inquiry Journal,*** p. 83<br>▪ Explore OCR Web site for theme connections | **Independent Activities**<br>▪ Concept/Question Board<br>▪ Complete Independent Practice in Supporting the Investigation, p. 93D<br>▪ Diagrams, ***Inquiry Journal,*** p. 103 | **Independent Activities**<br>▪ Concept/Question Board<br>▪ Use ***Research Assistant CD-ROM*** to continue investigation |
| **Teacher Directed**<br>▪ Grammar, Usage, and Mechanics, ***Intervention Guide,*** p. 220<br>▪ Comparative and Superlative Adverbs, ***Reteach,*** p. 123<br>**Independent Activities**<br>▪ Vocabulary: Money Words, ***Spelling and Vocabulary Skills,*** pp. 94–95<br>▪ Comparative and Superlative Adverbs, ***Challenge,*** p. 108 | **Teacher Directed**<br>▪ Writing Activity, ***Intervention Guide,*** p. 221<br>▪ Vocabulary: ***Reteach,*** p. 122<br>**Independent Activities**<br>▪ Spelling: Compound Words, ***Spelling and Vocabulary Skills,*** p. 96<br>▪ Vocabulary: ***Challenge,*** p. 107<br>▪ Writer's Craft: Supporting Details, ***Comprehension and Language Arts Skills,*** pp. 120–121 | **Teacher Directed**<br>▪ Writer's Craft: Supporting Details, ***Reteach,*** p. 124<br>▪ Writing Activity, ***Intervention Guide,*** p. 221<br>▪ Spelling: Compound Words, ***Reteach,*** p. 121<br>**Independent Activities**<br>▪ Spelling: Compound Words<br>• ***Spelling and Vocabulary Skills,*** p. 97<br>• ***Challenge,*** p. 106 | **Independent Activities**<br>▪ Seminar: Edit/Proofread and Publish a Persuasive Poster, p. 93J<br>▪ Penmanship: Practice Cursive Letters *Z* and *V,* p. 93J<br>▪ Writer's Craft: Supporting Details, ***Challenge,*** p. 109 |

ASSESSMENT

# Formal Assessment Options

Use these summative assessments along with your informal observations to assess student progress.

Name ______ Date ______ Score ______

UNIT 4 Money • Lesson 6

LESSON ASSESSMENT

**The Go-Around Dollar**

**Read the following questions carefully. Then completely fill in the bubble of each correct answer. You may look back at the story to find the answer to each of the questions.**

1. This story is mostly about
   - Ⓐ where dollar bills are made
   - ● the life of a dollar bill
   - Ⓒ why the dollar bill is green
2. Water does not hurt a dollar bill because dollar bills are
   - ● made with strong paper
   - Ⓑ made to weigh little
   - Ⓒ made with two kinds of ink

**Read the following questions carefully. Use complete sentences to answer the questions.**

3. What causes dollar bills to wear out so quickly?
   They go from person to person so many times.
4. Why do store owners sometimes put a dollar bill inside of a frame?
   It is their first dollar and has special meaning.
5. Who had the dollar bill just before Kathy?
   Rob had it and paid her to take the dog for a walk.

22 Unit 4 • Lesson 6 *The Go-Around Dollar* • Unit 4 Assessment

**Unit 4 Assessment p. 22**

The Go-Around Dollar *(continued)*

LESSON ASSESSMENT

6. Why did the ticket seller make a phone call?
   The ticket seller thought a dollar he was given seemed fake.
7. What makes dollar bills easy to lose?
   They are light and easy to drop without noticing.
8. Why is the formula for the dollar bill's ink a secret?
   It helps prevent people from making fake bills.

**Read the following questions carefully. Then completely fill in the bubble of each correct answer.**

9. Which of these is not on the one-dollar bill?
   - ● an owl
   - Ⓑ a pyramid
   - Ⓒ an eagle
10. What does Kathy decide to do with the dollar?
    - Ⓐ buy some bubble gum
    - ● buy an ice cream cone
    - Ⓒ buy a funny hat

Unit 4 Assessment • *The Go-Around Dollar* Unit 4 • Lesson 6 23

**Unit 4 Assessment p. 23**

The Go-Around Dollar *(continued)*

LESSON ASSESSMENT

**Read the questions below. Use complete sentences in your answers.**

**Linking to the Concepts** According to the story, how is the dollar bill a useful part of everyday life?
Answers will vary. Accept all reasonable answers.

**Personal Response** If you got the dollar bill in this story, how would you decide to spend it and why?
Answers will vary. Accept all reasonable answers.

24 Unit 4 • Lesson 6 *The Go-Around Dollar* • Unit 4 Assessment

**Unit 4 Assessment p. 24**

The Go-Around Dollar *(continued)*

LESSON ASSESSMENT

**Vocabulary**

**Read the following questions carefully. Then completely fill in the bubble of each correct answer.**

1. Dollars go into circulation after they reach banks in cities, small towns, and neighborhoods. **Circulation** means
   - Ⓐ the dollars are used so often they wear out
   - Ⓑ the dollars have a round shape on them
   - ● the dollars are used again and again
2. There is a notice on each dollar that says, "This note is legal tender for all debts, public and private." In this sentence, **tender** is another word for
   - Ⓐ gentle
   - ● money
   - Ⓒ ticket
3. The Great Seal is an official symbol of our country. Another word for **official** is
   - ● legal
   - Ⓑ fake
   - Ⓒ simple
4. The formula for the ink used on the dollar bill is a secret. A **formula** tells you how to
   - Ⓐ find something
   - Ⓑ buy something
   - ● make something
5. The bald eagle, our national emblem, is holding arrows and an olive branch. An **emblem** is
   - Ⓐ an idea that no one understands
   - Ⓑ a bird that is no longer living
   - ● a sign that stands for something

Unit 4 Assessment • *The Go-Around Dollar* Unit 4 • Lesson 6 25

**Unit 4 Assessment p. 25**

Name ______ Date ______ Score ______

UNIT 4 Money • Lesson 6 *The Go-Around Dollar*

LESSON ASSESSMENT

**Spelling Pretest: Compound Words**

**Fold this page back on the dotted line. Take the Pretest. Then correct any word you misspelled by crossing out the word and rewriting it next to the incorrect spelling.**

| | | | |
|---|---|---|---|
| 1. | ______ | 1. | playground |
| 2. | ______ | 2. | underground |
| 3. | ______ | 3. | chalkboard |
| 4. | ______ | 4. | cardboard |
| 5. | ______ | 5. | spacewalk |
| 6. | ______ | 6. | sidewalk |
| 7. | ______ | 7. | rainbow |
| 8. | ______ | 8. | anything |
| 9. | ______ | 9. | campfire |
| 10. | ______ | 10. | eyelash |
| 11. | ______ | 11. | shoelaces |
| 12. | ______ | 12. | something |
| 13. | ______ | 13. | overprinting |
| 14. | ______ | 14. | neighborhood |
| 15. | ______ | 15. | sometimes |

40 Unit 4 • Lesson 6 *Spelling Pretest: Compound Words* • Unit 4 Assessment

**Unit 4 Assessment p. 40**

Name ______ Date ______ Score ______

UNIT 4 Money • Lesson 6 *The Go-Around Dollar*

LESSON ASSESSMENT

**Spelling Final Test: Compound Words**

**Mark the letter next to the underlined word that is misspelled. Focus on the underlined word.**

1. ● A slide is found on a plaground.
   Ⓑ Teachers write on a chalkboard.
   Ⓒ An eyelash is a small hair.
   Ⓓ Correct as is.
2. Ⓔ A cardboard box is strong.
   ● A sidewallk is made of cement.
   Ⓗ People tie shoelaces in bows.
   Ⓙ Correct as is.
3. Ⓐ Trash is anything thrown away.
   Ⓑ Families live in a neighborhood.
   Ⓒ Chalk can write on a chalkboard.
   ● Correct as is.
4. Ⓕ It is safe to walk on a sidewalk.
   ● Many shoes have sholaces.
   Ⓗ A rainbow is a spectrum.
   Ⓙ Correct as is.
5. ● A sandwich is somthing to eat.
   Ⓑ A neighborhood has neighbors.
   Ⓒ An eyelash can fall out.
   Ⓓ Correct as is.
6. Ⓕ A game is something to play.
   Ⓖ Some tunnels go underground.
   Ⓗ A sidewalk is a cement path.
   ● Correct as is.

Unit 4 Assessment • *Spelling Final Test: Compound Words* Unit 4 • Lesson 6 41

**Unit 4 Assessment p. 41**

**Online Assessment** for ***Open Court Reading*** helps teachers differentiate classroom instruction based on students' scores from the weekly and end-of-unit assessments. It provides exercises best suited to meet the needs of each student. For more information, visit SRAonline.com.

ASSESSMENT

# Informal Comprehension Strategies Rubrics

## Asking Questions

- The student asks questions about ideas or facts presented in the text and attempts to answer these questions by reading the text.

## Making Connections

- The student activates prior knowledge and related knowledge.
- The student uses prior knowledge to explain something encountered in text.
- The student connects ideas presented later in the text to ideas presented earlier in the text.
- The student notes ideas in the text that are new or conflict with what he or she thought previously.

## Summarizing

- The student paraphrases the text, reporting main ideas and a summary of what is in the text.
- The student decides which parts of the text are important in his or her summary.
- The student draws conclusions from the text.
- The student makes global interpretations of the text, such as recognizing the genre.

# Research Rubrics

During Workshop, assess students using the rubrics below. The rubrics range from 1 to 4 in most categories, with 1 being the lowest score. Record each student's score on the inside back cover of the ***Inquiry Journal.***

## Revising Problems and Conjectures

**1** No revision.

**2** Produces new problems or conjectures with little relation to earlier ones.

**3** Tends to lift problems and conjectures directly from reference material.

**4** Progresses to deeper, more refined problems and conjectures.

### Objectives

- Students practice recognizing base words and the suffix *-ment*.
- Students practice recognizing antonyms.
- Students practice recognizing related words.
- Students review special spellings: the /nk/ sound, the /n/ sound spelled *gn_*, the /t/ sound spelled *bt*.
- Students practice recognizing compound words.

### Materials

- Student Anthology, Book 2, pp. 72–93
- Sound/Spelling Cards
- Decodable Book 34
- Routine Card 1, Routines 1–2

**Teacher Tip** SYLLABICATION To help students blend words and build fluency, use the syllabication below of the words in the word lines.

gov•ern, gov•ern•ment, pave, pave•ment, en•ter•tain, en•ter•tain•ment, in•volve, in•volve•ment, black, white, hot, cold, big, small, real, coun•ter•feit, dol•lar, bills, mon•ey, buy, pay, ten•der, bank, pink, sign, de•sign, doubt, debt, some•times, neigh•bor•hood, some•thing, shoe•lac•es

### Differentiating Instruction

| If... | Then... |
|---|---|
| Students need extra help with antonyms or synonyms | Use *Online Phonics* |
| Students need extra help with base words and the suffix *-ment* | Use *Intervention Guide* pages 215–216 |

**Spelling**
See pages 93E–93J for the corresponding spelling lesson for compound words.

**Routine Card**
Refer to *Routine 1* for whole-word blending and *Routine 2* for sentence blending.

WORD KNOWLEDGE

## Word Knowledge

### Reading the Words and Sentences

- Use direct teaching to teach the following lesson.
- Use the established procedure as you have students read each line of words and the sentences in this and in subsequent lessons. The words in **boldface** are from the selection.

Line 1: govern **government** pave pavement
Line 2: entertain entertainment involve involvement
Line 3: **black** **white** hot cold big small **real** **counterfeit**
Line 4: **dollar** **bills** **money** **buy** **pay** **tender**
Line 5: **bank** pink **sign** **design** doubt debt
Line 6: **sometimes** **neighborhood** **overprinting** **something** **shoelaces**
Sentence 1: The United States **government** has laws about the way dollar bills can be shown.
Sentence 2: For instance, a dollar drawn as an illustration for a book must be in black and white, not in full color.
Sentence 3: Dollar bills are used to buy things, pay back money that was borrowed, or pay for a service such as a bus ride.
Sentence 4: **Sometimes** people can trip if their **shoelaces** are untied.

### About the Words and Sentences

- **Lines 1 and 2:** The words in Lines 1 and 2 have base words with the suffix *-ment* added. Ask students to generalize about how the suffix changes the part of speech of the word *(verb to noun)* and to use each word in a sentence. Ask students to explain what the suffix *-ment* means *(action or process)*.
- **Line 3:** The words in Line 3 are antonyms. Ask students to think of other antonyms *(asleep/awake, kind/mean, quiet/loud)*.
- **Line 4:** The words in Line 4 are all related words that have to do with money. Ask students to think of other related words *(cents, borrow, rich, poor, bank)*.
- **Line 5:** The words in this line review words with the sound /nk/, /n/ spelled *gn_*, and /t/ spelled *bt*. After reading each word, have students underline the special elements in the word.
- **Line 6:** These words are found in "The Go-Around Dollar" and review compound words. After reading the words, have the students identify the two words that make up the compound word. Ask if knowing the two words helps us understand the meaning.

- **Sentences 1–3:** These sentences are from the story students are about to read. Ask students to identify words with a suffix *(government).* Ask students to identify antonyms *(black/white, pay/borrow).* Ask students to identify related words *(dollar, bills, pay, money).*
- **Sentence 4:** Have students identify the compound words.

## Developing Oral Language

To review the words, do one or both of the following activities. Use these activities to help students practice the words aloud.

- Write the following words on the board: *sour, happy, messy.* Have students make a list of synonyms for each word and share the lists with the class.
- Point to a word on the board and select a student to read the word and use it in a sentence. Then that student can point to a word on the board and choose another student to read it and use it in a sentence. Erase the words as they are selected and continue until all the words have been used.

## Building Fluency

***Decodable Books*** are used to help develop fluency for students who need extra practice. The only way to gain fluency is to read. Students will have many opportunities to read, including the ***Student Anthology,*** the ***Leveled Classroom Library,*** and their own reading. The ***Decodable Books*** can be used to practice the phonics and fluency elements being reviewed. Refer to the Appendix for the procedure on using these books. For this lesson, use ***Decodable Book 34,*** *Peace and Quiet.*

***Decodable Book 34***

WORD KNOWLEDGE

**Teacher Tip FLUENCY** Gaining a better understanding of the spellings of sounds and structure of words will help students as they encounter unfamiliar words in their reading. By this time in Grade 3, students should be reading approximately 123 words per minute with fluency and expression. As students read, you may notice that some need work in building fluency. During Workshop, have these students select a section of the text (a minimum of 160 words) to read several times in order to build fluency.

## Objectives

- Students will understand the selection vocabulary before reading, using strategies such as suffixes and structural cues.
- Students will recognize antonyms, related words, and base words with the suffix *-ment.*
- Students will connect prior knowledge to subjects discussed in text.
- Students will use comprehension strategies such as Asking Questions, Making Connections, and Summarizing to construct meaning from the text and monitor reading.
- Students will use the comprehension skill Sequence as they read the story the second time.
- Students will discuss personal reactions to the story to begin identifying their own personal reading preferences.
- Students link the selection's key concepts to their investigations.

## Materials

- Student Anthology, Book 2, pp. 72–93
- Program Assessment
- Reading Transparencies 28, 46
- Inquiry Journal, p. 85
- Home Connection, p. 55
- Comprehension and Language Arts Skills, pp. 116–117
- Unit 4 Assessment, pp. 22–25
- Routine Card 1, 2, Routines 3–6
- Science/Social Studies Connection Center Card 32

| Clues | Problems | Wonderings |
|---|---|---|
| Title is "The Go-Around Dollar" | Treasury | How does money get made? |

SRA Open Court Reading — Reading Transparency 46

***Reading Transparency 46***

**Teacher Tip** INVESTIGATION
Remind students to think about the questions their investigation group has about money and to see whether the selection answers any of those questions. Students can also check the Concept/Question Board for questions the selection might answer.

# Build Background

## Activate Prior Knowledge

Discuss the following with students to find out what they may already know about the selection and have already learned about money.

- Preteach "The Go-Around Dollar" by determining students' prior knowledge by asking, "What do you know about how paper money is made?"
- Discuss how a dollar bill can pass from person to person through our society.
- Ask students what they think happens to money that gets damaged.

## Background Information

The following information may help students understand the selection they are about to read.

- Point out to students that the selection they will be reading is realistic fiction, but there are text boxes interspersed with the story that give factual information. This selection is a combination of fiction and nonfiction.
- The Federal Reserve is the central banking authority in the United States. It distributes paper currency, makes loans to banks, and financially protects accounts in banks.

# Preview and Prepare

## Browse

- Have a student read aloud the title. Point out and read the name of the author and illustrator to students. Have them preview the selection by browsing the first page or two of the story. Discuss what they think this story might teach them about money.
- Have the students search for clues that tell them something about the story. Also, have them look for any problems, such as unfamiliar words or long sentences, they notice while reading. Use ***Reading Transparency 46*** to record their observations as they browse. For example, a student might notice the fact that the title "The Go-Around Dollar" is a clue that the story is about a dollar that travels from person to person. For the Problems column, students might point out that they are unfamiliar with the term *Treasury.* They might wonder how new money is made. To save time and to model note taking, write students' observations as brief notes rather than as complete sentences.
- As students prepare to read the selection, have them browse the Focus Questions on the first page of the selection. Tell them to keep these questions in mind as they read.

## Set Purposes

Encourage students to set their own purposes for reading this selection. As they read, have students think about who shows money in this story, how they show it, and what it leads them to do.

# Selection Vocabulary

As students study vocabulary, they will use a variety of skills to determine the meaning of a word. These include context clues, word structure, and apposition. Students will apply these same skills while reading to clarify additional unfamiliar words. Students can write their definitions in their Writer's Notebooks.

Display ***Reading Transparency 28*** before reading the selection to introduce and discuss the following words and their meanings.

**circulation:** movement around many different places or people (page 73)
**tender:** money, payment (page 76)
**formula:** set method for doing something (page 80)
**official:** formal and proper (page 85)
**pyramid:** object with triangular sides that meet at a point at the top (page 85)
**emblem:** sign or figure that stands for something (page 85)

Have students read the words, stopping to blend any words that they have trouble reading. Help students decode multisyllabic words by breaking the words into syllables and blending the syllables. If students still have trouble, refer them to the ***Sound/Spelling Cards.*** If the word is not decodable, give the students the pronunciation.

Have students read the sentences on the transparency to determine the meaning of the underlined words. Each word has two sentences that students will read and from which they should be able to derive the meaning of the underlined word. Remind them to use one or more of the skills they have learned—context clues, word structure, or apposition—to figure out the meaning before using a dictionary. Be sure students explain which skills they are using and how they figured out the meanings of the words. Have students reread the sentence, substituting the definition to see if the sentence makes sense. Have a volunteer create a new sentence using the underlined word.

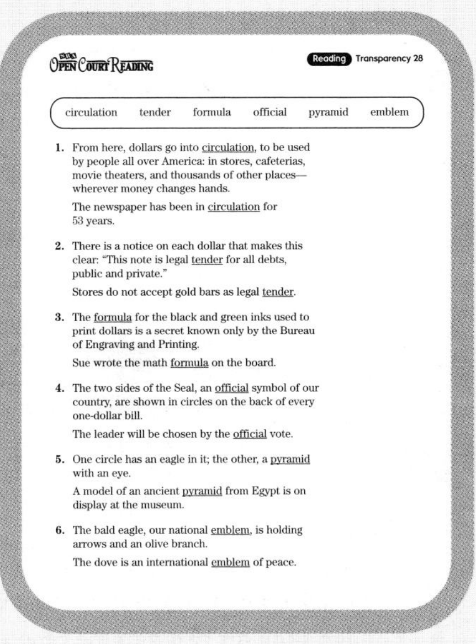
Open Court Reading — Reading Transparency 28

circulation tender formula official pyramid emblem

1. From here, dollars go into circulation, to be used by people all over America: in stores, cafeterias, movie theaters, and thousands of other places—wherever money changes hands.
   The newspaper has been in circulation for 53 years.
2. There is a notice on each dollar that makes this clear: "This note is legal tender for all debts, public and private."
   Stores do not accept gold bars as legal tender.
3. The formula for the black and green inks used to print dollars is a secret known only by the Bureau of Engraving and Printing.
   Sue wrote the math formula on the board.
4. The two sides of the Seal, an official symbol of our country, are shown in circles on the back of every one-dollar bill.
   The leader will be chosen by the official vote.
5. One circle has an eagle in it; the other, a pyramid with an eye.
   A model of an ancient pyramid from Egypt is on display at the museum.
6. The bald eagle, our national emblem, is holding arrows and an olive branch.
   The dove is an international emblem of peace.

***Reading Transparency 28***

**Teacher Tip SELECTION VOCABULARY** To help students decode words, divide them into syllables when you are saying them, as shown below. The information following each word tells how students can figure out the meaning of each word. When writing words on the board, do not divide them into syllables.

| | |
|---|---|
| cir • cu • la • tion | context clues |
| ten • der | context clues |
| for • mu • la | context clues |
| of • fi • cial | context clues |
| pyr • a • mid | context clues |
| em • blem | context clues |

## Differentiating Instruction

| If... | Then... |
|---|---|
| Students need extra help with selection vocabulary | Use *Intervention Guide* pages 216–217 |

**Routine Card**
Refer to ***Routine 3*** for the vocabulary procedure.

**Teacher Tip** Have students practice using each of the vocabulary words from the selection in context in a sentence. If students have trouble at first, give them an example. For instance, if the word is *pyramid,* say, "A pyramid is on the back of the one-dollar bill."

**Teacher Tip COMPREHENSION STRATEGIES** Remind students on the second day as they read the story to summarize what they learned from the first day.

**Routine Card**
Refer to ***Routine 5*** for the procedure on reading the selection.

During Workshop, and after the selection has been read at least once, have students listen to the recording of this lesson's selection on the ***Listening Library Audiocassette/CD.*** After students have listened, have them discuss their personal preferences of the selections read. Ask them what other things they have listened to and like to listen to on the radio, on audiocassettes, or on CDs.

### DIFFERENTIATING INSTRUCTION

| If... | Then... |
|---|---|
| Students need extra help with summarizing | Use ***Intervention Guide*** pages 217–218 |

# Reading Recommendations

## Oral Reading

The dialogue and informational sections inserted into the story make this a good selection for oral reading. In addition, reading this story aloud will give you the opportunity to continue modeling comprehension strategies for students and give students practice using the strategies aloud. Students should read aloud fluently with appropriate expression and intonation. Make sure that students attend to punctuation and read in phrases. Tell students to add a sense of feeling or anticipation as they read.

Have students make use of the comprehension strategies listed below to help them understand the selection. Have them stop reading periodically or wait until they have completed the selection to discuss the reading strategies. After the students have finished reading the selection, use the Discussing the Selection questions on page 91A to see if they understand what they have read.

## Using Comprehension Strategies 

Comprehension strategy instruction allows students to become aware of how good readers read. Good readers constantly check their understanding as they are reading and ask themselves questions. In addition, skilled readers recognize when they are having problems and stop to use various comprehension strategies to help them make sense of what they are reading.

During the first reading of "The Go-Around Dollar," teacher model and prompt the use of the following comprehension strategies.

- **Asking Questions** helps readers focus attention on what they are reading and engages them in a deeper understanding of themes, concepts, and ideas.
- **Making Connections** requires readers to activate prior knowledge and connect what they know or have experienced to what they are reading.
- **Summarizing** prompts readers to keep track of what they are reading and to focus their minds on important information.

As students read, they should be using a variety of strategies to help them understand the selection. Encourage students to use the strategies listed above as the class reads the story aloud. Do this by stopping at the points indicated by the numbers in the magenta circles on the reduced student page and modeling for students the use of a particular strategy. Students can also stop reading periodically to discuss what they have learned and what problems they may be having.

## Building Comprehension Skills 

Revisiting or rereading a selection allows readers to apply skills that give them a more complete understanding of the text. Some follow-up comprehension skills help students organize information. Others lead to deeper understanding—to "reading between the lines," as mature readers do.

An extended lesson on the comprehension skill, Sequence, can be found in the Supporting the Reading section on pages 91C–91D. This lesson is intended to give students extra practice with Sequence. However, it may be used at this time to introduce the comprehension skill to students.

- **Sequence:** Readers place events in the time order in which they occur in the story.

### Reading with a Purpose

Have students look for ways the story characters learn about money throughout the selection.

COMPREHENSION

This selection is broken into two parts.
On the first day, read pages 72–81.
On the second day, read pages 82–91.

## Comprehension Strategies

Read the story aloud, taking turns with the students. Start by teacher modeling the use of strategies for the students.

### Teacher Modeling

**1 Asking Questions** *I have a question here. Is this a nonfiction text? I'll reread again to see. All the information on this page is factual, so it is nonfiction. But here it says "might have happened to a dollar." The "might" means that part is made up, or fiction. I think this selection is a combination of nonfiction and fiction. Let's keep asking questions as we read.*

### Word Knowledge

**SCAFFOLDING** The skills students are reviewing in Word Knowledge should help them in reading the selection. This lesson focuses on base words with the suffix *-ment,* antonyms, related words, the /nk/ sound, the /n/ sound spelled *gn,* the /t/ sound spelled *bt,* and compound words.

**related words:** **dollar**
**money**
**treasury**
**bills**
**banks**

**Teacher Tip** **FLUENCY** Remind students to read with feeling. Encourage them to change the pitch of their voices to reflect the flow of the story and to not read in a monotone. As you take turns reading aloud with students, model reading with expression.

**First Reading Recommendation**

**ORAL • CHORAL**

*Focus Questions* How do you think paper money is made? Who do you think makes paper money? What do you think the symbols on the one-dollar bill represent?

# The Go-Around Dollar

Barbara Johnston Adams
*illustrated by Joyce Audy Zarins*

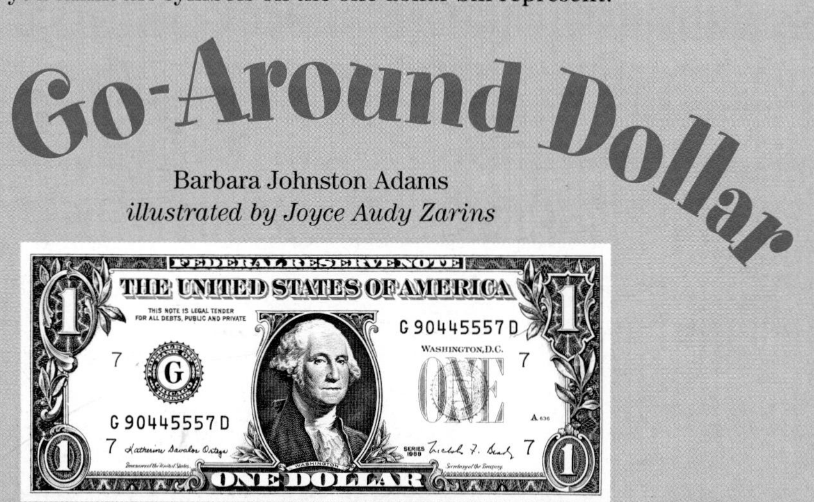


Every dollar travels from person to person in a different way. But each dollar starts out in the same place—the Bureau of Engraving and Printing in Washington, D.C. Since 1862, this is where our nation's paper money has been produced. The Bureau is part of the United States Treasury Department. At the Bureau, huge printing presses run around the clock, turning out dollar bills. In twenty-four hours, ten million one-dollar bills can be printed.

Dollars are printed in big sheets of thirty-two bills. First the basic design is printed. Then the sheets are cut in half and go back to the presses for an overprinting. This second printing adds information such as the serial numbers and the Treasury seal.

72

### Informal Assessment

Observe individual students as they read, and use the Teacher Observation Log, found in the ***Program Assessment Teacher's Edition,*** to record anecdotal information about each student's strengths and weaknesses.

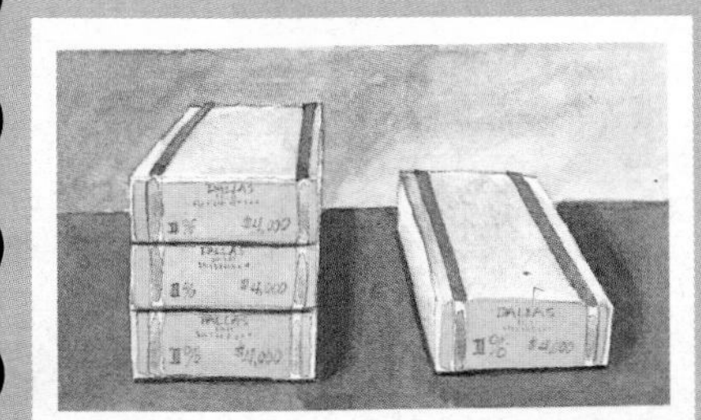

As bills are made, they're checked by people and machines over and over again to make sure they are perfect.

Finally, the sheets are cut into stacks of individual bills called bricks. Bricks are sent to one of twelve banks, located in different parts of the United States, called Federal Reserve Banks. Federal Reserve Banks, in turn, send dollars to banks in cities, small towns, and neighborhoods. From here, dollars go into circulation, to be used by people all over America: in stores, cafeterias, movie theaters, and thousands of other places—wherever money changes hands. Here's what might have happened to one dollar. . . . (1)

FEDERAL RESERVE

THE UNITED STATES OF

The United States government has laws about the way dollar bills can be shown. For instance, a dollar drawn as an illustration for a book must be in black and white, not in full color. A dollar must also be shown either larger than one and one-half times the size of a real dollar, or smaller than three-quarters the size of a real dollar.

73

## Comprehension Skills

COMPREHENSION

### Sequence

Tell students to look for clues that tell the order in which events happen. Paying careful attention to sequence helps readers fully understand what they are reading and anticipate what might happen next. Sometimes illustrations can help establish the sequence of events in a story.

- Ask students to point out the sequence of the fiction part of the text. *First, a girl loses money. Then David and Eric approach the place where the money fell.*
- Ask students to tell the order of events in the nonfiction part. *When money is printed, the basic design is printed. Then cut sheets go back for a second printing. Next, the bills are checked, sorted into bundles, and sent to Federal Reserve Banks. Finally, those banks send them into circulation.*

Encourage students to use time-order words in their explanation of the sequence of events in the selection. Record story events in order on the board or on an overhead transparency.

Sequence

Introduced in Grade 1.

Scaffolded throughout Grades 2 and 3.

**REINTRODUCED:** Unit 1, Lesson 6

**REINFORCED:** Unit 4, Lesson 6
Unit 5, Lesson 1
Unit 5, Lesson 7

**TESTED:** Unit 4 Assessment

**Second Reading Recommendation**

ORAL • **SILENT**

### Differentiating Instruction

| If... | Then... |
|---|---|
| English Learners need extra help with vocabulary | Use ***English Learner Support Guide*** pages 326–327 |
| English Learners need extra help with sequence | Use ***English Learner Support Guide*** pages 326–328 |

### Word Knowledge

**suffix *-ment*:** government

COMPREHENSION

## Comprehension Strategies

Begin prompting students for responses. Praise answers that are appropriate, even if they do not match the student sample. This will encourage students to use strategies as they read.

### Prompting

② **Asking Questions** *I see some things here that look a little confusing. I know I have some questions. Who else has any questions here?*

### Student Sample

**Asking Questions** *Is this section part of the story? I see the words that are part of the story; they go with the illustration. But this paragraph is in its own section. This information isn't a part of the story, but it does give facts that have to do with the story.*

### Word Knowledge

**antonyms:**
**hard** (easy)
**many** (few)
**lost** (found)

**Teacher Tip** COMPREHENSION STRATEGIES Students' own think-alouds are always preferred to the teacher's. Encourage students to model for one another when they work out problems or as they come up with ideas when they read.

**Teacher Tip** Remind students to use context clues, apposition, or word structure to figure out the meaning of difficult words as they are reading.

As Matt and Eric were walking home from school one day . . .

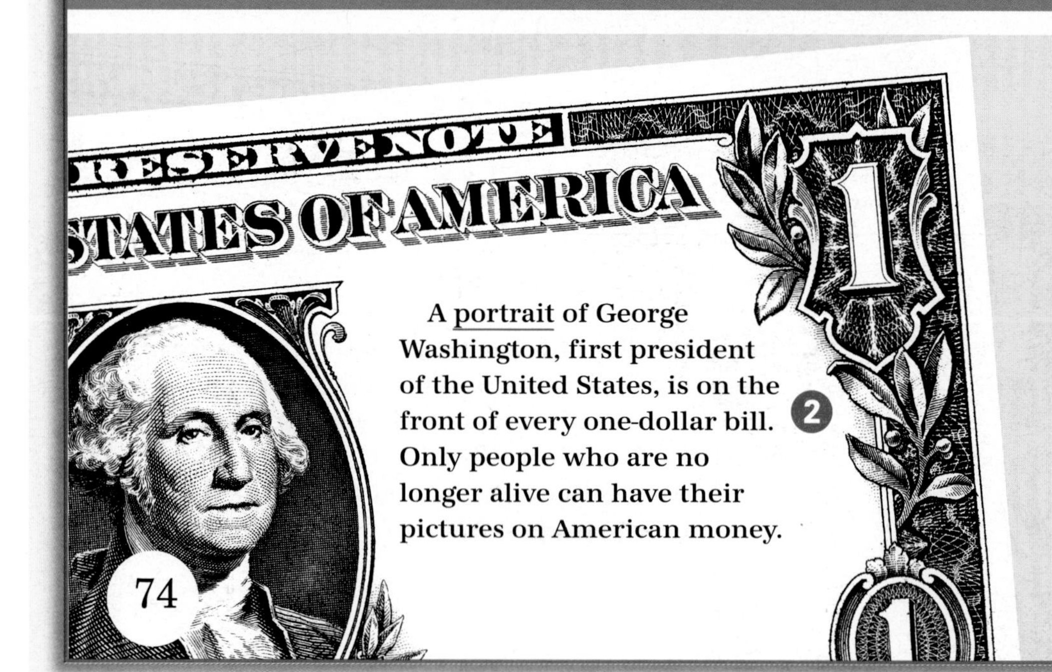


A portrait of George Washington, first president of the United States, is on the front of every one-dollar bill. ② Only people who are no longer alive can have their pictures on American money.

74

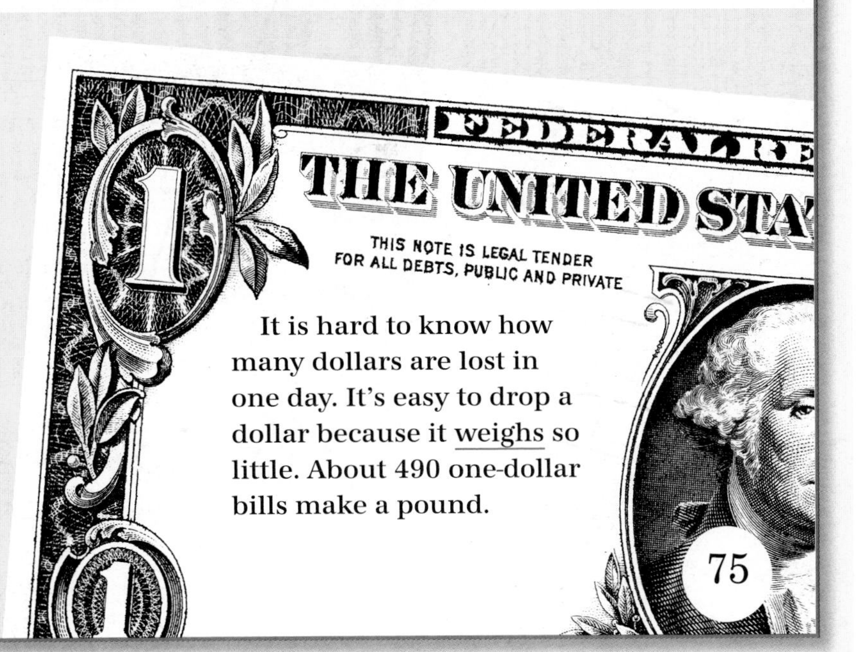


It is hard to know how many dollars are lost in one day. It's easy to drop a dollar because it weighs so little. About 490 one-dollar bills make a pound.

75

## Comprehension Skills

COMPREHENSION

### Sequence

Remind students that time-order words are clues to the sequence of events in a text. They include words such as *first, then, next, after, before,* and *finally.*

- What is the sequence of events in the story so far? *(After the girl dropped her money, Matt and Eric found it on the ground on their way home from school.)*

### Word Knowledge

**antonyms:** **first** (last)
**every** (none)
**alive** (dead)

**Teacher Tip** Tell students that good readers keep thinking about the questions that come up about the topic, and they keep coming back to those questions. As they read, tell them to keep the questions on the Concept/Question Board in mind. Have them make notes to themselves in the Response Journal section of their Writer's Notebooks about which questions seem most important. Tell them that good readers always think about what is important in selections, and they try to remember this important information.

### Differentiating Instruction

| If... | Then... |
|---|---|
| English Learners need extra help with vocabulary | Use ***English Learner Support Guide*** pages 328–329 |
| English Learners need extra help with sequence | Use ***English Learner Support Guide*** pages 329–330 |

COMPREHENSION

## Comprehension Strategies

### Teacher Modeling

**3 Making Connections** *I have a connection here. I have noticed that number before and always wondered what it meant. I've noticed the star too, but no one I asked knew what that meant. Now I have an explanation for something I wondered about. What other connections to the story can we make?*

#### Word Knowledge

**related words:** **dollar**
**bills**
**tender**

**Teacher Tip** Ask students to pay attention to the way characters in the story use money. Do their actions remind students of any other stories they have read?

**Teacher Tip COMPREHENSION** Good readers are active readers. They interact with the text as they read by emoting, reacting, responding, and problem solving in their efforts to construct and maintain meaning.

Matt offered to buy Eric's shoelaces for the dollar.

Dollar bills are used to buy things, pay back money that was borrowed, or pay for a service, such as a bus ride. There is a notice on each dollar that makes this clear: "This note is legal tender for all debts, public and private."

76

Eric used the dollar to buy some bubble gum . . .

SERVE NOTE
TES OF AMERICA
G 90445557 D

The front of every dollar has a long number in green ink, which appears in two different places. This is called the serial number. No two dollars have the same serial number. If a dollar is damaged while it is printed, it is replaced by a bill with a star where the last letter of the serial number would usually be. ❸ These bills are called star notes.

DOLLAR

77

## Comprehension Skills

COMPREHENSION

### Sequence

Ask students to keep track of the sequence of the story as they read. Keeping track of events is especially important in a text such as this one, in which the story action is broken up by factual inserts. Remind students to use time-order words to keep events in order.

- *After Matt found the dollar, he bought Eric's shoelaces.*
- *Next, Eric took the dollar to the store to buy bubble gum.*

What is the sequence of the factual information?

- *First a dollar is damaged during printing. Then it's replaced by a bill with a star replacing the last letter of the serial number.*

**Word Knowledge**

**related words:** **dollar** **note**

**Teacher Tip** The more you think aloud while you read, the more comfortable students will become with doing the same.

COMPREHENSION

## Comprehension Strategies

### Prompting

**4 Making Connections** *I see things here that I have a connection with. Does anyone else?*

### Student Sample

**Making Connections** *I have a connection here. This reminds me of one time when I did the exact same thing. My Grandma had given me money and I put it in my pocket. Then I forgot about it until later when Mom found it in the washing machine. The dollar was okay once it dried.*

### Word Knowledge

**related words:** **dollar**
**change**

**Teacher Tip** Encourage students to think aloud, practicing the strategies they have learned. Tell students that their ideas about the story are very important to the whole class's understanding of the story.

. . . and Jennifer received the dollar as part of her change from a five-dollar bill.

78

If dollars are in water a short time, they usually aren't damaged. They can't be ripped easily, either. This is because dollars are printed on especially strong paper made of cotton, linen, and silk. If you look closely, you can see the red and blue silk threads. 4

79

## Comprehension Skills

COMPREHENSION

### Sequence

Ask students to continue keeping track of story events. Remind them that tracking the order of events helps them better understand what they read.

- *After Eric bought the gum, Jennifer got the same dollar back as change for what she bought.*
- *Then she put the dollar in her pocket and forgot about it.*
- *After that, her Mom washed the jeans with the dollar in them.*

**Word Knowledge**

**antonyms:** **Mom** (Dad)
**my** (your)

COMPREHENSION

## Comprehension Strategies

### Prompting

**5 Summarizing** *Let's stop here and summarize all the important things that have happened so far. Who else would like to summarize the story?*

### Student Sample

**Summarizing** *First a runner lost a dollar out of her pocket. Then Matt and Eric saw the dollar on their way home from school. Matt kept the dollar and used it to buy Eric's shoelaces. Then Eric used the dollar to buy gum. Jennifer got the same dollar back as change at the store. She left the dollar in her pocket and it got thrown in the laundry with her jeans. Then Jennifer bought a hat from Rob at the flea market.*

### Word Knowledge

**related words:** **dollar**
**counterfeit**
**bills**

**Teacher Tip** Remind students that responses to texts are very individual. Each person responds in a unique way. Explain to students that this is natural and remind them to be respectful of the contributions of others.

Jennifer went to a flea market and bought a funny hat from Rob with the dollar. At a booth near Rob's, a ticket seller was handed an odd-looking dollar bill. 5



The formula for the black and green inks used to print dollars is a secret known only by the Bureau of Engraving and Printing. The secret is important; it keeps people from making fake, or counterfeit, bills exactly like the real ones.

80

81

## Comprehension Skills

COMPREHENSION

### Sequence

Students should continue placing the story events in sequence, using time-order words when possible.

- *After Jennifer got her dollar back out of the laundry, she used it to buy a hat from Rob at the flea market. Then a man handed a strange-looking dollar to a person in a booth near Rob's.*

**Teacher Tip** Good readers constantly evaluate their understanding of what they read. Stop often to make sure students are doing this.

### Differentiating Instruction

| If... | Then... |
| --- | --- |
| English Learners need extra help with vocabulary | Use ***English Learner Support Guide*** pages 330–331 |
| English Learners need extra help with sequence | Use ***English Learner Support Guide*** pages 331–332 |

COMPREHENSION

## Comprehension Strategies

### Prompting

**6 Asking Questions** *I see things here that I have questions about. Who else has any questions here?*

### Student Sample

**Asking Questions** *I have a question. Why did the lady ask the man with the odd-looking dollar to step aside? What happened to him? I'm going to reread the last page. The man from the booth called someone. I bet whoever he called asked him to take the man aside and ask him some questions. I think he might be in trouble if the dollar is fake.*

### Word Knowledge

**antonyms:** **We** (They)
**questions** (answers)
**few** (many)

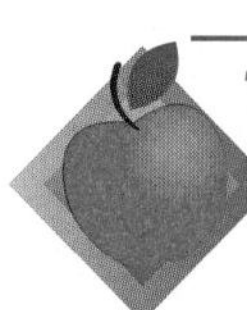

**Teacher Tip** Remind students to use the different reading strategies they have learned as they need to. They can use several at a time in whatever order they need to fully understand the text.

**Teacher Tip** Be sure students answer questions with appropriate elaboration.

**"We want to ask you a few questions about this dollar. Could you step over here for a minute?"** 6

82

Sometimes people called counterfeiters *do* make fake money. But it's very hard to make a dollar that looks and feels like a real one. When counterfeiters are caught, they're fined and sent to jail.

83

## Comprehension Skills

### Sequence

Students should continue placing story events in sequential order, using time-order words.

- *After the man gave the person at the booth an odd-looking dollar, the person behind the booth made a phone call. Then he and a lady asked the man to step aside so they could talk to him about the dollar.*

### Word Knowledge

**antonyms:** **fake** (real)
**hard** (easy)

**Teacher Tip** It may be helpful to list time-order words, such as *then, after, before, later,* or *next,* on the board when discussing sequence.

COMPREHENSION

COMPREHENSION

## Comprehension Strategies

### Prompting

**7 Making Connections** *I see things here that I have a connection with. Does anyone else?*

### Student Sample

**Making Connections** *Yes, I have a connection here. Sometimes our neighbor, Mrs. Francis, asks me and my brother to do chores for money. Sometimes we rake leaves for her or take care of her dog when she's away.*

### Word Knowledge

**antonyms:** **give** (take)

**Teacher Tip** Watch to see if students' application of a given strategy is becoming more effective over time.

Back at home, Rob asked his sister Kathy to do a chore for him. . . . 7

84

When a dollar changes hands, many people don't realize they're holding the Great Seal of the United States. The two sides of the Seal, an official symbol of our country, are shown in circles on the back of every one-dollar bill. One circle has an eagle in it; the other, a pyramid with an eye. The bald eagle, our national emblem, is holding arrows and an olive branch. The arrows stand for war and the olive branch for peace. The eagle faces the olive branch, which means the United States wants peace, not war. The pyramid stands for strength and growth; the eye, spiritual values.

85

# Comprehension Skills

## Sequence

Students should continue to place events from the story in sequential order, using time-order words to do so.

- *After Jennifer bought the hat from Rob, he took the dollar home and gave it to his sister for walking the dog. Then Kathy dropped the dollar.*

### Word Knowledge

**related words:** **Great Seal**
**symbol**
**emblem**

### Science/Social Studies Connection Center

Refer to the ***Science/Social Studies Connection Center*** Card 32 for a social studies activity that students can investigate.

COMPREHENSION

## Differentiating Instruction

| If... | Then... |
| --- | --- |
| Students have an understanding of the selection and would enjoy a challenge | Have them bring in foreign currency, such as a Canadian penny that they might have received accidentally in a store. Then have them find out the origins and significance of the symbols on the coin or bill. |

COMPREHENSION

## Comprehension Strategies

### Prompting

**8 Asking Questions** *Does anyone have questions here they would like to ask?*

### Student Sample

**Asking Questions** *I do. Why does a government official have to inspect some dollars? I'll read the section again to see if I missed something the first time. I see that an official inspects dollars if less than half of it remains. Why is that, I wonder? Maybe it's easier to fool someone with a part of a dollar bill. That must be it. Only an official could inspect a tiny part of a dollar bill and know for sure if it was real or fake.*

**Word Knowledge**

**antonyms:** **come** (go)
**here** (there)

**Teacher Tip** Whenever possible, allow students to generate and direct discussion and to take over the process of instruction.

86

## Comprehension Skills

COMPREHENSION

### Sequence

Sometimes story illustrations fill in the sequence of events more than the text of the story. Ask students to use these illustrations to put story events in sequence.

- *After Kathy dropped the dollar, the dog grabbed it and ran with it. Then Rob and Kathy caught the dog and got the dollar back. While they were taking the dollar back, it ripped in the dog's mouth.*

### Word Knowledge

**suffix *-ment*:** **government**

### Differentiating Instruction

| If... | Then... |
|---|---|
| English Learners need extra help with vocabulary | Use ***English Learner Support Guide*** pages 333–334 |
| English Learners need extra help with sequence | Use ***English Learner Support Guide*** pages 334–335 |

COMPREHENSION

## Comprehension Strategies

### Prompting

**9 Making Connections** *I see things here that I have a connection with. Does anyone else?*

### Student Sample

**Making Connections** *I have a connection here. The way Kathy is making a list of things she might buy reminds me of one time when I got a lot of money for my birthday. I wanted to think about how to spend it before I went to the store. I made a list then, too. Except I couldn't decide what to spend it on, so I saved it instead. Now I have a savings account.*

### Word Knowledge

**related words:** owls<br>spiders<br>creatures

**Teacher Tip** Remind students that in some selections, illustrations tell as much as words. If students feel confused, ask them to reread and to look carefully at illustrations to supply any missing information.

Lots of people say they see pictures of tiny owls or spiders near the corners of dollar bills. But the Bureau of Engraving and Printing says there are no such creatures on our money.

88

Kathy thought about different ways to spend the dollar. 9

89

## Comprehension Skills

### Sequence

Ask students to continue placing story events in sequential order, using time-order words to do so.

- *After Rob and Kathy got the dollar back from the dog, Kathy made a list of things she could buy with the dollar.*

**Word Knowledge**

**related words:** **spend**
**dollar**

COMPREHENSION

COMPREHENSION

## Comprehension Strategies

### Prompting

**10 Summarizing** *Let's summarize all that's happened in the story since we last stopped to summarize. The last thing that happened then was that Jennifer bought a hat from Rob at the flea market. Who would like to finish the summary?*

### Student Sample

**Summarizing** *A man at the flea market gave someone an odd-looking dollar, and then he had to step aside to talk to some people. Then Rob gave the dollar to his sister for walking the dog. After that, Kathy dropped the dollar, and the dog ran away with it. Then the dollar tore when Rob and Kathy tried to get it back. Next Kathy taped it together and used it to buy the first ice cream cone from Carl's Cones, who put it in a frame on the wall.*

### Discussing Strategy Use

After students read the selection, encourage them to share any problems encountered and to tell what strategies they used.

- What connections did they make between the reading and what they already know?
- What questions did they ask as they read?
- Where did they pause in the reading to summarize?

These are questions good readers ask after they read a text. After reading, the students should always be asking, "What did I find interesting? What is important here?" Later, remind the students again that whenever they conclude a reading, they should ask themselves questions about what was in the text.

90

**Teacher Tip BUILDING FLUENCY** As students read, you may notice that some need work in building fluency. During Workshop, have these students select a section of the text (a minimum of 160 words) to read several times in order to build fluency.

One-dollar bills wear out in about eighteen months because they are passed from person to person so often. Banks collect worn-out bills and send them to one of the Federal Reserve Banks. There they are shredded by machine into little pieces too small to be put together again. But once in a while, people will keep a dollar because it has special meaning for them. 10

91

## Comprehension Skills

### Sequence

Remind students that sometimes they must supply the time-order words to place events in sequential order. This is especially important in stories that use illustrations to explain story events. Have students place the final story events in order.

- *After Kathy made her list, she decided to buy an ice-cream cone. Then she bought a cone from Carl's Cones, where she was the first customer. Finally, the storeowner placed the dollar bill in a frame and hung it on a wall.*

### Checking Comprehension

Ask students the following questions to check their comprehension of the story.

- Why do you think the author of this selection combined fiction and nonfiction? How does the structure of the selection affect the reader? *(To make the informational part more interesting and to show how money passes from person to person.)*
- Who is responsible for printing and distributing money? *(The federal government is in charge of printing and distributing paper money.)*
- Why is special ink and paper used for making money, and why do bills have serial numbers? *(So that the government can tell the difference between real and fake money, and so that making fake money is more difficult.)*

COMPREHENSION

**Formal Assessment**

See pages 22–25 in ***Unit 4 Assessment*** to test student's comprehension of "The Go-Around Dollar."

### Differentiating Instruction

| If... | Then... |
| --- | --- |
| English Learners need extra help reviewing the selection | Use ***English Learner Support Guide*** pages 335–337 |

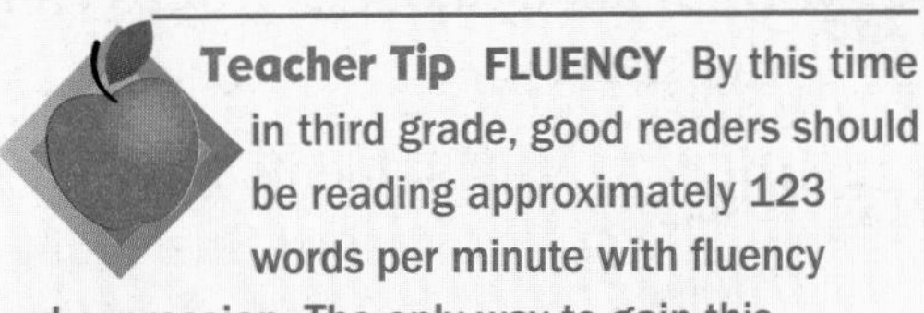

**Teacher Tip** **FLUENCY** By this time in third grade, good readers should be reading approximately 123 words per minute with fluency and expression. The only way to gain this fluency is through practice. Have students reread the selection to you and to each other during Workshop to help build fluency.

**Teacher Tip** **DISCUSSION** When you call on a student, allow him or her a few seconds to consider your question and arrive at an answer.

**Routine Card**
Refer to ***Routine 6*** for the *handing-off process.*

| Clues | Problems | Wonderings |
|---|---|---|
| Title is "The Go-Around Dollar" | Treasury | How does money get made? |

SRA Open Court Reading — Reading Transparency 46

***Reading Transparency 46***

**www.sra4kids.com**
**Web Connection**
Some students may choose to conduct a computer search for additional books or information about money. Invite them to make a list of these books and sources of information to share with classmates and the school librarian. Check the Reading link of the SRA Web page for additional links to the theme-related Web site.

## Discussing the Selection

After the first read, the whole group discusses the selection and any personal thoughts, reactions, problems, or questions that it raises. To stimulate discussion, students can ask one another the kinds of questions good readers ask themselves about a text: *How does it connect to money? What have I learned that is new? What did I find interesting about this story? What is important here? What was difficult to understand? Why would someone want to read this?*

**Handing-Off Process** Seeing you as a contributing member of the group sets a strong example for students. To emphasize that you are part of the group, actively participate in the *handing-off process:* Raise your hand to be called on by the last speaker when you have a contribution to make. Point out unusual and interesting insights verbalized by students so that these insights are recognized and discussed. As the year progresses, students will take more and more responsibility for discussions of the selections.

Engage students in a discussion to determine whether they have grasped the following ideas:

- how money is circulated
- what things are done to prevent people from making fake money
- how money changes hands from person to person
- what happens to damaged bills

During this time, have students return to the clues, problems, and wonderings they noted during browsing to determine whether the clues were borne out by the selection, whether and how their problems were solved, and whether their wonderings were answered or deserve further discussion and investigation. Let students decide which items deserve further discussion.

Also have students return to the Focus Questions on the first page of the selection. Select a student to read the questions aloud, and have volunteers answer the questions. If students do not know the answers to the questions, have them return to the text to find the answers.

You may wish to review the elements of realistic fiction and expository text with the students at this time. Ask the students how they can tell which section of the selection is realistic fiction and which section is expository text.

Have students break into small groups to discuss what this story tells them about money. Groups can then share their ideas with the rest of the class.

If students have ever found or lost money, encourage them to record this event.

## Review Selection Vocabulary

Have students review the definitions of the selection vocabulary words that they wrote in the vocabulary section of their Writer's Notebooks. Remind them that they discussed the meanings of these words before reading the selection. Have students write sentences for each of the vocabulary words after the definitions in the same section of their Writer's Notebooks. They can use the definitions and the sentences to study for the vocabulary portion of their Lesson Assessments. Have them add to the personal dictionary section of their Writer's Notebooks any other interesting words that they clarified while reading. Encourage students to refer to the selection vocabulary words throughout the unit. The words from the selection are:

**circulation** **formula** **pyramid** **tender** **official** **emblem**

If you created a Word Bank of key words related to the theme Money, remind students to find words from other resources, from their activities, and from family discussions and add them to the Word Bank. Students may also place synonyms and antonyms in the Word Bank, organizing words by number of syllables.

## View Fine Art

Have students reflect on the photo of the Daric coin on page 56 of the ***Student Anthology*** and share their thoughts and reactions with the class. Explain that this coin was found in Persia, now known as Iran. The coin was created by a skilled laborer who placed a sheet of metal between two plates with carved images. A mallet was used to hammer the plates together so that the design would be embossed onto the metal. The Daric coin is named after Darius I, the emperor of Persia from 522 B.C.E.–486 B.C.E. The artist also included a lance and bow, both symbols of power, and gave the coin the name of "archer." This Daric coin is one of the most valuable ancient coins.

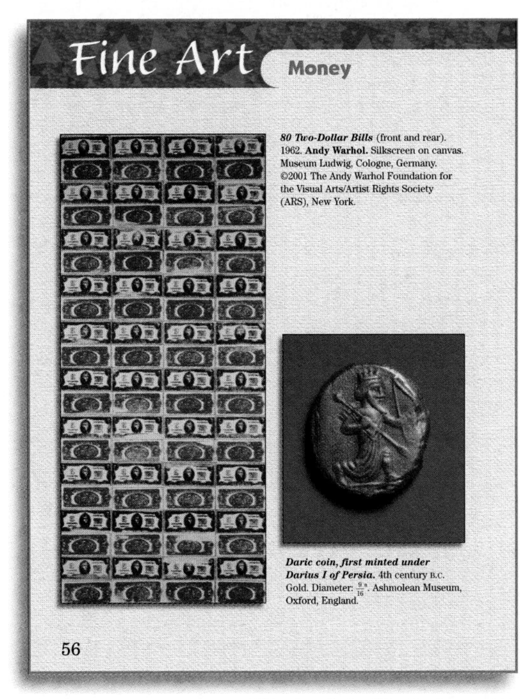
Fine Art Money

*80 Two-Dollar Bills* (front and rear). 1962. **Andy Warhol.** Silkscreen on canvas. Museum Ludwig, Cologne, Germany. ©2001 The Andy Warhol Foundation for the Visual Arts/Artist Rights Society (ARS), New York.

*Daric coin, first minted under Darius I of Persia.* 4th century B.C. Gold. Diameter: $\frac{9}{16}$". Ashmolean Museum, Oxford, England.

56

***Student Anthology* p. 56**

## Home Connection

Distribute ***Home Connection,*** page 55. Encourage students to discuss "The Go-Around Dollar" with their families. Students will have the opportunity to discuss money with their families. ***Home Connection*** is also available in Spanish, page 56.

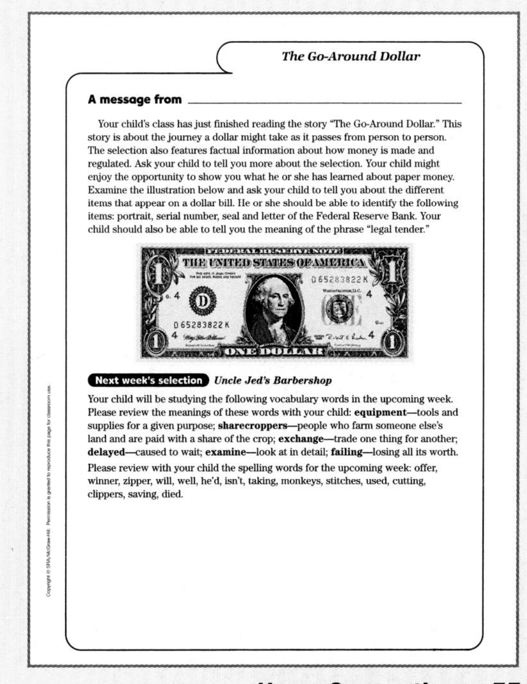
*The Go-Around Dollar*

**A message from** ______________________

Your child's class has just finished reading the story "The Go-Around Dollar." This story is about the journey a dollar might take as it passes from person to person. The selection also features factual information about how money is made and regulated. Ask your child to tell you more about the selection. Your child might enjoy the opportunity to show you what he or she has learned about paper money. Examine the illustration below and ask your child to tell you about the different items that appear on a dollar bill. He or she should be able to identify the following items: portrait, serial number, seal and letter of the Federal Reserve Bank. Your child should also be able to tell you the meaning of the phrase "legal tender."



**Next week's selection** ***Uncle Jed's Barbershop***

Your child will be studying the following vocabulary words in the upcoming week. Please review the meanings of these words with your child: **equipment**—tools and supplies for a given purpose; **sharecroppers**—people who farm someone else's land and are paid with a share of the crop; **exchange**—trade one thing for another; **delayed**—caused to wait; **examine**—look at in detail; **failing**—losing all its worth.

Please review with your child the spelling words for the upcoming week: offer, winner, zipper, will, well, he'd, isn't, taking, monkeys, stitches, used, cutting, clippers, saving, died.



***Home Connection* p. 55**

**Teacher Tip** This selection is an excellent time to teach sequence because of the two concurrent story lines. Students could present a skit where they reenact the events of the story. One group could act as lecturers on the symbolism of the dollar bill. The other group could act out the passing of the dollar bill in the realistic fiction section.

## Supporting the Reading

### Comprehension Skills: Sequence

**Teach** Young students sometimes find placing plot developments in order is a difficult task. This is because they do not yet have a firm grasp of time-and-order sequence. Remind them to pay special attention to time-order words and what they mean. For example, in the sentence "Before we ate dinner, we went to the store," make sure students understand that going to the store came first. Being able to place plot events in the correct sequential order adds to students' comprehension of what they read.

**Guided Practice** Display the list of story events that you created with the class. Have students take turns explaining the order of two events using either of the words *before* or *after*. For example, a student might say "Before Matt bought Eric's shoelaces, he found a dollar," or "After Matt found a dollar, he bought Eric's shoelaces." This exercise will help students develop an understanding of time-and-order sequence.

**Independent Practice** Read through the Focus section of ***Comprehension and Language Arts Skills,*** page 116, with students. Guide them through the Identify portion, and help them come up with examples found in the story. Then have students complete the Practice and Apply portions of ***Comprehension and Language Arts Skills,*** page 117.

**Link to Writing** Ask students to write about a special day they have had and to write about the events of that day. Remind students to use time-order words to explain the order in which events took place.

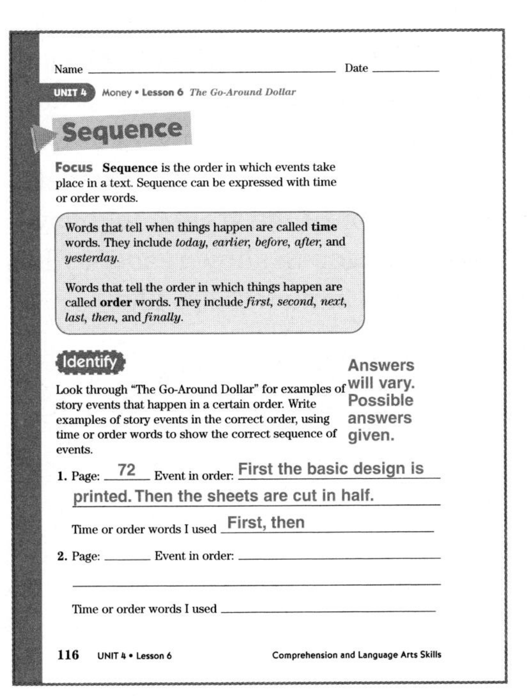

Name ____________ Date ______

UNIT 4 Money • Lesson 6 *The Go-Around Dollar*

## Sequence

**Focus** **Sequence** is the order in which events take place in a text. Sequence can be expressed with time or order words.

Words that tell when things happen are called **time** words. They include *today, earlier, before, after,* and *yesterday.*

Words that tell the order in which things happen are called **order** words. They include *first, second, next, last, then,* and *finally.*

**Identify**

Look through "The Go-Around Dollar" for examples of story events that happen in a certain order. Write examples of story events in the correct order, using time or order words to show the correct sequence of events. Answers will vary. Possible answers given.

1. Page: 72 Event in order: First the basic design is printed. Then the sheets are cut in half.

   Time or order words I used First, then

2. Page: ______ Event in order: ____________

   Time or order words I used ____________

116 UNIT 4 • Lesson 6 Comprehension and Language Arts Skills

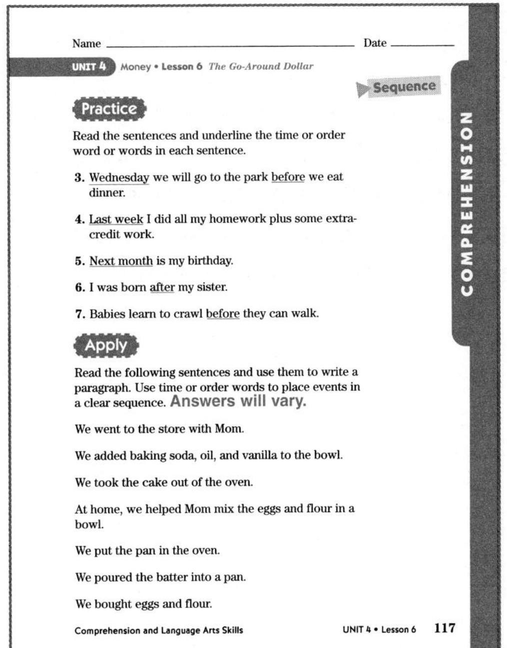

Name ____________ Date ______

UNIT 4 Money • Lesson 6 *The Go-Around Dollar*

Sequence

COMPREHENSION

**Practice**

Read the sentences and underline the time or order word or words in each sentence.

3. Wednesday we will go to the park before we eat dinner.
4. Last week I did all my homework plus some extra-credit work.
5. Next month is my birthday.
6. I was born after my sister.
7. Babies learn to crawl before they can walk.

**Apply**

Read the following sentences and use them to write a paragraph. Use time or order words to place events in a clear sequence. Answers will vary.

We went to the store with Mom.

We added baking soda, oil, and vanilla to the bowl.

We took the cake out of the oven.

At home, we helped Mom mix the eggs and flour in a bowl.

We put the pan in the oven.

We poured the batter into a pan.

We bought eggs and flour.

Comprehension and Language Arts Skills UNIT 4 • Lesson 6 117

***Comprehension and Language Arts Skills pp. 116–117***

## Differentiating Instruction

| If... | Then... |
|---|---|
| Students need extra help with sequence | Use ***Reteach*** pages 119–120 |
| Students have an understanding of sequence and would enjoy a challenge | Use ***Challenge*** page 105 |

**Teacher Tip** **WRITING** Encourage students to exchange papers with a peer to practice proofreading skills. Have students look for initial capital letters at the beginning of each sentence and end punctuation at the end of each sentence.

Sequence

Introduced in Grade 1.

Scaffolded throughout Grades 2 and 3.

**REINTRODUCED:** Unit 1, Lesson 6

**REINFORCED:** Unit 4, Lesson 6
Unit 5, Lesson 1
Unit 5, Lesson 7

**TESTED:** Unit 4 Assessment

**Differentiating Instruction**

| If... | Then... |
|---|---|
| Students need extra practice identifying dialogue | Have them look back at selections they have read in their ***Anthologies*** and find other examples of dialogue |

## Literary Elements

### Dialogue

**Teach** Ask students what they already know about dialogue in stories. If necessary remind students that dialogue is spoken words in a text. Writers use dialogue primarily for characterization and also at important points in the plot to help move the action along. Remind students that dialogue is enclosed in quotation marks, starts with a capital letter, and ends with end punctuation. Each time the speaker changes in a story, a new paragraph begins.

**Guided Practice** Ask students to find examples of dialogue in "The Go-Around Dollar." Ask them to explain how the dialogue helps them better understand the story characters. Point out that dialogue can move the plot along in a way that is sometimes more interesting than a description of the action could be. For example, when Jennifer left her dollar bill in her jeans, the narrator of the story could have explained what happened. Instead, the writer used dialogue to show readers what happened. Ask students how dialogue tells us what the characters are like.

**Independent Practice** Have students look in their Writer's Notebooks at the stories they wrote. Ask students to consider how dialogue could be used in their stories.

## Social Studies Connection

### Government and Money

In "The Go-Around Dollar," students read about the journey a dollar bill might have taken as it passed from person to person. They also learned about how money is made and regulated by the government. Now ask students to consider how the government generates money for its own income. Ask students questions such as the following: *Why does the government need money? What services does the government provide? Who pays police officers and postal workers? Who pays for libraries? Who pays for national parks and monuments? How does the government make money to provide services? Throughout history, who has paid for national structures such as palaces, temples, and tombs?*

Ask students to investigate these questions further. Students may choose between investigating these issues in a modern context or investigating a particular place and time in ancient history. Students may work alone, in pairs, or in small groups. Ask students to prepare a presentation of their findings, accompanied by visuals. Visuals can include a diagram that shows the flow of money to government from various sources and out through goods and services. Or the visual could be an illustration of a great monument from ancient times, for example.

**Teacher Tip MATERIALS**
- ✓ poster board
- ✓ colored pencils or markers

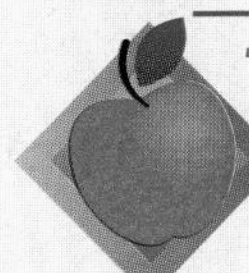

**Teacher Tip PURPOSE** To learn about how the government generates income and why it generates income.

**Teacher Tip** This activity could be linked to whatever historical period you are studying.

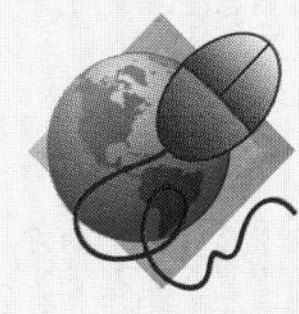

**www.sra4kids.com**
**Web Connection**
**For additional support, have students visit the Money Web site at www.sra4kids.com.**

## Concept Connections

### Linking the Selection

- Students might mention the picture of George Washington or the pyramid with an eye.
- The Bureau of Engraving and Printing prints paper money.

### Exploring Concept Vocabulary

The concept word for this lesson is ***currency.*** Write the word on the board. Work with students to develop a definition that clearly links to the unit theme. Have students copy the word and definition into the Vocabulary section of their Writer's Notebooks.

***Currency:*** the money that is used in a country as a means of exchange. For example, the currency in Japan is the yen.

- The official currency of the United States is the U.S. dollar.
- There are laws about how currency is made and reproduced so people cannot counterfeit, or copy, it to use as real, or legal, money.

Explain that the sentences students create should show an understanding of the word ***currency*** as well as the selection vocabulary word that they choose to use.

### Expanding the Concept

You may want to do a whole-group discussion to help students continue to develop their ability to engage in meaningful dialogue. However, students may conduct these dialogues in small groups. If the students work in small groups, bring the groups together and have them share their ideas with the whole class.

As students complete their discussions, have them record their ideas and impressions about the selection on page 85 of their ***Inquiry Journals.***

# The Go-Around Dollar

## Concept Connections

### Linking the Selection

Think about the following questions, and then record your responses in the Response Journal section of your Writer's Notebook.

- What types of symbols appear on the U.S. one-dollar bill?
- What role does the government play in making and maintaining paper money?

### Exploring Concept Vocabulary

The concept word for this lesson is ***currency.*** If you do not know what this word means, look it up in a dictionary. Answer these questions:

- What is the official ***currency*** of the United States?
- Why are there laws about how ***currency*** is made and how it is shown in illustrations?

In the Vocabulary section of your Writer's Notebook, write a sentence using the word ***currency*** and a selection vocabulary word.

### Expanding the Concept

Think about "The Go-Around Dollar." What did you learn about money that you did not already know? Compare the way Kathy spent her dollar to the way Alexander in "Alexander, Who Used to Be Rich Last Sunday" spent his dollar.

Try to use the word ***currency*** in your discussion.

Add new ideas about money to the Concept/Question Board.

92

**Informal Assessment**

**This may be a good time to observe students working in small groups and to mark your observations in the Teacher Observation Log, found in the *Program Assessment Teacher's Edition.***

**Teacher Tip CONCEPT VOCABULARY** Developing a repertoire of concept-related vocabulary will help students deepen their understanding of theme concepts, help facilitate class discussions, and help students formulate ideas, problems, and questions for inquiry.

## Meet the Author

**Barbara Johnston** and her family live in Virginia. She writes nonfiction books for children. She has even written a book about the life of the famous comedian, Bill Cosby. Another book, which she wrote under a different name, is about women who have won the Nobel Prize. Her books have been chosen for the Child Study Association of America's Children's Books of the Year.

## Meet the Illustrator

**Joyce Audy Zarins** has written as well as illustrated children's books. On a regular basis, she illustrates for children's magazines. Readers can find her illustrations in books such as *Log Cabin in the Woods; Toasted Bagels; Sand Dollar, Sand Dollar; Mrs. Peloki's Snake;* and *Piskies, Spriggans, and Other Magical Beings*. Currently, Zarins lives in Massachusetts.

93

## Meet the Author

After students read the information about Barbara Johnston, discuss the following questions with them.

- Why do you think Johnston chose the topic of women and the Nobel Prize for a children's book? *(Possible answer: She thought it was important for children to know about successful women.)*
- Why might an author, like Johnston, write a book using a different name? *(Possible answer: Maybe she thought one name sounded more professional than her real name.)*

## Meet the Illustrator

After students read the information about Joyce Audy Zarins, discuss the following questions with them.

- How might illustrating for a children's magazine be different from illustrating for a children's book? *(Possible answer: Maybe Zarins has to draw more often, because a magazine comes out more often than a book.)*
- How might the fact that Zarins both writes and illustrates children's books be beneficial to her career? *(Possible answer: Zarins probably has more jobs because she is able to work as either a writer or an artist. She can also understand what the other person, either the author or the illustrator, is going through and can help on both sides.)*

### Objectives

- Students come to a deeper understanding of money.
- Students will gain a deeper understanding of issues related to money.
- Student groups begin investigation and make revisions as necessary.

### Materials

- Student Anthology, Book 2, pp. 72–93
- Inquiry Journal, pp. 102–103
- Reading Transparency 29
- Research Assistant CD-ROM

**Teacher Tip** Federal Reserve Banks are located in the following cities: Boston, New York, Philadelphia, Chicago, San Francisco, and in Cleveland, Ohio; Richmond, Va.; Atlanta, Ga.; St. Louis, Mo.; Minneapolis, Minn.; Kansas City, Mo.; and Dallas, Texas.

Name________________ Date________

UNIT 4 Money

**Varieties of Money Chart**

Many different things have been used as money across the ages. As you read the selections in this unit and as you do your investigation, record the names of things that have been used as money, and when and where they were used.

Answers will vary.

| Things Used as Money | When | Where |
|---|---|---|
| | | |
| | | |
| | | |
| | | |
| | | |
| | | |

102 UNIT 4 *Varieties of Money Chart* • Inquiry Journal

***Inquiry Journal* p. 102**

INVESTIGATION

## Investigating Concepts Beyond the Text

Throughout the remaining time in this unit, meet with each group to arrange schedules and update calendars, discuss problems that students are encountering in their investigations, hear preliminary presentations and discussions of interesting findings, and arrange more formal presentations of students' investigations. As students progress, meet informally with them during Workshop. During these individual conferences, you might ask questions such as the following: *What did you look up? What are you finding out? What else might you need to find out? Can you give me more details about that fact or idea? How does this information help you? What does this information tell you that you didn't already know? How does new information change your initial problem, question, or conjecture? How can you revise or restate your initial conjecture? How might you present this information?* Remind students that the Research Cycle is recursive. Provide guidance to groups to ensure that they progress through the phases of the Research Cycle: obtaining information; revising problems, conjectures, needs, and plans (perhaps with input resulting from a presentation to the class); and proceeding to a further cycle of problem, conjecture, and so forth. Make sure students are effectively using titles, tables of contents, chapter headings, and glossaries of texts to aid in this cycle.

Have the groups meet to discuss questions or ideas they might have about the selection they have just read. Does the selection tell them something about money they did not know before? Does the selection make them wonder about something? After reading "The Go-Around Dollar," students might wish to create a story or miniplay about how money passes from person to person in our society. Alternatively, students might wish to investigate the different things that have been used for money in different places and times throughout history. Students can use page 102 of the ***Inquiry Journal*** to help them organize information. If students live near a city that has a Federal Reserve Bank, you might want to schedule an educational field trip for your class.

INVESTIGATION

## Concept/Question Board

Tell students this is a good time to post on the Concept/Question Board any new questions they have about money that "The Go-Around Dollar" might have raised. Remind them of your earlier discussion about the Concept/Question Board and ask them to tell what they remember about that discussion.

After reading each selection, students should use the Concept/Question Board to:

- Post any questions they asked about a selection before reading that have not yet been answered.
- Refer to as they formulate statements about concepts that apply to their investigations.
- Post general statements formulated by each collaborative group.
- Continue to post news articles or other items that they find during the unit investigation.
- Read and think about posted questions, articles, or concepts that interest them and provide answers to the questions.
- Students might wish to bring in articles or questions about how money is regulated or how it passes from person to person in our society.

Concept/Question Board

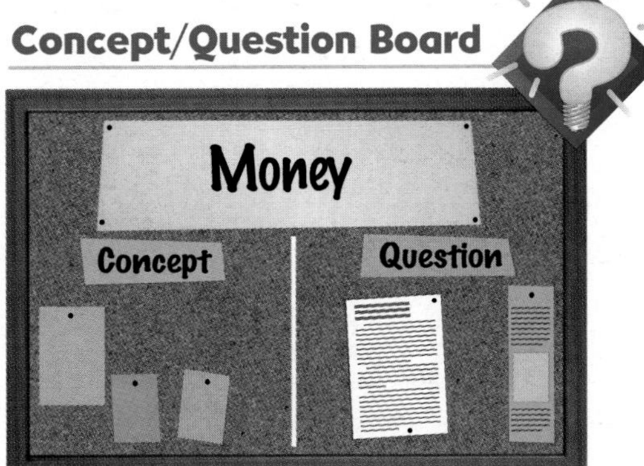


## Unit 4 Investigation Management

| | |
|---|---|
| Lesson 1 | Brainstorm questions related to the theme. Investigate alternatives to money, such as barter. |
| Lesson 2 | Groups form based on areas of shared interest. Investigate choices related to spending and saving money. |
| Lesson 3 | Begin forming conjectures. Brainstorm about how to turn hobbies into businesses. |
| Lesson 4 | Discuss conjectures in groups and begin plans. Look for stories or illustrations about the ways that money can change people and things that money cannot buy. |
| Lesson 5 | Students revise their plans as necessary and continue investigations. Groups can debate on borrowing and lending money. |
| Lesson 6 | Collaborative Investigation<br>**Continue investigations and prepare final presentations.**<br>Supplementary Activity<br>**Create a story or miniplay about how money passes from person to person, or plan a field trip to a Federal Reserve Bank.** |
| Lesson 7 | Groups give formal presentations. Students discuss saving money for personal goals or investigate the Great Depression further. |

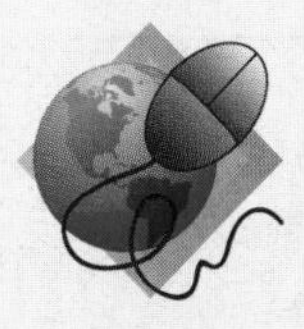

**Teacher Tip** Continue to encourage use of the Concept/Question Board by recognizing and thanking students for their contributions. Incorporate discussion of those items into classroom discussions whenever appropriate.

**www.sra4kids.com**
**Web Connection**
Students may wish to use the Money connections found on the Reading Web site.

Encourage students to use ***TechKnowledge*** to learn more about how to use a computer to complete various investigation tasks.

**Teacher Tip** Remind students that their investigations are ongoing. The unit investigations are not performed to find final conclusions or come to final decisions regarding any one topic. Instead, they are designed to stimulate further thinking and investigation, lasting past the end of a unit or the end of the school year.

**Formal Assessment**

Use the Research Rubrics on page 72J to assess students' ability to revise problems and conjectures.

**Teacher Tip** As students prepare for their presentations, have them use the contributions from you or from classmates to establish goals to improve their speaking and better their presentations.

INVESTIGATION

## Revising Conjectures

Now that students have been investigating the theme Money for several weeks, they may have new insights they would like to discuss with others or record for themselves. Looking over the entries they have made in their ***Inquiry Journals*** will show them how far they have come in their investigations. As students are concluding their investigations and preparing formal presentations, remind them to look at questions and ideas they had at the beginning of the unit. Have those ideas changed? If so, in what ways have they changed? What do they know now that they did not know before? Students should be using questions such as these to revise their initial conjectures. Have students work in their groups on revising and restating their investigation conjectures. Then have them proceed with plans for their presentations.

Name ______ Date ______

Money UNIT 4

### Recording Concept Information

As I read each selection, I learned these facts about money.

- "A New Coat for Anna" by Harriet Ziefert

Answers will vary.

- "Alexander, Who Used to Be Rich Last Sunday" by Judith Viorst

Answers will vary.

Inquiry Journal • *Recording Concept Information* UNIT 4 83

***Inquiry Journal p. 83***

## Diagrams

**Teach** Ask students what they remember about diagrams. If necessary, remind them that a diagram is a drawing that shows and labels the parts of something or explains how something works. Labels are used with the diagram to identify the parts of what is being shown.

**Guided Practice** Display ***Reading Transparency 29.*** Ask students what the diagram shows. *(a penny)*

Point to the features on the penny and ask students to tell what they are. Have students match the features to the answers written below the diagram. Label the four parts of the penny on the transparency as you discuss the diagram with the class. Have several real coins available for students to examine.

**Independent Practice** Ask students to draw an object that is made up of different parts (for example: a car, a computer keyboard, a television, etc.) After they have drawn the picture, ask them to label all of the parts of the object. For additional practice with diagrams, have students complete ***Inquiry Journal,*** page 103.

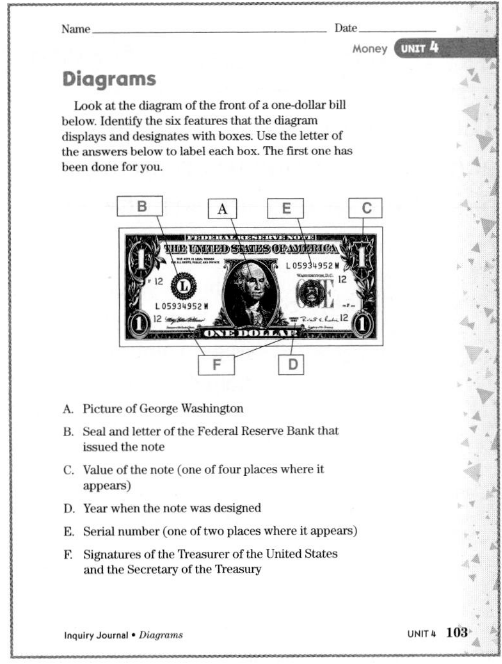
Name ______ Date ______

Money UNIT 4

Diagrams

Look at the diagram of the front of a one-dollar bill below. Identify the six features that the diagram displays and designates with boxes. Use the letter of the answers below to label each box. The first one has been done for you.



A. Picture of George Washington
B. Seal and letter of the Federal Reserve Bank that issued the note
C. Value of the note (one of four places where it appears)
D. Year when the note was designed
E. Serial number (one of two places where it appears)
F. Signatures of the Treasurer of the United States and the Secretary of the Treasury

Inquiry Journal • *Diagrams* UNIT 4 103

***Inquiry Journal* p. 103**

SUPPORTING THE INVESTIGATION

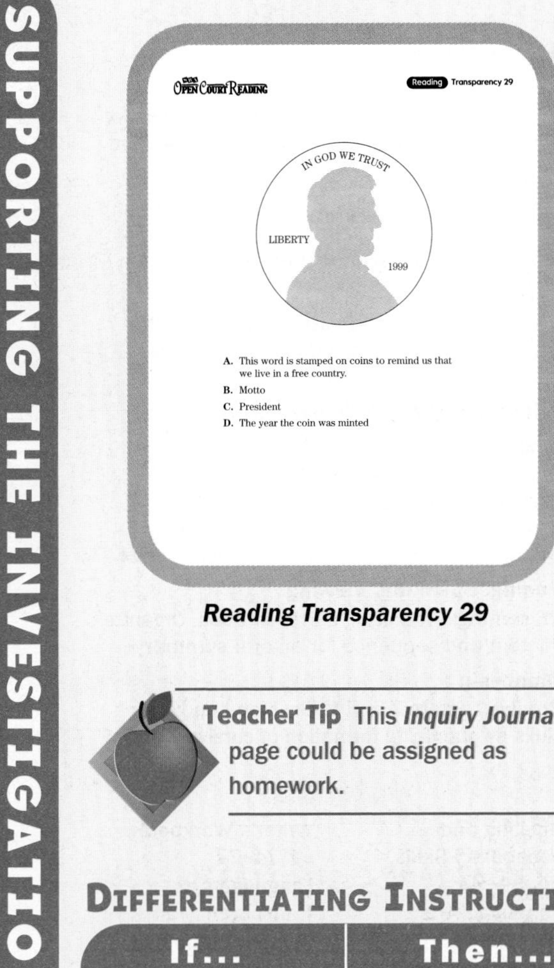


A. This word is stamped on coins to remind us that we live in a free country.
B. Motto
C. President
D. The year the coin was minted

***Reading Transparency 29***

**Teacher Tip** This ***Inquiry Journal*** page could be assigned as homework.

### Differentiating Instruction

| If... | Then... |
| --- | --- |
| Students are having difficulty with the Independent Practice portion of this activity | • Review ***Reading Transparency 29*** with them during Workshop<br>• Help them brainstorm a list of objects that are made up of different parts, and then help them create a diagram for one of the objects<br>• Work with them on ***Inquiry Journal*** page 103 |

### Objectives

**Word Analysis**

**Spelling**

- **Compound Words.** Develop an understanding of how compound words are formed and spelled.

**Vocabulary**

- **Money Words.** Using words from "The Go-Around Dollar," learn the meanings of words that relate to math and currency.

**Writing Process Strategies**

- **Persuasive Writing—Poster.** Building on the idea of ways to spend a dollar, learn to use persuasive writing to create a poster.

**English Language Conventions**

**Grammar, Usage, and Mechanics**

- **Comparative and Superlative Adverbs.** Understand the use and formation of comparative and superlative adverbs. Find examples of adverbs in "The Go-Around Dollar."

**Listening, Speaking, Viewing**

- **Presenting: Organizing a Presentation.** Organize content and sequence for an oral summary.

**Penmanship**

- **Cursive Letters *Z* and *V*.** Develop handwriting skills by practicing formation of cursive *Z* and *V*.

### Materials

- Spelling and Vocabulary Skills, pp. 94–97
- Language Arts Handbook
- Comprehension and Language Arts Skills, pp. 116–121
- Writer's Workbook, pp. 74–77
- Language Arts Transparency 24
- Student Anthology

### Differentiating Instruction

***Reteach, Challenge,*** and ***Intervention*** lessons are available to support the language arts instruction in this lesson.

### Research in Action

The proportion of difficult words in a text is the single most powerful predictor of text difficulty, and a reader's general vocabulary knowledge is the single best predictor of how well that reader can understand text.
*(William E. Nagy,* Vocabulary Instruction and Reading Comprehension)

OVERVIEW

# Language Arts Overview

## Word Analysis

**Spelling** The Spelling activities expand upon how a compound word is formed from two complete words. Unlike a contraction, a compound word retains the original spellings of the two base words, as in *newspaper.*

### Selection Spelling Words

These words from "The Go-Around Dollar" are compound words.

**sometimes neighborhood overprinting something shoelaces**

**Vocabulary** The Vocabulary activities extend the instruction of the Vocabulary Skill Words from "The Go-Around Dollar" to recognize the meanings of economic terms and words that relate to money.

### Vocabulary Skill Words

**treasury circulation* tender* debts formula***

**Also Selection Vocabulary*

**Additional Materials:** dictionary

## Writing Process Strategies

The Writing Process Strategies lesson involves instruction in using persuasive writing to create a poster. Visual composition—colors, placement of text and art, design—is used as an important part of a persuasive poster.

To teach spreadsheet applications in the writing process, show students how to display spreadsheet data in a bar graph and a line graph. You might want to help students create a bar graph to persuade people to help those less fortunate. ***TechKnowledge,*** Level 3, Lesson 72, teaches these spreadsheet application skills.

## English Language Conventions

**Grammar, Usage, and Mechanics** **Comparative and Superlative Adverbs.** This lesson develops an understanding of comparative and superlative adverbs.

**Listening, Speaking, Viewing** **Presenting: Organizing a Presentation.** In this Presenting lesson, students will work together to decide the appropriate content and sequence for an oral summary.

**Penmanship** **Cursive Letters *Z* and *V*.** This lesson develops handwriting skills by having students learn formation of *Z* and *V*. Students then write words from the literature selection.

# DAY 1

## Word Analysis

### Spelling

**Assessment: Pretest**

**Compound Words**

**Teach**

Give students the Pretest on page 40 of ***Unit 4 Assessment.*** Have them proofread and correct any misspelled words.

**Pretest Sentences**

1. **playground** A slide is part of a **playground**.
2. **underground** A subway is **underground**.
3. **chalkboard** Teachers write on a **chalkboard**.
4. **cardboard** A television is packed in **cardboard**.
5. **spacewalk** Astronauts can take a **spacewalk**.
6. **sidewalk** Bikes are ridden on a **sidewalk**.
7. **rainbow** A **rainbow** is made from water and light.
8. **anything** In a dream, you can do **anything**.
9. **campfire** A **campfire** is warm.
10. **eyelash** An **eyelash** protects the eye.
11. **shoelaces** Most tennis shoes have **shoelaces**.
12. **something** A goal is **something** you work toward.
13. **overprinting** Printing too much is **overprinting**.
14. **neighborhood** A **neighborhood** is where people live.
15. **sometimes** Wind **sometimes** causes damage.

Diagnose any misspellings by determining if students misspelled the way the compound word was formed or some other part of the word. Then use the Pretest as a take-home list to study spellings for compound words.

## Writing Process Strategies

### Getting Ideas

**Persuasive Poster**

**Teach**

Review ***Language Arts Handbook,*** pages 156–157, on persuasive writing.

**Inspiration**

Teacher Model: *"I often find money when I take a walk after school. I put it in a jar and then give it to the local animal shelter to help pay for the cost of feeding the animals. I am going to make a poster persuading others to give to the animal shelter too."*

**Brainstorming**

Using the many ways in which money is used as a springboard for ideas, encourage students to suggest what they would encourage others to do with their money. Make a list of these ideas on the board.

### Guided Practice

**Getting Ideas**

Have students write ideas for a persuasive poster in their Writer's Notebooks.

Persuasive Writing

Persuasive writing does two things. It can make readers think or feel a certain way. It can also make readers do something. Sometimes persuasive writing can do both of these things at the same time. Advertisements are one kind of persuasive writing. You will learn about other kinds in the following lessons.

156 Persuasive Writing

*Language Arts Handbook p. 156*

## English Language Conventions

### Grammar, Usage, and Mechanics

**Grammar: Comparative and Superlative Adverbs**

**Teach**

- Use ***Language Arts Handbook,*** page 266, for the definitions and examples of comparative and superlative adverbs.
- Write these sentences on the board and ask students to fill in the correct adverb.
  - Jennifer runs ______ than me. She runs the ______ of all. *(faster/fastest)*
  - Sam is ______ at reading, but he's even ______ at spelling. *(good/better)*
  - Joan is the ______ talented at drawing. *(most)*

### Independent Practice

Use ***Comprehension and Language Arts Skills,*** pages 118–119, to identify comparative and superlative adverbs.

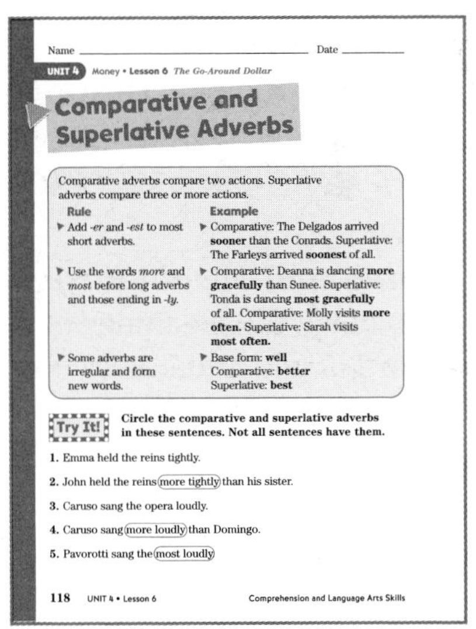

Name ______ Date ______

UNIT 4 Money • Lesson 6 *The Go-Around Dollar*

Comparative and Superlative Adverbs

Comparative adverbs compare two actions. Superlative adverbs compare three or more actions.

| Rule | Example |
| --- | --- |
| Add *-er* and *-est* to most short adverbs. | Comparative: The Delgados arrived **sooner** than the Conrads. Superlative: The Farleys arrived **soonest** of all. |
| Use the words *more* and *most* before long adverbs and those ending in *-ly*. | Comparative: Deanna is dancing **more gracefully** than Sunee. Superlative: Tonda is dancing **most gracefully** of all. Comparative: Molly visits **more often.** Superlative: Sarah visits **most often.** |
| Some adverbs are irregular and form new words. | Base form: **well** Comparative: **better** Superlative: **best** |

Try It! **Circle the comparative and superlative adverbs in these sentences. Not all sentences have them.**

1. Emma held the reins tightly.
2. John held the reins (more tightly) than his sister.
3. Caruso sang the opera loudly.
4. Caruso sang (more loudly) than Domingo.
5. Pavorotti sang the (most loudly)

118 UNIT 4 • Lesson 6 Comprehension and Language Arts Skills

***Comprehension and Language Arts Skills p. 118***

# DAY 2

## Word Analysis

### Spelling

**Compound Words**

#### Board Work

- Write *thing* on the board. Review that a compound word is formed from two words. Ask a student to spell a compound word using *any* and *thing. (anything)*
- Discuss other compound words with *thing.* (*something, nothing, everything)*

### Vocabulary

**Money Words**

#### Teach

- Write *Treasury* ("The Go-Around Dollar," p. 72) on the board, and ask students what *treasure* means *(riches, gold, money).*
- Explain that *treasury* is "money owned by a group." When *treasury* is capitalized *(Treasury)*, it means the department of finances.
- Ask students to look in "The Go-Around Dollar" for words related to *treasury (Treasury seal, Treasury Department).*

#### Guided Practice

Use ***Spelling and Vocabulary Skills,*** page 94, to teach the meanings of money-related words. Ask students to complete page 95 as independent practice.

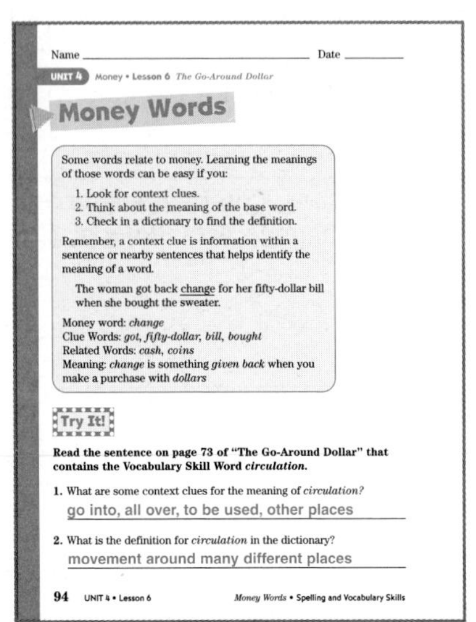

Name ______ Date ______

UNIT 4 Money • Lesson 6 *The Go-Around Dollar*

**Money Words**

Some words relate to money. Learning the meanings of those words can be easy if you:

1. Look for context clues.
2. Think about the meaning of the base word.
3. Check in a dictionary to find the definition.

Remember, a context clue is information within a sentence or nearby sentences that helps identify the meaning of a word.

The woman got back change for her fifty-dollar bill when she bought the sweater.

Money word: *change*
Clue Words: *got, fifty-dollar, bill, bought*
Related Words: *cash, coins*
Meaning: *change* is something *given back* when you make a purchase with *dollars*

**Try It!**

**Read the sentence on page 73 of "The Go-Around Dollar" that contains the Vocabulary Skill Word *circulation.***

1. What are some context clues for the meaning of *circulation?*
go into, all over, to be used, other places
2. What is the definition for *circulation* in the dictionary?
movement around many different places

94 UNIT 4 • Lesson 6 *Money Words* • Spelling and Vocabulary Skills

***Spelling and Vocabulary Skills p. 94***

## Writing Process Strategies

### Prewriting

**Persuasive Poster**

#### Teach

- **Review** the ideas for a persuasive poster that students wrote on Day 1.
- Read ***Writer's Workbook,*** page 74, on prewriting for a persuasive poster.

#### Independent Practice

**Prewriting**

- Have students write their audience and purpose on ***Writer's Workbook,*** page 74. Also have students sketch any ideas about the visual aspect of their posters at the bottom of the page.
- Have students complete the graphic organizer on ***Writer's Workbook,*** page 75, to help them organize their thoughts.

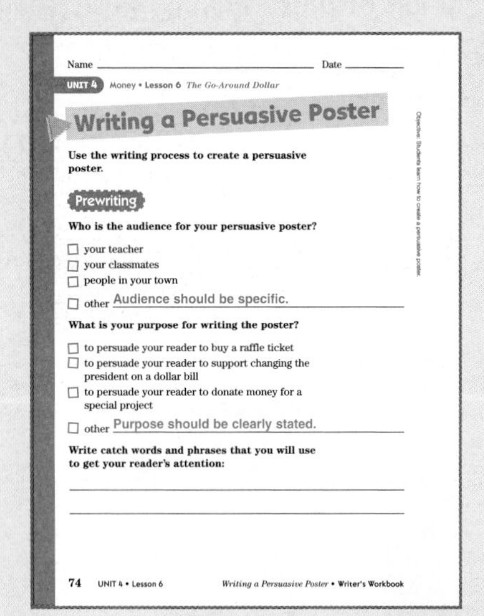

Name ______ Date ______

UNIT 4 Money • Lesson 6 *The Go-Around Dollar*

**Writing a Persuasive Poster**

**Use the writing process to create a persuasive poster.**

Prewriting

**Who is the audience for your persuasive poster?**

- ☐ your teacher
- ☐ your classmates
- ☐ people in your town
- ☐ other Audience should be specific.

**What is your purpose for writing the poster?**

- ☐ to persuade your reader to buy a raffle ticket
- ☐ to persuade your reader to support changing the president on a dollar bill
- ☐ to persuade your reader to donate money for a special project
- ☐ other Purpose should be clearly stated.

**Write catch words and phrases that you will use to get your reader's attention:**

Objective: Students learn how to create a persuasive poster.

74 UNIT 4 • Lesson 6 *Writing a Persuasive Poster* • Writer's Workbook

***Writer's Workbook p. 74***

**Professional Development**

***Teacher Resource Library CD-ROMs*** or ***Online Professional Development*** provides courses that help you better understand the Writing instruction in ***Open Court Reading.*** For more information about this program, visit SRAonline.com.

## English Language Conventions

### Grammar, Usage, and Mechanics

**Grammar: Comparative and Superlative Adverbs**

#### Teach

- Review comparative and superlative adverbs using ***Language Arts Handbook,*** page 266, from Day 1.
- Write the following sentences on the board. Have students read them and identify the comparative and superlative adverbs.
  - Larry thinks Robin Williams is funnier than Billy Crystal. (funnier *is comparative)*
  - Josephine arrived the latest of all the guests. (the latest *is superlative)*
  - Dmitri tried the sushi more reluctantly than Yukio. (more reluctantly *is comparative)*
  - Of all the guests, Yukio tried the caviar most reluctantly. (most reluctantly *is superlative)*

#### Guided Practice in Reading

Ask students to identify adverbs in "The Go-Around Dollar." Write them on the board with the corresponding page number from the story. For each adverb, have students turn to the page, ask volunteers to read the sentence aloud, then ask the students to change the adverb to the comparative and superlative forms.

# DAY 3

## Word Analysis

### Spelling

**Compound Words**

**Teach**

- Introduce the five compound words found in "The Go-Around Dollar."
- Ask students to think of sporting goods that are compound words *(baseball, softball, football).*

**Guided Practice**

Have students complete page 96 from ***Spelling and Vocabulary Skills*** to get familiar with spelling common compound words.

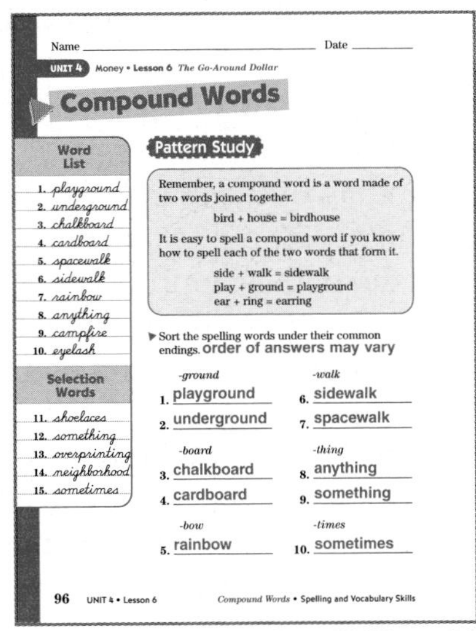
Name ____ Date ____
UNIT 4 Money • Lesson 6 *The Go-Around Dollar*

**Compound Words**

**Word List**
1. playground
2. underground
3. chalkboard
4. cardboard
5. spacewalk
6. sidewalk
7. rainbow
8. anything
9. campfire
10. eyelash

**Selection Words**
11. shoelaces
12. something
13. overprinting
14. neighborhood
15. sometimes

**Pattern Study**

Remember, a compound word is a word made of two words joined together.

bird + house = birdhouse

It is easy to spell a compound word if you know how to spell each of the two words that form it.

side + walk = sidewalk
play + ground = playground
ear + ring = earring

▶ Sort the spelling words under their common endings. order of answers may vary

*-ground*
1. playground
2. underground

*-board*
3. chalkboard
4. cardboard

*-bow*
5. rainbow

*-walk*
6. sidewalk
7. spacewalk

*-thing*
8. anything
9. something

*-times*
10. sometimes

96 UNIT 4 • Lesson 6 *Compound Words* • Spelling and Vocabulary Skills

***Spelling and Vocabulary Skills* p. 96**

### Vocabulary (continued)

**Money Words**

- Write *tender* ("The Go-Around Dollar," p. 76) on the board. Explain that *tender* has many meanings, but *tender* in this story relates to money.
- Read the sentence with *tender.* Point out that *dollar* and *note* describe *tender*. Ask a student what *legal tender* is for *("all debts, public and private").*
- Ask a student to find *tender* in the dictionary *(an unconditional offer of money).* Discuss why a dollar is *legal* tender *(our government offers this promise of money).*

## Writing Process Strategies

### Drafting

**Persuasive Poster**

**Teach**

Read ***Writer's Workbook,*** page 75, on drafting a persuasive poster.

**Writer's Craft**

**Supporting Details**

- Tell students you have come up with the following reasons to support giving money to animal shelters, but one just doesn't seem right. Ask them to identify the one that doesn't fit.
  - Animals can't help themselves.
  - Shelters take all kinds of animals.
  - Just one dollar a day can feed three animals.
- Read ***Language Arts Handbook,*** page 183, on staying on topic.
- Read ***Comprehension and Language Arts Skills,*** pages 120–121, on supporting details.

**Guided Practice**

**Drafting**

- Have students create drafts of their persuasive posters in their Writer's Notebooks.
- If you have computers in the classroom, you may want to give students the option of using word processing software to make their drafts.

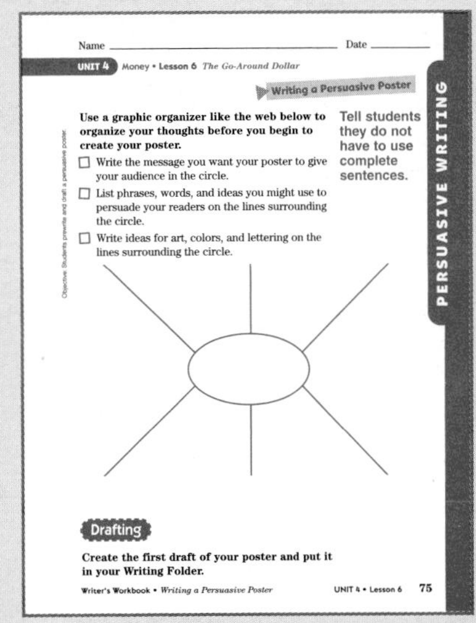
Name ____ Date ____
UNIT 4 Money • Lesson 6 *The Go-Around Dollar*

**Writing a Persuasive Poster**

PERSUASIVE WRITING

**Use a graphic organizer like the web below to organize your thoughts before you begin to create your poster.**

- ☐ Write the message you want your poster to give your audience in the circle.
- ☐ List phrases, words, and ideas you might use to persuade your readers on the lines surrounding the circle.
- ☐ Write ideas for art, colors, and lettering on the lines surrounding the circle.

Tell students they do not have to use complete sentences.

Objective: Students prewrite and draft a persuasive poster.

**Drafting**

**Create the first draft of your poster and put it in your Writing Folder.**

Writer's Workbook • *Writing a Persuasive Poster* UNIT 4 • Lesson 6 75

***Writer's Workbook* p. 75**

## English Language Conventions

### Grammar, Usage, and Mechanics

**Grammar: Comparative and Superlative Adverbs**

**Teach**

- Review adverbs using ***Comprehension and Language Arts Skills,*** pages 118–119.
- Read the following sentences aloud. Give students time to write them down. Ask students to identify the adverb and write down the comparative and superlative forms for each.
  - Jessie climbed carefully up the tree. *(Adverb is* carefully. *Comparative,* more carefully; *superlative,* the most carefully)
  - He rocked steadily on the camel. *(Adverb is* steadily. *Comparative,* more steadily; *superlative,* the most steadily)
  - Her dog acts nice. *(Adverb is* nice. *Comparative,* nicer; *superlative,* the nicest)
  - We arrived late for church. *(Adverb is* late. *Comparative,* later; *superlative,* the latest)

**Guided Practice in Writing**

Have students create posters persuading people to give money and/or time to help others. Encourage students to include adverbs in their posters.

**Informal Assessment**

Check students' writing to make sure they are using adverbs correctly.

# DAY 4

## Word Analysis

### Spelling

**Compound Words**

**Teach**

Explain that these exercises in ***Spelling and Vocabulary Skills*** are designed to help them realize how to spell compound words by knowing how to spell the two words that form them.

**Guided Practice**

Have students complete page 97 of ***Spelling and Vocabulary Skills*** to reinforce how to spell compound words.

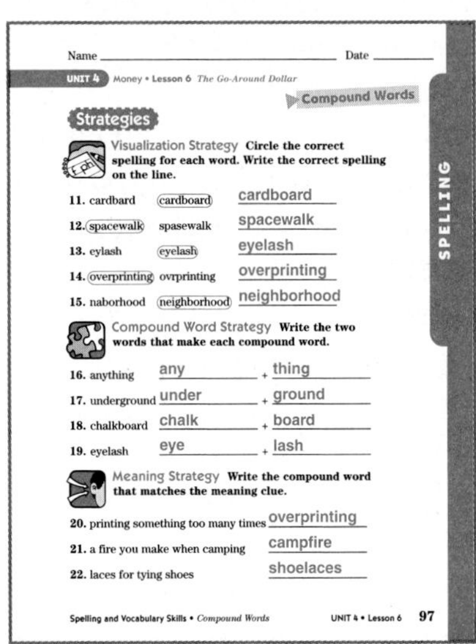

Name ______________ Date ________

UNIT 4 Money • Lesson 6 *The Go-Around Dollar*

Compound Words

SPELLING

Strategies

Visualization Strategy **Circle the correct spelling for each word. Write the correct spelling on the line.**

11. cardbard (cardboard) cardboard
12. (spacewalk) spasewalk spacewalk
13. eylash (eyelash) eyelash
14. (overprinting) ovrprinting overprinting
15. naborhood (neighborhood) neighborhood

Compound Word Strategy **Write the two words that make each compound word.**

16. anything any + thing
17. underground under + ground
18. chalkboard chalk + board
19. eyelash eye + lash

Meaning Strategy **Write the compound word that matches the meaning clue.**

20. printing something too many times overprinting
21. a fire you make when camping campfire
22. laces for tying shoes shoelaces

Spelling and Vocabulary Skills • *Compound Words* UNIT 4 • Lesson 6 97

***Spelling and Vocabulary Skills* p. 97**

### Vocabulary (continued)

**Money Words**

- Write *debts* ("The Go-Around Dollar," p. 76) on the board.
- Ask the class what *debts* are or what it means if someone is in *debt* *(something owed, money)*. Ask a student to find *debt* in a dictionary *(something that is owed to another)*. Discuss how *debt* relates to the job of the American dollar *(dollars pay for debt, a lack of dollars means debt, dollars can be paid to end debt)*.

## Writing Process Strategies

**Revising**

**Persuasive Poster**

**Teach**

- Read ***Writer's Workbook,*** page 76, on revising a persuasive poster.
- Remind students to view their posters with their audience and purpose in mind. They should ask themselves, "Will the look of this poster appeal to my readers? Does my message come through loud and clear? Have I persuaded them to care about my message?"
- Discuss ***Language Arts Transparency 24,*** Revising: Word Choice.

**Troubleshooting**

- There is no focal point to grab the reader's eye.
- Too few words on the poster may make it difficult for readers to understand the point. Too many words will make the poster look cluttered.
- The art should support the message.

**Guided Practice**

**Revising**

- Have students revise their posters.
- Have students use the checklist on ***Writer's Workbook,*** page 76, to help them.

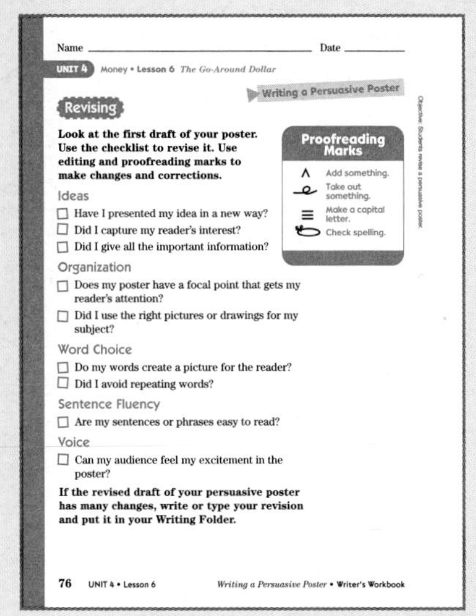

Name ______________ Date ________

UNIT 4 Money • Lesson 6 *The Go-Around Dollar*

Writing a Persuasive Poster

Revising

**Look at the first draft of your poster. Use the checklist to revise it. Use editing and proofreading marks to make changes and corrections.**

Ideas

- ☐ Have I presented my idea in a new way?
- ☐ Did I capture my reader's interest?
- ☐ Did I give all the important information?

Organization

- ☐ Does my poster have a focal point that gets my reader's attention?
- ☐ Did I use the right pictures or drawings for my subject?

Word Choice

- ☐ Do my words create a picture for the reader?
- ☐ Did I avoid repeating words?

Sentence Fluency

- ☐ Are my sentences or phrases easy to read?

Voice

- ☐ Can my audience feel my excitement in the poster?

**If the revised draft of your persuasive poster has many changes, write or type your revision and put it in your Writing Folder.**

Proofreading Marks

- ^ Add something.
- Take out something.
- ≡ Make a capital letter.
- Check spelling.

Objective: Students revise a persuasive poster.

76 UNIT 4 • Lesson 6 *Writing a Persuasive Poster* • Writer's Workbook

***Writer's Workbook* p. 76**

## English Language Conventions

**Listening, Speaking, Viewing**

**Presenting: Organizing a Presentation**

**Teach**

- Explain to the class that summarizing a story is a way of making a presentation. A summary includes the most important ideas or details in a story.
- Explain that the organization of a presentation is very important. An audience is better able to follow a presentation when related details are grouped together, and events are retold with a beginning, a middle, and an end.

**Guided Practice**

- In small groups, have students refer to "The Go-Around Dollar" to make a summary of the story. What details or events are important to our understanding of the story? Which details can be left out? Students should organize the details appropriately, according to sequence, grouping them into a beginning, middle, and end.
- As a class, discuss which details students would include in their presentations and which they would omit. Have students share why they would include or omit certain details.

**Informal Assessment**

Observe whether students can choose the appropriate content and sequence of events for an oral summary.

# DAY 5

## Word Analysis

### Spelling

#### Assessment: Final Test

**Compound Words**

#### Teach

Repeat the Pretest or use the Final Test on page 41 of ***Unit 4 Assessment*** as summative assessment of student understanding of spelling compound words.

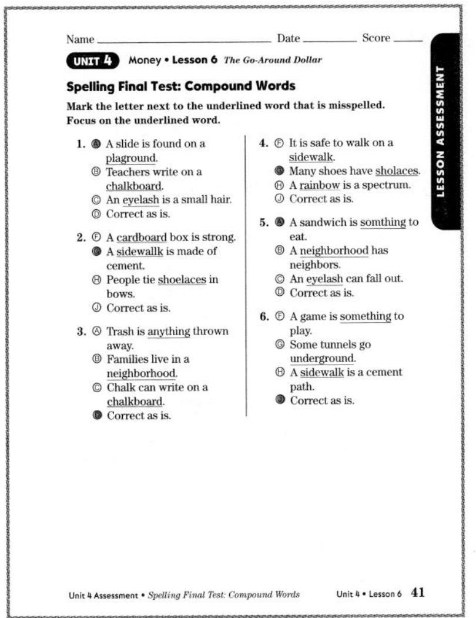

Name ____ Date ____ Score ____

UNIT 4 Money • Lesson 6 *The Go-Around Dollar*

LESSON ASSESSMENT

**Spelling Final Test: Compound Words**

**Mark the letter next to the underlined word that is misspelled. Focus on the underlined word.**

1. Ⓐ A slide is found on a <u>plaground</u>.
   Ⓑ Teachers write on a <u>chalkboard</u>.
   Ⓒ An <u>eyelash</u> is a small hair.
   Ⓓ Correct as is.
2. Ⓕ A <u>cardboard</u> box is strong.
   Ⓖ A <u>sidewallk</u> is made of cement.
   Ⓗ People tie <u>shoelaces</u> in bows.
   Ⓙ Correct as is.
3. Ⓐ Trash is <u>anything</u> thrown away.
   Ⓑ Families live in a <u>neighborhood</u>.
   Ⓒ Chalk can write on a <u>chalkboard</u>.
   Ⓓ Correct as is.
4. Ⓕ It is safe to walk on a <u>sidewalk</u>.
   Ⓖ Many shoes have <u>sholaces</u>.
   Ⓗ A <u>rainbow</u> is a spectrum.
   Ⓙ Correct as is.
5. Ⓐ A sandwich is <u>somthing</u> to eat.
   Ⓑ A <u>neighborhood</u> has neighbors.
   Ⓒ An <u>eyelash</u> can fall out.
   Ⓓ Correct as is.
6. Ⓕ A game is <u>something</u> to play.
   Ⓖ Some tunnels go <u>underground</u>.
   Ⓗ A <u>sidewalk</u> is a cement path.
   Ⓙ Correct as is.

Unit 4 Assessment • *Spelling Final Test: Compound Words* Unit 4 • Lesson 6 41

***Unit 4 Assessment* p. 41**

#### Guided Practice

Have students categorize any mistakes they made on the Final Test as careless errors or lesson-pattern problems.

### Vocabulary

**Informal Assessment**

Periodically check to see if students are applying and understanding the Vocabulary Skill Words related to money in their writing. Offer praise and encouragement as needed. Have students add any new words to the running Vocabulary Word List in the Writer's Notebook.

## Writing Process Strategies

### Editing/Proofreading and Publishing

**Persuasive Poster**

#### Teach

- Read ***Writer's Workbook,*** page 77, on editing/proofreading and publishing a persuasive poster.

#### Guided Practice

**Editing/Proofreading and Publishing**

- Have students edit/proofread their letters.
- Direct students to use the checklist on ***Writer's Workbook,*** page 77.
- Refer to the ***Grammar, Usage, and Mechanics*** comparative and superlative adverbs lesson on page 93F.
- Discuss with students some possibilities for displaying the posters. If appropriate, you may wish to display them in local businesses.

**Formal Assessment**

Total Point Value: 10

1. The main idea is clearly stated. (2 points)
2. Reasons supporting the main idea are clear and precise. (2 points)
3. Adverbs have been used effectively. (2 points)
4. The mechanics are correct. (2 points)
5. Art supports the poster's message. (2 points)

Name ____ Date ____

UNIT 4 Money • Lesson 6 *The Go-Around Dollar*

Writing a Persuasive Poster

PERSUASIVE WRITING

Objective: Students edit/proofread and publish a persuasive poster.

Editing/Proofreading

**Edit your persuasive poster on paper or a computer. Then make a clean copy of your letter, and put it in your Writing Folder. Read your persuasive poster carefully. Use the checklist to help you correct any mistakes.**

Conventions

- ☐ Make sure your words are spelled correctly.
- ☐ Make sure you have used adverbs correctly.
- ☐ Make sure all sentences have end punctuation.

Publishing

**Use this checklist to get your poster ready to show others.**

Presentation

- ☐ Make sure your writing says exactly what you want it to say.
- ☐ Make a clean copy. You may want to use the computer.
- ☐ Add drawings or pictures to make your poster more appealing.

Writer's Workbook • *Writing a Persuasive Poster* UNIT 4 • Lesson 6 77

***Writer's Workbook* p. 77**

## English Language Conventions

### Penmanship

**Cursive Letters *Z* and *V***

#### Teach

- **Teacher Model:** Introduce formation of uppercase *Z* and *V* as curve forward letters by demonstrating on the board.

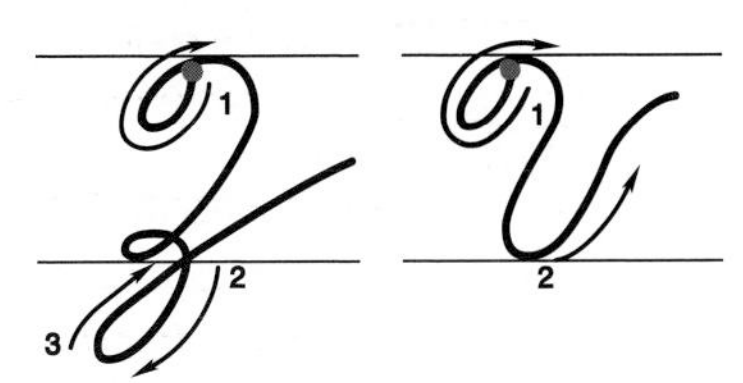

**Z** Starting point, loop
Curve forward, slant down,
Overcurve, curve down
Loop into overcurve:
capital *Z*

**V** Starting point, loop
Curve forward and slant down
Undercurve up, overcurve:
capital *V*

- **Teacher Model:** Write the words *Zimbabwe* and *Victor* to model proper letter formation.
- Tell students their letters all have to slant to the right in order to be legible. A consistent slant is one of the keys to legibility.

#### Guided Practice

- Have students practice writing rows of *Zs* and *Vs* in their Writer's Notebooks.
- From "The Go-Around Dollar," have students write three words of their choice.
- Have students draw slanted lines through their letters to check for proper slant.

**Informal Assessment**

Check students' handwriting for proper formation of *Z* and *V* and a consistent slant to the right.

# Reading and Language Arts Skills Traces

## Language Arts

### WORD ANALYSIS

Skills Trace

**Spelling: Compound Words**

Introduced in Grade 1.
Scaffolded throughout Grades 2–5.

**REINTRODUCED:** **Unit 4, Lesson 6,** p. 93E
**PRACTICED:** **Unit 4, Lesson 6,** pp. 93F–93J
*Spelling and Vocabulary Skills,* pp. 96–97
**TESTED:** **Unit 4, Lesson 6,** p. 93F (Pretest)
**Unit 4, Lesson 6,** p. 41 (Final Test)
**Unit 4 Assessment**

Skills Trace

**Vocabulary: Money Words**

Introduced in Grade 3.
Scaffolded throughout Grades 3–5.

**INTRODUCED:** **Unit 4, Lesson 6,** p. 93G
**PRACTICED:** **Unit 4, Lesson 6,** pp. 93G–93J
*Spelling and Vocabulary Skills,* pp. 94–95
**TESTED:** **Unit 4 Assessment**

### WRITING PROCESS STRATEGIES

Skills Trace

**Persuasive Writing: Persuasive Poster**

Introduced in Grade K.
Scaffolded throughout Grades 1–3, 5.

**REINTRODUCED:** **Unit 4, Lesson 6,** p. 93F
**PRACTICED:** **Unit 4, Lesson 6,** pp. 93G–93J
*Writer's Workbook,* pp. 74–77
**TESTED:** **Unit 4, Lesson 6,**
Formal Assessment, p. 93J
**Unit 4 Assessment**

Skills Trace

**Writer's Craft: Supporting Details**

Introduced in Grade 2.
Scaffolded throughout Grades 3–6.

**REINTRODUCED:** **Unit 4, Lesson 6,** p. 93H
**PRACTICED:** **Unit 4, Lesson 6,** p. 93H
*Comprehension and Language Arts Skills,* pp. 120–121
**TESTED:** **Unit 4 Assessment**

### ENGLISH LANGUAGE CONVENTIONS

Skills Trace

**Grammar: Comparative and Superlative Adverbs**

Introduced in Grade 2.
Scaffolded throughout Grades 3–6.

**REINTRODUCED:** **Unit 4, Lesson 6,** p. 93F
**PRACTICED:** **Unit 4, Lesson 6,** p. 93G
**Unit 4, Lesson 6,** p. 93H
*Comprehension and Language Arts Skills,* pp. 118–119
**TESTED:** **Unit 4, Lesson 6,**
Informal Assessment, p. 93H
**Unit 4 Assessment**

Skills Trace

**Listening, Speaking, Viewing Presenting: Organizing a Presentation**

Introduced in Grade 2.
Scaffolded throughout Grades 3–6.

**REINTRODUCED:** **Unit 4, Lesson 6,** p. 93I
**TESTED:** **Unit 4, Lesson 6**
Informal Assessment, p. 93I

Skills Trace

**Penmanship: Cursive Letters *Z* and *V***

Introduced in Grade 3.
Scaffolded throughout Grades 4–6.

**INTRODUCED:** **Unit 4, Lesson 6,** p. 93J
**TESTED:** **Unit 4, Lesson 6**
Informal Assessment, p. 93J

## Reading

### COMPREHENSION

**Sequence**

Introduced in Grade 1.
Scaffolded throughout Grades 2 and 3.

**REINTRODUCED:** **Unit 1, Lesson 6**
**REINFORCED:** **Unit 4, Lesson 6**
**Unit 5, Lesson 1**
**Unit 5, Lesson 7**
**TESTED:** **Unit 4 Assessment**

# Professional Development: Writing

## Developing Writers One Day at a Time: A Picture of the Writing Classroom

Each day, a writing community brings new growth as well as new challenges. It is a dynamic time with writers working busily. On a typical day, some students will be holding conferences about their drafts or revisions with the teacher, others will be drafting or revising, pairs might be editing in preparation for publishing, and others will be planning and researching. How does this all come together?

### Getting Started

Writing should be natural, and developing ideas for writing should grow naturally out of everyday activities. While students should be choosing their own topics, many teachers feel this is one of the most difficult aspects of getting started on writing. How do students come up with topics? What do you do when students think they have no ideas?

The group can brainstorm about where to get ideas for writing (for example, from books, family, places students have gone, things they want to learn more about, things they like to do, and so on). Then they can start a list of ideas and keep it prominently displayed in the classroom. Teacher modeling here is valuable: "I might write about Washington, D.C., because I just took a trip there;" or "I think I might try writing a mystery, because I've been reading some and really like them." As students read new stories, as ideas are shared in Seminar, and as ideas come up from content-area reading or at any time in the day, they should be added to the list. In addition, the Concept/Question Board may be a valuable source of ideas not just for research but for writing, as well.

Discuss with students how they think the authors whose stories they read find their ideas for writing. During Seminar, encourage student authors to share how they found ideas for their stories. In one first-grade classroom, an author read her story about geese migrating to the South. When the teacher asked what made her write that story, the student said she had seen something about it on the news the previous evening. In this way, the news became a resource not just for this particular student, but for the rest of the class as well.

Professional writers keep journals and/or notebooks of writing ideas. Writers put down all kinds of ideas—some good, some not so good—because they never know when these ideas will be useful. For example, a writer might jot down a few lines of dialogue they had with a friend, a brief description of a man's tie, or a line from a popular song. The writer may never use these bits in a story. Or, she or he may find months later that a line of dialogue or a descriptive detail is perfect for a character being developed in a story.

Students can make notes of writing ideas at any time, with a special time being set aside following the discussion of each reading selection. The writing ideas students get from a discussion might concern the topic of the selection they have just read or an aspect of the author's style. Teachers should keep such a list of writing ideas also, thinking aloud occasionally while writing idea notes. This will model for students the kind of notes they should make. For example, the teacher might say something like the following:

- *This selection reminds me of a time when I felt very sad about my friend moving away. I think I might write a poem about that.*
- *I want to explain how archaeologists can tell how old a building is. That might make a good photoessay.*

**Professional Development**

***Teacher Resource Library CD-ROMs*** or ***Online Professional Development*** provides courses that help you better understand the Writing instruction in ***Open Court Reading.*** For more information about this program, visit SRAonline.com.

Additional information about writing as well as resource references can be found in the ***Professional Development Guide: Writing.***

*Focus Questions* What is it like to save for a long time for something you really want? How would you feel if you saved a lot of money for something you wanted and then had to spend it on something else? How would you feel if that something else was very important and your money was going to a good cause?

# UNCLE JED'S BARBERSHOP

Margaree King Mitchell
*illustrated by James Ransome*

Jedediah Johnson was my granddaddy's brother. Everybody has their favorite relative. Well, Uncle Jedediah was mine.

He used to come by our house every Wednesday night with his clippers. He was the only black barber in the county. Daddy said that before Uncle Jed started cutting hair, he and Granddaddy used to have to go thirty miles to get a haircut.

94

SELECTION INTRODUCTION

## Selection Summary

### Genre: Historical Fiction

"Uncle Jed's Barbershop" is the story of a determined man who was also a loving uncle. Uncle Jed had a dream that was challenged by a family crisis and the Great Depression. This is his story, told from the viewpoint of his loving niece.

Historical fiction is a type of realistic fiction that is set in some specific period of the past.

Some elements of historical fiction include:

- The setting occurs sometime in the past.
- The plot reflects events or problems of the period.
- The details about clothing, tools, and food are authentic to the period.
- Often, but not always, the story is based on actual historical events and people of the period.

## About the Author

**Margaree King Mitchell** not only writes children stories, but television scripts and plays as well. When volunteering at her son's school, she found the inspiration to become a writer. *"I thought if I could somehow write a book that would inspire children to achieve their dreams, then maybe children would be motivated to stay in school and look to the future for a better life for themselves,"* she says. After reading "Uncle Jed's Barbershop" to a group of eight year olds, a girl approached Mitchell to say that she learned that she could accomplish anything, even her dream of becoming a doctor. Mitchell is currently researching the Buffalo Soldiers for a future work.

Students can read more about writer Margaree King Mitchell on page 105 of the ***Student Anthology.***

## About the Illustrator

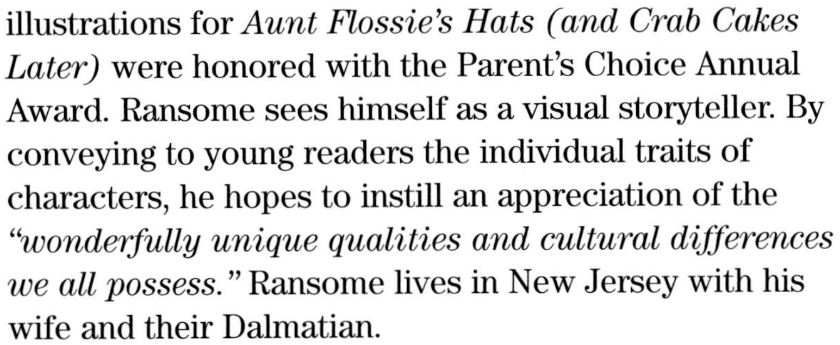

**James E. Ransome** was born in North Carolina. Like Uncle Jed, Ransome's father worked for many years as a barber before he opened his own shop. A graduate of the prestigious Pratt Institute in Brooklyn, Ransome is a two-time winner of the Coretta Scott King Award for Illustration. Ransome's illustrations for *Do Like Kayle* received *Parenting Magazine's* Reading Magic Award. His illustrations for *Aunt Flossie's Hats (and Crab Cakes Later)* were honored with the Parent's Choice Annual Award. Ransome sees himself as a visual storyteller. By conveying to young readers the individual traits of characters, he hopes to instill an appreciation of the *"wonderfully unique qualities and cultural differences we all possess."* Ransome lives in New Jersey with his wife and their Dalmatian.

Students can read more about illustrator James E. Ransome on page 105 of the ***Student Anthology.***

## Inquiry Connections

"Uncle Jed's Barbershop" is a warm and uplifting story about the power of a dream. The story also illustrates the fact that many dreams require money to get them going. The theme of determination expresses itself through the story.

- Many dreams require money to get them started.
- Everybody can save money, even after facing setbacks.
- Saving money and making a dream happen require strong determination and patience.

Before reading the selection:

- Point out that students may post a question, concept, word, illustration, or object on the Concept/Question Board at any time during the course of their unit investigation. Be sure that students include their name or initials on the items they post so that others will know to whom to go if they have an answer or if they wish to collaborate on a related activity.
- Students should feel free to write an answer or a note on someone else's question or to consult the Board for ideas for their own investigations throughout the unit.
- Encourage students to read about money at home and to bring in articles or pictures that are good examples to post on the Board.

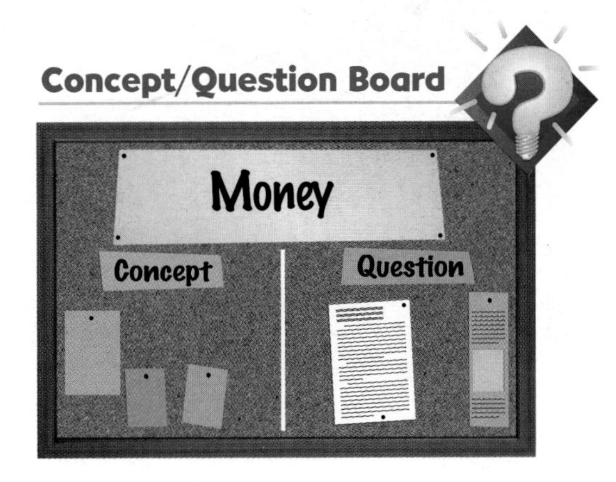

## Leveled Practice

### Reteach
**Pages 125–128**

### Challenge
**Pages 110–113**

### English Learner Support Activities

### Intervention Workbook

### Decodable Book 35

## Leveled Classroom Library*

Encourage students to read at least 30 minutes daily outside of class. Have them read books in the ***Leveled Classroom Library*** to support the unit theme and help students develop their vocabulary by reading independently.

### *The Treasure*

BY URI SHULEVITZ. FARRAR, STRAUS & GIROUX, 1978.

In this traditional English tale of a journey to find treasure, a man follows the instructions of his dream, which takes him away from his home. Upon arrival, he learns the treasure is really at his home. (Caldecott Honor Book) **(Easy)**

### *Saturday Sancocho*

BY LEYLA TORRES. FARRAR, STRAUS & GIROUX, 1995.

Every Saturday, Maria Lili shares a meal with her grandparents, eating Chicken Sancocho, until the weekend comes when money is tight and they are missing essential ingredients. Mama Ana barters with her eggs for the final ingredients, saving the day. **(Average)**

### *Our Money*

BY KAREN BORNEMANN SPIES. THE MILLBROOK PRESS, 1994.

Chronicling the changes American money has undergone, this book explains money ranging from wampum to today's currency. Also discussed are counterfeiting and minting procedures. **(Advanced)**

* These books, which all support the unit theme Money, are part of a 36-book ***Leveled Classroom Library*** available for purchase from SRA/McGraw-Hill. Note: Teachers should preview any trade books for appropriateness in their classrooms before recommending them to students.

## SRA TECHNOLOGY

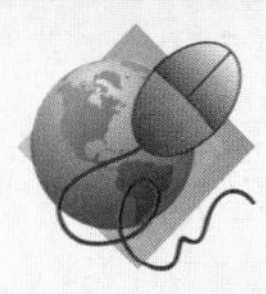

### Web Connections

- Money Web Site
- Online Professional Development
- Online Phonics
- Online Assessment

### CD-ROMs

- Research Assistant
- Spelling
- Teacher Resource Library

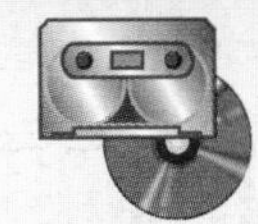

### Audiocassette/CD

Listening Library: Money

### Computer Skills

TechKnowledge

Materials are available through SRA/McGraw-Hill.

LESSON PLANNER

Suggested Pacing: 3–5 days

| | DAY 1 | DAY 2 |
|---|---|---|
| | DAY 1 | DAY 2 |
| **1 Preparing to Read**<br><br>**Materials**<br>■ Student Anthology, Book 2, pp. 94–105<br>■ Sound/Spelling Cards<br>■ Decodable Book 35<br>■ Routine Card 1, Routines 1–2 | **Word Knowledge,** p. 94K<br>■ Compound words<br>■ Suffixes *-ment, -tion,* and *-sion*<br>**About the Words and Sentences,** p. 94K | **Developing Oral Language,** p. 94L |
| **2 Reading & Responding**<br><br>**Materials**<br>■ Student Anthology, Book 2, pp. 94–105<br>■ Reading Transparencies 30, 46<br>■ Inquiry Journal, p. 86<br>■ Routine Cards 1, 2, Routines 3–6<br>■ Science/Social Studies Connection Center Card 33<br>■ Home Connection, p. 57<br>■ Unit 4 Assessment Guide, pp. 26–29<br>■ Writer's Notebook | **Build Background,** p. 94M<br>**Preview and Prepare,** pp. 94M–94N<br>**Selection Vocabulary,** p. 94N<br>**Reading Recommendations,** p. 94O | **Student Anthology,** pp. 94–103 First Read<br>✓ **Comprehension Strategies**<br>■ Monitoring and Adjusting Reading Speed, pp. 94, 96, 100<br>■ Predicting, pp. 98, 102<br>■ Summarizing, p. 102<br>**Discussing Strategy Use,** p. 102<br>**Discussing the Selection,** p. 103A<br>**Supporting the Reading,** p. 103C<br>■ Monitoring and Adjusting Reading Speed |
| **Inquiry**<br><br>**Materials**<br>■ Student Anthology, Book 2, pp. 94–105<br>■ Inquiry Journal, p. 104<br>■ Research Assistant CD-ROM | **Investigation**<br>■ Investigating Concepts Beyond the Text, p. 105A | **Investigation**<br>■ Concept/Question Board, p. 105B |
| **3 Language Arts**<br><br>**Materials**<br>■ Spelling and Vocabulary Skills, pp. 98–101<br>■ Comprehension and Language Arts Skills, pp. 122–125<br>■ Spelling Software<br>■ The Ultimate Writing and Creativity Center<br>■ Language Arts Handbook<br>■ Writer's Workbook, pp. 78–81<br>■ Language Arts Transparency 28<br>■ Student Anthology<br>■ Routine Card 2, Routine 7 | **Word Analysis**<br>✓■ Spelling: Unit 4 Review Pretest, p. 105F<br>**Writing Process Strategies**<br>■ Persuasive Writing: Paragraph, p. 105F<br>**English Language Conventions**<br>■ Grammar: Unit Review, p. 105F | **Word Analysis**<br>■ Spelling: Unit 4 Review, p. 105G<br>■ Vocabulary: Unit 4 Review, p. 105G<br>**Writing Process Strategies**<br>■ Persuasive Writing: Paragraph, p. 105G<br>**English Language Conventions**<br>■ Grammar: Unit Review, p. 105G |



P Phonics ✓ Informal Assessment Available ✓ Formal Assessment Available

| DAY 2 continued | DAY 3 | |
|---|---|---|
| **DAY 3** | **DAY 4** | **DAY 5** |
| **General Review** | **General Review** | **Review Word Knowledge** |
| **Student Anthology,** pp. 94–103 (Second Read)<br>**Comprehension Skills**<br>■ Cause and Effect, pp. 95, 97, 99, 101, 103<br>**Checking Comprehension,** p. 103<br>**Math Connection**<br>■ The Interest Game II, p. 103E | **Literary Elements,** p. 103D<br>■ Characterization<br>**Student Anthology**<br>✓■ Concept Connections, p. 104<br>■ Meet the Author/Illustrator, p. 105<br>**Review Selection Vocabulary,** p. 103B | ✓**Selection Assessment**<br>■ "Uncle Jed's Barber Shop," pp. 26–29<br>**Home Connection,** p. 103B<br>**Social Studies Connection**<br>■ Hard Times, p. 103F |
| ✓**Investigation**<br>✓■ Presentations, p. 105C | **Supporting the Investigation**<br>■ Time Lines, p. 105D | **Investigation**<br>■ Unit Investigation Continued<br>■ Update Concept/Question Board |
| **Word Analysis**<br>■ Spelling: Unit 4 Review, p. 105H<br>■ Vocabulary: Unit 4 Review, p. 105H<br>**Writing Process Strategies**<br>■ Persuasive Writing: Paragraph, p. 105H<br>■ Writer's Craft: Effective Beginnings and Endings, p. 105H<br>**English Language Conventions**<br>✓■ Grammar: Unit Review, p. 105H | **Word Analysis**<br>■ Spelling: Unit 4 Review, p. 105I<br>■ Vocabulary: Unit 4 Review, p. 105I<br>**Writing Process Strategies**<br>■ Persuasive Writing: Paragraph, p. 105I<br>**English Language Conventions**<br>✓■ Listening, Speaking, Viewing Interacting: Engaging an Audience, p. 105I | **Word Analysis**<br>✓■ Spelling: Unit 4 Review Final Test<br>✓■ Vocabulary: Unit 4 Review, p. 105J<br>**Writing Process Strategies**<br>✓■ Persuasive Writing: Paragraph, p. 105J<br>**English Language Conventions**<br>✓■ Penmanship: Cursive Letters *X* and *W*, p. 105J |

Below are suggestions for differentiating instruction. These are the same skills shown in the Lesson Planner; however, these pages provide extra practice opportunities or enriching activities to meet the varied needs of students.

WORKSHOP

# Differentiating Instruction

## Teacher Directed: Individual and Small-Group Instruction

Spend time each day with individuals and small groups to individualize instruction. Each day:

- preteach students who need help with the next lesson.
- reteach students who need to solidify their understanding of content previously taught.
- listen to students read to check their fluency.
- hold writing and inquiry conferences.

Use the following program components to support instruction:

- ***Reteach*** with students who need a bit more practice
- ***Intervention*** for students who exhibit a lack of understanding of the lesson concepts
- ***English Learner Support*** with students who need language help
- ***Differentiating Instruction Support Activities*** with students who need alternative activities to strengthen skill and strategy instruction

## Student: Independent Activities

Students can work alone, with a partner, or in small groups on such activities as:

- Review sound/spellings
- Practice dictation words
- Partner reading
- Practice fluency
- Independent reading
- Reading Roundtable
- Concept vocabulary
- Selection vocabulary
- Writing in progress
- Conference
- Language Arts
- Challenge activities
- Inquiry and Investigation activities
- Listening Library
- Online Phonics

For Workshop Management Tips, see Appendix pages 41–42.

| | DAY I |
|---|---|
| **Word Knowledge** | **Teacher Directed**<br>▪ Reading Words: Suffix *-tion*, ***Intervention Guide,*** p. 223<br>**Independent Activities**<br>▪ ***Online Phonics*** |
| **Fluency** | **Independent Activities**<br>▪ Self-test fluency rate<br>▪ Partner reading |
| **Comprehension** | **Teacher Directed**<br>▪ Preteach "Uncle Jed's Barbershop," ***Intervention Guide,*** pp. 224–225<br>▪ Preteach Intervention Selection One, ***Intervention Guide,*** pp. 225–226<br>▪ ***English Learner Support Guide***<br>• Vocabulary, pp. 340–341<br>• Comprehension Skill: Cause and Effect, pp. 341–342<br>**Independent Activities**<br>▪ Browse ***Leveled Classroom Library***<br>▪ Add vocabulary in Writer's Notebook |
| **Inquiry** | **Independent Activities**<br>▪ Investigating Concepts Beyond the Text, p. 105A<br>▪ Concept/Question Board<br>▪ Explore OCR Web site for theme connections |
| **Language Arts** | **Teacher Directed**<br>▪ Grammar, Usage, and Mechanics, ***Intervention Guide,*** p. 228<br>**Independent Activities**<br>▪ Review, ***Comprehension and Language Arts Skills,*** pp. 122–123 |

| DAY 2 | DAY 3 | DAY 4 | DAY 5 |
|---|---|---|---|
| **Teacher Directed**<br>▪ Developing Oral Language, ***Intervention Guide,*** p. 223<br>**Independent Activities**<br>▪ ***Online Phonics***<br>▪ Read ***Decodable Book 35,*** *School Days Long Ago* | **Teacher Directed**<br>▪ Dictation and Spelling: Suffix *-tion,* ***Intervention Guide,*** pp. 223–224<br>**Independent Activities**<br>▪ ***Online Phonics*** | **Teacher Directed**<br>▪ General Review<br>**Independent Activities**<br>▪ ***Online Phonics*** | **Teacher Directed**<br>▪ General Review<br>**Independent Activities**<br>▪ ***Online Phonics*** |
| **Independent Activities**<br>▪ Oral reading of "Uncle Jed's Barbershop" for fluency<br>▪ Partner reading of ***Decodable Book 35,*** *School Days Long Ago* | **Independent Activities**<br>▪ Partner reading of selection<br>▪ Reread ***Decodable Book 35,*** *School Days Long Ago* | **Independent Activities**<br>▪ Reread "Uncle Jed's Barbershop"<br>▪ Partner reading of ***Decodable Book 35,*** *School Days Long Ago* | **Teacher Directed**<br>▪ Repeated Readings/Fluency Check, ***Intervention Guide,*** p. 228<br>**Independent Activities**<br>▪ Reread ***Decodable Book 35,*** *School Days Long Ago* |
| **Teacher Directed**<br>▪ Preteach "Uncle Jed's Barbershop," ***Intervention Guide,*** pp. 224–225<br>▪ Comprehension Strategies, ***Intervention Guide,*** p. 226<br>▪ Reread Intervention Selection One, ***Intervention Guide,*** pp. 225–226<br>▪ ***English Learner Support Guide***<br>• Vocabulary, pp. 342–344<br>• Comprehension Skill: Cause and Effect, p. 344<br>**Independent Activities**<br>▪ Choose a ***Leveled Classroom Library*** book for independent reading<br>▪ Record response to selection in Writer's Notebook<br>▪ Complete Link to Writing in Supporting the Reading, p. 103C | **Teacher Directed**<br>▪ Reread "Uncle Jed's Barbershop," ***Intervention Guide,*** pp. 224–225<br>▪ Preteach Intervention Selection Two, ***Intervention Guide,*** pp. 226–227<br>▪ ***English Learner Support Guide***<br>• Vocabulary, pp. 345-346<br>• Comprehension Skill: Cause and Effect, pp. 346-347<br>▪ Math Connection, p. 103E<br>**Independent Activities**<br>▪ Read ***Leveled Classroom Library*** book<br>▪ ***Listening Library Audiocassette/CD*** | **Teacher Directed**<br>▪ Discuss Concept Connections, p. 104<br>▪ Reread "Uncle Jed's Barbershop," ***Intervention Guide,*** pp. 224–225<br>▪ Comprehension Strategies, ***Intervention Guide,*** p. 227<br>▪ Reread Intervention Selection Two, ***Intervention Guide,*** pp. 226–227<br>▪ ***English Learner Support Guide***<br>• Vocabulary, pp. 347–349<br>• Comprehension Skill: Cause and Effect, p. 349<br>**Independent Activities**<br>▪ Reread ***Leveled Classroom Library*** book<br>▪ Add words to Word Bank<br>▪ Complete Independent Practice in Literary Elements, p. 103D | **Teacher Directed**<br>▪ Informal Assessment for Intervention<br>▪ ***English Learner Support Guide***<br>• Review Vocabulary, p. 350<br>• Comprehension Skill: Cause and Effect, pp. 350-351<br>▪ ***Differentiating Instruction Support Activities,*** pp. 22–25<br>**Independent Activities**<br>▪ Read ***Leveled Classroom Library*** book as independent reading<br>▪ Reading Roundtable<br>▪ Social Studies Connection, p. 103F<br>▪ ***English Learner Support Activities,*** p. 44 |
| **Independent Activities**<br>▪ Concept/Question Board<br>▪ Use ***Research Assistant CD-ROM*** to continue investigation<br>▪ Explore OCR Web site for theme connections | **Independent Activities**<br>▪ Presentations and proposal questions, p. 105C<br>▪ Concept/Question Board<br>▪ Explore OCR Web site for theme connections | **Independent Activities**<br>▪ Concept/Question Board<br>▪ Complete Independent Practice in Supporting the Investigation, p. 105D<br>▪ Time Lines, ***Inquiry Journal,*** p. 104 | **Independent Activities**<br>▪ Final preparations for presentations<br>▪ Record responses to investigation<br>▪ Continue work on investigation |
| **Teacher Directed**<br>▪ Grammar, Usage, and Mechanics, ***Intervention Guide,*** p. 228<br>▪ Spelling: Word Sort, p. 105G<br>▪ Review, ***Reteach,*** p. 127<br>**Independent Activities**<br>▪ Vocabulary: Unit 4 Review, ***Spelling and Vocabulary Skills,*** pp. 98–99<br>▪ Review, ***Challenge,*** p. 112<br>▪ Seminar: Plan a Persuasive Paragraph, p. 105G | **Teacher Directed**<br>▪ Writing Activity, ***Intervention Guide,*** p. 229<br>▪ Vocabulary: ***Reteach,*** p. 126<br>**Independent Activities**<br>▪ Spelling: Unit 4 Review, ***Spelling and Vocabulary Skills,*** p. 100<br>▪ Vocabulary: ***Challenge,*** p. 111<br>▪ Writer's Craft: Effective Beginnings and Endings, ***Comprehension and Language Arts Skills,*** pp. 124-125 | **Teacher Directed**<br>▪ Writer's Craft: Effective Beginnings, ***Reteach,*** p. 128<br>▪ Writing Activity, ***Intervention Guide,*** p. 229<br>▪ Spelling: Review, ***Reteach,*** p. 125<br>**Independent Activities**<br>▪ Spelling: Unit 4 Review<br>• ***Spelling and Vocabulary Skills,*** p. 101<br>• ***Challenge,*** p. 110 | **Teacher Directed**<br>▪ ***Differentiating Instruction Support Activities,*** pp. 26–28<br>**Independent Activities**<br>▪ Seminar: Edit/Proofread and Publish a Persuasive Paragraph, p. 105J<br>▪ Penmanship: Practice Cursive Letters *X* and *W*, p. 105J<br>▪ Writer's Craft: Effective Beginnings and Endings, ***Challenge,*** p. 113 |

ASSESSMENT

# Formal Assessment Options

Use these summative assessments along with your informal observations to assess student progress.

Name ______ Date ______ Score ______

UNIT 4 Money • Lesson 7

LESSON ASSESSMENT

**Uncle Jed's Barbershop**

**Read the following questions carefully. Then completely fill in the bubble of each correct answer. You may look back at the story to find the answer to each of the questions.**

1. Who is the person telling this story?
   - Ⓐ Uncle Jed
   - ● Sarah Jean
   - Ⓒ Sarah's mama
2. Where does the girl in the story live?
   - Ⓐ in the city
   - ● on a farm
   - Ⓒ in a forest

**Read the following questions carefully. Use complete sentences to answer the questions.**

3. Why didn't anyone believe Uncle Jed would someday have his own shop?
   They thought it was just an impossible dream.
4. Why did it take so long for the doctors to look at Sarah?
   It took so long because the doctors looked at all of the white patients first.
5. Why did Sarah almost not have the operation?
   Sarah's parents needed three hundred dollars to pay for the operation, but they did not have the money.

26 Unit 4 • Lesson 7 *Uncle Jed's Barbershop* • Unit 4 Assessment

**Unit 4 Assessment p. 26**

**Uncle Jed's Barbershop** *(continued)*

LESSON ASSESSMENT

6. What did Uncle Jed do when his customers could not pay him?
   He cut their hair anyway, and they shared what they had with him.
7. How is Uncle Jed different from Sarah's doctors?
   Uncle Jed helped people for free, but the doctors did not help Sarah for free.
8. What caused Uncle Jed to work all night in his new shop?
   He was so happy to have a shop that he did not want to stop cutting hair.

**Read the following questions carefully. Then completely fill in the bubble of each correct answer.**

9. Who paid for Sarah's operation?
   - ● Uncle Jed
   - Ⓑ Sarah's Daddy
   - Ⓒ the doctors
10. Which of these best describes Uncle Jed?
    - Ⓐ proud and intelligent
    - Ⓑ friendly but careless
    - ● hardworking and kind

Unit 4 Assessment • *Uncle Jed's Barbershop* Unit 4 • Lesson 7 27

**Unit 4 Assessment p. 27**

**Uncle Jed's Barbershop** *(continued)*

LESSON ASSESSMENT

**Read the question and statement below. Use complete sentences in your answers.**

**Linking to the Concepts** What does this story teach about being patient and working hard to make dreams come true?
Answers will vary. Accept all reasonable answers.

**Personal Response** Tell about a time when you wanted something very badly but you had to wait for it. How long did you have to wait? Are you still waiting?
Answers will vary. Accept all reasonable answers.

28 Unit 4 • Lesson 7 *Uncle Jed's Barbershop* • Unit 4 Assessment

**Unit 4 Assessment p. 28**

**Uncle Jed's Barbershop** *(continued)*

LESSON ASSESSMENT

**Vocabulary**

**Read the following questions carefully. Then completely fill in the bubble of each correct answer.**

1. Uncle Jed talks about the fancy equipment that will be in his shop one day. **Equipment** is a word for
   - Ⓐ haircuts and hair styles
   - Ⓑ hats and purses
   - ● tools and supplies
2. The new shop was delayed because of a lack of money. When something is **delayed**, you have to
   - ● wait longer for it
   - Ⓑ forget all about it
   - Ⓒ get advice about it
3. Most people in the story are sharecroppers. **Sharecroppers** are people who
   - Ⓐ don't grow crops on their land anymore
   - ● work on someone else's land for a share of the crops
   - Ⓒ buy land and work hard to grow crops on it
4. When the doctors examined the girl, they said she needed an operation. In this sentence, **examined** means
   - Ⓐ took a difficult test
   - Ⓑ ignored for a while
   - ● looked at carefully
5. Mr. Ernest Walters is the person who tells Uncle Jed about the banks failing. When a bank **fails**, it
   - ● loses its money
   - Ⓑ gives money back
   - Ⓒ makes more money

Unit 4 Assessment • *Uncle Jed's Barbershop* Unit 4 • Lesson 7 29

**Unit 4 Assessment p. 29**

Name ______ Date ______ Score ______

UNIT 4 Money • Lesson 7 *Uncle Jed's Barber Shop*

LESSON ASSESSMENT

**Spelling Pretest: Unit 4 Review**

**Fold this page back on the dotted line. Take the Pretest. Then correct any word you misspelled by crossing out the word and rewriting it next to the incorrect spelling.**

| | | | |
|---|---|---|---|
| 1. | ______ | 1. | offer |
| 2. | ______ | 2. | winner |
| 3. | ______ | 3. | zipper |
| 4. | ______ | 4. | will |
| 5. | ______ | 5. | well |
| 6. | ______ | 6. | he'd |
| 7. | ______ | 7. | isn't |
| 8. | ______ | 8. | taking |
| 9. | ______ | 9. | monkeys |
| 10. | ______ | 10. | stitches |
| 11. | ______ | 11. | used |
| 12. | ______ | 12. | cutting |
| 13. | ______ | 13. | clippers |
| 14. | ______ | 14. | saving |
| 15. | ______ | 15. | died |

42 Unit 4 • Lesson 7 *Spelling Pretest: Unit 4 Review* • Unit 4 Assessment

**Unit 4 Assessment p. 42**

Name ______ Date ______ Score ______

UNIT 4 Money • Lesson 7 *Uncle Jed's Barber Shop*

LESSON ASSESSMENT

**Spelling Final Test: Unit 4 Review**

**Mark the letter next to the underlined word that is misspelled. Focus on the underlined word.**

1. ● Restaurant hosts ofer menus.
   - Ⓑ A used car is not new.
   - Ⓒ An ill person doesn't feel well.
   - Ⓓ Correct as is.
2. Ⓔ Some computers will crash.
   - ● Many monkeies have long tails.
   - Ⓖ Rescuers like saving lives.
   - Ⓩ Correct as is.
3. Ⓐ Loose stitches come undone.
   - Ⓑ Some zoos have monkeys.
   - Ⓒ Pianos are used for music.
   - ● Correct as is.
4. Ⓔ Nail clippers cut nails.
   - ● Coupons are for saveing money.
   - Ⓖ A banana isn't a vegetable.
   - Ⓩ Correct as is.
5. ● A needle sews stitchs in fabric.
   - Ⓑ If you try, you're a winner.
   - Ⓒ Tadpoles will grow legs.
   - Ⓓ Correct as is.
6. Ⓔ Mowers are for cutting grass.
   - Ⓖ Snakes will lose their skin.
   - ● A fish is'nt a mammal.
   - Ⓩ Correct as is.

Unit 4 Assessment • *Spelling Final Test: Unit 4 Review* Unit 4 • Lesson 7 43

**Unit 4 Assessment p. 43**

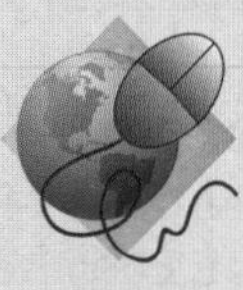

**Online Assessment** for ***Open Court Reading*** helps teachers differentiate classroom instruction based on students' scores from the weekly and end-of-unit assessments. It provides exercises best suited to meet the needs of each student. For more information, visit SRAonline.com.

## Informal Comprehension Strategies Rubrics

### Monitoring and Adjusting Reading Speed

The student changes reading speed in reaction to text, exhibiting such behavior as:

- skimming parts of the text that are not important or relevant.
- purposely reading more slowly because of difficulty in comprehending the text.

### Predicting

- The student makes predictions about what the text is about.
- The student updates predictions during reading, based on information in the text.

### Summarizing

- The student paraphrases the text, reporting main ideas and a summary of what is in the text.
- The student decides which parts of the text are important in his or her summary.
- The student draws conclusions from the text.
- The student makes global interpretations of the text, such as recognizing the genre.

## Research Rubrics

During Workshop, assess students using the rubrics below. The rubrics range from 1 to 4 in most categories, with 1 being the lowest score. Record each student's score on the inside back cover of the ***Inquiry Journal.***

### Overall Assessment of Research

**1** A collection of facts related in miscellaneous ways to a topic.

**2** An organized collection of facts relevant to the research problem.

**3** A thoughtful effort to tackle a research problem, with some indication of progress toward solving it.

**4** Significant progress on a challenging problem of understanding.

### Objectives

- Students practice recognizing compound words.
- Students practice recognizing base words and the suffixes *-ment, -tion,* and *-sion.*

### Materials

- Student Anthology, Book 2, pp. 94–105
- Sound/Spelling Cards
- Decodable Book 35
- Routine Card 1, Routines 1–2

**Teacher Tip SYLLABICATION** To help students blend words and build fluency, use the syllabication below of the words in the word lines.

| | | |
|---|---|---|
| hair • cut | bar • ber • shop | share • crop • pers |
| night • gown | bed • clothes | ship • wreck |
| e • quip | e • quip • ment | im • pris • on |
| im • pris • on • ment | | seg • re • ga • tion |
| o • pe • ra • tion | de • pres • sion | used |
| cut • ting | clip • pers | sav • ing |
| died | | |

### Differentiating Instruction

| If... | Then... |
|---|---|
| Students need extra help recognizing the suffix *-sion* | Use ***Online Phonics*** |
| Students need extra help with the suffix *-tion* | • Use ***Online Phonics***<br>• Use ***Intervention Guide*** pages 223–224 |

**Spelling**
See pages 105E–105J for the corresponding spelling lesson for Unit 4 review.

**Routine Card**
Refer to ***Routine 1*** for whole-word blending and ***Routine 2*** for sentence blending.

WORD KNOWLEDGE

## Word Knowledge

### Reading the Words and Sentences

- Use direct teaching to teach the following lesson.
- Use the established procedure as you have students read each line of words and the sentences in this and in subsequent lessons. The words in **boldface** are from the selection.

| | | | | | |
|---|---|---|---|---|---|
| Line 1: | **haircut** | **barbershop** | **sharecroppers** | | |
| Line 2: | **nightgown** | **bedclothes** | shipwreck | | |
| Line 3: | equip | **equipment** | imprison | imprisonment | |
| Line 4: | **segregation** | **operation** | **depression** | | |
| Line 5: | used | cutting | clippers | saving | **died** |

Sentence 1: When he was done, he would pick me up and sit me in his lap and tell me about the barbershop he was going to open one day and about all the fancy equipment that would be in it.
Sentence 2: When the doctors did examine me, they told my daddy that I needed an operation and that it would cost three hundred dollars.
Sentence 3: That was the beginning of the Great Depression.
Sentence 4: The tailor used clippers for cutting the hem of the dress.

### About the Words and Sentences

- **Lines 1 and 2:** These words are compound words. Ask students to read the words and tell what the two words are that make up the compounds. Ask if the two words help with the meaning of the compound word.
- **Line 3:** The words in Line 3 are base words with the suffix *-ment* added. Ask students to read the words and use them in a sentence.
- **Line 4:** The words in Line 4 all have the suffix *-tion* or *-sion.* Ask students to identify the base words and to explain how the suffixes change the part of speech of the word *(verb to noun).*
- **Line 5:** The words in the last line are found in "Uncle Jed's Barbershop" and review the spelling patterns learned in Unit 4.
- **Sentences 1–3:** These sentences are from the story students are about to read. Ask students to identify the compound word *(barbershop).* Ask students to identify the word with the suffix *-ment (equipment).* Ask students to identify the word with the suffix *-sion (Depression).* Have a student underline the suffix in each word.
- **Sentence 4:** Have students identify the words in the last sentence that review the suffixes *-ed, -ing,* and *-s.*

WORD KNOWLEDGE

## Developing Oral Language

Use direct teaching to review the words. Use one or both of the following activities to help students practice the words aloud.

- Point to a line on the board. Ask a student to read a word from the line and use it in a sentence. Then ask that student to choose another student to pick a word from the line and use it in a sentence. Continue until all the words have been used in a sentence.
- Ask a student to find a word by naming its location. For example, Line 2, Word 3 is *shipwreck.* Then ask the student to identify the word by reading it aloud and using it in a sentence. Erase the word and ask the student to choose a volunteer to continue. Continue the activity until all the words have been erased.

## Building Fluency

***Decodable Books*** are used to help develop fluency for students who need extra practice. The only way to gain fluency is to read. Students will have many opportunities to read, including the ***Student Anthology,*** the ***Leveled Classroom Library,*** and their own reading. The ***Decodable Books*** can be used to practice the phonics and fluency elements being reviewed. Refer to the Appendix for the procedure on using these books. For this lesson, use ***Decodable Book 35,*** *School Days Long Ago.*

***Decodable Book 35***

**Teacher Tip** **FLUENCY** Gaining a better understanding of the spellings of sounds and structure of words will help students as they encounter unfamiliar words in their reading. By this time in Grade 3 students should be reading approximately 123 words per minute with fluency and expression. As students read, you may notice that some need work in building fluency. During Workshop, have these students select a selection of the text (a minimum of 160 words) to read several times in order to build fluency.

### Differentiating Instruction

| If... | Then... |
|---|---|
| Students need help building fluency | Have them read ***Decodable Book 35,*** *School Days Long Ago,* with partners |

**Teacher Tip** **FLUENCY** Using ***Unit 4 Assessment*** pages 52A and 52, administer the Oral Fluency Assessment individually to students. Use the Accuracy Rate chart to determine the student's accuracy rate. If the student reads the entire passage in one minute, 17 errors equates to 90% accuracy.

### Objectives

- Students will understand the selection vocabulary before reading, using strategies such as suffixes and structural cues.
- Students will recognize compound words and base words with the suffixes *-ment, -tion,* and *-sion.*
- Students will connect prior knowledge to subjects discussed in text.
- Students will use comprehension strategies such as Monitoring and Adjusting Reading Speed, Predicting, and Summarizing to construct meaning from the text and monitor reading.
- Students will use the comprehension skill Cause and Effect as they read the story the second time.
- Students will discuss personal reactions to the story to begin identifying their own personal reading preferences.
- Students link the selection's key concepts to their investigations.

### Materials

- Student Anthology, Book 2, pp. 94–105
- Teacher Observation Log
- Reading Transparencies 30, 46
- Inquiry Journal, p. 86
- Home Connection, p. 57
- Unit 4 Assessment, pp. 26–29
- Routine Card 1, 2, Routines 3–6
- Science/Social Studies Connection Center Card 33

### Differentiating Instruction

| If... | Then... |
|---|---|
| Students need extra help with selection vocabulary | Use ***Intervention Guide*** pages 224–225 |

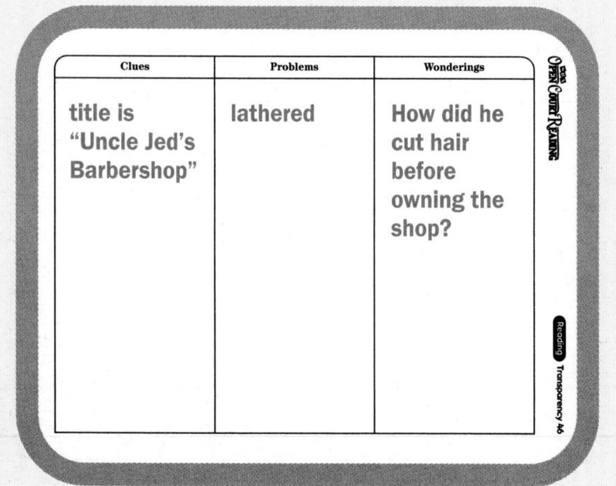

| Clues | Problems | Wonderings |
|---|---|---|
| title is "Uncle Jed's Barbershop" | lathered | How did he cut hair before owning the shop? |

***Reading Transparency 46***

## Build Background

### Activate Prior Knowledge

Discuss the following with students to find out what they may already know about the selection and have already learned about money.

- Preteach "Uncle Jed's Barbershop" by determining students' prior knowledge by asking, "What do you know about the Great Depression?"
- Discuss how working to make a dream happen takes patience and determination. Ask students to relate personal stories of when they have had to work hard for something.
- Ask students what they know about saving money.

### Background Information

The following information may help students understand the selection they are about to read.

- Point out to students that the selection they will be reading is historical fiction. The events are made up but could actually happen in real life during an actual time period—the Great Depression.
- Explain that the Great Depression began in this country and spread to other countries in Europe. It was a time when banks collapsed and people lost the money they kept there. Most people had no money or a way to earn money. People had to find ways to feed their families and meet their needs without money. This happened between 1929 and 1939.

## Preview and Prepare

### Browse

- Have a student read aloud the title and the name of the author and illustrator. Have them preview the selection by browsing the first page or two of the story. Discuss what they think this story might teach them about money.
- Have the students search for clues that tell them something about the story. Also, have them look for any problems, such as unfamiliar words, they notice while reading. Use ***Reading Transparency 46*** to record their observations as they browse. For example, a student might notice the fact that the title "Uncle Jed's Barbershop" is a clue the story is about Uncle Jed's dream. For the Problems column, students might point out they are unfamiliar with the term *lathered.* They might wonder how Uncle Jed cut hair before he had the barbershop. To save time and model note taking, write students' observations as brief notes rather than as complete sentences.
- As students prepare to read the selection, have them browse the Focus Questions on the first page of the selection. Tell them to keep these questions in mind as they read.

## Set Purposes

Encourage students to set their own purposes for reading this selection. As they read, have students think about saving and sharing money.

## Selection Vocabulary

As students study vocabulary, they will use a variety of skills to determine the meaning of a word. These include context clues, word structure, and apposition. Students will apply these same skills while reading to clarify additional unfamiliar words. Students can write definitions of new words in their Writer's Notebooks.

Display ***Reading Transparency 30*** before reading the selection to introduce and discuss the following words and their meanings.

**equipment:** tools and supplies used for a given purpose (page 95)
**sharecroppers:** people who farm someone else's land and are paid with a share of the crops (page 96)
**exchange:** trade one thing for another (page 96)
**examine:** look in detail (page 97)
**delayed:** caused to wait (page 99)
**failing:** losing all its money (page 100)

Have students read the words, stopping to blend any words that they have trouble reading. Help students decode multisyllabic words by breaking the words into syllables and blending the syllables. If students still have trouble, refer them to the ***Sound/Spelling Cards.*** If the word is not decodable, give the students the pronunciation.

Have students read the sentences on the transparency to determine the meaning of the underlined words. Each word has two sentences that students will read and from which they should be able to derive the meaning of the underlined word. Remind them to use one or more of the skills they have learned—context clues, word structure, or apposition—to figure out the meaning before using a dictionary. Be sure students explain which skills they are using and how they figured out the meanings of the words. Have students reread the sentence, substituting the definition to see if the sentence makes sense. Have a volunteer create a new sentence using the underlined word.

**Teacher Tip INVESTIGATION** Tell students that some of their grandparents or great grandparents might remember the Great Depression. People who were born before 1930 will likely have many stories to tell about that time. Ask students to think about their investigation questions and to decide whether interviewing a grandparent might help answer some of the questions they have. If students cannot interview grandparents, people in a local retirement home or senior community might agree to be interviewed.

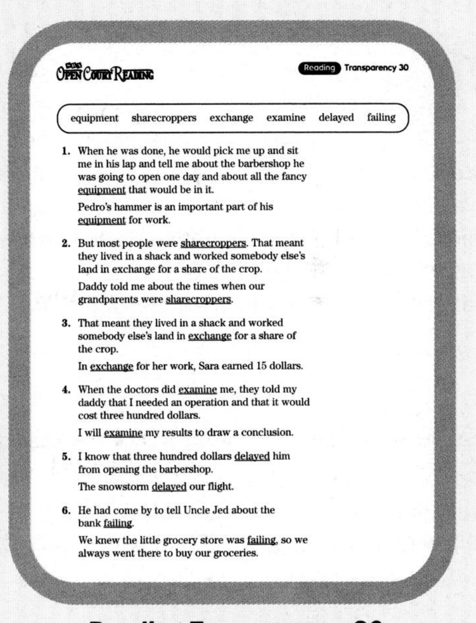

Open Court Reading    Reading Transparency 30

equipment sharecroppers exchange examine delayed failing

1. When he was done, he would pick me up and sit me in his lap and tell me about the barbershop he was going to open one day and about all the fancy equipment that would be in it.
   Pedro's hammer is an important part of his equipment for work.
2. But most people were sharecroppers. That meant they lived in a shack and worked somebody else's land in exchange for a share of the crop.
   Daddy told me about the times when our grandparents were sharecroppers.
3. That meant they lived in a shack and worked somebody else's land in exchange for a share of the crop.
   In exchange for her work, Sara earned 15 dollars.
4. When the doctors did examine me, they told my daddy that I needed an operation and that it would cost three hundred dollars.
   I will examine my results to draw a conclusion.
5. I know that three hundred dollars delayed him from opening the barbershop.
   The snowstorm delayed our flight.
6. He had come by to tell Uncle Jed about the bank failing.
   We knew the little grocery store was failing, so we always went there to buy our groceries.

***Reading Transparency 30***

**Teacher Tip SELECTION VOCABULARY** To help students decode words, divide them into syllables when you are saying them, as shown below. The information following each word tells how students can figure out the meaning of each word. When writing words on the board, do not divide them into syllables.

| | |
|---|---|
| **e • quip • ment** | context clues |
| **share • crop • pers** | apposition |
| **ex • change** | context clues |
| **ex • am • ine** | context clues |
| **de • layed** | context clues |
| **fail • ing** | context clues |

**Routine Card**
Refer to ***Routine 3*** for the vocabulary procedure.

**Teacher Tip** COMPREHENSION STRATEGIES Remind students on the second day as they read the story to summarize what they learned from the first day.

**Routine Card**
Refer to ***Routine 5*** for the procedure on reading the selection.

During Workshop, and after the selection has been read at least once, have students listen to the recording of this lesson's selection on the ***Listening Library Audiocassette/CD.*** After students have listened, have them discuss their personal preferences of the selections read. Ask them what other things they have listened to and like to listen to on the radio, on audiocassettes, or on CDs.

### DIFFERENTIATING INSTRUCTION

| If... | Then... |
|---|---|
| Students need extra help with summarizing | Use ***Intervention Guide*** pages 225–227 |

**Teacher Tip** For extra practice in oral fluency, have individual students read aloud to you a selection they have previously read, either from a ***Decodable Book*** or a passage from the ***Student Anthology.*** Time each student for one minute. If the student reads more than 123 words correctly, have the student retell the selection he or she has just read. Use one prompt if the student seems to be stuck, and allow a maximum of one minute for the student to retell the story. If the student does not read more than 123 words correctly, have the student try reading from an earlier ***Decodable Book*** to help you determine where the problem lies.

# Reading Recommendations

## Oral Reading

The captivating narrative style of this story makes this a good selection for oral reading. In addition, reading this story aloud will give you the opportunity to continue modeling comprehension strategies for students and give students practice using the strategies aloud. Students should read aloud fluently with appropriate expression and intonation. Make sure that students attend to punctuation and read in phrases. Tell students to add a sense of feeling or anticipation as they read.

Have students make use of the comprehension strategies listed below to help them understand the selection. Have them stop reading periodically or wait until they have completed the selection to discuss the reading strategies.

After the students have finished reading the selection, use the Discussing the Selection questions on page 103A to see if they understand what they have read.

## Using Comprehension Strategies 

Comprehension strategy instruction allows students to become aware of how good readers read. Good readers constantly check their understanding as they are reading and ask themselves questions. In addition, skilled readers recognize when they are having problems and stop to use various comprehension strategies to help them make sense of what they are reading.

An extended lesson on the comprehension strategy, Monitoring and Adjusting Reading Speed, can be found in the Supporting the Reading section on page 103C. This lesson is intended to give students extra practice with Monitoring and Adjusting Reading Speed. However, it may be used at this time to introduce the comprehension strategy to students.

During the first reading of "Uncle Jed's Barbershop," teacher model and prompt the use of the following comprehension strategies:

- **Monitoring and Adjusting Reading Speed** is sometimes necessary for readers to slow down and reread in order to obtain all of the information.
- **Predicting** causes readers to analyze information given about story events and characters in the context of how it may logically connect to the story's conclusion.
- **Summarizing** prompts readers to keep track of what they are reading and to focus their minds on important information.

As students read, they should be using a variety of strategies to help them understand the selection. Encourage students to use the strategies listed above as the class reads the story aloud. Do this by stopping at the points indicated by the numbers in the magenta circles on the reduced student page and modeling for students the use of a particular strategy. Students can also stop reading periodically to discuss what they have learned and what problems they may be having.

## Building Comprehension Skills 

Revisiting or rereading a selection allows readers to apply skills that give them a more complete understanding of the text. Some follow-up comprehension skills help students organize information. Others lead to deeper understanding—to "reading between the lines," as mature readers do. In this selection, students will review the following comprehension skill:

- **Cause and Effect:** Readers identify what causes events to happen or what causes characters to behave in certain ways, which helps readers put together logical explanations in the text.

### Reading with a Purpose

Have students look for ways the story characters learn about money throughout the selection.

## Research in Action

Stories are universal. They are an integral part of all cultures. From the moral of a traditional folktale to the complex psychology of a character in a modern novel, stories have much to teach us about ourselves and others. We use stories to interpret and understand our social world and ourselves. Stories tell of human actions and intentions and link them to consequences. Although "thinking narratively" has been given short shrift in our highly technological, scientific world, it is often the best way to explore universal themes—such as . . . Journeys and Quests/Risks and Consequences/Friendship, etc. My research has shown that by explicitly teaching children the components of plot structure they are better able to analyze and craft stories, that is, to understand and express how and why people act as they do, and to explore contexts, characters, and conflicts that are an essential part of the human condition.
*(Anne McKeough)*

COMPREHENSION

Read pages 94–103.

## Comprehension Strategies

First Read

Read the story aloud, taking turns with the students. Start by modeling the use of strategies for the students.

### Teacher Modeling

**1 Monitoring and Adjusting Reading Speed** *I started reading this story pretty fast. But so far there's already been a lot of information. Since this is still the beginning of the story, I want to make sure I don't miss any important information. I'm going to slow down here and reread the first few paragraphs.*

### Word Knowledge

**SCAFFOLDING** The skills students are reviewing in Word Knowledge should help them in reading the story. This lesson focuses on compound words and base words with the suffixes *-ment, -tion,* and *-sion.*

**compound words:** **haircut**

**Teacher Tip** Remind students to share their think alouds with the class. When they stop to use a strategy on their own, encourage them to share their thoughts with the class.

### Informal Assessment

Observe individual students as they read and use the Teacher Observation Log, found in the ***Program Assessment Teacher's Edition,*** to record anecdotal information about each student's strengths and weaknesses.

**First Reading Recommendation**

**ORAL • CHORAL**

*Focus Questions* What is it like to save for a long time for something you really want? How would you feel if you saved a lot of money for something you wanted and then had to spend it on something else? How would you feel if that something else was very important and your money was going to a good cause?

# UNCLE JED'S BARBERSHOP

Margaree King Mitchell
*illustrated by James Ransome*

Jedediah Johnson was my granddaddy's brother. Everybody has their favorite relative. Well, Uncle Jedediah was mine.

He used to come by our house every Wednesday night with his clippers. He was the only black barber in the county. Daddy said that before Uncle Jed started cutting hair, he and Granddaddy used to have to go thirty miles to get a haircut.

94

### Differentiating Instruction

| If... | Then... |
|---|---|
| English Learners need extra help with vocabulary | Use ***English Learner Support Guide*** pages 340–341 |
| English Learners need extra help with cause and effect | Use ***English Learner Support Guide*** pages 341–342 |

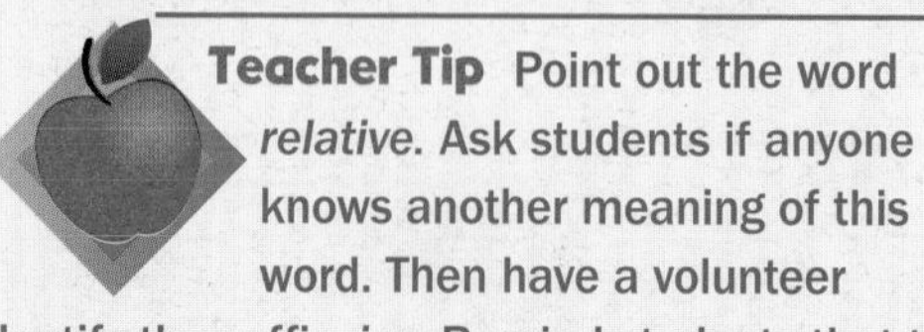

**Teacher Tip** Point out the word *relative.* Ask students if anyone knows another meaning of this word. Then have a volunteer identify the suffix *-ive.* Remind students that the suffix *-ive* means, "performs an action." Ask students if they can think of words to which the suffix *-ive* has been added.

After Uncle Jed cut my daddy's hair, he lathered a short brush with soap and spread it over my daddy's face and shaved him. Then he started over on my granddaddy.

I always asked Uncle Jed to cut my hair, but Mama wouldn't let him. So he would run the clippers on the back of my neck and just pretend to cut my hair. He even spread lotion on my neck. I would smell wonderful all day.

When he was done, he would pick me up and sit me in his lap and tell me about the barbershop he was going to open one day and about all the fancy equipment that would be in it. The sinks would be so shiny they sparkled, the floors so clean you could see yourself. He was going to have four barber chairs. And outside was going to be a big, tall, red-and-white barber pole. He told me he was saving up for it. **1**

95

## Comprehension Skills

### Cause and Effect

Identifying causes and effects helps students gain a deeper understanding of what they read. Review cause and effect with students and ask them to look for such relationships during the second read of the story. Students should attempt to make inferences and draw conclusions when considering cause and effect. Record students' answers on the board or on an overhead transparency.

- **Cause:** *Her mama didn't want him to cut her hair.*
  **Effect:** *Uncle Jed only pretended to cut the little girl's hair.*
- **Cause:** *He didn't own his own barbershop.*
  **Effect:** *Uncle Jed came to the family's house to cut their hair.*

Remind students that words called *causal indicators* express cause-and-effect relationships. They include *since, because, so, therefore, as a result of, in order to.*

**Cause and Effect**

Introduced in Grade 1.
Scaffolded throughout Grades 2 and 3.

| | |
|---|---|
| **REINTRODUCED:** | Unit 1, Lesson 2 |
| **REINFORCED:** | Unit 1, Lesson 4 |
| | Unit 2, Lesson 4 |
| | Unit 2, Lesson 5 |
| | Unit 4, Lesson 2 |
| | Unit 4, Lesson 7 |
| | Unit 6, Lesson 6 |
| **TESTED:** | Unit 4 Assessment |

**Second Reading Recommendation**

**ORAL • SILENT**

COMPREHENSION

### Word Knowledge

**compound words:** **barbershop**

**Teacher Tip** Students who have trouble identifying causes and effects might find it easier if they begin by stating the effect, or *what happened.* Then they can look in the text to find *why* it happened.

COMPREHENSION

## Comprehension Strategies

Begin prompting students for responses. Recognize answers that are appropriate, even if they do not match the student sample. This will encourage students to use strategies as they read.

### Prompting

**2 Monitoring and Adjusting Reading Speed** *This paragraph doesn't seem to be part of the events in the story, but it seems to have important information. Who else needs to adjust their reading speed here to make sure they understand all the information?*

**Monitoring and Adjusting Reading Speed** *I need to slow down and reread this part carefully. I think this paragraph is important because it shows what the lives of the people were like. Rereading this more slowly gives me a chance to form a clear picture of what is being described.*

### Word Knowledge

**compound words:** sharecroppers
nightgown
bedclothes

**Teacher Tip** Tell students that good readers keep thinking about the questions that come up about the topic, and they keep coming back to those questions. As they read, tell them to keep the questions on the Concept/Question Board in mind. Have them make notes to themselves in the Response Journal section of their Writer's Notebooks about which questions seem most important. Tell them that good readers always think about what is important in selections, and they try to remember this important information.

He had been saying the same things for years. Nobody believed him. People didn't have dreams like that in those days.

We lived in the South. Most people were poor. My daddy owned a few acres of land and so did a few others. But most people were sharecroppers. That meant they lived in a shack and worked somebody else's land in exchange for a share of the crop. **2**

When I was five years old, I got sick. This particular morning, I didn't come into the kitchen while Mama was fixing breakfast. Mama and Daddy couldn't wake me up. My nightgown and the bedclothes were all wet where I had sweated.

96

**Teacher Tip** Remind students that each person might have a different response to literature and to think-alouds. Hearing what other people think can make discussing literature more interesting.

**Science/Social Studies Connection Center**
Refer to the ***Science/Social Studies Connection Center*** Card 33 for a social studies activity that students can investigate.

Mama wrapped me in a blanket while Daddy went outside and hitched the horse to the wagon. We had to travel about twenty miles into town to the hospital. It was midday when we got there. We had to go to the colored waiting room. In those days, they kept blacks and whites separate. There were separate public rest rooms, separate water fountains, separate schools. It was called segregation. So in the hospital, we had to go to the colored waiting room.

Even though I was unconscious, the doctors wouldn't look at me until they had finished with all the white patients. When the doctors did examine me, they told my daddy that I needed an operation and that it would cost three hundred dollars.

97

## Comprehension Skills

### Cause and Effect

Ask students to continue looking for cause-and-effect relationships in the story. Remind them to use causal indicators, if they like, as they are discussing causes and effects.

- *The nightgown and bedclothes were wet because the little girl had a fever.*
- *The girl and her daddy had to wait in a separate waiting room at the hospital because of segregation.*
- *The girl needed an operation, so her family had to find a way to get three hundred dollars.*

### Word Knowledge

**suffix *-tion*:** **segregation**
**operation**

**Effective Beginnings and Endings**

Tell students that it is important to have an effective beginning to catch their readers' attention and make them want to read to the end. It's important to have an effective ending to leave the reader thinking. Explain to students that the beginning of the story is effective because it makes the reader wonder why Uncle Jed was her favorite relative. The ending is effective because the writer has summed up her reasons and given the reader something to think about—not giving up on your dreams. See Writer's Craft, page 105H.

COMPREHENSION

### Differentiating Instruction

| If... | Then... |
| --- | --- |
| English Learners need extra help with vocabulary | Use ***English Learner Support Guide*** pages 342–344 |
| English Learners need extra help with cause and effect | Use ***English Learner Support Guide*** page 344 |

COMPREHENSION

## Comprehension Strategies

### Teacher Modeling

**3 Predicting** *I have a prediction here. I think that Uncle Jed is going to give Sarah Jean's family the money they need for her operation. I also predict that because he lends them the money, he'll have to wait longer to open his barbershop. Does anyone else have any predictions?*

**4 Confirming Predictions** *My prediction was confirmed. I see here that Uncle Jed did give the family the money and that it did cause him to wait longer to open the barbershop.*

**Word Knowledge**

**suffix *-tion*:** **operation**

**Teacher Tip** Ask students to pay attention to the way characters in the story use money. Do their actions remind students of any other stories they have read?

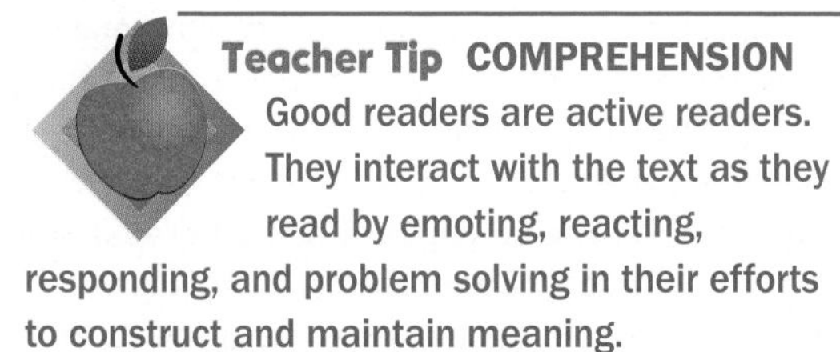

**Teacher Tip COMPREHENSION** Good readers are active readers. They interact with the text as they read by emoting, reacting, responding, and problem solving in their efforts to construct and maintain meaning.

Three hundred dollars was a lot of money in those days. My daddy didn't have that kind of money. And the doctors wouldn't do the operation until they had the money. 

My mama bundled me back up in the blanket and they took me home. Mama held me in her arms all night. She kept me alive until Daddy found Uncle Jed. He found him early the next morning in the next county on his way to cut somebody's hair. Daddy told him about me.

Uncle Jed leaned on his bent cane and stared straight ahead. He told Daddy that the money didn't matter. He couldn't let anything happen to his Sarah Jean. 4

98

Well, I had the operation. For a long time after that, Uncle Jed came by the house every day to see how I was doing. I know that three hundred dollars delayed him from opening the barbershop.

Uncle Jed came awfully close to opening his shop a few years after my operation. He had saved enough money to buy the land and build the building. But he still needed money for the equipment.

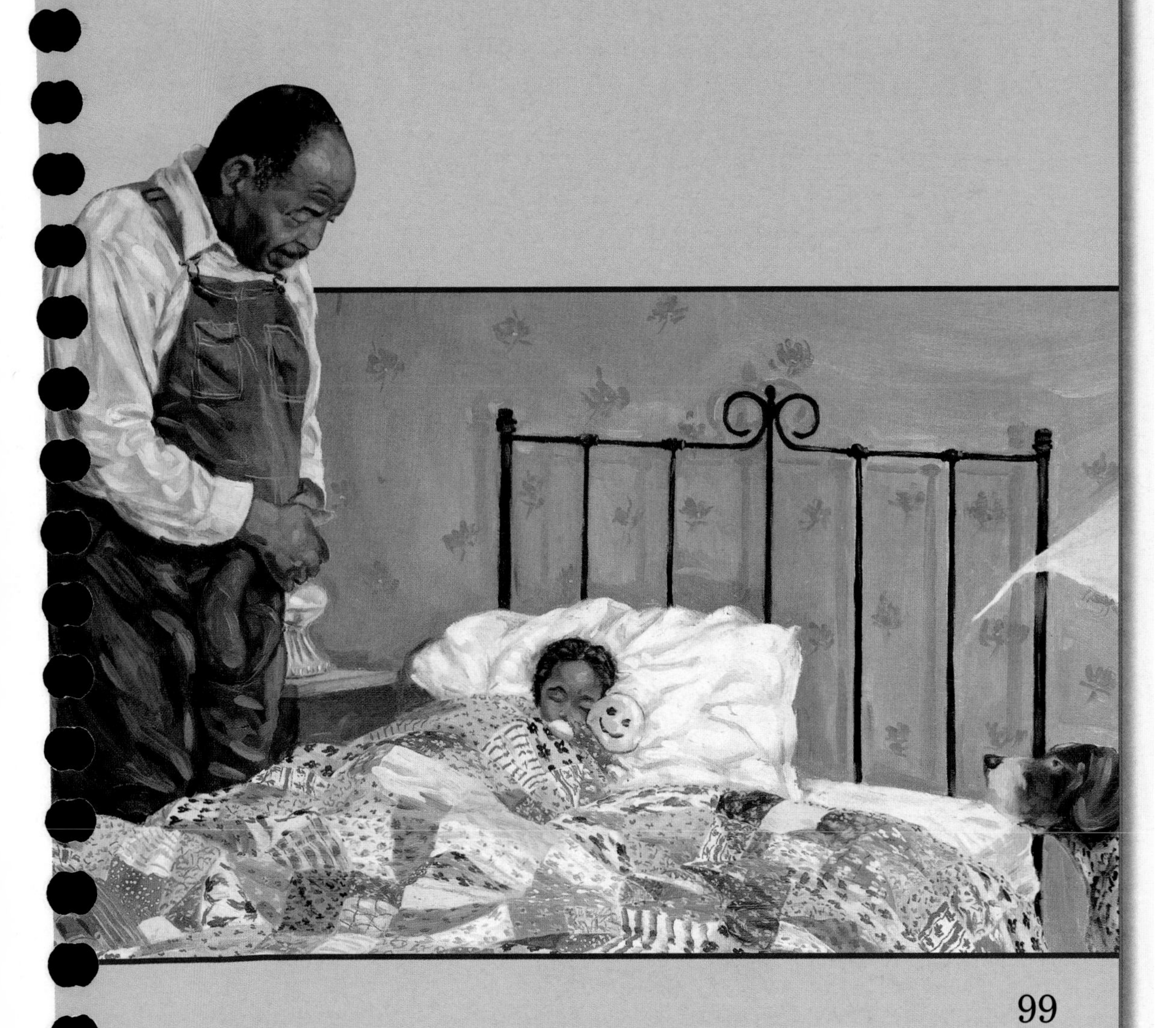

99

## Comprehension Skills

### Cause and Effect

Ask students to continue identifying causes and effects in the story. Remind them that authors do not always specifically point out cause-and-effect relationships, but careful readers can identify them.

- *Uncle Jed gave Sarah Jean's family three hundred dollars so that she could have the operation she needed.*
- *Uncle Jed had to delay opening his barbershop because he gave his money for Sarah Jean's operation.*

#### Word Knowledge

**suffix *-ment*:** **equipment**

**Teacher Tip** Good readers constantly evaluate their understanding of what they read. Stop often to make sure students are doing this.

COMPREHENSION

COMPREHENSION

## Comprehension Strategies

### Teacher Modeling

**5 Monitoring and Adjusting Reading Speed** *There is a lot of information in these paragraphs. I think I need to slow down and reread these paragraphs to make sure I understand all that has happened. Mr. Walters told Uncle Jed that all of their money in the bank was gone. It was the start of the Great Depression. Now Uncle Jed is going to have to start all over again to save money for his barbershop.*

### Word Knowledge

**suffix *-sion:*** **depression**

**Teacher Tip** You may want to review information regarding the Great Depression with the students.

**Teacher Tip** Remind students to use context clues, apposition, or word structure to figure out the meaning of difficult words as they are reading.

Anyway, Uncle Jed had come by the house. We had just finished supper when there was a knock on the door. It was Mr. Ernest Walters, a friend of Uncle Jed's. He had come by to tell Uncle Jed about the bank failing. That was where Mr. Walters and Uncle Jed had their money. Uncle Jed had over three thousand dollars in the bank, and it was gone.

Uncle Jed just stood there a long time before he said anything. Then he told Mr. Walters that even though he was disappointed, he would just have to start all over again. 

100

Talk about some hard times. That was the beginning of the Great Depression. Nobody had much money.

But Uncle Jed kept going around to his customers cutting their hair, even though they couldn't pay him. His customers shared with him whatever they had—a hot meal, fresh eggs, vegetables from the garden. And when they were able to pay again, they did.

And Uncle Jed started saving all over again.

101

## Comprehension Skills

Second Read

### Cause and Effect

Ask students to continue identifying causes and effects in the story. A major turning point occurs at this part of the story. Have students identify the cause-and-effect aspects at this point.

- *Uncle Jed lost all of the money he had in the bank because the banks failed.*
- *Uncle Jed would have to start saving money for his barbershop all over again because of the Great Depression.*
- *Uncle Jed's customers had no money to pay him so they paid him with meals and food.*

### Word Knowledge

**compound word:** **whatever**

COMPREHENSION

### Differentiating Instruction

| If... | Then... |
| --- | --- |
| English Learners need extra help with vocabulary | Use ***English Learner Support Guide*** pages 345–346 |
| English Learners need extra help with cause and effect | Use ***English Learner Support Guide*** pages 346–347 |

COMPREHENSION

## Comprehension Strategies

### Prompting

**6 Confirming Predictions** *Does the text confirm or refute anyone's prediction here?*

### Student Sample

**Confirming Predictions** *I predicted that Uncle Jed would some day open his own barbershop. The story says here that he did.*

### Prompting

**7 Summarizing** *Would anyone like to summarize all that's happened in the story?*

### Student Sample

**Summarizing** *Uncle Jed used to come to Sarah Jean's house to cut people's hair. He was saving money for his own barbershop. He gave Sarah Jean money to pay for the operation. Then later the Great Depression came and he lost all his money. He kept cutting hair and saving money, and finally opened his shop.*

### Discussing Strategy Use

After students read the selection, encourage them to share any problems encountered and to tell what strategies they used.

- Where did they pause in the reading to summarize?
- What predictions did they make?
- How did they adjust their reading speed?

These are questions good readers ask after they read a text. After reading, the students should always be asking, "What did I find interesting? What is important here?" Later, remind the students again that whenever they conclude a reading, they should ask themselves questions about what was in the text.

Ol' Uncle Jed finally got his barbershop. He opened it on his seventy-ninth birthday. It had everything, just like he said it would—big comfortable chairs, four cutting stations. You name it! The floors were so clean, they sparkled. 6

On opening day, people came from all over the county. They were Ol' Uncle Jed's customers. He had walked to see them for so many years. That day they all came to him.

I believe he cut hair all night and all the next day and the next night and the day after that! That man was so glad to have that shop, he didn't need any sleep.

102

### Word Knowledge

**compound word:** **barbershop**

**Teacher Tip** Encourage students to think aloud, practicing the strategies they have learned. Tell students that their ideas about the story are very important to the whole class's understanding of the story.

Of course, I was there, too. I wouldn't have missed it for the world. When I sat in one of the big barber chairs, Uncle Jed patted the back of my neck with lotion like he always did. Then he twirled me round and round in the barber chair.

Uncle Jed died not long after that, and I think he died a happy man. You see, he made his dream come true even when nobody else believed in it. 7

He taught me to dream, too.

103

## Comprehension Skills

### Cause and Effect

Ask students to identify the cause-and-effect relationships in this story.

- *Uncle Jed saved money so he could some day open his own barbershop.*
- *Uncle Jed had to save money for many years because he was helping his family, and the Great Depression took his savings.*

### Checking Comprehension

Ask students the following questions to check their comprehension of the story.

- Why did Uncle Jed walk to his customers' homes? *(Because he didn't have his own barbershop.)*
- Why didn't anyone believe he would ever have his own shop? *(During segregation and the Great Depression, no one thought he could save all the money he would need.)*
- Why did all Uncle Jed's customers come to his shop the day it opened? *(He had always walked to see them, and they were happy for him.)*

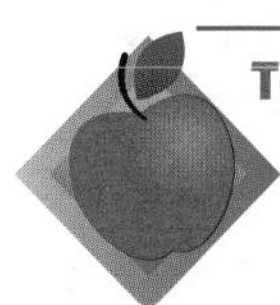

**Teacher Tip** By this time in third grade, good readers should be reading approximately 123 words per minute with fluency and expression. The only way to gain this fluency is through practice. Have students reread the selection to you and to each other during Workshop to help build fluency. As students read, you may notice that some need work in building fluency. During Workshop, have these students select a section of the text (a minimum of 160 words) to read several times in order to build fluency.

**Formal Assessment**

See pages 26–29 in ***Unit 4 Assessment*** to test students' comprehension of "Uncle Jed's Barbershop."

COMPREHENSION

### Differentiating Instruction

| If... | Then... |
|---|---|
| English Learners need extra help with vocabulary | Use ***English Learner Support Guide*** pages 347–349 |
| English Learners need extra help with cause and effect | Use ***English Learner Support Guide*** page 349 |
| English Learners need extra help reviewing "Uncle Jed's Barbershop" | Use ***English Learner Support Guide*** pages 350–351 |

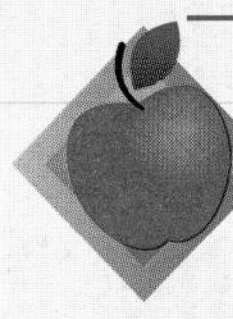

**Teacher Tip** **DISCUSSION** When you call on a student, allow him or her a few seconds to consider your question and to arrive at an answer.

**Routine Card**
Refer to ***Routine 6*** for the *handing-off process.*

| Clues | Problems | Wonderings |
| --- | --- | --- |
| title is "Uncle Jed's Barbershop" | lathered | How did he cut hair before owning the shop? |

***Reading Transparency 46***

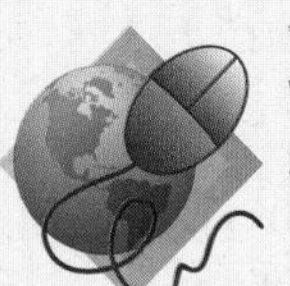

**www.sra4kids.com**
**Web Connection**
**Some students may choose to conduct a computer search for additional books or information about money. Invite them to make a list of these books and sources of information to share with classmates and the school librarian. Check the Reading link of the SRA Web page for additional links to the theme-related Web site.**

## Discussing the Selection

After the first read, the whole group discusses the selection and any personal thoughts, reactions, problems, or questions that it raises. The underlying theme should be discussed after students give their personal responses to the story. To stimulate discussion, students can ask one another the kinds of questions good readers ask themselves about a text: *What did I find interesting about this story? What is important here? What was difficult to understand? Why would someone want to read this?*

**Handing-Off Process** Seeing you as a contributing member of the group sets a strong example for students. To emphasize that you are part of the group, actively participate in the *handing-off process:* Raise your hand to be called on by the last speaker when you have a contribution to make. Point out unusual and interesting insights verbalized by students so that these insights are recognized and discussed. As the year progresses, students will take more and more responsibility for the discussions of the selections.

Engage students in a discussion to determine whether they have grasped the following ideas:

- what Uncle Jed's dream was
- what he did to make his dream a reality
- how he helped his family
- why he was a happy man in the end

During this time, have students return to the clues, problems, and wonderings they noted during browsing to determine whether the clues were borne out by the selection, whether and how their problems were solved, and whether their wonderings were answered or deserve further discussion and investigation. Let students decide which items deserve further discussion.

Also have students return to the Focus Questions on the first page of the selection. Select a student to read the questions aloud, and have volunteers answer the questions. If students do not know the answers to the questions, have them return to the text to find the answers. You may wish to review the elements of realistic fiction at this time. Ask students to explain how they know "Uncle Jed's Barbershop" is a piece of historical fiction.

Have students break into small groups to discuss what this story tells them about money. Groups can then share their ideas with the rest of the class.

If students have ever known someone that reminds them of Uncle Jed, or if they are planning their own dream, encourage them to write about these things.

## Review Selection Vocabulary

Have students review the definitions of the selection vocabulary words that they wrote in the vocabulary section of their Writer's Notebooks. Remind them that they discussed the meanings of these words before reading the selection. Have students write sentences for each of the vocabulary words after the definitions in the same section of their Writer's Notebooks. They can use the definitions and the sentences to study for the vocabulary portion of their Lesson Assessments. Have them add to the personal dictionary section of their Writer's Notebooks any other interesting words that they clarified while reading. Encourage students to refer to the selection vocabulary words throughout the unit. The words from the selection are:

**equipment exchange delayed sharecroppers examine failing**

If you created a Word Bank of key words related to the theme Money, remind students to find words from other resources, from their activities, and from family discussions and add them to the Word Bank. Students may also place synonyms and antonyms in the Word Bank.

## Home Connection

Distribute ***Home Connection,*** page 57. Encourage students to discuss "Uncle Jed's Barbershop" with their families. Students will have the opportunity to discuss with their families any relatives who made a dream happen. ***Home Connection*** is also available in Spanish, page 58.

*Uncle Jed's Barbershop*

**A message from** ______________________

Your child's class has just finished reading the story "Uncle Jed's Barbershop." This story is about a man who, in spite of the Great Depression and many other setbacks, turned his lifelong dream into a reality. Ask your child to tell you more about the story.

With your child, discuss members of your family who worked to make a dream come true. Who were they? Where did they live? What was their dream? What was the world like at the time they were working toward their dream? Did they work to make the dream come true? What did they do? Did they face difficulties? If so, what were they? Did the dream become a reality? Did the dream change? Allow your child's questions to direct the discussion. If necessary, use the questions here for guidance. Your child can record answers to his or her questions on this page. If necessary, use another piece of paper to record information.

***Home Connection p. 57***

### Differentiating Instruction

| If... | Then... |
| --- | --- |
| Students are having difficulty with vocabulary | • Invite volunteers to give definitions of their own<br>• Invite volunteers to use the words in sentences |

**Teacher Tip WRITING** Encourage students to exchange papers with a peer to practice proofreading skills. Have students look for initial capital letters at the beginning of each sentence and end punctuation at the end of each sentence.

**Teacher Tip CLASSROOM LIBRARY** Invite the students to read from the ***Leveled Classroom Library***. As they read, have them take notes on their reading speed. Ask them if they noticed if certain selections caused them to slow their reading down or if they were able to quickly read others.

# Supporting the Reading

## Comprehension Strategies: Monitoring and Adjusting Reading Speed

**Teach** Explain to students that monitoring their own comprehension means paying attention to how well they are understanding what they read. When they notice that a part of the text is challenging or has a lot of information, students can improve comprehension by reading more slowly and paying attention to details.

**Guided Practice** Copy a page or two from a nonfiction book, a newspaper, or a magazine article onto a transparency. Introduce the selection and display the transparency for several minutes, giving students a chance to read silently. Ask students to focus on monitoring and adjusting reading speed when reading. Then ask volunteers to indicate places where they slowed down to read more carefully. Place a star by those sections. Discuss with students how they were able to identify places where it was necessary to slow down and read more carefully.

**Independent Practice** Have students focus on the strategy Monitoring and Adjusting Reading Speed as they read selections in the ***Student Anthology,*** classroom library, and bibliography.

**Link to Writing** Ask students to write two short pieces that they believe should be read at different speeds for comprehension purposes. This can be completed as homework. Examples include a narrative and a poem, an informational text and a fairy tale, and a rhyming poem and a biography. Students should exchange their pieces to have other students read them aloud. The writer should note if the reader read one of the pieces slower than the other and if their original intent to slow the reader down was applied.

## Literary Elements

### Characterization

**Teach** Ask students what they remember about how a writer reveals a character to his readers. Review with students that *characterization* is the way a writer shows what the characters in his or her story are like. Writers do this by telling what the characters do, say, think, and feel.

**Guided Practice** Call on a volunteer to identify the main character in "Uncle Jed's Barbershop" *(Uncle Jed)*. Remind students that in most stories, the main characters go through some kind of change because of experiences they have.

Invite volunteers to give characteristics of Uncle Jed. Then ask students to tell what actions of Uncle Jed revealed his character. Record students' responses on the board.

**Independent Practice** Ask students to look in their ***Writing Folders*** for a story they have written. Can the reader tell what the characters are really like? If not, what words or actions might reveal what they are like? Have students think about revisions they can make to their stories.

**Teacher Tip** CHARACTERIZATION Teaching characterization is key to introducing students to literary elements that extend beyond mere comprehension.

**Differentiating Instruction**

| If... | Then... |
|---|---|
| Students need extra help with characterization | Have them reread the story with you, stopping at the end of each page, and point out things Uncle Jed says, thinks, feels, or does that reveal his character |

**Teacher Tip** Have the class generate a set of criteria or a rubric to evaluate the effectiveness of a piece of writing. Have them use this rubric to evaluate their own writing.

**Teacher Tip** MATERIALS
- ✔ chalk
- ✔ board

**Teacher Tip** PURPOSE To teach students the value of savings and the positive effects of interest when one deposits money instead of taking loans. To show students the importance of saving money.

**Teacher Tip** If this lesson is too complicated for your students, modify it to meet your students' math needs.

## Math Connection

### The Interest Game II

Just as in Lesson 5 of this unit, the students will learn about interest but, this time, it will involve savings. Explain that just as banks can charge interest on a loan, they will give you interest when you put your savings in the bank. Ask students if they know how this works and why banks would want to do this. Explain that when you deposit money in the bank, you essentially give the bank a loan.

As in the Interest Game I, perform some basic interest problems together on the board, this time concentrating on the amount of money a person can earn. It would be beneficial to complete problems that are comparative, for example:

*If Uncle Jed invests $1,500 dollars in a bank that pays $20 a month in interest, and Mr. Walters invests $1,700 in a bank that pays $10 a month in interest, who will reach $2,000 first? (Uncle Jed, in 25 months)*

Again, break the classroom into two teams and have one representative from each team come to the board to complete math problems involving interest and savings. Each team gets a point for the right answer. Make sure all students get an opportunity to participate.

When the game is finished, discuss with the students what they have learned through these two games involving interest. Ask them if they have any final comments or questions on the subject of interest.

## Social Studies Connection

### Hard Times

In "Uncle Jed's Barbershop," students read about a man who made his dream happen in spite of the Great Depression. The Great Depression did, however, cause him to delay the dream. For years, he accepted food in exchange for work because his customers had no money.

Ask students to investigate the effects of the Great Depression. Have them identify at least one example of a decision that was made due to the lack of money during that time. For example, they might interview a person who lived during that time and be able to provide an example of a family decision that was made due to economic conditions. Or they might investigate a national decision that was made at that time, such as when the United States began massive national works projects to help put people back to work. Ask students to create a brief presentation of their findings.

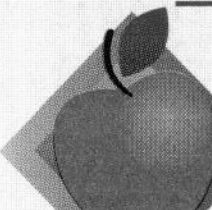

**Teacher Tip MATERIALS**

- ✔ poster boards
- ✔ colored pencils or markers
- ✔ interview recorded on video or audiocassette

**Teacher Tip PURPOSE** To learn about a time in history when scarcity impacted personal or national decisions.

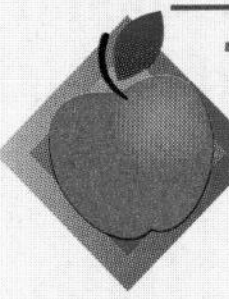

**Teacher Tip** You may want to invite a guest speaker who is an expert on the Great Depression to your class.

## Concept Connections

### Linking the Selection

- Most people were not able to save money because they were poor.
- Sarah Jean was more important than money to Uncle Jed.

### Exploring Concept Vocabulary

The concept word for this lesson is ***savings.*** Write the word on the board. Work with students to develop a definition that clearly links to the unit theme. Have students copy the word and definition into the Vocabulary section of their Writer's Notebooks.

***Savings:*** money saved, or set aside, for use in the future. For example, Alexander had no savings in "Alexander, Who Used to Be Rich Last Sunday."

- It was important for Uncle Jed to have a savings because he would need a large amount of money to open his own barbershop.
- Uncle Jed's savings dwindled when he paid for Sarah Jean's operation. His savings disappeared when the bank failed.

Remind students that the sentences they create should include the concept word as well as a selection vocabulary word.

### Expanding the Concept

You may want to do a whole-group discussion to help students further develop their ability to engage in meaningful dialogue. However, students may conduct these dialogues in small groups. If the students work in small groups, bring the groups together and have them share their ideas with the whole class.

As students complete their discussions, have them record their ideas and impressions about the selection on page 86 of their ***Inquiry Journals.***

# UNCLE JED'S BARBERSHOP

## Concept Connections

### Linking the Selection

Think about the following questions, and then record your responses in the Response Journal section of your Writer's Notebook.

- Why did no one believe that Uncle Jed could save enough money to open a barbershop?
- Why did money not matter to Uncle Jed when Sarah Jean needed an operation?

### Exploring Concept Vocabulary

The concept word for this lesson is ***savings.*** If you do not know what this word means, look it up in a dictionary. Answer these questions:

- Why was it important for Uncle Jed to have ***savings?***
- How did Uncle Jed's ***savings*** dwindle and then later disappear?

Think about the word ***savings*** and the selection vocabulary words. Then make up an oral sentence using ***savings*** and one of the selection vocabulary words.

### Expanding the Concept

Think about the selections you have read in this unit. How was Uncle Jed similar to other characters in the selections you read? How was he different? What conclusions can you draw about money?

Try to use the word ***savings*** in your discussion.

Add new ideas about money to the Concept/Question Board.

104

**Informal Assessment**

This may be a good time to observe students working in small groups and to mark your observations in the Teacher Observation Log found in the ***Program Assessment Teacher's Edition.***

## Meet the Author

**Margaree King Mitchell** writes not only children's stories, but television scripts and plays as well. When volunteering at her son's school, she found the inspiration to become a children's book writer. *"I thought if I could somehow write a book that would inspire children to achieve their dreams, then maybe children would be motivated to stay in school and look to the future for a better life for themselves,"* she says. After reading "Uncle Jed's Barbershop" to a group of eight year olds, a girl approached Mitchell to say that she learned she could accomplish everything, even her dream of being a doctor. Mitchell feels that this is the measure of success in writing.

## Meet the Illustrator

**James Ransome** was born in North Carolina. He became interested in art when he was just a child and loved to look at the illustrations in superhero comic books. He was also influenced by television cartoons and *Mad* magazine. Now that he is an illustrator, the characters he draws are all very different and special. James Ransome's characters show the cultural and racial differences that make us who we are. Sometimes James Ransome's illustrations appear on book jackets for young adult books.

105

## Meet the Author

After students read the information about Margaree King Mitchell, discuss the following questions with them.

- Why does Mitchell feel she has succeeded in being a writer? *(Possible answer: A reader found the inspiration to follow her dreams in one of Mitchell's books.)*
- What might have happened at her son's school to cause Mitchell to write books that inspire children? *(Possible answer: Maybe she read the books at the school and didn't think they were inspirational.)*
- Why do you think that inspiring children in Mitchell's books is her measure of success? *(Possible answer: Mitchell wants to provide children with quality literature that involves them instead of just entertaining them.)*

## Meet the Illustrator

After students read the information about James E. Ransome, discuss the following questions with them.

- How did James Ransome become interested in art? *(Possible answer: By seeing pictures in comic books when he was a child.)*
- Other than inside picture books, where else might you see James Ransome's illustrations? *(Possible answer: On book jackets for young adults.)*
- What is it that makes James Ransome's characters so special? *(Possible answer: He draws his characters to show their differences.)*

### Objectives

- Students come to a deeper understanding of money.
- Students will gain a deeper understanding of issues related to money.
- Student groups make final preparations and begin formal presentations.

### Materials

- Student Anthology, Book 2, pp. 94–105
- Inquiry Journal, p. 104
- Research Assistant CD-ROM

**Teacher Tip** If students choose to conduct interviews, remind them of the interview skills they have learned. Students should schedule an interview with the person and prepare questions ahead of time. Recording the interview frees students up to listen instead of writing notes, but they must always obtain permission from the person they are interviewing before recording. Ask students to send a thank-you note to people who give them an interview.

INVESTIGATION

## Investigating Concepts Beyond the Text

At this point, students should be concluding their investigations. Groups should begin putting presentations together, although some revision might be necessary before the final presentation. As the unit comes to an end, you might consider providing additional class time for the students to finish their investigations, complete the visual or written portion of their investigations, and present their findings. Arrange ample time for formal presentations, spreading them out over several days. After the presentations, have the students record new information in their ***Inquiry Journals*** and on the Concept/Question Board. Remind students that investigation often generates as many questions as it answers; learning is an ongoing process. Encourage students always to consider new information in light of what they already know and to think about how it changes or adds to their existing ideas. Some groups may wish to continue investigating a problem or question after the unit.

Have the groups meet to discuss questions or ideas they might have about the story they have just read. Does the story tell them something about money they didn't know before? Does the story make them wonder about something? After reading "Uncle Jed's Barbershop," students might wish to discuss the issue of saving money and keeping sight of goals even during hard times. They might wish to further investigate the Great Depression through investigation or interviews.

Remind students that they can use these discussion questions and ideas to revise their problems, questions, and conjectures at any time. Revising a presentation at the last minute shows that investigations are truly recursive, open to change at any time, and that the investigation is ongoing.

INVESTIGATION

## Concept/Question Board

Tell students this is a good time to post on the Concept/Question Board any new questions they have about money that "Uncle Jed's Barbershop" might have raised. Remind them of your earlier discussion about the Concept/ Question Board and ask them to tell what they remember about that discussion.

After reading each selection, students should use the Concept/Question Board to:

- Post any questions they asked about a selection before reading that have not yet been answered.
- Refer to as they formulate statements about concepts that apply to their investigations.
- Post general statements formulated by each collaborative group.
- Continue to post news articles or other items that they find during the unit investigation.
- Read and think about posted questions, articles, or concepts that interest them and provide answers to the questions.
- Students might wish to bring in articles or questions about how money is regulated or how it passes from person to person in our society.

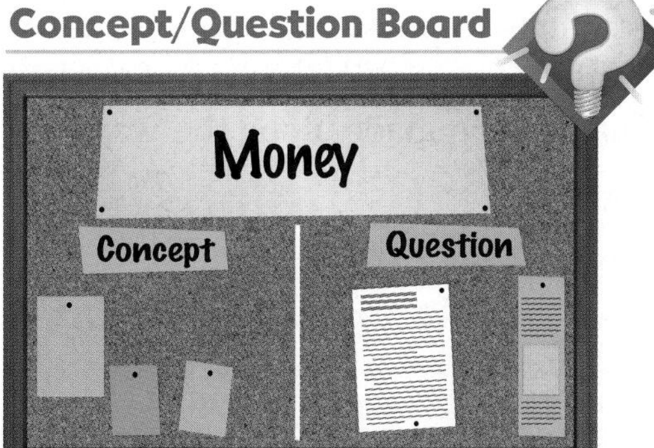


## Unit 4 Investigation Management

| | |
|---|---|
| Lesson 1 | Brainstorm questions related to the theme. Investigate alternatives to money, such as barter. |
| Lesson 2 | Groups form based on areas of shared interest. Investigate choices related to spending and saving money. |
| Lesson 3 | Begin forming conjectures. Brainstorm about how to turn hobbies into businesses. |
| Lesson 4 | Discuss conjectures in groups and begin plans. Look for stories or illustrations about the ways that money can change people and things that money cannot buy. |
| Lesson 5 | Students revise their plans as necessary and continue investigations. Groups can debate on borrowing and lending money. |
| Lesson 6 | Continue investigations and prepare final presentations. Create a story or miniplay about how money passes from person to person, or plan a field trip to a Federal Reserve Bank. |
| Lesson 7 | Collaborative Investigation<br>**Groups give formal presentations.**<br>Supplementary Activity<br>**Students discuss saving money for personal goals or investigate the Great Depression further.** |

**Teacher Tip** Continue to encourage use of the Concept/Question Board by recognizing and thanking students for their contributions. Incorporate discussion of those items into classroom discussions whenever appropriate.

**Teacher Tip** Have the students choose a book to read from the library relating to the theme. This book should identify their preference in either literary or nonfiction texts. Encourage students to read often from their preferred genre. Make sure students utilize the appropriate areas of the library to select reading materials. If necessary, review these areas with students before they visit the library.

### Research Assistant

**The *Research Assistant CD-ROM* can assist students with their investigations.**

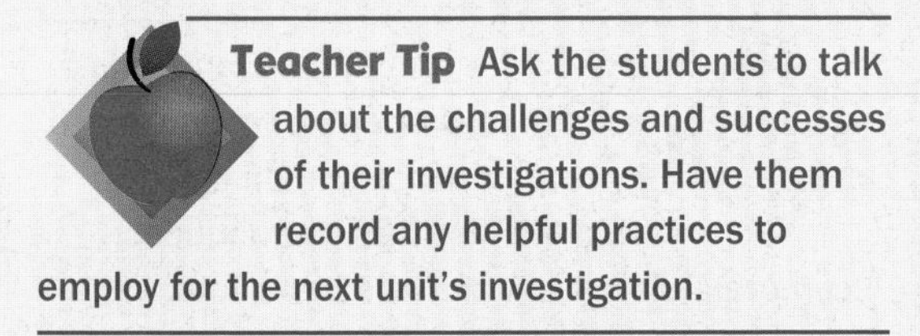

**Teacher Tip** Ask the students to talk about the challenges and successes of their investigations. Have them record any helpful practices to employ for the next unit's investigation.

**Informal Assessment**

Observe and assess students during their oral presentations. Record your observations in the Teacher Observation Log found in the ***Program Assessment Teacher's Edition.***

**Formal Assessment**

Use the Research Rubrics on page 94J as an overall assessment of the students' research.

INVESTIGATION

## Presentations

Now that students have been investigating money and related issues for several weeks, students may have new insights they would like to discuss with others or record for themselves. Looking over the entries they have made in their ***Inquiry Journals*** will show them how far they have come in their investigations.

As students are concluding their investigations and giving formal presentations, remind them to look at questions and ideas they had at the beginning of the unit. Have those ideas changed? If so, in what ways have they changed? What do they know now that they did not know before? What did they learn from working on the group investigations?

Have students propose new questions and form new conjectures based on their readings, activities, and investigations of this unit's theme. Encourage students to pursue these questions on their own if they desire. Remind them of the never-ending nature of research and investigation and of the discoveries that will be made along the way.

## Time Lines

**Teach** Review time lines with the class. Remind students that time lines are a way of organizing information according to when things take place. When we make a time line, we list information in the order in which events happened. Time lines can be organized by year, month, week, day, or hour.

**Guided Practice** Explain to students that they will be making a time line that shows what happened on a Saturday. Draw a horizontal line on the board. Divide the line into 30-minute increments from 9:00 A.M. to 4:00 P.M. and label the times.

List the following Saturday activities on the board:

| | | |
|---|---|---|
| **put basket in the car** | **drive home** | **set up picnic** |
| **clean up picnic area** | **eat lunch** | **play ball** |
| **wake up** | **go swimming** | **unpack car** |
| **put basket back in car** | **drive to park** | **make lunch** |
| **pack lunch in basket** | **eat breakfast** | **get dressed** |

Ask students to help you put the activities in the correct order on the time line. Begin at 9:00 A.M., and discuss which of the activities occurred at that time. When the class has agreed upon an activity, write it on the time line under the corresponding time. Complete the time line.

If resources are available, suggest students also make a time line using computer technology.

For additional practice with time lines, have students complete ***Inquiry Journal,*** page 104.

**Independent Practice** Ask students to think about the investigation topic they just completed. Would a time line have been an effective visual for any portion of the presentation? If so, have them complete a time line that corresponds to their investigations or to the selection, "Uncle Jed's Barbershop." Remind them to think about incorporating time lines in their future investigations and presentations.

SUPPORTING THE INVESTIGATION

### Differentiating Instruction

| If... | Then... |
|---|---|
| Students have shown an understanding of time lines and would enjoy a challenge | Have them make an additional time line for an imaginary "first day of summer vacation" |

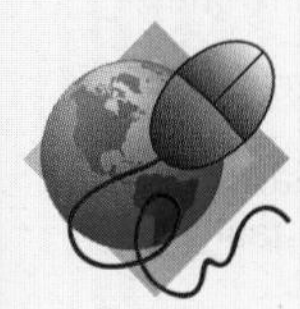

**www.sra4kids.com**
**Web Connection**
Students may wish to use the Money connections found on the Reading Web site.

Encourage students to use ***TechKnowledge*** to learn more about how to use a computer to complete various investigation tasks.

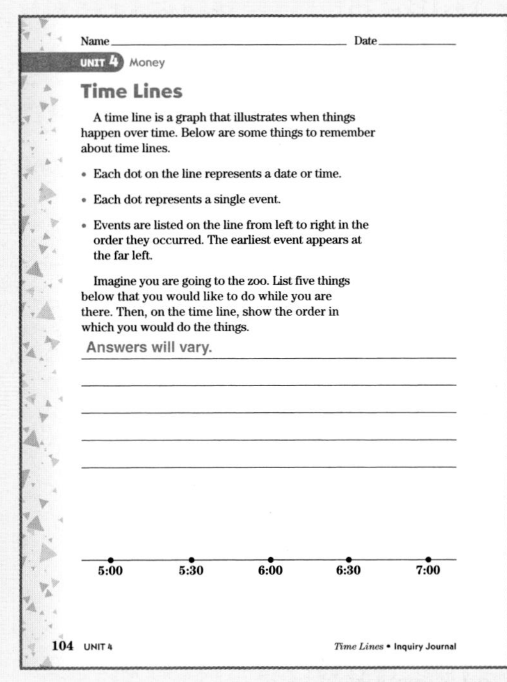
Name ____________ Date ________

UNIT 4 Money

Time Lines

A time line is a graph that illustrates when things happen over time. Below are some things to remember about time lines.

- Each dot on the line represents a date or time.
- Each dot represents a single event.
- Events are listed on the line from left to right in the order they occurred. The earliest event appears at the far left.

Imagine you are going to the zoo. List five things below that you would like to do while you are there. Then, on the time line, show the order in which you would do the things.

Answers will vary.

5:00 5:30 6:00 6:30 7:00

104 UNIT 4 Time Lines • Inquiry Journal

***Inquiry Journal p. 104***

### Objectives

**Word Analysis**

**Spelling**

- **Spelling Review.** Review double consonants, words with final double consonants, contractions, how to add *-ed*, *-ing*, *-s*, or *-es*, and how to form compound words.

**Vocabulary**

- **Vocabulary Review.** Using words from "Uncle Jed's Barbershop," review base word families, the suffix *-ly*, business vocabulary, the endings *-ed* and *-ing*, compound words, and money-related words.

**Writing Process Strategies**

- **Persuasive Writing—Paragraph.** Learn the form and function of writing a persuasive paragraph.

**English Language Conventions**

**Grammar, Usage, and Mechanics**

- **Review.** Display knowledge and understanding of Lessons 1–6 skills. Find examples of as many of these items/concepts as possible in "Uncle Jed's Barbershop."

**Listening, Speaking, Viewing**

- **Interacting: Engaging an Audience.** Practice using gestures and making eye contact when communicating with others.

**Penmanship**

- **Cursive Letters *X* and *W*.** Develop handwriting skills by practicing cursive *X* and *W*.

### Materials

- Spelling and Vocabulary Skills, pp. 98–101
- Language Arts Handbook
- Comprehension and Language Arts Skills, pp. 122–125
- Writer's Workbook, pp. 78–81
- Language Arts Transparency 28
- Student Anthology
- Spelling Software
- Routine Card 2, Routine 7

### Differentiating Instruction

***Reteach, Challenge,*** and ***Intervention*** lessons are available to support the language arts instruction in this lesson.

### Research in Action

It is important to recognize that style and voice are not exactly the same thing. Style . . . is a feature of genre. . . . Voice, on the other hand, transcends style.
(*James D. Williams*, Preparing to Teach Writing: Research, Theory, and Practice)

OVERVIEW

# Language Arts Overview

## Word Analysis

**Spelling** The Spelling activities review words with double consonants and final double consonants. The activities also review how contractions and compound words, are formed. Spelling patterns for how to add *-ed* and *-ing* to words are also reviewed. The activities also include a review of how to make words plural by adding *-s* or *-es*.

### Selection Spelling Words

These words from "Uncle Jed's Barbershop" review spelling patterns from Unit 4.

**used** **cutting** **clippers** **saving** **died**

**Vocabulary** The Vocabulary activities review student understanding of base word families, the suffix *-ly*, business vocabulary, the endings *-ed* and *-ing*, compound words, and money-related words as taught in Unit 4.

### Vocabulary Skill Words

**unconscious** **equipment*** **failing*** **sharecroppers*** **exchange***
**Also Selection Vocabulary*

**Additional Materials:** dictionary

## Writing Process Strategies

The Writing Process Strategies lesson involves instruction in writing a persuasive paragraph. Emphasis is given to including a topic sentence, supporting sentences that give reasons or feelings, and a closing sentence.

To reinforce spreadsheet applications in the writing process, and to show understanding of the material presented in the Spreadsheet unit, help students create a spreadsheet and a line graph. ***TechKnowledge,*** Level 3, Lessons 67–72, teach these spreadsheet application skills.

## English Language Conventions

**Grammar, Usage, and Mechanics** **Review.** This lesson reviews the skills learned in Lessons 1–6.

**Listening, Speaking, Viewing** **Interacting: Engaging an Audience.** In this Interacting lesson, students will use gestures and make eye contact to develop their communication skills.

**Penmanship** **Cursive letters *X* and *W*.** This lesson develops handwriting skills by having students learn formation of *X* and *W*. Students then write words from the literature selection.

# DAY 1

## Word Analysis

### Spelling

**Assessment: Pretest**
**Unit 4 Review**

**Teach**

Give students the Pretest on page 42 of ***Unit 4 Assessment.*** Have them proofread and correct any misspelled words.

**Pretest Sentences**

1. **offer** Volunteers **offer** to work.
2. **winner** The **winner** of a sprint runs the fastest.
3. **zipper** A plastic **zipper** is not as strong as a metal one.
4. **will** Elections **will** be held every four years.
5. **well** A fever is a sign that the body is not **well**.
6. **he'd** If a boy was the son of the king, **he'd** be the next king.
7. **isn't** Chocolate mousse **isn't** a type of animal.
8. **taking** Stealing is **taking** what is not yours.
9. **monkeys** Gorillas and **monkeys** are in the same species.
10. **stitches** A surgeon sews **stitches**.
11. **used** Some plants can be **used** to flavor foods.
12. **cutting** Shears are for **cutting**.
13. **clippers** Scissors for cutting nails are called **clippers**.
14. **saving** Firefighters continue **saving** lives every year.
15. **died** The old tree **died**.

Diagnose any misspellings by determining whether students misspelled the spelling pattern or some other part of the word. Then use the Pretest as a take-home list to study the spelling patterns learned in Unit 4.

## Writing Process Strategies

### Getting Ideas

**Persuasive Paragraph**

**Teach**

**Persuasive Paragraphs**

- Read ***Language Arts Handbook,*** page 187, to introduce or review persuasive paragraphs.
- Share the formal assessment rubrics with students (see Day 5 of this lesson).

**Inspiration**

Teacher Model: *"When I was a child, I wanted to save for roller skates. I am going to write a persuasive paragraph to convince my parents to raise my allowance so I can save."*

**Brainstorming**

Using the idea of working and saving toward a goal, encourage students to generate ideas for how they could work to make money to save for something important to them. Make a list of their ideas on the board.

**Guided Practice**

**Getting Ideas**

Have students write ideas for a persuasive paragraph in their Writer's Notebooks.

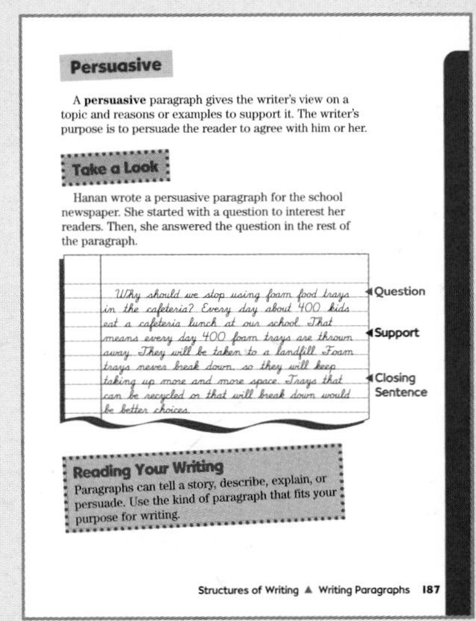

**Persuasive**

A **persuasive** paragraph gives the writer's view on a topic and reasons or examples to support it. The writer's purpose is to persuade the reader to agree with him or her.

**Take a Look**

Hanan wrote a persuasive paragraph for the school newspaper. She started with a question to interest her readers. Then, she answered the question in the rest of the paragraph.

*Why should we stop using foam food trays in the cafeteria? Every day about 400 kids eat a cafeteria lunch at our school. That means every day 400 foam trays are thrown away. They will be taken to a landfill. Foam trays never break down, so they will keep taking up more and more space. Trays that can be recycled or that will break down would be better choices.*

Question
Support
Closing Sentence

**Reading Your Writing**
Paragraphs can tell a story, describe, explain, or persuade. Use the kind of paragraph that fits your purpose for writing.

Structures of Writing ▲ Writing Paragraphs 187

***Language Arts Handbook p. 187***

## English Language Conventions

### Grammar, Usage, and Mechanics

**Skills Review**

**Teach**

- Review the skills from Lessons 1–6.
  - Lesson 1, Prepositions: Make sure students know what a preposition is.
  - Lesson 2, Subjects and Predicates: Make sure students understand that every sentence needs a subject and a predicate.
  - Lesson 3, Periods with Abbreviations, Titles, and Initials; Use of Parentheses: Make sure students are using correctly.
  - Lesson 4, Pronouns: Singular and Plural Possessive: Make sure students can identify the different types.
  - Lesson 5, Subject/Verb Agreement: Make sure students know that if the subject is singular the verb must be singular, and if the subject is plural the verb must be plural.
  - Lesson 6, Comparative and Superlative Adverbs: Make sure students know to create them properly.

**Independent Practice**

Have students complete ***Comprehension and Language Arts Skills,*** pages 122–123, which review all the skills in the unit.

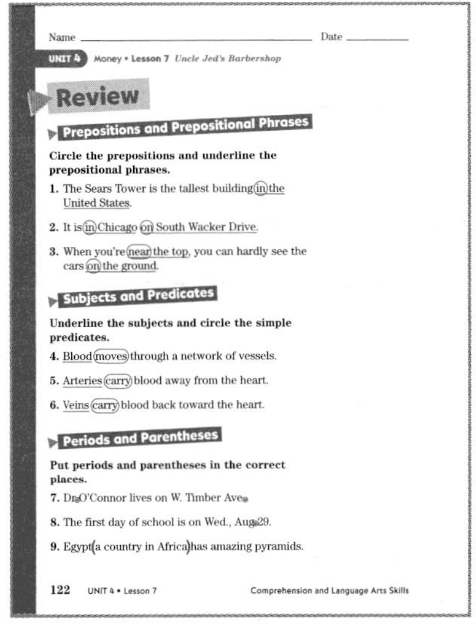

Name ______________________ Date __________

UNIT 4 Money • Lesson 7 *Uncle Jed's Barbershop*

**Review**

**Prepositions and Prepositional Phrases**

**Circle the prepositions and underline the prepositional phrases.**

1. The Sears Tower is the tallest building in the United States.
2. It is in Chicago on South Wacker Drive.
3. When you're near the top, you can hardly see the cars on the ground.

**Subjects and Predicates**

**Underline the subjects and circle the simple predicates.**

4. Blood moves through a network of vessels.
5. Arteries carry blood away from the heart.
6. Veins carry blood back toward the heart.

**Periods and Parentheses**

**Put periods and parentheses in the correct places.**

7. Dr. O'Connor lives on W. Timber Ave.
8. The first day of school is on Wed., Aug. 29.
9. Egypt (a country in Africa) has amazing pyramids.

122 UNIT 4 • Lesson 7 Comprehension and Language Arts Skills

***Comprehension and Language Arts Skills p. 122***

# DAY 2

## Word Analysis

### Spelling

**Spelling Review: Double Consonants**

Ask the class to say *diner* and *dinner* and listen for the short-vowel sound in *dinner*. Write the words on the board. Ask a student to circle *nn* in *dinner*. Remind the class that double consonants come after short-vowel sounds and can be in the middle or at the end of a word.

### Vocabulary

**Vocabulary Review: Money Words**

#### Teach

- Write *exchange* ("Uncle Jed's Barbershop," page 96) on the board. Ask what *exchange* means *(trade, barter, swap)*.
- Review that the word *exchange* is related to payment or money. Ask a student to read the sentence with *exchange*.
- Discuss what sharecroppers exchanged, and what can be exchanged today. *(work for profit from the land; money, lunches, cars)*

#### Guided Practice

Use ***Spelling and Vocabulary Skills,*** page 98, to review the meanings of the endings *-ed* and *-ing*. Ask students to complete page 99 as independent practice.

Name ______ Date ______

UNIT 4 Money • Lesson 7 *Uncle Jed's Barbershop*

Unit 4 Review

Remember, when the endings *-ed* and *-ing* are added to a base word, the meaning of the base word changes.
The *-ed* ending shows an action in the past.
The *-ing* ending shows an action in the present.

play + -ed = played The children played yesterday.
play + -ing = playing The children are playing now.

Remember how adding the endings *-ed* and *-ing* to some base words changes the spelling of the words.

Try It! The word *failing* on page 100 of "Uncle Jed's Barbershop" has the *-ing* ending.

1. Circle *fail*, meaning "to not succeed, lose," in the word below: failing
2. Knowing how the ending *-ing* changes the meaning of a word, what does the word *failing* mean? not succeeding, losing
3. Did the spelling of *fail* change when *-ing* was added? no
4. How would you spell the word formed by *fail* + *ed*? failed
5. Write sentences for the two words that show their meanings.
   failing: answers will vary
   failed: ______

98 UNIT 4 • Lesson 7 *Unit 4 Review* • Spelling and Vocabulary Skills

*Spelling and Vocabulary Skills p. 98*

## Writing Process Strategies

### Prewriting

**Persuasive Paragraph**

#### Teach

- Read ***Writer's Workbook,*** page 78, on prewriting for a persuasive paragraph.
- Review ideas students generated for persuasive paragraphs on Day 1.
- Model generating supporting reasons or feelings. *"I will have to persuade my parents that it will be worth it to them, as well as to me, to raise my allowance. Maybe I can tell them that I will do extra chores, watch my little sister, and feed the dog without being asked. I could also tell them that when I get my roller skates, it will be good exercise."* You may wish to put your ideas in a web to model this for your students.

#### Independent Practice

**Prewriting**

- Have students write their audience and purpose on ***Writer's Workbook,*** page 78.
- Have students fill in the graphic organizer on ***Writer's Workbook,*** page 79.

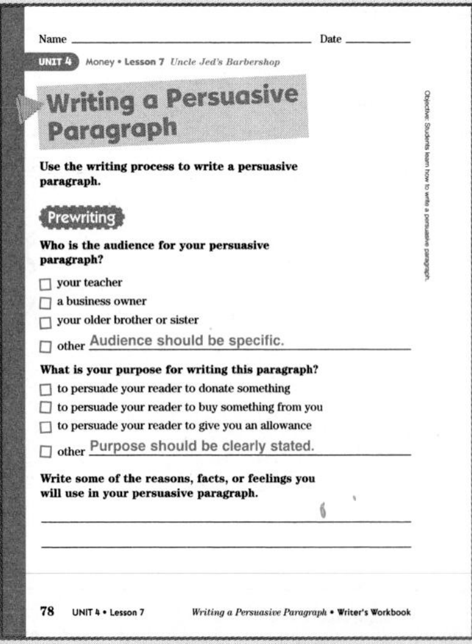

Name ______ Date ______

UNIT 4 Money • Lesson 7 *Uncle Jed's Barbershop*

Writing a Persuasive Paragraph

Use the writing process to write a persuasive paragraph.

Prewriting

Who is the audience for your persuasive paragraph?

- your teacher
- a business owner
- your older brother or sister
- other Audience should be specific.

What is your purpose for writing this paragraph?

- to persuade your reader to donate something
- to persuade your reader to buy something from you
- to persuade your reader to give you an allowance
- other Purpose should be clearly stated.

Write some of the reasons, facts, or feelings you will use in your persuasive paragraph.

78 UNIT 4 • Lesson 7 *Writing a Persuasive Paragraph* • Writer's Workbook

*Writer's Workbook p. 78*

## English Language Conventions

### Grammar, Usage, and Mechanics

**Skills Review**

#### Teach

- Review prepositions and prepositional phrases by writing *about, across, between,* and *beside* on the board and asking students to come up with sentences using these prepositions.
- Review subjects and predicates by writing these sentences on the board and asking students to identify the subject and predicate.
  - Donna likes Chicago. *(subject,* Donna; *predicate,* likes)
  - Gordon and Daniel have new bikes. *(compound subject,* Gordon and Daniel; *predicate,* have)
- Review periods and parentheses using ***Language Arts Handbook,*** pages 270 and 274.
- Review pronouns by writing these sentences on the board and calling on students to change the noun to a pronoun.
  - Why does Lucy like cheese? *(she)*
  - Harriet and William are both late. *(they)*
  - Raymond's sister runs fast. *(his)*
- Review subject/verb agreement by reading ***Language Arts Handbook,*** pages 176 and 264–265.
- Review adverbs by writing these sentences on the board and asking students to identify the adverbs as comparative or superlative.
  - Melissa likes to read the most. *(superlative)*
  - She reads more than Brett does. *(comparative)*

#### Guided Practice in Reading

Have students look for the skills from Lessons 1–6 in "Uncle Jed's Barbershop." *(It may not be possible for them to find all of the skills in this literature selection.)*

# DAY 3

## Word Analysis

### Spelling

**Spelling Review**

**Teach**

- Remind students that the letter *-s* is added to most words to make them plural and *-es* is added to words that end in *ch*, *sh*, *s*, *ss*, *x*, *z*, or *zz*.
- Have students complete the Spelling Bee activity for Unit 4 on the ***Spelling Software.***

**Guided Practice**

Have students complete page 100 from the ***Spelling and Vocabulary Skills*** to review the spelling strategies.

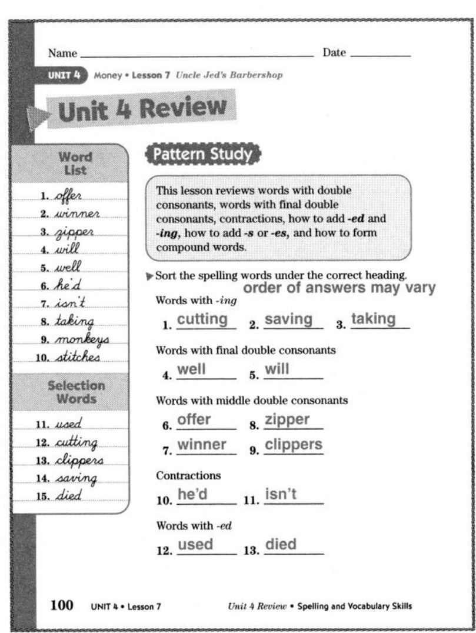

Name ______________________ Date ________

UNIT 4 Money • Lesson 7 *Uncle Jed's Barbershop*

**Unit 4 Review**

**Word List**

1. offer
2. winner
3. zipper
4. will
5. well
6. he'd
7. isn't
8. taking
9. monkeys
10. stitches

**Selection Words**

11. used
12. cutting
13. clippers
14. saving
15. died

**Pattern Study**

This lesson reviews words with double consonants, words with final double consonants, contractions, how to add ***-ed*** and ***-ing***, how to add ***-s*** or ***-es***, and how to form compound words.

▶ Sort the spelling words under the correct heading.
order of answers may vary

Words with *-ing*
1. cutting 2. saving 3. taking

Words with final double consonants
4. well 5. will

Words with middle double consonants
6. offer 8. zipper
7. winner 9. clippers

Contractions
10. he'd 11. isn't

Words with *-ed*
12. used 13. died

100 UNIT 4 • Lesson 7 *Unit 4 Review* • Spelling and Vocabulary Skills

***Spelling and Vocabulary Skills* p. 100**

### Vocabulary (continued)

**Vocabulary Review: Business Vocabulary**

- Write *equipment* on the board.
- Ask a student to read the sentences in "Uncle Jed's Barbershop" (p. 95) near *equipment*. Discuss examples of *equipment* for a barber *(sinks, pole, scissors).*
- Ask a student to find the definition of *equip (to provide what is needed).* Discuss how *equipment* and *equip* relate to one another *(equipment is the tool that equips).*

## Writing Process Strategies

**Drafting**

**Persuasive Paragraph**

**Teach**

Read ***Writer's Workbook,*** page 79, on drafting a persuasive paragraph.

**Writer's Craft**

**Effective Beginnings and Endings**

- Discuss how the beginning must grab the reader's attention, and that if beginnings are always the same, the writing may become boring.
- Explain that telling about an interesting fact, a problem, or something that happened to someone, and asking questions, are all ways to write good beginnings.
- Explain that the ending is just as important as the beginning, since it summarizes the main point.
- Read ***Language Arts Handbook,*** pages 202–205, on effective beginnings and endings.
- Read ***Comprehension and Language Arts Skills,*** pages 124–125 on effective beginnings and endings.

**Guided Practice**

**Drafting**

Have students draft their persuasive paragraphs.

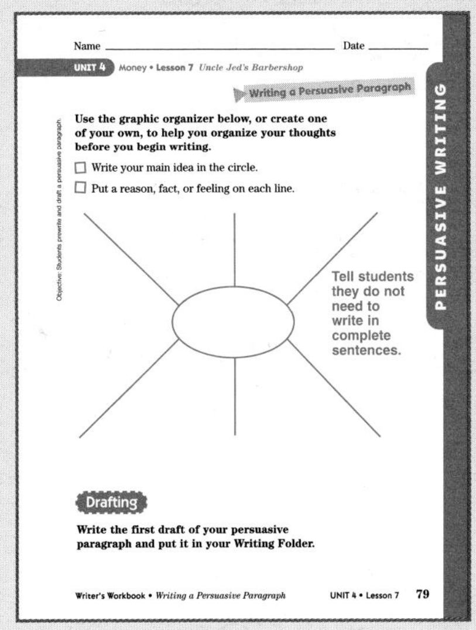

Name ______________________ Date ________

UNIT 4 Money • Lesson 7 *Uncle Jed's Barbershop*

Writing a Persuasive Paragraph

PERSUASIVE WRITING

Objective: Students prewrite and draft a persuasive paragraph.

**Use the graphic organizer below, or create one of your own, to help you organize your thoughts before you begin writing.**

☐ Write your main idea in the circle.

☐ Put a reason, fact, or feeling on each line.

Tell students they do not need to write in complete sentences.

**Drafting**

**Write the first draft of your persuasive paragraph and put it in your Writing Folder.**

Writer's Workbook • *Writing a Persuasive Paragraph* UNIT 4 • Lesson 7 79

***Writer's Workbook* p. 79**

## English Language Conventions

**Grammar, Usage, and Mechanics**

**Skills Review**

**Teach**

Write these sentences on the board and point out the rules you are illustrating.

- *Jennifer sits across from T.J. and Steve. She likes to sing to them. She sings better than they do.* (Preposition, *across;* prepositional phrase, *across from T.J.;* periods in initials, *T.J.;* subjects, *Jennifer/she;* predicates, *sits/sings;* pronouns, *she/they;* subject/verb agreement, *Jennifer sits/she likes/she sings;* adverb, *better than* [comparative])

**Guided Practice in Writing**

Have students write a persuasive paragraph to their parents, asking for a raise in their allowance. Instruct students to include reasons they deserve a raise or things they can do to deserve one.

**Informal Assessment**

Check students' writing for the correct use of skills learned in Lessons 1–6.

# DAY 4

## Word Analysis

### Spelling

**Spelling Review: Contractions**

#### Teach

Review how a contraction is formed by writing *is* and *not* on the board. Ask a student to explain what an apostrophe is *(a symbol that marks the spot where letters are taken out)*. Ask another student to spell the contraction *can't* .

#### Guided Practice

Have students complete page 101 of ***Spelling and Vocabulary Skills*** to reinforce the spelling strategies learned in Unit 4.

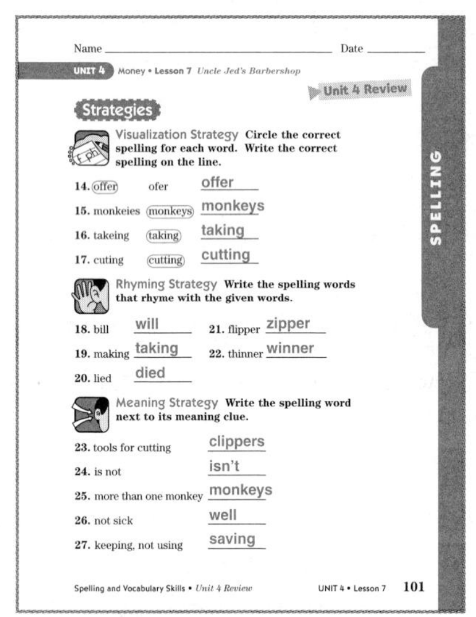

Name ______ Date ______

UNIT 4 Money • Lesson 7 *Uncle Jed's Barbershop*

Unit 4 Review

Strategies

Visualization Strategy **Circle the correct spelling for each word. Write the correct spelling on the line.**

14. (offer) ofer offer
15. monkeies (monkeys) monkeys
16. takeing (taking) taking
17. cuting (cutting) cutting

Rhyming Strategy **Write the spelling words that rhyme with the given words.**

18. bill will
19. making taking
20. lied died
21. flipper zipper
22. thinner winner

Meaning Strategy **Write the spelling word next to its meaning clue.**

23. tools for cutting clippers
24. is not isn't
25. more than one monkey monkeys
26. not sick well
27. keeping, not using saving

SPELLING

Spelling and Vocabulary Skills • *Unit 4 Review* UNIT 4 • Lesson 7 101

*Spelling and Vocabulary Skills p. 101*

### Vocabulary (continued)

**Vocabulary Review: Base Word Families**

- Write *unconscious* on the board. Ask the class to find the base word in *unconscious (conscious)*.
- Ask what the prefix *un-* means (*not, opposite of)*.
- Ask a student to find *conscious* in the dictionary (*awake, able to see and feel things)*.
- Ask a student what *unconscious* means *(not awake, not able to feel or see)*. Discuss what it is like to be *unconscious (not awake, a deep sleep, serious condition)*.

## Writing Process Strategies

### Revising

**Persuasive Paragraph**

#### Teach

Read ***Writer's Workbook,*** page 80, on revising a persuasive paragraph.

**Troubleshooting**

- Topic sentence does not catch the reader's interest. Your reader will be more likely to keep reading if you catch his or her interest right away.
- Supporting reasons do not matter to your audience. Use only reasons that your audience will find important, or they will not be persuaded by your argument.
- The closing sentence does not suggest what the writer wants the reader to do or think. This is the writer's last chance to clearly state what action they want the reader to take.

**Routine Card**

Refer to ***Routine 7*** for Writing Conferences.

#### Guided Practice

**Revising**

- Have students revise their paragraph and put it in their ***Writer's Folders.***
- Have students use the checklist on ***Writer's Workbook,*** page 80, to revise their persuasive paragraphs.

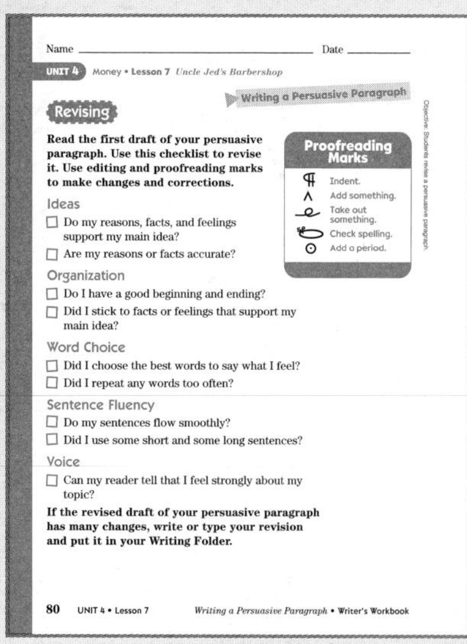

Name ______ Date ______

UNIT 4 Money • Lesson 7 *Uncle Jed's Barbershop*

Writing a Persuasive Paragraph

Revising

**Read the first draft of your persuasive paragraph. Use this checklist to revise it. Use editing and proofreading marks to make changes and corrections.**

Ideas

- ☐ Do my reasons, facts, and feelings support my main idea?
- ☐ Are my reasons or facts accurate?

Organization

- ☐ Do I have a good beginning and ending?
- ☐ Did I stick to facts or feelings that support my main idea?

Word Choice

- ☐ Did I choose the best words to say what I feel?
- ☐ Did I repeat any words too often?

Sentence Fluency

- ☐ Do my sentences flow smoothly?
- ☐ Did I use some short and some long sentences?

Voice

- ☐ Can my reader tell that I feel strongly about my topic?

**If the revised draft of your persuasive paragraph has many changes, write or type your revision and put it in your Writing Folder.**

Proofreading Marks

¶ Indent.
^ Add something.
Take out something.
Check spelling.
⊙ Add a period.

Objective: Students revise a persuasive paragraph.

80 UNIT 4 • Lesson 7 *Writing a Persuasive Paragraph* • Writer's Workbook

*Writer's Workbook p. 80*

## English Language Conventions

### Listening, Speaking, Viewing

**Interacting: Engaging an Audience**

#### Teach

- Remind the class that while money is an important part of life, family, friends, and loved ones are what really matter.
- Explain why Uncle Jed's gift was so selfless. Uncle Jed had a dream to own and run his own barbershop. He worked very hard to make the money, but the money or the barbershop was not as important to him as Sarah Jean. He put his dream on hold in order to help a loved one, and that is more important than anything.

#### Guided Practice

- As a class, discuss "Uncle Jed's Barbershop" and Uncle Jed's incredible act of kindness. Have students use good listening and speaking skills: listen attentively, face the speaker, make eye contact, and use hand gestures in order to make their comments more meaningful.
- Invite the students to share what kinds of things they would do for a loved one. Could they act as selflessly as Uncle Jed did? What kinds of amazing things have others done for them?

**Informal Assessment**

Observe whether students use eye contact and hand gestures when communicating with one another.

# DAY 5

## Word Analysis

### Spelling

#### Assessment: Final Test

**Spelling Review**

#### Teach

Repeat the Pretest or use the Final Test on page 43 of ***Unit 4 Assessment*** as summative assessment of student understanding of spelling patterns from Unit 4.

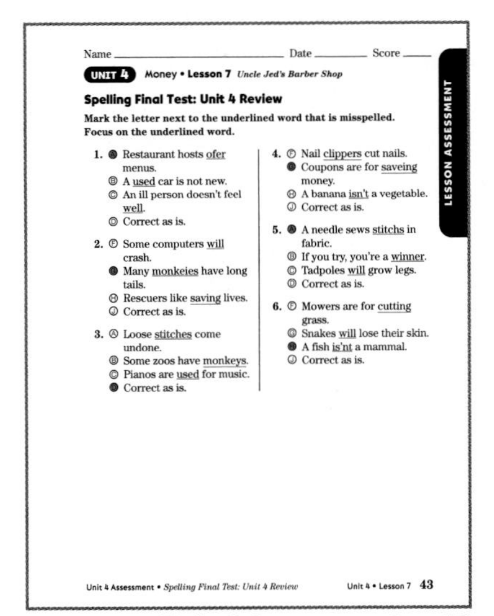

Name ____________ Date ______ Score ____

UNIT 4 Money • **Lesson 7** *Uncle Jed's Barber Shop*

**Spelling Final Test: Unit 4 Review**

**Mark the letter next to the underlined word that is misspelled. Focus on the underlined word.**

1. Ⓐ Restaurant hosts ofer menus.
   Ⓑ A used car is not new.
   Ⓒ An ill person doesn't feel well.
   Ⓓ Correct as is.
2. Ⓕ Some computers will crash.
   Ⓖ Many monkeies have long tails.
   Ⓗ Rescuers like saving lives.
   Ⓙ Correct as is.
3. Ⓐ Loose stitches come undone.
   Ⓑ Some zoos have monkeys.
   Ⓒ Pianos are used for music.
   Ⓓ Correct as is.
4. Ⓕ Nail clippers cut nails.
   Ⓖ Coupons are for saveing money.
   Ⓗ A banana isn't a vegetable.
   Ⓙ Correct as is.
5. Ⓐ A needle sews stitchs in fabric.
   Ⓑ If you try, you're a winner.
   Ⓒ Tadpoles will grow legs.
   Ⓓ Correct as is.
6. Ⓕ Mowers are for cutting grass.
   Ⓖ Snakes will lose their skin.
   Ⓗ A fish is'nt a mammal.
   Ⓙ Correct as is.

LESSON ASSESSMENT

Unit 4 Assessment • *Spelling Final Test: Unit 4 Review* Unit 4 • Lesson 7 43

***Unit 4 Assessment p. 43***

#### Guided Practice

Have students categorize any mistakes they made on the Final Test as careless errors or lesson-pattern problems.

### Vocabulary

**Informal Assessment**

Write *sharecroppers* "Uncle Jed's Barbershop" (p. 96) on the board. Discuss how *sharecroppers* explains exactly what *sharecroppers* did *(shared the value of the crops with the land owner)*. Check in students' writing to see if they are correctly forming compound words. Have students add any new words to the running word list in the Writer's Notebook.

## Writing Process Strategies

### Editing/Proofreading and Publishing

**Persuasive Paragraph**

#### Teach

- Read ***Writer's Workbook,*** page 81, on editing/proofreading and publishing a persuasive paragraph.
- Discuss ***Language Arts Transparency 28,*** Editing: Grammar and Punctuation.

#### Guided Practice

**Editing/Proofreading and Publishing**

- Have students edit/proofread their persuasive paragraphs.
- Direct students to use the checklist on ***Writer's Workbook,*** page 81, to help them edit/proofread their writing.
- Have students make a clean copy of their paragraphs in their best cursive handwriting.

**Formal Assessment**

Total Point Value: 10

1. Topic sentence grabs the reader's attention. (2 points)
2. All of the reasons support the topic sentence. (2 points)
3. The strongest reason is given last. (2 points)
4. Mechanics are correct. (2 points)
5. The paragraph is indented. (2 points)

Name ____________ Date ______

UNIT 4 Money • **Lesson 7** *Uncle Jed's Barbershop*

Writing a Persuasive Paragraph

**Editing/Proofreading**

Objective: Students edit/proofread and publish a persuasive paragraph.

**Edit your persuasive paragraph on paper or a computer. Then make a clean copy of your paragraph, and put it in your Writing Folder. Read your persuasive paragraph carefully. Use the checklist to help you correct any mistakes.**

Conventions

- ☐ Does every sentence have a subject and a predicate?
- ☐ Did I use pronouns and adverbs correctly?
- ☐ Does every sentence have end punctuation?
- ☐ Did I capitalize all proper nouns and the first word of every sentence?
- ☐ Is my paragraph indented?
- ☐ Are the words spelled correctly?

**Publishing**

**Use the checklist to get your persuasive paragraph ready for your reader.**

Presentation

- ☐ Make sure your writing says exactly what you want it to say.
- ☐ Make a clean copy. You may want to use the computer.
- ☐ Practice reading your persuasive paragraph out loud if you plan to give an oral presentation.

PERSUASIVE WRITING

Writer's Workbook • *Writing a Persuasive Paragraph* UNIT 4 • Lesson 7 81

***Writer's Workbook p. 81***

## English Language Conventions

### Penmanship

**Cursive Letters *X* and *W***

#### Teach

- **Teacher Model:** Introduce formation of uppercase *X* and *W* as curve forward letters by demonstrating on the board.

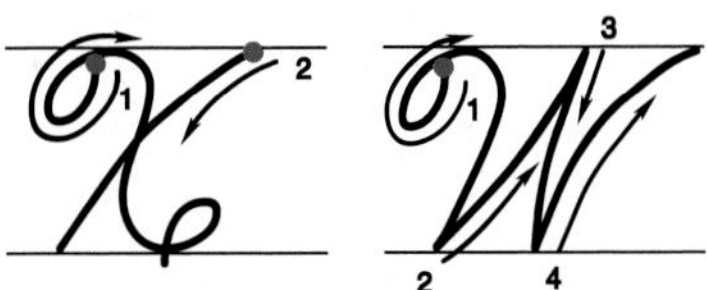

**X** Starting point, loop
Curve forward, slant down
Undercurve to end point
Starting point, slant down: capital *X*

**W** Starting point, loop, curve forward
Slant down into undercurve
Slant down into overcurve
Overcurve: capital *W*

- **Teacher Model:** Write the words *Xavier* and *Washington* to model proper letter formation.
- Remind students that they should keep their letters within neat margins on the paper.

#### Guided Practice

- Have students practice writing rows of *X*s and *W*s in their Writer's Notebooks.
- From "Uncle Jed's Barbershop," have students write the words *when, was,* and *fixing* to practice letter formation.
- Ask students to correct any instances where they may have written over a margin.

**Informal Assessment**

Check students' handwriting for proper formation of *X* and *W* and for neat margins.

# Reading and Language Arts Skills Traces

## Language Arts

### WORD ANALYSIS

Skills Trace

**Spelling: Unit 4 Review**

Introduced in Grade 3.
Scaffolded throughout Grades 3–5.

**INTRODUCED:** Unit 4, Lessons 1–6
**PRACTICED:** Unit 4, Lesson 7, pp. 105F–105J
*Spelling and Vocabulary Skills,* pp. 100–101
**TESTED:** Unit 4, Lesson 7, p. 105F (Pretest)
Unit 4, Lesson 7, p. 43 (Final Test)
Unit 4 Assessment

Skills Trace

**Vocabulary: Unit 4 Review**

Introduced in Grade 3.
Scaffolded throughout Grades 3–5.

**INTRODUCED:** Unit 4, Lessons 1–6
**PRACTICED:** Unit 4, Lesson 7, pp. 105G–105J
*Spelling and Vocabulary Skills,* pp. 98–99
**TESTED:** Unit 4 Assessment

### WRITING PROCESS STRATEGIES

Skills Trace

**Persuasive Writing: Persuasive Paragraph**

Introduced in Grade 1.
Scaffolded throughout Grades 2–5.

**REINTRODUCED:** Unit 4, Lesson 7, p. 103F
**PRACTICED:** Unit 4, Lesson 7, pp. 103G–103J
*Writer's Workbook,* pp. 78–81
**TESTED:** Unit 4, Lesson 7, Formal Assessment, p. 103J
Unit 4 Assessment

Skills Trace

**Writer's Craft: Effective Beginnings and Endings**

Introduced in Grade 2.
Scaffolded throughout Grades 3–6.

**REINTRODUCED:** Unit 4, Lesson 7, p. 103H
**PRACTICED:** Unit 4, Lesson 7, p. 103H
*Comprehension and Language Arts Skills,* pp. 124–125
**TESTED:** Unit 4 Assessment

### ENGLISH LANGUAGE CONVENTIONS

Skills Trace

**Listening, Speaking, Viewing Interacting: Engaging an Audience**

Introduced in Grade K.
Scaffolded throughout Grades 1–6.

**REINTRODUCED:** Unit 4, Lesson 7, p. 105I
**TESTED:** Unit 4, Lesson 7
Informal Assessment, p. 105I

**Penmanship: Cursive Letters *X* and *W***

Introduced in Grade 3.
Scaffolded throughout Grades 4–6.

**INTRODUCED:** Unit 4, Lesson 7, p. 105J
**TESTED:** Unit 4, Lesson 7
Informal Assessment, p. 105

## Reading

### COMPREHENSION

**Cause and Effect**

Introduced in Grade 1.
Scaffolded throughout Grade 2.

**REINTRODUCED:** Unit 1, Lesson 2
**REINFORCED:** Unit 1, Lesson 4
Unit 2, Lesson 4
Unit 2, Lesson 5
Unit 4, Lesson 2
Unit 4, Lesson 7
Unit 6, Lesson 6
**TESTED:** Unit 4 Assessment

# Professional Development: Assessment

## What Assessment Looks Like in the Classroom

### Informal Assessment

***Observation*** Observation of students' progress is a part of the everyday classroom routine. Before class begins, assemble the materials you will need, decide which students to observe, and decide which aspect of student performance to monitor.

During a lesson, keep your Informal Observation Log from the ***Program Assessment*** nearby to record information quickly as you observe students' performance. You may wish to extend your observations over several days, until you have had a chance to observe each student's performance in a particular area. Often, you may want to observe the same student more than once to gauge progress or identify specific difficulties.

As part of your observations, encourage students to talk about any confusion they might be experiencing. By identifying areas of confusion, you can gain valuable insight into an individual student's specific needs.

Observe students as part of the regular lesson, either with the entire class or in small groups. Do this instead of pulling students aside individually, unless it is to check their oral fluency.

***Written Work*** Regularly monitor students' written work in workbooks, Writer's Notebooks, and so forth. These pieces of writing provide invaluable information about how well students understand a concept or can apply a particular skill.

Also keep portfolios of students' written work as a way to follow their progress. In addition, use portfolios as a way to help build students' self-confidence. Collecting, commenting on, and keeping student work indicates to students that their writing has value.

***Reading*** Each day during Workshop, sit with individual students and invite them to read aloud from an appropriate selection. As a student reads, note how well he or she applies reading skills and strategies. For example, with young students, note their ability to apply sound/spelling relationship information to decode unknown words. With students of all ages, note their attempts—successful or not—to use reading strategies to clarify, predict, summarize, or otherwise make sense of what they are reading.

From time to time, also check students' oral reading fluency by timing their reading and noting how well they are able to sustain the reading without faltering.

### Formal, Standardized Assessment

Administer standardized tests—whether mandated by the school, district, state, or nation—to obtain a picture of student achievement or aptitude in a specific area.

Prepare for the administration of standardized assessments by making students comfortable with the format of the particular test—multiple-choice answers, fill-in-the-blanks, and so forth. This enables students to focus on the content of the questions on the test and not on the way in which they are asked. Go over sample questions with students to make sure they understand what to do.

Additional information about assessment as well as resource references can be found in the ***Professional Development Guide: Assessment.***

## Review the Concepts

After all of the groups have presented their findings, lead students in a large-group discussion about the unit activity. Ask students which part of the investigation they enjoyed most. Which part was the most challenging? What parts of their investigation can they use in their everyday lives?

Review with students the following key concepts:

- Money has changed over time and is still changing.
- People can trade things of value to acquire things they need.
- Understanding your market is important to doing business.
- Money management is important.
- Borrowing and credit must be handled very carefully.
- Money cannot buy happiness.
- Money can be used to help others.
- If necessary, remind students of the questions they raised throughout the unit and ask them to discuss each one.
- As always, students' ideas should determine the discussion.
- Remind students that they can continue to investigate money even though they have completed the unit.

### Tips for Reviewing the Concepts

- If necessary, remind students of the questions they raised throughout the unit and ask them to discuss each one.
- As always, students' ideas should determine the discussion.
- Remind students that they can continue to investigate money even though they have completed the unit.

Have students refer to page 82 of the ***Inquiry Journal*** to remind themselves of what their ideas about money were when the unit began and also of what they expected to learn from the unit. Ask them to describe the new ideas they have acquired and the new information they have learned.

## Evaluating the Unit

- Have students conduct an evaluation of the unit selections, identifying those selections they found most interesting and those they found least interesting.
- Have students evaluate the different activities in which they participated throughout the unit. Which activities did they find the most enjoyable and informative?
- Ask students to evaluate the overall unit. Have them answer questions such as the following: How well did the unit cover the theme? Which selections added something new to your knowledge of imagination?
- Have students suggest ideas related to money to explore further, possibly beginning with any questions left on the Concept/Question Board.

Name ________ Date ________

UNIT 4 Money

**Knowledge About Money**

- This is what I know about money before reading the unit.

Answers will vary.

- These are some things that I would like to know about money.

Answers will vary.

Reminder: When I get to the end of the unit, I should read this page again to see how much I have learned about money.

82 UNIT 4 *Knowledge About Money* • Inquiry Journal

***Inquiry Journal* p. 82**

## Evaluating Participation

In their small groups, have students discuss the unit activity. Encourage them to talk about the importance of teamwork. Have the groups consider the following: What things did we do well as a team? What things could we do better next time? Why is teamwork important?

Throughout this unit investigation into Money, you have been informally assessing student progress. Go over your notes to see who has been contributing to the group's investigation and how students have helped each other during this process. Talk with each group to get their feedback about how they felt working as a team. Use your observation notes, feedback from the group, and the Research Rubrics to assess the groups as well as individual student participation in the groups. Record each student's score on the inside back cover of the ***Inquiry Journal***.

### Research Rubrics

#### Collaborative Group Work

(this rubric is applied to groups, not individuals)

**1** Group members work on separate tasks with little interaction.

**2** Work-related decisions are made by the group, but there is little interaction related to ideas.

**3** Information and ideas are shared, but there is little discussion concerned with advancing understanding.

**4** The group clearly progresses in its thinking beyond where individual students could have gone.

#### Participation in Collaborative Inquiry

(this rubric is applied to individual students)

**1** Does not contribute ideas or information to team or class.

**2** Makes contributions to Concept/Question Board or class discussions when specifically called upon to do so.

**3** Occasionally contributes ideas or information to other students' inquiries.

**4** Takes an active interest in the success of the whole class's knowledge-building efforts.

## Informal Assessment

### Self-Evaluation

- Give students the opportunity to evaluate their personal learning experiences during this unit by completing ***Inquiry Journal***, pages 105–106.
- The students can also complete the self-evaluation questions on the ***Research Assistant CD-ROM***.

Name ______________________ Date ________

Money UNIT 4

**Unit Wrap-Up**

- How did you feel about this unit?
  - ☐ I enjoyed it very much. ☐ I liked it.
  - ☐ I liked some of it. ☐ I didn't like it.
- How would you rate the difficulty of the unit?
  - ☐ easy ☐ medium ☐ hard
- How would you rate your performance during this unit?
  - ☐ I learned a lot about money.
  - ☐ I learned some new things about money.
  - ☐ I didn't learn much about money.
- Why did you choose these ratings?
  Answers will vary.
- What was the most interesting thing you learned about money?
  Answers will vary.

Inquiry Journal • *Unit Wrap-Up* UNIT 4 105

**Unit Wrap-Up** *(continued)*

- What did you learn about money that you didn't know before?
  Answers will vary.
- What did you learn about yourself as a learner?
  Answers will vary.
- What do you need to work on to improve your skills as a learner?
  Answers will vary.
- What resources (books, films, magazines, interviews, other) did you use on your own during this unit? Which of these were the most helpful? Why?
  Answers will vary.

106 UNIT 4 *Unit Wrap-Up* • Inquiry Journal

***Inquiry Journal pp. 105–106***

# Formal Assessment

Use these summative assessments along with your informal observations to assess student mastery.

Name ______________ Date ________ Score ____

UNIT 4 Money

**Connecting Unit Selections**

**Read the following questions carefully. Then answer each one in complete sentences. You may want to refer back to the stories.**

1. What are the different ways that people earn money in the stories in this unit?
   Answers will vary.

2. How are Uncle Jed and the cobbler different? What information in the stories helps you answer this question?
   Uncle Jed uses his money in a good way. The cobbler just worries about his money. Uncle Jed earned his money, but the cobbler was given his. Answers will vary about information in the stories.

END OF UNIT ASSESSMENT Short Answer

44 *Connecting Unit Selections* • Unit 4 Assessment

**Unit 4 Assessment p. 44**

**Connecting Unit Selections** *(continued)*

3. How did Shorty and Widow Macrae get their money? How is this different from the young people in "Kids Did It! in Business"?
   Shorty and Widow Macrae got a reward for recovering stolen money. The young people earned their money in business.

4. Think about the story "The Go-Around Dollar." What are some of the things you learned about money? How is this story like "Alexander, Who Used to Be Rich Last Sunday"?
   Answers will vary. The two stories show lots of ways that money can be spent.

END OF UNIT ASSESSMENT Short Answer

Unit 4 Assessment • *Connecting Unit Selections* 45

**Unit 4 Assessment p. 45**

Name ______________ Date ________ Score ____

UNIT 4 Money

**Comprehension Assessment**

**Read the story silently. Then answer the questions about the story.**

**Money Matters**

It's fun to earn a little extra money. Let's say you do some special chores, and your mom offers to pay you. You reach out your hand, and she fills it with salt.

That would seem strange today, but hundreds of years ago, it would not. Before there was money, people used things like salt for money. Salt was valuable, so people traded with it.

This kind of trade is called barter. Early cultures bartered with things besides salt. They also used beads, cocoa beans, animals, and other useful things. Barter was a difficult way of doing business. What are fifty cocoa beans worth? How many pots are worth a piece of cloth? Everything had to be counted and measured, and everyone paid differently.

The first coins were made in Lydia, in an area that is now Turkey, over two thousand years ago. They were shaped like beans and made of gold and silver. They even had a government stamp which made them official. At last, everyone was using the same kind of money. Soon, other places were making their own coins.

Paper money was invented in China about a thousand years later. It took Europe another thousand years to catch on. Today, almost every country has its own form of paper money and coins.

Remarkably, many people do not buy things with coins and bills any more. They write checks or use credit cards. Even so, money will probably be with us for a long, long time.

1. Where were the first coins invented?
   Ⓐ China
   Ⓑ the United States
   ● Lydia

END OF UNIT ASSESSMENT Multiple Choice

46 *Comprehension Assessment* • Unit 4 Assessment

**Unit 4 Assessment p. 46**

**Comprehension Assessment** *(continued)*

2. All of these were used for barter except
   Ⓕ cocoa beans
   ● plastic cards
   Ⓗ animals

3. Who probably made the coins of Lydia?
   Ⓐ the shops
   Ⓑ the banks
   ● the government

**Read the following questions carefully. Use complete sentences to answer the questions.**

4. What was the trouble with bartering?
   Bartering made business difficult, because everything had to be counted or measured.

5. According to the story, what are ways other than coins and bills to pay for things today?
   People write checks and use credit cards.

END OF UNIT ASSESSMENT Multiple Choice/Short Answer

Unit 4 Assessment • *Comprehension Assessment* 47

**Unit 4 Assessment p. 47**

Name ______________ Date ________ Score ____

UNIT 4 Money

**Spelling Assessment**

**Read each line carefully. Look for the underlined word that is misspelled. Then completely fill in the bubble of the line where the word is misspelled. If no word is misspelled, fill in the bubble of the line marked "Correct as is."**

1. ● People should walk on the sidewak.
   Ⓑ Counselors offer advice.
   Ⓒ Teachers know you'll succeed.
   Ⓓ Correct as is.

2. Ⓕ A potter works with clay.
   Ⓖ A raisin is a grape that's dried.
   ● Quarterbacks try pasing the ball.
   Ⓙ Correct as is.

3. Ⓐ Painting can make a mess.
   ● Some cowboyes wear boots.
   Ⓒ June is a summer month.
   Ⓓ Correct as is.

4. ● Winners think theyl'l be best.
   Ⓖ Frozen ponds are skated upon.
   Ⓗ A cliff is made of rock.
   Ⓙ Correct as is.

5. Ⓐ A hammer drives in a nail.
   Ⓑ A snake defends itself by biting.
   ● Sledding down a hil can be fun.
   Ⓓ Correct as is.

6. Ⓕ A poncho is something to wear.
   Ⓖ Some berries can be eaten.
   Ⓗ Young babies drink milk.
   ● Correct as is.

END OF UNIT ASSESSMENT Multiple Choice

48 *Spelling Assessment* • Unit 4 Assessment

**Unit 4 Assessment p. 48**

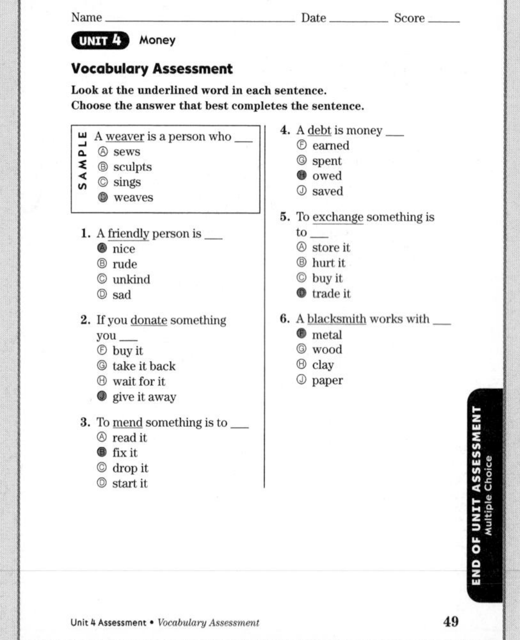

Name ______________ Date ________ Score ____

UNIT 4 Money

**Vocabulary Assessment**

**Look at the underlined word in each sentence. Choose the answer that best completes the sentence.**

SAMPLE: A weaver is a person who ___
Ⓐ sews
Ⓑ sculpts
Ⓒ sings
● weaves

1. A friendly person is ___
   ● nice
   Ⓑ rude
   Ⓒ unkind
   Ⓓ sad

2. If you donate something you ___
   Ⓕ buy it
   Ⓖ take it back
   Ⓗ wait for it
   ● give it away

3. To mend something is to ___
   Ⓐ read it
   ● fix it
   Ⓒ drop it
   Ⓓ start it

4. A debt is money ___
   Ⓕ earned
   Ⓖ spent
   ● owed
   Ⓙ saved

5. To exchange something is to ___
   Ⓐ store it
   Ⓑ hurt it
   Ⓒ buy it
   ● trade it

6. A blacksmith works with ___
   ● metal
   Ⓖ wood
   Ⓗ clay
   Ⓙ paper

END OF UNIT ASSESSMENT Multiple Choice

Unit 4 Assessment • *Vocabulary Assessment* 49

**Unit 4 Assessment p. 49**

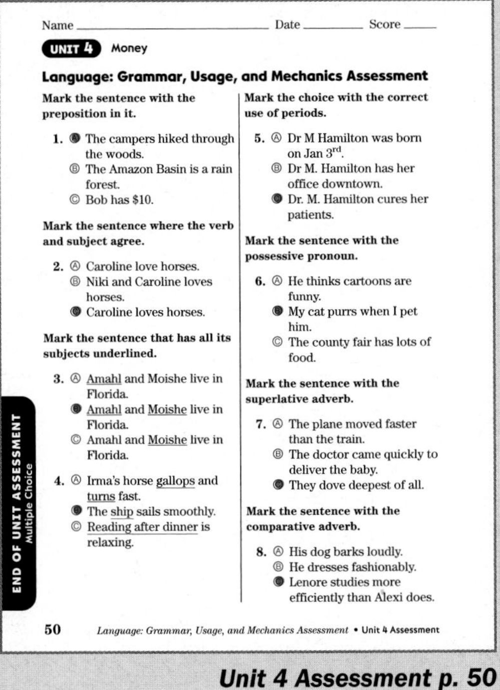

Name ______ Date ______ Score ______

UNIT 4 Money

**Language: Grammar, Usage, and Mechanics Assessment**

**Mark the sentence with the preposition in it.**

1. ● The campers hiked through the woods.
   Ⓑ The Amazon Basin is a rain forest.
   Ⓒ Bob has $10.

**Mark the sentence where the verb and subject agree.**

2. Ⓐ Caroline love horses.
   Ⓑ Niki and Caroline loves horses.
   ● Caroline loves horses.

**Mark the sentence that has all its subjects underlined.**

3. Ⓐ Amahl and Moishe live in Florida.
   ● Amahl and Moishe live in Florida.
   Ⓒ Amahl and Moishe live in Florida.

4. Ⓐ Irma's horse gallops and turns fast.
   ● The ship sails smoothly.
   Ⓒ Reading after dinner is relaxing.

**Mark the choice with the correct use of periods.**

5. Ⓐ Dr M Hamilton was born on Jan 3rd.
   Ⓑ Dr M. Hamilton has her office downtown.
   ● Dr. M. Hamilton cures her patients.

**Mark the sentence with the possessive pronoun.**

6. Ⓐ He thinks cartoons are funny.
   ● My cat purrs when I pet him.
   Ⓒ The county fair has lots of food.

**Mark the sentence with the superlative adverb.**

7. Ⓐ The plane moved faster than the train.
   Ⓑ The doctor came quickly to deliver the baby.
   ● They dove deepest of all.

**Mark the sentence with the comparative adverb.**

8. Ⓐ His dog barks loudly.
   Ⓑ He dresses fashionably.
   ● Lenore studies more efficiently than Alexi does.

END OF UNIT ASSESSMENT Multiple Choice

50 *Language: Grammar, Usage, and Mechanics Assessment* • Unit 4 Assessment

**Unit 4 Assessment p. 50**

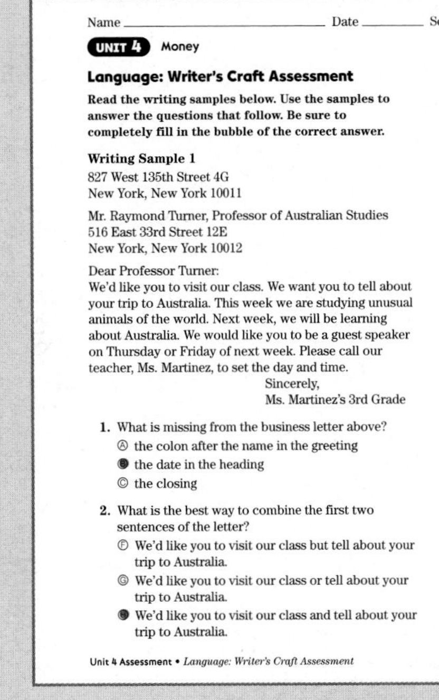

Name ______ Date ______ Score ______

UNIT 4 Money

**Language: Writer's Craft Assessment**

**Read the writing samples below. Use the samples to answer the questions that follow. Be sure to completely fill in the bubble of the correct answer.**

**Writing Sample 1**

827 West 135th Street 4G
New York, New York 10011

Mr. Raymond Turner, Professor of Australian Studies
516 East 33rd Street 12E
New York, New York 10012

Dear Professor Turner:
We'd like you to visit our class. We want you to tell about your trip to Australia. This week we are studying unusual animals of the world. Next week, we will be learning about Australia. We would like you to be a guest speaker on Thursday or Friday of next week. Please call our teacher, Ms. Martinez, to set the day and time.

Sincerely,
Ms. Martinez's 3rd Grade

1. What is missing from the business letter above?
   Ⓐ the colon after the name in the greeting
   ● the date in the heading
   Ⓒ the closing

2. What is the best way to combine the first two sentences of the letter?
   Ⓕ We'd like you to visit our class but tell about your trip to Australia.
   Ⓖ We'd like you to visit our class or tell about your trip to Australia.
   ● We'd like you to visit our class and tell about your trip to Australia.

END OF UNIT ASSESSMENT Multiple Choice

Unit 4 Assessment • *Language: Writer's Craft Assessment* 51

**Unit 4 Assessment p. 51**

Name ______ Date ______ Score ______

UNIT 4 Money

**Oral Fluency Assessment**

*Treasure in Your Pocket*

Everyone likes finding a treasure. But not all treasure is gold or jewels. Some treasure can look pretty common. You might be holding a fortune and not even know it! Some coins can be worth a lot of money. You just have to know what to look for.

The hobby of coin collecting is very popular. People all over the world collect coins. You don't have to have a lot of time or money to start a collection. All you need is a pile of change.

When you start your treasure hunt, there are a few things to watch for. First, check out the condition of the coin. If it's beat-up, scratched, bent, or really dirty, it's probably not worth much. If it looks shiny and new, the coin is more valuable.

You should also look at the date. Some dates are more valuable than others. Most dates will have a letter beside them. This letter is called the "mint mark." It tells you where the coin was made. For example, "P" is for Philadelphia and "D" is for Denver.

END OF UNIT ASSESSMENT Teacher-Directed

Unit 4 Assessment • *Oral Fluency Assessment* 52

**Unit 4 Assessment p. 52**

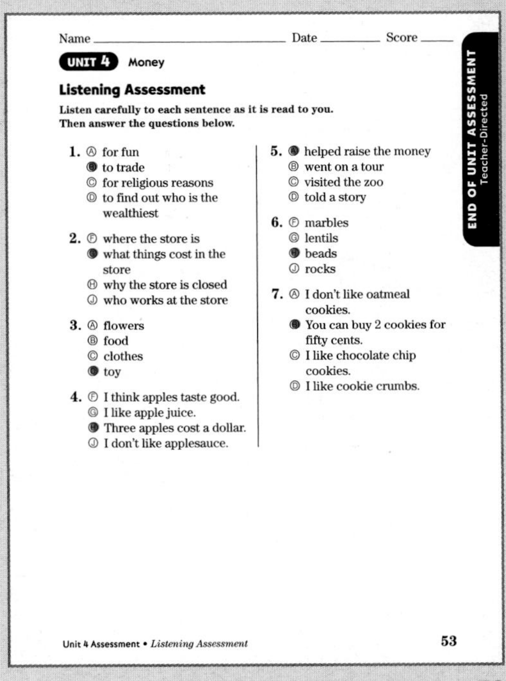

Name ______ Date ______ Score ______

UNIT 4 Money

**Listening Assessment**

**Listen carefully to each sentence as it is read to you. Then answer the questions below.**

1. Ⓐ for fun
   ● to trade
   Ⓒ for religious reasons
   Ⓓ to find out who is the wealthiest

2. Ⓕ where the store is
   ● what things cost in the store
   Ⓗ why the store is closed
   Ⓙ who works at the store

3. Ⓐ flowers
   Ⓑ food
   Ⓒ clothes
   ● toy

4. Ⓕ I think apples taste good.
   Ⓖ I like apple juice.
   ● Three apples cost a dollar.
   Ⓙ I don't like applesauce.

5. ● helped raise the money
   Ⓑ went on a tour
   Ⓒ visited the zoo
   Ⓓ told a story

6. Ⓕ marbles
   Ⓖ lentils
   ● beads
   Ⓙ rocks

7. Ⓐ I don't like oatmeal cookies.
   ● You can buy 2 cookies for fifty cents.
   Ⓒ I like chocolate chip cookies.
   Ⓓ I like cookie crumbs.

END OF UNIT ASSESSMENT Teacher-Directed

Unit 4 Assessment • *Listening Assessment* 53

**Unit 4 Assessment p. 53**

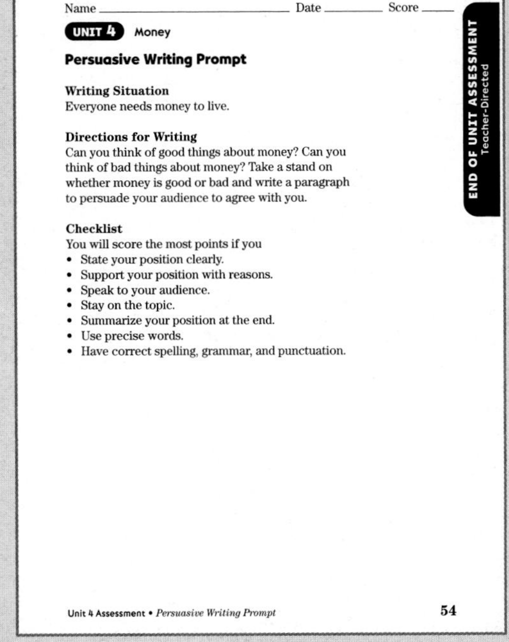

Name ______ Date ______ Score ______

UNIT 4 Money

**Persuasive Writing Prompt**

**Writing Situation**
Everyone needs money to live.

**Directions for Writing**
Can you think of good things about money? Can you think of bad things about money? Take a stand on whether money is good or bad and write a paragraph to persuade your audience to agree with you.

**Checklist**
You will score the most points if you
- State your position clearly.
- Support your position with reasons.
- Speak to your audience.
- Stay on the topic.
- Summarize your position at the end.
- Use precise words.
- Have correct spelling, grammar, and punctuation.

END OF UNIT ASSESSMENT Teacher-Directed

Unit 4 Assessment • *Persuasive Writing Prompt* 54

**Unit 4 Assessment p. 54**

## Also included:

- **Writing Rubrics (Four Point and Six Point)**
- **Writing Portfolio Assessment and Rubrics**
- **Directions for Listening Assessment**
- **Teacher's Record of Oral Fluency**
- **Formal Assessment Record**

**Online Assessment** for ***Open Court Reading*** helps teachers differentiate classroom instruction based on students' scores from the weekly and end-of-unit assessments. It provides exercises best suited to meet the needs of each student. For more information, visit SRAonline.com.

## Responding to Results

***Differentiating Instruction Support Activities*** is designed for students who need quick alternative activities to strengthen or extend their skills.

# Anthology Glossary

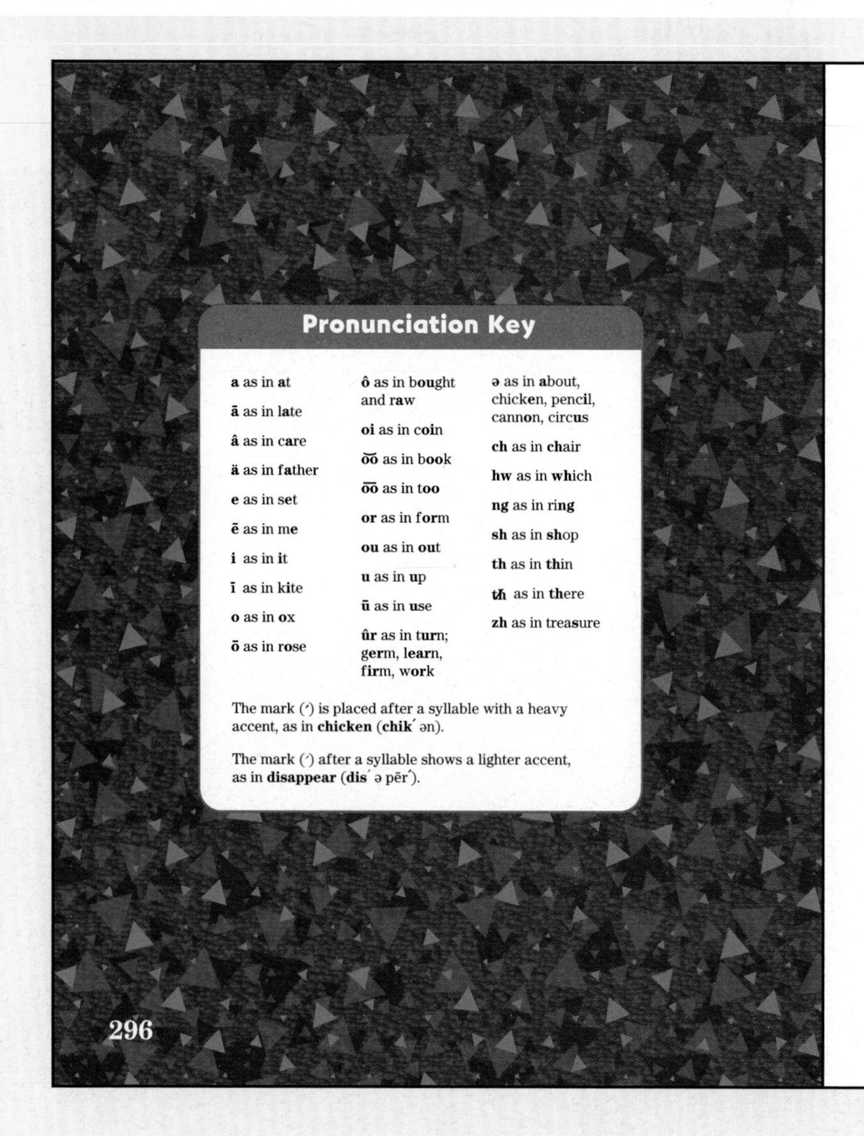

## Pronunciation Key

**a** as in **a**t
**ā** as in l**a**te
**â** as in c**a**re
**ä** as in f**a**ther
**e** as in s**e**t
**ē** as in m**e**
**i** as in **i**t
**ī** as in k**i**te
**o** as in **o**x
**ō** as in r**o**se
**ô** as in b**ou**ght and r**aw**
**oi** as in c**oi**n
**o͝o** as in b**oo**k
**o͞o** as in t**oo**
**or** as in f**or**m
**ou** as in **ou**t
**u** as in **u**p
**ū** as in **u**se
**ûr** as in t**ur**n; g**er**m, l**ear**n, f**ir**m, w**or**k
**ə** as in **a**bout, chick**e**n, penc**i**l, cann**o**n, circ**u**s
**ch** as in **ch**air
**hw** as in **wh**ich
**ng** as in ri**ng**
**sh** as in **sh**op
**th** as in **th**in
**t͟h** as in **th**ere
**zh** as in trea**s**ure

The mark (ˊ) is placed after a syllable with a heavy accent, as in **chicken** (**chik**ˊ ən).

The mark (ˊ) after a syllable shows a lighter accent, as in **disappear** (**dis**ˊ ə pērˊ).

296

# Glossary

## A

**absolutely** (abˊ sə lo͞otˊ lē) *adv.* Certainly; for sure.

**advise** (əd vīzˊ) *v.* To give information.

**adze** (adz) *n.* A tool shaped like an axe. It is used by the **Tsimshian** tribe to create a pattern on the surface of a wood carving. The adze handle is handmade from the elbow of a yew or alder branch. The blade is made of steel.

**allergic** (ə lûrˊ jik) *adj.* Having an unpleasant reaction to certain things.

**ambition** (am biˊ shən) *n.* A strong desire for success.

**amidst** (ə midstˊ) *prep.* In the middle of.

**analyze** (anˊ l īzˊ) *v.* To examine the parts of something.

**ancestor** (anˊ ses tər) *n.* A parent, grandparent, great-grandparent, and so on.

**artificial** (ärˊ tə fishˊ əl) *adj.* Made by people rather than nature.

**auction** (ôkˊ shôn) *n.* A public sale where each item is sold to the person who will pay the highest price.

**automatic** (ô tə maˊ tik) *adj.* Operating by itself.

**away** (ə wāˊ) *v.* To go somewhere.

## B

**babushka** (bə bo͞oshˊ kə) *n.* A head scarf shaped like a triangle.

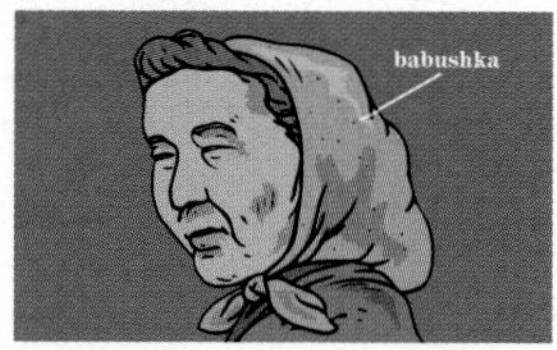


**bale** (bāl) *n.* A large bundle of hay, packed tightly and tied together.

**banquet** (bangˊ kwit) *n.* A feast; a large dinner.

297

Pronunciation Key: **at**; **lāte**; **câre**; **fäther**; **set**; **mē**; **it**; **kīte**; **ox**; **rōse**; **ô** in **bought**; **coin**; **bŏŏk**; **tōō**; **form**; **out**; **up**; **ūse**; **tûrn**; **ə** sound in **about**, **chicken**, **pencil**, **cannon**, **circus**; **chair**; **hw** in **which**; **ring**; **shop**; **thin**; **there**; **zh** in **treasure**.

**befriend** (bi frend′) *v.* To become friends with.

**blacksmith** (blak′ smith′) *n.* A person who makes horseshoes.

**boisterous** (boi′ stə rəs) *adj.* Lively and noisy.

**bold** (bōld) *adj.* Very easy to see; standing out clearly.

**bolt** (bōlt) *n.* A roll of cloth.

**bosom** (bŏŏz′ əm) *n.* The chest; the heart.

**botherment** (both′ ər mənt) *n.* A feeling of worry.

**bough** (bou) *n.* One of the major branches of a tree.

**bouquet** (bōō′ kā) *n.* A bunch of flowers.

**boutique** (bōō tēk′) *n.* A small shop.

**bowie knife** (bō′ ē nīf′) *n.* A thick-handled knife named for James Bowie.

**brandish** (bran′ dish) *v.* To swing or shake an object in a way that signals possible danger.

**brave** (brāv) *adj.* Having courage.

**britches** (brich′ iz) *n.* Breeches; pants; trousers.

**bronco** (brong′ kō) *n.* A wild horse.

**buckboard** (buk′ bord′) *n.* A horse-drawn carriage made from a long, wooden board or simple frame.

**bugler** (bū′ glər) *n.* A person who plays the bugle or trumpet.

**butternut** (bə′ tər nət′) *n.* A type of sweet nut that comes from a tree in the walnut family and can be eaten.

butternut

## C

**calabash** (kal′ ə bash′) *n.* The shell of a dried gourd, used as a bowl.

**card** (kärd) *v.* To comb wool.

**cater** (ka′ tər) *v.* To prepare and serve food for a private occasion.

**challah** (hä′ lə) *n.* A bread, which is often braided, made with eggs. Challah is eaten on the Jewish Sabbath.

challah





**charity** (châr′ ə tē) *n.* 1. A group that gives help to the needy and operates without making any money. 2. Generosity and helpfulness.

**chore** (chor) *n.* A small job done regularly.

**circulation** (sər′ kyə lā′ shən) *n.* Movement around many different places or people.

**clan** (klan) *n.* A group of families with one common ancestor. The **Tsimshian** have four major clans: the Eagles, Wolves, Ravens, and Killer Whales.

**clench** (klench) *v.* To close the teeth or fingers tightly.

**cobbler** (kob′ lər) *n.* A person who repairs shoes and boots.

**coffin** (kô′ fin) *n.* The box in which a dead body is buried.

**collect** (kə lekt′) *v.* To receive payment for a debt.

**condescend** (kon′ də send′) *v.* To act as if one is too good to do something.

**condescending** (kon′ də sen ding) *adj.* With an attitude of superiority.

**conquer** (kon′ kər) *v.* To overcome.

**constantly** (kän′ stənt lē) *adv.* All the time.

**converge** (kən vûrj′) *v.* To come together from different places.

**core** (kor) *n.* The central part of something.

**corpse** (korps) *n.* A dead body.

**corral** (kə ral′) *n.* A fenced-in area for cattle or horses.

**country** (kun′ trē) *n.* An area with fields and fewer houses than a city or town.

**course** (kors) *n.* A number of lessons given on a subject; a class.

**crackerjack** (krak′ ər jak′) *adj.* Extremely good.

**creation** (krē ā′ shən) *n.* Something that is made.

**crimson** (krim′ zən) *adj.* Deep red.

**cultivate** (kəl′ tə vāt′) *v.* To help plants grow better by breaking up the soil around them.

## D

**dainty** (dān′ tē) *n.* A special, delicious food.—*adj.* Delicately beautiful.

**deadbeat** (ded′ bēt′) *n.* A person who owes money and doesn't pay.

**debt** (det) *n.* The condition of owing money.

**decade** (de′ kād′) *n.* A period of ten years.

**decent** (dē′ sənt) *adj.* Proper.

**defenseless** (di fense′ ləs) *adj.* Helpless.

**delay** (di lā′) *v.* To cause to wait.

**delicious** (di li′ shəs) *adj.* Pleasing to taste; tasty.

Pronunciation Key: **a**t; l**ā**te; c**â**re; f**ä**ther; s**e**t; m**ē**; **i**t; k**ī**te; **o**x; r**ō**se; **ô** in b**ou**ght; c**oi**n; b**o͝o**k; t**o͞o**; f**or**m; **ou**t; **u**p; **ū**se; t**û**rn; **ə** sound in **a**bout, chick**e**n, penc**i**l, cann**o**n, circ**u**s; **ch**air; **hw** in **wh**ich; ri**ng**; **sh**op; **th**in; **th**ere; **zh** in trea**s**ure.

**descendant** (di sen′ dənt) *n.* A person's child or the child's child, and so on; anyone born from a particular family line.

**detective** (di tek′ tiv) *n.* A person who searches for information and gathers clues.

**determined** (di tûr′ mənd) *adj.* Firm and unwilling to change.

**diamond** (dī′ mənd) *n.* A valuable, clear-colored gem that sparkles in the light.

**disappear** (di′ sə pēr′) *v.* To vanish; to no longer be seen.

**disappointed** (di′ sə point′ əd) *adj.* Unhappy that something expected did not occur.

**divider** (di vī′ dər) *n.* Anything that cuts a thing into parts.

**divvy** (div′ ē) *v.* To divide for sharing.

**donate** (dō′ nāt) *v.* To give.

**dorsal** (dor′ səl) *adj.* On the upper side of the body; on the back.

**dreadful** (dred′ fəl) *adj.* Terrible; very bad.

**drench** (drench) *v.* To soak completely.

**drift** (drift) *n.* A mound formed by blowing wind.

**drought** (drout) *n.* Dry weather that lasts a very long time.

**drowsily** (drou′ zə lē) *adv.* Sleepily; in a sleepy way.

**dugout** (dug′ out′) *n.* A crude shelter made by digging a hole in the ground or on the side of a hill.

## E

**eager** (ē′ gər) *adj.* Filled with excitement or interest.

**earnings** (ûr′ ningz) *n.* Money that is paid for doing a job.

**ebb** (eb) *v.* To flow away.

**educational** (e′ jə kā′ shnəl) *adj.* Helping one to gain knowledge or a skill.

**elder** (el′ dər) *n.* An official in certain churches.

**elevated** (el′ ə vā′ tid) *adj.* Raised up.

**elevator** (el′ ə vā′ tər) *n.* A building in which grain is handled and stored.

**emblem** (em′ bləm) *n.* A sign or figure that stands for something.

**endure** (en do͝or′) *v.* To put up with; to bear.

**equipment** (i kwip′ mənt) *n.* Tools and supplies used for a given purpose.

**errand** (er′ ənd) *n.* A short trip to do something.

**etch** (ech) *v.* To outline clearly.

**examine** (ig za′ mən) *v.* To look at in detail.

**exchange** (iks chānj′) *v.* To trade one thing for another.

## F

**fail** (fā′ əl) *v.* To lose worth.

**fashion** (fa′ shn) *n.* A style of clothing or jewelry that is popular at a given time. *adj.* To be in style.

**feature** (fē′ chər) *v.* To have in an important place.

**fertile** (fûr′ tl) *adj.* Fruitful; productive.

**flamboyant** (flam boi′ ənt) *adj.* Showy; bold; striking.

**flavor** (flā′ vər) *n.* Taste or specific quality.

**folk** (fōk) *n.* People or relatives; coming from or belonging to the common people.

**folklore** (fōk′ lor′) *n.* The legends, beliefs, and customs of a people.

**forestry** (for′ ə strē) *n.* The science of maintaining a forest.

**formula** (for′ myə lə) *n.* A set method for doing something.

**forsaken** (for sā′ kən) *v.* A past tense of **forsake:** To abandon; to give up.

**foundation** (foun dā′ shən) *n.* The base of a house.

**frisky** (fris′ kē) *adj.* Full of energy, playful, active.

**frolic** (frol′ ik) *n.* A party at which work is done. —*v.* To behave playfully.

**frond** (frond) *n.* A very large leaf.

**frontlet** (frənt′ lət) *n.* A carved wooden mask worn over the forehead as a part of a headdress, usually carved with the crest of the wearer.

**fruit** (fro͞ot) *n.* Any kind of food that is grown and picked by hand.

**furious** (fyûr′ ē əs) *adj.* Violently angry.

## G

**gadget** (ga′ jət) *n.* An invention for a special purpose.

**garnet** (gär′ nit) *n.* A deep red jewel.

**generation** (jen′ ə rā′ shən) *n.* A group of people who are about the same age.

**girth** (gûrth) *n.* A strap that goes around the body of a horse, usually to fasten a saddle.

**Pronunciation Key:** **at**; **lāte**; **câre**; **fäther**; **set**; **mē**; **it**; **kīte**; **ox**; **rōse**; **ô** in **bought**; **coin**; **bo͝ok**; **to͞o**; **form**; **out**; **up**; **ūse**; **tûrn**; **ə** sound in **about**, **chicken**, **pencil**, **cannon**, **circus**; **chair**; **hw** in **which**; **ring**; **shop**; **thin**; **there**; **zh** in **treasure**.

**glitch** (glich) *n.* Something that doesn't work quite right.

**gourd** (gord) *n.* A hard-rinded fruit that can be dried, scooped out, and used as a bowl.

**government** (gə´ vərn mənt) *n.* The act or process of ruling a group of people.

**grain** (grān) *n.* A seed of corn, wheat, oats, rye, or other cereal plant.

**graze** (grāz) *v.* To eat grass.

**grieve** (grēv) *v.* To feel sadness because of loss or bad fortune.

**griot** (grē ō´) *n.* A person in a tribe whose job is to remember the oral history of all the families in the tribe or village.

**gully** (gu´ lē) *n.* A narrow ditch made by flowing water.

## H

**haltingly** (hôl´ ting lē) *adv.* In a slow way.

**handkerchief** (hang´ kər chəf) *n.* A cloth used to wipe the nose or face.

**harvest** (här´ vəst) *v.* To bring the crops in from the field.

**haul** (hôl) *v.* To pull or move with force.

**herd** (hûrd) *n.* A group of animals.

**hired** (hī´ ərd) *adj.* Paid to work.





**hitch** (hich) *v.* To fasten with a loop or a hook.

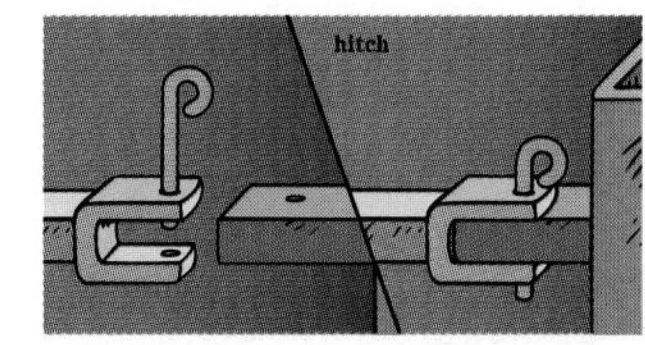


**holler** (ho´ lər) *v.* To call out loudly.

**hue** (hū) *n.* A shade of color.

***huppa*** (ho͞o´ pə) *n.* A covering that stands like a tent above the bride and groom in a Jewish wedding.

## I

**illustration** (i´ ləs trā´ shən) *n.* A picture used to explain something written.

**incite** (in sīt´) *v.* To urge or bring to action.

**inherit** (in her´ it) *v.* To receive another person's property after his or her death.

**inspect** (in spekt´) *v.* To look at closely and carefully.

**inspired** (in spī´ ûrd) *adj.* Filled with a strong encouraging feeling.

**install** (in stôl´) *v.* To place a thing where it is going to be used.

**invent** (in vent´) *v.* To come up with a new idea for.

## K

**Klallam** (klä´ lum) *n.* A coast Salish Indian tribe who live on a reservation called Little Boston, near Port Gamble, Washington.

## L

**ladle** (lād´ l) *n.* A long-handled cup for serving liquids.

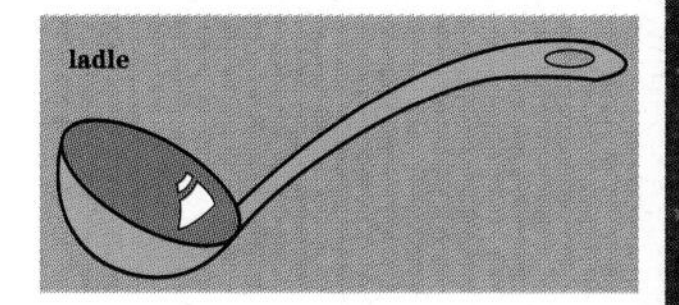


**latex gum** (lā´ teks gum´) *n.* A sticky liquid taken from a plant.

**lather** (la´ thər) *v.* To spread a foam made from soap and water over something.

**launch** (lônch) *v.* To get something started.

**lean-to** (lēn´ to͞o´) *n.* A crude shelter with a sloping top that extends from a post or tree to the ground.

**lease** (lēs) *n.* An agreement to rent something.

**legal** (lē´ gəl) *adj.* Allowed by the rules or laws.

**legend** (le´ jənd) *n.* A story passed down that is not entirely true.

Pronunciation Key: at; lāte; câre; fäther; set; mē; it; kīte; ox; rōse; ô in bought; coin; bŏŏk; tōō; form; out; up; ūse; tûrn; ə sound in about, chicken, pencil, cannon, circus; chair; hw in which; ring; shop; thin; there; zh in treasure.

**lingonberry** (ling′ ən ber′ ē) *n.* A bright red berry related to the cranberry.

**livelihood** (līv′ lē hŏŏd′) *n.* A way of making a living.

**lox** (loks) *n.* A form of salmon for eating.

**lug** (lug) *v.* To pull; to drag.

**lump** (lump) *n.* A piece; a chunk.

## M

**malfunction** (mal′ fung′ shən) *v.* To break down or work badly.

**mandarin** (man′ də rən) *adj.* Orange or reddish-yellow.

**mathematician** (math′ ə mə tish′ ən) *n.* A person who works with numbers.

**measurement** (mezh′ ər mənt) *n.* The size of something.

**memory** (me mə rē) *n.* A thing or time remembered.

**mend** (mend) *v.* To fix or repair.

**merchandise** (mûr′ chən dīz) *n.* Items to be bought or sold.

**merge** (mûrj) *v.* To be mixed together.

**message** (me′ sij) *n.* A sign of what may be coming.

**mode** (mōd) *n.* A way.

**model** (mo′ dl) *v.* To wear in order to show others.

**morsel** (mor′ səl) *n.* A small piece of food.

**mortgage** (mor′ gij) *n.* The money borrowed to buy a house.

**mosey** (mō′ zē) *v.* To walk slowly; to stroll.

**myth** (mith) *n.* A story or legend from olden days that tries to explain something.

## N

**natural** (na′ chə rəl) *n.* Not artificial or made by humans.

**nestle** (ne′ səl) *v.* To settle safely; to snuggle.

**non-returnable** (nän′ ri tûr′ nə bəl) *adj.* Something that cannot be taken or given back.

## O

**official** (ə fi′ shəl) *adj.* Formal and proper.

**operation** (ä′ pə rā′ shən) *n.* An action performed with instruments on a living body to fix damage or improve health.

**oral** (or′ əl) *adj.* Spoken.





**orchard** (or′ chərd) *n.* An area containing fruit trees.

***Ordnung*** (ord′ nəng) *n.* The Amish laws.

**organdy** (or′ gən dē) *n.* A smooth, stiff cotton material.

**outwit** (out′ wit′) *v.* To beat by being sly.

**oval** (ō′ vəl) *adj.* Egg-shaped.

**overcome** (ō′ vər kəm′) *v.* To beat or conquer.

## P

**padlock** (pad′ lok′) *n.* A lock that can be taken off and put back on by unlocking a curved piece of metal.

**parlor** (pär′ lər) *n.* A somewhat private room used for business, conversation, entertaining, or receiving visitors.

**partial** (pär′ shəl) *adj.* Not complete.

**pasture** (pas′ chər) *n.* A field of grass in which cattle, horses, or sheep graze.

**pattern** (pat′ ərn) *n.* A model to follow when making clothes.

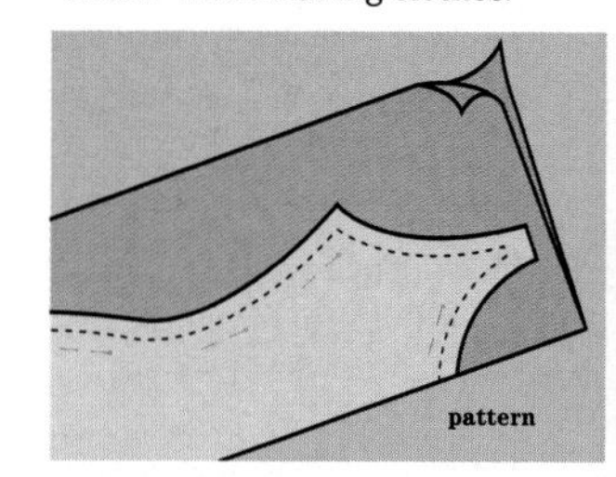


**pesky** (pes′ kē) *adj.* Causing trouble.

**petunia** (pi tōōn′ yə) *n.* A popular garden plant bearing funnel-shaped, colorful flowers.

**pitch** (pich) *n.* A dark, sticky substance used to make things waterproof.

**pitifully** (pit′ i flē) *adv.* Sadly.

**pleasure** (plezh′ ər) *v.* To please; to satisfy.

**porcelain** (por′ sə lin) *n.* A fine, delicate china.

**portrait** (por′ trət) *n.* A picture of someone.

**positively** (poz′ i tiv lē) *adv.* Certainly; for sure.

**posse** (pos′ ē) *n.* A group of people who gather to help a sheriff, usually on horses.

**poverty** (pov′ ər tē) *n.* The state of being poor.

**Pronunciation Key:** **at**; **lāte**; **câre**; **fäther**; **set**; **mē**; **it**; **kīte**; **ox**; **rōse**; **ô** in **bought**; **coin**; **bo͝ok**; **to͞o**; **form**; **out**; **up**; **ūse**; **tûrn**; **ə** sound in **a**bout, chick**e**n, penc**i**l, cann**o**n, circ**u**s; **chair**; **hw** in **wh**ich; **ring**; **shop**; **thin**; **th**ere; **zh** in trea**s**ure.

**prairie** (prâr′ ē) *n.* Flat or rolling land covered with grass.

**pretend** (pri tend′) *v.* To make believe.

**preserve** (pri zûrv′) *v.* To keep safe.

**profitable** (prof′ i tə bəl) *adj.* Making money; gainful.

**propose** (prə pōz′) *v.* To offer a plan; to suggest.

**pyramid** (pēr′ ə mid′) *n.* An object with triangular sides that meet at a point at the top.

## Q

**quantity** (kwän′ tə tē) *n.* A number or amount.

**quote** (kwōt) *v.* To state a price for something.

## R

**rampage** (ram′ pāj) *v.* To act wild.

**rawhide** (rô′ hīd′) *n.* A piece of cattle hide, or skin, that has not been tanned, or turned into leather.

**realty** (rē′ əl tē) *n.* Property, including land and buildings; real estate.

**recite** (ri sīt′) *v.* To tell aloud.

**reckon** (rek′ ən) *v.* To think; to suppose.

**recognize** (re′ kig nīz′) *v.* To be aware that someone or something is familiar.

**recollection** (re′ kə lek′ shən) *n.* Something remembered; memories.

**record** (rek′ ərd) *n.* A piece of writing that tells a memory of some facts or events. —*v.* (ri kord′) To write down facts or information about events.

**reflection** (ri flek′ shən) *n.* An image or likeness seen in a surface such as water or glass.

**reign** (rān) *v.* To rule.

**rein** (rān) *n.* A strap used for control by a rider of a horse or the driver of a carriage.

**rein in** (rān′ in′) *v.* To stop a horse by pulling the reins.

**relative** (re′ lə tiv) *n.* A person who is related by either blood or marriage to another.

**relieve** (ri lēv′) *v.* To comfort.

**reluctantly** (ri luk′ tənt lē) *adv.* Not willingly.

**remain** (ri mān) *v.* To stay the same or to stay in the same place.

**rent** (rent) *v.* To provide the use of something for a fee; to pay a fee in order to use something.

**repeat** (ri pēt′) *n.* Something that is done again.

**replenish** (ri ple′ nish) *v.* Fill up again.

**rescue** (res′ kū) *v.* To save or free.

**reservation** (re zər vā′ shən) *n.* 1. Public land set aside for the use of Native American tribes. 2. Something that is kept back or withheld.

**reserve** (ri zûrv′) *v.* To set aside for later use.

**rolling pin** (rō′ ling pin′) *n.* A cylinder with handles, used to roll dough flat.

rolling pin

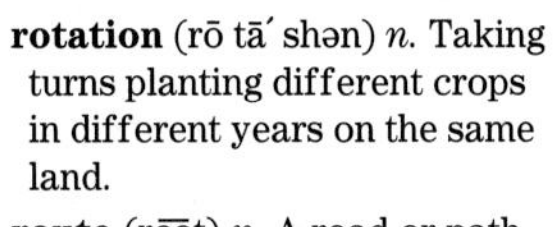

**rotation** (rō tā′ shən) *n.* Taking turns planting different crops in different years on the same land.

**route** (rōōt) *n.* A road or path.

## S

**saddle** (sa′ dəl) *n.* A leather seat for riding a horse.

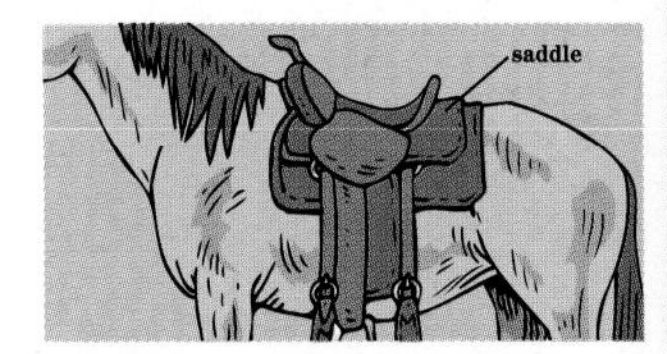


**safekeeping** (sāf′ kē′ ping) *n.* The act of protecting something.

**sagebrush** (sāj′ brush′) *n.* A grayish-green shrub that grows in the dry West.

**scarcely** (skârs′ lē) *adv.* Barely.

**scurry** (skûr′ ē) *v.* To move quickly as if in a great hurry.

**seasonal** (sē′ zə nl) *adj.* Ripe at a certain time of the year.

**seedling** (sēd′ ling) *n.* A very young plant.

**sensible** (sen′ sə bəl) *adj.* Having or showing good sense.

**serial** (sēr′ ē əl) *adj.* Arranged in a sequence or series.

**Pronunciation Key:** **a**t; l**ā**te; c**â**re; f**ä**ther; s**e**t; m**ē**; **i**t; k**ī**te; **o**x; r**ō**se; **ô** in bought; c**oi**n; b**o͝o**k; t**o͞o**; f**o**rm; **ou**t; **u**p; **ū**se; t**û**rn; **ə** sound in **a**bout, chick**e**n, penc**i**l, cann**o**n, circ**u**s; **ch**air; **hw** in **wh**ich; ri**ng**; **sh**op; **th**in; **th**ere; **zh** in trea**s**ure.

**sharecropper** (shâr′ krä′ pər) *n.* A person who farms someone else's land and is paid with a share of the crops.

**shear** (shēr) *v.* To clip; to cut.

**shun** (shun) *v.* To keep away from.

**silage** (sī′ lij) *n.* Feed for farm animals.

**silo** (sī′ lō) *n.* A tall building for storing food for animals on a farm.

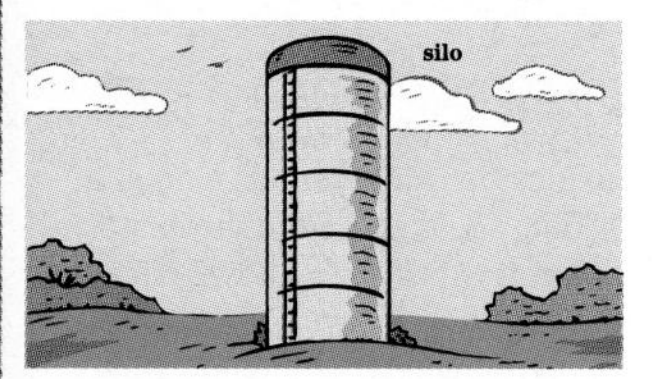


**skillet** (skil′ it) *n.* A frying pan.

**software** (sôft′ wâr′) *n.* Written programs and data used to operate a computer.

**sow** (sou) *n.* An adult female pig.

**spade** (spād) *n.* A digging tool with a flat blade and a long handle.

**speaker stick** (spē′ kər stik) *n.* A long, straight pole that is carved with the crest of the chief and shows that he is the leader of the tribe. When the chief holds it, the people listen to his words of advice or wisdom.

**splendid** (splen′ dəd) *adj.* Magnificent; glorious.

**sprawl** (sprôl) *v.* To spread out.

**spread** (spred) *v.* To stretch out in different directions.

**station** (stā′ shən) *n.* A place where a service is performed.

**string** (string) *v.* To stretch from one place to another.

**strongbox** (strông′ boks′) *n.* A sturdy box with a lock for holding money or other valuable items.

**suction** (suk′ shən) *n.* A pulling force that uses a sucking action.

**support** (sə port′) *v.* To provide all the money needed.

**surplus** (sûr′ plus) *n.* An amount more than is needed; an extra amount.

**suspicion** (sə spish′ ən) *n.* An idea that something is wrong, but without proof.

**swift** (swift) *adj.* Able to move quickly.

**symbol** (sim′ bəl) *n.* Something that represents or stands for something else.

## T

**tailor** (tā′ lər) *n.* A person who makes clothing.

**tatter** (tat´ ər) *v.* To tear.

**teeming** (tē´ ming) *adj.* Swarming; filled with.

**tempting** (temp´ ting) *adj.* Attractive; desirable.

**tender** (ten´ dər) *n.* Money, payment.

**terrapin** (ter´ ə pin) *n.* A type of turtle.

**thrive** (thrīv) *v.* To survive; to do well.

**tinker** (ting´ kər) *v.* To repair in a clumsy or makeshift way; to putter.

**toil** (toil) *v.* To work hard.

**token** (tō´ kən) *n.* A piece of metal shaped like a coin, used instead of money.

**totem** (tō´ təm) *n.* An animal or object from which a family traces its clan origins.

**totem pole** (tō´ təm pōl) *n.* A tall pole carved from a single log with a design showing several **totems** stacked one upon the other. Totem poles are made to honor an individual or to tell a legend or story.

**tractor** (trak´ tər) *n.* A farm vehicle that can pull wagons, plows, or other farming equipment.

**tradition** (trə dish´ ən) *n.* A custom handed down through many generations; the handing down of customs or beliefs from one generation to another.

**tranquil** (tran´ kwəl) *adj.* Calm and quiet.

**traveller** (tra´ və lər) *n.* A person who goes on a trip or a journey.

**treasure** (tre´ zhər) *n.* Something valuable.

**treasured** (trezh´ ərd) *adj.* Regarded as being of great value.

**tribe** (trīb) *n.* A group of persons or clans with one common language and living under a leader or chief.

**trickster** (trik´ stər) *n.* A character or person who delights in playing tricks on others and is skilled at doing so. In the **Tsimshian** stories, Raven was a well-known trickster.

**trillion** (tril´ yən) *n.* The number 1,000,000,000,000; a very large number.

**trinket** (trin´ kət) *n.* A small ornament.

**Tsimshian** (tsim´ shē an) *n.* A tribe of Northwest Coast Indians who came from the banks of the Nass and Skeena Rivers of British Columbia.

**turpentine** (tûr´ pən tīn´) *n.* An oil used to thin paint.

**twirl** (twûrl) *v.* To spin around.





**Pronunciation Key:** **a**t; l**ā**te; c**â**re; f**ä**ther; s**e**t; m**ē**; **i**t; k**ī**te; **o**x; r**ō**se; **ô** in b**ou**ght; c**oi**n; b**o͝o**k; t**o͞o**; f**o**rm; **ou**t; **u**p; **u**se; t**û**rn; **ə** sound in **a**bout, chick**e**n, penc**i**l, cann**o**n, circ**u**s; **ch**air; **hw** in **wh**ich; ri**ng**; **sh**op; **th**in; **th**ere; **zh** in trea**s**ure.

## U

**udder** (ud´ ər) *n.* The part of a cow's body from which it gives milk.

**unharness** (un här´ nis) *v.* To take off the leather straps that fasten a horse to a buggy.

**unpredictable** (un´ pri dik´ tə bəl) *adj.* Not able to be planned; not certain.

**unite** (ū nīt´) *v.* To work together as a group.

**untangle** (un tang´ gəl) *v.* To remove tangles or knots.

## V

**vanish** (van´ ish) *v.* To disappear.

**vital** (vīt´ l) *adj.* Necessary.

**volunteer** (vol´ ən tēr´) *v.* To offer to do something.

## W

**weaver** (wē´ vər) *n.* A person who makes fabric from thread or yarn.

**weigh** (wā) *v.* To measure how heavy something is.

**whinny** (hwi´ nē) *n.* A sound made by a horse.

**widow** (wid´ ō) *n.* A woman whose husband has died.

**willies** (wil´ ēz) *n. pl.* A nervous fear.

**wilt** (wilt) *v.* To droop; to fade.

**workbench** (wûrk´ bench´) *n.* A strong table used for working with tools and materials.

**wound** (wound) *v.* Past tense of **wind**: To wrap around and around.

## Y

**yam** (yam) *n.* A type of sweet potato.

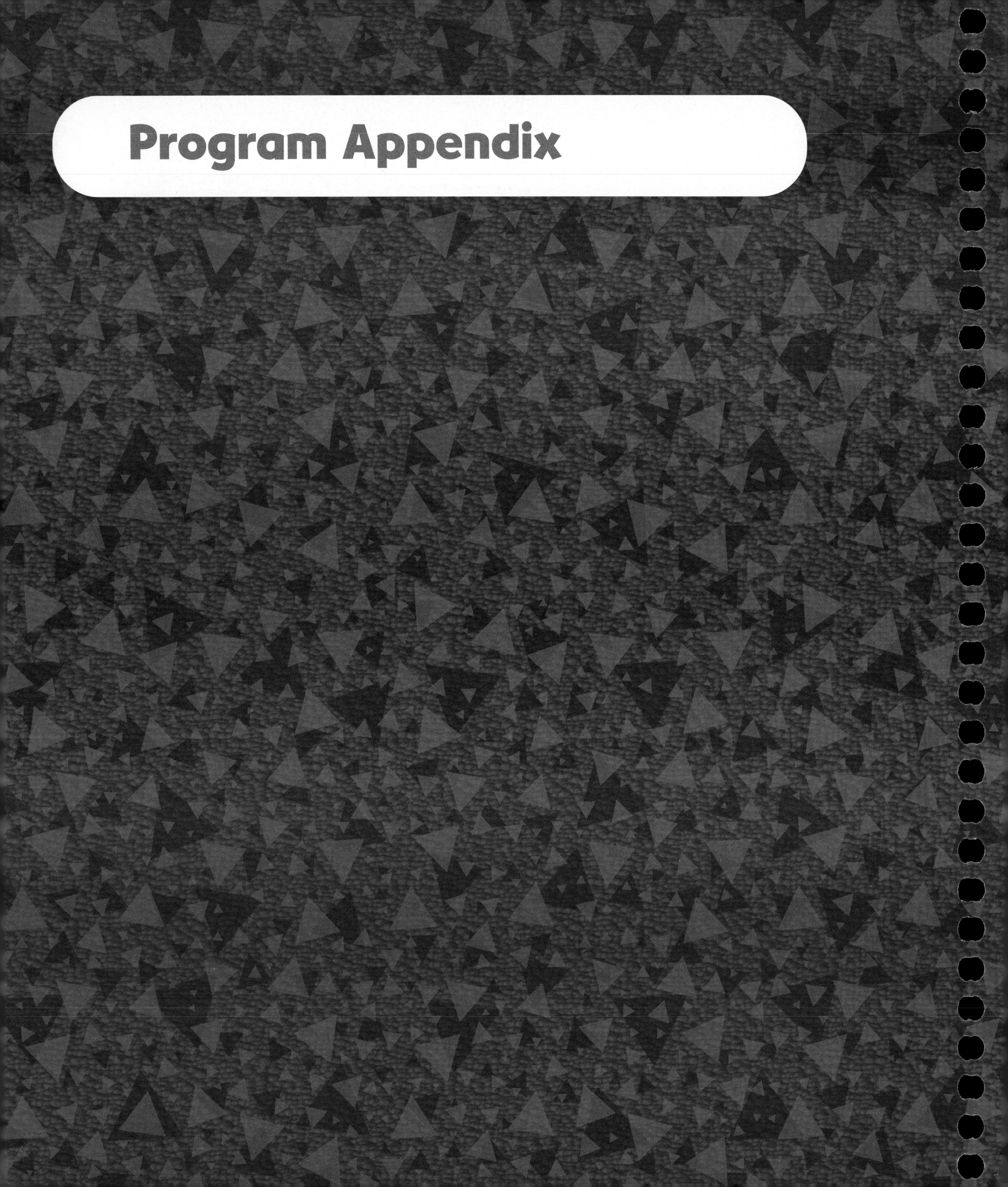

# Program Appendix

# Program Appendix

PROGRAM APPENDIX

The Program Appendix includes a step-by-step explanation of procedures for research-based, effective practices in reading instruction that are repeatedly used throughout ***SRA/Open Court Reading.*** These practices may also be used in other instructional materials.

## Table of Contents

### Effective Teaching Practices



### Teacher References

# Reading Materials and Techniques

PROGRAM APPENDIX

Different reading materials and techniques are appropriate at different stages of reading development. The purpose of this section is to discuss different types of reading materials and how they may be used most effectively.

## Reading Big Books

### Purpose

Many students come from homes where they are read to often, but a significant number of other students have not had this valuable experience. Big Books (Levels K and 1) offer all students crucial opportunities to confirm and expand their knowledge about print and reading. They are especially useful for shared reading experiences in the early grades.

The benefits of reading Big Books include engaging even nonreaders in:

- unlocking the books' messages.
- developing print awareness.
- participating in good reading behaviors.
- observing what a good reader does: remarking on the illustrations and the title, asking questions about the content and what might happen, making predictions, and clarifying words and ideas.
- promoting the insight that a given word is spelled the same way every time it occurs as high-frequency words are pointed out.
- reinforcing the correspondence between spoken and written words and spelling patterns.
- enjoying the illustrations and connecting them to the text to help students learn to explore books for enjoyment and information.
- interpreting and responding to literature and expository text before they can read themselves.

### Procedure for Reading Big Books

During the first reading of the Big Books, you will model reading behaviors and comprehension strategies similar to those that will later be taught formally. During the second reading, you will address print awareness and teach comprehension skills such as classifying and categorizing or sequencing, which help the reader organize information. In addition, you will teach skills such as making inferences and drawing conclusions, which help the reader focus on the deeper meaning of the text. At first, teachers should expect to do all of the reading but should not prevent students from trying to read on their own or from reading words they already know.

- **Activate Prior Knowledge.** Read the title of the selection and the author's and illustrator's names. At the beginning of each Big Book, read the title of the book and discuss what the whole book is about before going on to reading the first selection.
- **Discuss Prior Knowledge.** Initiate a brief discussion of any prior knowledge the students have that might help them understand the selection.
- **Browse the Selection.** Ask students to tell what they think the story might be about just from looking at the illustrations. This conversation should be brief so that the students can move on to a prereading discussion of print awareness.

***Big Books offer all students crucial opportunities to confirm and expand their knowledge about print and reading.***

- **Develop Print Awareness.** The focus of browsing the Big Books is to develop awareness of print. Urge students to tell what words or letters they recognize rather than what they expect the selection to be about.

  To develop print awareness, have students look through the selection page by page and comment on whatever they notice in the text. Some students may know some of the words, while others may only recognize specific letters or sounds. The key is to get the students to look at the print separately from the illustrations even before they have heard the actual text content. This process isolates print awareness so that it is not influenced by content. It also gives you a clearer idea of what your students do or do not know about print.
- **Read Aloud.** Read the selection aloud expressively. The reading enables the students simply to hear and enjoy the text as it is read through once. With this reading, you will model behaviors and comprehension strategies that all students will need to develop to become successful readers—for example, asking questions; clarifying unfamiliar words, first by using the pictures and later by using context; or predicting what might happen next.
- **Reread.** Read the selection expressively again. During the second reading of the stories, you will focus on teaching comprehension skills. Also, to develop print awareness, point to each word as it is read, thus demonstrating that text proceeds from left to right and from top to bottom and helping advance the idea that words are individual spoken and written units. Invite the students to identify the rhyming words in a poem or chime in on repetitive parts of text as you point to the words. Or students can read with you on this second reading, depending on the text.
- **Discuss Print.** Return to print awareness by encouraging discussion of anything the students noticed about the words. Young students should begin to realize that you are reading separate words that are separated by spaces. Later, students will begin to see that each word is made up of a group of letters. The students should be encouraged to discuss anything related to the print. For example, you might ask students to point to a word or count the number of words on a line. Or you might connect the words to the illustrations by pointing to a word and saying it and then asking the students to find a picture of that word.
- **Responding.** Responding to a selection is a way of insuring comprehension. Invite students to tell about the story by asking them what they like about the poem or story or calling on a student to explain in his or her own words what the poem or story tells about. Call on others to add to the telling as needed. For nonfiction selections, this discussion might include asking students what they learned about the topic and what they thought was most interesting.

### Tips for Using Big Books

- Make sure the entire group is able to see the book clearly while you are reading.
- If some students are able to read or predict words, encourage them to do so during the rereading.
- Encourage students to present and use their knowledge of print.
- Allow students to look at the Big Books whenever they wish.
- Provide small versions of the Big Books for students to browse through and try to read at their leisure.
- The reader of the Big Book should try to be part of the collaborative group of learners rather than the leader.

# Using the Pre-Decodable Books

## Purpose

**Pre-Decodable Books** play an important role in students' early literacy development by providing them with meaningful "reading" experiences before they are actually reading on their own and by expanding their awareness of the forms and uses of print. By following along as you read aloud a **Pre-Decodable Book,** students learn about the left-to-right and top-to-bottom progression of print on a page, the clues that indicate the beginnings and endings of sentences, the connections between pictures and words, and important book conventions, such as front and back covers, authors' and illustrators' names, title pages, and page numbers.

The **Pre-Decodable Books** provide students with opportunities to apply their growing knowledge of letter names, shapes, and sounds, and to become familiar with individual words.

Through retelling the story in a **Pre-Decodable Book,** predicting or wondering about what will happen, and asking and responding to questions about the book, students not only learn about the relationship between spoken and written language, they learn to think about what they have read.

## About the Pre-Decodable Books

Each **Pre-Decodable Book** contains a story that engages students' interest as it provides them with opportunities to practice what they are learning in their lessons. These "Pre-Decodable" stories each contain several high-frequency words that most students already have in their spoken vocabularies and that are a basic part of all meaningful stories. Learning to identify high-frequency words quickly, accurately, and effortlessly is a critical part of students' development as fluent, independent readers. The inside back cover of each **Pre-Decodable Book** contains a list of high-frequency words.

### How to Read the Pre-Decodable Books

- Before reading a **Pre-Decodable Book,** take time to familiarize students with any new **high-frequency words** in the book and to review previously introduced words. To reinforce the idea that it is important to know these words because they are used so often in print, always point out the words in context. For example, focus students' attention on the words in Big Book selections or on signs and posters around the classroom.
- Give each student a copy of the book. Tell students that you will read the book together. Hold up your book. Read the title. If the title has a rebus picture, point to it and tell the students what it is. Then point to the word beneath it and explain that the picture represents that word. Point to and read the names of the author and illustrator, reminding students that an author writes a book and an illustrator draws the pictures. Page through the book, pointing to and naming the rebus pictures. Have the students say the name of each rebus. To avoid confusion, always *tell* them the *exact* word that a rebus represents. *Don't encourage them to guess at its meaning.*
- Allow students time to browse through the book on their own, commenting on what they see in the illustrations and making predictions about what they think the book will be about. Encourage them to comment on anything special they notice about the story, the illustrations, or the words in the book.
- Help the students to find page 3. Read the book aloud without stopping. As you read, move your hand beneath the words to show the progression of print. Pause at each rebus as you say the word it represents, pointing first to the rebus, then to the word beneath it.
- Reread the book. This time, ask the students to point to and read the high-frequency words.
- Tell the students to follow along in their books as you read the story again. Read the title aloud, and then have the students read it with you. Reread page 3. Point to each rebus picture and ask a volunteer to "read" it. Point to the word beneath the picture and remind students that the picture shows what the word is. Continue through each page of the book, calling on volunteers to "read" and stopping as necessary to clarify and help students with words.
- After reading, answer any questions the students might have about the book. Encourage them to discuss the illustrations and to explain what is happening in each one.

# Reading Decodables and Building Fluency

## Purpose

The most urgent task of early reading instruction is to make written thoughts intelligible to students. This requires a balanced approach that includes systematic instruction in phonics as well as experiences with authentic literature. Thus, from the very beginning, ***Open Court Reading*** includes the reading of literature. At the beginning of first grade, when students are learning phonics and blending as a tool to access words, the teacher reads aloud. During this time students are working on using comprehension strategies and skills and discussing stories. As students learn the code and blend words, recognize critical sight words, and develop some level of fluency, they take more responsibility for the actual reading of the text.

This program has a systematic instruction in phonics that allows the students to begin reading independently. This instruction is supported by ***Open Court Reading*** **Decodable Books.**

## Practice

The ***Open Court Reading*** **Decodable Books** are designed to help the students apply, review, and reinforce their expanding knowledge of sound/spelling correspondences. Each story supports instruction in new phonic elements and incorporates elements and words that have been learned earlier. There are eight page and sixteen page **Decodable Books.** Grade K has eight-page **Decodable Books.** In Grade 1 the eight-page books focus on the new element introduced in the lesson, while the sixteen-page books review and reinforce the elements that have been taught since the last sixteen-page book. They review sounds from several lessons and provide additional reading practice. Grades 2–3 have eight-page **Decodable Books** in Getting Started, and sixteen-page books in the first 4–5 units of the grade level. The primary purpose is to provide practice reading the words. It is important that the students also attach meaning to what they are reading. Questions are often included in the ***Teacher's Edition*** to check both understanding and attention to words.

### Fluency

Fluency is the effortless ability to read or access words with seemingly little attention to decoding. It also involves grouping words into meaningful units and using expression appropriately. Fluency is critical but not sufficient for comprehension.

To become proficient readers who fully understand what they read, the whole process of decoding must become as automatic as possible. The students need to be so familiar with the sound/spellings and with the most common nondecodable sight words that they automatically process the letters or spellings and expend most of their energy on comprehending the meaning of the text.

While fluency begins in first grade, many students will continue to need practice in building fluency in second and third grades. Initially, students can use the ***Open Court Reading* Decodable Books** in grades 2 and 3, but fluency practice should include using materials from actual literature the students are reading.

## Procedure

### Preparing to Read

- Introduce and write on the board any nondecodable high-frequency or story words introduced or reviewed in the story. Tell the students how to pronounce any newly introduced high-frequency words. Then point to each new word and have the students say it. Have them read any previously introduced sight word in the Word Bank list. All of the ***Open Court Reading* Decodable Books** contain high-frequency words that may not be decodable. For example, the word *said* is a very common high-frequency word that is not decodable. Including words like *said* makes the language of the story flow smoothly and naturally. The students need to be able to recognize these words quickly and smoothly.
- Read the title. At the beginning of the year, you may need to read the title of the book to the students, but as the year goes on, you should have a student read it whenever possible. The sixteen-page ***Open Court Reading* Decodable Books** contain two related chapters, each using the same sounds and spellings. In such cases, read the title of the **Decodable** book, and then point out the two individual chapter titles. Have volunteers read the title of the chapter you are about to read.
- Browse the story. Have the students look through the story, commenting on whatever they notice in the text or illustrations and telling what they think the story will tell them.

### Reading the Story

After this browsing, the students will read the story a page at a time. Again, these books are designed to support the learning of sounds and spellings. The focus should not be on comprehension. Students should understand what they are reading, and they should feel free to discuss anything in the story that interests them. Any areas of confusion are discussed and clarified as they arise, as described below.

- Have the students read a page to themselves. Then call on one student to read the page aloud, or have the whole group read it aloud.
- If a student has difficulty with a word that can be blended, help her or him blend the word. Remind the student to check the **Sound/Spelling Cards** for help. If a word cannot be blended using the sound/spellings learned so far, pronounce the word for the student.
- If a student has trouble with a word or sentence, have the reader call on a classmate for help, and then continue reading after the word or sentence has been clarified. After something on a page has been clarified or discussed, have that page reread by a different student before moving on to the next page.
- Repeat this procedure for each page.
- Reread the story twice more, calling on different students to read or reading it in unison. These readings should go more quickly, with fewer stops for clarification.

### Responding to the Story

Once the story has been read aloud a few times, have the students respond as follows:

- Ask the students what hard words they found in the story and how they figured them out. They may mention high-frequency words they didn't recognize, words they had to blend, and words whose meanings they did not know.
- Invite the students to tell about the story, retelling it in their own words, describing what they liked about it, or citing what they found interesting or surprising. Specific suggestions to use are listed in the ***Teacher's Edition.***
- Questions are provided in the ***Teacher's Edition.*** They are designed to focus the students' attention on the words and not just the pictures. The questions require answers that cannot be guessed by looking at the pictures alone, such as a name, a bit of dialogue, or an action or object that is not pictured. Have the students point to the words, phrases, or sentences that answer the questions.

### Building Fluency

Building fluency is essential to gaining strong comprehension. The more fluent the students become, the more they can attend to the critical business of understanding the text. Opportunities for students to build fluency may include:

- Have students "partner read" the most recent ***Open Court Reading* Decodable Book** twice, taking turns reading a page at a time. The partners should switch the second time through so they are reading different pages from the ones they read the first time. If there is time left, the partners should choose any of the previously read stories to read together. Use this time for diagnosis, having one student at a time read with you.
- Making sure that the ***Open Court Reading* Decodable Books** are readily available in the classroom.
- Reading **Decodable Books** with as many students as possible one at a time.
- Reminding the students that they may read with partners during Workshop.

The only way the students can become fluent readers is to read as much and as often as possible.

# Reading the Student Anthologies

## Purpose

Reading is a complex process that requires students not only to decode what they read but also to understand and respond to it. The purpose of this section is to help you identify various reading behaviors used by good readers and to encourage those behaviors in your students.

## Reading Behaviors and Comprehension Strategies

There are four basic behaviors that good readers engage in during reading. These behaviors include the application of certain comprehension strategies, which are modeled while reading the Student Anthology (Levels 1–6).

### Setting Reading Goals and Expectations

Good readers set reading goals and expectations before they begin reading. This behavior involves a variety of strategies that will help students prepare to read the text.

- **Activate prior knowledge.** When good readers approach a new text, they consider what they already know about the subject or what their experiences have been in reading similar material.
- **Browse the text.** To get an idea of what to expect from a text, good readers look at the title and the illustrations. They may look for potential problems, such as difficult words. When browsing a unit, have students glance quickly at each selection, looking briefly at the illustrations and the print. Have them tell what they think they might be learning about as they read the unit.
- **Decide what they expect from the text.** When reading for pleasure, good readers anticipate enjoying the story or the language. When reading to learn something, they ask themselves what they expect to find out.

### Responding to Text

Good readers are active readers. They interact with text by using the following strategies:

- **Making connections.** Good readers make connections between what they read and what they already know. They pay attention to elements in the text that remind them of their own experiences.
- **Visualizing, or picturing.** Good readers visualize what is happening in the text. They form mental images as they read. They picture the setting, the characters, and the action in a story. When reading expository text, good readers picture the objects, processes, or events described. Visualizing helps readers understand descriptions of complex activities or processes.
- **Asking questions.** Good readers ask questions that may prepare them for what they will learn. If their questions are not answered in the text, they may try to find answers elsewhere and thus add even more to their store of knowledge.
- **Predicting.** Good readers predict what will happen next. When reading fiction, they make predictions about what they are reading and then confirm or revise those predictions as they go.
- **Thinking about how the text makes you feel.** Well-written fiction touches readers' emotions; it sparks ideas.

### Checking Understanding

One of the most important behaviors good readers exhibit is the refusal to continue reading when something fails to make sense. Good readers continually assess their understanding of the text with strategies such as:

- **Interpreting.** As they read, good readers make inferences that help them understand and appreciate what they are reading.
- **Summing up.** Good readers sum up to check their understanding as they read. Sometimes they reread to fill in gaps in their understanding.
- **Monitoring and adjusting reading speed.** Good readers monitor their understanding of what they read. They slow down as they come to difficult words and passages. They speed up as they read easier passages.

### Monitoring and Clarifying Unfamiliar Words and Passages

- **Apply decoding skills** to sound out unknown words.
- **Determine what is unclear** to find the source of the confusion.
- **Apply context clues** in text and illustrations to figure out the meanings of words or passages.
- **Reread the passage** to make sure the passage makes sense.
- **Check a dictionary or the glossary** to understand the meanings of words not clarified by clues or rereading.

## Procedures

### Modeling and Thinking Aloud

Modeling and encouraging students to think aloud as they attempt to understand text can demonstrate for everyone how reading behaviors are put into practice. The most effective models will be those that come from your own reading. Using questions such as the following, as well as your students' questions and comments, will make both the text and the strategic reading process more meaningful to students.

- What kinds of things did you wonder about?
- What kinds of things surprised you?
- What new information did you learn?
- What was confusing until you reread or read further?

Model comprehension strategies in a natural way, and choose questions and comments that fit the text you are reading. Present a variety of ways to respond to text.

- Pose questions that you really do wonder about.
- Identify with characters by comparing them with yourself.
- React emotionally by showing joy, sadness, amusement, or surprise.
- Show empathy with or sympathy for characters.
- Relate the text to something that has happened to you or to something you already know.
- Show interest in the text ideas.
- Question the meaning or clarity of the author's words and ideas.

### Encouraging Students' Responses and Use of Strategies

Most students will typically remain silent as they try to figure out an unfamiliar word or a confusing passage. Encourage students to identify specifically what they are having difficulty with. Once the problem has been identified, ask the students to suggest a strategy for dealing with the problem. Remind students to:

- Treat problems encountered in text as interesting learning opportunities.
- Think out loud about text challenges.
- Help each other build meaning. Rather than tell what a word is, students should tell how they figured out the meanings of challenging words and passages.
- Consider reading a selection again with a partner after reading it once alone. Partner reading provides valuable practice in reading for fluency.
- Make as many connections as they can between what they are reading and what they already know.
- Visualize to clarify meanings or enjoy descriptions.
- Ask questions about what they are reading.
- Notice how the text makes them feel.

PROGRAM APPENDIX

# Reading Techniques

## Reading Aloud

### Purpose

Adults read a variety of materials aloud to students. These include Big Books, picture books, and novels. Research has shown that students who are read to are more likely to develop the skills they need to read successfully on their own.

In every grade level of **Open Court Reading** there are opportunities for teachers to read aloud to students. At the beginning of each unit is a Read-Aloud selection tied to the unit theme. This Read-Aloud selection allows students the opportunity to think about the unit theme before reading selections on their own.

Reading aloud at any age serves multiple purposes. Reading aloud:

- Provokes students' curiosity about text.
- Conveys an awareness that text has meaning.
- Demonstrates the various reasons for reading text (to find out about the world around them, to learn useful new information and new skills, or simply for pleasure).
- Exposes students to the "language of literature," which is more complex than the language they ordinarily use and hear.
- Provides an opportunity to teach the problem-solving strategies that good readers employ. As the students observe you interacting with the text, expressing your own enthusiasm, and modeling your thinking aloud, they perceive these as valid responses and begin to respond to text in similar ways.

### Procedures

The following set of general procedures for reading aloud is designed to help you maximize the effectiveness of Read-Aloud sessions.

- **Read-aloud sessions.** Set aside time each day to read aloud.
- **Introduce the story.** Tell the students that you are going to read a story aloud to them. Tell its title and briefly comment on the topic. To allow the students to anticipate what will happen in the story, be careful not to summarize.
- **Activate prior knowledge.** Ask whether anyone has already heard the story. If so, ask them to see if this version is the same as the one they have heard. If not, activate prior knowledge by saying, "First, let's talk a little about _____." If the story is being read in two (or more) parts, before reading the second part, ask the students to recall the first part.
- **Before reading.** Invite students to interrupt your reading if there are any words they do not understand or ideas they find puzzling. Throughout the reading, encourage them to do this.
- **Read the story expressively.** Occasionally react verbally to the story by showing surprise, asking questions, giving an opinion, expressing pleasure, or predicting events. Think-aloud suggestions are outlined below.
- **Use Comprehension Strategies.** While reading aloud to the students, model the use of comprehension strategies in a natural, authentic way. Remember to try to present a variety of ways to respond to text. These include visualizing, asking questions, predicting, making connections, clarifying, and summarizing.
- **Retell.** When you have finished reading the story, call on volunteers to retell it.
- **Discuss.** After reading, discuss with the students their own reactions: how the story reminded them of things that have happened to them, what they thought of the story, and what they liked best about the story.
- **Reread.** You may wish to reread the selection on subsequent occasions focusing the discussion on the unit theme.

#### Think-Aloud Responses

The following options for modeling thinking aloud will be useful for reading any story aloud. Choose responses that are most appropriate for the selection you are reading.

- **React emotionally** by showing joy, sadness, amusement, or surprise.
- **Ask questions** about ideas in the text. This should be done when there are points or ideas that you really do wonder about.
- **Identify with characters** by comparing them to yourself.
- **Show empathy with or sympathy for** characters.
- **Relate the text to something** you already know or something that has happened to you.
- **Show interest** in the text ideas.
- **Question the meaning and/or clarity** of the author's words and ideas.

#### Questions to Help Students Respond

At reasonable stopping points in reading, ask the students general questions in order to get them to express their own ideas and to focus their attention on the text.

- What do you already know about this?
- What seems really important here? Why do you think so?
- Was there anything that you didn't understand? What?
- What did you like best about this?
- What new ideas did you learn from this?
- What does this make you wonder about?

## Reading Roundtable

### Purpose

Adult readers discuss their reading, give opinions on it, and recommend books to each other. Reading Roundtable, an activity students may choose to participate in during **Workshop**, provides the same opportunity for students in the classroom. Sessions can be small or large. During Reading Roundtable, students share the reading they do on their own. They can discuss a book they have all read, or one person can review a book for the others and answer questions from the group.

During Reading Roundtable, students can discuss and review a variety of books:

- Full-length versions of Anthology selections.
- Classroom Library selections.
- Books that students learn about when discussing authors and illustrators.
- Books related to the investigations of unit concepts can be shared with others who might want to read them.
- Interesting articles from magazines, newspapers, and other sources.

### Procedures

#### Encouraging Reading

- Read aloud to your students regularly. You can read Classroom Library selections or full-length versions of Student Anthology selections.
- Provide a time each day for students to read silently. This time can be as short as 10–15 minutes but should be strictly observed. You should stop what you are doing and read. Students should be allowed to choose their own reading materials during this time and record their reactions in the Response Journal section of their Writer's Notebook.
- Establish a classroom library and reading center with books from the school or local library or ask for donations of books from students, parents, and community members.
- Take your students to the school library or to the public library.

#### Conducting a Reading Roundtable

- When a student reviews a book others have not read, he or she can use some of the sentence starters to tell about the book. These may include, "This book is about . . . , I chose this book because. . . , What I really like/don't like about this book is . . . " and so on.
- When several students read the same book and discuss it during Reading Roundtable, they can use discussion starters. If the book is from the Classroom Library, they can discuss how it relates to the unit concepts.

# Introducing Sounds and Letters



## Purpose

In ***SRA/Open Court Reading***, students learn to relate sounds to letters in Kindergarten through the use of thirty-one **Alphabet Sound Cards** (Level K). In the upper grade levels, **Sound Spelling Cards** (Levels 1–3) are used to relate sounds and spellings. The purpose of the **Alphabet Sound Cards** is to remind the students of the sounds of the English language and their letter correspondences. These cards are a resource for the students to use to remember sound-letter associations for both reading and writing.

Each card contains the capital and small letter, and a picture that shows the sound being produced. For instance, the **Monkey** card introduces the /m/ sound and shows a monkey looking at bananas and saying */m/ /m/ /m/*. The name of the picture on each card contains the target sound at the beginning of the word for the consonants and in the middle for most of the vowels. Vowel letters are printed in red and consonants are printed in black. In addition, the picture associates a sound with an action. This action-sound association is introduced through a short, interactive story found in the ***Teacher's Edition*** in which the pictured object or character "makes" the sound of the letter. Long vowels are represented by a tall—or "long"—picture of the letters themselves, rather than by a picture for action-sound association.

## Procedures

- Display the cards 1–26 with the picture sides to the wall. Initially post the first twenty-six cards in alphabetical order so that only the alphabet letters show. The short vowel cards may be posted as they are introduced later. As you introduce the letter sound, you will turn the card to show the picture and the letter on the other side. Once the cards are posted, do not change their positions so that the students can locate the cards quickly.
- Before turning a card, point to the letter. Ask students to tell what they know about the letter. For example, they are likely to know its name and possibly its sound if the letter is one they have already worked with.
- Turn the card and show the picture. Tell the students the name of the card, and explain that it will help them to remember the sound the letter makes.
- Read the story that goes with the letter. Read it expressively, emphasizing the words with the target sound and the isolated sound when it occurs. Have the students join in to produce the sound.
- Repeat the story a few times, encouraging all students to say the sound along with you.
- Follow the story with the cards for the target sound. (These are listed within the lessons.)
- Name each picture, and have students listen for the target sound at the beginning of the word. Ask students to repeat the words and the sound.
- For every letter sound, a listening activity follows the introduction of the cards. Lead the students in the "Listening for the Sound" activity to reinforce the letter sound.
- To link the sound and the letter, demonstrate how to form the uppercase and lowercase letter by writing on the board or on an overhead transparency. The students practice forming the letter and saying the sound as they write.

### Alphabet Sound Cards

The pictures and letters on the **Alphabet Sound Cards (Wall Cards)** also appear on the small sets of **Alphabet Sound Cards (Individual)**. The Teacher's Edition specifically suggests that you use the **Individual Alphabet Sound Cards** for some activities. You may also use the small cards for review and for small-group reteaching and practice sessions. Have sets of the cards available for the students to use during **Workshop** either alone or with partners. Add each small card to the Activity Center after you have taught the lesson in which the corresponding **Alphabet Sound Card** is introduced. Here are some suggestions for activities using the **Alphabet Sound Cards**:

1. **Saying sounds from pictures.** The leader flashes pictures as the others say the sound each picture represents.
2. **Saying sounds.** The leader flashes the letters on the cards as the others say the sound that the letters represent.
3. **Naming words from pictures.** The leader flashes pictures. The others say the sound, and then say a word beginning with that sound.
4. **Writing letters from the pictures.** Working alone, a student looks at a picture and then writes the letter for the sound that picture represents.

## Tips

- Throughout the beginning lessons, help students remember that vowels are special by reminding them that vowels sometimes say their names in words. For example, the picture of the *a* on the long *a* **Alphabet Sound Card** is long because the long *a* says its name. The short *a* **Alphabet Sound Card** pictures the lamb, because the lamb makes the short *a* sound, and you can hear the sound in the word, *lamb*. In the later lessons, students will use both sets of cards to help them remember that the vowels have both a short and a long sound.
- From the very beginning, encourage students to use the **Alphabet Sound Cards** as a resource to help them with their work.
- Mastery of letter recognition is the goal students should reach so that they will be prepared to link each letter with its associated sound. If students have not yet mastered the names of the letters, it is important to work with them individually in **Workshop**, or at other times during the day.
- The *Kk* card is a little tricky. A camera makes the /k/ sound when it clicks, and the word *camera* begins with the /k/ sound. However, the word *camera* is not spelled with a *k*. While you need not dwell on this, be aware that some students may be confused by the fact that the *Cc* and *Kk* cards have the same picture.
- The picture on the *Qq* card depicts ducks, *quacking ducks*. Make sure that the students consistently call them *quacking ducks*, not *ducks*, and that they focus on the /kw/ sound.

# The Alphabetic Principle

## Purpose

A major emphasis in the kindergarten program is on letter recognition and attending to sounds. Students need to learn the alphabetic principle: that letters work together in a systematic way to connect spoken language to written words. This understanding is the foundation for reading. Students are not expected to master letter/sound correspondence at the beginning of kindergarten, nor are they expected to blend sounds into words themselves. They are only expected to become an "expert" on their Special Letter as they learn how the alphabet works. Through this introduction to the alphabetic principle, the students will have the basic understanding required to work through the alphabet letter by letter, attaching sounds to each.

Key concepts of the Alphabetic Principle include:

- A limited number of letters combine in different ways to make many different words.
- Words are composed of sounds and letters represent those sounds.
- Anything that can be pronounced can be spelled.
- Letters and sounds can be used to identify words.
- Meaning can be obtained by using letters and sounds to figure out words.

## Procedures for Kindergarten

The following steps can be used for introducing letters and sounds in Kindergarten. These steps may be adapted for students at other grades if they do not understand the alphabetic principle. The tone of these activities should be informal, fun, and fast-paced. The purpose of these activities is to familiarize the students with how the alphabet works by having them participate in group play with letters and sounds.

### Introducing Letters

- Reinforce the idea that anything that can be pronounced can be spelled with the letters of the alphabet.
- Tell the students that you can spell any word. Have them give you words to spell.
- Write the words on the board, and show students that the words contain the letters displayed on the **Alphabet Sound Cards**.
- Have students help you spell the words by pointing to letters as you say them and then write them.
- Encourage students to spell each word letter by letter.

### Letter Expert Groups

- Have **Letter Cards** (Levels K and 1) available for the following set of letters: *b, d, f, h, l, m, n, p, s, t*. You will need two or three cards for each letter. (You will not need the **Alphabet Sound Cards** until later.)
- You will be the letter expert for the vowels.
- Divide the class into groups of two or three and assign each group a letter. Give each student the appropriate **Letter Card**.
- Tell the students that they are now in their Letter Expert groups and that they are going to become experts on their Special Letter's name, shape, and sound.

***Students need to learn the alphabetic principle: that letters work together in a systematic way to connect spoken language to written words. This understanding is the foundation for reading.***

### Making Words

- Begin each lesson with a rehearsal of each group's letter name.
- Demonstrate how letters work by writing a word in large letters on the board.
- Tell the students the experts for each letter in the word should hold up their **Letter Cards** and name the letter. One member of the group should stand in front of their letter on the board.
- Continue until all letters in the word are accounted for. Remember that you are responsible for the vowels.
- Demonstrate that you can make different words by changing a letter or by changing the letter order.

### Identifying Sounds in Words

- Use the **Alphabet Sound Cards** to demonstrate that every letter has at least one sound.
- Give each student the **Alphabet Sound Card** for his or her Special Letter.
- Point out the pictures on the cards. Explain that each card has a picture of something that makes the letter's sound. The picture will help them remember the sound.
- Tell each group the sound for its letter. (Remember, you are the expert for the vowels.)
- Quickly have each group rehearse its letter's name and sound.
- Write a word on the board in large letters. Say the word first sound-by-sound and then blend the word.
- For each letter/sound in the word, have one student from each Letter Expert group come forward, stand in front of the appropriate letter, and hold their cards. Although only one member of the group may come forward with the **Letter Card** or **Alphabet Sound Card,** all students in a Special Letter group should say the name and/or sound of their letter when it occurs in words.
- Say the word again, pointing to the **Alphabet Sound Cards**.
- Ask students who are not already standing to help you hold the vowel cards.
- Vary the activity by changing one letter sound and having an expert for that letter come forward.
- End the activity for each word by saying the sounds in the words one by one and then saying the entire word. Encourage the students to participate.

## Tips

- Remind the students to use the picture on the **Alphabet Sound Card** for their Special Letter to help them remember the letter's sound. The students are expected only to "master" their own Special Letter and share the information with their classmates. At this point in the year, they are not expected to blend and read the words by themselves. These are group activities in which you work with the students to help them gain insight into the alphabet.
- Have students note that what they learn about the letters and words applies to the words they work with in Big Book selections.
- Occasionally, have students find their special letters in a Big Book selection. Play some of the letter replacement and rearrangement games with words encountered in the Big Books.

# Developing the Alphabetic Principle

## Purpose

The following activities are extended to provide kindergarten students with a more thorough understanding of how sounds "work" in words. In this group of exercises, the students are introduced to specific letter/sound correspondences, consonants and short vowels. The students have previously been introduced to vowels and their special characteristics. This understanding is extended by introducing students to the convention that a vowel has a short sound in addition to its long sound. With this information and a carefully structured set of activities, the students can begin to explore and understand the alphabetic principle in a straightforward and thorough manner. The students not only listen for sounds in specified positions in words; they also link sounds to their corresponding letters. The activities in this group of lessons lay the groundwork for students to work their way through the entire alphabet as they learn letter-sound associations and to understand the purpose and the value of this learning.

Move the students quickly through these activities. Do not wait for all the students to master each letter/sound correspondence before going on. The students will have more opportunities to achieve mastery. The goal of these activities is for the students to obtain a basic understanding of the alphabetic principle.

## Procedures

### Introducing Consonant Letters and Sounds

- Point to the **Alphabet Sound Card** and name the letter.
- Point to the picture. Tell the students the sound of the letter and how the picture helps them to remember the sound. Repeat the sound several times.
- Tell the students you will read them the short story or an alliterative sentence to help them remember the sound of the letter. Read the story several times, emphasizing the words with the target sound. Have the students join in and say the sound.
- After introducing and reviewing a letter/sound correspondence, summarize the information on the **Alphabet Sound Card**.

### Generating Words with the Target Sound

- Brainstorm to create a list of words that begin with the target sound. Write the words on the board or on a chart. Include any of the students' names that begin with the target sound.
- Play the *I'm Thinking of Something That Starts With* game. Begin with the target sound and add clues until the students guess the word. If the students guess a word that does not begin with the target sound, emphasize the beginning sound and ask if the word begins with the target sound.
- Silly Sentences. Make silly sentences with the students that include many words with the target sound. Encourage the students to participate by extending the sentences: *Mary mopes. Mary mopes on Monday. Mary and Michael mope on Monday in Miami.*

### Listening for Initial Sounds

- Give each student a **Letter Card** for the target sound, /s/.
- Point to the picture on the **Alphabet Sound Card**, and have the students give the sound, /s/.
- Tell the students to listen for the first sound in each word you say. If it is /s/, they should hold up their *s* cards. Establish a signal so that the students know when to respond.
- Read a list of words, some beginning with /s/, some beginning with other sounds.

### Listening for Final Sounds

The procedure for listening for the final sound of a word is the same as that for listening for the initial sound. The students may need to be reminded throughout the activity to pay attention to the *final* sound.

- Read a list of words, some ending with the target sound and some ending with other sounds. Avoid words that begin with the target sound.

### Linking the Sound to the Letter

- **Word Pairs (initial sounds).** Write pairs of words on the board. One of each pair should begin with the target sound. Say the word beginning with the target sound, and ask the students to identify it. Remind them to listen for the target sound at the beginning of the word, to think about which letter makes that sound, and to find the word that begins with that letter. For example,
  Target sound: /s/
  Word pair: *fit sit*
  Which word is *sit*?
- **Word Pairs (final sounds).** Follow the same procedure used for initial sounds, and direct the students to think about the sound that they hear at the end of the word. Since it is often more difficult for the students to attend to the ending sound, you may need to lead them through several pairs of words. Remind the students to listen for the target sound and to think about which letter makes that sound.
- **Writing Letters.** Using either of the handwriting systems outlined in the Program Appendix of ***SRA/Open Court Reading***, or the system in use at your school, have students practice writing uppercase and lowercase letters. Remind the students about the letter sound, and have them repeat it.

### Comparing Initial Consonant Sounds

This activity is exactly like **Listening for Initial Sounds** except that the students must discriminate between two sounds. They are given **Letter Cards** for both sounds and must hold up the appropriate card when they hear the sound.

### Comparing Final Consonant Sounds

This activity is exactly like listening for final sounds except that the students must discriminate between two sounds. They are given **Letter Cards** for both sounds and must hold up the appropriate card when they hear the sound.

### Linking the Consonant Sound to the Letter

In this activity to help students link sounds and letters, the students will make words either by adding initial consonants to selected word parts or by adding a different final consonant to a consonant-vowel-consonant combination.

## The Alphabetic Principle: How the Alphabet Works (continued)



### Introducing Short Vowel Sounds

- Tell the students that the vowels are printed in red to remind them that they are special letters. (They are not special because they are printed in red.) They are special because they have more than one sound, and every word must have a vowel sound.
- Point to the long *Aa* **Alphabet Sound Card,** and remind the students that this letter is called a *vowel.* Vowels sometimes say their names in words: for example, *say, day, tray.* This vowel sound is called long *a.*
- Have the students repeat the sound.
- Sometimes vowels say different sounds. Point to the picture of the lamb on the short *Aa* card, and tell students that *a* also makes the sound heard in the middle of *lamb.* This is the short *a.* Read the short vowel story to help the students remember the short *a.*
- Have all the students join in saying /a/ /a/ /a/.

### Listening for Short Vowel Sounds Versus Long Vowel Sounds

- Tell the students that you will read words with long *a* and short *a.* Review the two sounds.
- Give the students a signal to indicate when they hear the vowel sound. You may want one signal for short *a,* such as scrunching down, and another for long *a,* such as stretching up tall.
- Continue with lists of words such as: *add, back, aid, tan, bake, tame.*

### Linking the Vowel Sound to the Letter

- Writing Letters. Have students practice writing the letter and review the sound of the letter.
- In this activity to help students link sounds and letters, the students will make words either by adding initial consonants to selected word parts or by adding a different final consonant to a consonant-vowel-consonant combination. Change the beginning of the word or the word ending, but retain the vowel sound to make new words:

| | | | |
|---|---|---|---|
| *at* | *hat* | *mat* | *pat* |
| *ap* | *map* | *tap* | *sap* |
| *am* | *Sam* | *Pam* | *ham* |

### Comparing Short Vowel Sounds

This activity requires students to discriminate between short vowel sounds in the middle of words. Review the vowel sounds.

- Say a word, and have the students repeat it. Establish a signal to indicate whether they hear short *a* or short *o* in the middle of the word. For example, they can hold up the appropriate **Letter Card** when they hear a sound. Sample words: *cap, cot, rat, rot, rack, rock.*

### Linking the Sound to the Letter

- In this activity write a word on the board, and help the students say it.
- Change the word by changing the vowel. Help the students say the new word, for example, *map, mop; hot, hat; pot, pat.*
- For a variation of this activity, write the pairs of words, and simply have the students say which word is the target word. For example, the students see *tap* and *top.* Ask which word *top* is, directing the students' attention to the vowel.

## Tips

- Lead and model the exercises as necessary until the students begin to catch on and can participate with confidence.
- To keep the students focused on the various activities, have them tell you the task for each activity. For example, after telling the students to listen for final sounds, ask the students what they will be listening for.
- Actively involve the students by giving them opportunities to tell what they know rather than supplying the information for them. Do they know the letter name? Do they know the sound? Can they think of words that begin with the sound?
- Keeping the students focused on the idea that they are learning about sounds and letters so they can read these books themselves makes the lessons more relevant for the students.

# Phonemic Awareness

The basic purpose of providing structured practice in phonemic awareness is to help the students hear and understand the sounds from which words are made. Before students can be expected to understand the sound/symbol correspondence that forms the base of written English, they need to have a strong working knowledge of the sound relationships that make up the spoken language. This understanding of spoken language lays the foundation for the transition to written language.

Phonemic awareness activities provide the students with easy practice in discriminating the sounds that make up words. Phonemic awareness consists of quick, gamelike activities designed to help students understand that speech is made up of distinct, identifiable sounds. The playful nature of the activities makes them appealing and engaging, while giving the students practice and support for learning about language. Once the students begin reading and writing, this experience with manipulating sounds will help them use what they know about sounds and letters to sound out and spell unfamiliar words when they read and write.

The two main formats for teaching phonemic awareness are oral blending and segmentation. These are supported by occasional discrimination activities and general wordplay. Oral blending encourages students to combine sounds to make words. Segmentation, conversely, requires them to isolate sounds from words. Other activities support discrimination, or recognition, of particular sounds. Sometimes simple songs, rhymes, or games engage students in wordplay. In these, the students manipulate words in a variety of ways. From these playful activities, the students derive serious knowledge about language.

As the students progress through different phonemic awareness activities, they will become proficient at listening for and reproducing the sounds they hear. It is essential for their progression to phonics and reading that they are able to hear the sounds and the patterns used to make up recognizable words. The phonemic awareness activities support the phonics instruction, but the activities are oral and do not focus on sound/spelling correspondences. Because the students are not expected to read the words they are experimenting with, any consonant and vowel sounds may be used, even if the students have not been formally taught the sound and its spellings.

## Oral Blending

### Purpose

In oral blending, the students are led through a progression of activities designed to help them hear how sounds are put together to make words.

Until students develop an awareness of the component parts of words, they have no tools with which to decode words or put letters together to form words. Oral blending helps students master these component parts of words, from syllables down to single sounds, or phonemes. Oral blending is not to be confused with the formal blending of specific sounds whose spellings the students will be taught through phonics instruction. Oral blending does not depend on the recognition of written words; it focuses instead on hearing the sounds.

Oral blending focuses on hearing sounds through a sequence that introduces the most easily distinguished word parts and then systematically moves to sound blending that contains all the challenges of phonic decoding (except letter recognition). This sequence provides support for the least-prepared student—one who comes to school with no concept of words or sounds within words. At the same time, the lively pace and playful nature of oral blending activities hold the interest of students who already have some familiarity with words and letters.

Oral blending prepares students for phonics instruction by developing an awareness of the separate sounds that make up speech. Oral blending activities then continue in concert with phonics instruction to reinforce and extend new learning. And, because these activities involve simply listening to and reproducing sounds, oral blending need not be restricted to the sounds students have been or will be taught in phonics.

The tone of the activities should be playful and informal and should move quickly. Although these activities will provide information about student progress, they are not diagnostic tools. Do not expect mastery. Those students who have not caught on will be helped more by varied experiences than by more drilling on the same activity.

### Procedures

Following is a description of the progression of oral blending activities.

#### Syllable Blending

Syllables are easier to distinguish than individual sounds (phonemes), so students can quickly experience success in forming meaningful words. Tell the students that you are going to say some words in two parts. Tell them to listen carefully so that they can discover what the words are. Read each word, pronouncing each part distinctly with a definite pause between syllables broken by. . . . The lists of words that follow are arranged in sequence from easy to harder. They cover different types of cues. At any point where they fit in the sequence, include multisyllable names of students in the class.

***Model***

**TEACHER:** *dino . . . saur. What's the word?*

**STUDENTS:** *dinosaur*

***Example Words***

- First part of the word cues the whole word:
  *vita . . . min* *vaca . . . tion*
  *hippopot . . . amus* *ambu . . . lance*
- Two distinct words easily combined:
  *butter. . . fly* *straw. . . berry*
  *surf . . . board* *basket . . . ball*

## Phonemic Awareness (continued)



- Two distinct words, but first word could cue the wrong ending:
  *tooth . . . ache tooth . . . paste*
  *water . . . fall water . . . melon*
- First part, consonant + vowel, not enough to guess whole word:
  *re . . . member re . . . frigerator*
  *bi . . . cycle bi . . . ology*
- Identifying clues in second part:
  *light . . . ning sub . . . ject in . . . sect*
- Last part, consonant + vowel sound, carries essential information:
  *yester . . . day rain . . . bow*
  *noi . . . sy pota . . . to*
- Changing the final part changes the word:
  *start . . . ing start . . . er start. . . ed*

### Initial Consonant Sounds

Initial consonant blending prepares students for consonant replacement activities that will come later. Tell the students that you will ask them to put some sounds together to make words. Pronounce each word part distinctly, and make a definite pause at the breaks indicated. When a letter is surrounded by slash marks, pronounce the letter's sound, not its name. When you see /s/, for example, you will say "ssss," not "ess." The words that follow are arranged from easy to harder. At any point where they fit in the sequence, include names of students in the class.

***Model***

**Teacher:** /t/ . . . iger. What's the word?

**Students:** tiger

***Example Words***

- Separated consonant blend, with rest of word giving strong cue to word identity:
  */b/ . . . roccoli /k/ . . . racker*
  */f/ . . . lashlight /k/ . . . reature*
- Held consonant that is easy for students to hear, with rest of word giving strong cue:
  */s/ . . . innamon /l/ . . . adybug*
  */s/ . . . eventeen /n/ . . . ewspaper*
- Stop consonant that is harder for students to hear preceding vowel, with rest of word giving strong cue:
  */t/. . . adpole /p/ . . . iggybank*
  */d/ . . . ragonfly /b/ . . . arbecue*
- Single-syllable words and words in which the second part gives a weaker cue:
  */s/ . . . ing /l/ . . . augh /v/ . . . ase*

### Final Consonant Sounds

In this phase of oral blending, the last sound in the word is separated.

***Model***

**Teacher:** cabba . . . /j/. What's the word?

**Students:** cabbage

***Example Words***

- Words that are easily recognized even before the final consonant is pronounced:
  *bubblegu . . . /m/ Columbu . . . /s/*
  *crocodi . . . /l/ submari . . . /n/*
- Multisyllable words that need the final consonant for recognition:
  *colle . . . /j/ (college) come . . . /t/ (comet)*
- Single-syllable words:
  *sa . . . /d/ gra . . . /s/ snai . . . /l/*

### Initial Consonant Sound Replacement

This level of oral blending further develops awareness of initial consonant sounds. The activity begins with a common word, then quickly changes its initial consonant sound. Most of the words produced are nonsense words, which helps keep the focus on the sounds in the word. Note that the words are written on the board, but the students are not expected to read them. The writing is to help the students see that when the sounds change, the letters change, and vice versa.

***Model***

**Teacher:** [Writes word on board.] This word is *magazine*. What is it?

**Students:** *magazine*

**Teacher:** Now I'm going to change it. [Erases initial consonant.] Now it doesn't start with /m/, it's going to start with /b/. What's the new word?

**Students:** *bagazine*

**Teacher:** That's right . . . [Writes b where m had been.] It's *bagazine*. Now I'm going to change it again. . . .

Repeat with different consonant sounds. Then do the same with other words, such as: *remember, Saturday, tomorrow, lotion*, and *million*. Continue with single-syllable words, such as: *take, big, boot, cot, seat, look, tap, ride*, and *late*. There are two stages in using written letters:

- The replacement letter is not written until *after* the new "word" has been identified.
- Later, the replacement letter is written *at the same time* the change in the initial phoneme is announced. For example, the teacher erases *d* and writes *m* while saying, "Now it doesn't start with /d/, it starts with /m/."

You may wish to alter the procedure when the consonants used have already been introduced in phonics by writing the replacement letter and having students sound out the new word. Feel free to switch between the two procedures within a single exercise. If the students are not responding orally to written spellings that have been introduced in phonics, don't force it. Proceed by saying the word before writing the letter, and wait until another time to move on to writing before pronouncing.

### One-Syllable Words

The students now begin blending individual phonemes to form words. This important step can be continued well into the year. Continued repetitions of this activity will help the students realize how they can use the sound/spellings they are learning to read and write real words.

At first, the blended words are presented in a story context that helps the students identify the words. They soon recognize that they are actually decoding meaningful words. However, the context must not be so strong that the students can guess the word without listening to the phonemic cues. Any vowel sounds and irregularly spelled words may be used, since there is no writing involved.

***Model***

**Teacher:** *When I looked out the window, I saw a /l/ /ī/ /t/. What did I see?*

**Students:** *A light.*

**Teacher:** *Yes, I saw a light. At first I thought it was the /m/ /o͞o/ /n/. What did I think it was?*

**Students:** *The moon.*

**Teacher:** *But it didn't really look like the moon. Suddenly I thought, maybe it's a space /sh/ /i/ /p/. What did I think it might be?*

**Students:** *A space ship!*

Once the students are familiar with this phase of oral blending, they can move to blending one-syllable words without the story context.

***Example Words***

- CVC (consonant/vowel/consonant) words beginning with easily blended consonant sounds (/sh/, /h/, /r/, /v/, /s/, /n/, /z/, /f/, /l/, /m/):
  *nip nap*
- CVC words beginning with any consonant:
  *ten bug lip*
- Add CCVC words:
  *flap step*
- Add CVCC words:
  *most band went*
- Add CCVCC words:
  *stamp grand scuffs*

### Final Consonant Sound Replacement

Final consonant sounds are typically more difficult for students to use than initial consonants.

- Begin with multisyllable words, and move to one-syllable words.
- As with initial consonants, first write the changed consonant after students have pronounced the new word.
- Then write the consonant as they pronounce it.
- For sound/spellings introduced in phonics instruction, write the new consonant spelling, and have students identify and pronounce it.

*Model*

**TEACHER:** *[Writes word on board.] This word is* teapot. *What is it?*

**STUDENTS:** *teapot*

**TEACHER:** *Now I'm going to change it.* [Erases final consonant.] *Now it doesn't end with /t/, it ends with /p/. What's the word now?*

**STUDENTS:** *teapop*

**TEACHER:** *That's right . . .* [Writes *p* where *t* had been.] *It's* teapop. *Now I'm going to change it again. . . .*

***Example Words***

- Words that are easily recognized even before the final consonant is pronounced:
  *picnic picnit picnis picnil picnid*
  *airplane airplate airplabe airplafe*
- Multisyllable words that need the final consonant for recognition:
  *muffin muffil muffim muffip muffit*
  *amaze amate amake amale amade*
- Single-syllable words:
  *neat nean neap neam neaj nead neaf*
  *broom broot brood broof broop broon*

### Initial Vowel Replacement

Up to now, oral blending has concentrated on consonant sounds because they are easier to hear than vowels. As you move to vowel play, remember that the focus is still on the sounds, not the spellings. Use any vowel sounds.

*Model*

**TEACHER:** [Writes word on board.] *This word is* elephant. *What is it?*

**STUDENTS:** *elephant*

**TEACHER:** *Now I'm going to change it.* [Erases initial vowel.] *Now it doesn't start with /e/, it starts with /a/. What's the word now?*

**STUDENTS:** *alephant*

**TEACHER:** *That's right . . .* [Writes *a* where *e* had been.] *It's alephant. Now I'm going to change it again. . . .*

***Example Words***

- Multisyllable words:
  *angry ingry oongry ungry engry*
  *ivy avy oovy evy ovy oivy*
- One-syllable words:
  *ink ank oonk unk onk oink*
  *add odd idd oudd edd udd*

# Segmentation

## Purpose

Segmentation and oral blending complement each other: Oral blending puts sounds together to make words, while segmentation separates words into sounds. Oral blending will provide valuable support for decoding when students begin reading independently.

## Procedure

### Syllables

The earliest segmentation activities focus on syllables, which are easier to distinguish than individual sounds, or phonemes. Start with students' names, then use other words. As with the oral blending activities, remember to move quickly through these activities. Do not hold the class back waiting for all students to catch on. Individual progress will vary, but drilling on one activity is less helpful than going on to others. Return to the same activity often. Frequent repetition is very beneficial and allows students additional opportunities to catch on.

- Say, for example, "Let's clap out Amanda's name. A-man-da."
- Have the students clap and say the syllables along with you. Count the claps.
- Tell the students that these word parts are called *syllables*. Don't try to explain; the idea will develop with practice. Once you have provided the term, simply say, "How many syllables?" after the students clap and count.
- Mix one-syllable and multisyllable words:
  *fantastic tambourine good*
  *imaginary stand afraid*

### Comparative Length of Words

Unlike most phonemic awareness activities, this one involves writing on the board or on an overhead transparency. Remember, though, that the students are not expected to read what is written. They are merely noticing that words that take longer to say generally look longer when written.

- Start with students' names. Choose two names, one short and one long, with the same first initial (for example, *Joe* and *Jonathan*).
- Write the two names on the board, one above the other, so that the difference is obvious.
- Tell the students that one name is *Jonathan* and one is *Joe*. Have them pronounce and clap each name. Then, have them tell which written word they think says *Joe*.
- Move your finger under each name as they clap and say it, syllable by syllable.
- Repeat with other pairs of names and words, such as: *tea/telephone, cat/caterpillar, butterfly/bug*. Be sure not to give false clues. For example, sometimes write the longer word on top, sometimes the shorter one; sometimes ask for the shorter word, sometimes the longer; sometimes ask for the top word, sometimes the bottom; sometimes point to a word and ask the students to name it, and sometimes name the word and ask the students to point to it.

### Listen for Individual Sounds

Activities using a puppet help the students listen for individual sounds in words. Use any puppet you have on hand. When you introduce the puppet, tell the students that it likes to play word games. Each new activity begins with the teacher speaking to and for the puppet until the students determine the pattern. Next, students either speak for the puppet or correct the puppet. To make sure all the students are participating, alternate randomly between having the whole group or individuals respond. The activities focus on particular parts of words, according to the following sequence:

1. **Repeating last part of word.** Use words beginning with easy-to-hear consonants, such as *f, l, m, n, r, s,* and *z*. The puppet repeats only the rime, the part of the syllable after the initial consonant.

*Model*

**TEACHER:** *farm*

**PUPPET:** *arm*

Once the pattern is established, the students respond for the puppet.

**TEACHER:** *rope*

**STUDENTS:** *ope*

***Example Words***

Use words such as the following: *mine . . . ine soup . . . oup feet . . . eet*

2. **Restoring initial phonemes.** Now the students correct the puppet. Be sure to acknowledge the correction.

*Model*

**TEACHER:** *lake*

**PUPPET:** *ake*

**TEACHER:** *No, lllake. You forgot the /l/.*

**TEACHER:** *real*

**PUPPET:** *eal*

**TEACHER:** *What did the puppet leave off?*

**STUDENTS:** */r/. It's supposed to be* real.

**TEACHER:** *That's right. The word is* real.

***Example Words***

Use words such as the following:
*look . . . ook mouse . . . ouse sand . . . and*

3. **Segmenting initial consonants.** The puppet pronounces only the initial consonant.

***Model***

**TEACHER:** *pay*

**PUPPET:** */p/*

***Example Words***

Use words such as the following:

*moon . . . /m/*   *nose . . . /n/*   *bell . . . /b/*

4. **Restoring final consonants.** The students correct the puppet. Prompt if necessary: *"What's the word? What did the puppet leave off?"*

***Model***

**TEACHER:** *run*

**PUPPET:** *ru*

**STUDENTS:** *It's run! You left off the /n/.*

**TEACHER:** *That's right. The word is* run.

***Example Words***

Use words such as the following:

*meet. . . mee*   *cool . . . coo*   *boot. . . boo*

5. **Isolating final consonants.** The puppet pronounces only the final consonant.

***Model***

**TEACHER:** *green*

**PUPPET:** */n/*

***Example Words***

Use words such as the following:

*glass . . . /s/*   *boom . . . /m/*   *mice . . . /s/*

6. **Segmenting initial consonant blends.** The sounds in blends are emphasized.

***Model***

**TEACHER:** *clap*

**PUPPET:** *lap*

Next have students correct the puppet.

**TEACHER:** *stain*

**PUPPET:** *tain*

**STUDENTS:** *It's* stain! *You left off the /s/.*

**TEACHER:** *That's right. The word is stain.*

***Example Words***

Use words such as the following:

*blaze . . . laze*   *draw. . . raw*   *proud . . . roud*

# Discrimination

## Purpose

Discrimination activities help students focus on particular sounds in words.

**Listening for long vowel sounds** is the earliest discrimination activity. Vowel sounds are necessary for decoding, but young students do not hear them easily. This is evident in students' invented spellings, where vowels are often omitted. Early in the year, the students listen for long vowel sounds, which are more easily distinguished than short vowel sounds:

- Explain to the students that vowels are special, because sometimes they say their names in words.
- Tell the students which vowel sound to listen for.
- Have them repeat the sound when they hear it in a word. For example, if the target vowel sound is long e, the students will say long e when you say *leaf* but they should not respond when you say *loaf*.
- Initially the students should listen for one long vowel sound at a time. Later they can listen for two vowel sounds. All **Example Words**, however, should contain one of the target vowels.

## Procedure

**Listening for short vowel sounds** discrimination activities should be done once the short vowels /a/ and /i/ have been introduced. Short vowels are very useful in reading. They are generally more regular in spelling than long vowels, and they appear in many short, simple words. However, their sounds are less easily distinguished than those of long vowels. Thus, the activities focus only on /a/ and /i/. All the words provided have one or the other of these sounds. Either have the students repeat the sound of a specified vowel, or vary the activity as follows: Write an *a* on one side of the board and an *i* on the other. Ask the students to point to the *a* when they hear a word with the /a/ sound and point to the *i* when they hear a word with the /i/ sound. Use words such as the following:

*bat*   *mat*   *sat*   *sit*   *spit*
*pit*   *pat*   *pan*   *pin*   *spin*

**Consonant sounds in multisyllable words.** Discriminating these sounds helps students attend to consonant sounds in the middle of words.

- Say the word *rib*, and have the students repeat it. Ask where they hear the /b/ in *rib*.
- Then say *ribbon* and ask the students where they hear the /b/ in *ribbon*.
- Tell the students that you will say some words and they will repeat each word.
- After they repeat each word, ask what consonant sound they hear in the middle of that word. Use words such as the following:

*famous*   *message*   *picky*
*jogger*   *flavor*   *zipper*

# Phonemic Play

## Purpose

Wordplay activities help the students focus on and manipulate sounds, thus supporting the idea that words are made of specific sounds that can be taken apart, put together, or changed to make new words. Through wordplay, students gain important knowledge about language.

## Procedure

**Producing rhymes.** Many phonemic play activities focus on producing rhymes. A familiar or easily learned rhyme or song is introduced, and the students are encouraged to substitute words or sounds. An example is "*Willaby Wallaby Woo*," in which students change the rhyming words in the couplet "*Willaby Wallaby Woo/An elephant sat on you*" so that the second line ends with a student's name and the first line ends with a rhyme beginning with W (for example, "*Willaby Wallaby Wissy/An elephant sat on Missy*").

**Generate alliterative words.** Students can also say as many words as they can think of that begin with a given consonant sound. This is a valuable complement to discrimination activities in which the teacher produces the words and the students identify them.

The purpose of phonics instruction is to teach students the association between the sounds of the language and the written symbols—spellings—that have been chosen to represent those sounds.

As with all alphabetic languages, English has a limited number of symbols—twenty-six—that are combined and recombined to make the written language. These written symbols are a visual representation of the speech sounds we use to communicate. This is simply a code. The faster the students learn the code and how it works, the faster the whole world of reading opens to them.

Students are introduced to the sounds and spellings of English in a very systematic, sequential manner. This allows them to continually build on what they learned the day before. As each sound/symbol relationship is introduced, students learn about and practice with words containing the target sound/spelling and then reinforce their learning through the use of engaging text specifically written for this purpose.

It can be very difficult for students to hear the individual sounds, or phonemes, that make up words. When phonics instruction is explicit—students are told the sounds associated with the different written symbols—there is no guesswork involved. They know that this sound /b/ is spelled *b*. Therefore, students in an SRA/Open Court Reading classroom spend time learning to discriminate individual speech sounds, and then they learn the spellings of those sounds. This systematic, explicit approach affords students the very best chance for early and continuing success.

## Sound/Spelling Cards

### Purpose

The purpose of the **Sound/Spelling Cards** (Levels 1–3) is to remind the students of the sounds of English and their spellings. The name of the picture on each card contains the target sound at the beginning for the consonants and in the middle for most vowels. In addition, the picture associates a sound with an action. This association is introduced through an interactive story in which the pictured object or character "makes" the sound. These cards are a resource for the students to use to remember sound/spelling associations for both reading and writing.

### Procedure

#### Posting the Cards

Initially, post the first twenty-six cards with the picture to the wall so that only the alphabet letters on the backs show. As you introduce each card, you will turn it to show the picture and the spellings on the front of the card. If, however, most of your students already have some knowledge of the letters—this is a second- or third-grade classroom and students are reviewing what they learned the year before—you may want to go ahead and place the cards with the picture and the spellings facing forward to provide support as they begin writing. Make sure that the cards are positioned so that you can touch them with your hand or with a pointer when you refer to them and so that all of the students can see them easily. The cards should be placed where the students can readily see them during reading and writing.

#### Special Devices

- Vowel spellings are printed in red to draw attention to them. Consonants are printed in black. The blank line in a spelling indicates that a letter will take the place of the blank in a word. For example, the replacement of the blank with *t* in the spelling *a_e* makes the word *ate.* The blank lines may also indicate the position of a spelling in a word or a syllable. The blank in *h_* for example, means that the spelling occurs at the beginning of a word or a syllable.
- The blanks in *_ie_* indicate that the *ie* spelling comes in the middle of a word or a syllable, while the blank in *_oy* shows that the *oy* spelling comes at the end of a word or a syllable. Uses of blanks in specific spellings are in the lessons. Please note now, however, that when you write a spelling of a sound on the board or an overhead transparency, you should include the blanks.
- The color of the background behind the spellings also has a meaning. Consonants have a white background. The colors behind vowel spellings are pronunciation clues. Short vowel spellings have a green background, which corresponds to the green box that appears before some consonant spellings. Thus, before *ck* or *x* you will see a green box, which indicates that a short vowel always precedes that spelling. Long vowel spellings have a yellow background; other vowel spellings, such as r-controlled vowels and diphthongs, have a blue background. The color code reinforces the idea that vowels are special and have different pronunciations.

#### Introducing the Sound/Spelling Cards

In first grade, each sound and spelling is introduced by using a see/hear/say/write sequence. In grades two and three the same sequence is used in the review of the cards.

1. **See:** Students see the spelling or spellings on the **Sound/Spelling Card** and the board or an overhead transparency.
2. **Hear:** Students hear the sound used in words and in isolation in the story. The sound is, of course, related to the picture (and the action) shown on the **Sound/Spelling Card.**
3. **Say:** Students say the sound.
4. **Write:** Students write the spelling(s) for the sound.

There are a number of important points to remember about this technique.

- The first item written on the board or an overhead transparency is the spelling of the sound being introduced. This gives the spelling a special emphasis in the mind of the student. It is the "see" part of the sequence.
- One of the causes of blending failure is the failure to teach sounds thoroughly during introduction of the **Sound/Spelling Card** and during initial sounding and blending. To help ensure success for all students, make certain that every student is able to see the board or screen.
- After you present the sound and spelling, have several students go to the board to write the spelling. Have them say the sound as they write the spelling. After they have written the spelling of the sound, give them a chance to proofread their own work. Then give the other

PROGRAM APPENDIX

students the opportunity to help with proofreading by noting what is good about the spelling and then suggesting how to make it better.

### Sample Lesson, Using the Letter m and the Sound /m/

- Point to the **Sound/Spelling Card 13 Monkey** and have students tell you whether it is a vowel or a consonant. Have them tell the name of the card. If they do not know it, tell them it is Monkey. Point to the *monkey* in the picture and say the word monkey, emphasizing the initial consonant sound—*mmmonkey*.
- Point to the spelling *m*. Tell students that /m/ is spelled *m*.
- If you wish, make up an alliterative sentence about the Monkey, or use the alliterative story that accompanies the card. (In first grade this story is printed on the page on which the card is introduced and in the Appendix. In grades two and three, the cards are printed in the Appendix of the ***Teacher's Edition.***) For example, *When Muzzie the monkey munches bananas, the sound she makes is /mmmmmm/.*
- If students had ***SRA/Open Court Reading*** before, you can ask them if they learned an action such as rubbing their tummies to help them remember the sound. If your students don't have an action they associate with the cards already, make some up with your students. They will have fun, and it will be another way for them to remember the sound/spelling relationships.
- Write *m* on the board or on an overhead transparency and say the sound. Write the letter again and ask the students to say the sound with you as they write the letter on slates, on paper, or with their index finger on a surface. Repeat this activity several times.
- Have the students listen for words beginning with /m/, indicating by some signal, such as thumbs-up or thumbs-down, whether they hear the /m/ sound and saying /m/ when they hear it in a word. Repeat with the sound in various positions in words. Encourage students to tell you and the class words with /m/ at the beginning and end as well as in the middle of words.
- Check students' learning by pointing to the card. Have students identify the sound, name the spelling, and discuss how the card can help them remember the sound.

### Individual Sound/Spelling Cards

Use the **Individual Sound/Spelling Cards** for review and for small-group reteaching and practice sessions. Students can use them alone or with partners. Here are some suggestions for activities using the **Individual Sound/Spelling Cards**:

1. **Saying sounds from pictures.** The leader flashes pictures as the others say the sound each picture represents.
2. **Saying sounds.** The leader flashes the spellings on the cards as the others say the sound that the spellings represent.

***The faster the students learn the code and how it works, the faster the whole world of reading opens to them.***

3. **Naming spellings from pictures.** The leader flashes pictures. The others name the card, say the sound, and then name as many spellings as they can.
4. **Writing spellings from the pictures.** Working alone, a student looks at a picture and then writes as many spellings for that **Sound/Spelling Card** as he or she can remember.
5. **Saying words from pictures.** The leader presents a series of pictures. The others form words by blending the sounds represented.

## Blending

### Purpose

The purpose of blending is to teach the students a strategy for figuring out unfamiliar words. Initially, students will be blending sound by sound. Ultimately, the students will sound and blend only those words that they cannot read. Eventually, the blending process will become quick and comfortable for them.

### Procedure

Learning the sounds and their spellings is only the first step in learning to read and write. The second step is learning to blend the sounds into words.

### Blending Techniques

Blending lines are written on the board or an overhead transparency as the students watch and participate. The lines and sentences should not be written out before class begins. It is through the sound-by-sound blending of the words and the sentences that the students learn the blending process.

### Sound-by-Sound Blending

- Write the spelling of the first sound in the word. Point to the spelling, and say the sound.
- Have the students say the sound with you as you say the sound again. Write the spelling of the next sound. Point to the spelling, and say the sound. Have the students say the sound with you as you say the sound again. After you have written the vowel spelling, blend through the vowel (unless the vowel is the first letter of the word), making the blending motion—a smooth sweeping of the hand beneath the sounds, linking them from left to right, for example, *ba*. As you make the blending motion, make sure that your hand is under the letter that corresponds to the sound you are saying at the moment.
- Have the students blend through the vowel. Write the spelling of the next sound. Point to the spelling and say the sound. Have the students say the sound with you as you touch the letter and say the sound again.
- Continue as described above through the word. After pronouncing the final sound in the word, make the blending motion from left to right under the word as you blend the sounds. Then have the students blend the word. Let them be the first to pronounce the word normally.
- Ask a student to read the word again and use it in a sentence. Ask another student to extend the sentence—that is, make it longer by giving more information. Help the student by asking an appropriate question about the sentence, using, for example, *How? When? Where?* or *Why?* Continue blending the rest of the words.

### Whole-Word Blending

Once students are comfortable with sound-by-sound blending, they are ready for whole-word blending.

- Write the whole word to be blended on the board or an overhead transparency.
- Ask the students to blend the sounds as you point to them.
- Then have the students say the whole word.
- Ask the students to use the word in a sentence and then to extend the sentence.
- When all of the words have been blended, point to words randomly and ask individuals to read them.

### Blending Syllables

In reading the ***Student Anthologies,*** students will often encounter multisyllabic words. Some students are intimidated by long words, yet many multisyllabic words are easily read by reading and blending the syllables rather than the individual sounds. Following a set of rules for syllables is difficult since so many of the rules have exceptions. Students need to remember that each syllable in a word contains one vowel sound.

- Have students identify the vowel sounds in the word.
- Have students blend the first syllable sound by sound if necessary or read the first syllable.
- Handle the remaining syllables the same way.
- Have students blend the syllables together to read the word.

### Blending Sentences

Blending sentences is the logical extension of blending words. Blending sentences helps students develop fluency, which is critical to comprehension. Encourage students to reread sentences with phrasing and natural intonation.

- Write the sentence on the board or on a transparency, underlining any high-frequency sight words—words that the students cannot decode either because they are irregular or because they contain sounds or spellings that the students have not yet learned or reviewed. If the students have not read these words before, write the words on the board or an overhead transparency and introduce them before writing the sentence. These words should not be blended but read as whole words.

### Building for Success

A primary cause of students' blending failure is their failure to understand how to use the **Sound/Spelling Cards**. Students need to practice sounds and spellings when the **Sound/Spelling Cards** are introduced and during initial blending. They also need to understand that if they are not sure of how to pronounce a spelling, they can check the cards.

Early blending may be frustrating. You must lead the group almost constantly. Soon, however, leaders in the group will take over. Watch to see whether any students are having trouble during the blending. Include them in small-group instruction sessions. At that time you may want to use the vowel-first procedure described below to reteach blending lines.

### Extra Help

In working with small groups during **Workshop**, you may want to use some of the following suggestions to support students who need help with blending.

### Vowel-First Blending

Vowel-first blending is an alternative to sound-by-sound and whole-word blending for students who need special help. Used in small-group sessions, this technique helps students who have difficulty with the other two types of blending to focus on the most important part of each word, the vowels, and to do only one thing at a time. These students are not expected to say a sound and blend it with another at virtually the same time. The steps to use in vowel-first blending follow:

> ***Blending is the heart of phonics instruction and the key strategy students must learn to open the world of written language.***

1. Across the board or on an overhead transparency, write the vowel spelling in each of the words in the line. For a short vowel, the line may look like this:
   a a a
   For a long vowel, the line may look like this:
   ee ea ea
2. Point to the spelling as the students say the sound for the spelling.
3. Begin blending around the vowels. In front of the first vowel spelling, add the spelling for the beginning sound of the word. Make the blending motion, and have the students blend through the vowel, adding a blank to indicate that the word is still incomplete. Repeat this procedure for each partial word in the line until the line looks like this:
   ma__ sa__ pa__
   see__ mea__ tea__
4. Have the students blend the partial word again as you make the blending motion and then add the spelling for the ending sound.
5. Make the blending motion, and have the students blend the completed word—for example, *mat* or *seed*.
6. Ask a student to repeat the word and use it in a sentence. Then have another student extend the sentence.
7. Repeat steps 4, 5, and 6 for each word in the line, which might look like this:
   *mat sad pan*
   or
   *seed meat team*

## Tips

- In the early lessons, do blending with as much direction and dialogue as is necessary for success. Reduce your directions to a minimum as soon as possible. You have made good progress when you no longer have to say, "Sound—Sound—Blend," because the students automatically sound and blend as you write.
- Unless the line is used to introduce or to reinforce a spelling pattern, always ask a student to use a word in a sentence and then to extend the sentence immediately after you've developed the word. If the line is used to introduce or to reinforce a spelling pattern, however, ask the students to give sentences at the end of the line. Students will naturally extend sentences by adding phrases to the ends of the sentences. Encourage them to add phrases at the beginning or in the middle of the sentence.
- Use the vowel-first procedure in small group preteaching or reteaching sessions with students who are having a lot of trouble with blending. Remember that you must adapt the blending lines in the lessons to the vowel-first method.
- The sight words in the sentences cannot be blended. The students must approach them as sight words to be memorized. If students are having problems reading sight words, tell them the words.
- Cue marks written over the vowels may help students.
  - ✓ Straight line cue for long vowels
    EXAMPLES: *āpe, mē, fīne, sō, ūse*
  - ✓ Curved line cue for short vowels
    EXAMPLES: *căt, pĕt, wĭn, hŏt, tŭg*
  - ✓ Tent cue for variations of a and o
    EXAMPLES: *âll, ôff*
  - ✓ Dot cue for schwa sound with multiple-syllable words
    EXAMPLES: *salȧd, planėt, pencil, wagȯn*

# Dictation and Spelling

## Purpose

The purpose of dictation is to teach the students to spell words based on the sounds and spellings. In addition, learning dictation gives students a new strategy for reflecting on the sounds they hear in words to help them with their own writing.

As the students learn that sounds and spellings are connected to form words and that words form sentences, they begin to learn the standard spellings that will enable others to read their writing. As students learn to encode correctly, they develop their visual memory for words (spelling ability) and hence increase their writing fluency. Reinforcing the association between sounds and spellings and words through dictation gives students a spelling strategy that provides support and reassurance for writing independently. Reflecting on the sounds they hear in words will help students develop writing fluency as they apply the strategy to writing unfamiliar words.

A dictation activity is a learning experience; it is not a test. The students should be encouraged to ask for as much help as they need. The proofreading techniques are an integral part of dictation. Students' errors lead to self-correction and, if need be, to reteaching. The dictation activities must not become a frustrating ordeal. The students should receive reinforcement and feedback.

There are two kinds of dictation: Sounds-in-Sequence Dictation and Whole-Word Dictation. The two types differ mainly in the amount of help they give the students in spelling the words. The instructions vary for each type.

## Procedure

### Sounds-in-Sequence Dictation

Sounds-in-Sequence Dictation gives the students the opportunity to spell words sound by sound, left to right, checking the spelling of each sound as they write. (Many students write words as they think they hear and say the words, not as the words are actually pronounced or written.)

- Pronounce the first word to be spelled. Use the word in a sentence and say the word again (word/sentence/word). Have students say the word.
- Tell students to think about the sounds they hear in the word. Ask, "What's the first sound in the word?"
- Have students say the sound.
- Point to the **Sound/Spelling Card**, and direct the students to check the card. Ask what the spelling is. The students should say the spelling and then write it.
- Proceed in this manner until the word is complete.
- Proofread. You can write the word on the board as a model, or have a student do it. Check the work by referring to the **Sound/Spelling Cards**. If a word is misspelled, have the students circle the word and write it correctly, either above the word or next to it.

### Whole-Word Dictation

Whole-Word Dictation gives the students the opportunity to practice this spelling strategy with less help from the teacher.

- Pronounce the word, use the word in a sentence, and then repeat the word (word/sentence/word). Have the students repeat the word. Tell the students to think about the word. Remind the students to check the **Sound/Spelling Cards** for spellings and to write the word.
- Proofread. Write or have a volunteer write the word on the board as a model. Check the word by referring to the **Sound/Spelling Cards**.

### Sentence Dictation

**Writing dictated sentences**. Help students apply this spelling strategy to writing sentences. Dictation supports the development of fluent and independent writing. Dictation of a sentence will also help the students apply conventions of written language, such as capitalization and punctuation.

- Say the complete sentence aloud.
- Dictate one word at a time following the procedure for Sounds-in-Sequence Dictation.

Continue this procedure for the rest of the words in the sentence. Remind the students to put a period at the end. Then proofread the sentence, sound by sound, or word by word. When sentences contain sight words, the sight words should be dictated as whole words, not sound by sound. As the students learn to write more independently, the whole sentence can be dictated word by word.

### Proofreading

Whenever the students write, whether at the board or on paper, they should proofread their work. Proofreading is an important technique because it allows the students to learn by self-correction and it gives them an immediate second chance for success. It is the same skill students will use as they proofread their writing. Students should proofread by circling—not by erasing—each error. After they circle an error, they should write the correction beside the circle. This type of correction allows you and the students to see the error as well as the correct form. Students also can see what needs to be changed and how they have made their own work better.

You may want to have students use a colored pencil to circle and write in the correction. This will make it easier for them to see the changes.

### Procedure for Proofreading

- Have a student write the word or sentence on the board or on an overhead transparency.
- Have students tell what is good.
- Have students identify anything that can be made better.
- If there is a mistake, have the student circle it and write it correctly.
- Have the rest of the class proofread their own work.

### The Word Building Game

The major reason for developing writing alongside reading is that reading and writing are complementary communicative processes. Decoding requires that students blend the phonemes together into familiar cohesive words. Spelling requires that students segment familiar cohesive words into separate phonemes. Both help students develop an understanding of how the alphabetic principle works.

The Word Building game gives the students a chance to exercise their segmentation abilities and to practice using the sounds and spellings they are learning. The game is a fast-paced activity in which the students spell related sets of words with the teacher's guidance. (Each successive word in the list differs from the previous one by one sound.)

For the Word Building game, the students use their ***Individual Letter Cards*** (Levels K and 1) to build the words. (As an alternative they can use pencil and paper.) You will be writing at the board.

Give the students the appropriate ***Letter Cards.*** For example, if the list for the Word Building game is *am, at, mat,* they will need their *a, m,* and *t* ***Letter Cards.***

- Say the first word, such as *am.* (Use it in a sentence if you wish.) Have the students repeat the word. Say the word slowly, sound by sound. Tell the students to look at the ***Sound/Spelling Cards*** to find the letters that spell the sounds. Touch the first sound's card, in this case the Lamb card, and have students say the sound. Continue the process with the second sound. Write the word on the board while the students use their ***Letter Cards*** to spell it. Have students compare their words with your word, make changes as needed, and then blend and read the word with you.
- The students will then change the first word to make a different word. Say the next word in the list, (*at*). Segment the sounds of the word, and have students find the ***Sound/Spelling Cards*** that correspond. Write the new word (*at*) under the first word (*am*) on the board and have the students change their cards to spell the new word. Have them compare their words to yours and make changes as needed. Blend and read the word with the students. Continue in a like manner through the word list.

# Spelling Strategies

## Spelling

Many people find English difficult, because English sound/spelling patterns seem to have a million exceptions. The key to becoming a good speller, however, is not just memorization. The key is recognizing and internalizing English spelling patterns. Some people do this naturally as they read and develop large vocabularies. They intuitively recognize spelling patterns and apply them appropriately. Others need explicit and direct teaching of vocabulary and spelling strategies and spelling patterns before they develop spelling consciousness.

## Purpose

Spelling is a fundamental skill in written communication. Although a writer may have wonderful ideas, he or she may find it difficult to communicate those ideas without spelling skills. Learning to spell requires much exposure to text and writing. For many it requires a methodical presentation of English spelling patterns.

## English Spelling Patterns

A basic understanding of English spelling patterns will help provide efficient and effective spelling instruction. Just as the goal of phonics instruction is to enable students to read fluently, the goal of spelling instruction is to enable students to write fluently so they can concentrate on ideas rather than spelling.

- **Sound Patterns** Many words are spelled the way they sound. Most consonants and short vowels are very regular. Once a student learns the sound/spelling relationships, he or she has the key to spelling many words.
- **Structural Patterns** Structural patterns are employed when adding endings to words. Examples of structural patterns include doubling the final consonant, adding *–s* or *–es* to form plurals, and dropping the final *e* before adding *–ing*, *-ed*, *-er*, or *–est.* Often these structural patterns are very regular in their application. Many students have little trouble learning these patterns.
- **Meaning Patterns** Many spelling patterns in English are *morphological;* in other words, the meaning relationship is maintained regardless of how a sound may change. Prefixes, suffixes, and root words that retain their spellings regardless of how they are pronounced are further examples of meaning patterns.
- **Foreign Language Patterns** Many English words are derived from foreign words and retain those language patterns. For example, *kindergarten* (German), *boulevard* (French), and *ballet* (French from Italian) are foreign language patterns at work in English.

## Developmental Stages of Spelling

The most important finding in spelling research in the past thirty years is that students learn to spell in a predictable developmental sequence, much as they learn to read. It appears to take the average student three to six years to progress through the developmental stages and emerge as a fairly competent, mature speller.

**Prephonemic** The first stage is the *prephonemic* stage, characterized by random letters arranged either in continuous lines or in word-like clusters. Only the writer can "read" it, and it may be "read" differently on different days.

**Semiphonemic** As emergent readers learn that letters stand for sounds, they use particular letters specifically to represent the initial consonant sound and sometimes a few other very salient sounds. This marks the discovery of *phonemic awareness* that letters represent speech sounds in writing.

**Phonemic** When students can represent most of the sounds they hear in words, they have entered the *phonemic* stage of spelling. They spell what they hear, using everything they know about letter sounds, letter names, and familiar words. Many remedial spellers never develop beyond this stage and spell a word the way it sounds whenever they encounter a word they can't spell.

**Transitional or Within Word Pattern** As they are exposed to more difficult words, students discover that not all words are spelled as they sound. They learn that they must include silent letters, spell past tenses with *–ed*, include a vowel even in unstressed syllables, and remember how words look. The *transitional* stage represents the transition from primarily phonemic strategies to rule-bound spelling.

**Derivational** The *derivational* stage occurs as transitional spellers accumulate a large spelling vocabulary and gain control over affixes, contractions, homophones and other meaning patterns. They discover that related or derived forms of words share spelling features even if they do not sound the same. As spellers gain control over these subtle word features and spell most words correctly, they become conventional spellers.

## Procedures

The spelling lessons are organized around different spelling patterns, beginning with phonetic spelling patterns and progressing to other types of spelling patterns in a logical sequence. Word lists including words from the literature selection focus on the particular patterns in each lesson. In general, the sound patterns occur in the first units at each grade, followed by structural patterns, meaning patterns, and foreign language patterns in the upper grade levels.

- As you begin each new spelling lesson, have students identify the spelling pattern and how it is like and different from other patterns.
- Give the pretest to help students focus on the lesson pattern.
- Have students proofread their own pretests immediately after the test, crossing out any misspellings and writing the correct spelling.
- Have them diagnose whether the errors they made were in the lesson pattern or in another part of the word. Help students determine where they made errors and what type of pattern they should work on to correct them.
- As students work through the spelling pages from the ***Spelling and Vocabulary Skills*** book, encourage them to practice the different spelling strategies in the exercises.

### Sound Pattern Strategies

✓ **Pronunciation Strategy** As students encounter an unknown word, have them say the word carefully to hear each sound. Encourage them to check the **Sound/Spelling Cards.** Then have them spell each sound. (/s/ + /i/ + /t/: *sit)*

✓ **Consonant Substitution** Have students switch consonants. The vowel spelling usually remains the same. *(bat, hat, rat, flat, splat)*

✓ **Vowel Substitution** Have students switch vowels. The consonant spellings usually remain the same. (CVC: *hit, hat, hut, hot;* CVCV: *mane, mine;* CVVC: *boat, beat, bait, beet)*

✓ **Rhyming Word Strategy** Have students think of rhyming words and the rimes that spell a particular sound. Often the sound will be spelled the same way in another word. *(cub, tub, rub)*

### Structural Pattern Strategies

✓ **Conventions Strategy** Have students learn the rule and exceptions for adding endings to words (dropping *y*, dropping *e*, doubling the final consonant, and so on).

✓ **Proofreading Strategy** Many spelling errors occur because of simple mistakes. Have students check their writing carefully and specifically for spelling.

✓ **Visualization Strategy** Have students think about how a word looks. Sometimes words "look" wrong because a wrong spelling pattern has been written. Have them double-check the spelling of any word that looks wrong.

### Meaning Pattern Strategies

✓ **Family Strategy** When students are not sure of a spelling, have them think of how words from the same base word family are spelled. *(critic, criticize, critical; sign, signal, signature)*

## Spelling and Vocabulary Strategies (continued)



✓ **Meaning Strategy** Have students determine a homophone's meaning to make sure they are using the right word. Knowing prefixes, suffixes, and base words will also help.

✓ **Compound Word Strategy** Tell students to break a compound apart and spell each word. Compounds may not follow conventions rules for adding endings. *(homework, nonetheless)*

✓ **Foreign Language Strategy** Have students think of foreign language spellings that are different from English spelling patterns. *(ballet, boulevard, sauerkraut)*

✓ **Dictionary Strategy** Ask students to look up the word in a dictionary to make sure their spelling is correct. If they do not know how to spell a word, have them try a few different spellings and look them up to see which one is correct. *(fotograph, photograph)* This develops a spelling consciousness.

Use the Final Test to determine understanding of the lesson spelling pattern and to identify any other spelling pattern problems. Encourage student understanding of spelling patterns and use of spelling strategies in all their writing to help transfer spelling skills to writing.

# Vocabulary Strategies

## Purpose

Strong vocabulary skills are correlated to achievement throughout school. The purpose of vocabulary strategy instruction is to teach students a range of strategies for learning, remembering, and incorporating unknown vocabulary words into their existing reading, writing, speaking, and listening vocabularies.

## Procedures

The selection vocabulary instruction in the first and second part of the lesson focuses on teaching specific vocabulary necessary for understanding the literature selection more completely. The weekly vocabulary instruction in the Language Arts part of each lesson is geared toward teaching vocabulary skills and strategies to build and secure vocabulary through word relationships or develop vocabulary strategies for unknown words.

### General Strategies

There is no question that having students read and reading to students are effective vocabulary instructional strategies. Most word learning occurs through exposure to words in listening and reading. Multiple exposures to words, particularly when students hear, see, say, and write words, is also effective. Word play, including meaning and dictionary games, helps to develop a word consciousness as well.

### Vocabulary Skills and Strategies

**Word Relationships** People effectively learn new words by relating them to words they already know. An understanding of different word relationships enables students to quickly and efficiently secure new vocabulary. The weekly vocabulary lessons are organized around these types of word groups. Word relationships include:

- **Antonyms** Words with opposite or nearly opposite meanings. *(hot/cold)*
- **Synonyms** Words with similar meanings. *(cup, mug, glass)*
- **Multiple Meanings** Words that have more than one meaning. *(run, dressing, bowl)*
- **Shades of Meaning** Words that express degrees of a concept or quality. *(like, love, worship)*
- **Levels of Specificity** Words that describe at different levels of precision. *(living thing, plant, flower, daffodil)*
- **Analogies** Pairs of words that have the same relationship. *(ball is to baseball as puck is to hockey)*
- **Compound Words** Words comprised of two or more words. *(daylight)*
- **Homographs** Words that are spelled the same but have different meanings and come from different root words. *(bear, count)*
- **Homophones** Words that sound the same but have different spellings and meanings. *(mane/main, to/two/too)*
- **Base Word Families** Words that have the same base word. *(care, careless, careful, uncaring, carefree)*
- **Prefixes** An affix attached before a base word that changes the meaning of the word. *(misspell)*
- **Suffixes** An affix attached to the end of a base word that changes the meaning of the word. *(careless)*
- **Concept Vocabulary** Words that help develop understanding of a concept. *(space, sun, Earth, satellite, planet, asteroid)*
- **Classification and Categorization** Sorting words by related meanings. *(colors, shapes, animals, foods)*

**Contextual Word Lists** Teaching vocabulary in context is another way to secure understanding of unknown words. Grouping words by subject area such as science, social studies, math, descriptive words, new words, and so on enables students to connect word meanings and build vocabulary understanding.

- **Figurative Language** Idioms, metaphors, similes, personification, puns, and novel meanings need to be specifically taught, especially for English language learners.
- **Derivational Word Lists** Presenting groups of words derived from particular languages or with specific roots or affixes is an effective way to reinforce meanings and spellings of foreign words and word parts.

### Vocabulary Strategies for Unknown Words

Different strategies have been shown to be particularly effective for learning completely new words. These strategies are included in the ***Spelling and Vocabulary Skills*** activities.

**Key Word** This strategy involves providing or having students create a mnemonic clue for unknown vocabulary. For example, the word *mole* is defined in chemistry as a "gram molecule." By relating *mole* to *molecule*, students have a key to the meaning of the word.

**Definitions** Copying a definition from a dictionary is somewhat effective in learning new vocabulary. Combining this with using the word in writing and speaking adds to the effectiveness of this strategy. Requiring students to explain a word or use it in a novel sentence helps to ensure that the meaning is understood.

**Context Clues** Many words are learned from context, particularly with repeated exposure to words in reading and listening. Without specific instruction in consciously using context clues, however, unknown words are often ignored.

- **Syntax** How a word is used in a sentence provides some clue to its meaning.
- **External Context Clues** Hints about a word's meaning may appear in the setting, words, phrases, or sentences surrounding a word in text. Other known words in the text may be descriptive, may provide a definition (apposition), may be compared or contrasted, or may be used synonymously in context. Modeling and teaching students to use context to infer a word's meaning can help in learning unknown words.

**Word Structure** Examining the affixes and roots of a word may provide some clue to its meaning. Knowing the meaning of at least part of the word can provide a clue to its meaning. (For example, *unenforceable* can be broken down into meaningful word parts.)

**Semantic Mapping** Having students create a semantic map of an unknown word after learning its definition helps them to learn it. Have students write the new word and then list in a map or web all words they can think of that are related to it.

**Semantic Feature Analysis** A semantic feature analysis helps students compare and contrast similar types of words within a category to help secure unknown words. Have students chart, for example, the similarities and differences between different types of sports, including new vocabulary such as *lacrosse* and *cricket*.

# Developing Vocabulary

## Purpose

Vocabulary is closely connected to comprehension. Considerable vocabulary growth occurs incidentally during reading. A clear connection exists between vocabulary development and the amount of reading a person does, and there are strong indications that vocabulary instruction is important and that understanding the meaning of key words helps with comprehension.

In ***Open Court Reading***, vocabulary is addressed before, during, and after reading. Before reading, the teacher presents vocabulary words from the selection. Students use skills such as context clues, apposition, and structural analysis to figure out the meaning of the words. These selection vocabulary words are not only important to understanding the text but are also high-utility words that can be used in discussing and writing about the unit theme.

During reading, students monitor their understanding of words and text. When they do not understand something, they stop and clarify what they have read. Students will use these same skills—context clues, apposition, structural elements, and the like—to clarify the meanings of additional words encountered while reading. Figuring out the meanings of words while reading prepares students for the demands of independent reading both in and out of school.

After reading, students review the vocabulary words that they learned before reading the selection. They also review any interesting words that they identified and discussed during reading. Students record in their Writer's Notebook both the selection vocabulary words and the interesting words they identified during their reading and are encouraged to use both sets of words in discussion and in writing.

## Procedure

Before students read a selection, the teacher uses an overhead transparency to introduce the selection vocabulary to the class. The transparency contains two sentences for each selection vocabulary word. Students must use context clues, apposition, or word structure in the sentences to figure out the meaning of the underlined vocabulary words. If students cannot figure out the meaning of the word using one of these skills, they can consult the glossary or dictionary.

Below are suggestions for modeling the use of context clues, apposition, or word structure to figure out the meaning of a word.

### Modeling Using Context Clues

Have students read the sentences on the transparency. Explain to students that they will use *context clues*, or other words in the sentence, to figure out the meaning of the underlined word. For example, if the word is "treacherous," the sentences might include:

1. Mrs. Frisby must undertake a treacherous journey to bring her son some medicine.
2. We took a treacherous walk near a swamp filled with crocodiles.

Have students look for clues in the sentences that might help them understand the meaning of the underlined word. Point out that a good clue in the second sentence is "near a swamp filled with crocodiles." This clue should help them understand that *treacherous* probably has something to do with danger. Guide students until they can give a reasonable definition of *treacherous*. To consolidate understanding of the word, ask another student to use the definition in a sentence.

### Modeling Using Apposition

Have students read the sentences on the transparency. Explain to students that they will use *apposition* to figure out the meaning of the word. In apposition, the word is followed by the definition, which is set off by commas. For example, if the word is "abolitionist," the sentences might include the following:

1. The conductor thought he was an abolitionist, a person who wanted to end slavery.
2. John Brown was a famous abolitionist, a person who wanted to end slavery.

It should be pretty clear to students using apposition that the definition of the word *abolitionist* is "a person who wanted to end slavery."

### Modeling Using Word Structure

Have students read the sentences on the transparency. Explain to students that they will use *word structure*, or parts of the selection vocabulary word, to figure out the meaning. For example, if the word is "uncharted," the sentences might include:

1. The strong wind blew Ivan's ship away into uncharted seas.
2. The explorers Lewis and Clark went into uncharted territory.

Have students look at the word *uncharted* and break it into parts: the prefix *un-*, *chart*, and the suffix *–ed*. Students should know that the suffix *un-* means "not," and that the suffix *–ed* usually indicates the past tense of a verb. However, you may need to remind students about the meanings of these affixes. Ask students for the meaning of the word *chart*. Students should know that a chart could be a "map" or a "table." Guide them as they put together the definitions of the word parts, *un-* (not), *charted* (mapped or tabled). They should be able to come up with the definition "not mapped" or "unmapped" or even "unknown." Have them substitute their definition in the sentences to see if the definition makes sense. So, for instance, the first sentence would read "The strong wind blew Ivan's ship away into unmapped (or unknown) seas." Confirm with students that the new sentence makes sense, and then repeat the same process for the second sentence.

# Reading Comprehension

PROGRAM APPENDIX

Everything the students learn about phonemic awareness, phonics, and decoding has one primary goal—to help them understand what they are reading. Without comprehension, there is no reading.

## Reading Comprehension Strategies

### Purpose

The primary aim of reading is comprehension. Without comprehension, neither intellectual nor emotional responses to reading are possible—other than the response of frustration. Good readers are problem solvers. They bring their critical faculties to bear on everything they read. Experienced readers generally understand most of what they read, but just as importantly, they recognize when they do not understand, and they have at their command an assortment of strategies for monitoring and furthering their understanding.

The goal of comprehension strategy instruction is to turn responsibility for using strategies over to the students as soon as possible. Research has shown that students' comprehension and learning problems are not a matter of mental capacity but rather their inability to use strategies to help them learn. Good readers use a variety of strategies to help them make sense of the text and get the most out of what they read. Trained to use a variety of comprehension strategies, students dramatically improve their learning performance. In order to do this, the teacher models strategy use and gradually incorporates different kinds of prompts and possible student think-alouds as examples of the types of thinking students might do as they read to comprehend what they are reading.

#### Setting Reading Goals

Even before they begin reading and using comprehension strategies, good readers set reading goals and expectations. Readers who have set their own goals and have definite expectations about the text they are about to read are more engaged in their reading and notice more in what they read. Having determined a purpose for reading, they are better able to evaluate a text and determine whether it meets their needs. Even when the reading is assigned, the reader's engagement is enhanced when he or she has determined ahead of time what information might be gathered from the selection or how the selection might interest him or her.

#### Comprehension Strategies

Descriptions of strategies good readers use to comprehend the text follow.

***Summarizing***

Good readers sum up to check their understanding as they read. Sometimes they reread to fill in gaps in their understanding. Good readers use the strategy of summarizing to keep track of what they are reading and to focus their minds on important information. The process of putting the information in one's own words not only helps good readers remember what they have read, but also prompts them to evaluate how well they understand the information. Sometimes the summary reveals that one's understanding is incomplete, in which case it might be appropriate to reread the previous section to fill in the gaps. Good readers usually find that the strategy of summarizing is particularly helpful when they are reading long or complicated text.

***Monitoring and Clarifying***

Good readers constantly monitor themselves as they read in order to make sure they understand what they are reading. They note the characteristics of the text, such as whether it is difficult to read or whether some sections are more challenging or more important than others are. In addition, when good readers become aware that they do not understand, they take appropriate action, such as rereading, in order to understand the text better. As they read, good readers stay alert for problem signs such as loss of concentration, unfamiliar vocabulary, or lack of sufficient background knowledge to comprehend the text. This ability to self-monitor and identify aspects of the text that hinder comprehension is crucial to becoming a proficient reader.

***Asking Questions***

Good readers ask questions that may prepare them for what they will learn. If their questions are not answered in the text, they may try to find answers elsewhere and thus add even more to their store of knowledge. Certain kinds of questions occur naturally to a reader, such as clearing up confusion or wondering why something in the text is as it is. Intentional readers take this somewhat informal questioning one step further by formulating questions with the specific intent of checking their understanding. They literally test themselves by thinking of questions a teacher might ask and then by determining answers to those questions.

***Predicting***

Good readers predict what will happen next. When reading fiction, they make predictions about what they are reading and then confirm or revise those predictions as they go.

***Making Connections***

Good readers make connections between what they are reading and what they already know from past experience or previous reading.

***Visualizing***

Good readers visualize what is happening in the text. They form mental images as they read. They picture the setting, the characters, and the action in a story. Visualizing can also be helpful when reading expository text. Visualizing helps readers understand descriptions of complex activities or processes. When a complex process or an event is being described, the reader can follow the process or the event better by visualizing each step or episode. Sometimes an author or an editor helps the reader by providing illustrations, diagrams, or maps. If no visual aids have been provided, it may help the reader to create one.

***Monitoring and Adjusting Reading Speed***

Good readers understand that not all text is equal. Because of this, good readers continuously monitor what they are reading and adjust their reading speed accordingly. They skim parts of the text that are not important or relevant to their reading goals and they purposely slow down when they encounter difficulty in understanding the text.

### Procedures

#### Modeling and Thinking Aloud

One of the most effective ways to help students use and understand the strategies good readers use is to make strategic thinking public. Modeling these behaviors and encouraging students to think aloud as they attempt to understand text can demonstrate for everyone in a class how these behaviors are put into practice. Suggestions for think-alouds are provided throughout the **Teacher's Edition.**

The most effective models you can offer will be those that come from your own reading experiences. What kinds of questions did you ask yourself? What kinds of things surprised you the first time you read a story? What kinds of new information did you learn? What kinds of things were confusing until you reread or read further? Drawing on these questions and on your students' questions and comments as they read will make the strategic reading process more meaningful to the students. Below are suggestions for modeling each of the comprehension strategies.

- **Modeling Setting Reading Goals.** To model setting reading goals, engage students in the following:

- **Activate prior knowledge.** As you approach a new text, consider aloud what you already know about the subject or what your experiences have been in reading similar material.
- **Browse the text.** To get an idea of what to expect from a text, look at the title and the illustrations. Look for potential problems, such as difficult words. Have students glance quickly at the selection, looking briefly at the illustrations and the print. Have them tell what they think they might be learning about as they read the selection.
- **Decide what to expect from the text.** Anticipate enjoying the story, the language of the text, or the new information you expect to gain from the selection.

- **Modeling Summarizing.** Just as the strategy of summarizing the plot and then predicting what will happen next can enhance a student's reading of fiction, so too can the same procedure be used to the student's advantage in reading nonfiction. In expository text, it is particularly logical to stop and summarize at the end of a chapter or section before going on to the next. One way to model the valuable exercise of making predictions and at the same time expand knowledge is to summarize information learned from a piece of expository writing and then predict what the next step or category will be. Appropriate times to stop and summarize include the following:
  - when a narrative text has covered a long period of time or a number of events
  - when many facts have been presented
  - when an especially critical scene has occurred
  - when a complex process has been described
  - any time there is the potential for confusion about what has happened or what has been presented in the text
  - when returning to a selection
- **Modeling Monitoring and Clarifying.** A reader may need clarification at any point in the reading. Model this strategy by stopping at points that confuse you or that may confuse your students. Indicate that you are experiencing some confusion and need to stop and make sure you understand what is being read. Difficulty may arise from a challenging or unknown word or phrase. It may also stem from the manner in which the information is presented. Perhaps the author did not supply needed information. As you model this strategy, vary the reasons for stopping to clarify so that the students understand that good readers do not simply skip over difficult or confusing material—they stop and figure out what they don't understand.
- **Modeling Asking Questions.** Learning to ask productive questions is not an easy task. Students' earliest experiences with this strategy take the form of answering teacher-generated questions. However, students should be able to move fairly quickly to asking questions like those a teacher might ask. Questions that can be answered with a simple yes or no are not typically very useful for helping them remember and understand what they have read. Many students find it helpful to ask questions beginning with *Who? What? When? Where? How?* or *Why?* As students become more accustomed to asking and answering questions, they will naturally become more adept at phrasing their questions. As their question-asking becomes more sophisticated, they progress from simple questions that can be answered with explicit information in the text to questions that require making inferences based on the text.

***Good readers use a variety of strategies to help them make sense of the text and get the most out of what they read.***

- **Modeling Predicting.** Predicting can be appropriate at the beginning of a selection—on the basis of the titles and the illustrations—or at any point while reading a selection. At first, your modeling will take the form of speculation about what might happen next, but tell students from the start what clues in the text or illustrations helped you predict, in order to make it clear that predicting is not just guessing. When a student makes a prediction—especially a far-fetched one—ask what in the selection or in his or her own experience the prediction is based on. If the student can back up the prediction, let the prediction stand; otherwise, suggest that the student make another prediction on the basis of what he or she already knows. Often it is appropriate to sum up before making a prediction. This will help students consider what has come before as they make their predictions about what will happen next. When reading aloud, stop whenever a student's prediction has been confirmed or contradicted. Have students tell whether the prediction was correct. If students seem comfortable with the idea of making predictions but rarely do so on their own, encourage them to discuss how to find clues in the text that will help them.
- **Modeling Making Connections.** To model making connections, share with students any thoughts or memories that come to mind as you read the selection. Perhaps a character in a story reminds you of a childhood friend, allowing you to better identify with interactions between characters. Perhaps information in an article on Native-American life in the Old West reminds you of an article that you have read on the importance of the bison to Native Americans. Sharing your connections will help students become aware of the dynamic nature of reading and show them another way of being intentional, active learners.
- **Modeling Visualizing.** Model visualizing by describing the mental images that occur to you as you read. A well-described scene is relatively easy to visualize, and if no one does so voluntarily, you may want to prompt students to express their own visualizations. If the author has not provided a description of a scene, but a picture of the scene would make the story more interesting or comprehensible, you might want to model visualizing as follows: "Let's see. The author says that the street was busy, and we know that this story is set during the colonial period. From what I already know about those times, there were no cars, and the roads were different from the roads of today. The street may have been paved with cobblestones. Horses would have been pulling carriages or wagons. I can almost hear the horses' hoofs going clip-clop over the stones." Remind students that different readers may picture the same scene quite differently, which is fine. Every reader responds to a story in her or his own way.
- **Modeling Monitoring and Adjusting Reading Speed.** Just as readers need to monitor for problems, they need to be aware that different texts can be approached in different ways. For example, if reading a story or novel for enjoyment, the reader will typically read at a relaxed speed that is neither so fast as to be missing information nor as slow as they might read a textbook. If on the other hand, the reader is reading a textbook, he or she will probably decrease speed to assure understanding and make sure that all important information is read and understood. When modeling this strategy, be sure you indicate why you, as the reader, have chosen to slow down or speed up. Good readers continually monitor their speed and ability to understand throughout reading.

## Reading Comprehension (continued)



### Reading Aloud

At the beginning of the year, students should be encouraged to read selections aloud. This practice will help you and them understand some of the challenges posed by the text and how different students approach these challenges.

Reading aloud helps students build fluency, which in turn will aid their comprehension. Students in grades K–3 can use **Decodable Books** to build fluency, while students in grades 4–6 can use the literature from the **Student Anthologies.** Fluent second graders read between 82 and 124 words per minute with accuracy and understanding, depending on the time of the year (fall/spring). Fluent third graders can be expected to read between 107 and 142 words per minute; fourth (125/143); fifth (126/151); sixth (127/153).

Make sure that you set aside time to hear each student read during the first few days of class—the days devoted to Getting Started are perfect for this—so that you can determine students' abilities and needs. **Workshop** is also a good time to listen to any students who do not get to read aloud while the class is reading the selection together.

If your students have not previously engaged in the sort of strategic thinking aloud that is promoted throughout the ***SRA/Open Court Reading*** program, you will have to do all or most of the modeling at first, but encourage the students to participate as soon as possible.

As the year progresses, students should continue reading aloud often, especially with particularly challenging text. Model your own use of strategies, not only to help students better understand how to use strategies, but also to help them understand that actively using strategies is something that good, mature readers do constantly.

Most students are unaccustomed to thinking out loud. They will typically stand mute as they try to figure out an unfamiliar word or deal with a confusing passage. When this happens, students should be encouraged to identify specifically what they are having difficulty with. A student might identify a particular word, or he or she may note that the individual words are familiar but the meaning of the passage is unclear.

### Active Response

Not only are good readers active in their reading when they encounter problems, but they respond constantly to whatever they read. In this way they make the text their own. As students read they should be encouraged to:

- Make as many connections as they can between what they are reading and what they already know.
- Visualize passages to help clarify their meanings or simply to picture appealing descriptions.
- Ask questions about what they are reading. The questions that go through their minds during reading will help them to examine, and thus better understand, the text. Doing so may also interest them in pursuing their own investigations. The questions may also provide a direction for students' research or exploration.
- Summarize and make predictions as a check on how well they understand what they are reading.

## Tips

- Remember that the goal of all reading strategies is comprehension. If a story or article does not make sense, the reader needs to choose whatever strategies will help make sense of it. If one strategy does not work, the reader should try another.
- Always treat problems encountered in text as interesting learning opportunities rather than something to be avoided or dreaded.
- Encourage students to think out loud about text challenges.
- Encourage students to help each other build meaning from text. Rather than telling each other what a word is or what a passage means, students should tell each other how they figured out the meanings of challenging words and passages.
- Assure students that these are not the only strategies that can be used while reading. Any strategy that they find helpful in understanding text is a good useful strategy.
- Encourage students to freely share strategies they have devised on their own. You might want to write these on a large sheet of paper and tape them to the board.
- An absence of questions does not necessarily indicate that students understand what they are reading. Be especially alert to students who never seem to ask questions. Be sure to spend tutorial time with these students occasionally, and encourage them to discuss specific selections in the context of difficulties they might have encountered and how they solved them as well as their thoughts about unit concepts.
- Observing students' responses to text will enable you to ascertain not only how well they understand a particular selection but also their facility in choosing and applying appropriate strategies. Take note of the following:

✓ Whether the strategies a student uses are effective in the particular situation.

✓ Whether the student chooses from a variety of appropriate strategies or uses the same few over and over.

✓ Whether the student can explain to classmates which strategies to use in a particular situation and why.

✓ Whether the student can identify alternative resources to pursue when the strategies she or he has tried are not effective.

✓ Whether students' application of a given strategy is becoming more effective over a period of time.

Becoming familiar and comfortable with these self-monitoring techniques gives readers the confidence to tackle material that is progressively more difficult. A good, mature reader knows that he or she will know when understanding what he or she is reading is becoming a problem and can take steps to correct the situation.

# Reading Comprehension Skills

## Purpose

An important purpose of writing is to communicate thoughts from one person to another. The goal of instruction in reading comprehension skills is to make students aware of the logic behind the structure of a written piece. If the reader can discern the logic of the structure, he or she will be more able to understand the author's logic and gain knowledge both of the facts and the intent of the selection. By keeping the organization of a piece in mind and considering the author's purpose for writing, the reader can go beyond the actual words on the page and make inferences or draw conclusions based on what was read. Strong, mature readers utilize these "between the lines" skills to get a complete picture of not only what the writer is saying, but what the writer is trying to say.

Effective comprehension skills include:

### Author's Point of View

Point of view involves identifying who is telling the story. If a character in the story is telling the story, that one character describes the action and tells what the other characters are like. This is first-person point of view. In such a story, one character will do the talking and use the pronouns *I*, *my*, *me*. All other characters' thoughts, feelings, and emotions will be reported through this one character.

If the story is told in third-person point of view, someone outside the story who is aware of all of the characters' thoughts and feelings and actions is relating them to the reader. All of the characters are referred to by their names or the pronouns *he/she*, *him/her*, *it*.

If students stay aware of who is telling a story, they will know whether they are getting the full picture or the picture of events as seen through the eyes of only one character.

### Sequence

The reader can't make any decisions about relationships or events if he or she has no idea in which order the events take place. The reader needs to pay attention to how the writer is conveying the sequence. Is it simply stated that first this happened and then that happened? Does the writer present the end of the story first and then go back and let the reader know the sequence of events? Knowing what the sequence is and how it is presented helps the reader follow the writer's line of thought.

### Fact and Opinion

Learning to distinguish fact from opinion is essential to critical reading and thinking. Students learn what factors need to be present in order for a statement to be provable. They also learn that an opinion, while not provable itself, should be based on fact. Readers use this knowledge to determine for themselves the validity of the ideas presented in their reading.

### Main Idea and Details

An author always has something specific to say to his or her reader. The author may state this main idea in different ways, but the reader should always be able to tell what the writing is about.

To strengthen the main point or main idea of a piece, the author provides details to help the reader understand. For example, the author may use comparison and contrast to make a point, provide examples, provide facts, give opinions, give descriptions, give reasons or causes, or give definitions. The reader needs to know what kinds of details he or she is dealing with before making a judgment about the main idea.

### Compare and Contrast

Using comparison and contrast is one of the most common and easiest ways a writer uses to get his or her reader to understand a subject. Comparing and contrasting unfamiliar thoughts, ideas, or things with familiar thoughts, ideas, and things gives the reader something within his or her own experience base to use in understanding.

### Cause and Effect

What made this happen? Why did this character act the way he or she did? Knowing the causes of events helps the reader to see the whole story. Using this information to identify the probable outcomes (effects) of events or actions will help the reader anticipate the story or article.

### Classify and Categorize

The relationships of actions, events, characters, outcomes, and such in a selection should be clear enough for the reader to see the relationships. Putting like things or ideas together can help the reader understand the relationships set up by the writer.

### Author's Purpose

Everything that is written is written for a purpose. That purpose may be to entertain, to persuade, or to inform. Knowing why a piece is written—what purpose the author had for writing the piece—gives the reader an idea of what to expect and perhaps some prior idea of what the author is going to say.

If a writer is writing to entertain, then the reader can generally just relax and let the writer carry him or her away. If, on the other hand, the purpose is to persuade, it will help the reader understand and keep perspective if he or she knows that the purpose is to persuade. The reader can be prepared for whatever argument the writer delivers.

### Drawing Conclusions

Often, writers do not directly state everything—they take for granted their audience's ability to "read between the lines." Readers draw conclusions when they take from the text small pieces of information about a character or event and use this information to make a statement about that character or event.

### Making Inferences

Readers make inferences about characters and events to understand the total picture in a story. When making inferences, readers use information from the text, along with personal experience or knowledge, to gain a deeper understanding of a story event and its implications.

## Procedure

### Read the Selection

First, have students read the selection using whatever strategies they need to help them make sense of the selection. Then discuss the selection to assure that students did, indeed, understand what they read. Talk about any confusion they may have, and make any necessary clarifications.

### Reread

Revisiting or rereading a selection allows the reader to note specific techniques that authors use to organize and present information in narratives and expository genres. Once students have a basic understanding of the piece, have them reread the selection in whole or in part, concentrating on selected skills. Choose examples of how the writer organized the piece to help the reader understand.

Limit this concentration on specific comprehension/writing skills to one or two that can be clearly identified in the piece. Trying to concentrate on too many things will just confuse students and make it harder for them to identify any of the organizational devices used by the writer. If a piece has many good examples of several different aspects, then go back to the piece several times over a span of days.

### Write

Solidify the connection between how an author writes and how readers make sense of a selection by encouraging students to incorporate these organizational devices into their own writing. As they attempt to use these devices, they will get a clearer understanding of how to identify them when they are reading.

Remind students often that the purpose of any skill exercise is to give them tools to use when they are reading and writing. Unless students learn to apply the skills to their own reading—in every area of reading and study—then they are not gaining a full understanding of the purpose of the exercise.

# Grammar, Usage, and Mechanics

PROGRAM APPENDIX

*Writing is a complicated process. A writer uses handwriting, spelling, vocabulary, grammar, usage, genre structures, and mechanics skills with ideas to create readable text. In addition, a writer must know how to generate content, or ideas, and understand genre structures in order to effectively present ideas in writing. Many students never progress beyond producing a written text that duplicates their everyday speech patterns. Mature writers, however, take composition beyond conversation. They understand the importance of audience and purpose for writing. They organize their thoughts, eliminating those that do not advance their main ideas, and elaborating on those that do so that their readers can follow a logical progression of ideas in an essay or story. Mature writers also know and can use the conventions of grammar, usage, spelling, and mechanics. They proofread and edit for these conventions, so their readers are not distracted by errors.*

## Purpose

### The Study of English Conventions

Over the years the study of grammar, usage, and mechanics has gone in and out of favor. In the past century much research has been done to demonstrate the effectiveness of traditional types of instruction in the conventions of English. Experience and research have shown that learning grammatical terms and completing grammar exercises have little effect on the student's practical application of these skills in the context of speaking or writing. These skills, in and of themselves, do not play a significant role in the way students use language to generate and express their ideas—for example during the prewriting and drafting phases of the writing process. In fact, emphasis on correct conventions has been shown to have a damaging effect when it is the sole focus of writing instruction. If students are evaluated only on the proper use of spelling, grammar, and punctuation, they tend to write fewer and less complex sentences.

Knowledge of English conventions is, however, vitally important in the editing and proofreading phases of the writing process. A paper riddled with mistakes in grammar, usage, or mechanics is quickly discounted. Many immature writers never revise or edit. They finish the last sentence and turn their papers in to the teacher. Mature writers employ their knowledge of English language conventions in the editing phase to refine and polish their ideas.

The study of grammar, usage, and mechanics is important for two reasons.

1. Educated people need to know and understand the structure of their language, which in large part defines their culture.
2. Knowledge of grammar gives teachers and students a common vocabulary for talking about language and makes discussions of writing tasks more efficient and clearer.

## Procedure

The key issue in learning grammar, usage, and mechanics is *how* to do it. On the one hand, teaching these skills in isolation from writing has been shown to be ineffective and even detrimental if too much emphasis is placed on them. On the other hand, not teaching these skills and having students write without concern for conventions is equally ineffective. The answer is to teach the skills in a context that allows students to directly apply them to a reading or writing activity. Students should be taught proper use of punctuation or subject/verb agreement at the same time they are taught to proofread for those conventions. As they learn to apply their knowledge of conventions during the final stages of the writing process, they will begin to see that *correcting* errors is an editorial, rather than a composition skill.

## History of English

A basic understanding of the history and structure of the English language helps students understand the rich but complex resource they have for writing.

### Old English

The English language began about AD 450 when the Angles, Jutes, and Saxons—three tribes that lived in northern Europe—invaded the British Isles. Much of their language included words that had to do with farming (*sheep, dirt, tree, earth*). Many of their words are the most frequently used words in the English language today. Because of Latin influences, English became the first of the European languages to be written down.

### Middle English

In 1066 William the Conqueror invaded England and brought Norman French with him. Slowly Old English and Norman French came together, and Middle English began to appear. Today 40% of Modern English comes from French. With the introduction of the printing press English became more widespread.

### Modern English

With the Renaissance and its rediscovery of classical Greek and Latin, many new words were created from Greek and Latin word elements. This continued intensively during the Early Modern English period. This rich language was used in the writings of Shakespeare and his contemporaries and profoundly influenced the nature and vocabulary of English. With dictionaries and spelling books, the English language became more standardized, although it continues to be influenced by other languages and new words and trends. These influences continue to make English a living, dynamic language.

## Punctuation

Early writing had no punctuation or even spaces between words. English punctuation had its beginning in ancient Greece and Rome. Early punctuation reflected speaking, rather than reading. By the end of the eighteenth century, after the invention of printing, most of the rules for punctuation were established, although they were not the same in all languages.

## The Structure of English

**Grammar** is the sound, structure, and meaning system of language. People who speak the same language are able to communicate because they intuitively know the grammar system of that language, the rules of making meaning. All languages have grammar, and yet each language has its own grammar.

Traditional grammar study usually involves two areas:

- **Parts of speech** (nouns, verbs, adjectives, adverbs, pronouns, prepositions, conjunctions) are typically considered the content of grammar. The parts of speech involve the *form* of English words.
- **Sentence structure** (subjects, predicates, objects, clauses, phrases) is also included in grammar study. Sentence structure involves the *function* of English.

**Mechanics** involves the conventions of punctuation and capitalization. Punctuation helps readers understand writers' messages. Proper punctuation involves marking off sentences according to grammatical structure. In speech students can produce sentences as easily and unconsciously as they can walk, but in writing they must think about what is and what is not a sentence.

In English there are about 14 punctuation marks (period, comma, quotation marks, question mark, exclamation point, colon, semicolon, apostrophe, hyphen, ellipsis, parentheses, brackets, dash, and underscore). Most immature writers use only three: period, comma, and question mark. The experienced writer or poet with the command of punctuation adds both flexibility and meaning to his or her sentences through his or her use of punctuation.

**Usage** is the way in which we speak in a given community. Language varies over time, across national and geographical boundaries, by gender, across age groups, and by socioeconomic status. When the variation occurs within a given language, the different versions of the same language are called *dialects.* Every language has a *prestige dialect* associated with education and financial success. In the United States, this *dialect* is known as Standard English and is the language of school and business.

Usage involves the word choices people make when speaking certain dialects. Word choices that are perfectly acceptable in conversation among friends may be unacceptable in writing. Usage is often the most obvious indicator of the difference between conversation and composition. Errors in word usage can make a writer seem ignorant and thus jeopardize his or her credibility, no matter how valid or important his or her overall message might be. Usage depends on a student's cultural and linguistic heritage. If the dialect students have learned is not the formal language of school settings or if it is not English, students must master another dialect or language in order to write Standard English.

The English Language Conventions lessons in ***Open Court Reading*** are structured to focus on grammar and usage or mechanics skills presented in a logical sequence. A skill is introduced on the first day of the lesson with appropriate models and then practiced in reading and writing on subsequent days to ensure that skills are not taught in isolation. Encourage students to use the focused English language convention presented in each lesson as they complete each Writing Process Strategies activity. Also encourage them to reread their writing, checking for proper use of the conventions taught. With practice, students should be able to apply their knowledge of conventions to any writing they do.

### Tips

- Some of the errors students make in writing are the result simply of not carefully reading their final drafts. Many errors occur because the writer's train of thought was interrupted and a sentence is not complete or a word is skipped. These may look like huge errors that a simple rereading can remedy. Most often the writer can correct these types of errors on his or her own. A major emphasis of any English composition program should be to teach the editing and proofreading phases of the writing process so students can eliminate these types of errors themselves. This involves a shift in perception—from thinking of grammar as a set of discrete skills that involve mastery of individual rules, to understanding grammar as it applies to the act of communicating in writing.
- As students learn English language conventions, they should be expected to incorporate them into their written work. A cumulative student checklist of the grammar, usage, and mechanics skills covered in a grade level appears in the back of the ***Writer's Workbook.***
- Sometimes, students write sentences that raise grammatically complex problems that require a deep understanding of English grammar. Use the Sentence Lifting strategies outlined in the **Proofreading** part of the Appendix to identify and discuss these more sophisticated types of errors that can include:
  - **Faulty Parallelism.** Parts of a sentence parallel in meaning are not parallel in structure.
  - **Nonsequitors.** A statement does not follow logically from something said previously.
  - **Dangling Modifiers.** A phrase or clause does not logically modify the word next to it.
  - **Awkwardness.** Sentences are not written simply.
  - **Wordiness.** Thoughts are not written in as few words as possible.
  - **Vocabulary.** Precise words are not used.

## Listening, Speaking, Viewing

*Some people are naturally good listeners, and others have no trouble speaking in front of groups. Many people, however, need explicit instruction on how to tune in for important details and how to organize and make an oral presentation. While some people naturally critique what they read, hear, and see, many others need specific guidance to develop skills for analyzing what they encounter in images and the media. The abilities to listen appropriately and to speak in conversations and in groups, as well as to critically evaluate the information with which they are presented, are fundamental skills that will serve students throughout their lives.*

### Purpose

In addition to reading and writing, listening, speaking, and viewing complete the language arts picture. Through the development of these language arts skills, students gain flexibility in communicating orally, visually, and in writing. When speaking and listening skills are neglected, many students have difficulty speaking in front of groups, organizing a speech, or distinguishing important information they hear. A top anxiety for many adults is speaking in front of groups. Much of this anxiety would not exist if listening, speaking, and viewing skills were taught from the early years.

The Listening, Speaking, and Viewing instruction focuses on the literature selection or the Writing Process Strategies to provide context, reinforce other elements of the lesson, and integrate the other language arts. Many of the Listening, Speaking, and Viewing skills are very similar to reading or writing skills. For example, listening for details is the same type of skill as reading for details. Preparing an oral report employs many of the same skills as preparing a written report. Learning to use these skills effectively gives students flexibility in how they approach a task.

### Procedure

Listening, speaking, and viewing skills are presented with increasing sophistication throughout every grade level of ***Open Court Reading*** in the Language Arts part of each lesson. Every unit includes at least one lesson on each of the following skills so that students encounter the skills again and again throughout a grade level:

- **Listening.** Listening skills include comprehending what one hears and listening for different purposes, such as to identify sequence or details, to summarize or draw conclusions, or to follow directions.
- **Speaking.** Speaking skills include speaking formally and conversationally, using appropriate volume, giving oral presentations, and using effective grammar. Speaking skills also include using descriptive words, using figurative language, and using formal and informal language.
- **Viewing.** Viewing skills include comprehending main ideas and messages in images, mass media, and other multimedia.
- **Interaction.** Interaction instruction focuses on a combination of listening and speaking skills. These include asking and responding to questions, nonverbal cues such as eye contact, facial expression, and posture, and contributing to and interacting in group settings.
- **Presenting Information.** The last Listening, Speaking, and Viewing lesson in every unit usually focuses on presentation skills. These include sharing ideas, relating experiences or stories, organizing information, and preparing for speeches. These lessons often parallel the Writing Process Strategies instruction, so that students can prepare their information in written or oral form.

### Tips

- Point out the parallels among the language arts skills: providing written and oral directions, telling or writing a narrative, and so on. Encourage students to see that they have choices for communicating. Discuss the similarities and differences between different forms of communication, and determine whether one is preferable in a given situation.
- Ensure that all students have opportunities to speak in small groups and whole-class situations.
- Provide and teach students to allow appropriate wait time before someone answers a question.

# Writing

PROGRAM APPENDIX

The ability to write with clarity and coherence is essential to students' success in school as well as in life. Communicating through writing is becoming more and more important in this age of computers. Yet, writing remains a major problem for students at all levels, as well as adults in the workplace.

## Purpose

Writing is a complex process. It requires the ability to use a variety of skills (penmanship, grammar, usage, mechanics, spelling, vocabulary) fluently and appropriately at the same time one's creative and critical thinking processes create and structure an idea. Familiarity with the structures of writing and different genres, audiences, and purposes is necessary to write appropriately as well. The art of writing well also involves writer's craft, the ability to manipulate words and sentences for effect.

As strange as it may seem, the better a writer is, the *harder* he or she works at writing. The best writers are not the best because they are naturally talented. They are the best usually because they work the hardest. Good writers really do take *more* time than others in the planning and revising stages of the writing process. Poorer writers make writing look easy by writing without planning and typically build a composition sentence by sentence. They turn in their papers with little or no correction.

***The best writers are not the best because they are naturally talented. They are the best usually because they work the hardest. Good writers really do take* more *time than others in the planning and revising stages of the writing process.***

The goals of writing instruction have many facets:

- To model and practice writing in a variety of writing genres so that students can choose and write in an appropriate form.
- To model and practice a writing process to help students develop routines for planning their work and then revising and editing it.
- To practice using spelling, vocabulary, and English language conventions skills in writing so that students can use them fluently.
- To develop writing traits: ideas, organization, voice, word choice, sentence fluency, and presentation so that students become effective writers.

Just as the goal of phonics instruction is to teach students to read, the Writing Process Strategies instruction in ***Open Court Reading*** focuses on skills, structures, and strategies for writing. The goal of this instruction is to learn how to write, rather than to develop a particular idea. From this instruction, students will have a comprehensive bank of tools for writing, which they can then employ in the development of their Research and Inquiry investigations in each unit or in any other writing application.

## Procedures

### Writing Genres

There are several different genres students are typically asked to write. These usually include many creative stories and a few reports. The only narrative writing most adults do, however, is summaries of meetings. The bulk of adult writing consists of writing reports, letters, analyses, memos, and proposals. College students, as well, typically write research reports or critiques. A literate student needs to be able to choose and write in an appropriate genre.

- Narrative writing is story writing, which has a beginning, middle, and end. It includes myth, realistic fiction, historical fiction, biography, science fiction, fantasy, folktale, and legend.
- Expository writing is informational writing. It includes research reports, scientific investigation, summaries, and explanations of a process.
- Descriptive writing is observational writing that includes details. It has descriptive paragraphs that may be part of narrative or expository writing.
- Poetry writing involves particular attention to word choice and rhythm. Poetry may be free form, ballad, rhyming, or a variety of other forms.
- Personal writing is functional writing to help record ideas, thoughts, or feelings or to communicate with others and may include E-mail, journals, lists, and messages.
- Persuasive writing involves the development of a persuasive argument. It includes posters, persuasive essays, and advertisements.

In ***Open Court Reading*** the first unit of every grade teaches the writing process and traits of writing. Each subsequent unit focuses on a particular genre appropriate for the unit content. Expository and persuasive writing are typically in the units with research themes such as medicine or business; personal, narrative, descriptive, and poetry writing are in units with universal themes, such as friendship and courage. Exemplary models of each form of writing are included either in the literature selection, on the ***Language Arts Transparencies,*** or in the ***Language Arts Handbook.***

Each genre has its own form and function. For example:

- A personal narrative is probably best ordered as a straightforward chronological retelling of events. Dialogue may help to tell the story.
- A process description should be told in a step-by-step order. The draft should include as much information as possible; each step must be clear. If the piece needs cutting, the student can always do it later.
- A persuasive piece appeals to feelings. It requires facts as well as expert opinions.
- An interview could be written as a series of questions and answers.
- The order of details in a descriptive piece must be easy to follow—from left to right, top to bottom, or whatever order makes sense.
- A fictional story must include details describing characters, setting, and the characters' actions. Dialogue also helps to tell the story.

The goal is not to develop full-blown novels and compositions, but to experience the structures of different forms of writing.

### Structures of Writing

Structures of writing involve the effective development of sentences, paragraphs, and compositions. In ***Open Court Reading*** structures of writing are taught within the context of the Writing Process Strategies activities rather than in isolation, so that students integrate their practice of writing structures as they develop different writing genres.

### Writer's Craft

Writer's Craft involves the elements and choices writers make to add drama, suspense, or lightheartedness to a written work. These elements may include foreshadowing, use of figurative language, dialogue, or enhancement of setting or use of description to affect the mood and tone. In ***Open Court Reading,*** along with structures of writing, the writer's craft is pointed out in the literature selection and then taught and practiced within the context of the Writing Process Strategies activities.

### Writing Traits

Writing traits are those elements and qualities in a composition that enhance the effectiveness of the writing. These include:

- Ideas/Content. Not only the quality of the idea, but the development, support, and focus of the idea makes a strong composition.

- Organization. In quality writing, the organization develops the central idea. The order and structure move the reader through the text easily. The beginning grabs the reader's attention and the conclusion adds impact.
- Voice. Voice is the overall tone of a piece of writing. Good writers choose a voice appropriate for the topic, purpose, and audience. As students develop writing skills, a unique style begins to emerge. The writing is expressive, engaging, or sincere, demonstrating a strong commitment to the topic.
- Word Choice. In quality writing words convey the intended message in an interesting, precise, and natural way appropriate to audience and purpose.
- Sentence Fluency. Sentence fluency enhances the flow and rhythm of a composition. In good writing sentence patterns are somewhat varied, contributing to ease in oral reading.
- Conventions. Good writers demonstrate consistent use and awareness of English language conventions.
- Presentation. A quality piece of writing includes an impressive presentation with attention to format, style, illustration, and clarity.

In ***Open Court Reading***, the traits of writing are taught in the first unit and then practiced in every Writing Process Strategies activity as an integral part of the writing process.

### The Writing Process

Providing a routine or process for students to follow will help them to learn a systematic approach to writing. By following the steps of the writing process, students will learn to approach everything they write with purpose and thought. They learn that although writing takes time and thought, there are steps they can take to make their writing clear, coherent, and appealing to their audience.

In ***Open Court Reading***, the first unit of every grade provides an overview and teaching of the writing process, including strategies and examples for getting ideas, determining audience and purpose for writing, organizing writing, drafting, revising, editing, and presenting. The vehicle used to apply this instruction is a student autobiography. The autobiographies can be collected in a school portfolio to assess writing development over the course of the elementary years.

# Prewriting

## Purpose

Prewriting is that phase of the writing process when students think through an idea they want to write about. To improve their writing, students should think about their ideas, discuss them, and plan how they want readers to respond. It is important for students to take time before writing to plan ahead so that they can proceed from one phase of the writing process to another without spending unnecessary time making decisions that should have been made earlier. Prewriting is the most time-consuming phase of the writing process, but it may be the most important.

***The goal is not to develop full-blown novels and compositions, but to familiarize and practice the structures of different forms of writing.***

## Procedure

### Good student writers

- Listen to advice about time requirements and plan time accordingly.
- Spend time choosing, thinking about, and planning the topic.
- Spend time narrowing the topic.
- Determine the purpose for writing.
- Consider the audience and what readers already know about the topic.
- Conduct research, if necessary, before writing.
- Get information from a lot of different sources.
- Use models for different types of writing, but develop individual plans.
- Organize the resource information.
- Make a plan for writing that shows how the ideas will be organized.
- Elaborate on a plan and evaluate and alter ideas as writing proceeds.

### Noting Writing Ideas

Students can make notes of writing ideas at any time, with a special time being set aside following the discussion of each reading selection. The writing ideas students get from a discussion might be concerned with the topic of the selection they just read or with an aspect of the author's style. You should keep such a list of writing ideas also, and think aloud occasionally as you make writing idea notes.

Students must make many decisions during the prewriting phase of the writing process. Most students can benefit from talking with a partner or a small group of classmates about these decisions. They may want to discuss some of the following points.

- **Genre** or format of each writing piece. Having decided to use a writing idea such as "a misunderstanding on the first day of school," the student must decide how to use it—for example, as a personal narrative, a realistic fiction story, a poem, a fantasy story, a play, a letter, and so on.
- **Audience**. Although students' writing pieces will be shared with classmates and with you, some may ultimately be intended for other audiences.
- **Writing Purpose**. Each student should write a sentence that tells the purpose of the piece he or she plans to write. The purpose statement should name the intended audience and the effect the writer hopes to have on that audience. For example, a writer may want to describe her first day in school. The intended audience is kindergarten students, and she intends her story to be humorous. Her purpose statement would read, "I want to write a funny story for other students about my first day in kindergarten."
- **Planning**. Some writers may find it helpful to brainstorm with a partner or small group to list words and phrases they might use in a piece of writing. Sometimes this list can be organized into webs of related ideas or details. This kind of prewriting activity might be particularly useful for planning a descriptive piece. For planning a comparison/contrast piece, a writer might use another kind of visual organizer, such as a Venn diagram. Students planning fiction pieces might use a story frame or plot line.

## Tips

- Circulate as students make notes on writing ideas or work in small groups on prewriting activities.
- Notice which students are having difficulty coming up with writing ideas. It may help to pair these students with students who have many ideas.
- Do not worry if this phase of the process seems noisy and somewhat chaotic. Students must be allowed to let their imaginations roam in free association and to play around with words and ideas until they hit on something that seems right. They must be permitted to share ideas and help each other.
- Do not worry if, in the early sessions, the class as a whole seems to have few ideas. Through the reading and discussion of selections in the reading anthology, most students will soon have more writing ideas than they can use.

PROGRAM APPENDIX

# Drafting

## Purpose

During the drafting phase of the writing process, students shape their planning notes into main ideas and details. They devote their time and effort to getting words down on paper. Whether students are drafting on scrap paper or on computer screens, your role is to encourage each writer to "get it all down." You must also provide a suitable writing environment with the expectation that there will be revision to the draft and to the original plan.

### Good Student Writers

- Express all their ideas in the first draft.
- Stop and think about what is being written while drafting.
- Evaluate and alter ideas while drafting.
- Change or elaborate on original plans while drafting.
- Discover that they need more information about certain parts of their writing.
- Learn a lot more about the topic while drafting.

## Procedure

Here are some points to share with students before they begin drafting:

- Drafting is putting your ideas down on paper for your own use. Writers do not need to worry about spelling or exact words. They just need to get their ideas down.
- Write on every other line so that you will have room to make revisions.
- Write on only one side of a page so that when you revise you can see all of your draft at once.
- As you draft, keep in mind your purpose for writing this piece and your intended audience.
- Use your plan and your notes from research to add details.

### Using Word Processors for Drafting

Many students enjoy drafting on the screen of a computer more than drafting on paper. Once they have mastered the keyboard, they may find it easier to think as they write. Their first attempts look less sloppy, and they are often more willing to make changes and experiment as they draft. They will certainly find it neater to use the delete key on the word processor than to correct their mistakes by crossing out. The Basic Computer Skills instruction in the Language Arts Overview of every lesson provides instruction on using the computer.

## Tips

Sometimes the hardest part of drafting is getting the first sentence down on paper. It may help a student even before she or he starts writing to begin a story in the middle or to write the word "Draft" in big letters at the top of the paper.

- If a student feels stuck during drafting, he or she may need to go back and try a different prewriting technique.
- After an initial fifteen or twenty minutes of imposed silence, some students may work better and come up with more ideas if they share as they write.
- You may find that it is difficult to get students to "loosen up" as they draft. Remember, most students have been encouraged to be neat and to erase mistakes when they write. It may help to share some of your own marked-up manuscripts with students.

# Revising

## Purpose

The purpose of revising is to make sure that a piece of writing expresses the writer's ideas clearly and completely. It has been said that there is no good writing, just good rewriting. A major distinction between good writers and poor writers is the amount of time and effort they put into revision. Poor writers look for spelling and grammatical errors if they do read their work.

### Good Student writers

- Evaluate what has been written.
- Read the draft as a reader, not the writer.
- Identify problems with focus, giving enough information, clarity, and order.
- Think of solutions to problems and understand when solutions will and won't work.
- Recognize when and how the text needs to be reorganized.
- Eliminate sentences or paragraphs that don't fit the main idea.
- Identify ideas that need elaboration.
- Do more research if needed to support or add ideas.
- Identify and eliminate unnecessary details.
- Ask for feedback from peer and teacher conferences.
- Take advantage of classroom and outside resources.
- Check the accuracy of facts and details.
- Give credit for any ideas from other people or sources.

## Procedure

Model asking questions like the following when revising various kinds of writing:

- About a narrative:
  - ✓ Does my first sentence get my readers' attention?
  - ✓ Are events in the story told in an order that makes sense?
  - ✓ Have I included dialogue to help move the story along?
  - ✓ Does the story have a clear focus?
- About a description:
  - ✓ Have I used details that appeal to the senses?
- About a comparison/contrast piece:
  - ✓ Have I made a separate paragraph for each subject discussed?
- About an explanation:
  - ✓ Will readers understand what I am saying?
  - ✓ Are the steps of the explanation in a clear order?
  - ✓ Have I made effective use of signal words?
  - ✓ Have I included enough information?
- About fiction:
  - ✓ Have I described my characters and setting?
  - ✓ Does the plot include a problem, build to a climax, and then describe the resolution of the problem?
- About persuasive writing:
  - ✓ Have I made my position clear?
  - ✓ Does my evidence support my position?
  - ✓ Have I used opinions as well as facts, and have I said whose opinions I used?
  - ✓ Have I directed my writing to my audience?

Help students understand the value of asking questions such as the following as they revise:

- About each paragraph:
  - ✓ Does each sentence belong in it?
  - ✓ Does each sentence connect smoothly with the next?
  - ✓ Does each sentence say something about the main idea?
- About each sentence:
  - ✓ Do the sentences read smoothly?
  - ✓ Have I combined sentences that were too short?
  - ✓ Have I broken sentences that were too long into two shorter sentences?
  - ✓ Have I varied the beginnings of the sentences?
- About the words:
  - ✓ Have I changed words that were repeated too often?
  - ✓ Do transition words connect ideas?

## Tips

- Use the student Writing Folder to review student progress. Check first drafts against revised versions to see how each student is able to apply revision strategies.
- You may find that some students are reluctant to revise. You might then try the following:

  ✓ If a student doesn't see anything that needs to be changed or doesn't want to change anything, get him or her to do something to the paper—number the details in a description or the steps in a process, circle exact words, underline the best parts of the paper. Once a paper is marked, the student may not be so reluctant to change it.

  ✓ One reason many students do not like to revise is that they think they must recopy everything. This is not always necessary. Sometimes writers can cut and paste sections that they want to move. Or they can use carets and deletion marks to show additions and subtractions from a piece.

  ✓ Give an especially reluctant student a deadline by which she or he must revise a piece or lose the chance to publish it.

  ✓ Students will hopefully be writing in other classes and on a variety of topics. Revision techniques can be used to improve writing in any curriculum area. Stress to students the importance of focusing on their intended audience as they revise.

# Proofreading

## Purpose

Writing that is free of grammatical, spelling, and technical mistakes is clearer and easier for readers to understand. By proofreading their pieces, students will also notice which errors they make repeatedly and will learn not to make them in the future.

After a piece of writing has been revised for content and style, students must read it carefully line by line to make sure that it contains no errors. This activity, the fourth phase of the writing process, is called proofreading and is a critical step that must occur before a piece of writing can be published. Students can begin proofreading a piece when they feel that it has been sufficiently revised.

### Good Student Writers

- Edit the work to allow the reader to understand and enjoy the words.
- Correct most errors in English language conventions.
- Use resources or seek assistance to address any uncertainties in English language conventions.

## Procedure

### Using What They Have Learned

Students should be expected to proofread at a level appropriate to their grade. Young authors should not be held responsible for skills they have not yet learned. Older students will be able to check for a greater variety of errors than younger students and should be expected to take greater responsibility for their proofreading. For example, students in first grade can be expected to check for and correct omitted capital letters at the beginning of sentences, but they should not necessarily be expected to understand and correct capital letters in proper nouns or in names of organizations. Older students will have mastered many more grammatical, mechanical, usage, and spelling skills and can be expected to perform accordingly. When you spot an error related to a skill beyond a student's level, make clear to the student that you do not expect her or him to be responsible for the mistake, but do explain that the error still needs to be corrected. The following suggestions may be useful as you introduce proofreading to the students and help them develop their proofreading skills.

### Proofreading Checklist

Have students use a proofreading checklist similar to the one shown here to help them remember the steps for effective proofreading.

✓ Read each sentence.

✓ Does each sentence begin with a capital letter and end with correct punctuation?

✓ Do you notice any sentence fragments or run-on sentences?

✓ Are words missing from the sentence?

✓ Is any punctuation or capitalization missing from within the sentence?

✓ Do you notice any incorrect grammar or incorrect word usage in the sentence?

✓ Do you notice any misspelled words?

✓ Are the paragraphs indented?

✓ Can very long paragraphs be broken into two paragraphs?

✓ Can very short paragraphs be combined into one paragraph?

## Tips

- **Proofreader's Marks** Students should use standard Proofreader's Marks to indicate the changes they wish to make. Explain to students that these marks are a kind of code used to show which alterations to make without a long explanation. Students may also be interested to know that professional writers, editors, and proofreaders use these same marks. You may want to review these marks one by one, illustrating on the board how to use them. For example, they may insert a word or a phrase by using a caret (^). If students wish to insert more text than will fit above the line, they may write in the margin or attach another sheet of paper. It may be a good idea, when such extensive corrections are made, for students to proofread their final copy carefully to make sure they have included all their alterations.
- **Sentence lifting** is a very effective method of showing students how to proofread their own work. Because students are working on their own sentences, they will be more inclined to both pay attention to what is going on and better understand the corrections that are made.

  ✓ Choose several pieces of student writing and look for common errors.

  ✓ On an overhead transparency, write several sentences. Include at least one sentence that has no errors.

  ✓ Tell students that you are going to concentrate on one type of error at a time. For example, first you will concentrate on spelling.

  ✓ Ask students to read the first sentence and point out any words they feel are spelled incorrectly. Do not erase errors. Cross them out and write the correctly spelled word above the crossed out word.

  ✓ Next move to a different type of error. Ask students to check for capitalization and punctuation.

  ✓ Continue in this way, correcting errors as you go through the sample sentences.
- **Using a Word Processor.** If the students are using a word processor to write their pieces, they may wish to run a spell check on their document. Caution them, however, that even the most sophisticated computer cannot catch every spelling error. Misuse of homophones and typographical errors may not be caught by the computer if the misused words appear in the computer's dictionary. For example, if a student types *form* instead of *from*, the computer will not register a mistake because *form* is also a word.

Circulate as students are proofreading on their own or in pairs.

✓ Are students able to check references when they are unsure of a spelling or usage?

✓ Are students criticizing each other's work constructively?

✓ Does a student no longer omit end punctuation because he or she noticed this error repeatedly during proofreading?

✓ Note students who are having difficulty. You may wish to address these difficulties during individual conferences.

# Publishing

## Purpose

Publishing is the process of bringing private writing to the reading public. The purpose of writing is to communicate. Unless students are writing in a journal, they will want to present their writing to the public. Such sharing helps students to learn about themselves and others, provides an opportunity for them to take pride in their hard work, and thus motivates them to further writing.

Publishing their work helps motivate students to improve such skills as spelling, grammar, and handwriting. Publishing can be as simple as displaying papers on a bulletin board or as elaborate as creating a class newspaper. Publishing will not—indeed should not—always require large blocks of class time. Students will wish to spend more time elaborately presenting their favorite pieces and less time on other works. If students take an inordinate amount of time to publish their work, you may want to coach them on how to speed up the process.

### Good Student Writers

- Present the work in a way that makes it easy to read and understand.
- Consider format, style, illustration, and clarity in the presentation of the work.
- Show pride in the finished work.

## Procedure

### Preparing the Final Copy

When students feel that they have thoroughly proofread their pieces, they should copy the work onto another sheet of paper, using their best handwriting, or type the work on a computer or typewriter. They should then check this copy against the proofread copy to make sure that they made all the changes correctly and did not introduce any new errors. You may need to proofread and correct students' papers one final time before publishing to make sure that they have caught all errors.

### Publishing Choices

In publishing, students need to decide

✓ how to prepare the piece for publication.
✓ what form the published work should take.
✓ whether to illustrate their writing with photographs, drawings, or charts with captions, as necessary.
✓ where to place any art they are using.

### Publishing Checklist

The following checklist will help students when they are publishing their work. (Not every question applies to every form of publishing.)

✓ Have I revised my work to make it better?
✓ Have I proofread it carefully?
✓ Have I decided upon my illustrations?
✓ Have I recopied my piece carefully and illustrated it?
✓ Have I numbered the pages?
✓ Have I made a cover that tells the title and my name?

## Tips

- Read through the piece, and tell the student if any corrections still need to be made. Also make some suggestions about the best way to publish a piece if a student has trouble coming up with an idea.
- Make suggestions and give criticism as needed, but remember that students must retain ownership of their publishing. Leave final decisions about form and design of their work up to individual students.
- Remind students to think about their intended audience when they are deciding on the form for their published piece. Will the form they have selected present their ideas effectively to the people they want to reach?

# Writing Seminar

## Purpose

The purpose of Writing Seminar (Levels 1–6) is for students to discuss their work in progress and to share ideas for improving it.

Writing Seminar is one of the activities in which students may choose to participate during Workshop. Students will meet in small groups to read and discuss one another's writing. One student reads a piece in progress. Other students comment on the writing and ask questions about the ideas behind the writing. The student whose work is being critiqued writes down the comments made by his or her classmates and decides how to use these comments to make the writing better.

## Procedure

To begin the seminar, have one student writer read his or her revised draft as other students listen carefully. When the student has finished, invite other students to retell the story in their own words. If they have trouble retelling the story, the writer knows that he or she must make some ideas clearer.

Then have listeners who wish to comment raise their hands. The writer calls on each in turn. The listeners ask questions or make comments about the writing, telling, for example, what they like about it or what they might change to make it better. After several comments have been made, the writer notes any information that she or he might use. Another student then reads his or her piece.

### Guidelines for Peer Conferencing

In an early session, work with students to establish guidelines for peer conferencing. You might suggest rules such as the following:

✓ Listen quietly while someone else is speaking.
✓ Think carefully before you comment on another person's work.
✓ Make your comments specific.
✓ Comment on something that you like about the piece before you comment on something that needs to be improved.
✓ Discuss your work quietly so as not to disturb the rest of the class.

### Modeling Seminar Behavior

You may need to model meaningful comments and questions. For example:

✓ What was your favorite part?
✓ I like the part where (or when)
✓ I like the way you describe
✓ What happened after . . . ?
✓ I'd like to know more about
✓ Why did ________ happen?
✓ What do you think is the most important part?

### Teacher Conferencing

During Writing Seminar, you will want to schedule individual conferences with students to help them evaluate their writing so that they can recognize problems and find ways to solve them. Teacher conferences are useful during all phases of the writing process, but they are crucial during the revising phase. Conferences give you an opportunity to observe students as they evaluate their writing, solve problems, make decisions about their work, and take responsibility for the development and completion of their work. The basic procedure for conferences is:

- Have the student read his or her work aloud.
- Review any feedback the student has received so far.
- Identify positive elements of the work.
- Use one or more of these strategies to help the student improve his or her work.
  ✓ Have students explain how they got their ideas.
  ✓ Have students think aloud about how they will address the feedback they have received.
  ✓ Ask students to help you understand any confusion you may have about their writing.
  ✓ Have the student add, delete, or rearrange something in the work and ask how it affects the whole piece.
  ✓ Think aloud while you do a part of what the student was asked to do. Ask the student to compare what you did to what he or she did.
  ✓ Have the student prescribe as if to a younger student how to revise the work.

- Ask two or three questions to guide students through revising (see below).
- Conclude by having the student state a plan for continuing work on the piece.

## Writing Conference Questions

### Ideas

- Who is your audience?
- What is your purpose for writing?
- How does the reader know the purpose?
- Is there enough information about the topic?
- Do you like one part of your work more than the rest? Why?
- Is your main idea clear?
- Is there a better way to express this idea?
- Is this a good topic sentence?
- Is your introduction engaging?
- Are any important details left out?
- Are any not-so-important details left in?
- Do you use specific details and examples?
- Are your ideas accurate and, if necessary, supported by research?
- Does your conclusion sum up or restate your purpose for writing?
- What might be another way to end the work?

### Organization

- Is the writing organized in a way that makes the most sense based on the main idea?
- Is the structure clear for the reader? Is there a clear beginning, middle, and end?
- Are there smooth transitions from one part to the next?
- Are supporting details ordered in the most logical way?
- Can you combine any smaller paragraphs or separate larger ones?

### Voice

- Do you sound confident and knowledgeable?
- Does the voice you use reflect the purpose of your writing? Does your writing sound funny or serious when you want it to be?
- Is your voice appropriate for your audience?
- Do you sound interested in the subject?
- Have you confidently stated your opinion? Have you used the pronoun "I" if appropriate?
- Does your writing sound like you?
- Is your voice too formal or informal?
- Will this writing get a strong response from the reader?
- Does your writing make the reader care about your topic?

### Word Choice

- Do you use the same word/phrase repeatedly?
- Could you say the same thing with different words?
- Have you defined words your audience may not understand?
- Have you used precise words to describe or explain?
- Is there a better word to express this idea?
- Have you used your own words when summarizing information from another text?
- Do you use time and order words such as *first*, *next*, *then*, and *last* to help the reader understand when events take place?

### Sentence Fluency

- Are your sentences clear and to the point?
- Have you used different kinds and lengths of sentences to effectively present your ideas?
- Could any of your sentences be combined?
- Is there a rhythm to your sentences?
- Does each sentence introduce a new idea or a new piece of information?
- Do some sentences repeat what has already been stated? If so, cut or change them.
- Have you used transition words such as *in contrast*, *however*, and *on the other hand* to move smoothly from one subject to the other?
- Have you used transitional phrases, such as *according to*, *in addition to*, or *at the same time* to link sentences?
- Have you used conjunctions such as *and*, *but*, and *or* to combine short, choppy sentences?

## Tips

- Completed pieces as well as works in progress can be shared during Writing Seminar.
- Concentrate on one phase of the writing process at a time.
- Remember to keep conferences brief and to the point. If you are calling the conference, prepare your comments in advance. Be sure that you confer regularly with every student if only to check that each one is continuing to write, revise, and publish.
- During teacher conferences, you might use the following responses to student writing.
  - ✓ To open communication with the writer:
    - How is the writing going?
    - Tell me about your piece.
    - How did you get your ideas?
  - ✓ To give encouragement:
    - I like the part where . . . .
    - I like the way you open your piece by . . . .
    - I like your description of . . . .
  - ✓ To get the writer to clarify meaning:
    - I wonder about . . . .
    - What happened after . . . .
    - Why did . . . ?
  - ✓ To get the writer to think about direction and about writing strategies:
    - What do you plan to do with your piece?
    - How will you go about doing that?
    - What could I do to help you?
- As you confer with students, also recognize growth—evidence in the text that a student has applied what he or she learned in earlier conferences to another piece of writing.
- Some cues to look for when evaluating a student's growth as a writer include:
  - ✓ The writer identifies problems.
  - ✓ The writer thinks of solutions to a problem.
  - ✓ The writer recognizes when and how the text needs to be reorganized.
  - ✓ The writer identifies ideas in the text that need elaboration.
  - ✓ The writer makes thoughtful changes and pays attention to detail.
  - ✓ The writer takes advantage of peer and teacher conferences, books, and other resources to improve his or her writing.

### Teaching Strategies for Writing

The teacher's role in writing instruction is critical. Certain strategies have been shown to be particularly effective in teaching writing.

**Teacher Modeling** Students learn best when they have good models. Models for the forms of writing appear in the literature selections, ***Language Arts Transparencies,*** and ***Language Arts Handbook.*** The Writing Process Strategies include instruction and models for all phases of the writing process. Teachers can also model the writing process for students every time they write.

**Feedback.** The most effective writing instruction is the feedback good teachers give to individual student work. Unfortunately many teachers simply mark errors in spelling, grammar, usage, and mechanics. The ***Routine Card*** and the ***Writer's Workbook*** provide questions that teachers can consider to offer constructive and meaningful feedback to students.

**Clear Assignments.** A well-written assignment makes clear to students what they are supposed to do, how they are supposed to do it, who the students are writing for, and what constitutes a successful response. When students have this information, they can plan, organize, and produce more effective work.

**Instruction.** Having students write a lot does not make them good writers. Few people become good writers, no matter how much they write. For many, the effect of years of practice is simply to produce increasingly fluent bad writing. Students need specific instruction and practice on different forms of writing and on different phases of the writing process, which they receive with instruction, modeling, practice, and feedback.

# Classroom Discussion

PROGRAM APPENDIX

The more students are able to discuss what they are learning, voice their confusions, and compare perceptions of what they are learning, the deeper and more meaningful their learning becomes.

## Purpose

It is in discussions that students are exposed to points of view different from their own, and it is through discussion that they learn how to express their thoughts and opinions coherently. Through discussion, students add to their own knowledge that of their classmates and learn to explain themselves coherently. They also begin to ask insightful questions that help them better understand what they have read and all that they are learning through their inquiry/research and explorations. The purpose of classroom discussion is to provide a sequence through which discussion can proceed.

## Procedure

### Reflecting on the Selection

After students have finished reading a selection, provide an opportunity for them to engage in **whole-group** discussion about the selection. Students should:

- Check to see whether the questions they asked before reading have been answered. Encourage them to discuss whether any unanswered questions should still be answered and if so have them add those questions to the Concept/Question Board.
- Discuss any new questions that have arisen because of the reading. Encourage students to decide which of these questions should go on the Concept/Question Board.
- Share what they expected to learn from reading the selection and tell whether expectations were met.
- Talk about whatever has come to mind while reading the selection. This discussion should be an informal sharing of impressions of, or opinions about, the selection; it should never take on the aspects of a question-and-answer session about the selection.
- Give students ample opportunity to ask questions and share their thoughts about the selection. Participate as an active member of the group, making your own observations about information in a selection or modeling your own appreciation of a story. Be especially aware of unusual and interesting insights suggested by students so that these insights can be recognized and discussed. To help students learn to keep the discussion student-centered, have each student choose the next speaker instead of handing the discussion back to you.

### Recording Ideas

As students finish discussions about their reactions to a selection, they should be encouraged to record their thoughts, feelings, reactions, and ideas about the selection or the subject of the selection in their Writer's Notebooks. This will not only help keep the selections fresh in students' minds; it will strengthen their writing abilities and help them learn how to write about their thoughts and feelings.

Students may find that the selection gave them ideas for their own writing, or it could have reminded them of some person or incident in their own lives. Perhaps the selection answered a question that has been on their minds or raised a question they had never thought before. Good, mature writers—especially professional writers—learn the value of recording such thoughts and impressions quickly before they fade. Students should be encouraged to do this also.

### Handing Off

Handing off (Levels 1–6) is a method of turning over to students the primary responsibility for controlling discussion. Often, students who are taking responsibility for controlling a discussion tend to have all "turns" go through the teacher. The teacher is the one to whom attention is transferred when a speaker finishes, and the teacher is the one who is expected to call on the next speaker—the result being that the teacher remains the pivotal figure in the discussion.

Having the students "hand off" the discussion to other students instead of the teacher encourages them to retain complete control of the discussion and to become more actively involved in the learning process. When a student finishes his or her comments, that student should choose (hand the discussion off to) the next speaker. In this way, students maintain a discussion without relying on the teacher to decide who speaks.

When handing off is in place, the teacher's main roles are to occasionally remind students to hand off and to monitor the discussion to ensure that everyone gets a chance to contribute. The teacher may say, for example, "Remember, not just boys (or girls)," or "Try to choose someone who has not had a chance to talk yet."

In order for handing off to work effectively, a seating arrangement that allows students to see one another is essential. A circle or a semicircle is effective. In addition, all of the students need to have copies of the materials being discussed.

Actively encourage this handing-off process by letting students know that they, not you, are in control of the discussion.

If students want to remember thoughts about, or reactions to, a selection, suggest that they record these in the Writing Journal section of the Writer's Notebook. Encourage students to record the thoughts, feelings, or reactions that are elicited by any reading they do.

### Exploring Concepts Within the Selection

To provide an opportunity for collaborative learning and to focus on the concepts, have students form small groups and spend time discussing what they have learned about the concepts from this selection. Topics may include new information that they have acquired or new ideas that they have had.

Students should always base their discussions on postings from the Concept/Question Board as well as on previous discussions of the concept. The small-group discussions should be ongoing throughout the unit; during this time students should continue to compare and contrast any new information with their previous ideas, opinions, and impressions about the concepts. Does this selection help confirm their ideas? Does it contradict their thinking? Has it changed their outlook?

As students discuss the concepts in small groups, circulate around the room to make sure that each group stays focused upon the selection and the concepts. After students have had some time to discuss the information and the ideas in the selection, encourage each group to formulate some statements about the concept that apply to the selection.

### Sharing Ideas about Concepts

Have a representative from each group report and explain the group's ideas to the rest of the class. Then have the class formulate one or more general statements related to the unit concepts and write these statements on the Concept/Question Board. As students progress through the unit, they will gain more and more confidence in suggesting additions to the Concept/Question Board.

**Visual Aids** During this part of the discussion, you may find it helpful to use visual aids to help students as they build the connections to the unit concepts. Not all units or concepts will lend themselves to this type of treatment; however, aids such as time lines, charts, graphs, or pictographs may help students see how each new selection adds to their growing knowledge of the concepts.

Encourage students to ask questions about the concepts that the selection may have raised. Have students list on the Concept/Question Board those questions that cannot be answered immediately and that they want to explore further.

### Exploring Concepts Across Selections

As each new selection is read, encourage students to discuss its connection with the other selections and with the unit concepts. Also encourage students to think about selections that they have read from other units and how they relate to the concepts for this unit.

Ultimately, it is this ability to make connections between past knowledge and new knowledge that allows any learner to gain insights into what is being studied. The goal of the work with concepts and the discussions is to help students to start thinking in terms of connections—how is this like what I have learned before? Does this information confirm, contradict, or add a completely different layer to that which I already know about this concept? How can the others in the class have such different ideas than I do when we just read the same selection? Why is so much written about this subject?

Learning to make connections and to delve deeper through self-generated questions gives students the tools they need to become effective, efficient, lifelong learners.

## Tips

- Discussions offer a prime opportunity for you to introduce, or seed, new ideas about the concepts. New ideas can come from a variety of sources: students may draw on their own experiences or on the books or videos they are studying; you may introduce new ideas into the discussion; or you may, at times, invite experts to speak to the class.
- If students do not mention an important idea that is necessary to the understanding of some larger issue, you may "drop" that idea into the conversation and, indeed, repeat it several times to make sure that it does get picked up. This seeding may be subtle ("I think that might be important here.") or quite direct ("This is a big idea, one that we will definitely need to understand and one that we will return to regularly.").

***Discussion is an integral part of learning.***

- In order to facilitate this process for each unit, you must be aware of the unit concepts and be able to recognize and reinforce them when they arise spontaneously in discussions. If central unit concepts do not arise naturally, then, and only then, will you seed these ideas by direct modeling. The more you turn discussions over to students, the more involved they will become, and the more responsibility they will take for their own learning. Make it your goal to become a participant in, rather than the leader of, class discussions.
- Help students to see that they are responsible for carrying on the discussion. After a question is asked, always wait instead of jumping in with a comment or an explanation. Although this wait time may be uncomfortable at first, students will come to understand that the discussion is their responsibility and that you will not jump in every time there is a hesitation.
- As the year progresses, students will become more and more adept at conducting and participating in meaningful discussions about what they have read. These discussions will greatly enhance students' understanding of the concepts that they are exploring.

## Discussion Starters

- I didn't know that . . . .
- Does anyone know . . . .
- I figured out that . . . .
- I liked the part where . . . .
- I'm still confused about . . . .
- This made me think . . . .
- I agree with ____________ because . . . .
- I disagree with ____________ because . . . .
- The reason I think . . . .

# Inquiry and Investigation

PROGRAM APPENDIX

Research and Investigation form the heart of the ***SRA/Open Court Reading*** program. In order to encourage students to understand how reading can enhance their lives and help them to become mature, educated adults, they are asked in each unit to use what they are learning in the unit as the basis for further exploration and research. The unit information is simply the base for their investigations.

There are two types of units in the ***SRA/Open Court Reading*** program—units based on universal topics of interest such as Friendship, Perseverance, and Courage and research units that provide students a very solid base of information upon which they can begin their own inquiry and research. Units delving into such areas as fossils, astronomy, and medicine invite students to become true researchers by choosing definite areas of interest—problems or questions to research in small cooperative groups and then to present to their classmates. In this way, students gain much more knowledge of the subject than they would have simply by reading the selections in the unit.

The selections in the units are organized so that each selection will add more information or a different perspective to students' growing bodies of knowledge.

## Investigating through Reflective Activities

### Purpose

The units in ***SRA/Open Court Reading*** that deal with universal topics will be explored through reflective activities. These units—such as Courage, Friendship, and Risks and Consequences—are organized to help students expand their perspectives in familiar areas. As they explore and discuss the unit concepts related to each topic, students are involved in activities that extend their experiences and offer opportunities for reflection. Such activities include writing, drama, art, interviews, debates, and panel discussions. Throughout each unit, students may be involved in a single ongoing investigative activity, or they may participate in a number of different activities. They may choose to produce a final written project or a visual aid. They will share with the rest of the class the new knowledge that they have gained from their reflective activities. During **Workshop** students will work individually or in collaborative groups on their investigation and/or projects.

The reflective activities will be activities of students' own choosing that allow them to explore the unit concepts more fully. They are free, of course, to make other choices or to devise activities of their own.

### Procedure

#### Choosing an Area to Investigate

Students may work on activities alone, in pairs, or in small groups. They have the option of writing about or presenting their findings to the whole group upon completion. Before choosing a reflective activity, students should decide what concept-related question or problem they wish to explore. Generally, it is better for students to generate questions or problems after they have engaged in some discussion but before they have had a chance to consult source materials. This approach is more likely to bring forth ideas that students actually wonder about or wish to understand. Students may also look at the questions posted on the Concept/Question Board or introduce fresh ideas inspired by material they have just finished reading. Students who are working in pairs or in small groups should confer with one another before making a decision about what to explore. Some of the students may need your assistance in deciding upon, or narrowing down, a question or a problem so that it can be explored more easily. A good way to model this process for students is to make webs for a few of your own ideas on the board and to narrow these ideas down to a workable question or problem.

#### Organizing the Group

After a question or a problem has been chosen, the students may choose an activity that will help them to investigate that problem or question. The students' next responsibility is to decide who is going to investigate which facet of the question or the problem (when they are conducting a literature search, for example) or who is going to perform which task related to the particular reflective activity (when they are writing and performing an original playlet or puppet show, for example). Lastly, students need to decide how, or if, they want to present their findings. For instance, after conducting a literature search, some students may want to read and discuss passages from a book with a plot or theme that relates to a unit concept. Other students may prefer acting out and discussing scenes from the book.

#### Deciding How to Investigate

The following suggestions may help you and your students choose ways in which to pursue their investigations. You may want to post this list in the classroom so that groups have access to it as they decide what they want to investigate and how they want to proceed.

### Investigation Activities

- Conduct a literature search to pursue a question or a problem. Discussion or writing may follow.
- Write and produce an original playlet or puppet show based on situations related to the concepts.
- Play a role-playing game to work out a problem related to the concepts.
- Stage a panel discussion with audience participation on a question or problem.
- Hold a debate on an issue related to the concept.
- Write an advice column dealing with problems related to the concepts.
- Write a personal-experience story related to the concepts.
- Invite experts to class. Formulate questions to ask.
- Conduct an interview with someone on a subject related to the concepts.
- Produce and carry out a survey on an issue or question related to the concept.
- Produce a picture or photo essay about the concept.

**EXAMPLE:** In the Heritage unit in grade 5 of ***SRA/Open Court Reading,*** students read "In Two Worlds: A Yup'ik Eskimo Family." This selection is about how three generations of Eskimos living in Alaska near the Arctic strive to adopt the best of modern ways without abandoning their traditional values. During the class discussion, some students may note that Alice and Billy Rivers want their students to learn both the new and the old ways of living. As the discussion continues, many students may conclude from the story that the older generations hope that future generations will continue to value their roots and their cultural traditions. Students then relate this story to their own heritage. Some students may share information about their customs or traditions.

Students choose some reflective activities that will help them learn more about family heritage and that will answer some of their questions about the unit concepts. Some students may be interested in interviewing family members or close family friends about their cultural traditions and heritages. These students review what they know about interviewing. They proceed by:

- Contacting in advance the person(s) they want to interview.
- Preparing a list of questions to ask.
- Preparing a list of subjects to discuss, deciding how to record the interview (by audiotape, videotape, or taking notes).
- Deciding whether to photograph the person and, if so, getting permission to do so in advance—collecting the equipment necessary for conducting the interview.

After they conduct the interviews, students decide how they wish to present the information that they have collected.

***Investigating through reflective activities allows students to gain a wider perspective on a concept by relating it to their own experiences. Students quickly become aware that it is their responsibility to learn and to help their peers learn more about the unit concepts.***

**EXAMPLE:** Another group of students in the same fifth-grade class may be more interested in planning a photo essay about one family or about a neighborhood with many families belonging to a particular culture. These students may decide to re-examine "In Two Worlds" to notice how the text and the photographs complement each other and what information is conveyed in each photograph. They may also decide to examine some photo essays listed in the unit bibliography. These students will need to make some advance preparations as well. They proceed by:

- Determining which neighborhood and which family or families to photograph.
- Contacting in advance the persons to be interviewed and photographed.
- Touring the neighborhood in advance of the photo shoot.
- Making a list of questions to ask the family or families about their heritage or about their neighborhood.
- Thinking about what information to include in their essay so that they can determine what photographs to take.
- Collecting the equipment necessary for conducting interviews and photographing subjects.

After students collect the information and take photographs, they may write and organize the photo essay and present it to the class. The teacher should remind students of the phases of the writing process, and encourage them to revise and proofread their work until they are completely pleased with it. Students can continue discussing family heritage and raising any new questions that they wish to investigate. The teacher should remind them that as they read further, they may think of a variety of ways to explore the unit concepts. The teacher should then ask students to post on the Concept/Question Board any new questions they have about family heritage. Students should sign or initial their questions so that they can identify classmates with similar interests and exchange ideas with them. The teacher should encourage students to feel free to write an answer or a note on someone else's question or to consult the board for ideas for their own explorations. From time to time, the teacher should post his or her own questions on the Concept/Question Board.

## Tips

- The ***Leveled Classroom Library*** contains books related to the unit concepts. Remind students that these are good sources of information and that they should consult them regularly— especially when they are investigating concept-related ideas and questions.
- Some students work better within a specified time frame. Whenever they are beginning a new activity, discuss with the students a reasonable period of time within which they will be expected to complete their investigations. Post the completion date somewhere in the classroom so that students can refer to it and pace themselves accordingly. At first, you may have to help them determine a suitable deadline, but eventually they should be able to make this judgment on their own.

PROGRAM APPENDIX

# Investigating through Research

## Purpose

Students come to school with a wealth of fascinating questions. Educators need to capitalize on this excitement for learning and natural curiosity. A classroom in which only correct answers are accepted and students are not allowed to make errors and consider alternative possibilities to questions can quickly deaden this natural curiosity and enthusiasm. The purpose of the research aspect of this program is to capitalize on students' questions and natural curiosity by using a proven structure. This structure helps students to not get lost or bogged down but at the same time to preserve the open-ended character of real research, which can lead to unexpected findings and to questions that were not originally considered.

There is a conventional approach to school research papers that can be found, with minor variations, in countless textbooks. It consists of a series of steps such as the following: select a topic, narrow the topic, collect materials, take notes, outline, and write. By following these steps, a student may produce a presentable paper, but the procedure does not constitute research in a meaningful sense and indeed gives students a distorted notion of what research is about. We see students in universities and even in graduate schools still following this procedure when they do library research papers or literature reviews; we see their dismay when their professors regard such work as mere cutting and pasting and ask them where their original contribution is.

Even elementary school students can produce works of genuine research—research that seeks answers to real questions or solutions to real problems. This skill in collecting and analyzing information is a valuable tool in the adult world in which adults, as consumers, are constantly analyzing new information and making informed decisions on the basis of this information. Preparing students for the analytic demands of adult life and teaching them how to find answers to their questions are goals of education.

## Procedure

In order to make the research productive, the following important principles are embodied in this approach:

1. Research is focused on problems, not topics.
2. Conjectures—opinions based on less than complete evidence or proof—guide the research; the research does not simply produce conjectures.
3. New information is gathered to test and revise conjectures.
4. Discussion, ongoing feedback, and constructive criticism are important in all phases of the research but especially in the revising of problems and conjectures.
5. The cycle of true research is essentially endless, although presentations of findings are made from time to time; new findings give rise to new problems and conjectures and thus to new cycles of research.

### Following a Process

While working with the research units, students are encouraged to follow a set pattern or cycle in order to keep their research activities focused and on track. Students may go through these steps many times before they come to the end of their research. Certainly for adult researchers, this cycle of question, conjecture, research, and reevaluation can go on for years and in some cases lifetimes.

This cycle uses the following process:

1. **Decide on a problem or question to research.** Students should identify a question or problem that they truly wonder about or wish to understand and then form research groups with other students who have the same interests.
   - My problem or question is ________
2. **Formulate an idea or conjecture about the research problem.** Students should think about and discuss with classmates possible answers to their research problems or questions and meet with their research groups to discuss and record their ideas or conjectures.
   - My idea/conjecture/theory about this question or problem is ________
3. **Identify needs and make plans.** Students should identify knowledge needs related to their conjectures and meet with their research groups to determine which resources to consult and to make individual job assignments. Students should also meet periodically with the teacher, other classmates, and research groups to present preliminary findings and make revisions to their problems and conjectures on the basis of these findings.
   - I need to find out ________
   - To do this, I will need these resources ________
   - My role in the group is ________
   - This is what I have learned so far ________
   - This is what happened when we presented our findings ________
4. **Reevaluate the problem or question based on what we have learned so far and the feedback we have received.**
   - My revised problem or question is ________
5. **Revise the idea or conjecture.**
   - My new conjecture about this problem is ________
6. **Identify new needs and make new plans.**
   - Based on what I found out, I still need to know ________
   - To do this, I will need these resources ________
   - This is what I have learned ________
   - This is what happened when we presented our new findings ________

### Procedure for Choosing a Problem to Research

1. Discuss with students the nature of the unit. Explain to students that the unit they are reading is a research unit and that they will produce and publish in some way the results of their explorations. They are free to decide what problems or questions they wish to explore, with whom they want to work, and how they want to present their finished products. They may publish a piece of writing, produce a poster, write and perform a play, or use any other means to present the results of their investigations and research. They may work with partners or in small groups.
2. Discuss with students the schedule you have planned for their investigations: how long the project is expected to take, how much time will be available for research, when the first presentation will be due. This schedule will partly determine the nature of the problems that students should be encouraged to work on and the depth of the inquiry students will be encouraged to pursue.
3. Have students talk about things they wonder about that are related to the unit subject. For example, in the grade 3 unit, Money, students might wonder where money in the money machine comes from or how prices are determined. Conduct a free-floating discussion of questions about the unit subject.
4. Brainstorm possible questions for students to think about. It is essential that the students' own ideas and questions be the starting point of all inquiry. *Helpful hint:* For the first research unit, you might wish to generate a list of your own ideas, having students add to this list and having them choose from it.

5. Using their wonderings, model for students the difference between a research topic and a research problem or question by providing several examples. For example, have them consider the difference between the topic California and the problem, *Why do so many people move to California?* Explain to them that if they choose to research the topic California, everything they look up under the subject heading or index entry *California* will be related in some way to their topic. Therefore, it will be quite difficult to choose which information to record. This excess of information also creates problems in organizing their research. Clearly, then, this topic is too broad and general. Choosing a specific question or problem, one that particularly interests them, helps them narrow their exploration and advance their understanding. Some possible ideas for questions can be found in the unit introduction. Ideas can also be generated as you and your students create a web of their questions or problems related to the unit concept. For example, questions related to the subject California might include the following:
   - Why do so many people move to California?
   - How have the different groups of people living in California affected the state?
6. A good research problem or question not only requires students to consult a variety of sources but is engaging and adds to the groups' knowledge of the concepts. Furthermore, good problems generate more questions. Help students understand that the question, *Why do so many people move to California?* is an easy one to research. Many sources will contribute to an answer to the question, and all information located can be easily evaluated in terms of usefulness in answering the question. *Helpful hint:* Students' initial responses may indeed be topics instead of problems or questions. If so, the following questions might be helpful:
   - What aspect of the topic really interests you?
   - Can you turn that idea into a question?
7. Remember that this initial problem or question serves only as a guide for research. As students begin collecting information and collaborating with classmates, their ideas will change, and they can revise their research problem or question. Frequently, students do not sufficiently revise their problems until after they have had time to consider their conjectures and collect information.
8. As students begin formulating their research problems, have them elaborate on their reasons for wanting to research their stated problems. They should go beyond simple expressions of interest or liking and indicate what is puzzling, important, or potentially informative, and so forth, about the problems they have chosen.
9. At this stage, students' ideas will be of a very vague and limited sort. The important thing is to start them thinking about what really interests them and what value it has to them and the class.
10. Have students present their proposed problems or questions, along with reasons for their choices, and have an open discussion of how promising proposed problems are. As students present their proposed problems, ask them what new things they think they will be learning from their investigations and how that will add to the group's growing knowledge of the concepts. This constant emphasis on group knowledge building will help set a clear purpose for students' research.

***Even elementary school students can produce works of genuine research—research that seeks answers to real questions or solutions to real problems.***

11. Form research groups. To make it easier for students to form groups, they may record their problems on the board or on self-sticking notes. Final groups should be constituted in the way you find best for your class—by self-selection, by assignment on the basis of common interests, or by some combination of methods. Students can then meet during **Workshop** to agree on a precise statement of their research problem, the nature of their expected research contributions, and lists of related questions that may help later in assigning individual roles. They should also record any scheduling information that can be added to the planning calendar.

### Using Technology

The **Research Assistant CD-ROM** (Levels 2–6), an interactive software program, supports student research by helping them plan, organize, present, and assess their research.

Students and teachers can access the Web site **www.sra4kids.com** to find information about the themes in their grade level.

## Tips

- If students are careful about the problems or questions they choose to research, they should have few problems in following through with the research. If the problem is too broad or too narrow, they will have problems.
- Have students take sufficient time in assessing their needs—both knowledge needs and physical needs in relation to their research. Careful preplanning can help the research progress smoothly with great results.
- Encourage students to reevaluate their needs often so they are not wasting time finding things they already have or ignoring needs that they haven't noticed.
- Interim presentations of material are every bit as important, if not more so, than final presentations. It is during interim presentations that students have the opportunity to rethink and reevaluate their work and change direction or decide to carry on with their planned research.

# Workshop

PROGRAM APPENDIX

Every teacher and every student needs time during the day to organize, take stock of work that is done, make plans for work that needs doing, and finish up incomplete projects. In addition, time is needed for differentiating instruction and for peer conferencing.

## Purpose

**Workshop** is the period of time each day in which students work independently or collaboratively to practice and review material taught in the lessons.

A variety of activities may occur during this time. Students may work on a specific daily assignment, complete an ongoing project, work on unit exploration activities, focus on writing, or choose from among a wide range of possibilities. With lots of guidance and encouragement, students gradually learn to make decisions about their use of time and materials and to collaborate with their peers.

A goal of **Workshop** is to get students to work independently. This is essential since **Workshop** is also the time during which the teacher can work with individuals or groups of students to reinforce learning, to provide extra help for those having difficulties, to extend learning, or to assess the progress of the class or of individuals.

## Procedure

Initially, for many students, you will need to structure **Workshop** carefully. Eventually, students will automatically go to the appropriate areas, take up ongoing projects, and get the materials they will need. **Workshop** will evolve slowly from a very structured period to a time when students make choices and move freely from one activity to the next.

Adhere firmly to **Workshop** guidelines. By the time the students have completed the first few weeks of school, they should feel confident during **Workshop**. If not, continue to structure the time and limit options. For young students, early periods of **Workshop** may run no more than five to eight minutes. The time can gradually increase to fifteen minutes or longer as the students gain independence. Older students may be able to work longer and independently from the very beginning of the school year.

### Introducing Workshop

Introduce **Workshop** to students by telling them that every day there will be a time when they are expected to work on activities on their own or in small groups. For young students in the beginning, you will assign the **Workshop** activities to help them learn to work on their own. Point out the shelf or area of the classroom where **Workshop** materials are stored. Tell students that when they finish working with the materials for one activity, they will choose something else from the **Workshop** shelf. New activity materials will be added to the shelf from time to time. Make sure that the students know that they may always look at books during **Workshop**.

Tell older students that they will have an opportunity each day to work on their unit explorations, their writing, and other projects. Students will be working independently and collaboratively during this time.

### Guidelines

- Make sure each student knows what he or she needs to do during **Workshop**.
- Demonstrate for the whole group any activity assigned for **Workshop**; for example, teaching the students a new game, introducing new materials or projects, or explaining different areas.
- For young students, it is essential to introduce and demonstrate different activities and games before the students do them on their own. With games, you may want to have several students play while the others watch. Make sure that all the students know exactly what is expected of them.
- In the beginning, plan to circulate among the students providing encouragement and help as necessary.
- Once students are engaged in appropriate activities and can work independently, meet with those students who need your particular attention. This may include individual students or small groups.
- Let the students know that they need to ask questions and clarify assignments during **Workshop** introduction, so that you are free to work with small groups.
- Be sure that students know what they are to do when they have finished an activity and where to put their finished work.

Establish and discuss rules for **Workshop** with the students. Keep them simple and straightforward. You may want to write the finalized rules on the board or on a poster. You may want to review these rules each day at the beginning of **Workshop** for the first few lessons or so. You may also wish to revisit and revise the rules from time to time. Suggested rules include:

✓ Be polite.
✓ Share.
✓ Whisper.
✓ Take only the materials you need.
✓ Return materials.

### Setting Up Your Classroom for Workshop

Carefully setting up your classroom to accommodate different **Workshop** activities will help assure that the **Workshop** period progresses smoothly and effectively. While setting up your classroom, keep the primary **Workshop** activities in mind. During **Workshop** the students will be doing independent and collaborative activities. In kindergarten and first grade, these activities may include letter recognition and phonemic awareness activities and writing or illustrating stories or projects. In addition, they will be working on individual or small group projects.

Many classrooms have centers that the students visit on a regular or rotating basis. Center time can be easily and efficiently incorporated into the **Workshop** concept. For example, the activities suggested during **Workshop** can be incorporated into reading and writing areas. Other typical classroom areas include an art center, math center, science table, play area, etc.

The following are suggestions for space and materials for use during **Workshop**:

1. **Reading Area** supplied with books and magazines. The materials in the Reading Area should be dynamic—changing with students' abilities and reflecting unit themes they are reading. You may wish to add books suggested in the ***Leveled Classroom Libraries*** and unit bibliographies available with each unit.
2. **Writing Area** stocked with various types and sizes of lined and unlined paper, pencils, erasers, markers, crayons, small slates, and chalk. The area should also have various **Letter Cards**, other handwriting models, and worksheets for those students who want to practice letter formation or handwriting. Students should know that this is where they come for writing supplies. In addition to the supplies described above, the Writing Area can also have supplies to encourage the students to create and write on their own:
   ✓ magazines and catalogs to cut up for pictures; stickers, paint, glue, glitter, etc. to decorate books and book covers; precut and stapled blank books for the students to write in. (Some can be plain and some cut in special shapes.)
   ✓ cardboard, tag board, construction paper, etc., for making book covers. (Provide some samples.)

- ✓ tape, scissors, yarn, hole punches for binding books.
- ✓ picture dictionaries, dictionaries, thesaurus, word lists, and other materials that may encourage independence.

3. **Listening Area** supplied with tape recorder, CD player, optional headphones, and tapes of stories, poems, and songs for the students to listen to and react to. You might also want to provide blank tapes and encourage the students to retell and record their favorite stories or make up and tell stories for their classmates to listen to on tape. You may also want to make available the ***Listening Library Audiocassettes/CDs*** that are available with the program.
4. **Workshop Activity Center** supplied with **Alphabet Flash Cards,** individual **Alphabet Sound Card** sets (Kindergarten), **Individual Sound/Spelling Cards** and **High-Frequency Word Flash Cards** (Grades 1-3), and other materials that enhance what the students are learning. Other commonly used classroom materials that enhance reading can be included (for example, plastic letters, puzzles, workbooks).

Since students will be working on their inquiry/investigations during **Workshop**, make sure there are adequate supplies to help them with their research. These might include dictionaries, encyclopedias, magazines, newspapers, and computers—preferably with Internet capability.

***Workshop is the period of time each day in which students work independently or collaboratively to practice and review material taught in the lessons.***

Students thrive in an environment that provides structure, repetition, and routine. Within a sound structure, the students will gain confidence and independence. This setting allows you to differentiate instruction in order to provide opportunities for flexibility and individual choice. This will allow students to develop their strengths, abilities, and talents to the fullest.

### Suggestions for English Learners

**Workshop** affords students who are English Learners a wealth of opportunities for gaining proficiency in English. It also encourages them to share their backgrounds with peers. Since you will be working with all students individually and in small groups regardless of their reading ability, students who need special help with language will not feel self-conscious about working with you. In addition, working in small groups made up of students with the same interests rather than the same abilities will provide them with the opportunity to learn about language from their peers during the regular course of **Workshop** activities.

Some suggestions for meeting the special needs of students with diverse backgrounds follow:

- Preread a selection with English Learners to help them identify words and ideas they wish to talk about. This will prepare them for discussions with the whole group.
- Preteach vocabulary and develop selection concepts that may be a challenge for students.
- Negotiate the meaning of selections by asking questions, checking for comprehension, and speaking with English Learners as much as possible.
- Draw English Learners into small group discussions to give them a sense that their ideas are valid and worth attention.
- Pair English Learners with native English speakers to share their experiences and provide new knowledge to other students.
- Have English Learners draw or dictate to you or another student a description of a new idea they may have during **Workshop** activities.

## Workshop Management Tips

Use the following **Workshop** management tips to ensure that **Workshop** runs smoothly. Note that these suggestions for a weekly unit/lesson may not exactly correspond to a particular unit/lesson in a given grade level, but will give you a sense of how **Workshop** should progress.

**Unit 1, Lesson 1** Introduce **Workshop** to students. Make sure they know where materials are located. Post the rules on the board or other prominent place in the classroom. Keep **Workshop** time short (less than thirty minutes) and very directed during the first few weeks until students can work independently.

**Unit 1, Lesson 2** Discuss using small groups for pre/reteaching purposes and how you will indicate who will be in the groups. Start by forming one small group randomly and having other students do something specific such as a writing assignment. When you have finished with the small group, send them to do independent work. Call another small group of students to work with you. Continue this each day until students are accustomed to forming groups and working independently.

**Unit 1, Lesson 3 Reading Roundtable** is a student-formed and student-run book discussion. Encourage students participating in Reading Roundtable to choose a book that they all will read and discuss. Several different Reading Roundtable groups may form on the basis of the books students choose.

**Unit 1, Lesson 4** For the first few weeks of the school year, make sure each student has a plan for using **Workshop** time.

**Unit 1, Lesson 5** Allot time for presentation and discussion of research activities. Use a whole **Workshop** day and have all groups present their findings, or split the presentations over several days, depending on the small-group needs of your class.

**Unit 1, Lesson 6** Review how students have used **Workshop** during this unit. Have they used their time well? Do they have the materials they need? Discuss suggestions for improving their use of this time. Take a few minutes at the beginning of each **Workshop** to make sure students know what they will be doing.

**Unit 2, Lesson 1** Form small extra-practice groups with the more advanced students from time to time, as they also need special attention.

**Unit 2, Lesson 2** To keep the whole class informed about the independent research being done, every other day or so invite a research group to explain what it is doing, how the research is going, and any problems they are encountering.

## Workshop (continued)



**Unit 2, Lesson 3** Discuss the use of **Workshop** time for doing inquiry and research projects. Introduce students to the activities provided for use with this unit at **www.sra4kids.com.**

**Unit 2, Lesson 4** Make sure small extra-practice groups are formed based on your observations of students' work on the different daily lessons. Small groups should be fluid and based on demonstrated need rather than becoming static and unchanging.

**Unit 2, Lesson 5** One purpose of **Workshop** is to help students learn independence and responsibility. Assign students to monitor **Workshop** materials. They should alert you whenever materials are running low or missing, and they can be responsible for checking on return dates of library books and making sure the books are either returned or renewed.

**Unit 2, Lesson 6** Students sometimes have difficulty starting discussions in Reading Roundtable. Try some of these discussion starters with students, and print them on a poster paper for student use.

I didn't know that . . . I liked the part where . . .

Does anyone know . . . I'm still confused by . . .

I figured out that . . . This made me think . . .

I agree/disagree with __________ because . . .

**Unit 3, Lesson 1** By this time students should be accustomed to the routines, rules, expectations, and usage of **Workshop** time and be moving smoothly from small teacher-led groups to independent work. Monitor small groups occasionally to see that they are on task and making progress on their activities.

**Unit 3, Lesson 2** Make a practice of reading aloud to students. All students enjoy being read to, no matter their age or grade. Encourage them to discuss the shared reading in Reading Roundtable groups and to bring books and read them aloud to their classmates.

**Unit 3, Lesson 3** Encourage cooperation and collaboration by providing students with opportunities to engage in small groups.

**Unit 3, Lesson 4** Spend a few minutes each day circulating around the room and monitoring what students are doing independently or in small groups. Students can then share any questions or problems they are having with you on a timely basis.

**Unit 3, Lesson 5** Take note of different small groups. Make sure that quieter students are able to participate in the discussions. Often the stronger, more confident students dominate such discussions. Encourage them to give all participants a chance to share their ideas.

**Unit 3, Lesson 6** If students are not productive during **Workshop**, keep them in the small group you are working with until they can successfully benefit from independent work. Discuss strategies they could use to become more independent.

**Unit 4, Lesson 1** Different students can monitor **Workshop** materials and alert you when materials or supplies are running low or missing and can check that library books are either returned or renewed.

**Unit 4, Lesson 2** From time to time, join a Reading Roundtable group, and take part in their discussion. Make sure students lead the discussion.

**Unit 4, Lesson 3** Encourage responsibility and independence by reminding students to show respect for each other and the materials provided.

**Unit 4, Lesson 4** Be sure students discuss during Reading Roundtable what they like or dislike about a book, why they wanted to read it, and how the book either lived up to their expectations or disappointed them. Discussions should not be about basic comprehension but should help students think more deeply about the ideas presented in the book.

**Unit 4, Lesson 5** Make sure students continue to use the activities provided for use with this unit at **www.sra4kids.com.**

**Unit 4, Lesson 6** If students are not productive in **Workshop**, keep them in the small group you are working with until they can successfully benefit from independent work. Discuss strategies they could use to become more independent.

**Unit 5, Lesson 1** Students often make great tutors for other students. They are uniquely qualified to understand problems that others might be having. Encourage students to pair up during **Workshop** to help each other with their daily lessons.

**Unit 5, Lesson 2** Form small extra-practice groups with the more advanced students from time to time, as they also need special attention.

**Unit 5, Lesson 3** In order to keep the whole class informed about the independent research being done, every other day or so, invite a research/investigation group to explain what it is doing, how the research is going, and any problems they are encountering.

**Unit 5, Lesson 4** Most of the authors of the student anthology selections are well known and have written many, many pieces of fine literature. Encourage students who enjoy the anthology selections to find other books by the same author. Encourage them to think about and discuss what about that particular author's work attracts them.

**Unit 5, Lesson 5** Share your impressions of books from the ***Leveled Classroom Library*** or other reading during Reading Roundtable. Note which students initiate sharing and which are reluctant to share.

**Unit 5, Lesson 6** Review with students the time they have used in **Workshop**. Have they used their time well? Do they have the materials they need? Discuss suggestions for improving the use of this time.

**Unit 6, Lesson 1** Spend a few minutes each day circulating around the room and monitoring what students are doing independently or in small groups. Students can share any questions or problems they are having with you on a timely basis.

**Unit 6, Lesson 2** Students should be accustomed to the routines, rules, expectations, and usage of **Workshop** time and be moving smoothly from small teacher-led groups to independent work. Make sure to monitor small groups occasionally to see that they are on task and making progress with their activities.

**Unit 6, Lesson 3** Make sure students continue to use the activities provided for use with this unit at **www.sra4kids.com.**

**Unit 6, Lesson 4** Allot time for presentation and discussion of research activities. You may want to use a whole **Workshop** day and have all groups present their findings or split the presentations over several days, depending on the urgency of the small-group instruction your class needs.

**Unit 6, Lesson 5** Students often make great tutors for other students. The fact that they too are just learning the materials makes them uniquely qualified to understand problems that others might be having. Encourage students to pair up during **Workshop** to help each other on their daily lessons.

**Unit 6, Lesson 6** If the reading selection is an excerpt from a longer piece, encourage students to read the book from which the excerpt is taken and discuss how the excerpt fits into the larger work.

Assessment can be one of your most effective teaching tools if it is used with the purpose of informing instruction and highlighting areas that need special attention.

## Purpose

Assessment is a tool the teacher uses to monitor students' progress and to detect students' strengths and weaknesses. Evaluation of student learning is addressed in two ways: Informal Assessment and Formal Assessment. Informal, observational assessment, or a quick check of students' written work, is presented in the ***Teacher's Edition*** in the form of assessment suggestions. Formal Assessment consists of performance assessment (both reading and writing) and objective tests (multiple choice and essay).

## Procedure

### Informal Assessment

***Observation***

Observing students as they go about their regular classwork is probably the single most effective way to learn in depth your students' strengths and areas of need. The more students become accustomed to you jotting down informal notes about their work, the more it will become just another part of classroom life that they accept and take little note of. This gives you the opportunity to assess their progress constantly without the interference and possible drawback of formal testing situations.

In order to make informal assessment of student progress a part of your everyday classroom routine, you might want to start by preparing the materials you will need on hand.

- Enter students' names in the Teacher's Observation Log, found in ***Program Assessment.***
- Before each day's lesson begins, decide which students you will observe.
- Keep the Teacher's Observation Log available so that you can easily record your observations.
- Decide what aspect of the students' learning you wish to monitor.
- During each lesson, observe this aspect in the performances of several students.
- Record your observations.
- It may take four to five days to make sure you have observed and recorded the performance of each student. If you need more information about performance in a particular area for some of your students, you may want to observe them more than once.

### Progress Assessment

***Written Work***

Students are writing one thing or another all day long. Each of these pieces of writing can provide you with valuable information about your students' progress. Two very helpful resources that students will work in daily are the ***Comprehension and Language Arts Skills*** (Levels 1–6) and the ***Inquiry Journal*** (Levels 2–6).

- The ***Comprehension and Language Arts Skills*** include skills practice lessons that act as practice and reinforcement for the skills lessons taught during the reading of the lesson or in conjunction with the Language Arts lesson. These skill pages give you a clear picture of students' understanding of the skills taught. Use them as a daily assessment of student progress in the particular skills taught through the program. In ***Phonemic Awareness and Phonics Skills*** (K), and ***Phonics Skills*** (1), students practice each of the skills taught in Part 1 of the program.
- The ***Inquiry Journal*** can give you invaluable information on how students are progressing in many different areas. In the ***Inquiry Journal,*** students
  - ✓ Record what they know about the concepts and what they learn. You will be able to monitor their growing ability to make connections and use their prior knowledge to help them understand new concepts.
  - ✓ Keep a record of their research: what resources they need, what they have used, where they have looked, and what they have found. You can keep track of students' growing ability to find the resources and knowledge base they need to answer the questions they pose.
  - ✓ Keep track of their work with their collaborative groups. This will give you a good idea of students' growing ability to work with peers for a common goal—the acquisition of new knowledge.
  - ✓ Practice study and research skills that will help them in all of their schooling. You can easily keep track of how well they are learning to use such things as library resources, reference books, visual organizers, and much, much more.

***Dictation***

In grades 1–3, students use dictation to practice the sound/spelling associations they are learning and/or reviewing. Collect the dictation papers and look through them to see how the students are doing with writing and with proofreading their words. Record notes on the papers and keep them in the student portfolios.

***Portfolios***

Portfolios are more than just a collection bin or gathering place for student projects and records. They add balance to an assessment program by providing unique benefits to teachers, students, and families.

- Portfolios help build self-confidence and increase self-esteem as students come to appreciate the value of their work. More importantly, portfolios allow students to reflect on what they know and what they need to learn. At the end of the school year, each student will be able to go through their portfolios and write about their progress.
- Portfolios provide the teacher with an authentic record of what students can do. Just as important, portfolios give students a concrete example of their own progress and development. Thus, portfolios become a valuable source of information for making instructional decisions.
- Portfolios allow families to judge student performance directly. Portfolios are an ideal starting point for discussions about a student's achievements and future goals during teacher/family conferences.

You will find that there are many opportunities to add to students' portfolios.

## Assessment (continued)



***Reading***

- During partner reading, during **Workshop**, or at other times of the day, invite students, one at a time, to sit with you and read a story from an appropriate ***Decodable Book*** (grades 1–3) or from the ***Student Anthology.***
- As each student reads to you, follow along and make note of any recurring problems the student has while reading. Note students' ability to decode unknown words as well as any attempt—successful or not—to use strategies to clarify or otherwise make sense of what they are reading. From time to time, check students' fluency by timing their reading and noting how well they are able to sustain the oral reading without faltering.
- If the student has trouble reading a particular **Decodable Book**, encourage the student to read the story a few times on her or his own before reading it aloud to you. If the **Decodable Book** has two stories, use the alternate story to reassess the student a day or two later.
- If after practicing with a particular **Decodable Book** and reading it on his or her own a few times, a student is still experiencing difficulty, try the following:
  - Drop back two **Decodable Books.** (Continue to drop back until the student is able to read a story with no trouble.) If the student can read that book without problems, move up one book.
  - Continue the process until the student is able to read the current Decodable Book.

***Preparing for Formal Assessment***

**Written Tests**

- Have the students clear their desks.
- Make sure the students can hear and see clearly.
- Explain the instructions and complete one or two examples with students before each test to make sure they understand what to do.
- Give students ample time to finish each test.

***Observing students as they go about their regular classwork is probably the single most effective way to learn in depth your students' strengths and areas of need.***

The assessment components of ***Open Court Reading*** are designed to help teachers make appropriate instructional decisions. The variety of assessments is intended to be used continuously and formatively. That is, students should be assessed regularly as a follow-up to instructional activities, and the results of the assessment should be used to inform subsequent instruction.

**Program Assessment**

The Program Assessment is a series of three broad measures that are meant to be administered at the beginning of the school year, at midyear, and at the end of the year.

- The Pretest gives teachers a snapshot of students' entry-level skills. This information allows the teacher to provide supplemental instruction to students who have not mastered critical skills and to offer more challenging material to students who demonstrate advanced abilities. In addition, this Pretest can serve as a baseline against which to measure students' progress throughout the year.
- The Midyear Test reviews skills that were taught in the first half of the school year, allowing teachers to determine how well students are retaining what they have learned. In addition, the Midyear Test contains "anchor items" similar to those that appeared on the pretest. These items will allow teachers to measure student progress from the beginning of the year to the middle of the year.
- The Posttest is a review of the content that was taught throughout the year and is a summative measure that reflects exit-level skills. The Posttest also contains anchor items, so it is possible to compare students' performance on specific skills at three points in the school year.

In addition to the Pretest, Midyear Test, and Posttest, the Program Assessment also contains a Teacher's Observation Log. Informal assessment is a part of the everyday classroom routine. Teachers can record information quickly on this observation sheet, and they may extend their observations over several days, until they have had a chance to observe each student's performance in a particular area.

**Unit Assessments**

Unit Assessments, as the name implies, reflect the instructional content and reading selections in each unit. The various measures within a unit assessment allow the teacher to see how well students have learned the skills that have recently been taught and to provide any additional instruction that is necessary.

Unit Assessments include a variety of measures that vary in form and difficulty so they are both motivating and challenging. Some of the questions are relatively easy, and most students should answer them correctly. Others are more difficult, but none are beyond the abilities of the majority of the students in a class. The skills featured on unit assessments are tied to reading success and reflect both state and national standards.

**Unit Assessments include:**

- Individual lesson assessments that assess the skills taught in each lesson immediately after instruction is delivered. These assessments will help you determine how well students are grasping the skills and concepts as they are taught.
- End-of-unit assessments that assess all of the skills taught throughout the unit. These assessments will help determine the students' ability and growing bank of knowledge as well as their ability to retain concepts over a limited period of time—generally six to eight weeks per unit.

**Diagnostic Assessments**

For the majority of the students in a class, the Program Assessment component of ***Open Court Reading*** will provide the teacher with all the information needed to make appropriate instructional decisions. In certain circumstances, however, it may be necessary to gather additional information in order to provide students with appropriate instruction. Some students, for example, may have specific skill deficits that prevent them from making adequate progress. Other students may enter the class after the beginning of the school year. A third situation is when the teacher might want to group students who have the same skill deficit. For these circumstances, we provide Diagnostic Assessments.

The Diagnostic Assessments offer a variety of measures that allow the teacher to identify students' strengths and weaknesses. The results of the assessment can help the teacher develop intervention strategies and choose the right supplemental instruction that will meet each student's needs. General and specific instructions are provided so that the teacher can use the Diagnostic Assessments efficiently without disrupting the instructional routine.

## Tips

- When observing students, do not pull them aside; rather, observe students as part of the regular lesson, either with the whole class or in small groups.
- Encourage students to express any confusion they may be experiencing. The questions students ask can give you valuable insight into their progress and development.
- The more comfortable students become with standardized-test formats—usually multiple choice—the more confident you and they will be in the fact that the test is testing their knowledge of a subject rather than their test-taking skills.
- Make sure students know that the ultimate purpose of assessment is to keep track of their progress and to help them continue to do better.

# Assessment

## Rubrics

A rubric is an established rule or criterion. Rubrics provide criteria for different levels of performance. Rubrics established before an assignment is given are extremely helpful in evaluating the assignment. When students know what the rubrics for a particular assignment are, they can focus their energies on the key issues.

### Using Comprehension Strategies Rubrics

The following rubrics can be used to gauge the students' growing knowledge of the comprehension strategies and how adept they are becoming in their use. The rubrics are simply a guide. Students may and probably will develop strategies of their own. The important thing to consider is whether or not students are becoming strategic, active readers—do they employ these and other strategies, or do they continue to simply plough through text unaware of any problems they might be having? The rubrics indicate the types of behaviors strategic readers use and will help you identify the growing facility your students can gain in dealing with text of all sorts.

**Grade 1: Comprehension Strategies Rubrics**

**Predicting**

- The student makes predictions about what the text is about.
- The student updates predictions during reading, based on information in the text.

**Visualizing**

- The student visualizes ideas or scenes described in the text.

**Grades 2-6: Comprehension Strategies Rubrics**

**Summarizing**

- The student paraphrases text, reporting main ideas and a summary of what is in the text.
- The student decides which parts of the text are important in his/her summary.
- The student draws conclusions from the text.
- The student makes global interpretations of the text, such as recognizing the genre.

**Asking Questions**

- The student asks questions about ideas or facts presented in the text and attempts to answer these questions by reading the text.

**Predicting**

- The student makes predictions about what the text is about.
- The student updates predictions during reading, based on information in the text.

**Making Connections**

- The student activates prior knowledge and related knowledge.
- The student uses prior knowledge to explain something encountered in text.
- The student connects ideas presented later in the text to ideas presented earlier in the text.
- The student notes ideas in the text that are new to him/her or conflict with what he/she thought previously.

**Visualizing**

- The student visualizes ideas or scenes described in the text.

**Monitoring and Clarifying**

- The student notes characteristics of the text, such as whether it is difficult to read or whether some sections are more challenging or more important than others are.
- The student shows awareness of whether he/she understands the text and takes appropriate action, such as rereading, in order to understand the text better.
- The student rereads to reconsider something presented earlier in the text.
- The student recognizes problems during reading, such as a loss of concentration, unfamiliar vocabulary, or a lack of sufficient background knowledge to comprehend the text.

**Monitoring and Adjusting Reading Speed**

The student changes reading speed in reaction to text, exhibiting such behavior as

- Skimming parts of the text that are not important or relevant.
- Purposely reading more slowly because of difficulty in comprehending the text.

### Research Rubrics

Throughout each unit, students engage in research and inquiry activities based on the unit concepts. They will present the findings of their research to the class. In this way they exhibit the wealth of knowledge and understanding they have gained about that particular concept. In addition to gaining knowledge about the concepts, students will be honing their research skills. With each unit, they will progress with their research in the same manner in which professional researchers do.

With each new unit of study, students should also become more and more sophisticated in their ability to formulate questions, make conjectures about those questions, recognize their own information needs, conduct research to find that information, reevaluate their questions and conjectures as new information is added to their knowledge base, and communicate their findings effectively. In addition, they will become more and more adept at working as a team and being aware of the progress being made as individuals and as a group. The Research Rubrics will help you to assess the students' progress as researchers and as members of collaborative teams.

**Formulating Research Questions and Problems**

1. With help, identifies things she/he wonders about in relation to a topic.
2. Expresses curiosity about topics; with help, translates this into specific questions.
3. Poses an interesting problem or question for research; with help, refines it into a researchable question.
4. Identifies something she/he genuinely wonders about and translates it into a researchable question.

**Making Conjectures**

1. Offers conjectures that are mainly expressions of fact or opinion. ("I think the Anasazi lived a long time ago." "I think tigers should be protected.")
2. Offers conjectures that partially address the research question. ("I think germs make you sick because they get your body upset." "I think germs make you sick because they multiply really fast.")
3. Offers conjectures that address the research question with guesses. ("I think the Anasazi were wiped out by a meteor.")
4. Offers reasonable conjectures that address the question and that can be improved through further research.

**Recognizing Information Needs**

1. Identifies topics about which more needs to be learned. ("I need to learn more about the brain.")
2. Identifies information needs that are relevant though not essential to the research question. ("To understand how Leeuwenhoek invented the microscope, I need to know what size germs are.")
3. Identifies questions that are deeper than the one originally asked. (Original question: "How does the heart work?" Deeper question: "Why does blood need to circulate?")

**Finding Needed Information**

1. Collects information loosely related to topic.
2. Collects information clearly related to topic.
3. Collects information helpful in advancing on a research problem.
4. Collects problem-relevant information from varied sources and notices inconsistencies and missing pieces.

5. Collects useful information, paying attention to the reliability of sources and reviewing information critically.

**Revising Problems and Conjectures**

1. No revision.
2. Produces new problems or conjectures with little relation to earlier ones.
3. Tends to lift problems and conjectures directly from reference material.
4. Progresses to deeper, more refined problems and conjectures.

**Communicating Research Progress and Results**

1. Reporting is sparse and fragmentary.
2. Report is factual; communicates findings but not the thinking behind them.
3. Report provides a good picture of the research problem, of how original conjectures were modified in light of new information, and of difficulties and unresolved issues.
4. A report that not only interests and informs the audience but also draws helpful commentary from them.

**Overall Assessment of Research**

1. A collection of facts related in miscellaneous ways to a topic.
2. An organized collection of facts relevant to the research problem.
3. A thoughtful effort to tackle a research problem, with some indication of progress toward solving it.
4. Significant progress on a challenging problem of understanding.

**Collaborative Group Work**

1. Group members work on separate tasks with little interaction.
2. Work-related decisions are made by the group, but there is little interaction related to ideas.
3. Information and ideas are shared, but there is little discussion concerned with advancing understanding.
4. The group clearly progresses in its thinking beyond where individual students could have gone.

**Participation in Collaborative Inquiry**

1. Does not contribute ideas or information to team or class.
2. Makes contributions to Concept/Question Board or class discussions when specifically called upon to do so.
3. Occasionally contributes ideas or information to other students' inquiries.
4. Takes an active interest in the success of the whole class's knowledge-building efforts.

### Writing Rubrics

Rubrics are particularly effective for writing assignments, which do not have simple right or wrong answers. The rubrics included in the ***Unit Assessments*** for writing cover different elements of the writing. They are intended to help teachers provide criteria and feedback to students.

***Open Court Reading*** provides four-point rubrics for writing in each of four areas. This enables teachers to clearly distinguish among different levels of performance.

1. Point score indicates that a student is performing below basic level.
2. Point score indicates that a student's abilities are emerging.
3. Point score indicates that a student's work is adequate and achieving expectations.
4. Point score indicates that a student is exceeding expectations.

**Conventions**

The conventions rubrics provide criteria for evaluating a student's understanding and ability to use English language conventions, which include:

- Grammar and Usage
- Mechanics: Punctuation
- Mechanics: Capitalization
- Sentence Structure
- Spelling
- Overall grammar, usage, mechanics, and spelling

**Genre**

Genre rubrics, found in the ***Unit Assessment,*** enable evaluation of students' grasp of the different structures and elements of each of these different forms of writing:

- Descriptive Writing
- Expository Structure
- Genre
- Narrative
- Narrative Character
- Narrative Plot
- Narrative Setting
- Persuasive
- Personal
- Poetry

**Writing Process**

Writing process rubrics allow teachers to evaluate students' abilities in these areas:

- Getting Ideas
- Prewriting—Organizing Writing
- Drafting
- Revising
- Editing
- Presentation/Publishing
- Self-Management
- Language Resources

**Writing Traits**

Writing traits rubrics, found in the ***Unit Assessment,*** provide criteria for different elements of written composition to identify a student's strengths and weaknesses.

- Audience
- Citing Sources
- Elaboration (supporting details and examples that develop the main idea)
- Focus
- Ideas/Content
- Organization
- Sentence Fluency
- Voice
- Word Choice

## Responding to Results

***Open Court Reading*** provides several ways to differentiate instruction based on the results of the various assessments. These include

- ***Reteach*** for students who appear to grasp a given concept but need more instruction and practice to solidify their learning.
- ***Intervention*** for students who are struggling to understand the material and need significant help and support.
- ***English Learner Support*** for students who are having difficulty with the concepts because they lack the necessary English language background.
- ***Challenge*** for those students who are doing well and would enjoy a challenge.
- ***Differentiating Instruction Support Activities*** for students who need quick alternative activities to strengthen or extend their skills.

These materials, along with informal assessment suggestions, help ensure that assessment and instruction work together to meet each student's needs.

# Audiovisual and Technology Resource Directory

PROGRAM APPENDIX

This directory is provided for the convenience of ordering the Technology Resources listed on the Technology pages in each Unit Overview.

**100% Educational Videos, Inc.**
P.O. Box 4440
El Dorado Hills, CA 95762-0018
800-483-3383
FAX: 1-888-478-1426
**www.schoolvideos.com**

**AIMS Multimedia**
9710 De Soto Avenue
Chatsworth, CA 91311-4409
800-367-2467
**www.aimsmultimedia.com**

**Ambrose Video**
145 W. 45th Street, Suite 1115
NY, NY 10036
800-526-4663
FAX: 212-768-9282
**www.ambrosevideo.com**

**Atari, Inc. (Humongous Entertainment)**
3855 Monte Villa Parkway
Bothell, WA 98021
425-486-9258
**www.funkidsgames.com**

**Clearvue/eav**
6465 North Avondale Avenue
Chicago, IL 60631
800-CLEARVU
**www.clearvue.com**

**Communication Skills, Inc.**
49 Richmondville Ave.
Westport, CT 06880
800-824-2398
FAX: 203-226-8820
**www.comunicationskills.com**

**Devine Entertainment Corp.**
2 Berkeley St., Suite 504
Toronto, Ontario M5A 2W3, CANADA
416-364-2282

**Discovery Communications Incorporated**
One Discovery Place
Silver Springs, MD 20910
240-662-2000
**www.discovery.com**

**Dorling Kindersley**
375 Hudson Street
New York, NY 10014
800-788-6262
FAX: 800-227-9604
**www.dk.com**

**Dreams Come True Productions**
c/o Big Kids Productions Inc.
1606 Dywer Avenue
Austin, TX 78704
800-297-8787
**www.dreamscometrueprod.com**

**Fine Media Group**
9925 S. 76th Avenue, Suites A & B
Bridgeview, IL 60455
800-FMG-2000
**www.finemediagroup.com**

**Fort Fun Productions**
Fort Wayne, IN 46802
260-423-3373
**www.ftfun.com**

**Goldhil Home Media International**
137 E. Thousand Oaks Blvd., 2nd Floor
Thousand Oaks, CA 91360
800-250-8760
**www.goldhil.com**

**Great Plains National Instructional Television Library**
University of Nebraska—Lincoln
1800 North 33rd Street
Omaha, NE 68583
402-472-4076
**www.gpn.unl.edu**

**Grolier Incorporated**
90 Sherman Turnpike
Danbury, CT 06816
800-285-3140
**www.grolier.com**

**Home Vision Entertainment**
4423 North Ravenswood Avenue
Chicago, IL 60640-5802
**www.homevision.com**

**Innovative Educators**
P.O. Box 520
Montezuma, GA 31063
1-888-252-KIDS
FAX: 888-536-8553
**www.innovative-educators.com**

**Library Video Company**
P.O. Box 580
Wynnewood, PA 19096
800-843-3630
FAX: 610-645-4040
**www.libraryvideo.com**

**Little Mammoth Media**
704-563-3304
**http://www.littlemammoth.com**

**Live Oak Media**
P.O. Box 652
Pine Plains, NY 12567-0652
800-788-1121
FAX: 866-398-1070
**http://www.liveoakmedia.com**

**Macmillan/McGraw-Hill School Division**
220 East Danieldale Road
DeSoto, TX 75115-9960
800-442-9685
FAX: 972-228-1982
**www.mhschool.com**

**Mazon Productions, Inc.**
P.O. Box 2427
Northbrook, IL 60065
800-332-4344
**www.vpopmail.cx**

**MCA Video**
MCA Records/Universal Studios
100 Universal City Plaza
Universal City, CA 91608
818-777-1000

**Mindscape, Inc.**
88 Rowland Way
Novato, California 94945
415-895-2000
Fax: 415-895-2102
**www.mindscape.com**

**MPI Media Group**
16101 South 108th Ave.
Orland Park, IL 60467
800-777-2223
**www.mpimedia.com**

**Multimedia 2000 Inc.**
2017 Eighth Avenue, 3rd Floor
Seattle, WA 98101
800-850-7272
Fax: 206-622-4380
**www.m-2K.com**

**National Geographic School Publishing**
P.O. Box 10579
Des Moines, IA 50340
800-368-2728
**www.nationalgeographic.com/education**

**Orange Cherry New Media**
P.O. Box 390
69 Winchester Ave.
Pound Ridge, NY 10576
914-764-4104
FAX: 914-764-0104
**www.orangecherry.com**

**Paramount Studios**
5555 Melrose Ave.
Hollywood, CA 90038
323-956-5000
**www.paramount.com**

**PBS Home Video**
800-424-7963
**www.shoppbs.org**

**PPI Entertainment**
103 Eisenhower Parkway
Roseland, NJ 07068
800-272-4214
**www.peterpan.com**

**Phoenix Learning Group**
2349 Chaffee Drive
St. Louis, MO 63146
800-221-1274
**www.phoenixlearninggroup.com**

**Queue, Inc.**
1450 Barnum Avenue
Bridgeport, CT 06610
800-232-2224
FAX: 203-336-2481
**www.queueinc.com**

**Rainbow Educational Media**
4540 Preslyn Drive
Raleigh, NC 27616
800-331-4047
FAX: 919-954-7554
**www.rainbowedumedia.com**

**Scholastic, Inc.**
P.O. Box 7503
Jefferson City, MO 65102
800-SCHOLASTIC
**www.scholastic.com**

**Simon & Schuster Interactive**
1230 Avenue of Americas
New York, NY 10020
**www.simonsays.com**

**Sony Music Store**
P.O. Box 4000
Carrollton, GA 30017
800-338-7834
**www.sonymusicstore.com**

**SRA/McGraw-Hill**
220 East Danieldale Road
DeSoto, TX 75115-2490
888-SRA-4543
FAX: 972-228-1982
**www.sraonline.com**

**Stage Fright Productions**
P.O. Box 373
Geneva, IL 60134
800-979-6800
**E-mail: stagefright@bowe.ccm.net**

**Sunburst Technology**
1550 Executive Drive
Elgin, IL 60123
800-821-7511
**www.sunburst.com**

**Time-Life**
1450 E. Parham Road
Richmond, VA 23280
800-950-7887
**www.timelife.com**

**Tom Snyder Productions**
80 Coolidge Hill Road
Watertown, MA 02472
800-342-0236
FAX: 800-304-1254
**www.tomsnyder.com**

**Worldlink Media**
2955 Clay Street, Suite 7
San Francisco, CA 94115
415-561-2141

# Scope and Sequence

## Reading

| | Level K | 1 | 2 | 3 | 4 | 5 | 6 |
|---|---|---|---|---|---|---|---|
| **Print/Book Awareness (Recognize and understand the conventions of print and books)** | | | | | | | |
| Capitalization | ✔ | ✔ | ✔ | | | ✔ | ✔ |
| Constancy of Words | | | | | | ✔ | |
| End Punctuation | ✔ | ✔ | | | | ✔ | ✔ |
| Follow Left-to-right, Top-to-bottom | ✔ | ✔ | | | | | |
| Letter Recognition and Formation | ✔ | ✔ | | | | | |
| Page Numbering | | ✔ | | | | | |
| Picture/Text Relationship | ✔ | | | | ✔ | | |
| Quotation Marks | ✔ | ✔ | ✔ | | | ✔ | ✔ |
| Relationship Between Spoken and Printed Language | | ✔ | | | | | |
| Sentence Recognition | | | | | | | |
| Table of Contents | ✔ | ✔ | | | | | |
| Word Length | ✔ | | | | | | |
| Word Boundaries | | ✔ | | | | | |
| **Phonemic Awareness (Recognize discrete sounds in words)** | | | | | | | |
| Oral Blending: Words/Word Parts | ✔ | ✔ | ✔ | | | | |
| Oral Blending: Initial Consonants/Blends | ✔ | ✔ | ✔ | ✔ | | | |
| Oral Blending: Final Consonants | ✔ | ✔ | ✔ | ✔ | | | |
| Oral Blending: Initial Vowels | | ✔ | | | | | |
| Oral Blending: Syllables | | ✔ | | | ✔ | | |
| Oral Blending: Vowel Replacement | | | | | ✔ | | |
| Segmentation: Initial Consonants/Blends | ✔ | ✔ | ✔ | ✔ | | ✔ | |
| Segmentation: Final Consonants | ✔ | ✔ | ✔ | ✔ | | | |
| Segmentation: Words/Word Parts | ✔ | ✔ | ✔ | ✔ | ✔ | ✔ | |
| Rhyming | ✔ | ✔ | | | ✔ | ✔ | |
| **How the Alphabet Works** | | | | | | | |
| Letter Knowledge | ✔ | ✔ | ✔ | ✔ | | | |
| Letter Order (Alphabetic Order) | ✔ | ✔ | | | | | |
| Letter Sounds | ✔ | ✔ | ✔ | ✔ | ✔ | | |
| Sounds in Words | ✔ | ✔ | ✔ | ✔ | ✔ | | |
| **Phonics (Associate sounds and spellings to read words)** | | | | | | | |
| Blending Sounds into Words | ✔ | ✔ | | | | | |
| Consonant Clusters | | ✔ | | ✔ | | | |
| Consonant Digraphs | | ✔ | | ✔ | ✔ | | |
| Consonant Sounds and Spellings | ✔ | ✔ | ✔ | ✔ | | | |
| Phonograms | ✔ | ✔ | | ✔ | | | ✔ |
| Syllables | ✔ | ✔ | | | ✔ | | |
| Vowel Diphthongs | | ✔ | | ✔ | | | ✔ |
| Vowels: Long Sounds and Spellings | ✔ | ✔ | ✔ | ✔ | ✔ | ✔ | ✔ |
| Vowels: r-controlled | | ✔ | ✔ | ✔ | ✔ | ✔ | ✔ |
| Vowels: Short Sounds and Spellings | ✔ | ✔ | ✔ | ✔ | ✔ | ✔ | ✔ |

[shaded box] Skills, strategies, and other teaching opportunities    ✔ Formal, progress, or informal testing opportunities

# Reading (continued)

| | Level K | Level 1 | Level 2 | Level 3 | Level 4 | Level 5 | Level 6 |
|---|---|---|---|---|---|---|---|
| **Comprehension Strategies** | | | | | | | |
| Asking Questions/Answering Questions | | ✔ | ✔ | ✔ | ✔ | ✔ | ✔ |
| Making Connections | | ✔ | ✔ | ✔ | ✔ | ✔ | ✔ |
| Monitoring and Clarifying | | ✔ | ✔ | ✔ | ✔ | ✔ | ✔ |
| Monitoring and Adjusting Reading Speed | | | ✔ | ✔ | ✔ | ✔ | ✔ |
| Predicting/Confirming Predictions | ✔ | ✔ | ✔ | ✔ | ✔ | ✔ | ✔ |
| Summarizing | | ✔ | ✔ | ✔ | ✔ | ✔ | ✔ |
| Visualizing | | ✔ | ✔ | ✔ | ✔ | ✔ | ✔ |
| **Comprehension Skills** | | | | | | | |
| Author's Point of View | | | ✔ | ✔ | ✔ | ✔ | ✔ |
| Author's Purpose | | | ✔ | ✔ | ✔ | ✔ | ✔ |
| Cause and Effect | ✔ | ✔ | ✔ | ✔ | ✔ | ✔ | ✔ |
| Classify and Categorize | ✔ | ✔ | ✔ | ✔ | ✔ | ✔ | ✔ |
| Compare and Contrast | ✔ | ✔ | ✔ | ✔ | ✔ | ✔ | ✔ |
| Drawing Conclusions | ✔ | ✔ | ✔ | ✔ | ✔ | ✔ | ✔ |
| Fact and Opinion | | | ✔ | ✔ | ✔ | ✔ | ✔ |
| Main Idea and Details | ✔ | ✔ | ✔ | ✔ | ✔ | ✔ | ✔ |
| Making Inferences | | ✔ | ✔ | ✔ | ✔ | ✔ | ✔ |
| Reality/Fantasy | ✔ | ✔ | | ✔ | | | |
| Sequence | | ✔ | ✔ | ✔ | ✔ | ✔ | ✔ |
| **Vocabulary** | | | | | | | |
| Antonyms | ✔ | ✔ | ✔ | ✔ | ✔ | ✔ | ✔ |
| Comparatives/Superlatives | | ✔ | ✔ | ✔ | ✔ | ✔ | ✔ |
| Compound Words | ✔ | ✔ | ✔ | ✔ | ✔ | ✔ | ✔ |
| Connecting Words (Transition Words) | | | | | | ✔ | ✔ |
| Context Clues | | ✔ | ✔ | ✔ | ✔ | ✔ | ✔ |
| Contractions | | | ✔ | ✔ | ✔ | ✔ | |
| Figurative Language | | | | ✔ | | ✔ | |
| Greek and Latin Roots | | | | ✔ | ✔ | | |
| High-Frequency Words | ✔ | ✔ | ✔ | ✔ | ✔ | ✔ | ✔ |
| Homographs | | | ✔ | ✔ | ✔ | ✔ | |
| Homophones/Homonyms | | ✔ | ✔ | ✔ | ✔ | ✔ | ✔ |
| Idioms | | | | | ✔ | ✔ | ✔ |
| Inflectional Endings | | ✔ | ✔ | ✔ | ✔ | ✔ | ✔ |
| Irregular Plurals | | | | ✔ | | ✔ | ✔ |
| Multiple Meaning Words | | | ✔ | ✔ | ✔ | ✔ | ✔ |
| Multisyllabic Words | | | ✔ | ✔ | | ✔ | |
| Position Words | ✔ | ✔ | | | | ✔ | |
| Prefixes | | | ✔ | ✔ | ✔ | ✔ | ✔ |
| Question Words | | ✔ | | | | | |
| Base or Root Words | | ✔ | ✔ | ✔ | ✔ | ✔ | ✔ |
| Selection Vocabulary | ✔ | ✔ | ✔ | ✔ | ✔ | ✔ | ✔ |
| Suffixes | | ✔ | ✔ | ✔ | ✔ | ✔ | ✔ |
| Synonyms | | ✔ | ✔ | ✔ | ✔ | ✔ | ✔ |
| Time and Order Words (Creating Sequence) | | | | ✔ | ✔ | ✔ | ✔ |
| Utility Words (Colors, Classroom Objects, etc.) | ✔ | ✔ | | | | | |
| Word Families | | | ✔ | ✔ | ✔ | ✔ | ✔ |

## Scope and Sequence (continued)



# Inquiry and Research

| Study Skills | K | 1 | 2 | 3 | 4 | 5 | 6 |
|---|---|---|---|---|---|---|---|
| Charts, Graphs, and Diagrams/Visual Aids | | | ✔ | | ✔ | ✔ | ✔ |
| Collaborative Inquiry | | | ✔ | ✔ | ✔ | ✔ | ✔ |
| Communicating Research Progress Results | | | ✔ | ✔ | ✔ | ✔ | ✔ |
| Compile Notes | | | | | | ✔ | ✔ |
| Conducting an Interview | | | | | | | ✔ |
| Finding Needed Information | | | ✔ | ✔ | ✔ | ✔ | ✔ |
| Follow Directions | ✔ | | | ✔ | | | |
| Formulate Questions for Inquiry and Research | | | ✔ | | | ✔ | ✔ |
| Give Reports | | | | | ✔ | ✔ | ✔ |
| Make Outlines | | | | ✔ | | ✔ | ✔ |
| Making Conjectures | | | ✔ | ✔ | ✔ | ✔ | ✔ |
| Maps and Globes | | | | | ✔ | | ✔ |
| Note Taking | | | ✔ | ✔ | ✔ | ✔ | ✔ |
| Parts of a Book | | | ✔ | ✔ | ✔ | | |
| Planning Investigation | | | ✔ | ✔ | ✔ | ✔ | ✔ |
| Recognizing Information Needs | | | ✔ | ✔ | ✔ | ✔ | ✔ |
| Revising Questions and Conjectures | | | ✔ | ✔ | ✔ | ✔ | ✔ |
| Summarize and Organize Information | | | | | ✔ | ✔ | ✔ |
| Time Lines | | | | | ✔ | ✔ | ✔ |
| Use Appropriate Resources (Media Source, Reference Books, Experts, Internet) | | | | | ✔ | ✔ | ✔ |
| Using a Dictionary/Glossary | | ✔ | ✔ | ✔ | ✔ | ✔ | ✔ |
| Using a Media Center/Library | | | | | ✔ | | ✔ |
| Using a Thesaurus | | | ✔ | ✔ | ✔ | ✔ | ✔ |
| Using an Encyclopedia | | | | | ✔ | | ✔ |
| Using Newspapers and Magazines | | | | | ✔ | | ✔ |
| Using Technology | | | | | | | |

Skills, strategies, and other teaching opportunities (shaded) ✔ Formal, progress, or informal testing opportunities

# Language Arts

## Writing/Composition

| | Level K | 1 | 2 | 3 | 4 | 5 | 6 |
|---|---|---|---|---|---|---|---|
| **Approaches** | | | | | | | |
| Collaborative Writing | | ✔ | | | | | |
| Group Writing | | | | | | | |
| **Process** | | | | | | | |
| Brainstorming/Prewriting | ✔ | ✔ | | ✔ | ✔ | ✔ | |
| Drafting | ✔ | ✔ | | ✔ | ✔ | ✔ | |
| Revising | ✔ | ✔ | | ✔ | ✔ | ✔ | |
| Proofreading | ✔ | ✔ | | ✔ | ✔ | ✔ | |
| Publishing | ✔ | ✔ | | ✔ | ✔ | ✔ | |
| **Forms** | | | | | | | |
| Biography/Autobiography | ✔ | ✔ | ✔ | ✔ | ✔ | ✔ | ✔ |
| Business Letter | | | | ✔ | ✔ | ✔ | ✔ |
| Describe a Process | | ✔ | ✔ | ✔ | ✔ | | ✔ |
| Descriptive Writing | ✔ | ✔ | ✔ | ✔ | ✔ | ✔ | ✔ |
| Expository/Informational Text | ✔ | ✔ | ✔ | ✔ | ✔ | ✔ | ✔ |
| Folklore (Folktales, Fairy Tales, Tall Tales, Legends, Myths) | | | ✔ | ✔ | ✔ | | |
| Friendly Letter | | ✔ | ✔ | ✔ | ✔ | ✔ | ✔ |
| Historical Fiction | | | | | | ✔ | ✔ |
| Journal Writing | | ✔ | ✔ | ✔ | ✔ | ✔ | ✔ |
| Narrative | | ✔ | ✔ | ✔ | ✔ | ✔ | ✔ |
| Personal Writing | | ✔ | ✔ | ✔ | ✔ | ✔ | ✔ |
| Persuasive Writing | ✔ | ✔ | ✔ | ✔ | ✔ | ✔ | ✔ |
| Play/Dramatization | | | | ✔ | ✔ | ✔ | ✔ |
| Poetry | | ✔ | ✔ | ✔ | ✔ | ✔ | ✔ |
| Realistic Story | | | | ✔ | | | |
| **Writer's Craft** | | | | | | | |
| Characterization | | | ✔ | ✔ | ✔ | ✔ | ✔ |
| Descriptive Writing | ✔ | ✔ | ✔ | ✔ | ✔ | ✔ | ✔ |
| Dialogue | | ✔ | ✔ | ✔ | ✔ | ✔ | ✔ |
| Effective Beginnings | | | ✔ | ✔ | ✔ | ✔ | ✔ |
| Effective Endings | | | ✔ | ✔ | ✔ | ✔ | ✔ |
| Event Sequence | | ✔ | ✔ | ✔ | ✔ | ✔ | ✔ |
| Figurative Language | ✔ | | ✔ | ✔ | ✔ | ✔ | ✔ |
| Identifying Thoughts and Feelings | ✔ | | ✔ | ✔ | ✔ | ✔ | ✔ |
| Mood and Tone | | | | ✔ | ✔ | ✔ | ✔ |
| Plot (Problem/Solutions) | ✔ | ✔ | ✔ | ✔ | ✔ | ✔ | ✔ |
| Point of View | | | | ✔ | ✔ | ✔ | |
| Rhyme | ✔ | ✔ | ✔ | ✔ | ✔ | ✔ | |
| Sensory Details | | | | ✔ | | ✔ | ✔ |
| Sentence Variety | | | | ✔ | | ✔ | ✔ |
| Sentence Elaboration | | | | ✔ | | ✔ | ✔ |
| Setting | ✔ | | ✔ | ✔ | | ✔ | ✔ |
| Suspense and Surprise | | | ✔ | ✔ | ✔ | ✔ | |
| Topic Sentences | | | ✔ | ✔ | ✔ | ✔ | ✔ |
| Using Comparisons | | | | | | ✔ | |
| **Purposes** | | | | | | | |
| Determining Purposes for Writing | ✔ | ✔ | | | | ✔ | |

PROGRAM APPENDIX

# Language Arts

## Grammar

| | Level K | 1 | 2 | 3 | 4 | 5 | 6 |
|---|---|---|---|---|---|---|---|
| **Parts of Speech** | | | | | | | |
| Adjectives | ✔ | ✔ | ✔ | ✔ | ✔ | ✔ | ✔ |
| Adverbs | | | ✔ | ✔ | ✔ | ✔ | ✔ |
| Conjunctions | | | ✔ | ✔ | ✔ | ✔ | ✔ |
| Nouns | ✔ | ✔ | ✔ | ✔ | ✔ | ✔ | ✔ |
| Prepositions | ✔ | | | ✔ | ✔ | ✔ | ✔ |
| Pronouns | ✔ | ✔ | ✔ | ✔ | ✔ | ✔ | ✔ |
| Verbs | ✔ | ✔ | ✔ | ✔ | ✔ | ✔ | ✔ |
| **Sentences** | | | | | | | |
| Fragments | | | | | ✔ | ✔ | ✔ |
| Parts (Subjects/Predicates) | | ✔ | ✔ | ✔ | ✔ | ✔ | ✔ |
| Subject/Verb Agreement | ✔ | ✔ | ✔ | ✔ | ✔ | ✔ | ✔ |
| Structure (Simple, Compound, Complex) | | | | ✔ | ✔ | ✔ | ✔ |
| Types (Declarative, Interrogative, Exclamatory, Imperatives) | ✔ | ✔ | ✔ | ✔ | ✔ | ✔ | ✔ |
| Verb Tenses | ✔ | ✔ | ✔ | ✔ | ✔ | ✔ | ✔ |
| Verbs (Action, Helping, Linking, Regular/Irregular) | ✔ | ✔ | ✔ | ✔ | ✔ | ✔ | ✔ |
| **Usage** | | | | | | | |
| Adjectives | ✔ | ✔ | ✔ | ✔ | ✔ | ✔ | ✔ |
| Adverbs | | | ✔ | ✔ | ✔ | ✔ | ✔ |
| Articles | ✔ | ✔ | ✔ | ✔ | ✔ | ✔ | ✔ |
| Nouns | ✔ | ✔ | ✔ | ✔ | ✔ | ✔ | ✔ |
| Pronouns | ✔ | ✔ | ✔ | ✔ | ✔ | ✔ | ✔ |
| Verbs | ✔ | ✔ | ✔ | ✔ | ✔ | ✔ | ✔ |
| **Mechanics** | | | | | | | |
| Capitalization (Sentence, Proper Nouns, Titles, Direct Address, Pronoun "I") | ✔ | ✔ | ✔ | ✔ | ✔ | ✔ | ✔ |
| Punctuation (End Punctuation, Comma Use, Quotation Marks, Apostrophe, Colon, Semicolon, Hyphen, Parentheses) | ✔ | ✔ | ✔ | ✔ | ✔ | ✔ | ✔ |
| **Spelling** | | | | | | | |
| Contractions | | ✔ | ✔ | ✔ | | ✔ | |
| Inflectional Endings | | | ✔ | ✔ | ✔ | ✔ | |
| Irregular Plurals | | | ✔ | ✔ | ✔ | ✔ | ✔ |
| Long Vowel Patterns | | ✔ | ✔ | ✔ | ✔ | ✔ | ✔ |
| Multisyllabic Words | | | ✔ | ✔ | | ✔ | |
| Phonograms | | ✔ | ✔ | ✔ | | | ✔ |
| *r*-controlled Vowel Spellings | | ✔ | ✔ | ✔ | ✔ | ✔ | ✔ |
| Short Vowel Spellings | | ✔ | ✔ | ✔ | ✔ | ✔ | ✔ |
| Silent Letters | | | | ✔ | | | |
| Sound/Letter Relationships | | ✔ | ✔ | ✔ | | | |
| Special Spelling Patterns (*-ough, -augh, -all, -al, -alk, -ion,-sion, -tion*) | | ✔ | ✔ | ✔ | ✔ | ✔ | ✔ |



[shaded box] Skills, strategies, and other teaching opportunities   ✔ Formal, progress, or informal testing opportunities

# Language Arts (continued)

## Listening/Speaking/Viewing

| | Level K | 1 | 2 | 3 | 4 | 5 | 6 |
|---|---|---|---|---|---|---|---|
| **Listening/Speaking** | | | | | | | |
| Analyze/Evaluate Intent and Content of Speaker's Message | | ✔ | ✔ | ✔ | ✔ | ✔ | ✔ |
| Ask and Answer Questions | ✔ | ✔ | ✔ | ✔ | ✔ | ✔ | ✔ |
| Determine Purposes for Listening | | | ✔ | ✔ | ✔ | | |
| Follow Directions | ✔ | ✔ | ✔ | ✔ | ✔ | ✔ | ✔ |
| Learn about Different Cultures through Discussion | | | | | ✔ | ✔ | ✔ |
| Listen for Poetic Language (Rhythm/Rhyme) | ✔ | ✔ | ✔ | ✔ | | | |
| Participate in Group Discussions | | ✔ | ✔ | ✔ | ✔ | ✔ | ✔ |
| Respond to Speaker | ✔ | ✔ | ✔ | ✔ | ✔ | ✔ | ✔ |
| Use Nonverbal Communication Techniques | ✔ | ✔ | ✔ | ✔ | ✔ | ✔ | ✔ |
| **Speaking** | | | | | | | |
| Describe Ideas and Feelings | ✔ | ✔ | ✔ | ✔ | ✔ | ✔ | ✔ |
| Give Directions | | | | | ✔ | ✔ | ✔ |
| Learn about Different Cultures through Discussion | | | | ✔ | ✔ | ✔ | ✔ |
| Participate in Group Discussions | ✔ | ✔ | ✔ | ✔ | ✔ | ✔ | ✔ |
| Present Oral Reports | | | ✔ | ✔ | ✔ | ✔ | ✔ |
| Read Fluently with Expression, Phrasing, and Intonation | | | ✔ | ✔ | ✔ | ✔ | ✔ |
| Read Orally | | ✔ | ✔ | ✔ | ✔ | ✔ | ✔ |
| Share Information | ✔ | ✔ | ✔ | ✔ | ✔ | ✔ | ✔ |
| Speak Clearly at Appropriate Volume | ✔ | ✔ | ✔ | ✔ | ✔ | ✔ | ✔ |
| Summarize/Retell Stories | ✔ | ✔ | ✔ | ✔ | ✔ | ✔ | ✔ |
| Understand Formal and Informal Language | ✔ | ✔ | ✔ | ✔ | ✔ | ✔ | ✔ |
| Use Appropriate Vocabulary for Audience | | ✔ | ✔ | ✔ | ✔ | ✔ | ✔ |
| Use Elements of Grammar in Speech | | | | ✔ | ✔ | ✔ | ✔ |
| **Viewing** | | | | | | | |
| Analyze Purposes and Techniques of the Media | | | | ✔ | ✔ | ✔ | ✔ |
| Appreciate/Interpret Artist's Techniques | | | | | | | |
| Compare Visual and Written Material on the Same Subject | ✔ | | | | ✔ | | |
| Gather Information from Visual Images | ✔ | ✔ | ✔ | ✔ | ✔ | ✔ | ✔ |
| View Critically | | ✔ | ✔ | ✔ | ✔ | ✔ | ✔ |
| View Culturally Rich Materials | ✔ | ✔ | ✔ | | ✔ | ✔ | ✔ |
| **Penmanship** | | | | | | | |
| Cursive Letters | | | ✔ | ✔ | ✔ | ✔ | ✔ |
| Manuscript Letters | ✔ | ✔ | ✔ | | | | |
| Numbers | ✔ | ✔ | ✔ | ✔ | | | |

# Unit Themes



| | LEVEL K | LEVEL 1 | LEVEL 2 |
|---|---|---|---|
| **Unit 1** | School | Let's Read! | Sharing Stories |
| **Unit 2** | Shadows | Animals | Kindness |
| **Unit 3** | Finding Friends | Things That Go | Look Again |
| **Unit 4** | The Wind | Our Neighborhood at Work | Fossils |
| **Unit 5** | Stick to It | Weather | Courage |
| **Unit 6** | Red, White, and Blue | Journeys | Our Country and Its People |
| **Unit 7** | Teamwork | Keep Trying | |
| **Unit 8** | By the Sea | Games | |
| **Unit 9** | | Being Afraid | |
| **Unit 10** | | Homes | |

| LEVEL 3 | LEVEL 4 | LEVEL 5 | LEVEL 6 |
|---|---|---|---|
| Friendship | Risks and Consequences | Cooperation and Competition | Perseverance |
| City Wildlife | Dollars and Sense | Astronomy | Ancient Civilizations |
| Imagination | From Mystery to Medicine | Heritage | Taking a Stand |
| Money | Survival | Making a New Nation | Beyond the Notes |
| Storytelling | Communication | Going West | Ecology |
| Country Life | A Changing America | Journeys and Quests | A Question of Value |

# Leveled Classroom Library Books

PROGRAM APPENDIX

| LEVEL K | LEVEL 1 | LEVEL 2 | LEVEL 3 |
|---|---|---|---|
| **Unit 1 School:** *Mouse Views: What the Class Pet Saw; The 100th Day of School; Billy and the Big New School; Vera's First Day of School; Bea and Mr. Jones; The Kissing Hand*<br>**Unit 2 Shadows:** *Footprints and Shadows; Shadows Are About; I Have a Friend; My Shadow; What Makes Day and Night?; Sun Up, Sun Down*<br>**Unit 3 Finding Friends:** *My Friends; Yo! Yes?; Will You Be My Friend?; George and Martha One Fine Day; Friends; May I Bring a Friend?*<br>**Unit 4 The Wind:** *The Wind Blew; One Windy Wednesday; The Sun, the Wind, and the Rain; What Makes the Wind?; Millicent and the Wind; Feel the Wind*<br>**Unit 5 Stick to It:** *The Carrot Seed; Leo the Late Bloomer; You'll Soon Grow into Them, Titch; JoJo's Flying Side Kick; Paul Bunyan: A Tall Tale; Liang and the Magic Paintbrush*<br>**Unit 6 Red, White, and Blue:** *The Pledge of Allegiance; 'Night, America; This Land Is Your Land; Happy Birthday, America; The Flag We Love; Mr. Lincoln's Whiskers*<br>**Unit 7 Teamwork:** *Can I Help?; Animal Orchestra; Tippy Bear Hunts for Honey; Helping Out; Stone Soup; The Great Trash Bash*<br>**Unit 8 By the Sea:** *Oceans; In the Ocean; Tacky the Penguin; Fish Faces; The Seashore Book; Commotion in the Ocean* | **Unit 1 Let's Read!:** *America: My Land Your Land Our Land; I Read Signs; Miss Malarkey Doesn't Live in Room 10; The Old Woman Who Loved to Read; A Cake for Herbie; More Than Anything Else*<br>**Unit 2 Animals:** *Sweet Dreams: How Animals Sleep; Moo Moo, Brown Cow; Here Is the African Savanna; Is Your Mama a Llama?; A Pinky Is a Baby Mouse; Wolf Watch*<br>**Unit 3 Things That Go:** *I Spy a Freight Train; Wheels Around; This Plane; This Is the Way We Go to School; The Listening Walk; Firehorse Max*<br>**Unit 4 Our Neighborhood at Work:** *Communities; Night Shift Daddy; My Town; One Afternoon; Career Day; Mommy Works, Daddy Works*<br>**Unit 5 Weather:** *Snow; Snowballs; Rain; Red Rubber Boot Day; Twister; Snow Is Falling*<br>**Unit 6 Journeys:** *Rosie's Walk; The Train Ride; Amelia's Fantastic Flight; I'm Not Moving, Mama!; Ferryboat Ride!; The Josefina Story Quilt*<br>**Unit 7 Keep Trying:** *Flap Your Wings and Try; The Chick and the Duckling; One Duck Stuck; One Fine Day; The Purple Coat; The Story of a Blue Bird*<br>**Unit 8 Games:** *This Is Baseball; Take Me Out to the Ballgame; What's What? A Guessing Game; Leon and Bob; Moongame; James and the Rain*<br>**Unit 9 Being Afraid:** *Sheila Rae, the Brave; Henry and Mudge and the Bedtime Thumps; First Day Jitters; Let's Go Home Little Bear; Can't You Sleep, Little Bear?; Feelings*<br>**Unit 10 Homes:** *My House Mi Casa: A Book in Two Languages; To Market, To Market; The Someday House; Homeplace; The Little House; Livingstone Mouse* | **Unit 1 Sharing Stories:** *Just Like Me; Mouse Tales; The Wednesday Surprise; Dear Annie; Jeremiah Learns to Read; Painted Words*<br>**Unit 2 Kindness:** *Abe Lincoln's Hat; Jamaica's Find; The Bat in the Boot; The Giving Tree; Uncle Willie and the Soup Kitchen; A Chair for My Mother*<br>**Unit 3 Look Again:** *The Trek; Who's Hiding Here?; The Mixed-Up Chameleon; A Color of His Own; What Do You Do When Something Wants to Eat You?; Hiding Out*<br>**Unit 4 Fossils:** *Dinosaur Babies; The Day of the Dinosaur; A Boy Wants a Dinosaur; If the Dinosaurs Came Back; Archaeologists Dig for Clues; How Big Were the Dinosaurs?*<br>**Unit 5 Courage:** *White Dynamite and Curly Kidd; What's Under My Bed?; Ruth Law Thrills a Nation; Jamaica and the Substitute Teacher; Birdie's Lighthouse; The Buffalo Jump*<br>**Unit 6 Our Country and Its People:** *Dancing with the Indians; A Picnic in October; Amelia's Road; Dragon Parade; The Lotus Seed; Dumpling Soup* | **Unit 1 Friendship:** *Charlotte's Web; And To Think That We Thought That We'd Never Be Friends; Best Friends; Amigo; The Mountain that Loved a Bird; Alex Is My Friend*<br>**Unit 2 City Wildlife:** *Wild in the City; Come Back, Salmon: How a Group of Dedicated Kids Adopted Pigeon Creek and Brought It Back to Life; Farewell to Shady Glade; Coyotes in the Crosswalk: True Tales of Animal Life in the Wilds of the City!; City Park; Birds, Nests and Eggs*<br>**Unit 3 Imagination:** *Behind the Couch; My Life with the Wave; Maria's Comet; Frederick; How I Spent My Summer Vacation; Crocodile's Masterpiece*<br>**Unit 4 Money:** *Lemonade for Sale; Round and Round the Money Goes; Saturday Sancocho; The Treasure; Our Money; Screen of Frogs*<br>**Unit 5 Storytelling:** *Tell Me a Story, Mama; The Worry Stone; May'naise Sandwiches & Sunshine Tea; One Grain of Rice; A Storyteller's Story; Firetalking*<br>**Unit 6 Country Life:** *The Raft; Night in the Country; Mowing; Winter Wheat; A River Ran Wild; Unseen Rainbows, Silent Songs: The World Beyond Human Senses* |

| LEVEL 4 | LEVEL 5 | LEVEL 6 |
|---|---|---|
| **Unit 1 Risks and Consequences:** *The Big Balloon Race; A Day's Work; Poppy; Sarah, Plain and Tall; The Landry News; From the Mixed-Up Files of Mrs. Basil E. Frankweiler*<br>**Unit 2 Dollars and Sense:** *Max Malone Makes a Million; What's Cooking, Jenny Archer?; The Toothpaste Millionaire; Brainstorm! The Stories of Twenty American Kid Inventors; Odd Jobs; Better Than a Lemonade Stand!*<br>**Unit 3 From Mystery to Medicine:** *Germs Make Me Sick!; Pasteur's Fight Against Microbes; Marie Curie and the Discovery of Radium; Kids to the Rescue! First Aid Techniques for Kids; The First Woman Doctor; Fever: 1793*<br>**Unit 4 Survival:** *Harry the Poisonous Centipede; My Grandmother's Journey; Whichaway; Frozen Fire; Island of the Blue Dolphins; The Voyage of the Frog*<br>**Unit 5 Communication:** *Prairie Dogs Kiss and Lobsters Wave: How Animals Say Hello; Burton and Stanley; Dear Mr. Henshaw; The Chimpanzee Family Book; The Cat's Elbow and Other Secret Languages; Julie's Wolf Pack*<br>**Unit 6 A Changing America:** *Sleds on Boston Common: A Story from the American Revolution; The Discovery of the Americas; Stranded at Plimoth Plantation, 1626; . . . If You Traveled West in a Covered Wagon; The Louisiana Purchase; Gold Rush! The Young Prospector's Guide to Striking It Rich* | **Unit 1 Cooperation and Competition:** *The Big Bike Race; The Kid Who Ran For President; The Wheel on the School; Iditarod Dream: Dusty and His Sled Dogs Compete in Alaska's Jr. Iditarod; The View From Saturday; A World in Our Hands: In Honor of the 50th Anniversary of the United Nations*<br>**Unit 2 Astronomy:** *The Planets; Comets, Meteors, and Asteroids; Adventure in Space: The Flight to Fix the Hubble; The Young Astronomer; Edwin Hubble: American Astronomer; Tales of the Shimmering Sky: Ten Global Folktales with Activities*<br>**Unit 3 Heritage:** *Appalachia: The Voices of Sleeping Birds; This Land Is My Land; Going Back Home: An Artist Returns to the South; In the Year of the Boar and Jackie Robinson; The Great Ancestor Hunt: The Fun of Finding Out Who You Are; Do People Grow on Family Trees?*<br>**Unit 4 Making a New Nation:** *Samuel's Choice; Toliver's Secret; Johnny Tremain; A Young Patriot: The American Revolution as Experienced by One Boy; Mr. Revere and I; Come All You Brave Soldiers: Blacks in the Revolutionary War*<br>**Unit 5 Going West:** *Boom Town; Striking It Rich: The Story of the California Gold Rush; Black-Eyed Susan; By the Great Horn Spoon!; Children of the Wild West; Caddie Woodlawn*<br>**Unit 6 Journeys and Quests:** *Alicia's Treasure; Grass Sandals: The Travels of Basho; El Güero; Coast to Coast; Orphan Train Rider: One Boy's True Story; Call It Courage* | **Unit 1 Perseverance:** *The Most Beautiful Place in the World; Wilma Unlimited: How Wilma Rudolph Became the World's Fastest Woman; Littlejim's Dreams; The Circuit: Stories from the Life of a Migrant Child; Where the Lilies Bloom; The Wright Brothers: How They Invented the Airplane*<br>**Unit 2 Ancient Civilizations:** *Androcles and the Lion; Ancient Romans at a Glance; Painters of the Caves; Pyramids!; Dig This! How Archaeologists Uncover Our Past; Religions of the World*<br>**Unit 3 Taking a Stand:** *Aunt Harriet's Underground Railroad in the Sky; Jane Addams: Pioneer Social Worker; Number the Stars; Run Away Home; Kids at Work: Lewis Hine and the Crusade Against Child Labor; Red Scarf Girl: A Memoir of the Cultural Revolution*<br>**Unit 4 Beyond the Notes:** *The Jazz Man; A Mouse Called Wolf; Play Me a Story: Nine Tales about Musical Instruments; The Sea King's Daughter: A Russian Legend; Dragonsong; Music*<br>**Unit 5 Ecology:** *The Great Kapok Tree; Lifetimes; Elephant Woman: Cynthia Moss Explores the World of Elephants; The Missing 'Gator of Gumbo Limbo; Ecology for Every Kid: Easy Activities that Make Learning Science Fun; The Most Beautiful Roof in the World*<br>**Unit 6 A Question of Value:** *Abuelita's Heart; The Golden Bracelet; Lily's Crossing; The Black Pearl; The Monkey Thief; Wringer* |

# Glossary of Reading Terms

PROGRAM APPENDIX

**This glossary includes linguistic, grammatical, comprehension, and literary terms that may be helpful in understanding reading instruction.**

**acronym** a word formed from the initial letter of words in a phrase, **scuba (self-contained underwater breathing apparatus)**.

**acrostic** a kind of puzzle in which lines of a poem are arranged so that words or phrases are formed when certain letters from each line are used in a sequence.

**adjective** a word or group of words that modifies a noun.

**adventure story** a narrative that features the unknown or unexpected with elements of excitement, danger, and risk.

**adverb** a word or group of words that modifies a verb, adjective, or other adverb.

**affective domain** the psychological field of emotional activity.

**affix** a word part, either a prefix or a suffix, that changes the meaning or function of a word root or stem.

**affricate** a speech sound that starts as a stop but ends as a fricative, the /ch/ in **catch**.

**agreement** the correspondence of syntactically related words; subjects and predicates are in agreement when both are singular or plural.

**alliteration** the repetition of the initial sounds in neighboring words or stressed syllables.

**alphabet** the complete set of letters representing speech sounds used in writing a language.

**alphabet book** a book for helping young children learn the alphabet by pairing letters with pictures whose sounds they represent.

**alphabetic principle** the principle that there is an association between sounds and the letters that represent them in alphabetic writing systems.

**alveolar** a consonant speech sound made when the tongue and the ridge of the upper and lower jaw stop to constrict the air flow, as /t/.

**anagram** a word or phrase whose letters form other words or phrases when rearranged, for example, **add** and **dad**.

**analogy** a likeness or similarity.

**analytic phonics** also deductive phonics, a whole-to-part approach to phonics in which a student is taught a number of sight words and then phonetic generalizations that can be applied to other words.

**antonym** a word that is opposite in meaning to another word.

**appositive** a word that restates or modifies a preceding noun. For example, **my daughter**, **Charlotte**.

**aspirate** an unvoiced speech sound produced by a puff of air, as /h/ in **heart**.

**aspirated stop** a stop consonant sound released with a puff of air, as /k/, /p/, and /t/.

**auditory discrimination** the ability to hear phonetic likenesses and differences in phonemes and words.

**author's purpose** the motive or reason for which an author writes, includes to entertain, inform, persuade, and explain how.

**automaticity** fluent processing of information, requiring little effort or attention.

**auxiliary verb** a verb that precedes another verb to express time, mood, or voice, includes verbs such as **has**, **is**, **will**.

**ballad** a narrative poem, composed of short verses to be sung or recited, usually containing elements of drama and often tragic in tone.

**base word** a word to which affixes may be added to create related words.

**blank verse** unrhymed verse, especially unrhymed iambic pentameter.

**blend** the joining of the sounds of two or more letters with little change in those sounds, for example /spr/ in **spring**, also **consonant blend** or **consonant cluster**.

**blending** to combine the sounds represented by letters to sound out or pronounce a word, contrast with **oral blending**.

**breve** the symbol placed above a vowel to indicate that it is a short vowel.

**browse** to skim through or look over in search of something of interest.

**canon** in literature, the body of major works that a culture considers important at a given time.

**case** a grammatical category that indicates the syntactic/semantic role of a noun phrase in a sentence.

**cause-effect relationship** a stated or implied association between an outcome and the conditions that brought it about, also the comprehension skill associated with recognizing this type of relationship as an organizing principle in text.

**chapter book** a book long enough to be divided into chapters, but not long or complex enough to be considered a novel.

**characterization** the way in which an author presents a character in a story, including describing words, actions, thoughts, and impressions of that character.

**choral reading** oral group reading to develop oral fluency by modeling.

**cinquain** a stanza of five lines, specifically one that has successive lines of two, four, six, eight, and two syllables.

**cipher** a system for writing in code.

**clarifying** a comprehension strategy in which the reader rereads text, uses a dictionary, uses decoding skills, or uses context clues to comprehend something that is unclear.

**clause** a group of words with a subject and a predicate used to form a part of or a whole sentence, a dependent clause modifies an independent clause, which can stand alone as a complete sentence.

**collaborative learning** learning by working together in small groups.

**command** a sentence that asks for action and usually ends with a period.

**common noun** in contrast to **proper noun**, a noun that denotes a class rather than a unique or specific thing.

**comprehension** the understanding of what is written or said.

**comprehension skill** a skill that aids in understanding text, including identifying **author's purpose**, **comprehending cause and effect relationships**, **comparing and contrasting** items and events, **drawing conclusions**, distinguishing **fact from opinion**, identifying **main ideas**, making **inferences**, distinguishing **reality from fantasy**, and understanding **sequence**.

**comprehension strategy** a sequence of steps for understanding text, includes asking questions, clarifying, making connections, predicting, summarizing, and visualizing.

**conjugation** the complete set of all possible inflected forms of a verb.

**conjunction** a part of speech used to connect words, phrases, clauses, or sentences, including the words **and, but, or**.

**consonant** a speech sound, and the alphabet letter that represents that sound, made by partial or complete closure of part of the vocal tract, which obstructs air flow and causes audible friction.

**context clue** information from the immediate text that helps identify a word.

**contraction** a short version of a written or spoken expression in which letters are omitted, for example, **can't**.

**convention** an accepted practice in spoken or written language, usually referring to spelling, mechanics, or grammar rules.

**cooperative learning** a classroom organization that allows students to work together to achieve their individual goals.

**creative writing** prose and poetic forms of writing that express the writer's thoughts and feelings imaginatively.

**cuing system** any of the various sources of information that help to identify an unrecognizable word in reading, including phonetic, semantic, and syntactical information.

**cumulative tale** a story, such as The Gingerbread Man, in which details are repeated until the climax.

**dangling modifier** usually a participle that because of its placement in a sentence modifies the wrong object.

**decodable text** text materials controlled to include a majority of words whose sound/spelling relationships are known by the reader.

**decode** to analyze spoken or graphic symbols for meaning.

**diacritical mark** a mark, such as a breve or macron, added to a letter or graphic character, to indicate a specific pronunciation.

**dialect** a regional variety of a particular language with phonological, grammatical, and lexical patterns that distinguish it from other varieties.
**dialogue** a piece of writing written as conversation, usually punctuated by quotation marks.
**digraph** two letters that represent one speech sound, for example /sh/ or /ch/.
**diphthong** a vowel sound produced when the tongue glides from one vowel sound toward another in the same syllable, for example /oi/ or /ou/.
**direct object** the person or thing that receives the action of a verb in a sentence, for example, the word **cake** in this sentence: **Madeline baked a cake**.
**drafting** the process of writing ideas in rough form to record them.
**drama** a story in the form of a play, written to be performed.
**edit** in the writing process, to revise or correct a manuscript.
**emergent literacy** the development of the association of meaning and print that continues until a child reaches the stage of conventional reading and writing.
**emergent reading** a child's early interaction with books and print before the ability to decode text.
**encode** to change a message into symbols, for example, to change speech into writing.
**epic** a long narrative poem, usually about a hero.
**exclamatory sentence** a sentence that shows strong emotion and ends with an exclamation mark.
**expository writing** or **exposition** a composition in writing that explains an event or process.
**fable** a short tale that teaches a moral.
**fantasy** a highly imaginative story about characters, places, and events that do not exist.
**fiction** imaginative narrative designed to entertain rather than to explain, persuade, or describe.
**figure of speech** the expressive, nonliteral use of language usually through metaphor, simile, or personification.
**fluency** freedom from word-identification problems that hinder comprehension in reading.
**folktale** a narrative form of genre such as an epic, myth, or fable that is well-known through repeated storytellings.
**foreshadowing** giving clues to upcoming events in a story.
**free verse** verse with irregular metrical pattern.
**freewriting** writing that is not limited in form, style, content, or purpose, designed to encourage students to write.
**genre** a classification of literary works, including tragedy, comedy, novel, essay, short story, mystery, realistic fiction, poetry.
**grammar** the study of the classes of words, their inflections, and their functions and relations in sentences; includes phonological, morphological, syntactic, and semantic descriptions of a language.
**grapheme** a written or printed representation of a phoneme, such as **c** for /k/.
**guided reading** reading instruction in which the teacher provides the structure and purpose for reading and responding to the material read.
**handing off** a method of turning over to the students the primary responsibility for controlling discussion.
**indirect object** in a sentence, the person or thing to or for whom an action is done, for example, the word **dog** in this sentence: **Madeline gave the dog a treat**.
**inference** a conclusion based on facts, data, or evidence.
**infinitive** the base form of a verb, usually with the infinitive marker, for example, **to go**.
**inflectional ending** an ending that expresses a plural or possessive form of a noun, the tense of a verb, or the comparative or superlative form of an adjective or adverb.
**interrogative word** a word that marks a clause or sentence as a question, including **interrogative pronouns who**, **what**, **which**, **where**.
**intervention** a strategy or program designed to supplement or substitute instruction, especially for those students who fall behind.
**invented spelling** the result of an attempt to spell a word based on the writer's knowledge of the spelling system and how it works, often with overemphasis on sound/symbol relationships.
**irony** a figure of speech in which the literal meaning of the words is the opposite of their intended meaning.
**journal** a written record of daily events or responses.
**juvenile book** a book written for children or adolescents.
**legend** a traditional tale handed down from generation to generation.
**leitmotif** a repeated expression, event, or idea used to unify a work of art such as writing.
**letter** one of a set of graphic symbols that forms an alphabet and is used alone or in combination to represent a phoneme, also **grapheme**.
**linguistics** the study of the nature and structure of language and communication.
**literary elements** the elements of a story such as **setting**, **plot**, and **characterization** that create the structure of a narrative.
**macron** a diacritical mark placed above a vowel to indicate a long vowel sound.
**main idea** the central thought or chief topic of a passage.
**mechanics** the conventions of capitalization and punctuation.
**metacognition** awareness and knowledge of one's mental processes or thinking about what one is thinking about.
**metaphor** a figure of speech in which a comparison is implied but not stated, for example, **She is a jewel**.
**miscue** a deviation from text during oral reading in an attempt to make sense of the text.
**modeling** an instructional technique in which the teacher serves as an example of behavior.
**mood** the literary element that conveys the emotional atmosphere of a story.
**morpheme** a meaningful linguistic unit that cannot be divided into smaller units, for example, **word**; **a bound morpheme** is a morpheme that cannot stand alone as an independent word, for example, the prefix **re-**; a **free morpheme** can stand alone, for example, **dog**.
**myth** a story designed to explain the mysteries of life.
**narrative writing** or **narration** a composition in writing that tells a story or gives an account of an event.
**nonfiction** prose designed to explain, argue, or describe rather than to entertain with a factual emphasis, includes biography and autobiography.
**noun** a part of speech that denotes persons, places, things, qualities, or acts.
**novel** an extended fictional prose narration.
**onomatopoeia** the use of a word whose sound suggests its meaning, for example, **purr**.
**oral blending** the ability to fuse discrete phonemes into recognizable words; oral blending puts sounds together to make a word, **see also segmentation**.
**orthography** correct or standardized spelling according to established usage in a language.
**oxymoron** a figure of speech in which contrasting or contradictory words are brought together for emphasis.
**paragraph** a subdivision of a written composition that consists of one or more sentences, deals with one point, or gives the words of one speaker, usually beginning with an indented line.
**participle** a verb form used as an adjective, for example, **the skating party**.
**personification** a figure of speech in which animals, ideas, or things take on human characteristics.
**persuasive writing** a composition intended to persuade the reader to adopt the writer's point of view.
**phoneme** the smallest sound unit of speech, for example, the /k/ in **book**.
**phonemic awareness** the ability to recognize that spoken words are made up of discrete sounds and that those sounds can be manipulated.

## Glossary of Reading Terms (continued)



**phonetic spelling** the respelling of entry words in a dictionary according to a pronunciation key.

**phonetics** the study of speech sounds.

**phonics** a way of teaching reading that addresses sound/symbol relationships, especially in beginning instruction.

**phonogram** a letter or symbol that represents a phonetic sound.

**plot** the literary element that provides the structure of the action of a story, which may include rising action, climax, and falling action leading to a resolution or denouement.

**plural** a grammatical form of a word that refers to more than one in number; an **irregular plural** is one that does not follow normal patterns for inflectional endings.

**poetic license** the liberty taken by writers to ignore conventions.

**poetry** a metrical form of composition in which language is chosen and arranged to create a powerful response through meaning, sound, or rhythm.

**possessive** showing ownership either through the use of an adjective, an adjectival pronoun, or the possessive form of a noun.

**predicate** the part of the sentence that expresses something about the subject and includes the verb phrase; a **complete predicate** includes the principal verb in a sentence and all its modifiers or subordinate parts.

**predicting** a comprehension strategy in which the reader attempts to figure out what will happen and then confirms predictions as the text is read.

**prefix** an affix attached before a base word that changes the meaning of the word.

**preposition** a part of speech in the class of function words, such as **of**, **on**, **at**, that precede noun phrases to create prepositional phrases.

**prewriting** the planning stage of the writing process in which the writer formulates ideas, gathers information, and considers ways to organize them.

**print awareness** in emergent literacy, a child's growing recognition of conventions and characteristics of written language, including reading from left to right and top to bottom in English, and that words are separated by spaces.

**pronoun** a part of speech used as a substitute for a noun or noun phrase.

**proofreading** the act of reading with the intent to correct, clarify, or improve text.

**pseudonym** an assumed name used by an author, a pen name or nom de plume.

**publishing** the process of preparing written material for presentation.

**punctuation** graphic marks such as comma, period, quotation marks, and brackets used to clarify meaning and give speech characteristics to written language.

**question** an interrogative sentence that asks a question and ends with a question mark.

**realistic fiction** a story that attempts to portray characters and events as they actually are.

**rebus** the use of a picture or symbol to suggest a word or syllable.

**revise** in the writing process, to change or correct a manuscript to make its message more clear.

**rhyme** identical or very similar recurring final sounds in words, often at the ends of lines of poetry.

**rime** a vowel and any following consonants of a syllable.

**segmentation** the ability to break words into individual sounds; **see also oral blending**.

**semantic mapping** a graphic display of a group of words that are meaningfully related to support vocabulary instruction.

**semantics** the study of meaning in language, including the meanings of words, phrases, sentences, and texts.

**sentence** a grammatical unit that expresses a statement, question, or command; a **simple sentence** is a sentence with one subject and one predicate; a **compound sentence** is a sentence with two or more independent clauses usually separated by a comma and conjunction, but no dependent clause; a **complex sentence** is a sentence with one independent and one or more dependent clauses.

**sentence combining** a teaching technique in which complex sentence chunks and paragraphs are built from basic sentences.

**sentence lifting** the process of using sentences from children's writing to illustrate what is wrong or right to develop children's editing and proofreading skills.

**sequence** the order of elements or events.

**setting** the literary element that includes the time, place, and physical and psychological background in which a story takes place.

**sight word** a word that is taught to be read as a whole word, usually words that are phonetically irregular.

**simile** a figure of speech in which a comparison of two things that are unlike is directly stated usually with the words **like** or **as**, for example, **She is like a jewel**.

**spelling** the process of representing language by means of a writing system.

**statement** a sentence that tells something and ends with a period.

**study skills** a general term for the techniques and strategies that help readers comprehend text with the intent to remember, includes following directions, organizing, locating, and using graphic aids.

**style** the characteristics of a work that reflect the author's particular way of writing.

**subject** the main topic of a sentence to which a predicate refers, including the principal noun; a **complete subject** includes the principal noun in a sentence and all its modifiers.

**suffix** an affix attached at the end of a base word that changes the meaning of the word.

**summarizing** a comprehension strategy in which the reader constructs a brief statement that contains the essential ideas of a passage.

**syllable** a minimal unit of sequential speech sounds comprised of a vowel sound or a vowel-sound combination.

**symbolism** the use of one thing to represent something else in order to represent an idea in a concrete way.

**synonym** a word that means the same as another word.

**syntax** the grammatical pattern or structure of word order in sentences, clauses, and phrases.

**tense** the way in which verbs indicate past, present, and future time of action.

**text structure** the various patterns of ideas that are built into the organization of a written work.

**theme** a major idea or proposition that provides an organizing concept through which by study, students gain depth of understanding.

**topic sentence** a sentence intended to express the main idea of a paragraph or passage.

**tragedy** a literary work, often a play, in which the main character suffers conflicts and which presents a serious theme and has an unfortunate ending.

**usage** the way in which a native language or dialect is used by the members of the community.

**verb** a word that expresses an action or state that occurs in a predicate of a sentence; an **irregular verb** is a verb that does not follow normal patterns of inflectional endings that reflect past, present, or future verb tense.

**visualizing** a comprehension strategy in which the reader constructs a mental picture of a character, setting, or process.

**vowel** a voiced speech sound and the alphabet letter that represents that sound, made without stoppage or friction of the air flow as it passes through the vocal tract.

**vowel digraph** a spelling pattern in which two or more letters represent a single vowel sound.

**word calling** proficiency in decoding with little or no attention to word meaning.

**writing** also **composition** the process or result of organizing ideas in writing to form a clear message, includes persuasive, expository, narrative, and descriptive forms.

**writing process** the many aspects of the complex act of producing a piece of writing, including prewriting, drafting, revising, proofreading, and publishing.

***Open Court Reading*** develops handwriting skills through weekly Penmanship lessons. The instruction for these lessons appears in the Language Arts part of the lesson in every grade level. The purpose of these lessons is to develop important handwriting skills necessary for producing legible, properly spaced documents. Penmanship practice reinforces the vocabulary in the lesson selection.

In addition to the board, the overhead projector can be a very effective device for teaching penmanship. Students can move their pencils at the same time the teacher forms letters on the transparency. It also helps to recite the descriptions or chants that go with each letter.

## Penmanship in Levels K to 2

Beginning in kindergarten, the Penmanship lessons expand on the sound/spelling instruction by introducing letters the students study in Sounds and Letters. Students learn that those letters are made of four basic lines: curved lines, horizontal lines, vertical lines, and slanted lines.

Next, students learn letter and number formation. The students practice letter formation by writing the letter being studied and then words from the literature selection that contain the particular letter. This instruction continues in Level 1 and is tied to the letter formation instruction in Phonics and Fluency.

## Cursive Handwriting Models

Penmanship is developed and practiced through Level 6, with cursive instruction beginning in the final unit of Level 2. Students are taught that most cursive letters are comprised of four strokes: undercurve, downcurve, overcurve, and slanted lines. These lessons teach students the essentials of cursive handwriting, such as proper slant; loops; joining; and spacing between letters, words, and sentences. As in the earlier levels, the students practice letter formation by writing the letters in the Writer's Notebook and then words from the literature selection that contain the particular letter.

The writing exercises progress with each level. Students begin writing words in kindergarten and graduate to writing sentences by the end of Level 1 and into Level 2. Level 3 eases students into cursive by having them practice words from the literature, with a transition to sentences in Level 4, and paragraphs in Levels 5 and 6.

## Hand and Paper Positioning

The **hand and paper positioning** models are for teachers' reference and enhance the written instruction of positioning lessons. The diagrams give teachers a visual aid so that they may better understand and demonstrate an effective technique of positioning.

A right-handed student should hold the pencil loosely about one inch above the point, between the thumb and middle finger. A left-handed student should hold the pencil the same way, but up to one half inch farther away from the point. The index fingers of both writers should rest lightly on the top of the pencil. The wrist should be level and just slightly raised from the desk.

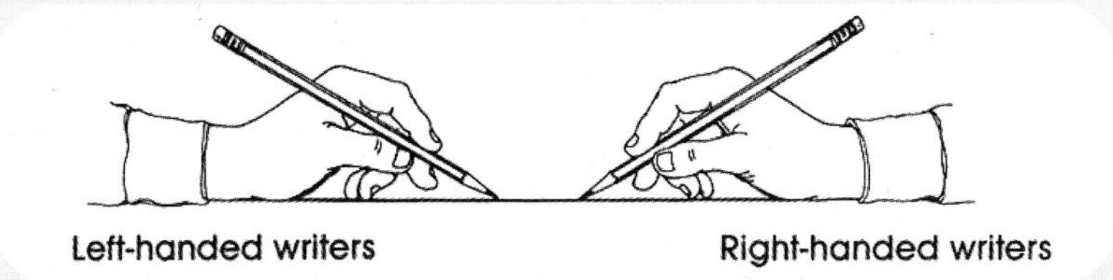

Left-handed writers Right-handed writers

For both kinds of writers, the paper should lie straight in front of the student with the edges parallel to the edges of the desk. A left-handed writer may find it easier to slant the paper slightly to the right and parallel to the left forearm. A right-handed writer's writing hand should be kept well below the writing. The left hand should hold down the paper.

Left-handed writers

Right-handed writers

## Cursive Handwriting Models

The models of cursive handwriting provide teachers with a systematic method for teaching students to form uppercase and lowercase letters of the alphabet. The dots on the letters indicate starting points for the students. The numbered arrows show the students in what order and what direction the line should go to form the particular letter. Teachers may use the chants to describe the letter step by step as he or she models the formation on the board. Students may also say the chants in unison as they practice the formation, whether they are writing the letter or tracing it on the board.

The four basic cursive strokes diagram aids teachers by giving examples of the strokes that recur frequently in cursive handwriting. Students can form most cursive letters by using one or more of these strokes. The letters in the Penmanship lessons are grouped according to the strokes particular to each letter.

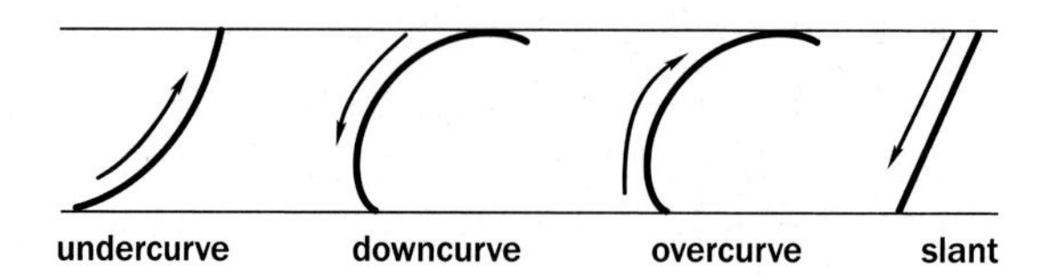


### Undercurve letters

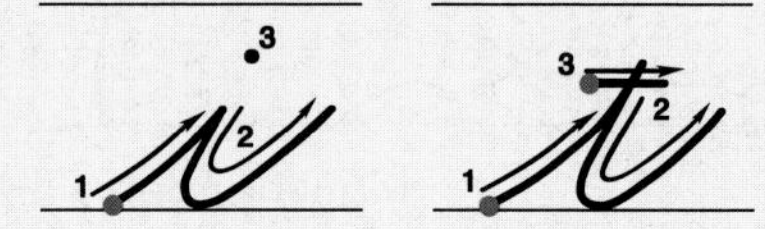

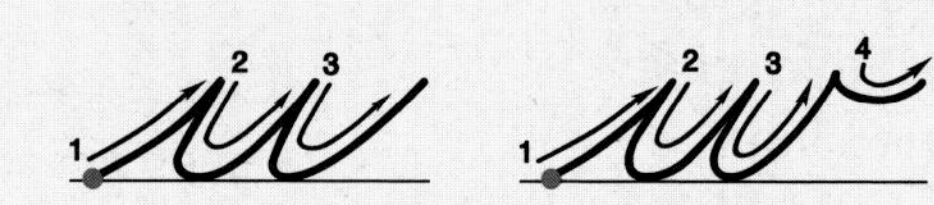

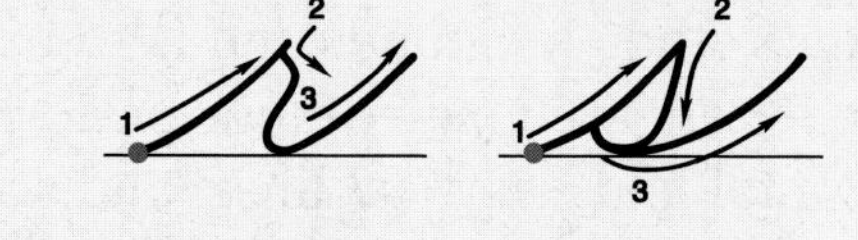

**i** Starting point, undercurve
Slant down, undercurve to endpoint, dot exactly above: small *i*

**t** Starting point, undercurve
Slant down, undercurve to endpoint
Starting point, straight across: small *t*

**u** Starting point, undercurve
Slant down, undercurve
Slant down, undercurve: small *u*

**w** Starting point, undercurve
Slant down, undercurve, slant down, undercurve, small curve to right: small *w*

**r** Starting point, undercurve
Slant right
Slant down, undercurve: small *r*

**s** Starting point, undercurve
Curve down and back, undercurve: small *s*

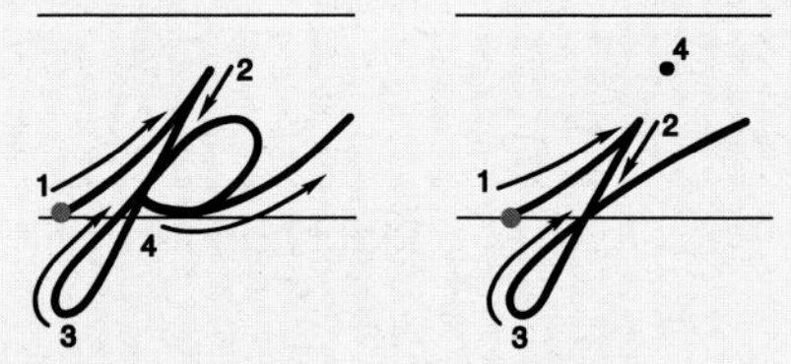

**p** Starting point, undercurve
Slant, loop back
Overcurve
Curve back, undercurve: small *p*

**j** Starting point, undercurve
Slant down
Loop back
Overcurve to endpoint
Dot exactly above: small *j*

### Downcurve letters

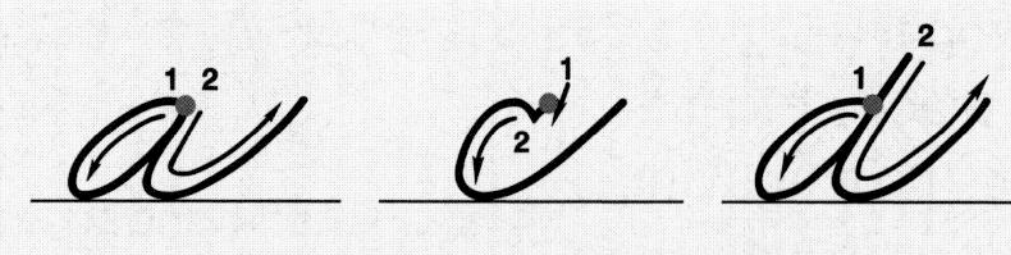

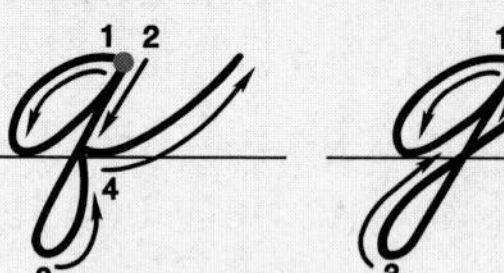

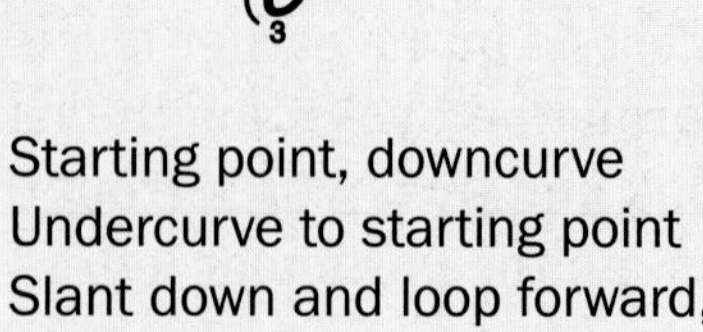

**a** Starting point, downcurve
Undercurve to starting point
Slant down, undercurve: small *a*

**c** Starting point, downcurve
Undercurve: small *c*

**d** Starting point, downcurve
Undercurve past starting point
Slant down, undercurve: small *d*

**q** Starting point, downcurve
Undercurve to starting point
Slant down and loop forward, undercurve:
small *q*

**g** Starting point, downcurve
Undercurve to starting point
Slant down and loop back, overcurve: small *g*

**o** Starting point, downcurve
Undercurve
Small curve to right: small *o*

## Cursive Handwriting Models

### Overcurve letters

**n** Starting point, overcurve
Slant down, overcurve
Slant down, undercurve: small *n*

**m** Starting point, overcurve
Slant down, overcurve
Slant down, overcurve
Slant down, undercurve: small *m*

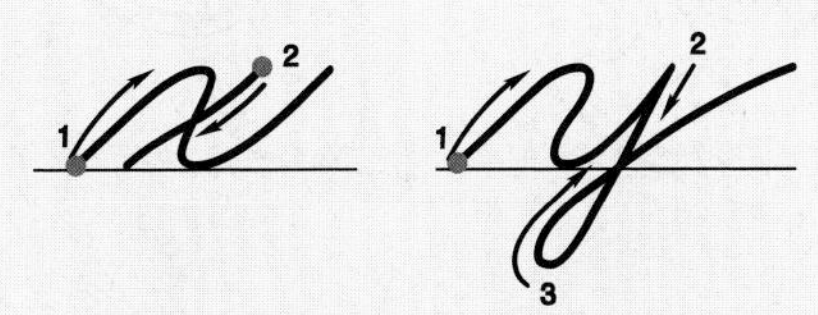

**x** Starting point, overcurve
Slant down, undercurve to endpoint
Starting point slant down: small *x*

**y** Starting point, overcurve
Slant down
Undercurve, slant down
Loop back into overcurve: small *y*

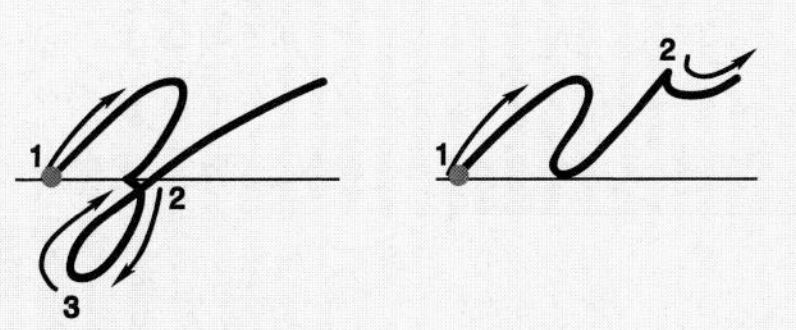

**z** Starting point, overcurve
Slant down, overcurve, down
Loop into overcurve: small *z*

**v** Starting point, overcurve
Slant down
Undercurve
Small curve to right: small *v*

### Letters with loops

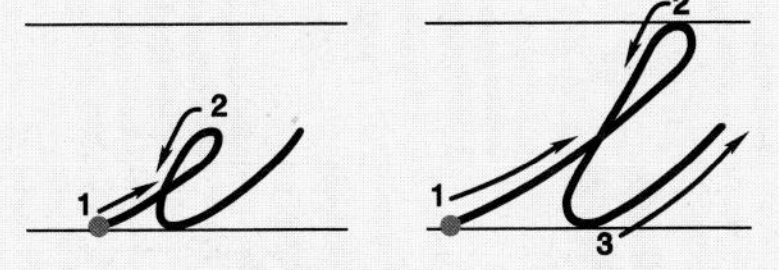

**e** Starting point, undercurve
Loop back, slant down
Undercurve: small e

**l** Starting point, undercurve
Loop back, slant down
Undercurve: small *l*

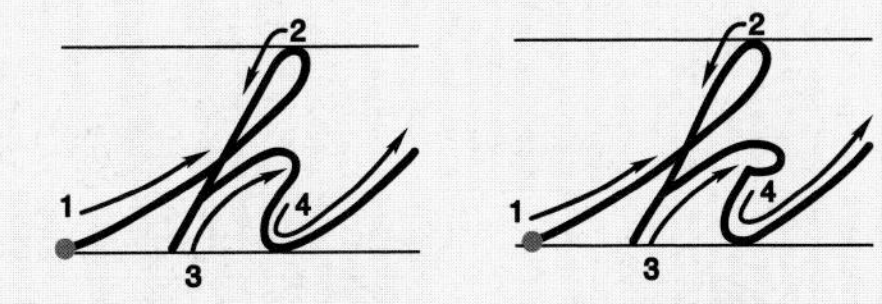

**h** Starting point, undercurve
Loop back, slant down
Overcurve, slant down
Undercurve: small *h*

**k** Starting point, undercurve
Loop back, slant down
Overcurve, curve forward and under
Slant down, undercurve: small *k*

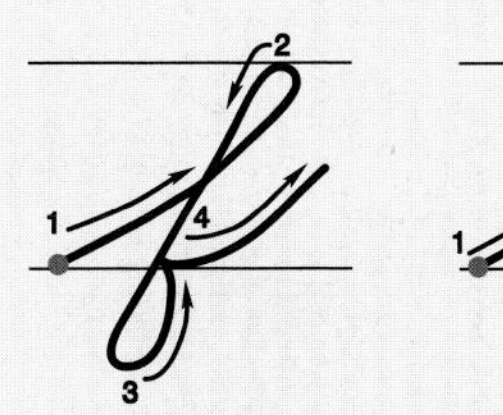

**f** Starting point, undercurve
Loop back, slant down
Loop forward into undercurve: small *f*

**b** Starting point, undercurve
Loop back, slant down
Undercurve, small curve to right:
small *b*

## Penmanship (continued)



### Cursive Handwriting Models

**Downcurve letters**

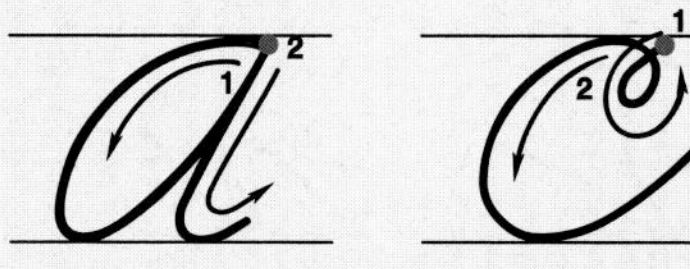

**A** Starting point, downcurve
Undercurve to starting point
Slant down, undercurve: capital *A*

**C** Starting point, loop
Downcurve, undercurve: capital *C*

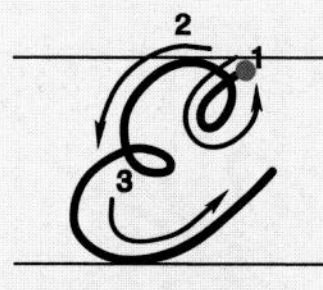

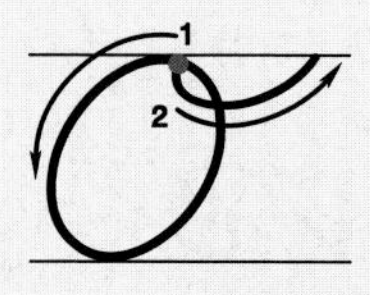

**E** Starting point, loop
Downcurve
Loop back, downcurve
Undercurve: capital *E*

**O** Starting point, downcurve
left into undercurve
Loop and curve right: capital *O*

**Curve forward letters**

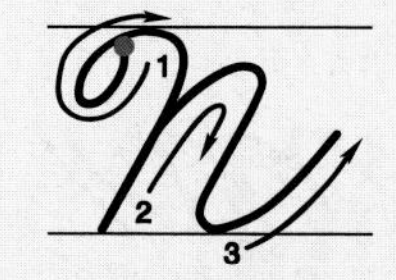

**N** Starting point, loop
Curve forward
Slant down
Retrace up slant
Overcurve down into undercurve:
capital *N*

**M** Starting point, loop
Curve forward, slant down
Retrace up slant, overcurve
Slant down, retrace up slant
Overcurve down into undercurve:
capital *M*

**Curve forward letters**

**K** Starting point, loop
Curve forward, slant down to end point
Starting point
Doublecurve back to slant
Curve forward
Undercurve up: capital *K*

**H** Starting point, loop
Curve forward, slant down to end point
Starting point
Curve back and slant down
Retrace up slant, loop left and
curve right: capital *H*

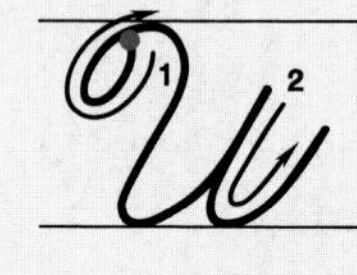

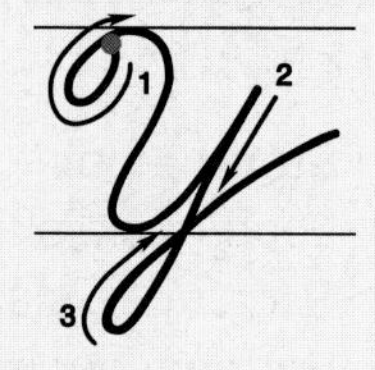

**U** Starting point, loop
Curve forward, slant down into
undercurve
Slant down, undercurve: capital *U*

**Y** Starting point, loop
Curve forward, slant down
Undercurve up, slant down
Loop back, overcurve: capital *Y*

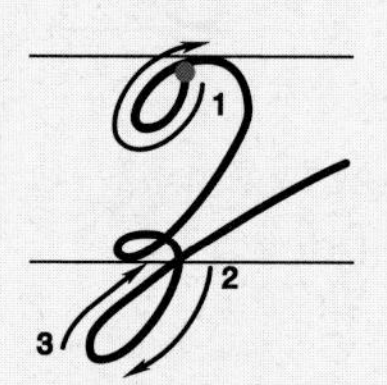

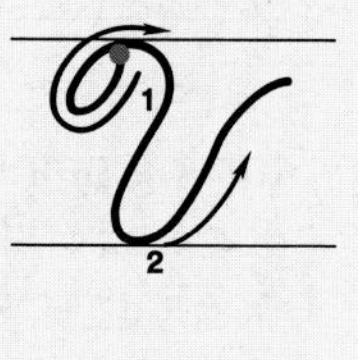

**Z** Starting point, loop
Curve forward, slant down
Overcurve, curve down
Loop into overcurve: capital *Z*

**V** Starting point, loop
Curve forward and slant down,
undercurve up and overcurve:
capital *V*

## Cursive Handwriting Models

**X** Starting point, loop
Curve forward, slant down
Undercurve to end point
Starting point, slant down: capital *X*

**W** Starting point, loop
Curve forward, slant down into undercurve
Slant down into undercurve
Overcurve: capital *W*

### Doublecurve letters

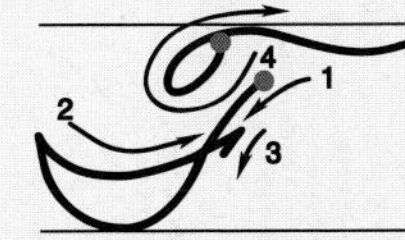

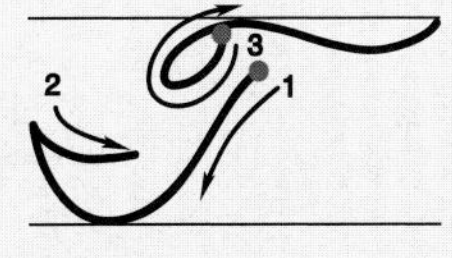

**F** Starting point, loop
Curve forward and right to endpoint
Starting point
Doublecurve, curve up
Curve right, slant down: capital *F*

**T** Starting point, loop
Curve forward to endpoint
Starting point
Doublecurve, curve up
Curve right: capital *T*

### Overcurve letters

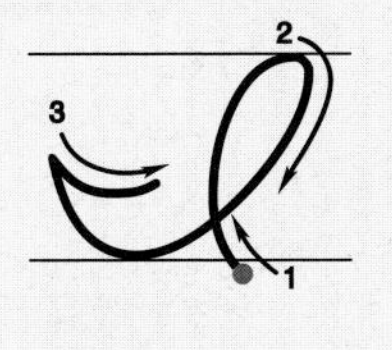

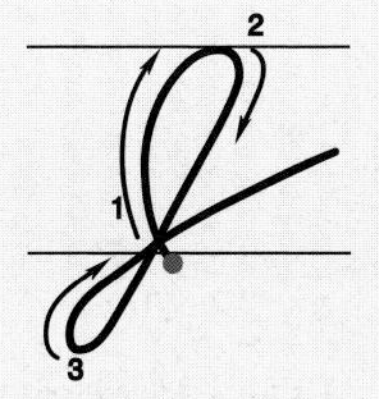

**I** Starting point, overcurve
Curve down and up
Curve right: capital *I*

**J** Starting point, overcurve
Slant down and loop back
Overcurve: capital *J*

**Q** Starting point, loop
Curve forward, slant down
Loop back, curve under: capital *Q*

### Letters with loops

**G** Starting point, undercurve
Loop, curve up
Double curve, curve up
Curve right: capital G

**S** Starting point, undercurve
Loop, curve down and up
Curve right: capital S

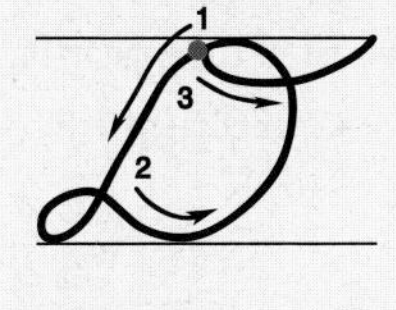

**L** Starting point, undercurve
Loop, curve down and loop
Curve under: capital *L*

**D** Starting point, slant down
Loop, curve down and up
Loop and curve right: capital *D*

### Undercurve-slant letters

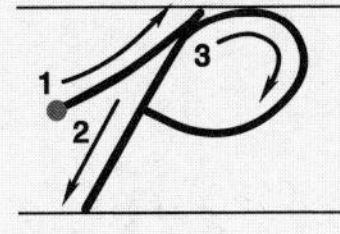

**P** Starting point, undercurve
Slant down, retrace up
Curve forward and back: capital *P*

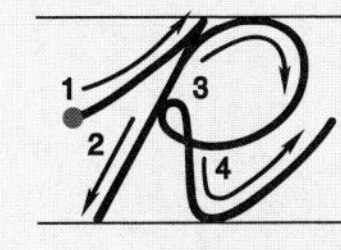

**R** Starting point, undercurve
Slant down, retrace up
Curve forward to slant
Curve forward
Undercurve: capital *R*

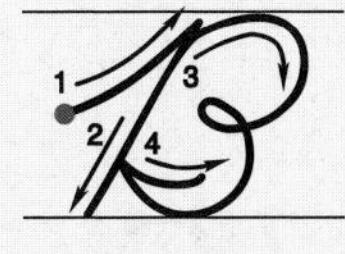

**B** Starting point, undercurve
Slant down, retrace up
Curve forward, loop
Curve forward and back
Curve right: capital *B*

## Penmanship (continued)



### Numbers

**1** Starting point, straight down: *1*

**2** Starting point, around right, slanting left and straight across right: *2*

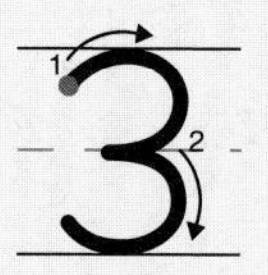

**3** Starting point, around right, in at the middle, around right: *3*

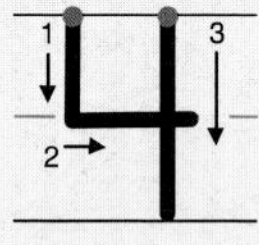

**4** Starting point, straight down
Straight across right
Starting point, straight down, crossing line: *4*

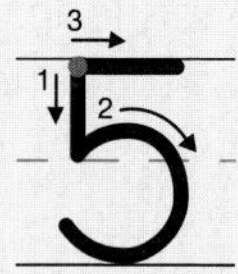

**5** Starting point, curving around right and up
Starting point, straight across right: *5*

**6** Starting point, slanting left, around the bottom curving up around right and into the curve: *6*

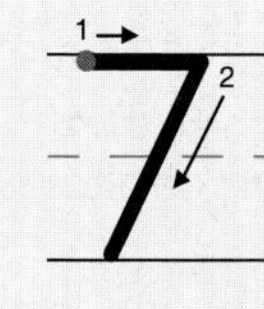

**7** Starting point, straight across right, slanting down left: *7*

**8** Starting point, curving left, curving down and around right, slanting up right to starting point: *8*

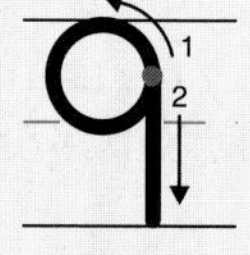

**9** Starting point, curving around left all the way, straight down: *9*

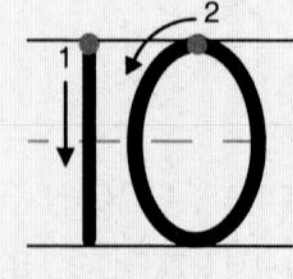

**10** Starting point, straight down
Starting point, curving left all the way around to starting point: *10*

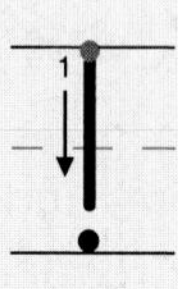

**!** Starting point, straight down
Dot exactly below: exclamation point

**?** Starting point, curving around right, straight down
Dot exactly below: question mark

# Introduction to Sounds



| LESSON | PHONICS SKILLS | DECODABLE BOOKS |
|---|---|---|
| **Getting Started** | | |
| DAY 1 | review /ā/ spellings; review /ē/ spellings | 1 Dave the Brave<br>2 Sleepy Steve |
| DAY 2 | review /ī/ spellings; review /ō/ spellings | 3 The Shy Bird's Trick<br>4 Chinlow of Singboat |
| DAY 3 | review /ū/ spellings; review /aw/ spelled *au_*, *aw* | 5 Mrs. Music<br>6 Paul, Aunt Maud, and Claude |
| DAY 4 | review /ow/ spelled *ou_*, *ow;* review /oi/ spelled *oi*, *_oy* | 7 Flower the Cow<br>8 Toy Store Explorer |
| DAY 5 | review /o͝o/ spelled *oo;* review /o͞o/ spelled *u*, *u_e*, *_ew*, *_ue*, *oo* | 9 A Book for Mr. Hook<br>10 Root Stew |
| **Unit 1** | | |
| LESSON 1 | /ī/ spelled *i_e*, *_y*, *igh;* endings *-ed*, *-ing*, *-s*, *-ful*, *-er;* review /a/; review short vowels | 11 The Frog Who Wanted to Fly |
| LESSON 2 | plural *–s;* inflectional endings; homographs; comparative and superlative adjectives; /e/ spelled *e;* special spelling pattern /m/ spelled *mb;* /e/ spelled *ea;* review short vowel;cvc – closed syllables | 12 Up to Bat |
| LESSON 3 | antonyms; homophones; prefix *re-;* related words; review /i/; /ā/ spelled *a*, *ai_*, *a_e*, *_ay* | 13 Baking Princess |
| LESSON 4 | suffixes *-ly*, *-ed*, *-ing;* contractions; /ŏ/; /ē/ spelled *e*, *ea*, *e_e*, *_y*, *ee*, *_ie_* | 14 City Girl |
| LESSON 5 | suffix *-tion;* prefixes and suffixes; frequently misspelled words; plural forms of nouns that end in *y;* /ū/ spellings; /ī/ spelled *i*, *_y*, *i_e*, *_ie*, *igh* | 15 The Prince's Foolish Wish |
| LESSON 6 | inflectional endings and suffixes added to base words; /k/ spelled *c;* nouns; review short vowels; /ō/ spelled *o*, *_ow*, *o_e*, *oa_*, *_oe* | 16 Rose, the Brave |
| **Unit 2** | | |
| LESSON 1 | antonyms; synonyms; compound words; suffix *-y;* prefix *un-;* spelling patterns /ar/ and *air;* review /ū/ spelled *u*, *u_e*, *_ue*, *_ew* | 17 Hugo Bugle |
| LESSON 2 | compound words; homophones; suffix *-tion;* suffix *-ly;* /er/ spelled *ur* and *ir;* /or/ spelled *or* and *ore;* review long vowels with open syllables | 18 Queen Kit |
| LESSON 3 | word families; synonyms; /əl/ spelled *-le;* open syllables with vowel digraphs | 19 Dead as a Dodo, Bald as an Eagle |
| LESSON 4 | compound words; related words; vivid verbs; /ow/ spelled *ou_* and *ow;* open syllables - vcv; closed syllables; multisyllabic words with long vowels; /s/ spelled *s*, *ce*, *ci_;* special spelling pattern: /s/ spelled *sc* | 20 The Lives of Sea Turtles |
| LESSON 5 | contractions; suffixes *-ly*, *-ing;* prefix *un-;* /oi/ spelled *oi* and *_oy;* multisyllabic words with long and short vowels ending *-le* | 21 Nesting and Burrowing Birds |
| LESSON 6 | compound words; suffix *-ed;* antonyms; vivid verbs; /əl/; /ow/; /oi/; /er/; multisyllabic words with long and short vowels | 22 Loop and Hook a Dream |

## Introduction to Sounds (continued)



| LESSON | PHONICS SKILLS | DECODABLE BOOKS |
|---|---|---|
| **Unit 3** | | |
| LESSON 1 | compound words; homophones; related words; /c/ spelled *s, ce, ci_;* /ā/ spelled *a, a_e, ai_, ay_;* review multisyllabic words with long and short vowels; special spelling patterns /n/ spelled *n, kn_,* and *gn_;* /m/ spelled *mb;* /g/ spelled *gh;* /l/ spelled *sl;* word families with spelling changes | 23 Sweet and Sour Soup |
| LESSON 2 | suffixes *-ful, -ly, -ing;* contractions; irregular past tense verbs; /ē/ spelled *ea, ee;* review diphthongs; /r/ spelled *er, ir, ur, ar;* /ə/ spelled *o* | 24 No Noise! |
| LESSON 3 | base words with suffixes; compound words; comparatives and superlatives (-er/-est); related words; /ī/ spelled *i_e, igh;* review diphthongs; suffixes *-ing, -ly, -er, -est* | 25 Summer Pen Pals |
| LESSON 4 | cardinal and ordinal numbers; suffixes; comparative and superlative endings *-er, -est;* /ō/ spelled *o* and *o_e;* diphthongs; prefixes *un-, re-, pre-, bi-, mis-, dis-* | 26 Joyce Writes a Good Story |
| LESSON 5 | prefixes and suffixes; /o͞o/ spelled *u_e, _ew;* diphthongs | 27 Little Hare |
| LESSON 6 | suffix *-ed;* comparatives; plural forms of words that end in *f;* homographs; related words; review long vowels; affixes as syllables | 28 Ralph, a Bug |
| **Unit 4** | | |
| LESSON 1 | homophones; base words and suffixes *-ed, -ment, -tion, -sion;* word families; double consonants | 29 Kitty and the Nothing Day |
| LESSON 2 | synonyms; base words with suffixes *-ly, -able;* final double consonants | 30 Traveling Star |
| LESSON 3 | compound words; /ā/ spelled *a_e, ai_, _ay;* contractions; base words with affixes; base words with suffixes: *-ful, -er, -tation* | 31 Whales |
| LESSON 4 | base words with suffixes *-ful, -ly, -ed, -ing;* /ē/ spelled *_ie_, ei* | 32 The Stone Wall |
| LESSON 5 | compound words; suffixes *-ed, -ing, -ial;* plural endings *-s* and *-es* | 33 Say It in Code |
| LESSON 6 | suffix *-ment;* antonyms; related words; special spelling patterns: *nk,* /t/ spelled *bt,* /n/ spelled *gn;* compound words | 34 Peace and Quiet |
| LESSON 7 | compound words; suffixes *-ment, -tion, -sion* | 35 School Days Long Ago |

## Introduction to Sounds (continued)

| LESSON | PHONICS SKILLS | DECODABLE BOOKS |
|---|---|---|
| **Unit 5** | | |
| **LESSON 1** | synonyms; hard *g;* /ā/ spelled *eigh,* consonant blends | |
| **LESSON 2** | antonyms; base words with suffixes *-ed, -able, -ation, -ative;* prefix *re-;* spellings *wr_, kn_, wh* | |
| **LESSON 3** | compound words; /wh/ spelled *wh-;* base words and suffix *-ness;* silent *l* in *lf;* /ch/ spelled ■*tch;* silent *g* in *gn* | |
| **LESSON 4** | homographs; /k/ spelled *c, k,* ■*ck;* base words with suffixes *-tion, -sion;* /ə/ | |
| **LESSON 5** | base words with prefixes and suffixes; /ā/ and /ī/; suffix *-ed;* /ē/ spelled *_ie;* /kw/ spelled *qu* | |
| **LESSON 6** | base words with prefix *be-, re-;* compound words; /s/ spelled *s* and *ce* and *ci_;* /j/ spelled *ge* | |
| **LESSON 7** | base words with suffixes *-ed, -ing, -y, -es;* review spelling patterns | |
| **Unit 6** | | |
| **LESSON 1** | vivid verbs; base words with suffixes *-ible* and *-ness;* irregular plurals | |
| **LESSON 2** | short vowel base words ending in *-tch* and the suffix *-ed;* long vowel base words ending in silent *e* with the suffix *-ing;* compound words; double consonants ending with *-y* | |
| **LESSON 3** | comparatives and superlatives; vivid verbs and adjectives; homophones; /f/ spelled *lf;* /m/ spelled *lm;* words ending in suffixes *-er, -est* | |
| **LESSON 4** | compound words; base words with the prefix *auto-;* plural words; Latin roots | |
| **LESSON 5** | compound words; prefix *un-;* suffix *-less;* Greek roots | |
| **LESSON 6** | compound words; suffix *-est;* prefix *re-;* French, Spanish, and German roots | |
| **LESSON 7** | contractions; vivid adjectives; irregular plurals | |

# High-Frequency Word List

LEVEL APPENDIX

| | | | | | |
|---|---|---|---|---|---|
| a | cold | grow | may | said | too |
| about | come | had | me | saw | try |
| after | could | has | much | say | two |
| again | cut | have | must | see | under |
| all | did | he | my | seven | up |
| always | do | help | myself | shall | upon |
| am | does | her | never | she | us |
| an | done | here | new | show | use |
| and | don't | him | no | sing | very |
| any | down | his | not | sit | walk |
| are | draw | hold | now | six | want |
| around | drink | hot | of | sleep | warm |
| as | eat | how | off | small | was |
| ask | eight | hurt | old | so | wash |
| at | every | I | on | some | we |
| ate | fall | if | once | soon | well |
| away | far | in | one | start | went |
| be | fast | into | only | stop | were |
| because | find | is | open | take | what |
| been | first | it | or | tell | when |
| before | five | its | our | ten | where |
| best | fly | jump | out | thank | which |
| better | for | just | over | that | white |
| big | found | keep | own | the | who |
| black | four | kind | pick | their | why |
| blue | from | know | play | them | will |
| both | full | laugh | please | then | wish |
| bring | funny | let | pretty | there | with |
| brown | gave | light | pull | these | work |
| but | get | like | put | they | would |
| buy | give | little | ran | think | write |
| by | go | live | read | this | yellow |
| call | goes | long | red | those | yes |
| came | going | look | ride | three | you |
| can | good | made | right | to | your |
| carry | got | make | round | today | |
| clean | green | many | run | together | |

## Card 1: /a/ Lamb

I'm Pam the Lamb, I am.
This is how I tell my Mommy where I am: /a/ /a/ /a/ /a/ /a/.

I'm Pam the Lamb, I am.
This is how I tell my Daddy where I am: /a/ /a/ /a/ /a/ /a/.

I'm Pam the Lamb, I am.
That young ram is my brother Sam.
This is how I tell my brother where I am: /a/ /a/ /a/ /a/ /a/.

I'm Pam the Lamb; I'm happy where I am.
Can you help me tell my family where I am? *(Have the children respond.)* /a/ /a/ /a/ /a/ /a/

## Card 2: /b/ Ball

Bobby loved to bounce his basketball.
He bounced it all day long.
This is the sound the ball made:
/b/ /b/ /b/ /b/ /b/.

One day, while Bobby was bouncing his basketball,
Bonnie came by on her bike.

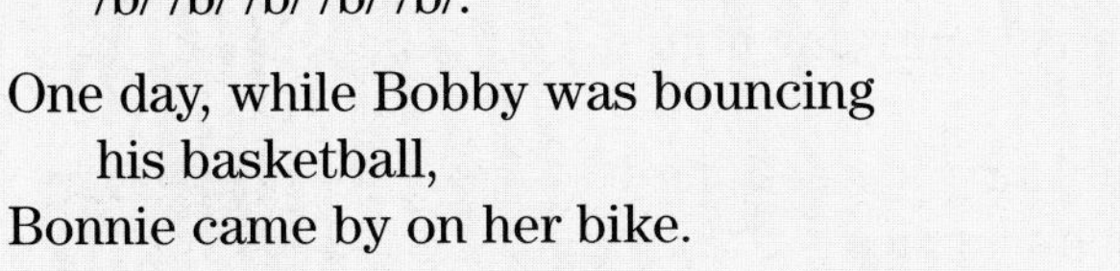

Bonnie said, "Hi, Bobby. I have a little bitty ball.
May I bounce my ball with you?"

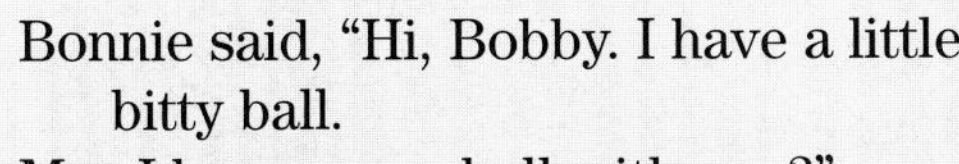

Bobby said, "Sure!" and Bonnie bounced her little bitty ball.

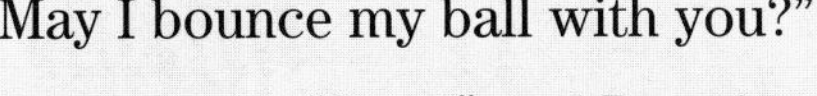

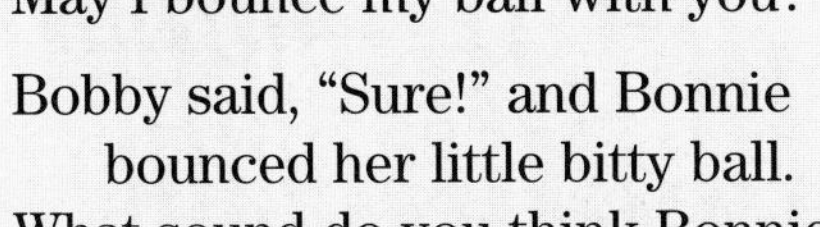

What sound do you think Bonnie's ball made?
*(Encourage a very soft reply.)* /b/ /b/ /b/ /b/ /b/

Soon Betsy came by. "Hi, Bobby. Hi, Bonnie," she said.
"I have a great big beach ball. May I bounce my ball with you?"

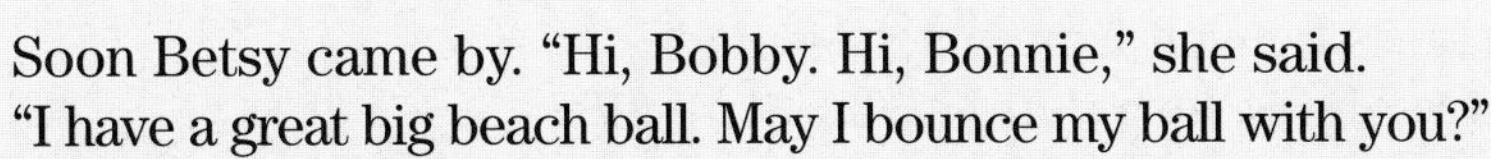

Bobby and Bonnie said, "Sure!" and Betsy bounced her big beach ball.
What sound do you think the beach ball made?
*(Encourage a louder, slower reply.)* /b/ /b/ /b/ /b/ /b/

*(Designate three groups, one for each ball sound.)*
Now when Bobby, Bonnie, and Betsy bounce their balls together, this is the sound you hear:

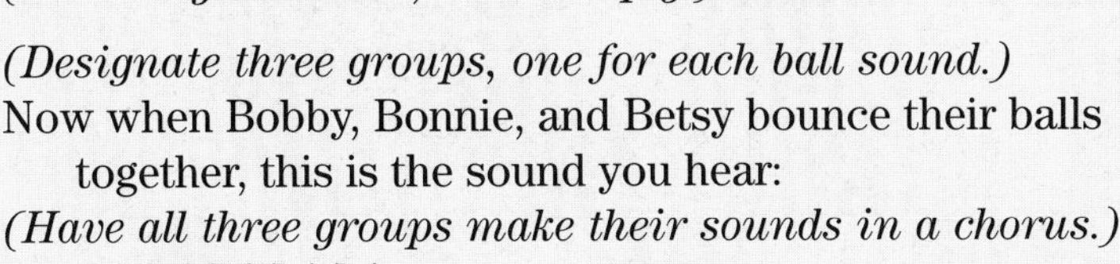

*(Have all three groups make their sounds in a chorus.)*
/b/ /b/ /b/ /b/ /b/

## Card 3: /k/ Camera

Carlos has a new camera. When he takes pictures, his camera makes a clicking sound like this:
/k/ /k/ /k/ /k/ /k/.

In the garden, Carlos takes pictures of caterpillars crawling on cabbage:
/k/ /k/ /k/ /k/ /k/.
At the zoo, Carlos takes pictures of a camel, a duck, and a kangaroo:
/k/ /k/ /k/.
In the park, Carlos takes pictures of his cousin flying a kite: /k/ /k/ /k/ /k/ /k/.
In his room, Carlos takes pictures of his cute kitten, Cozy: /k/ /k/ /k/ /k/ /k/.

Can you help Carlos take pictures with his camera?
*(Have the children join in.)* /k/ /k/ /k/ /k/ /k/ /k/ /k/

## Card 4: /d/ Dinosaur

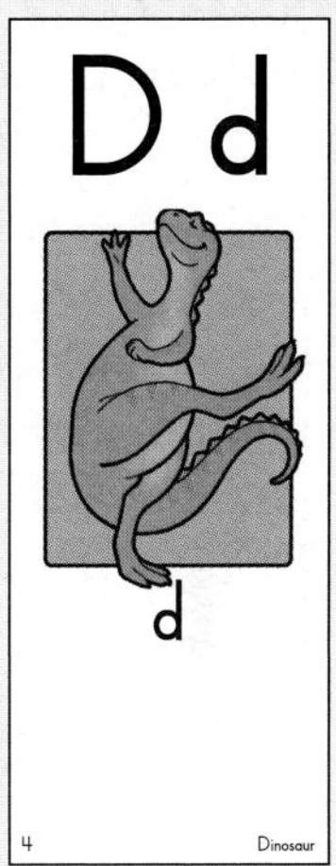


Dinah the Dinosaur loves to dance.
She dances whenever she gets the chance.
Whenever that dinosaur dips and whirls,
This is the sound of her dancing twirls:
/d/ /d/ /d/ /d/ /d/ /d/!

Dinah the Dinosaur dances all day.
From dawn to dark, she dances away.
And when Dinah dances, her dinosaur feet make a thundering, thudding, extremely loud beat:
*(loudly, with an exaggerated rhythm)*
/d/ /d/ /d/ /d/ /d/ /d/!

Now if you were a dinosaur just like Dinah,
you would certainly dance just as finely as she.
And if you were a Dino, and you had a chance,
what sound would your feet make when you did a dance?
*(Have the children join in.)* /d/ /d/ /d/ /d/ /d/ /d/

## Sound/Spelling Card Stories (continued)



### Card 5: /e/ Hen

Jem's pet hen likes to peck, peck, peck.
She pecks at a speck on the new red deck.
This is how her pecking sounds:
/e/ /e/ /e/ /e/ /e/.

Jem's pet hen pecks at corn in her pen.
She pecks ten kernels, then pecks again.
This is how her pecking sounds:
/e/ /e/ /e/ /e/ /e/.

Jem's hen pecks at a cracked egg shell.
She's helping a chick get out, alive and well.
This is how her pecking sounds:
/e/ /e/ /e/ /e/ /e/.

Can you help Jem's hen peck?
*(Have children say:)* /e/ /e/ /e/ /e/ /e/.

### Card 6: /f/ Fan

/f/ /f/ /f/ /f/ /f/—What's that funny sound?
It's Franny the Fan going round and round,
and this is the sound that old fan makes:
/f/ /f/ /f/ /f/ /f/.

When it gets too hot, you see,
Franny cools the family: /f/ /f/ /f/ /f/ /f/.
She fans Father's face
and Foxy's fur
and Felicity's feet.
Hear the Fan whir: /f/ /f/ /f/ /f/ /f/.

Can you make Franny the Fan go fast?
*(Have the children say quickly:)*
/f/ /f/ /f/ /f/ /f/.
Faster? /f/ /f/ /f/ /f/ /f/
Fastest? /f/ /f/ /f/ /f/ /f/

### Card 7: /g/ Gopher

Gary's a gopher.
He loves to gulp down food.
/g/ /g/ /g/ /g/ /g/, gulps the gopher.

Gary the Gopher gulps down grass
because it tastes so good.
/g/ /g/ /g/ /g/ /g/, gulps the gopher.

Gary the Gopher gulps down grapes—
gobs and gobs of grapes.
/g/ /g/ /g/ /g/ /g/, gulps the gopher.

Gary the Gopher gobbles green beans
and says once more,
/g/ /g/ /g/ /g/ /g/. He's such a hungry gopher!

Gary the Gopher gobbles in the garden
until everything is gone.

What sound does Gary the Gopher make?
*(Ask the children to join in.)* /g/ /g/ /g/ /g/ /g/

### Card 8: /h/ Hound

Harry the Hound dog hurries around.
Can you hear Harry's hurrying hound-
dog sound?
This is the sound Harry's breathing
makes when he hurries:
/h/ /h/ /h/ /h/ /h/ /h/!

When Harry the Hound dog sees a
hare hop by,
he tears down the hill, and his four
feet fly.
Hurry, Harry, hurry! /h/ /h/ /h/ /h/ /h/ /h/!

How Harry the Hound dog loves to hunt
and chase!
He hurls himself from place to place.
Hurry, Harry, hurry! /h/ /h/ /h/ /h/ /h/ /h/!

When Harry the Hound dog sees a big skunk roam,
He howls for help and heads for home.

What sound does Harry make when he hurries?
*(Have the children answer.)* /h/ /h/ /h/ /h/ /h/ /h/

## Card 9: /i/ Pig

This is Pickles the Pig.
If you tickle Pickles, she gets the giggles.
This is the sound of her giggling:
/i/ /i/ /i/ /i/ /i/.

Tickle Pickles the Pig under her chin.
Listen! She's giggling: /i/ /i/ /i/ /i/ /i/.
Wiggle a finger in Pickles' ribs.
Listen! She's giggling: /i/ /i/ /i/ /i/ /i/.

Give Pickles the Pig a wink,
and what do you think? First comes a grin.
Then listen!
She's giggling again: /i/ /i/ /i/ /i/ /i/.

Quick! Tickle Pickles the Pig. What will
she say? *(Have the children join in.)* /i/ /i/ /i/ /i/ /i/

## Card 10: /j/ Jump

J j
j ge
gi_
dge
10 Jump

When Jenny jumps her jump rope,
it sounds like this: /j/ /j/ /j/ /j/ /j/.
When Jackson jumps his jump rope,
it sounds like this: /j/ /j/ /j/ /j/ /j/.

The judges generally agree
that Jenny jumps most rapidly:
*(quickly)* /j/ /j/ /j/ /j/ /j/.

When Jenny jumps, she jumps to this jingle:
"Jump, jump, jump so quick.
Whenever I jump, I like to kick."
/j/ /j/ /j/ /j/ /j/

The Judges generally agree
that Jackson jumps most quietly:
*(quietly)* /j/ /j/ /j/ /j/ /j/.

When Jackson jumps, he jumps to this jingle:
"Jump, jump, nice and quiet.
See what happens when you try it." /j/ /j/ /j/ /j/ /j/

*(to the children)* Jump rope like Jenny.
*(quickly)* /j/ /j/ /j/ /j/ /j/
*(to the children)* Jump rope like Jackson.
*(quietly)* /j/ /j/ /j/ /j/ /j/

## Card 11: /k/ Camera

Carlos has a new camera. When he
takes pictures,
His camera makes a clicking sound like this:
/k/ /k/ /k/ /k/ /k/.

In the garden, Carlos takes pictures of
caterpillars crawling on cabbage:
/k/ /k/ /k/ /k/ /k/.
At the zoo, Carlos takes pictures of a camel,
a duck, and a kangaroo:
/k/ /k/ /k/.
In the park, Carlos takes pictures of his
cousin flying a kite: /k/ /k/ /k/ /k/ /k/
In his room, Carlos takes pictures of his
cute kitten, Cozy. /k/ /k/ /k/ /k/ /k/

Can you help Carlos take pictures with his camera?
*(Have the children join in.)* /k/ /k/ /k/ /k/ /k/ /k/ /k/

## Card 12: /l/ Lion

L l
l
12 Lion

Look! It's Leon the Lion.
Leon loves to lap water from lakes,
and this is the sound the lapping lion
makes: /l/ /l/ /l/ /l/ /l/.

Let's join Leon. Quick!
Take a little lick: /l/ /l/ /l/ /l/ /l/.

Are you a thirsty lass or lad?
Then lap until you don't feel bad:
/l/ /l/ /l/ /l/ /l/.

What sound do you make when you lap
like Leon the Lion?
*(Have the children say:)* /l/ /l/ /l/ /l/ /l/.

## Card 13: /m/ Monkey

For Muzzy the Monkey, bananas
are yummy.
She munches so many, they fill up
her tummy.
When she eats, she says:
/m/ /m/ /m/ /m/ /m/!

Bananas for breakfast, bananas
for lunch.
Mash them up, mush them up,
Munch, munch, munch, munch!
What does Muzzy the Monkey say?
*(Have the children say:)* /m/ /m/ /m/ /m/ /m/.

Bananas at bedtime? I have a hunch
Muzzy will mash them up, mush them up,
Munch, munch, munch, munch!
Then what will Muzzy the Monkey say?
*(Have the children say:)* /m/ /m/ /m/ /m/ /m/.

## Sound/Spelling Card Stories (continued)

LEVEL APPENDIX

### Card 14: /n/ Nose

When Norman Newsome has a cold,
his nose just won't work right.
It makes a noisy, stuffy sound
through morning, noon, and night.
When Norman has a cold, his nose goes:
/n/ /n/ /n/ /n/ /n/!

When Norman Newsome has a cold,
it's hard to just be quiet.
His nose just sniffs and snuffs
and snarls.
Norman wishes he could hide it!
Instead, his poor, sick, noisy nose just goes:
/n/ /n/ /n/ /n/ /n/!

Norman doesn't hate his nose;
It just does as it pleases!
Even when he sniffs a rose,
he nearly always sneezes.
Then Norman Newsome's nose
again goes *(Have the children say:)*
/n/ /n/ /n/ /n/ /n/.

### Card 15: /o/ Fox

Bob the Fox did not feel well at all.
He jogged to the doctor's office.
"Say /o/ Mr. Fox! /o/ /o/ /o/."

"My head is hot, and my throat hurts a lot,"
said the fox.
"Say /o/ Mr. Fox! /o/ /o/ /o/ /o/."

"Yes, you've got a rotten cold," said
the doctor.
"Say /o/ Mr. Fox! /o/ /o/ /o/."

"Find a spot to sit in the sun," said the doctor.
"Say /o/ Mr. Fox! /o/ /o/ /o/."

He sat on a rock in the sun.
Soon he felt much better.
*(with a satisfied sigh)* "/o/" said Mr. Fox.
/o/ /o/ /o/

### Card 16: /p/ Popcorn

Ping and Pong liked to pop corn. As
it cooked, it made this sound:
/p/ /p/ /p/ /p/ /p/ /p/ /p/.
One day Ping poured a whole package of
popcorn into the pot. It made this sound:
/p/ /p/ /p/ /p/ /p/ /p/ /p/.

The popcorn popped and popped. Ping filled
two pots, and still the popcorn popped:
/p/ /p/ /p/ /p/ /p/ /p/ /p/.
Pong filled three pails with popcorn, and still
it kept popping: /p/ /p/ /p/ /p/ /p/ /p/ /p/.

"Call all your pals," said their pop. "We'll have a party."
And the popcorn kept popping.
*(Have the children say the /p/ sound very fast.)*

### Card 17: /kw/ Quacking ducks

Quincy the Duck couldn't quite quack
like all the other quacking ducks.
Oh, he could say /kw/ /kw/ /kw/ /kw/,
but it never seemed just right.
When Quincy tried to quack quietly *(softly)*
/kw/ /kw/ /kw/ /kw/
his quack came out loudly *(loudly)*
/kw/ /kw/ /kw/ /kw/!
When he tried to quack slowly *(slowly)*
/kw/ . . . /kw/ . . . /kw/ . . . /kw/
his quack came out quickly *(quickly)*
/kw/ /kw/ /kw/ /kw/!
Quincy just couldn't quack right!

One day Quincy was practicing quacks.
His friend Quip quacked along with him.
"Repeat after me," said Quip
*(quietly)* /kw/ /kw/ /kw/ /kw/.
But Quincy quacked back,
*(in normal voice)* /kw/ /kw/ /kw/ /kw/ /kw/!
Quincy still couldn't quack quite right.
But Quincy kept quacking. He said, "I won't quit until I quack
like the best quackers around."
Can you show Quincy how quacking ducks quack?
*(Have the children join in.)*
/kw/ /kw/ /kw/ /kw/ /kw/ /kw/ /kw/ /kw/

Qq
qu_
17
Quacking ducks

### Card 18: /r/ Robot

Little Rosie Robot just runs and runs and runs.
She races round and round to get her chores
all done.
Here's how Rosie sounds when she's working:
/r/ /r/ /r/ /r/ /r/!

Rosie can rake around your roses.
Here comes that running robot!
/r/ /r/ /r/ /r/ /r/!

Rosie can repair your wrecked radio.
Here comes that racing robot!
*(softly)* /r/ /r/ /r/ /r/ /r/

Rosie can mend your round red rug.
Here comes that roaring robot!
*(loudly)* /r/ /r/ /r/ /r/ /r/!

Rosie rarely does anything wrong.
But there are two things that Rosie can't
do: rest and relax.
Here comes that roaring robot!
What does she say?
*(Have the children call out the answer:)*
/r/ /r/ /r/ /r/ /r/.

## Card 19: /s/ Sausages

Sue and Sammy had a nice place in the city.
On Saturday, Sue and Sammy decided to have sausages for supper.
Sammy put seven sausages in a skillet. /s/ /s/ /s/ /s/ /s/ /s/ /s/

Soon the smell of sausages filled the air.
/s/ /s/ /s/ /s/ /s/, sizzled the sausages.

"Pull up a seat, Sue," said Sammy.
"The sausages are almost ready to serve."
/s/ /s/ /s/ /s/ /s/, sizzled the sausages.

Sue and Sammy ate the delicious sausages.
Soon they wanted more, so Sam put six more sausages in the frying pan.
/s/ /s/ /s/ /s/ /s/ /s/, sizzled the sausages.

If you were cooking sausages with Sammy and Sue,
What sound would the sausages make as they sizzled?
*(Have the children join in:)* /s/ /s/ /s/ /s/ /s/ /s/.

## Card 20: /t/ Timer

When Tom Tuttle cooks, he uses his timer.
Tom Tuttle's timer ticks like this:
/t/ /t/ /t/ /t/ /t/ /t/ /t/

Tonight Tom Tuttle wants tomatoes on toast.
Tom turns on the oven.
Tom puts tomatoes on toast in the oven.
Tom sets the timer.
The timer will Ding! when Tom's toast and tomatoes are done.
Until the timer dings, it ticks: /t/ /t/ /t/ /t/ /t/ /t/ /t/.

Tomatoes on toast take ten minutes.
/t/ /t/ /t/ /t/ /t/ /t/ /t/
Tom can hardly wait. /t/ /t/ /t/ /t/ /t/ /t/ /t/
He taps out the time: /t/ /t/ /t/ /t/ /t/ /t/ /t/.

What is the sound of Tom Tuttle's ticking timer?
*(Have the children join in.)* /t/ /t/ /t/ /t/ /t/ /t/ /t/
Ding! Time for dinner, Tom Tuttle!

## Card 21: /u/ Tug

Tubby the Tugboat can huff and puff
and push and pull to move big stuff.
/u/ /u/ /u/ /u/ /u/ /u/ /u/
That's the sound of Tubby the Tug.

If a boat is stuck and will not budge,
Tubby the Tugboat can give it a nudge. /u/ /u/ /u/ /u/ /u/ /u/ /u/
It's Tubby the Trusty Tug.

If a ship is caught in mud and muck,
Tubby the Tugboat can get it unstuck.
/u/ /u/ /u/ /u/ /u/ /u/ /u/
It's Tubby the Trusty Tug.

Can you help Tubby push and pull?
*(Have the children join in.)*
/u/ /u/ /u/ /u/ /u/ /u/ /u/

## Card 22: /v/ Vacuum

Vinny the Vacuum is cleaning again.
Before visitors visit, he always begins.
This is the sound of his very loud voice:
/v/ /v/ /v/ /v/ /v/!
If only that Vinny could clean without noise!

Vinny sucks up the crumbs baby Vicki dropped.
/v/ /v/ /v/ /v/ /v/!
He visits nearly everywhere except the tabletop.
/v/ /v/ /v/ /v/ /v/!
Three vine leaves, two vitamins, part of a vase—
all vanish when Vinny goes over the place! /v/ /v/ /v/ /v/ /v/

As Vinny vacuums the velvety rug
a van full of visitors starts to drive up.
But Vinny's not done with the very last room!
Will you help Vinny the Vacuum vacuum?
*(Ask groups of children to say /v/ in a round to make the continuous sound of a vacuum cleaner.)*

## Card 23: /w/ Washer

Willie the Washer washed white clothes all week.
When he washed, he went:
/w/ /w/ /w/ /w/ /w/ /w/ /w/.

All winter, Willie worked well.
/w/ /w/ /w/ /w/ /w/ /w/ /w/
But last Wednesday, Willie was weak. *(softly)*
/w/ /w/ /w/ /w/ /w/ /w/ /w/
This week, he got worse. *(slower and slower)*
/w/. . . /w/. . . /w/. . .
Poor Willie was worn out. *(slowly)* /w/

Then a worker came and fixed Willie's wires.
Willie felt wonderful. *(more loudly)*
/w/ /w/ /w/ /w/ /w/ /w/ /w/!
Now Willie can wash and wash wildly!
*(quickly)* /w/ /w/ /w/ /w/ /w/ /w/ /w/!

How does Willie the Washer sound now when he washes?
*(Have the children join in.)* /w/ /w/ /w/ /w/ /w/ /w/ /w/
Can you wash just like Willie?
*(Children together:)* /w/ /w/ /w/ /w/ /w/ /w/ /w/.

## Sound/Spelling Card Stories (continued)

LEVEL APPENDIX

### Card 24: /ks/ Exit

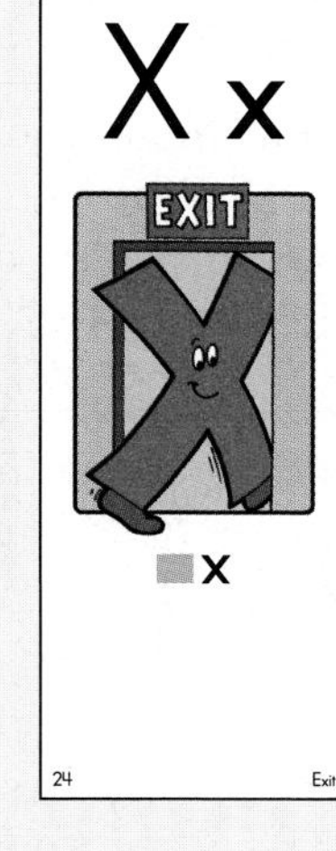


Rex is called the Exiting X;
he runs to guard the door.
To get past Rex, make the sound of X:
/ks/ /ks/ /ks/ /ks/.
That is what Rex expects!

The ox knows the sound of X,
so she says /ks/ /ks/ /ks/ /ks/
and gets past Rex.

The fox knows the sound of X,
so he says /ks/ /ks/ /ks/ /ks/
and gets past Rex.

Can you say /ks/ /ks/ /ks/ /ks/
and get past Rex the Exiting X?
*(Have the children respond:)* /ks/ /ks/ /ks/ /ks/!
Did we get past Rex?
*(Have the children say:)* Yes!

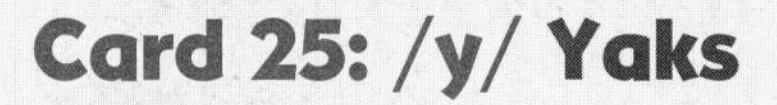

### Card 25: /y/ Yaks

Yolanda and Yoshiko are yaks.
They don't yell.
They don't yelp.
They don't yodel.
They don't yawn.
These young yaks just yak.
Yakety-yak, yakety-yak!
Can you hear the sound they make?
/y/ /y/ /y/ /y/ /y/ /y/ /y/.

Yolanda and Yoshiko yak in the yard.
/y/ /y/ /y/ /y/ /y/ /y/ /y/
They yak on their yellow yacht.
/y/ /y/ /y/ /y/ /y/ /y/ /y/
They yak in the yam patch.
/y/ /y/ /y/ /y/ /y/ /y/ /y/
These yaks yak all year!
/y/ /y/ /y/ /y/ /y/ /y/ /y/

Do you think these yaks like to yak?
*(Have the children answer:)* Yes!
*(Ask the children to yak like Yolanda and Yoshiko.)*

### Card 26: /z/ Zipper

Zack's jacket has a big long zipper.
The zipper zips like this: /z/ /z/ /z/ /z/.

When little Zack goes out to play,
he zips the zipper up this way:
/z/ /z/ /z/ /z/.
Later, when he comes back in,
Zack zips the zipper down again:
/z/ /z/ /z/ /z/.

Can you help Zack zip his jacket zipper?
*(Have the children join in.)* /z/ /z/ /z/ /z/

### Card 27: /ar/ Armadillo

Arthur Armadillo likes to whistle,
hum, and sing.
But when he gets a head cold,
his voice won't do a thing.

To sing and still sound charming—
and not sound so alarming—
Arthur has thought up the thing
of very often gargling.

Then Arthur Armadillo sounds like this:
/ar/ /ar/ /ar/ /ar/ /ar/.

Arthur gargles in the park. /ar/ /ar/ /ar/
/ar/ /ar/
He gargles in the dark. /ar/ /ar/ /ar/ /ar/ /ar/
He gargles on the farm. /ar/ /ar/ /ar/ /ar/ /ar/
He gargles in the barn. /ar/ /ar/ /ar/ ar/ /ar/
Arthur is great at gargling! /ar/ /ar/ /ar/ /ar/ /ar/

What does Arthur Armadillo's gargling sound like?
*(Have the children respond.)* /ar/ /ar/ /ar/ /ar/ /ar/

### Card 28: /hw/ Whales

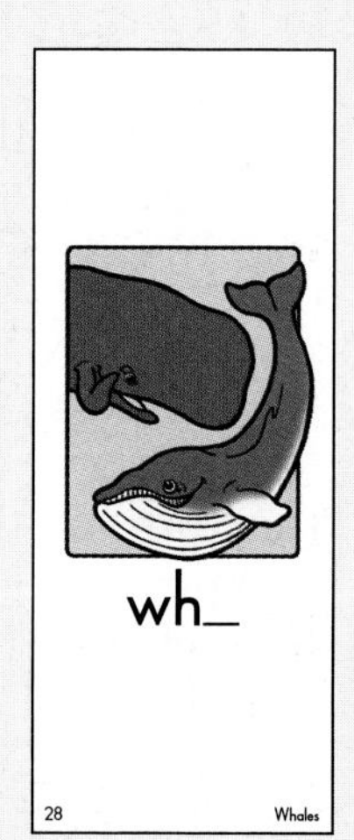


Look! It's Whitney the Whispering Whale!
Listen to her whisper: /hw/ /hw/ /hw/ /hw/ /hw/.

When Whitney meets with other whales,
she entertains them, telling tales.
She whispers: /hw/ /hw/ /hw/ /hw/ /hw/.
She's Whitney the Whispering Whale.

What ocean wonders does Whitney relate?
Does she whisper of whirlpools or whales
that are great?
We're only people, so we'll never guess.
She's Whitney the Whispering Whale!
/hw/ /hw/ /hw/.

Whatever Whitney whispers must be fun.
The other whales whistle when she's done.
They whoop and whack the white-capped waves.
They love Whitney the Whispering Whale! /hw/ /hw/ /hw/.

If you were Whitney, what sounds would you whisper
to your whale friends as they gathered to listen?
*(Have the children whisper:)* /hw/ /hw/ /hw/ /hw/ /hw/.

## Sound/Spelling Card Stories (continued)



### Card 29: /er/ Bird

Bertie the Bird is the oddest bird
that anyone has ever heard.
He doesn't caw like a crow or a gull,
or tweet like a robin or a wren.
Instead, he makes a chirping sound—
over and over again!
/er/ /er/ /er/ /er/ /er/ /er/!

Bert can't fly, since his wings are too short.
He arranges his feathers in curls.
He admits, "I've short wings and I don't really sing,
But I still am an interesting bird!"
/er/ /er/ /er/ /er/ /er/ /er/

Can you chirp like Bertie the Bird?
*(Have children say:)* /er/ /er/ /er/, /er/ /er/ /er/!

### Card 30: /sh/ Shell

Sheila and Sharon went to the seashore.
They saw lots of shells.
Sheila rushed from shell to shell.
Sharon held a shell to Sheila's ear.

"Do you hear anything?" asked Sharon.
"Yes, it sounds like the ocean crashing on
the shore," shouted Sheila,
"/sh/ /sh/ /sh/ /sh/ /sh/."

"Let's try different shaped shells," said Sharon.
She found a big shell. It made a loud /sh/
/sh/ /sh/ /sh/.
Sheila found a small shell. It made a soft /sh/ /sh/ /sh/ /sh/.
They found a thin shell. It made a high /sh/ /sh/ /sh/ /sh/.
They found a fat shell. It made a deep /sh/ /sh/ /sh/ /sh/.

Sheila and Sharon listened to lots of shells. But no matter
What the size and shape, what do you think Sheila and Sharon
Heard in every shell?
*(Have the children join in.)* /sh/ /sh/ /sh/ /sh/

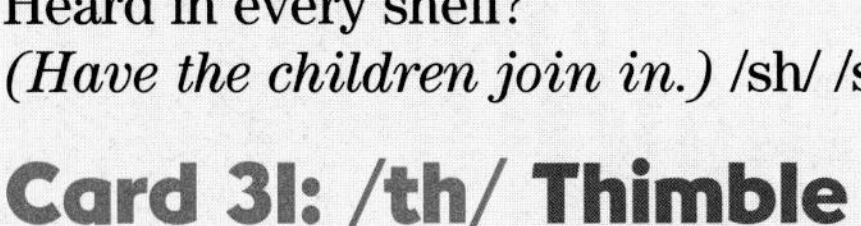

### Card 31: /th/ Thimble

Theodore Thimble is a thinker.
Theodore thinks and thinks and thinks.
And when he thinks, he rubs his head.
/th/ /th/ /th/ /th/ /th/ /th/ /th/ /th/ /th/

Theodore thinks of thumbs—
Thin thumbs
Thick thumbs
All different kinds of thumbs.
/th/ /th/ /th/ /th/ /th/ /th/ /th/ /th/ /th/

Theodore thinks of thread—
Red thread
Blue thread
All different color thread.
/th/ /th/ /th/ /th/ /th/ /th/ /th/ /th/ /th/

Thread and thumb
Thumb and thread
These are the thoughts
In Theodore's head.
/th/ /th/ /th/ /th/ /th/ /th/ /th/ /th/ /th/

### Card 32: /ch/ Chipmunk

Chipper the chipmunk is cheerful and chubby.
He chats and he chatters all day.
/ch/ /ch/ /ch/ /ch/ /ch/ /ch/
He sits on a chimney.
Can you hear him chat?
He chats and he chatters this way:
/ch/ /ch/ /ch/ /ch/ /ch/ /ch/.

Chipper stuffs cherries into his cheek.
Then he chatters /ch/ /ch/ /ch/ /ch/ /ch/ /ch/.
Chipper likes chestnuts and acorns to eat.
Then he chatters /ch/ /ch/ /ch/ /ch/ /ch/ /ch/.

Can you children chatter like Chipper?
*(Have the children answer.)*
/ch/ /ch/ /ch/ /ch/ /ch/ /ch/

Now chat with the chipmunk child beside you.
*(Ask partners to have chipmunk conversations.)*
/ch/ /ch/ /ch/ /ch/ /ch/ /ch/

### Card 38: /ng/ Gong

The young king has slept much
too long.
Let's go and awaken the king with
a gong.

A pinging gong? It makes a quiet song:
*(softly)* /ng/ /ng/ /ng/ /ng/ /ng/.

That gong is wrong.
*(softly)* /ng/ /ng/ /ng/ /ng/
We need a louder gong!

A dinging gong? It makes this song:
*(a bit louder)* /ng/ /ng/ /ng/ /ng/ /ng/ /ng/.

That, too, is wrong.
*(as before)* /ng/ /ng/ /ng/ /ng/
We need an even louder gong!

A clanging gong?
It makes this song: *(loudly)* /ng/ /ng/ /ng/ /ng/ /ng/!

That's just the thing! /ng/ /ng/ /ng/ /ng/ /ng/!
That's the gong we needed all along!

Now, which gong should we bring to awaken the King?
*(Have children make the /ng/ sound loud enough to wake the king.)* /ng/ /ng/ /ng/ /ng/ /ng/

**Note:** Cards 33 through 37 are long vowel cards and do not have corresponding stories.

## Sound/Spelling Card Stories (continued)



### Card 39: /ow/ Cow

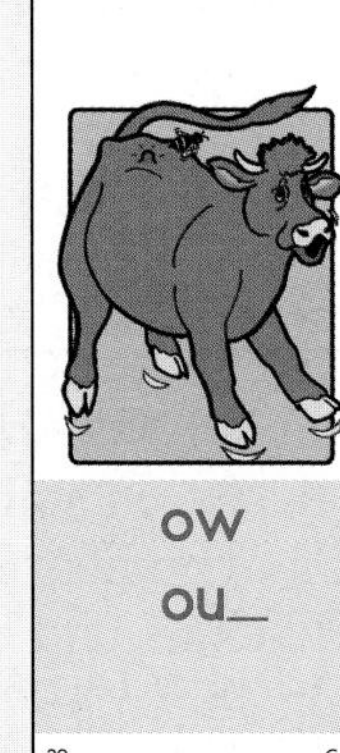


Wow! Can you see poor Brownie
the Cow?
She got stung by a bee and look at
her now!
She jumps up and down with an
/ow/ /ow/ /ow/ /ow/.

Poor Brownie found that a big buzzing sound
meant bees all around—in the air, on the ground.
Just one little bee gave Brownie a sting.
Now you can hear poor Brownie sing:
/ow/ /ow/ /ow/ /ow/.

Now if you were a cow and a bee found you
You'd probably jump and shout out too!
*(Have the children join in.)* /ow/ /ow/ /ow/ /ow/

### Card 40: /aw/ Hawk

Hazel the Hawk never cooks her food;
Instead, she eats it raw.
And when she thinks of dinnertime
She caws: /aw/ /aw/ /aw/ /aw/.

Hazel the Hawk likes rabbits and mice
and catches them with her claws.
In August, she flies high above the fields
and spies them below, in the straw.
Sometimes she even snatches a snake!
And when she's caught one, she caws:
/aw/ /aw/ /aw/ /aw/.

If you were a hawk thinking of dinnertime,
what do you think you'd say?
*(Have the children answer.)* /aw/ /aw/ /aw/ /aw/

### Card 41: /o͞o/ Goo

oo _ew
u_e _ue
u
41 Goo

/o͞o/ /o͞o/ /o͞o/ /o͞o/
What can be making that sound?
Could it be a new flute playing a tune?
No. It's goo!
/o͞o/ /o͞o/ /o͞o/ /o͞o/
The goo is oozing all over my hand.
/o͞o/ /o͞o/ /o͞o/ /o͞o/
The goo is oozing on my boots.
/o͞o/ /o͞o/ /o͞o/ /o͞o/
The goo is oozing off the roof.
The goo is oozing everywhere!
/o͞o/ /o͞o/ /o͞o/ /o͞o/
The goo is as sticky as glue.
It is as thick as stew.
/o͞o/ /o͞o/ /o͞o/ /o͞o/
Soon the goo will fill the school!
/o͞o/ /o͞o/ /o͞o/ /o͞o/
Soon the goo will reach the moon!
/o͞o/ /o͞o/ /o͞o/ /o͞o/
What sound does the oozing goo make?
*(Have the children join in.)* /o͞o/ /o͞o/ /o͞o/ /o͞o/

### Card 42: /o͝o/ Foot

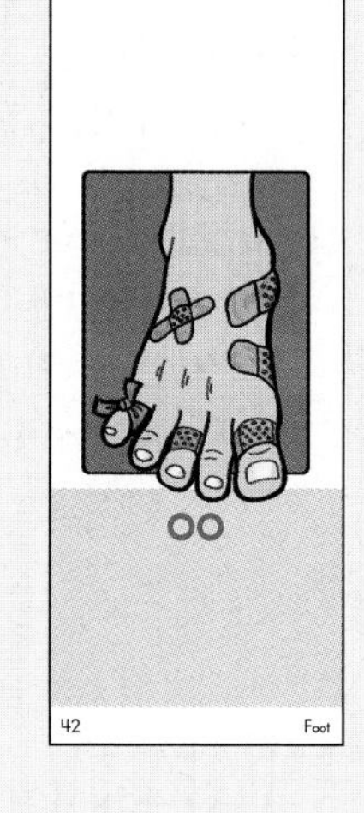


Mr. Hood took off his shoes and socks
And went out walking in the wood.
He kicked a rock and hurt his foot.
/o͝o/ /o͝o/ /o͝o/ /o͝o/
"Look, look!" said Mr. Hood. "There's a
babbling, bubbling brook. I'll walk
in the brook, so I won't hurt my foot."
So he stepped in the water, and guess what?
/o͝o/ /o͝o/ /o͝o/ /o͝o/
Mr. Hood stepped on a hook!
/o͝o/ /o͝o/ /o͝o/ /o͝o/
Mr. Hood stood. He shook his foot.
/o͝o/ /o͝o/ /o͝o/ /o͝o/
"This isn't good," said Mr. Hood.
"I think I'll go home and read a book.
At least that won't hurt my foot."
*(Have the children join in.)* /o͝o/ /o͝o/ /o͝o/ /o͝o/

### Card 43: /oi/ Coil

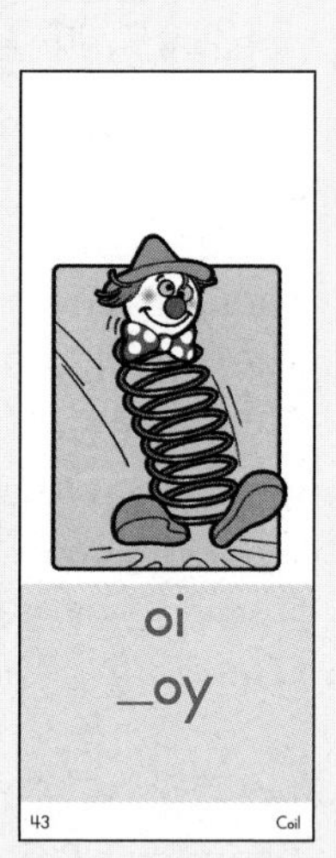


Boing! Boing! Boing! Boing!
Roy the Coil is a bouncing toy,
and this is the sound of his bounce:
/oi/ /oi/ /oi/ /oi/ /oi/.

Doing! Doing! Doing! Doing!
Roy the Coil just dances for joy.
This is the sound of his dance:
/oi/ /oi/ /oi/ /oi/ /oi/.

Ke-boing! Ke-boing!
Roy the Coil springs over a boy.
What springing sound does he make?
*(Have the children join in.)*
/oi/ /oi/ /oi/ /oi/ /oi/

## A

# B

INDEX



# E



# F

## G



## H



INDEX

# I



# J

## M



## N

# P



INDEX

# Index (continued)

INDEX



# S

INDEX

INDEX

INDEX



## T

INDEX

## Z

# Notes

Use this page to record lessons or elements that work well
or need to be adjusted for future reference.

## Lessons that work well.

## Lessons that need adjustments.

# Notes

Use this page to record lessons or elements that work well
or need to be adjusted for future reference.

## Lessons that work well.

## Lessons that need adjustments.

# Notes

Use this page to record lessons or elements that work well
or need to be adjusted for future reference.

## Lessons that work well.

## Lessons that need adjustments.

# Notes

Use this page to record lessons or elements that work well
or need to be adjusted for future reference.

## Lessons that work well.

## Lessons that need adjustments.

# Notes

Use this page to record lessons or elements that work well or need to be adjusted for future reference.

## Lessons that work well.

## Lessons that need adjustments.

# Notes

Use this page to record lessons or elements that work well
or need to be adjusted for future reference.

## Lessons that work well.

## Lessons that need adjustments.

# Notes

Use this page to record lessons or elements that work well
or need to be adjusted for future reference.

## Lessons that work well.

## Lessons that need adjustments.

# Notes

Use this page to record lessons or elements that work well
or need to be adjusted for future reference.

## Lessons that work well.

## Lessons that need adjustments.

# Notes

Use this page to record lessons or elements that work well
or need to be adjusted for future reference.

## Lessons that work well.

## Lessons that need adjustments.